MY FATHER'S PEOPLE

A HISTORY OF THE LUXTON FAMILY OF FROGPIT MOOR PETTON BAMPTON DEVON AND THEIR DESCENDANTS WORLDWIDE

BY
BRIAN C LUXTON

Best Wishes

Brian C. Luxton

A TIME-LINK PRODUCTION FOR THE
LUXTON FAMILY HISTORY SOCIETY
2018

Grosvenor House
Publishing Limited

This book is published by
Grosvenor House Publishing Ltd
Link House
140 The Broadway, Tolworth, Surrey, KT6 7HT.
www.grosvenorhousepublishing.co.uk

A CIP record for this book
is available from the British Library

ISBN 978-1-78623-425-4

First Printing: 2018

ISBN 978-0-244-41776-5

Brian C. Luxton, "Passat, 12, Coldbrook Road East, Barry, Vale of Glamorgan, CF63 1NF

email address>b.luxton@yahoo.co.uk

To my parents Burt & Beryl Luxton
&
For Renzo & Casper in the next generation

CONTENTS

ACKNOWLEDGEMENTS

No work such as this can be the work of one man. I must thank my cousin Malcolm Luxton who before I had a laptop typed up my early longhand version of this book and from my longhand version has typed out the tree. Malcolm has also contributed the chapter on his father. I am eternally grateful to my American cousins, Susan Freeborn in Calgary and Gail Mesplay in Denver for their research in Canada and the U.S.A. There are so many to thank, including late Willie Luxton in Wellington and his grandson David John Luxton in Taunton, late Dixon H. Luxton in Wiveliscombe and his brother Eddie in Winterbourne. Harold James Luxton and his daughter Gillian in Folkestone; late Geoffrey W. Luxton in Manchester; Frances Franklin, Marie Ronald; Marjorie Shaw, Queenie Luxton, Ian and Cynthia Green in Padstow, Cyril Luxton in Hove and his brother Wilfred George Luxton in Barry, Reginald James Luxton and family in Nailsea, Francis John Luxton, Portishead, Raymond James Luxton, Clevedon, Melvin Wallis, Rosemary Bryant, Nona E. Henderson, Murray Stewart, Eileen Bangay in Yeovil, Gordon Bond Luxton, Barbara Noble, Clive Luxton in Wrentham Suffolk, Marie Ann Visser in Amsterdam, Margaret Haagenaar in France, Edward S.W. Luxton in Brompton Regis, Susanna and Peter Nurse, Cannington, Somerset, Alfred W. Luxton, Doncaster, Brenda Joy Luxton in Burnham on Sea, Richard John Luxton, Winchmore Hill, David George Luxton in Nottingham and his son John in Leeds and Winifred Luxton in Maidstone, Kent.

I am also indebted to Mr and Mrs Jim Needs, Hutchings Farm, Frogpit Moor, Petton, Bampton, Maurice Hawkins of Venn Farm, Waterrow, Chipstable, Ralph and T. J. Budge, Brian Luxton in Toowomba, Queensland and Margaret Andrews in Plymouth for all their help. Thanks to Sue Passmore in New Quay, Ceredigion for reading and commenting on my book in draft format and to her son Guy, a professional photographer for taking photos of family items illustrated in the book. I am indebted also to Martin Baldwin- Edwards for his superb work in taking and improving the quality of photographs and to Aldon Grisdale for designing the book cover. Aldon, Martin and Andy Pridham patiently guided me in the use of my laptop. I give a big thank you to anyone else who has helped me in this venture. A big thanks to Becky Banning and her team at Grosvenor House Publishing and the typesetters for converting the pages on my laptop into the pages of this book. I could not have chosen a better team. I have done my best but any errors are my responsibility. I hope you all enjoy the read!

Brian C. Luxton

10th September 2018

FOREWORD

The acorn which grew into this family history was sown in my early life but I did not begin research until 1965, the year after I had settled into a teaching career. My big break came on the 31st May 1973 when I was fortunate to meet Mr and Mrs Jim Needs at Hutchings Farm, Frogpit Moor, Petton, Bampton. They kindly let me photocopy the farm deeds which begin in 1745 and from the deeds and other sources I soon had the outline of a tree back to 1704. I added to the general picture in July 1980 when Mr Maurice Hawkins of Venn Farm, Waterrow, Somerset, permitted me to make copious notes from his large collection of property deeds. Since that time there has been much filling in of details. I have taken a delight in collecting family oral tales. Some dating back more than one hundred and fifty years are but a whisper but they have added an authentic voice to the unfolding story told from documentary evidence.

Research has taken me to beautiful sylvan villages in the foothills of Exmoor on the Devon Somerset border- Clayhanger, Petton, Morebath, Skilgate, Raddington, Chipstable and Upton among them. These are places I had never heard of and would never have visited if it had not been for the fact I was bitten by the family tree bug! I have traced the family as it moved around Devon and across Somerset to Bristol, London, South Wales and the north of England. The more adventurous emigrated to Canada, the U. S. A. Australia and New Zealand. Research has taught me a great deal about my ancestors and I have learnt a lot about myself in the process. It's a journey I think we all need to make.

I have taken the family back to the marriage of Robert Luxton and Jane Daniell at St Peter's Clayhanger, Devon on the 28th August 1704. At this point I have hit a brick wall. Further research may turn up a lead that will take the family back to earlier generations. There is the possibility too that DNA analysis may link us to an earlier Luxton family in 16th or 17th century Winkleigh or Brushford. In places I have been unable to link up with living descendants who can provide oral evidence and family photographs. Much remains to be done in that direction but that must be the work of others.

I have compiled 44 family trees and readers interested in a particular branch will find chapter references directing them to the appropriate tree contained at the end of the book.

Brian C. Luxton

"Passat" 12, Coldbrook Road East, Barry, 10 September 2018

email b.luxton@yahoo.co.uk

1

I SEARCH FOR MY ANCESTRY

"Who am I? Where are my roots?" These are questions most people ask at some time in their lives. In the past it was the aristocracy and gentry who had the time and money to indulge in genealogy. In recent years the general populace have become more interested in the topic and their enthusiasm has been stimulated by Alex Haley's epic "Roots," first published in 1976, and T.V. series such as Gordon Honeycomb's "Family History," first transmitted on BBC2 in 1979, and currently by "Who Do You Think You Are?"

From an early age I had an identity crisis. I was born in Wales and when Wales played rugby against England at Cardiff Arms Park I was Welsh, but I was less certain of myself on St. David's Day, when as a non-Welsh speaker I became acutely aware of Welsh culture and history. I looked to my family for an answer. My father was born in Wales too, but his father was born in Somerset and his mother's family came from Lincolnshire and Lancashire. My mother was born in Queenstown (Cobh), Ireland of a Roman Catholic Irish mother, whose husband, James Reston Campbell, a Presbyterian, was born in Jarrow of a Geordie mother and a Scottish father who was born in Glasgow.

I was about four when my Irish grandmother opened an old chest in the box room at her home in Penarth to show me photographs of my Scottish and Geordie relatives. The memory of those photographs stayed with me and when my grandfather Campbell, died in 1978, they came into my possession.

In 1956 when I was fifteen, we were returning from a summer holiday in Torquay, when father made a detour to visit his uncle Fred Luxton who lived in Nailsea, Somerset. The visit made a lasting impression on me. Fred, a widower whose large family had left home, lived in Noah's Ark, one of a row of three cottages close by the village green in Nailsea. An inscribed plaque set high in the wall above his cottage gave the name Noah's Ark 1667, with the outline of an ark. Fred was no less interesting than the cottage. Around him were mementoes of a long and active life. A row of bright candlesticks stood on the mantelpiece. Talking of these led him to display a store of treasures, which brought back many memories and anecdotes. One unusual treasure was a silver watch weighing 8½ oz and a matching chain, which weighed a pound. It was illuminated by a battery, which lit a tiny bulb on the watch face. Next to the candlesticks stood a bugle – a reminder of the 1914-18 war. It was taken from a dead bugle boy and Fred said the stains on it were blood. A pipe for the ardent smoker hung on the wall. It was made of clay and held an ounce of tobacco. There was also a row of gleaming powder-and-shot flasks, and a "frying pan" clock, complete with knife and fork hands. These had been "collected" from a German captured while he was having breakfast in the trenches. Great Uncle Fred was one of Nailsea's best known characters. In his last years he became much attached to his pet turkey "Turk", who was quite a champion egg layer. This unusual pet stayed with Fred continually and even went for walks with him and his little dog, "Tiny". Turk clearly hailed from the West Country, for on returning from a walk she enjoyed a saucer of cider! Some years ago the Clevedon Mercury featured an amusing article entitled "Fred, Turk and Tiny in Noah's Ark". Fred died aged 87 in 1967.

I was researching local history in the reference room of Cardiff Central Library in 1966, when I came by chance upon my first documentary references to the Luxton family. They were contained in the will index of the British Record Society and revealed that the family came from Devon. Some of the 17th century Luxtons had grand sounding classical names- Scipio, Hannibal and Letitia- amusing names to our ears but, not so in that era.

Research confirmed that the Luxton family began in Winkleigh in the fourteenth century and spread from there throughout Devon, the rest of England and abroad. In 1566, in the reign of Elizabeth 1, Bernard Luxton of Winkleigh, yeoman, purchased the manor of Abbotsham, which included Brushford Barton from Sir Amyas Paulett. The Luxton family continued at Brushford Barton until early in the twentieth century.

However, all I had discovered on the Luxtons of Winkleigh and Brushford seemed a long way from my family who lived in Barry. My grandfather, E.A. Luxton, master baker, came to Barry in time for the almost Arctic winter of 1894-95 to work as an "improver" for John Spickett, who paid him a sovereign a week. He found the frozen, snow–bound town a miserable place and would have gone home to Clevedon, Somerset, if the trains had been running. However, he stayed and in time he set up his Golden Crust Bakery in Cadoxton. Was there a Devon connection I wondered? From Crockford's Clerical Directory in the Reference Room of the town library, I obtained the name and address of the Anglican priest in Clevedon, Somerset. I wrote and received a reply that my grandfather was born in 1875, son of George Luxton, stonemason. This George was not born in Clevedon, but from the 1871 census I established that he hailed from Chipstable, a pretty little village in the sylvan hills of western Somerset. Once more Crockford proved useful in establishing the name and address of the incumbent priest, who on searching the parish records, informed me that my great-grandfather George, was baptised in 1847, son of Jacob Luxton, stonemason. Jacob was not born in Chipstable, but the 1851 census revealed that he came from Bampton in Devon. This was the Devon connection I was seeking.

My knowledge of the family was enhanced by contact I made with older relatives. My great aunt Ida Laura Webber (nee Luxton 1884-1969), who lived at Marshfield to the east of Cardiff, provided much useful information and she gave me an ornately framed certificate that confirmed my  great grandfather Brother George Luxton had become a Legal Member of the Friendly Society of Stonemasons on the 26th March 1866. Ida and her husband Bert Webber, who spoke with a soft West Country burr and was possessed of a pleasing manner, are here pictured with a parrot at an agricultural show in the mid twentieth century.

By now my brother Ian and I were determined to visit the West Country. At Easter 1970 we spent a week at the Creech Castle Hotel in Taunton, which we used as a base to visit the record offices at Taunton and Exeter where we carried out further research into our Luxton forebears.

We also met relatives in Clevedon and Nailsea and saw other places associated with the family. In Nailsea we met Thomas John Luxton (1890-1972), our grandfather's youngest brother who gave me his father George's spirit level and brass ruler which he had used as a stonemason. Tom also gave me his own brass match box holder inscribed Sapper T. Luxton, Royal Engineers, 269. R.E. and on the reverse the names of battles he fought in – Vimy, Arras, Ypres.

The following year in April 1971 we arranged with the vicar of Bampton to examine the old parish registers which began in 1650. These proved disappointing as there were few references to the Luxtons and none to Jacob. We ascertained however that there was a hamlet named Petton, four miles to the east of Bampton, which possessed a church dedicated to the old Celtic Saint Petrock [1].

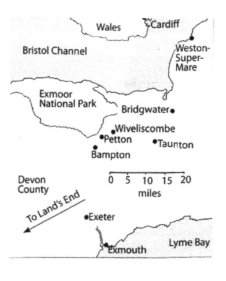

A visit revealed immediately that we had come to the right place as two gravestones bore Luxton inscriptions. Both the vicar and Mr Ellis, the church warden, who was the headmaster of the village school, were certain that the registers dated only from 1926. However, in the corner of the vestry was an old iron chest, where after scrummaging beneath a pile of papers we discovered the ancient registers which began in 1701. Examination revealed that my family were in the parish from 1707 and that they were well documented until about the time of the Great War. I learnt that my great-great grandfather Jacob was baptised there in 1800, the son of Isaac Luxton, a yeoman, living at Hutchings who died in 1834 aged 83.

---

[1] St. Petrock's Church was one of seven churches founded around Exmoor by the sixth century Celtic Saint Petroc before he travelled on to West Devon and mid Cornwall where he is far better known. Medieval hagiologists record Petroc as the uncle of the Welsh St Cadoc and he also has churches in Wales and Brittany.

The church is sited on a hill surrounded by fields and scattered farms. It was completely rebuilt in 1847 in the Victorian Gothic style by the Troyte family, the local landowners. Outside in the churchyard, Mr Ellis, the warden, pointed out a whitewashed eighteenth century farm in the valley below and identified it as the Hutchings mentioned in the burial register. On a later trip to the West Country I visited Hutchings, where the generous owners, Mr and Mrs James Needs, gave me a sumptuous Devon cream tea. With typical Devon hospitality they kindly allowed me to examine the old deeds, the earliest, dating from 1745, were written on sheepskin parchment. From the deeds and other documentary evidence, I discovered a great deal more about my family. For instance, Isaac in his will bequeathed to his son Jacob a nursery of young apple trees, and the orchard was still there when I visited in the 1970s. The old well from which the Luxtons obtained their water was still in existence too. Isaac I learnt was the son of Jacob Luxton (d. 1759), who was the son of Robert Luxton. This Robert Luxton (d.1751) and his wife Jane Daniell were my five times great grandparents.

Today from Robert and Jane Luxton, who were married in 1704, I have traced several hundred descendants living in various parts of Britain, Australia, Canada, U.S.A. and New Zealand. Having a rare surname like Luxton provides a valuable insight into the distribution and disbursement of families caused by economic trends and personal ambitions. Genealogy research also produces many surprises. On one occasion my enthusiasm led to my brother and myself being locked in a bank vault in Tiverton on market day. Still, the visit proved a very useful one as I obtained information which revealed that Mr Edward S.W. Luxton of Oatway Farm, Brompton Regis, Somerset, and I shared the same five times great grandparents.

Coincidences are always happening in genealogical research. In the autumn of 1974 I was studying documents in the Society of Genealogists' Library in London, when I noticed an elderly gentleman studying the same documents. It transpired that he was William John Luxton (1909-1992) of Guildford who was as enthusiastic as me on Luxton genealogy. He knew of my existence because we were tracing the same lines of research. "Bill" was in possession of a letter which I had sent to George Naismith Luxton, Bishop of Huron in Canada. He put me in touch with Eleanor Luxton in Canada who was the author of two books "Luxton's Pacific Crossing" and "Banff-Canada's First National Park". From reading the books I learnt that Eleanor's grandfather, William Fisher Luxton, emigrated from the West Country to Canada in 1855, where he had a distinguished career as a newspaperman. Looking over my research notes, I discovered that William Fisher Luxton was baptised in Skilgate, Somerset, in 1843 and he was related to me.

Research has taken me to beautiful places which I had never heard of and certainly would not have visited if I had not been bitten by the genealogy bug. I've made a pilgrimage to Winkleigh to see where the Luxton story began and to nearby St. Mary's Brushford and Brushford Barton, the home of the Luxton squires. My journey has taken me to Frogpit Moor, Petton, Bampton and the sequestered villages of Morebath, Raddington, Skilgate and Chipstable on the Devon Somerset border. I've been to bustling Tiverton and Taunton, with its fine churches. I've had the good fortune to meet relatives such as the late Dixon H. Luxton in Wiveliscombe, Edward S. W. Luxton in Brompton Regis and the late Willie Luxton in Wellington, Somerset. The family story I have traced starts at Hutchings Farm, Frogpit Moor, Petton, Bampton Devon, and that is where I will begin, but first I need to say something about the origins of the Luxton family.

2

THE ORIGINS OF THE LUXTON FAMILY

In England the majority of surnames did not become fixed until the years 1200 to 1400. Luxton is the name of two places in Devon, one in the parish of Winkleigh and the other in Upottery[2].The first was Luggeston in the reign of Henry 111(1216-1272) and the second was Luggestone in 1313.Both must mean "farm/place of (a man called) Lug" and there was a man called Nicholas Lug[3], a juror in Winkleigh Hundred in 1238. The surname Lugg, is found in the extreme s. w. of England but is predominately a Devon surname. It forms the first element in our surname and is a Devon variant of Lucas meaning "bright" "shining." It is not found in England before the Norman Conquest and seems to have come into use in the twelfth century in the Anglicized form of Luke and owed its popularity in the Middle Ages to St. Luke the Evangelist. The personal name was being adopted as a surname by the early thirteenth century so that Nicholas Lugg just means Nicholas son of Lugg. He in turn gave his name to the settlement he created at Winkleigh[4].

My research has confirmed Winkleigh as the aboriginal home of the family. It was one of the nucleated villages founded in the early Saxon occupation of Devon in the late seventh century, when Wineca cleared the woodland from the hill top. Land was abundant in Saxon Devon, but as the population grew in the Middle Ages, more and more of it was

---

[2] Today Luxton is the name of three farms, Higher, Middle and Lower Luxton, about two miles north of Upottery Church. The name of Nicholas de Loghston with twelve others is listed in the tithing of Sheldon in the Devonshire Lay Subsidy Roll of 1332.(Devon and Cornwall Record Society.N.S. Vol 14,1969).Sheldon is about five miles west of Upottery.Nicholas de Loghston was perhaps a descendant of Nicholas Lug of Winkleigh.If so the Upottery Luggeston was an outlier settlement hacked out of the Devon wilderness.The earliest concentration of the surname is in Winkleigh,a parish and a hundred in mid north Devon.

[3] Lugg survives as a separate surname today.

[4] Read more of my investigation into Lugg "an ugly monosyllabic word" in the appendix.

cleared and taken into individual ownership and cultivation. A great opportunity arose in 1204 when John (who was king 1199 to 1216) agreed to the deforestation of the whole of Devon, with the exception of Dartmoor and Exmoor in return for 5000 marks (roughly equivalent to £3400).

Enterprising individuals were enabled to make small piecemeal clearances of woodland, usually with the encouragement of the Lord of the manor. Nicholas Lug, the juror in Winkleigh Hundred in 1238, was such an enterprising individual who carved out his settlement at what is now called Luxton Barton, Winkleigh. It is perhaps significant that in the 1970s a silver coin of King John's reign was dug out of the cob wall in the barn at Luxton Barton. This building (in photo) is likely to have been the original Luggeston homestead built by Nicholas Lug.

The old building, which is now used as a barn, is a pretty basic structure, but is typical of medieval Devon farm houses. It still has two floors, with a fifteenth century wooden two light ogee headed window in one of its partition walls[5].(see photo below). The thatch roof has been replaced by corrugated iron, but it is remarkable to find the building still in use after perhaps 750 years. From their Winkleigh base the family spread throughout Devon, Cornwall, Somerset, the rest of England and abroad.

The present Luxton Barton, a brick house, (in photo below) was built in the eighteenth century over a well which was probably the main water supply for the old house which lies about twenty yards away. The well is actually a spring, and the cellars of the 'new' house are very damp.

---

[5] Sketch by Brian Blakeway (1920-2014)

More on Nicholas Lug, and the Lug family at Winkleigh has been derived from medieval Feet of Fines written in Latin on parchment with seals attached. They survive from the law offices of Coode and French Solicitors[6] of St Austell and can be dated 1216-1306. Nicholas Lug was most likely the leader (tithing man) of a tithing, originally a unit of ten households where the men stood security for each other when their tithing cleared the land and made an enclosure in the forest for their vill,[7] in this case at Luggeston. Recognition that Nicholas had successfully established the vill was made by Thomas de Lissors, who was perhaps his lord, when Nicholas was granted "the whole vill of Luggeston" for the sum of five shillings per year. The document is dated to the long reign of Henry111, but must be before 1238 for by then Nicholas was a juror, and jurors were invariably selected from property owners. As a juror, Nicholas would have been a member of a jury of presentment, a group that reviewed cases brought to its notice by the manor court.

Nicholas Lug seems to have died leaving Luggeston divided between two sons, Walter and Hugh Lug, and they too were almost certainly dead by the date of a second Feet of Fine, when Louisa Lug, daughter of Walter, conveyed to Nicholas son of Hugh Lug, all his right in the whole land of Luggeston which she held of Osbert de Liserne. This Nicholas Lug who was perhaps the grandson of the first Nicholas now held a reunited Luggeston. He is probably also the Nicholas named in two more feet of fines, perhaps dating to the reign of Edward1 (1272-1307). Three witnesses signed both documents, which suggests they were made in a comparatively short time of each other. Nicholas Lug gifts Richard de

---

[6] I am grateful to Mr Jim Luxon in San Diego California who has drawn my attention to these documents and freely discussed their significance with me.

[7] The term "vill" could be applied to a parish, a manor or tithing but a knowledge of Winkleigh's history makes tithing the most appropriate meaning here. Luxton lay in the parish of Winkleigh and was never a parish, likewise there was never a Luxton manor. Winkleigh appears to have been divided, not long after the Conquest, into two manors- Winkleigh Keynes and Winkleigh Tracey. At an early date too there was the manor of Hollacombe in Winkleigh.

Mileston 40 pence annually out of a tenement in Luggeston held by his brother Stephen and other lands there. Finally, Nicholas Lug conveys all his lands in Lugghesland to Richard, son of Richard de Mileston. In this way the Lugs gave up the lands of Luggeston to Richard de Mileston. In the fourteenth century, residents in the vill of Luggyston Winkleigh, adopted the surname Luggyston, the earliest spelling of the surname Luxton. Whether they were relatives of the original Lug family is unknown.

The fourteenth century, was a turbulent period in English history. The "mini" Ice Age in the 1300s caused a succession of major crop failures and widespread starvation. In addition in 1348-50, 1361 and in 1368-9 the Black Death wiped out perhaps three million people, nearly half of England's population. The sudden and over-whelming shortage of peasant labour gave those who survived an economic bargaining power unimaginable in previous centuries. Those who were left began to take advantage of the new opportunities for advancement which had opened up all around them. Survivors often relocated to places where they could obtain food or work.

Given the new mobility of labour and the enormous loss of life which had occurred, the rigid feudal structure was all but destroyed. Knowledge of neighbours and those in charge had gone. For all those wanting to be employed, or permitted to rent land, it was essential that they could be identified in the manor records. Thus what had been a trickle of surnames in 1200 had become a flood by 1400 to ensure clear identity. With the catastrophic fall in the number of people, many lords suffered a considerable decline in income and many cut losses by leasing out more of their estates to tenant farmers. The Peasants Revolt in 1381 reinforced the economic pressures, which led to the withering away of serfdom and the legal and social restrictions which went with it. The Luggystons at Winkleigh, along with others of the English peasantry, survived these tumults and the fourteenth and fifteenth centuries saw a period of slowly increasing prosperity for them.

Evidence for the Luggystons first substantial step up the property ladder is provided by a deed[8] made at East Luggyston on the Feast of the

---

[8] From the records of Coode & French.

Annunciation of the Blessed Virgin in the 9th year of HenryV(25March 1421).It refers to East Luggyston and Penston in the hundred of Wynkelegh, and to Walter and Roger Luggyston who were perhaps brothers born about 1400.East Luxton found on a nineteenth century map is now Luxton Barton.Penson is the next farm north of East Luxton.To the north of Penson lies Luxton Moor. The deed of 1421(in effect a will) is a complicated agreement, made between Roger Polerd of East Luggyston who lies ill "from the sickness", son and heir of Henry Polard, and Hugh Hyndeston, vicar of the parish church of Wynkelegh, to grant in fee, providing certain other provisions are met .....all Roger Polards property in East Luggyston to Roger Luggyston and his heirs for ever, with his property in Penston to Walter Luggyston and his heirs for ever.

Later documentation indicates that Roger Luggyston did in fact inherit East Luggyston in fee simple, for he is identified as the Roger Loggeston whose daughter and sole heir Joan married about 1450 to John Sawle of Penrice, a Cornish family. Their son Thomas Sawle of Polgrene, in the parish of St. Veep, Cornwall, a gentleman, in his will of 1511 identifies the property in Luggeston as part of his estates.

The male line of Roger Luggyston ended with his death when the property passed through his daughter Joan to the Sawle family in Cornwall.His brother Walter Luggyston, who by the terms of the 1421 deed, must have inherited Penson is the likely ancestor of the estimated thirty Luxtons who resided in Winkleigh in the first half of the sixteenth century. Their number included some substantial yeoman farmers by 1550.

Consequently, in the sixteenth century when the Reformation released the vast landed estates of the monasteries for sale, one branch of the family was able to purchase its share and make the step up into the gentry' class. In 1566, Barnard Luxton of Winkleigh, yeoman, purchased the manor of Hollacombe in Winkleigh and the manor of Abbotsham in the neighbouring parish of Brushford from Sir Amyas Paulet, who incidentally was the gaoler to Mary Queen of Scots when that ill-fated lady was imprisoned in England. Barnard was a prosperous farmer, who had accumulated the considerable sum of £400 to purchase the property, which before the Reformation had belonged to Hartland Abbey in north Devon. The Luxtons continued as lords at Brushford until early in the twentieth century and resided at Brushford Barton photographed here in 1904.

I have compiled family trees for the Luxtons at Winkleigh and Brushford, and elsewhere in Devon and further afield.

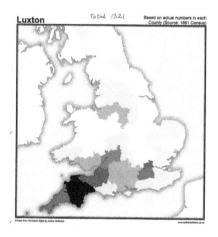

The original medieval spelling of the surname survived as late as the mid sixteenth century. A Latin deed dated 10th June 1552 granting lands for the maintenance of Winkleigh parish church, refers to Hugh, Bernard and Augustine Luggyston. The Winkleigh parish registers beginning in 1569 includes the present spelling "Luxton," but also offers Luxston (1586), Luxtone (1591), Luxstone (1594). As late as the middle of the nineteenth century, spelling was largely phonetic and enunciation, especially amongst the uneducated classes, far from perfect. This is why parish registers in eighteenth century Devon, taking Coldridge and Petton in Bampton, as random examples, contain the spelling "Luxen, Luxon". Indeed some branches, most notably in Cornwall and also at Clayhidon and Topsham in Devon, have retained the variant Luxon[9].

---

[9] At Petton the phonetic spelling Luxon first used in 1707 continued in usage until 1812 but Thomas Wood who was vicar of Bampton from early 1730s to early 1780s regularly spelt the name Luxen. The correct spelling Luxton first used in 1821 in the Petton baptismal register has continued to be used in entries since that date.

I founded the Luxton Family History Society in 1984 with the support and encouragement of the late Mr William John Luxton (1909-1992) of Guildford, who was descended from the Luxton family of Southmoor, Coldridge, a cadet branch of the Luxton squires at Brushford. Its aim is to promote research and the free exchange of information on the Luxton family. To advance the Society's aims, I write and edit a journal, "Time-Link", which I send out every Christmas. Since its first edition in 1984, Time-Link has proved a major success. In recent years its presentation has improved, thanks to the sterling work of the late Mr Alfred William Luxton (1920-1997) of Doncaster, and more lately by Mr Hubert Luxton.

1381 people surnamed Luxton are listed in the U.K. on the 1881 census. The distribution map reveals that the great majority still resided in Devon, but had spread throughout the South West, South of England, London, South Wales and the Midlands. Many too had emigrated to Britain's far flung Empire and the U.S.A.

I have compiled trees and written short narrative histories on many branches including the Luxtons at Winkleigh and Brushford, but this book is about my own branch of the Luxtons who lived at Frogpit Moor, in the hamlet of Petton in the parish of Bampton in Devon and I trace the family to the present day.

I will begin by describing a visit I made to Hutchings Farm, Frogpit Moor, Bampton, where my family story begins. This is an aerial view from the north c.1970.

3

HUTCHINGS FARM, FROGPIT MOOR, PETTON BAMPTON, DEVON.

When my brother Ian and I made our first visit in April 1971 to St. Petrock's Church Petton, in the parish of Bampton, we were disappointed that the tiny church surrounded by fields contained little of interest. It had been drastically rebuilt in 1847 in the neo-Romanesque style by over enthusiastic Victorian restorers. However, in the churchyard there were two surviving Luxton headstones. The oldest to Robert Luxton, a gunstock maker who died in 1831, was sited near the south west corner of the nave. The other headstone to John Luxton, of Forde Farm Cheriton Fitzpaine who died in 1906, lay near the northwest corner. We made rubbings of the epitaphs and took photographs of the headstones. Two medieval bells (in photograph) are visible in the gabled west end bell-cote above the rose window of the Church.

Mr Herbert Ellis, the churchwarden, impatiently played the organ while my brother Ian and I rummaged around in the vestry. Mr Coath, the vicar of Bampton, which includes Petton, and Mr Ellis said that the church registers only began in the 1920s, but at the bottom of an old iron chest, buried beneath a weight of jumbled books and papers, we triumphantly unearthed the ancient registers which commenced in the opening years of the eighteenth century. We carefully copied the numerous references to our family, including the burial in 1834 of our three times great grandfather Isaac Luxton, yeoman of Hutchings Farm.

At our request Mr Ellis led us to the north side of the churchyard where he pointed out the whitewashed shape of Hutchings in the valley below. A shaft of sunshine focused fleetingly on the farmhouse, as scudding clouds turned Frogpit Moor into a dappled patchwork of changing patterns. It was a mind branding moment which has left a permanent picture with me. I knew then that one day I would visit the farm.

My chance came at Whitsun two years later. I was staying at the Creech Castle Hotel and carrying out research in Taunton Record Office. The office closed at five on a fine sunny evening on Thursday 31st May 1973, when I decided to drive the seventeen miles to Petton. My nervous knock on the front door of Hutchings (photo above) was answered by Mrs Emily Needs in her working clothes and wellingtons. A dog was barking in the background. Despite this unpromising start I told Mrs Needs that my ancestor Isaac had lived at the farm. To my surprise she replied that she knew about Isaac and invited me into the living room. Turning to a sideboard, she brought out a large brown paper bag packed with the farm deeds and a copy of Isaac's Will. These she laid out on the table and with Mrs Needs chuckling at my excitement, I counted eight documents which directly related to my Luxton family who had resided at the farm for seven generations. The deeds spanned the years 1745 to 1912 and from them I was able to trace my descent from Robert Luxton and his wife Jane Daniell, who had married in the neighbouring parish of Clayhanger on the 28th August 1704.

Early the following morning, Friday 1st June, I returned to Hutchings and with Mrs Needs we took the property deeds into Taunton.

Mrs Needs did her shopping while the efficient staff at Taunton Record Office made photocopies of the documents. The comprehensive collection, which were in excellent condition, have been of paramount value in my efforts to compile a family tree and narrative history of the descendants of Robert Luxton, yeoman of Frogpit Moor, Petton, Bampton.

Hutchings was an attractive old property, which derived its name from Edward Hutchings, an early eighteenth century owner. Here is a photograph I took on its south side. When I visited it was a small holding of 5.51 acres, situated at Petton Cross, approximately six miles west of Wiveliscombe and four miles east of Bampton. The farmhouse, an eighteenth century stone building, had undergone little modernisation, although there was evidence it had incorporated some cob from an earlier structure. The exterior walls were partly whitewashed roughcast, with a slate and asbestos slate roof. On closer scrutiny I noted that the house was built of thousands of thin limestone slabs, excavated from the once numerous local Bampton quarries. Hutchings has the elements of the Devon longhouse, a building with accommodation for the farmer at one end and quarters for livestock at the other. Its design was a style favoured by peasant farmers in areas of small scale farming, above all in the poorer pastoral regions around the edges of Dartmoor and Exmoor. The family living quarters were

adjoined by a shippon (shelter) for animals and they were all placed under the one roof. In this way the bodies of the animals provided an additional source of heating for their human companions in winter. It also provided a greater security check on the livestock.

The ground plan, first revealed by the 1842 Bampton Tithe map, was an 'L' shape structure facing south, with the long wing of the L orientated on an east west line. It formed the main body of the house and was entered on the north side by a centrally placed front entrance, which opened into a small hall (1) giving access to the sitting room (2) on the south side of the house. The Needs, however, made greater use of the back entrance placed centrally on the south side[10]. This opened into a small square rear hall (3), from where a door on the left led to a pleasant living room (4) with views onto a lawn, with a large and productive vegetable garden. Another door on the right of the rear hall led to the sitting room (2), which had formerly been used as a kitchen.

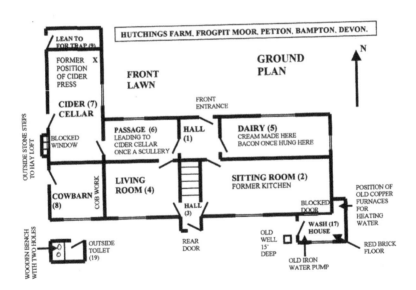

[10] Quite a few 16th or 17th century farm houses in the West Country were originally built to face north with their backs to the rain; but in the 18th or 19th centuries windows were inserted in the back wall so as to get the southern sun and a new front door was built to make the house face south. This accounts for the confusing arrangement of two front doors at Hutchings and leads me to suspect that part of the house might be of 17th century or earlier build. See Local History in England by W.G.Hoskins (1959) Page 126, published by Longmans, Green and Co. Ltd.

Both the living room and the sitting room had low ceilings and each possessed a door leading into a long passage room (5) and (6). The "passage room" (5) to the rear of the old kitchen had formally been used for hanging bacon. When Mr and Mrs Jim Needs became the owners in 1960, they found its floor was severely eroded by dripping salt from the bacon. They used this passage room (5) as a dairy and when I first visited, Mrs Needs generously gave me a pound of clotted cream to take home.

The passage room (6) entered from the living room had once been a scullery and on the left a door led off to the former cider house or cellar (7).

This brings us to the west side of the house, where a shorter north projecting wing gave the property its L shape plan. At ground level this consisted of a cow barn (8) and the old cider house (7).

The barn was entered on the outside by a west facing door, with a round headed archway. On the day of my first visit I watched as Mr Needs drove his two Guernsey and two Jersey cows into the barn for the night. The old cider cellar, or cider-house, in a room on the north  side of the barn, was also entered by an outside door on the west side of the house. The Needs chopped up the old cider press they found there for firewood. A lean-to building known as the 'Old Trap House (See photo) (9), rested against the north side of the cellar. It had a double folding wooden door and was used as a garage by the Needs, who found the old farm trap kept there when they moved in. They sold the trap and another link with the Luxtons left the farm.

The upstairs bedrooms were reached by a staircase of twelve steps in the rear hall (3). They opened out on a large hall landing (10), from where four doors led to four bedrooms and a box-room. The south facing bedrooms afforded fine panoramic views across the undulating hills of the Devon and Somerset border country, where fields formed a

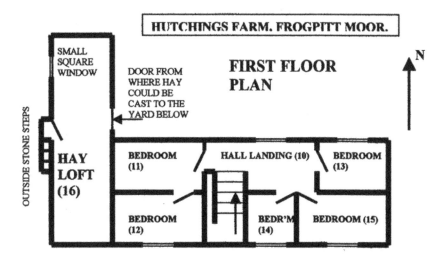

patchwork quilt of ploughed red soil and green pasture. On the day of my first visit a chorus of evening birdsong twittered a tranquil welcome, on a scene that would have been all too familiar to my ancestors.

A flight of external stone steps led up to the hay loft (16), which extended the length of the building above the cow barn and cider cellar. The stone steps were a later addition because they were built in front of a ground floor window in the cider cellar and blocked out most of its light.

Other evidence of structural alteration was in the cow barn, where the internal wall adjoining the living room revealed blocked up fire places, doors and windows. This wall was made of cob (that is clay gravel and straw), which was very old and indicated that the house incorporated an earlier building on the site. The photograph on right (next page) shows the barn's round headed archway entrance and external steps to the hay loft door, while the picture above shows the door where hay was cast down to the yard below.

A wash house (17) was built onto the south east corner of Hutchings during the nineteenth century. It is not marked on the 1842 Bampton

tithe map, but is clearly visible by
the date of the 1890, twenty five
inch to one mile, map of the area.
When Mr and Mrs Needs arrived
in 1960 a doorway linked the
wash house to the kitchen. They
blocked the doorway and converted
the kitchen into a sitting room.

Old copper furnaces used for
heating water were still in the
corner of the wash house, (in photograph below), but the Needs
removed them. Numerous square
cupboard holes, sunk into the internal stone walls of the washhouse,
were probably coeval with its construction. At the time of my visit,
the floor of the washhouse was
made of the original red brick, but
it was much worn. An old dilapi-
dated iron pump which stood in a
corner, was formerly used to pump
water from an outside well into a
sink. The well, (18) fifteen feet
deep, was situated outside the
washhouse and was full of water

when I looked into it. It was covered at ground level by a modern
iron cover with 'sunk in' hand grips. The water it supplied was
polluted, however, and the Needs sank a new well, twenty one feet
deep, at the top of the old apple orchard on the north west side of the
house. I found this old orchard particularly interesting as Isaac bequeathed
it in 1834 to his son Jacob Luxton, my great-great grandfather. It is
marked on the tithe map and more clearly on the 1890 25 inch to one
mile map. The quarter acre walled garden to the rear of the farm house
was used by the Luxton family as a vegetable plot and herb garden,
with the farm supplying its own meat, poultry, eggs, cheese, milk,
honey, apples and herbs. The Luxtons lived off their own resources
using money to purchase the few things they could not produce themselves. In the nineteenth century a line of fir trees were planted in the

hedged lane approach to Hutchings and they are indicated on the 1890 25 inch to one mile map.

The outside toilet placed in the garden near the south west corner of the house, was due for demolition at the time of my visit. It was a primitive structure, comprising a long wooden seat with two round holes cut into it so that people could sit side by side!

To the west of the west wing, and running parallel to its full length, lay a single storey stone outbuilding which appeared contemporary with the farm house. The eave of this outbuilding was overhanging on its west side by between eighteen inches to two feet, creating a sheltered corridor. I was fascinated by this feature, and Mr Needs explained that in former times it was used as a "pig-run". The Needs cat, captured in the photograph below sits in front of the old "pig-run," whilst an old apple tree in "Jacob's orchard" bears fruit.

I took a reel of coloured slides of the farmhouse and its outbuildings. I am thankful that I did, for on a later excursion in 1989 I discovered that new owners had drastically altered Hutchings and destroyed much of its distinctive character. The small front with its lawn and flower borders had survived intact, but the large rear garden comprising a level lawn and productive vegetable patch, enclosed by a substantial stone and grass embankment, had been swept away. Its place had been taken by a sunken lawn, which ignored the contours of the house and the land, while the stone and grass embankment had been replaced by trees which did not blend in with the rather austere style of the old house. The main building had also been modernised, with a "granny flat" on its west wing. The expensive facelift gave it the appearance of a prosperous newly built house on the outskirts of a town. The house and garden had been denuded of their quaint regional charm and the distinctive rural setting had been ignored.

In the pages which follow I write about the lives of the Luxtons who lived at Hutchings Farm and their other dwellings on Frogpit Moor, tracing their Luxton descendants to our own time. Below Hutchings is marked on the 25 inch to one mile map of 1890.

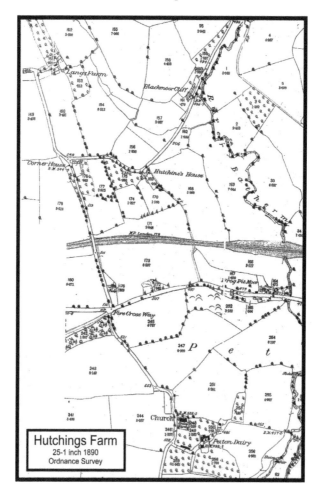

Hutchings Farm
25-1 inch 1890
Ordnance Survey

4

ROBERT LUXTON (C.1664/69-1751) OF FROGPIT MOOR, PETTON, BAMPTON

See tree 1

My branch of the Luxton family descends from humble yeoman stock, bearing neither coat of arms nor title. The family history begins with Robert Luxton and Jane Daniell who married at St. Peter's Church, Clayhanger, on Monday the 28th August 1704.

Clayhanger, which lies 26 miles from Winkleigh, as the crow flies, is the earliest known home of my Luxtons. It is a parish of rolling hills and many little lush combes, set in the rural landscape on Devon's north eastern border with Somerset. The 14th century tower of St. Peter's, the parish church, can be seen from miles away. Together with the 16th century manor house of Nutcombe, it nestles in a beautiful secluded valley some 800 feet above sea level.

Inside the church some of the most striking features are the 16th century carved pew-ends, which must have been familiar to Robert and Jane. They include a man with a trident and a harpy (a mythical monster with a woman's head and body, with bird's wings and claws). Behind the altar is part of the old rood screen and there is also an old oak alms box. The Norman font is built of Ham stone, while the church itself is built from hard grey limestone.The priest who celebrated Robert and Jane's marriage, or perhaps his parish clerk, entered their names phonetically in the register, "Robert Luxon and Jane Danell", a spelling which has preserved for us the unmistakable burr of their deep Devon accent.

Robert and Jane are my five times great grandparents. A Jane, baptised at Clayhanger on the 11th April 1675, the daughter of Robert and Hannah Daniell, who was buried on the 5th November the same year, was in all likelihood an elder sister to Jane Daniell who married Robert Luxton. Robert Daniell listed among the "Poor of Clayhanger," who paid on only one hearth in the 1674 Hearth Tax Returns for Clayhanger, must have been Jane's father. There is no reference to the Luxon/Luxton family in surviving records for seventeenth century Clayhanger, including the 1674 Hearth Tax.

Robert Luxton, his wife Jane and their young family, settled in the neighbouring hamlet of Petton in the parish of Bampton sometime in or before 1707. There are no references to the Luxton family in the surviving seventeenth century records for Bampton, and it seems that Robert was born and grew up elsewhere in Devon. The migration of labour at harvest was a common feature of the rural economy. It seems likely that Robert came to the district at the end of the 17th century in search of seasonal work. There he met and married Jane Daniell, a local girl and stayed to make a living in the locality.

William Henry Luxton (1893-1986), ironmonger in Wellington, Somerset, who descended from a senior line of our family, believed the Luxtons in Petton had originated in Rackenford. He may be right. Examination of parish registers in a twelve mile radius centred on Petton, reveals only one Luxton family living in the second half of the seventeenth century. These were the Luxtons residing at Puddington and its neighbouring parish of Rackenford, which lies high and remote in mid north Devon.

As he married in 1704, Robert Luxton, the founder of the Petton branch, was probably born within ten years either side of 1674. Unfortunately our knowledge of the Luxtons at Rackenford is incomplete, for pages have been cut out of the seventeenth century

Rackenford register. There is a suggestion that the register was called in by the Bishop of Exeter, who for some reason removed the pages. The strange jumble of letters before the removed pages may be the clue to why they were removed. Could it be they were a wizard's conjurations? The deficiency in the Rackenford registers is not wholly made up by the Bishops Transcripts, where the Easter returns for some vital years are found wanting. A further blow to research was struck on the 4th May 1942 when the Germans blitzed Exeter, in what has been nicknamed the "Baedecker Raids" after the famous guide book to places of architectural and historic significance. The probate registry containing six hundred years of private and public history, including Luxton family wills, lay in ashes. Another source which could have provided Robert Luxton's pedigree and other valuable information about him was destroyed.

A Robert Luxton and his wife Agnes were raising a family at Puddington and Rackenford at the very time Robert Luxton of Petton is believed to have been born, ten years either side of 1674. They buried a son Robert in 1664 at Puddington and baptised and buried a son Samuel at Rackenford in 1670. To give two sons the same name when the first died, was customary in our Petton family and it is highly likely that the Rackenford Luxtons had a second son, Robert, baptised sometime between 1664 and 1670 at either Puddington or Rackenford. Unfortunately the Rackenford register is defective for the years I think Robert was baptised there[11].

If my supposition is correct, Robert Luxton c.1664/69-1751 of Petton was the son of Robert Luxton and his wife Agnes. Robert Luxton senior was born in 1623 the son of George Luxton (churchwarden of Rackenford in 1631) and his wife Joan Frost, whom he married at Puddington in 1619. The Christian names of George Luxton's children, Thomazine, Robert, Jane, Frizwell, Mary, George and Beaton, indicate

---

[11] The rural population in Devon was very mobile at all times. In rural parishes, three families out of five disappear from their original villages within a hundred years and more than four in five disappear in the space of two hundred years. Most of these families seldom go far. We find that we pick them up again within a radius of five to ten miles of the place from which they started. Rackenford at a ten mile radius from Frogpit Moor is just on the outer ten miles limit. See W.G.Hoskins "Local History of England" (1959) P.49, published by Longmans.

a kinship with the Luxtons at Winkleigh. George may be the George Luxton baptised at Winkleigh in 1586 the son of Thomas Luxton.

If my hypothesis is correct, the Luxton family at Clayhanger and Petton originated in late sixteenth century Winkleigh, where they had begun in the early fourteenth century. From Winkleigh they moved with George Luxton to early seventeenth century Puddington and were settled in Rackenford in the middle years of the 1600s, from where a family member, Robert Luxton, moved to Clayhanger and Petton in the opening years of the eighteenth century.

I must stress that the foregoing is speculative, however, and Robert Luxton may have arrived in Clayhanger in the early eighteenth century from one of the other Luxton families in north Devon. One thing is apparent, Robert had received elementary schooling in his youth, for he signs deeds and other documents Robert Luxon, the phonetic spelling of his name which indicates he spoke in a strong Devon dialect. It is also evident that Robert and Jane had begun their family before their marriage. A son William was baptised at Clayhanger on the 15th December 1704, just over three months following their wedding, and six months after the marriage a son, John, was baptised there on 1st March 1705. These facts indicate William was illegitimate and that Jane was pregnant with John at the time of her marriage to Robert Luxton[12].

Robert and Jane settled with their young family sometime in the years 1705 to 1707 in the hamlet of Petton in the parish of Bampton, four miles from the market town. The couple had at least nine children, seven boys and two girls. William, the eldest son baptised at Clayhanger on the 15th December 1704, was buried at St. Petrock's Church in Petton Lane (in photograph) on the 6th July 1707. There is also no further record of a John baptised at Clayhanger on the 1st March 1705

---

[12] In spite of the fact that 'pre-nuptual fornication' was an offence punishable in the Archdeacon's Court there was a customary assumption among the peasantry that a contract to marry- an appraisal, a troth plight, a handfasting as it was called in some localities (what we would term an engagement) meant that freedom to copulate did not have to await the conclusion of a church marriage. Brides in Devon at this time must normally have gone to their weddings in the early and sometimes late stages of pregnancy. See Peter Laslett's, "The World We have Lost", Methuen and Co. Ltd, Second Edition 1971, Page 150.

and a second William baptised at Petton on the 24th June 1709, so it seems likely that they too died in childhood.

Their daughter Mary (1707-1766) baptised at Petton on the 26th October 1707, was the only one of their first four children to live to adulthood. A deed dated 27th November 1770 records that her father bequeathed her, "All that the Easter part or dwelling house together with the Garden Orchard and Appurtenances there unto belonging" at New House Tenement, Petton. Mary Luxon of Bampton, married James Blackmore at Clayhanger Devon, on the 16th June 1754. One of the witnesses was Joseph Luxon the bride's brother. Mary had married late in life, so there were no children and as Mary Blackmore she was buried at Petton on the 9th May 1766.

Robert is not recorded as owning land at Petton until 1738 and in the early years of his marriage the family may have moved to neighbouring parishes in search of work. Consequently the baptism of more of Robert and Jane's children may be recorded in parishes close to Petton. This may be the case with their sons Robert c.1710 and Abraham, who on an analysis of evidence in the Road Surveyor's Account Book for Bampton was possibly born c.1712. It is interesting too, that the children born later in the marriage were given Old Testament names. Abraham (c.1712-1782) was followed by Jacob (1715?-1759), whose baptism is almost certainly entered erroneously in the Bampton register,

27

"Jacob son of James and Joan Luxen baptised on the 25th March 1715". The name Jacob may have been chosen by Jane Daniell's side of the family, for Jacob was a popular Christian name in seventeenth century Clayhanger where it is recorded six times in the 1641/2 Protestation Returns. It is a Christian name found rarely among the Luxtons outside of the Petton branch of the family. Robert and Jane had a daughter Sarah, baptised at St. Michael's parish church, Bampton on Ash Wednesday 15th February 1716. Sarah was forty when she married Michael Wilson of Sampford Peverell at Bampton on the 3rd August 1756. The couple settled in Sampford Peverell, where Michael was buried on the 6th April 1766 and Sarah was buried on the 30th July 1773. Joseph (1719-1791), Robert and Jane's youngest son, was baptised at Bampton on the 5th June 1719.

With a growing family to feed, Robert and Jane struggled to pay their way, a fact revealed by the Bampton Churchwardens' accounts dated between 1712 and 1809[13]. They contain a reference in 1723 to Robert Luxton receiving five shillings from a charitable fund, known as Mr Mogridges Gift. This shows that the Luxtons were numbered among the deserving poor within the parish at this date.

1723 Mar 29th: "Mr Mogridges Gift distributed" by the two churchwardens "Robt Luxen: 5sh."

At some time in the mid 1730s there was a dramatic change in Robert's economic and social position in the parish when he purchased land at Frogpit Moor, Petton, which was to remain in his family for seven generations until the early twentieth century. The Bampton Pound Tax Book and Poor Rate (1708-1738) reveal that Frogpit Moor was in the possession of various other owners until at least the early 1730s. A reference in the Devon freeholders' annual return of 1738, as Robert Luxton yeoman of Bampton, indicates he owned land there by that date. Details of his purchase are wanting. Copies of earlier "deeds Evidences and Writings touching or concerning" the Cottage-house called Hutchings on Frogpit Moor,[14] which would clarify details of the purchase, and

---

[13] Devon Record Office:Bampton Parish Churchwardens Accounts1712-1809(1269A/PW1).
[14] Deeds examined at Hutchings Farm in 1973.

which Robert agreed to make available to his son Jacob by an indenture dated the 9th May 1745, are unfortunately no longer extant.

Confirmation for Robert's improved status comes from a search of the Bampton Constables Accounts between 1712 and 1781, which contain a reference to "Robert Luxon" authorising the Clothing Accounts for the Poor in the years 1737-1738.[15] This shows that within the fourteen years between 1723 and 1737, Robert Luxton had changed from being a recipient of charity to becoming part of the parish yeomanry who controlled local affairs. At this distance in time it would be difficult to establish how Robert had worked this transformation in his fortunes, but it's possible he inherited money through a relative's will.

The Bampton Workhouse Monthly Account Book 1732-1743[16] contain further references to Robert Luxon which reveal he was considered a trustworthy person, who had a useful contribution to make in his local community. It was the practice in the old Julian style calendar to end the year on the 24th March[17]. Robert was one of four people who examined the accounts for 1737 and he wrote the accounts himself in July, October, November and again in February and March 1737. The accounts for the year were finally completed on the 2nd April 1738, when it is recorded – Paid "Mr P.Badcocks and Mr Robert Luxons Bill: 8sh 4d". Robert Luxon signed the accounts.

There is a reference dated 1730 in the Bampton Churchwardens' Accounts[18] to a Frogpit Moor seat made within the new gallery in the parish church. It was almost certainly the seat in Bampton church that Robert and future generations of the family would have occupied on Sundays.

---

[15] Devon Record Office Bampton Parish Constable Accounts 1712-1781(PC1).
[16] Devon Record Office Bampton Parish Overseers of the Poor Monthly Account Books 1732-1823(PO 8-13)
[17] Until 1st January 1752 the year began on Lady Day, the 25th March and ended on the 24th March. An Act of Parliament replaced this old Julian Calendar by the Gregorian Calendar first introduced in 1582 by Pope Gregory X111. This was more accurate than the Julian Calendar but was eleven days ahead of it. To bring Britain into line, it was necessary to decree that the next day after the 3rd September 1752 would be the 14th September. So 1751 had only approximately nine months, starting on the 25th March and ending on the 31st December, and 1752 was eleven days short!
[18] Devon Record Office Bampton Churchwardens Accounts 1712-1809(PW1)

1730: "A Scheme for ascertaining the Rights of the Sittings in the Gallery lately erected in the Parish Church of Bampton"
"South Row seventh seat:6, Frogpits Moor: 1d"

The gallery was built in 1730 across the west end of the nave and box pews were installed when the rood screen was moved into the chancel arch. During a thorough restoration in the late 19th century, the gallery was taken down and the box pews went out and were replaced by the benches still in use today.

Roads in Tudor England were supposed to be maintained by the parishes through which they passed. The Highways Act of 1555 made each parish responsible for repairing its own roads, each parishioner being required to spend four days (later six days) a year on this task, under the direction of a surveyor appointed each year by election or rotation. This 'statute labour' was unpopular and in later years fines or compositions were paid in lieu from which the surveyor made payments to hired road workers for digging gravel, picking stones, filling in ruts and so forth. This system of road maintenance continued well into the eighteenth century.

Bampton, market town on the southern fringe of Exmoor, lay at the start of the eighteenth century, on the pack horse route along which Irish wool and other produce came from the port of Minehead on its way to Tiverton and Exeter. This north to south route which crossed the Batherm, a tributary of the River Exe, was met at the river crossing by another ancient trading route between Taunton in the east and Barnstaple in the west. The roads were kept in repair as they passed through Bampton and we learn more of Robert's activities from the Road Surveyors Account Book for the parish, which runs from 1735 to 1761.[19] In 1735 "Robert Luxon" paid 3 shillings and he paid the same amount every year after that until his death, excepting 1741 and 1742 when he did not pay and 1747 when he paid 2 shillings. He signs his name "Robert Luxon" in the account book on 26th December 1740 when taking office as one of the three surveyors "of the Highways for

---

[19] Devon Record Office Bampton Surveyors of Highways Rates & Accounts1735-1261(1269A/PS1)

the Burrough and parish of Bampton." This was a position that ended for the year on 26th December 1741.

Robert as waywarden or surveyor of Highways was an official holding an office to which only persons of property were appointed, as he was required to be the owner of an estate of £10 within the parish, or an occupier to the yearly value of £30. The surveyor's job was an unpopular one, as he was supposed to receive no payment for his year's work which was demanding in its nature. Robert was appointed in Christmas week by a warrant from the justices. His first duty was to interview his predecessor in office, taking over any cash balances and learning how the accounts were kept. Three times a year he had to view the roads and present their condition to the nearest justice. His duties included looking out for vehicles with more than the statutory number of horses, attending the highways sessions, the fixing of days when statute labour was to be performed and the supervising of his fellow parishioners in their road repairing duties. He had to collect all commutations and compositions and report all defaulters to the nearest justice. In many parishes the waywarden had the care of the parish bull, but Robert appears to have been mercifully spared this extra chore!

Annual returns of Devon freeholders were compiled in Registers from jurors' lists at the Michaelmas Sessions from 1711 to 1807. Robert Luxton, yeoman of Bampton, is listed for the years 1738, 1739, 1741, 1742, 1743 (spelt as Luxon) 1744, 1745.[20]

The Historic Bampton (Devon) Fair.

In north Devon while some corn was grown, mostly rye and oats, which was used to provide black bread and small beer until about 1800, the rolling landscape was best suited to sheep farming. In the late Middle Ages, the introduction of better breeds of sheep with finer fleeces produced abundant wool used in Devon's largest industry, the production of the coarse ribbed cloth known as kersey or 'Devon Dozen,' made by the cottagers in their homes.

---

[20] Devon Freeholders Returns in Devon Record Office

In the early eighteenth century, Bampton grew in importance as a market town known for its sheep fairs and its name was celebrated in a breed of sheep known as Bampton Notts. Robert and his sons at Frogpit Moor, because of their proximity to Bampton, were almost certainly involved in rearing sheep. Indeed, by the late 1700s the town's October fair was the largest in the West Country and in the peak years 14000 sheep were sold annually. Pigot's Directory 1844 states, "The vicinity of Bampton is remarkably pleasant; the land is in fine agricultural state, rather hilly, but exceedingly productive. The sheep fed in the neighbourhood are remarkable for their size, and large numbers are sold at the Bampton fairs." During the nineteenth century, however, the sale of sheep dramatically declined as the wool and cloth trade waned, but by then the Luxtons were breeding and dealing in cattle.

Robert and Jane were married for over 46 years when Jane Luxen died and was buried at St.Petrock's Church, Petton on the 23rd November 1750. Robert must have been heart broken and did not long survive his spouse's death, for within two months the Petton registers record the burial of Robert Luxen on the 14th January 1751.

The will of Robert Luxton, proved in 1751, was destroyed in May 1942 when the Germans blitzed Exeter. The destruction of the will is a grievous loss to our family archive, as much vital information has been obliterated. Fortunately, the Bampton Tithe Map and apportionment made in 1842,[21] over ninety years after Robert's demise reveals important information on his land holding, despite the passage of nearly a century. His Luxton descendants held 19 acres, 7 rods and 36 poles at Petton, all of which (save 3 acres and 2 rods) made one compact parcel of land, measuring 16 acres and 5 rods at Frogpit Moor. It may be reasonably argued that this land divided amongst Robert's descendants in 1842 had originally formed Robert's holding at Petton. Earlier documentation, the Land Tax Assessments for Petton which run annually from 1780 to 1832 confirm this idea of Frogpit Moor being subdivided among Robert's descendants for many of the tax entries simply refer to "The Luxons for Frogpit Moor".[22]

---

[21] Devon Record Office Bampton Tithe Map and apportionment 1842.
[22] Devon Record Office Bampton Land Tax Assessments1780-1832

Fortunately, Robert's bequest to his daughter Mary, already quoted, has been preserved in a deed dated 27th November 1770 which in July 1989 was in the possession of Mr Maurice Hawkins at Venn Farm, Waterrow, Chipstable.[23] Mr and Mrs Gathercole, the then owners at Hutchings Farm,[24] possessed other Luxton deeds including two dated the 8th and 9th May 1745. These earliest deeds are interesting because they reveal that Robert Luxton, husbandman, sold for £30 about 4 acres of his land at Frogpit Moor centred on Hutchings Farm, to his son Jacob Luxton husbandman. In this way Robert, who was probably too old to work, ensured an income from the purchase money. It is likely that he disposed of other parcels of his land at Petton to his sons Abraham and Joseph to raise further money for his old age, but details of these transactions are wanting.

Robert, who I believe was his eldest surviving son, returned to live in Petton in 1751 to inherit his father's property. When this second Robert died in 1792, the property passed in turn to his son Robert, the gunstock maker, who lived at Box Hedge, Frogpit Moor, which may originally have been his grandfather Robert Luxton's home too.

Sadly a visit I made in April 1971 to St. Petrock's Church, failed to indicate Robert and Jane's burial place, because no monumental inscription has survived. However, Robert and Jane are the ancestors of an extensive branch of the Luxton family, which has contributed its ample share of characters and enterprising pioneers. In the pages which follow I have striven to chronicle the history of these people who are my family.

---

[23] Consulted by the author in July 1989
[24] The Gathercoles succeeded the Needs as owners of Hutchings Farm

5

FOUR BROTHERS, HUSBANDMEN AT FROGPIT MOOR, PETTON, BAMPTON ROBERT (C.1710-1792), ABRAHAM (C.1712-1782), JACOB (1715?-1759), JOSEPH LUXTON (1719-1791).

See Tree 1

Robert Luxton, husbandman and his wife Jane Daniell who married at Clayhanger, Devon on the 28th August 1704, had at least nine children. There were seven boys, William (1704), John (1705), a second William (1709), Robert (c1710?) Abraham (1712?), Jacob (1715?) Joseph (1719) and two daughters, Mary (1707) and Sarah (1716).

William the eldest son, baptised at Clayhanger on the 15th December 1704, was buried at Petton, on the 6th July 1707 and as there is no further record of John baptised at Clayhanger on the 1st March 1705 and the second William, baptised at Petton on the 24th June 1709 it seems likely that they too died in childhood.

Robert and Jane who first settled at Petton sometime in the years 1705-1707, may have moved to other parishes in the area in search of work, but by the 1740s Robert had aquired over 19 acres of land at Petton. His four remaining sons, Robert, Abraham, Jacob and Joseph, survived their father as husbandmen at Frogpit Moor where the Land Tax Assessments record the "Luxons themselves" collectively paid the tax.

ROBERT LUXTON (C.1710-1792), HUSBANDMAN OF FROGPIT MOOR

Robert Luxton son of Robert Luxton and Jane Daniell, is a shadowy figure. This is because of the paucity of surviving records. I have no record of his baptism but believe he was the eldest of four sons who survived their parents to inherit Frogpit Moor. My hunch is, that like his brother Abraham he was possibly born in the years 1710-1715.

Robert had a son.The Bampton Surveyors of Highways Rates and Account Book states that "Robert Luxon and son paid to the surveyors 3sh..0d" in 1779[25].In that same year, the son Robert Luxton (1744-1831), the gunstock maker of Box Hedge Petton, was named Robert Luxon Junior of Frogpit Moor when Mary Bowden, a poor child, was apprenticed to him[26].

Further evidence for the existence of Robert Luxton comes from the Bampton Land Tax Assessments, which in the years 1780-1781 record the tax was paid by "Joseph and Robt Luxons etc Frogpit Moor". It was either Robert or his son Robert Luxton junior who signed his name "Robt Luxon" as a Land Tax Collector in 1785.

The Bampton Surveyors of Highways Rates and Accounts 1735-1761 and 1762-1816,[27] which record payments made towards the maintenance of the borough's roads contain a wealth of information on the activities of the Luxton's at Frogpit Moor in the eighteenth century. In the years 1735 to 1750 there is repeated reference to payments made to Robert's brothers Abraham, Jacob and Joseph for their maintenance work on the roads, but there is no mention of Robert himself being paid for such tasks. However, from 1751 the year his father died, Robert is often paid for carrying out various maintenance tasks on the roads in the Petton area. The omission of Robert's name in the years 1735-1750 is evidence enough that he was living elsewhere during this time, and the repeated references to him after 1751 is proof that he had returned home to reside at Frogpit Moor following the death of his father. I identify him as Robert Luxton who married Mary Pool (baptised 5th July1717) at St Michael's, Enmore, Somerset on the 20th June 1743. Their son Robert, baptised at Enmore on the 30th March 1744, became Robert Luxton (1744-1831) the gunstock maker who lived at Box Hedge on Frogpit Moor, and this too may have been the home Robert himself inherited in 1751 from his own father Robert Luxton (c.1664-1751) who first established the family on the moor in the early eighteenth century.

---

[25] D.R.O.Bampton Surveyors of Highways Rates and Accounts 1766-1804(1269A/P52)
[26] D.R.O. Apprentice Records.
[27] See D.R.O. Bampton Surveyors of Highways Rates and Accounts 1735-1761(1269A/P51) and 1762-1816(1269A/P52).

In 1751, his first year resident at Frogpit Moor, Robert paid a 4 shillings rate towards the up-keep of the Bampton Highways. He paid 1 shilling in 1755, 1756, 1759, 1760 and 1767 and one shilling and 6 pence in 1758, 2 shillings in 1752, 1753, 1757, 1761 to 1766, 1775 to1778 and 1780-1781, 3 shillings in 1754 (and with his son in 1779), 3 shillings and 6 pence in 1773 and 1782. Several men were needed to work on the road "near Robt Luxons" in October and December 1790 and this may be why he paid the surveyors the extra large sum of 10 shillings in 1791. One interesting record shown at the end of the Bampton Surveyors of Highways Rates and Accounts 1766-1816, was a list of occupiers that was unfortunately undated. It occurred, however, just after a section of receipts (dated between 1775 and 1781) that appeared at the end of this volume, separate from the disbursements for the same period. I have therefore tentatively given the year 1775 as the date for this list of occupiers. It includes a valuation of Robert's property:-

> Occupier: Robt Luxon
> Tenement: pt. Frogpit Moor
> Yearly value: £6..0sh..0d.
> Two 3rds value: £4..0sh..0d.
> Six days: 2sh..0d.

From 1751 onwards numerous payments were made to Robert Luxton for work he undertook in maintaining the Bampton highways. He was usually paid at the rate of 1 shilling and 2d a day for a variety of assignments, either working alone or with others. He was employed quarrying (called "drawing stones") around Petton at Rull in1757, Cornet Hill 1757, Hone 1759 and Dadiscombe in 1767. Other road building stints included, "drawing and spreading of stones", "beating rocks", "placing in the stone" and "laying in stones". Road drainage was improved by "laying in of wood & rounding the road", "let go the water from the rocks", "opening gutter holes". He was employed "to repair the road" or "mending the road". Another task was "cutting wallet and spreading stones". A wallet was a large bag used for carrying personal necessaries such as food on a journey. This and other references to wallet in the Bampton Highways accounts, suggests that roadside brushwood was cut and tied in faggots and packed into wallets for removal, perhaps as firewood. The photograph is of the lower quarry Cornet Hill.

The Petton burial register contains a final stark reference to Robert. "Robert Luxon was buried on the 19 October 1792"

Finally I enclose an extract of payments made to Robert for his work on the Bampton Highways:-

1751 Sep 4th: Paid "Robt Luxon and Thos Atkings laying in of wood and rounding the road": 2sh..4d.

Sep 6th: Paid "Thos Atkings, Robt Luxon, Jacob Luxon, James Tackel, John Southwood and John Blackmore 1 day in ye same road": 7sh..0d.

Sep 25th: Paid "James Hagly, Richd Melton and Robt Luxon rounding ye road in Petton Lane": 3sh..6d.

1754 June14th: Paid "Robt Luxon placing in the stone": 1sh..2d.

June 21st: Paid "Abm and Robt Luxon placing in ye stone": 2sh..4d.

Dec 6th : Paid "Robt Luxon, James Tatchel and James Hagly mending the road between Quartley Hill and Wey Down": 3sh..6d.

1755 Dec 8th: Paid "Robt Luxon laying in stones": 1sh..2d.

1756 June 2nd: Paid Robert Luxon for "placing in the stones": 1sh..0d.

1757 Mar 30th: Paid "Robt Luxon beating rocks in Quartly Lane": 1sh..2d.

Apr 2nd : Paid "Robt Luxon drawing stones at Rull": 1sh..2d.

Apr 3rd : Paid "Robt Luxon drawing stones at Cornet hill": 1sh..2d.

May 7th : Paid "Robt Luxon drawing stones at Cornet hill": 1sh..2d.

Dec 10th : Paid "James Hagley, Robt Luxon and Thos Stone drawing and spreading of stones": 3sh..6d.

Dec 12th : Paid "Henry Sulley, Robt Luxon and John Thorne drawing and spreading of stones": 3sh..6d.

1758 Nov 27th: Paid "Robt Luxon placing in of stones": 1sh..2d.

1759 Nov 15th: Paid "Abrm Luxon and Robt Luxon a day drawing stones at Hone": 2sh..4d.

1760 June 9th: Paid "Robt Luxon and James Hagly for working in the same road": 2sh..4d.

June 28th: Paid "Richd Melton, Robt Luxon and Abrm Luxon work in the same road": 3sh..6d.

1762 Oct 20th: Paid "Abram Luxon, Robt Luxon and John Thomas beating the rocks from Willm Cleeves up Cornwood Hill and let go the water from the rocks": 3sh..6d.

1763 Oct 13th: Paid "Robt Luxon cutting wallet and spreading stones between Hedge Mead End and Blackmores": 1sh..2d

1765 June 7th: Paid "to repair the road near Frogpit Moor towards Cornwood Hill: Edw Upham and Robt Luxon": 2sh..4d.

July 22nd : Paid "to repair the road between Doningstone Mill and Petton Chappell: Thos Hill, Edw Upham, Robert Luxon, John Thomas, John Southey and Thomas Atkins one day": 7sh.

July 23rd : Paid "to repair the road between Doningstone Mill and Petton Chappell: Edward Upham, Robt Luxon, Thos Atkins and John Thomas": 4sh..8d.

July 24th: Paid "to repair the road between Doningstone Mill and Petton Chappell: Edward Upham, Robt Luxon, Thos Hill and John Thomas": 4sh..8d.

July 25th : Paid "to repair the road between Doningstone Mill and Petton Chappell: Edward Upham, Robt Luxon, and Jas Hagley": 3sh..6d.

July 26th : Paid "to repair the road between Doningstone Mill and Petton Chappell: Edward Upham, Wm Sulley and Robt Luxon": 3sh..6d.

July 27th : Paid "to repair the road between Doningstone Mill and Petton Chappell: Rob[t] Luxon, Jas Hagley and John Southey": 3sh..6d.

July 29-30th: Paid "Rob[t] Luxon 2 days repairing the road between Tillet Bridge and Hayneridge": 2sh..4d.

Sept 13th: Paid "Rob[t] Luxon one day to repair the road from Mr Halls to Hedge Mead End": 1sh..2d

1766 Jan 14th: Paid "Abram Luxon, Rob[t] Luxon, John Southey and Elick Barrett repairing the road near Jos Luxons": 4sh..8d.

Nov 3rd : Paid "Rob[t] Luxon opening gutter holes from Petton Chappell towards Waterhouse": 1sh..2d.

1767: Mr Amos Pearse Disbursements:-

Mar 3rd: Paid "to repair the road between Petton Cross and Clayhanger Wood: Rob[t] Luxon, Henry Upham, Thos Hill and Benjamin Hill": 4sh..8d.

May 11th : Paid "Rob[t] Luxon and Geo Saunder drawing stones Dadiscombe": 2sh..4d.

July 18th : Paid "to repair the road at Blackmores Clift: Henry Upham, John Hawkins, Thos Hill and Rob[t] Luxon": 4sh..8d.

1779 Apr 24th: Paid "Rob[t] Luxon 3 days to repair near Frogpit Moor": 3sh..6d.

May 1st : Paid "Rob[t] Luxon 6 days to repair near Frogpit Moor": 7sh..0d.

May 8th : Paid "Rob[t] Luxon 6 days to repair near Frogpit Moor": 7sh..0d.

May 15th : Paid "Rob[t] Luxon 6 days to repair near Frogpit Moor": 7sh..0d.

May 22nd : Paid "Rob[t] Luxon 1 day to repair Stone Lane": 1sh..2d.

1790 Oct-Dec: Paid several men to work on road "near Rob[t] Luxons."

ABRAHAM LUXTON (c.1712-1782)
OF NEW HOUSE TENEMENT, PETTON, BAMPTON.

The Petton registers and Bishop's Transcipts have been imperfectly kept and preserved so that we do not have the baptism of Abraham. However, Mr Maurice Hawkins at Venn Farm, Waterrow, Chipstable in July 1989 possessed an indenture dated the 27th November 1770 which records that Abraham Luxon, husbandsman, living at the eastern part of New House Tenement, Petton, was a son of Robert.[28]

Abraham seems to have been the second eldest of Robert's four surviving sons. The Road Surveyor's Accounts for Bampton record Abraham Luxon paying 1 shilling towards the maintenance of the roads from the 26th December 1738. Abraham, together with his father Robert paid in each succeeding year and it was not until 1746 that they were joined by Abraham's brothers, Jacob and Joseph, in making these payments.

Abraham was perhaps born sometime between 1709 when a brother William was baptised at Petton but before 1716 when his sister Sarah was baptised at Bampton. It could be that the parents, Robert and Jane, who had not yet purchased property at Frogpit Moor, Petton, were temporarily residing and working in another parish in the vicinity in the years 1710-1715 and that Abraham's baptism is recorded there.

The indenture dated the 27th November 1770 in the possession of Mr Maurice Hawkins at Venn Farm records that Robert Luxton in his will proved in 1751 bequeathed his daughter Mary, baptised at Petton on the 26th October 1707, "All that the Easter part or dwelling house together with the Garden Orchard and Appurtenances there unto belonging" at New House Tenement, Petton. Mary before her death had granted the property to her brother Abraham Luxon (sic) husbandman at Petton. The indenture recites how Abraham's brother Joseph, in exchange for the New House Tenement entered into an agreement to pay Abraham and Mary "his now present wife" an annuity for life. This financial arrangement was a means of providing Abraham who was perhaps nearly ten years Joseph's senior with a small income in his old age.

---

[28] The author consulted this document in July 1989

Other valuable details are provided by the deed. Abraham and his brother Joseph are described as husbandmen which is information not recorded in other documentation. Husbandman was an extremely common description of men at this time because it was the description of what so many of them were engaged in, tending the animals and tilling the soil. Abraham signs the deed with a mark revealing that he was illiterate. This contrasts with his father Robert and younger brother Jacob who both boldly signed an indenture at Hutchings Farm, Petton in 1745 although they wrote their name Luxon in Devon dialect and not Luxton which is how the name is spelt by the more literate clerk drawing up the deed. It may be that because Abraham was one of the eldest surviving sons there was perhaps less money to provide him with an elementary education. Perhaps too the family were moving around working in different parishes in the years Abraham needed schooling.

Abraham Luxon of the parish of Bampton married Mary Upham in St James the parish church at Fitzhead Somerset on the 3rd June 1737[29]. There is no record of any children being baptised to the couple but a Mary Luxon of Bampton who married William Ashelford sojourner at Bampton on the 12th November 1761 was perhaps a daughter. She was too old to be the daughter of Abraham's younger brothers Jacob and Joseph. The fact too that Mary's husband, William Ashelford, later held Ashelford Plot[30], a part of the New House Tenement belonging to Abraham Luxton, gives added weight to the likelihood that Mary was indeed Abraham's daughter. William and Mary Ashelford had three children baptised at Petton beginning with Betty on the 6th November 1763, Isaac on the 7th August 1768 and Joseph on the 3rd March 1771. Mary's husband, William Ashelford was buried at Petton on the 11th February 1771.

It's tempting to think that an Abraham Luxton, sojourner, who married Hannah Hill at Wiveliscombe in 1799 and had a daughter Mary, was a son to Abraham Luxton but I have been unable to make a link.

---

[29] Fitzhead is almost part of Taunton today. A Mary Upham was baptised 5th Februa ry 1709/10 at Trull, Taunton daughter of Robert and Mary Upham or Mary baptised 10th July 1712 daughter of Walter, a blacksmith and Margaret Upham
[30] Ashelford's Plot was the site on which a house named Frogmore was built in 1858.

More knowledge of Abraham's activities is gleaned from reading the Bampton Surveyors of Highways Rates and Account Books covering the years 1735-1816. There we learn that 1s 2d was Abraham's usual rate of pay for a day's labour on the highways. Today Doddiscombe is the name of a farm which includes the site of an old quarry (in photograph) situated on the hill not far from St. Petrock's Church, Petton. The old quarry comes to life again in the account books where we read Abraham Luxon was paid 1sh...2d for "drawing stones" from "Dadiscombe Quarry" on the 30th April 1751 and he received the same sum for repeating the task on the 4th and 7th of June that year. He was employed in 1758 in quarrying ("drawing stones") in two other quarries in Petton, Little Rull and Hone. Other chores he undertook were "carrying stones & repairing the roads" "placing in of stones" & "spreading the gravel". He was hired to make improvements to road drainage. This included "rounding ye road" "making a drain and leveling ye road", "diging a new drain" "clensing the drains and gutter holes", "spreading stones and opening gutter holes" & "beating rocks... and let go the water from the roads".There were one-off jobs to fulfil. In 1754 he received payment for "carrying away a horse that fell in the road at Frogpit Moor" and in 1757 he "spent a day about Batherm Bridge" where he helped his brother Joseph to repair it.

Abraham Luxon (sometimes spelt Luxen) contributed his share in making payments to maintain the highways as they passed through Bampton. As I noted earlier he first paid the surveyor 1 shilling on the 26th December 1738 and he paid the same amount in the years 1739 to 1750, 1755, 1756, 1759, 1760 and 1767. He paid 1 shilling and 6d in 1754 & 1758 and 2 shillings in 1751, 1757, 1761 to 1766.

I conclude with a record of the labouring assignments fulfilled by Abraham in maintaining the highways as they passed through Bampton in the years 1747-1766 together with the payments he received:-

1747 Nov 2nd: Paid "Abra Luxon, Jos Luxon, Thos Actkings and John Crookham carrying stones and repairing the roads at Bampton Down, Dypfordown and Shillingford Lane": 7sh..2d.

1748 Sep 5th: Paid "Abrm Luxon, Jos Luxon, Thos Actkings and Jacob Luxon drawing stones at Dadiscombe Quarry and repairing the roads at Petton Lane and Frogpit Moore": 4sh..8d.

1751 Apr 30th: Paid "Abrm Luxon drawing stones Dadiscombe Quarry": 1sh..2d.

June 4th: Paid "Abrm Luxon one day drawing stones Dadiscombe Quarry": 1sh..2d.

June 7th: Paid "Abrm Luxon drawing stones Dadiscombe Quarry": 1sh..2d. (The photograph shows a close up of Doddiscombe Quarry.)

Aug 5th: Paid "Abrm Luxon making a drain in and leveling ye road from Hayne Ridge to the Water": 1sh..2d.

Aug 8th: Paid "Richard Melton and Abrm Luxon rounding ye road in Petton Lane": 2sh..4d.

1753 June 29th: Paid "Thos Stone and Abrm Luxon repairing the lane by Petton Chappel": 2sh..4d.

1754 June 21st: Paid "Abrm and Robt Luxon placing in ye stone": 2sh..4d.

Dec 6th: Paid "Abrm and Jacob Luxon clensing the drains and gutter holes from Frogpit Moor to Batherham Bridge yt leads to Radington": 2sh..4d.

Dec 10th: Paid "Abrm Luxon for carrying away of a horse that fell in the road at Frogpitt Moor": 1sh..2d.

1756 May 17th: Paid "Abr Luxon placing in of stones at Frogpitt Moor": 1sh..0d.

Dec 4th: Paid "Abrm Luxon for 2 days drawing stones near Little Rull": 2sh..0d.

1757 Feb 10th: Paid "Abrm Luxon a day about the bridge": 1sh..2d. (His brother Joseph with the aid of 2 horses was paid 2sh..6d the same day for carrying stones to repair Batherm Bridge).

1758 June 16th: Paid "William Webber, Abrm Luxon and Jos Luxon drawing stones at Little Rull": 3sh..6d.

June 24th: Paid "Abrm Luxon and Hum Honey Ball drawing stones at Little Rull": 2sh..4d.

1759 Nov 15th: Paid "Abrm Luxon and Robt Luxon a day drawing stones at Hone": 2sh..4d.

1760 June 20th: Paid "Abrm Luxon and John Thomas for "repairing the road at Frogpitt Moor": 2sh..4d.

June 28th: Paid "Richard Melton, Robt Luxon and Abrm Luxon work in the same road": 3sh..6d.

1761 Oct 9th: Paid "John Thomas and Abrm Luxon spreading stones and opening gutter holes": 2sh..4d.

Nov 4th: Paid "Abrm Luxon opening gutter holes from Hayn Beach towards Bampton Down": 1sh..2d.

1762 Oct 20th: Paid "Abrm Luxon, Robt Luxon and John Thomas beating the rocks from Willm Cleeves up Cornwood Hill and let go the water from the roads": 3sh..6d.

1763 Sep 18th: Paid "Abrm Luxon diging a new drain near Frogpitt Moor": 1sh..2d.

Oct 10th: Paid "Abrm Luxon cleansing ye drains from Petton to Radington Water": 1sh..2d.

Nov 11th: Paid "Abrm Luxon spreading the gravel": 1sh..2d. (with others)

1764 Nov 13th: Paid "Thos Chave and Abrm Luxon opening the gutters from Shillingford to Blackmores Cleft": 2sh..4d.

1765 Feb 4th: Paid "Abrm Luxon a day to repair the road between Shillingford and Hinkeley Bridge": 1sh.2d. (in photograph below)

Feb 8th: Paid "Abrm Luxon a day repairing the road from Hedge Mead End to Clayhanger Wood": 1sh..2d.

May 30th: Paid "to repair the road near Frogpit Moor towards Cornwood Hill: Thos Hill, Edw Upham, John Webber, James Tatchell, Abraham Luxon, John Baker and William Ashelford": 8sh..2d.

1766 Jan 14th: Paid"Abrm Luxon, Robt Luxon, John Southey and Elick Barrett repairing the road near Jos Luxons": 4sh..8d.

Nov 4th: Paid "Abrm Luxon and Elick Barrett repair the road from Hedge meadend towards Edw Halls": 2sh..4d.

The Bampton Surveyors of Highways Rates & Accounts continued in the same format until 1767 but then there was a gap until 1772. The rates and accounts reappeared in 1773, but under a different format, with receipts being given only for occasional years. There were no further references to Abraham Luxton.

Abraham Luxton had carried out arduous and back breaking work during his lifetime but towards its end when he was sick and poor he needed help. The Bampton Workhouse Monthly Account book

1775-1780[31] contains record of two payments made to him at this time.

1780	Jan-Feb:	"Paid the poor in sickness: Abraham Luxon: 4sh..0d".
1780	Feb-Mar:	"Paid the poor in sickness: Abraham Luxon: 2sh..0d".

Abraham Luxen was buried at Petton on the 1st December 1782. Mary Luxen (c.1723-1798) buried at Petton on the 18th May 1798 may have been his wife but her given age of 75 if correct would make her too young to have married Abraham in 1737. The reference in the New House indenture to Abraham's "now present wife" suggests he had married for a second time. This Mary may be that second wife. When I visited Petton for the first time in April 1971 there was no memorial stone marking the site of their grave.

JACOB LUXTON (1715?-1759), HUSBANDMAN OF HUTCHINGS FARM, PETTON, BAMPTON.

Jacob's baptism has been entered erroneously in the Bampton parish register as "Jacob son of James and Joan Luxen baptised 25 March 1715." An exhaustive search in the Bampton and neighbouring parish registers has failed to find any further reference to a James or Joan Luxton or their son Jacob. This in fact is yet another example of a careless entry in a Devon parish register[32]. That Jacob was the son of Robert Luxton and his wife Jane Daniell is proven from surviving property deeds. We know too that Robert and Jane Luxton were living in Bampton at the time for early in the following year their daughter Sarah was baptised in the church on Ash Wednesday, 15th February 1716 and their youngest child, Joseph, was baptised there on the 5th June 1719.

---

[31] D.R.O. Bampton Workhouse Monthly Account Book:1770-1780(1269A/PO9)

[32] That errors occurred in parish registers is well documented. Widecombe in the Moor baptismal register lists a Joshua Warren son of Edward and Joan on 2 October 1803. A note in the register makes it clear it should have been Joseph who was still alive in 1885. The Barnstaple register contains a baptism on the 23 November 1794 where the Christian name was corrected on the 29 June 1843.

Two well preserved indentures[33] belonging to Hutchings Farm Petton, dated the 8th and 9th May 1745 proves that Jacob was the son of Robert Luxton, husbandman at Petton. They read :-
"Between Robert Luxton of Petton within the parish of Bampton in the County of Devon husbandman of the one part And Jacob Luxton son of the said Robert of the same husbandman of the other part." By the second, dated the 9th May 1745, Robert "in Consideration of the sum of Thirty pounds of good and Lawful Money of Great Britain to him in hand well and truly paid," sold to Jacob his son "All that Cottage = house Gardens Orchards Land and premises heretofore in the possession of one Edward Hutchings husbandman Scituate Lying and being in the higher = East End of a certain Moor or premises called ffrogpits = Moor lying in Petton within the said parish of Bampton and containing in the whole about ffour acres of Ground (be the same more or less) together with all Ways paths passages profits previledges Advantages Emoluments hereditaments and Appurtenances," etc.

We learn more about Jacob from the Road Surveyor's Account Book, Bampton Vol 1 (1735-1762). With the purchase of Hutching's Farm

---

[33] Mrs Needs kept the old deeds in a brown paper parcel in their living room sideboard. The usual hiding place for deeds in Robert's day was a flat canvus bag which lay between the mattress and the sacking of the bed.

Jacob became liable for payment towards the maintenance of roads in the parish and for the year ending 26th December 1746 he paid 1 shilling. He did not pay in 1747 but paid a shilling in 1748, 1749, 1750, 1752, 1753, 1755, 1756; 1 shilling and 6d in 1754 and 1758 and 2 shillings in 1751, 1757. Jacob and his brothers supplemented their incomes by working as road menders. The usual rate of pay was 1shilling and 2 pence a day and in the ten years 1748-1758 he is mentioned as receiving payment for road works undertaken in the Frogpit Moor area. We find he was hired to quarry stone at Dadiscombe Quarry (1748) and in the lane near Mr Halls (1758). Other jobs included "placing stone", "beating the road", "beat the rocks at Cornwood Hill", "mending the roads" and "repairing the roads". To improve the drainage of the roads he was employed in "laying in of wood and rounding the road", "clensing the drains and gutter holes" and "opening gutter holes in the road[34]".The photograph shows a view from Cornet (or Cornwood) Hill looking towards Five Cross Way Petton.

This is the full record of Jacob's work on the Bampton highways, extracted from the surveyors of Highways Rates and Account books:-

1748 Sep 5th: Paid "Abrm Luxon, Jos Luxon, Thos Actkings and Jacob Luxon drawing stones at Dadiscombe Quarry and repairing the roads at Petton Lane and Frogpit Moore": 4sh..8d.

1749 Dec 6th: Paid "Jacob Luxon beating the road under Cornet Hill": 1sh..2d.

1750 June 12th: Paid "Jacob Luxon and Jos Luxon mending the road in Frogpit Moor": 2sh..4d.

1751 Sep 6th: Paid "Thos Atkings, Robt Luxon, Jacob Luxon, James Tackel, John Southwood and John Blackmore 1 day in ye same road": 7sh..0d.

---

[34] D.R.O.Bampton Surveyors of Highways Rates and Accounts1735-1761(1269A/ P51)

Sep 30th: Paid "Jacob Luxon, James Hagly and Richd Melton laying in of wood and rounding the road in Petton Lane": 3sh..6d.

1752 May 9th: Paid "James Hagly, Jacob Luxon, Jos Luxon and James Tatchill rounding the road": 4sh..8d.

1753 Sep 14th : Paid "Thos Atkins and Jacob Luxon placing stone": 2sh..4d.

1754 Dec 6th : Paid "Abrm and Jacob Luxons clensing the drains and gutter holes from Frogpit Moor to Batherham Bridge yt leads to Radington": 2sh..4d.

1755 July 7th: Paid "Jacob Luxon and James Tatchel beat the rocks at Cornwood hill": 2sh..4d.0

1756 Sep 7th : Paid "Jacob Luxon opening gutter holes in the road from Frogpitt moor to Wd Radington: 1sh..0d.

1758 Sep 30th: Paid "Jacob Luxon, John Thomas and Abraham Hodge drawing stones in the lane near Mr Halls": 3sh..6d.

Jacob Luxon married Susannah Lake at Bampton on Sunday the 6th December 1747. To eke out an existence Jacob almost certainly took on extra agricultural labouring work in neighbouring parishes. This may explain why the couple's first child, William Luxon, was baptised at Clayhanger, the parish adjoining Petton, on the 23rd July 1749. Bestowing his first son with the name William may have been an attempt to retain a family name for Jacob had two elder brothers named William who died in infancy. As Jacob's own son William is not mentioned again in Petton records, he too is most likely to have died in childhood. Isaac Luxen buried at Petton on the 8th October 1750 was maybe another infant son.

The family were in all likelihood residing in Clayhanger when a second Isaack Luxon (1751-1834) was baptised there on the 14th October 1751. Daniel Lyson's famous topographical work on Devon (1822)[35] states that Divine Service at St. Petrock's Chapel, Petton was held only once in the month and this may account for why a daughter,

---

[35] Daniel Lyson's Devon (1822).

Jenny Luxen, was baptised at Bampton on the 1st February 1754. She was buried at Petton on the 7th May 1775 aged about 21, possibly the victim of consumption or another of the killer diseases which plagued 18th century England. Jacob and Susannah had two more sons baptised at Petton, Thomas Luxen (1756-1817) on the 5th September 1756, and John Luxon on the 3rd February 1759. As no more is known about this sixth child, John, he too possibly died in infancy.

Jacob must have been in his mid forties when he died. As Jacob Luxen he was buried at Petton on the 27th May 1759, scarcely more than three months after the baptism of his youngest son, John. This must have been a difficult time for his widow Susannah who now had the sole responsibility of rearing their young family. Fortunately others too were thinking of the family's plight. The Bampton Vestry Minute Book (1756-1846)[36] contains a jotting at Christmas 1759 that "Jacob Luxons widow" was given a shilling from the "Pilemore money". The value of a shilling can be measured by the fact that a labourer in 1759 earned 1 shilling and 2 pence a day which in terms of today's money would be worth about £30.

Susannah Luxon, widow, signed the Bampton register with a mark when she married for a second time to John Merson, on the 4th September 1763. Susannah had a further five children by her second husband, John Merson. These were Betty Merson baptised at Petton on the 6th May 1764; John and Gertrude Merson baptised at Petton on the 1st March 1767, Gertrude was buried at Petton on the 1st January 1769. John died aged 31 and was buried at Petton on the 2nd May 1802. Mary Merson baptised at Petton on the 6th January 1771 was buried there on the 1st September that year. Susannah's eleventh child, William Merson, baptised at Petton on the 1st March 1772, married and had a family.

The Petton registers record that Susannah Merson[37] was buried at St. Petrock's Petton on the 19th July 1789, which is just five days after the storming of the Bastille in France. The curate at Bampton has printed a capital "P" enclosed in brackets after Susannah's burial entry in the

---

[36] D.R.O.Bampton Vestry Minute Book:1756-1846(1269A/PV1).
[37] If we assume that Susannah was aged 45 when her youngest child, William Merson, was born in 1772 she would have been born c.1727.

register. This usually means an abbreviation for "pauper", though it doesn't necessarily mean that persons concerned were destitute. At this time there was a levy brought in by the authorities[38] that a fee of 3d was to be paid at burials. The majority of parish priests were opposed to the tax so to get round it they would not charge it and simply wrote down the initial "P" for Pauper so that the tax could be avoided. Susannah's second husband, John Merson, aged 80 years, was buried at Petton on the 14th December 1800.

Jacob Luxton's smallholding at Hutchings Farm, Frogpit Moor, Petton, passed to his son Isaac Luxton (1751-1834) and the property was to remain in the Luxton family until 1923.

JOSEPH LUXTON (1719-1791) HUSBANDMAN OF PETTON, BAMPTON, DEVON

Joseph, the seventh son and youngest of nine children born to Robert Luxton, husbandman and his wife Jane Daniell was baptised Joseph Luxen at St. Michael's Church, Bampton on the 5th June 1719. The parish register at Bampton also records the marriage of Joseph Luxon to Dorothy Adams on Sunday the 25th August 1744.

The Luxtons were climbing the social ladder in Bampton during the 18th century. Joseph was twenty five in 1744 the year he married and he was also one of the two church wardens in Bampton that year. As churchwarden, Joseph, was a local official with many important responsibilities and it was a post only given to those thought capable and trustworthy. Joseph's ecclesiastical duties would have included the care of the parish finances, the care of the church building (except the chancel) and the presentation of offenders to the Ecclesiastical Courts. The job involved too a number of local government duties which included the supervision of pedlars, the testing of ale and the keeping down of vermin, which included not only crows, rooks and sparrows but also moles and foxes. He was responsible too for the simple fire fighting equipment stored in the church for communal use. Churchwardens were also associated with the officials responsible for

---

[38] The Stamp Act of 1783 granted the Crown a stamp duty of 3 pence upon every register entry of a burial, marriage, birth or christening. Unpopular, this legislation remained in force only until 1794 when it was repealed.

the administration of the Poor Law and the upkeep of the roads. Further evidence of Joseph's social standing in the community is revealed by the Bampton Vestry Minute Book 1756-1846. Joseph Luxon signed his name at Christmas 1772 as one of three parish officers authorising the provision of clothing to the poor in the workhouse[39].

Because Joseph owned property at Petton he is listed in the Bampton Land Tax Assessments, which are annual returns for the years 1780 to 1832. In the years 1780 and 1781 we find "Joseph & Robt. Luxon etc" paid £1..16..0. for Frogpit Moor which they occupied. Robert I identify as Robert Luxton (c.1710-1792), who lived at Frogpit Moor. He was, I believe, Joseph's eldest surviving brother.

Unfortunately, the precise location of Joseph's home on Frogpit Moor is not evident from surviving records. The later Land Tax Assessments are even less helpful, simply recording the tax paid by "The Luxons for Frogpit Moor". No more specific is a list of apprentices bound over to some Estates (1721-81) where we read a Jane Gardiner in 1754 and a James Tucker in 1769 were made apprentices to Joseph Luxon of Frogpit Moor[40]. A hint on the location of Joseph's abode is contained in the Bampton Surveyors of Highways books. In May 1762 there is a reference to work being carried out "repairing the *road between Joseph Luxons and Radington* and between Hedgemead End and Clayhanger Wood", and in September "from Shillingford to Hedgemead and from thence towards Jos Luxons". In November 1763 the road was repaired "between Petton Chapel and Joseph Luxons". Consequently, I'm inclined to think that Joseph and Dorothy lived at Corner House Frogpit Moor which lay on the road from Petton Cross to Raddington. Their son John Luxton (1747-1818) yeoman, resided at Corner House where he died in 1818. The site of the house is marked on the 1842 Bampton Tithe map and it is described in the apportionment as No. 1553, a Cottage garden and orchard measuring one acre, 1 rod and 5 poles. It was owned by Joseph's great grandson, James Luxton (1802-1853), a carpenter and joiner in Taunton.

---

[39] The Bampton Churchwardens' Accounts: 1712-1809 (1269A/PW1) preserved in the Devon Record Office contain, "The Account of Mr John Oxenham and Mr Joseph Luxen churchwardens" for the year 1744. See also the Bampton vestry minute Book: 1756-1846 (1269A/PV1).

[40] D.R.O. Apprentice Records 1719-1781

Joseph was a signatory to a fascinating agreement made on the 17th May 1754 by the "Parishioners of Bampton to defend the ancient custom of paying tythe[41]". By custom a tenth part of the main produce of the land (corn, oats, wood etc) and a tenth part of the produce of both stock and labour such as wool, pigs, milk etc were tithes paid to the church. However, over the years many tithes had been appropriated by lay owners and their payment was unpopular and frequently led to disputes.

Sir Thomas Dyke Acland, Baronet, heads a list of ten Trustees appointed to implement the Bampton agreement. The parishioners complain that they pay much more in tithes "than Comonly paid in the Neighbourhood for Many Miles Round" and the present owner has signified his "intentions to Alter and Augment" former agreements and to "wrest in his ffavour or litigate some of the said Customs whereby the parishioners are likely to be greatly Distressed and Angered". They consider such "attempts very unreasonable and to be an attack upon our lawful rights". They bind themselves to adhere strictly to the old customs for paying tithes and these are specified in a "paper writing hereto annexed" and in another copy to be deposited with the Governor of the Workhouse where it was to be left for the inspection of the parishioners.

Seventy signatures are at the foot of the agreement. "Occupyers and Renters of Lands" in Bampton sign their names in the three left hand columns. Five of the twenty-two signatories in this section sign with their mark. Joseph Luxon is one of a further forty eight "owners and possessors of lands" who sign their names in the three right hand columns. There are just three in this section who sign with their mark.

We learn more about Joseph in the Road Surveyor's Account Book for Bampton (1735 to 1761). As Joseph Luxon he is first mentioned as paying 1 shilling for the year ending December 26th, 1746. He paid 1 shilling in 1747,1748,1749,1750 and 1752, two shillings in 1751, 1753, 1755, 1756, 1759 and 1760; three shillings in 1754 and 1758; 3 shillings and 6 pence in 1773, 1781, 1782; four shillings in 1757, 1761 to 1764 and 1767; and eight shillings in 1765 and 1766. There is also reference to Joseph and his brother Jacob carrying out road repairs at Petton. For instance on the 12th June 1750 "Jacob Luxon & Joseph Luxon" received 2s..4d for, "mending the Road in the Frogpit Moor".

---

[41] D.R.O. Bampton Tithe Agreement 17 May 1754

Joseph was paid by the surveyor of the Bampton Highways 1 shilling and 2 pence a day for the work he undertook over 42 years from 1747 to 1789. He was the horse handler in the family and from 1754 onwards Joseph is often recorded working with two horses usually in teams with other horse handlers engaged in road repair work. The largest gang was in May 1765 when ten men and twenty horses were employed on repairing the road near Frogpit Moor. There is no mention of horse bells but I suspect they were used. Thomas Hardy in "The Woodlanders" (p81) refers to the work horses carrying bells on a frame above each animal's shoulders and tuned to scale. In narrow lanes before the days of turnpike roads the distinctive sound signals of a set of bells were a warning note to others coming from the opposite direction.

Joseph quarried stones too in the local quarries at Dadiscombe (1748), Hone (1754), Waterhouse (1756) and Little Rull (1758). Picking a100 seams of stones was another task. This was a great labour because a single "seam of stones" referred to the load carried by a pack horse. One hundred seams therefore equalled one hundred journeys or fifty if two horses were used. Joseph was also employed in "leveling the road", "rounding the road" and carrying stones to repair Batherm Bridge. He was also involved in collecting faggots of Browse (brushwood) and furze which were laid down in boggy parts of the highway on top of sheep skins used to soak up excess moisture. It was covered in earth and then stones to make firm ground. The view is of Batherm Bridge between Petton and Raddington.

I have extracted all references to Joseph Luxton contained in the Bampton Highways accounts and the payments he received:-

1747 Nov 2nd: Paid "Abra Luxon, Jos Luxon, Thos Actkings and John Crookham carrying stones and repairing the roads at Bampton Down, Dypfordown and Shillingford Lane": 7sh..2d.

1748 Sep 5th: Paid "Abrm Luxon, Jos Luxon, Thos Actkings and Jacob Luxon drawing stones at Dadiscombe Quarry and repairing the roads at Petton Lane and Frogpit Moore": 4sh..8d.

1749 May 2nd : Paid "Jos Luxon a day repairing ye same road" (Near Northhayne): 1sh..2d.

1750 June 12th: Paid "Jacob Luxon and Jos Luxon mending the road in Frogpit Moor": 2sh..4d.

1751 Oct 17th : Paid "Joseph Luxon leveling the road from Thos Thorne to Redington Bridge 2 days": 2sh..4d.

Nov 22nd-23rd: Paid "Jos Luxon for picking 100 seems of stones": 6sh..8d.

1752 May 8th: Paid "Jos Luxon and James Hagly rounding ye road": 2sh..4d.

May 9th: Paid "James Hagly, Jacob Luxon, Jos Luxon and James Tatchill rounding the road": 4sh..8d.

1754 Jan 28th : Paid "Jos Luxon drawing stone at Hone": 1sh..2d.

June 13-14th: Paid "Jos Luxon 2 days drawing stone at Hone": 2sh..4d.

June 21st: Paid "Jos Luxon drawing stone at Hone": 1sh..2d.

Oct 21st: Paid "Jos Luxon and 2 horses to repair placing in the stone": 2sh..6d.

1755 June 19th: Paid "Jos Luxon and James Haglay one day": 2sh..4d.

1756 June 2nd: Paid "Jos Luxon drawing stones at Waterhouse": 1sh..0d,

Dec 2nd :   Paid "William Cleeves man and 2 horses and Jos Luxons man and 2 horses carrying stone near Rull": 5sh..0d.

Dec 4th :   Paid "Jos Luxon and 2 horses, Willm Cleeve and 2 horses carrying stone near Frogpitt Moor": 5sh..0d.

1757 Feb 10th: Paid "Jos Luxon and 2 horses to carry stones to repair Batham Bridge": 2sh..6d.

Mar 30th :   Paid "William Cleeverinns man and 2 horses and Jos Luxon and 2 horses at Quartly Lane": 5sh..0d.

Apr 1st: Paid "Jos Luxon and 2 horses at Paton Lane": 2sh..6d.

Apr 2nd: Paid "Jos Luxon and 2 horses at Paton Lane": 2sh..6d.

May 6th :   Paid "Jos Luxon a day at CornetHill": 1sh..2d.

(The photograph shows lower quarry Cornet Hill)

1758 June 16th: Paid "Willm Webber, Abrm Luxon and Jos Luxon drawing stones at Little Rull": 3sh..6d.

June 17th: Paid "Jos Luxon and Alex Ballat placing stones": 2sh..4d.

Sep 30th : Paid "Jos Luxon cutting browse and laying in stones": 1sh..2d.

1759 Nov 23rd : Paid "Joseph Luxon and 2 horses and Thos Burton and 2 horses carrying stones between Cornet hill Gate and Wey Down": 5sh..0d.

1760 Apr 23rd : For repairing the road between Crimps and Cornwood Hill –
Paid "Thos Gale 1 man and 2 horses, Willm Cleeve 1 man and 2 horses, Jos Luxon 1 man and 2 horses, John Southwood 1 man and 2 horses, James Bessly 1 man and 2 horses": 12sh..6d.

Aug 5th: Paid "Jos Luxon work in the road near Blackmores Close": 1sh..2d.

1761 Oct 9th : Paid "Jos Luxon a man and 2 horses to carrying stones in the road between Hedge Mead End and Cornwood hill": 2sh..6d.

Nov 27th: Paid "William Cleeves man and 2 horses, William Cleeves junr man and two horses, James Besslys man and two horses, Jos Luxon a man and one horse carrying stones from Dadscombe Quarry to repair the road near Cornwood hill": 8sh..9d.

1762 May 14th: Paid "Thos Hill to cut wallet and spreading stones repairing the road between Joseph Luxons and Radington and between Hedgemead End, and Clayhanger Wood": 1sh..2d.

1762 May 15th: Paid "for drawing stone at Dadscombe":-
Mr John Hill a man and 2 horses, Mr Robt Norman a man and 2 horses, Mr Edwd Hall a man and 2 horses, Mr James Callard a man and 2 horses, Mr John Surridge a man and 2 horses, Mr Richd Upham a man and 2 horses, Mr Willm Cleeve a man and 2 horses, Mr Willm Cleeve junr a man and 2 horses, Mr Jos Luxon a man and 2 horses, Mr James Bessly a man and 2 horses": £1..5sh..0d.

1762 Sep 9th: Paid "Jas Hagley cutting wallet and spreading stones repairing the road from Shillingford to Hedgemead End and from thence towards Jos Luxons": 1sh..2d.

1763 Oct 13th: Paid "Wm Cleeves man and 2 horses, Wm Cleeve junr man and 2 horses, James Besslys man and 2 horses, Nath Bennett and 2 horses, Joseph Luxon and 2 horses, to repair the road between Hedge Mead End and Blackmore Cleft": 12sh..6d.

1763 Nov 4th : Paid "Mr John Hagleys man and 2 horses, Mr Edward Halls man and 2 horses, Mr Fran Mersons man and 2 horses, Edward Thomas and 2 horses, repairing the road between Petton Chappel and Joseph Luxons": 10sh-d.

1765 May 22nd: Paid "to repair the road near Frogpit Moor towards Cornwood Hill:

Mr John Hagleys man and 2 horses, Mr Edward Halls man and 2 horses, Thos Gales man and 2 horses, Willm Cleeves man and 2 horses, Willm Cleeve junr man and 2 horses, Joseph Luxon man and 2 horses, Richd Uphams man and 2 horses": 17sh..6d.

1765 May 23rd: Paid "to repair the road near Frogpit Moor towards Cornwood Hill:

Mr John Hagleys man and 2 horses, Mr James Surridge man and 2 horses, Mr Edward Hall man and 2 horses, Mr Thos Gales man and 2 horses, Mr Willm Cleeves man and 2 horses, Joseph Luxon man and 2 horses, Richd Uphams man and 2 horses, Elick Greenslade man and 2 horses": £1., 0sh..0d.

1765 May 30th: Paid "to repair the road near Frogpit Moor towards Cornwood Hill:

Mr James Surridge man and 2 horses, Mr Edward Halls man and 2 horses, Mr Thos Gales man and 2 horses, Mr William Bucknells

man and 2 horses, Mr Thos Allens man and 2
horses, Mr Richd Hills man and 2 horses, Richd
Uphams man and 2 horses, Henry Upham man
and 2 horses, Joseph Luxon man and 2 horses,
Alex Greenslade man and 2 horses": £1..5sh..0d.

1765 July 22nd: Paid "to repair the road between Doningstone
Mill and Petton Chappell:

Mr Willm Hills 2 men and 4 horses, Mr Thos
Gales man and 2 horses, Mr Richd Hills man
and 2 horses, Mr Thos Allens man and 2 horses,
Edward Thomas man and 2 horses, and Joseph
Luxon man and 2 horses": 17sh..6d.

1765 July 23rd: Paid "to repair the road between Doningstone
Mill and Petton Chappell:

Mr Willm Cleeves man and 2 horses, Joseph
Luxon man and 2 horses, Mr Thos Gales man
and 2 horses, Mr Thos Allens man and 2 horses,
Mr Willm Hills 2 men and 4 horses, Mr Geo
Blakes man and 2 horses, Edward Thomas man
and 2 horses": £1..0sh..0d.

1765 July 24th: Paid "to repair the road between Doningstone
Mill and Petton Chappell:

Mr Willm Hills man and 2 horses, Mr Edw
Halls man and 2 horses, Mrs Betty Moltons
man and 2 horses, Mr Amos Pearse man and 2
horses, Mr Thos Allens man and 2 horses,
Henry Uphams man and 2 horses, Joseph
Luxon man and 2 horses, Mr John Hills man
and 2 horses and Mr Geo Blakes man and 2
horses": £1..2sh..6d.

1765 Nov 4th: Paid "Edw Upham to repair the road near
Joseph Luxons": 1sh..2d.

1766 Jan 14th: Paid "Alexan Grenslades man and 2 horses,
Willm Cleeves man and 2 horses, Joseph
Luxons man and 2 horses repairing the road
near Jos Luxons": 7sh..6d.

1766 Jan 14th: Paid "Abram Luxon, Robt Luxon, John Southey and Elick Barrett repairing the road near Jos Luxons": 4sh..8d.

1766 Oct 1st: Paid "Willm Cleeves man and 2 horses, Willm Cleeve junr man and 2 horses, Alex Greenslade man and 2 horses, John Webber man and 2 horses, Joseph Luxon man and 2 horses, Thos Gales man and 2 horses, repairing the road near Jos Luxons": £1..5..0d.

1766 Oct 4th: Paid "Willm Cleeve man and 2 horses, Nath Bennett man and 2 horses and Jos Luxon man and 2 horses for repairing ye road near Cornwood Hill": 7sh..6d.

1789 Feb 21st: Paid "Joseph Luxon 50 fagots furze": 1sh..8d.

Furze was used to light domestic fires.In his "Return of the Native" (1878) p13 Thomas Hardy renders a vivid picture of the furze cutter.he carried a hook and leather gloves and his legs were sheathed in bulging leggings to protect him from the prickly gorse.The faggots held together by bramble bonds were carried upon the shoulder by means of a long stake sharpened at each end for impaling them easily-two in front and two behind.

In July 1989, on a beautiful Summer's day, Mr Maurice Hawkins of Venn Farm, Waterrow, Chipstable, kindly permitted me to study property deeds in his possession which threw further valuable light on Joseph's activities. Of particular interest was an indenture dated the 27th November 1770 made between Joseph Luxon husbandman of Petton and his brother, Abraham. Joseph purchased for 5 shillings in hand, paid to his brother Abraham, "All that the Easter part or dwelling house (which of late was and now is converted into two dwellings together with the Garden Orchard and Appurtenances….which….were sometimes heretofore in the possession of Thomas Atkins, then next of James Tatchel And now at this present in the possession of….Abraham Luxon….part of a cottage house or Tenement commonly called the New House….at Petton".

Joseph took "peaceful and quiet possession" of the dwelling on the 25th March 1771 and he agreed to pay "Abraham Luxon and Mary his now present wife and the longest lived of them yearly and every year during the term of their natural lives and the longest liver of them one annuity or yearly rent charge of one pound and two shillings a Year". This was to be paid by even and equal quarterly payments on the 24th June, 29th September, 25th December and the 25th March. The first payment was due on the 21st June 1771. It was agreed that if Joseph defaulted and did not pay within 21 days Abraham and Mary had the right to enter the premises and "distrain any Goods and Chattels to pay the arrears", and if there wasn't sufficient money to pay the debt Abraham and Mary could re-enter and repossess the property to "Enjoy as in his her or their former Estate". There was a shortage of ready money among some farmers particularly renters and warrants of distraint for the recovery of arrears were constantly being issued. Today such an agreement seems fraught with difficulty but matters must have transpired peacefully for the property passed to Joseph's son John (1747-1818) and grandson George Luxton (1802-1891), mason of Morebath.

Joseph Luxon and his wife Dorothy Adams were the parents of John Luxton (1747-1818) who was baptised John Luxen at Petton on the 14th August 1747. John, a yeoman farmer at Corner House, Petton, married Mary Redwood of Upton at Clatworthy, Somerset in 16th April 1779 and the couple had a large family whose descendants continue the Luxton surname. One descendant Edward Luxton of Oatway Farm, Brompton Regis in Somerset, possesses an old table which he believes could have belonged to Joseph himself.

Joseph Luxon was buried at St. Petrock's Church Petton on Sunday the 22nd May 1791 and his wife Dorothy Luxon followed him to the grave on Monday the 19th January 1795. When I visited St. Petrock's in April 1971 I was unable to locate the couple's burial place which is unmarked[42].

---

[42] For Joseph's descendants see chapters 48 to 74

6

ROBERT LUXON (LUXTON) 1744-1831 GUNSTOCK MAKER OF BOX HEDGE, PETTON BAMPTON, DEVON

See tree 2

Robert Luxton (1744 - 1831), the Gunstock Maker, was of the senior line of the family and was the third generation named Robert Luxton to live on Frogpit Moor. Robert (c1664-1751), his grandfather, had purchased the property sometime in the mid 1730s, and on his death in 1751, it had been sub-divided between his children including Robert (c1710-1792), the eldest of four surviving sons. This second Robert remains a shadowy figure due to the paucity of surviving records. He was born about 1710 and married his wife Mary Pool at St. Michael's, Enmore, Somerset on the 20th June 1743.Their son Robert Luxton (1744-1831), the gunstock maker of Box Hedge, Frogpit Moor, and the topic of this chapter, was baptised at Enmore, Somerset on the 30th March 1744.

In 1779 he was described as Robert Luxon, junior, of Frogpit Moor which means his father Robert Luxton, senior, was also alive in that year. The Bampton Surveyors of Highways Rates and Account Book for 1779 notes that "Robert Luxon and son paid to the surveyors 3sh.. od". Another document, the Bampton Workhouse Monthly Account Book, records that Robert Luxon, junior, of Frogpit Moor was paid 10 shillings when Mary Bowden a poor child was apprenticed to him between September and October of that year.[43] When Robert Luxton (c1710-1792), spelt Luxon in the register, was buried at Petton on 19th October 1792, his son Robert (1744-1831), the gunstock maker, inherited the lion's share of land belonging to the Luxton family at Frogpit Moor.

---

[43] One of the abuses meted out to pauper children in the parish was to apprentice them to 'husbandry' or 'housewifery' which might amount merely to unskilled menial farm or domestic service.

Robert Luxton was fifty when almost a year after his father's death he married Ann Evett at St Peter's Church, Clayhanger, on Monday 7th October 1793. The couple made their home at Box Hedge, Frogpit Moor, which lay close to the Turnpike Road from Wiveliscombe to Bampton. The property marked on the Bampton parish tithe map and apportionment, dated 22nd August 1842,[44] had belonged to his father and grandfather who may themselves have resided at Box Hedge (sometimes named Boxen Hedge).

Across the road from Box Hedge, a narrow deeply banked and hedged lane, common of the type found in Devon, climbed the hill to the Church of St Petrock's Petton. Robert and Ann had five children in the space of ten years and they were baptised in the tiny church which was rebuilt in 1847/1848. Their children were Mary Luxon baptised on 2nd February 1794, followed by Jane Luxon baptised on 6th November 1796, John Luxon baptised on 3rd February 1799, Martha Luxon on 7th June 1801 and Ann Luxon on 2nd December 1804. The family home at Box Hedge was demolished in 1917 when a modern property "Green Acres" was erected on the site.

The annual returns of Devon Freeholders list Robert Luxon for the years 1799 and 1807[45]. In an undated volume of circa 1807 he is referred to as Robert Luxon Joiner and Freeholder. Robert is mentioned too in the Bampton Land Tax Assessments which ran annually from 1780 to 1832. In 1780 and 1781 the tax was paid by his uncle and father "Joseph and Robert Luxons etc Frogpit Moor". The returns for 1782 to 1797 simply refer to the tax being paid by "The Luxons, Frogpit Moor". Robert's name as "Robert Luxon Frogpit Moor" first appears paying the tax in the 1799 return and continues until the final assessment year of 1832. In the years 1800, 1809, 1813, 1817 to 1832 his name is spelt as "Robert Luxton". Robert possessed the lion's share of land on Frogpit Moor for the 1830-1832 returns reveal he paid 18 shillings in tax compared to the 12 shillings and six shillings paid respectively by his kinsmen John Luxton and Isaac Luxton.

Robert Luxton was one of the 8000 Devon Freeholders who had the vote before the 1832 Reform Act. The Bampton Poll Books for 1816,

---

44 D.R.O. Bampton Parish tithe map 22nd August 1842
45 D.R.O. See Devon Freeholders Lists.

1818 and 1820 list Robert Luxton as an owner of "house and land" (1820 recites "houses and land"). In 1818 the property was occupied by "self and others" and in 1816 and 1820 it states "self occupied" or "self[46]".

The Bampton Surveyors of Highways Rates and Account Book 1766-1816 contains further references to Robert Luxton, the gunstock maker[47]. The first clear reference, as noted earlier, was in 1779 when with his father he paid 3 shillings towards the upkeep of the highways. The rates he paid varied. In 1792 "Mr Robert Luxon" paid the surveyors 6 shillings and 6p; 5 shillings in 1794, 1795; 6 shillings in 1796, 1797, 1799, 1800, 1802, 1803 and 1804; 3 shillings in 1798, 9 shillings in 1801; £1..4 shillings in 1805, 1810; 18 shillings in 1807, 12 shillings in 1809, £1..13 shillings in 1811, £1..16 shillings in 1812. The same sum was due again in 1813 but he was 14 shillings.. 9d in arrears and he paid £1..4 shillings in 1814.

Robert can be identified as receiving payment for his maintenance work undertaken on the Bampton roads in the 16 years 1799 to 1815. (I have attributed earlier payments to his father Robert Luxton c1710-1792). The first payment to "Mr Robert Luxon" was 2 shillings on 28th September 1799 "for repairing Cly (Clayhanger?) Bridge." The largest payment he received was £3..1 shilling and 6 pence on 26th August 1809 in settlement of "Robert Luxons bill." Payment in 1810 included 15 shillings and 6d for "cleaning drains" and 1 shilling for "repairing Tiller Bridge". His final payment was 2 shillings and 11 pence in 1815 for "cleaning water tables".

Like other parishes, Bampton was run by the 'vestry', a body consisting of the more substantial parishioners. By the Poor Law Act of 1597/98 each parish was responsible for its own poor and annually the vestry elected at least two persons as Overseers of the Poor – in rural areas usually farmers – who were responsible for giving relief to those unable to maintain themselves or their families. The money was raised through a poor rate levied on owners and occupiers of lands and buildings. The overseer was required to be a "substantial householder". Robert Luxon

---

[46] D.R.O.Bampton Poll Books for 1816,1818 & 1820.
[47] Bampton Surveyors of Highways Rates & Accounts1762-1816(1262-1816A/P32)

"junior" of Frogpit Moor was considered a valued and trustworthy member of his community fit to hold this office. The Bampton Vestry Minute Book 1756-1846 records that Robert was chosen as an overseer of the Poor in 1782[48]. At Michaelmas and again at Christmas 1782 Robert Luxon signed his name as one of the three or five parish officers authorising the provision of clothing to the poor in the Workhouse. For three months during 1782 "Mr Robert Luxon" also kept the accounts contained in the Bampton Workhouse Monthly Account Book 1780-1790[49]. Robert was involved too with another local task when he signed his name "Robt Luxon" as a Land Tax Collector in 1785.These public duties performed by Robert indicate he had the business expertise and the literacy and numerical skills needed to carry out the tasks.

In the last paragraph I referred to the vestry. This was the part of the Church where the clergy put on their vestments. It was also used by the parishioners when they met to decide local affairs. It was the beginning of local government before the Local Government Act of 1894  transferred the civil functions of the vestries to elected parish councils. "Robert Luxon" was one of those who signed his name to an agreement at a vestry meeting in St Michael's Bampton on 25th March 1799 which still impacts on the lives of people living in the town over two hundred years later. The vestry agreed that the church would pay to recast the five bells contained in the tower into six bells. Thomas Bilbie, a bell founder in Cullompton, recast the bells in 1800[50]. The bells are still in use and have a wonderful tone in full peal. They are incredibly heavy, the lightest being the treble which leads a peal, and is inscribed "When I call follow me all". The tenor weighs fifteen hundred weight, being the heaviest, and is more solemnly inscribed "I to the Church the living

---

[48] D.R.O. Bampton Vestry Minute Book1756-1846(1269A/PV1)
[49] Bampton Workhouse Monthly Account Book 1780-1790(1269/)
[50] The Bilbie family were bell-founders and clockmakers based initially in Chew Stoke in Somerset and later at Cullompton in Devon from the late 17th. century to early 19th century.

call, and to the grave do summon all." In May 1962 the oak frame holding the bells was weakening so the six huge bells were retuned and re-hung on a new metal bell frame. Robert continued to be interested in local affairs and he signed his name Robert Luxton as an attendee at a vestry meeting held on 26th March 1818.

Robert Luxton of Bampton, Gunstock Maker, made his will on 16th December 1830. Henry Sully of Wiveliscombe, Surgeon, and John Carew of Exeter, Attorney at Law, were appointed as trustees. They were to sell at a reasonable price or let for any term not exceeding seven years at a yearly rent "All my Freehold Messuages Lands and Premises with the Appurtenances in the parishes of Bampton and Clayhanger or elsewhere upon Trust". With the money raised they were to discharge his funeral and testamentary expenses and debts. The residue of the money was to be invested in stocks funds and securities. The dividends, interest and annual produce arising from this investment was to be paid to his widow, Ann, during her natural life for her use. After her decease the money was to be equally divided between his four daughters but it was his desire that Jane and Ann were each to receive an extra £5 above their shares.

Robert left his wife, Ann, "All my Personal and Testamentary Estates and Effects whatsoever." To Jane his daughter he left "my oak Bureau standing in my Bedroom and my large Family Bible in one volume". Martha received "my Desk and Coffer and Howard's Encyclopaedia[51] in two volumes." His daughter Ann was bequeathed "my watch, the Oak Bookcase standing in my Bedroom and one of the Bedsteads and its Furniture". Jane and Martha were to have "the other two Beds one each complete". Mary was to take "any one Article of Household Furniture which she may chuse Except those already specified". Jane, Martha, and Ann, his three youngest daughters, were to have "all the residue of my Household Furniture equally to be divided between them" and a Dictionary each. Robert appointed his wife Ann as sole executrix of his Will which was witnessed by Grace Haywood, James Haywood, and Richard Haywood. James Haywood was a tenant farmer on land belonging to the Luxtons at Frogpit Moor.

---

[51] The New Royal Encyclopaedia…by George Selby Howard LL. D. & F.R.S. was first published in London by Alex Hogg in 1788. It proved popular and new editions were produced. Published by the King's royal licence and authority it was sold in the early 1790s in 150 weekly numbers.

Within a month of making his Will Robert died at the grand age of 86 (his headstone gives his age as 87) on 8th January 1831. His wife Ann (1761-1834) who was some eighteen years his junior died aged 72 on 20th April 1834.

Their daughter, Martha, proved the will in the Archdeacon's Court of Exeter on 26th September 1837 when Robert's estate was valued under £200.

Robert and Ann lie buried together in the churchyard at Petton. In April 1971 I copied the inscription on their lichen blotched headstone which lay near the S. W. corner of the nave

<blockquote>
Sacred
To the memory of
John Luxton son of Robert
and Ann Luxton of this Parish,
who departed this life, January
20th 1829 aged 30 years

Robert Luxton departed
This life January 8th 1831 aged 87 years
Also Ann, the wife of Robert
Luxton, departed this life
April 20th 1834 aged 72 years.
Also Jane Luxton departed
This life January 28th
1867 aged 70 years.
Ann Luxton departed this
Life July 27th 1868 aged 63 years
</blockquote>

Sadly the old brown sandstone slab has been demolished and I have no record of why it was removed or what befell it.

In accordance with his will Robert's property at Bampton was auctioned at the White Horse Inn Bampton on Monday 16th July 1838 and the advert on the next page appeared in the press:-

BAMPTON, DEVON.

TO BE SOLD IN FEE,

Either in one Lot, or in such Lots as may be determined
on at the Auction,

TWO MESSUAGES or TENEMENTS, with the
Gardens, Orchards, and Fields thereto attached, called.

CALLS and BOXEN HEDGE;

Containing altogether about eleven acres,

And late in the occupation of Mr. Luxton, the proprietor.

☞ These premises lie in the parish of BAMPTON,
adjoining the Turnpike Road between Bampton and Wiveliscombe, about three and a half miles from the former, and
seven from the latter Town ; and would form a most
desirable Residence for any person of moderate means,
being well known for their neatness, comfort and convenience, and being situate in a healthy and cheap Country.

For sale of which premises,

An AUCTION will be held at the White Horse Inn, in
Bampton, on Monday the 16th day of July next, precisely at one o'clock in the afternoon.

For viewing the premises, application may be made at
Boxen Hedge ; and for further particulars, to Mr. MER-
SON, Petton, near Bampton ; or to Messrs. CAREW and
JONES, Exeter.

Dated 20th June, 1838.

Eleven years after his death the house and land occupied by Robert and
his family is shown and described in greater detail on the Bampton tithe
map and apportionment of 1842. His property on Frogpit Moor was a
corner piece at Five Crossway on the north side of the road to
Wiveliscombe. In 1842 it was owned by his daughter Jane and son in
law Robert Brimicombe, husband of his daughter Martha. Together
with plot No 1513 which was owned by Robert Luxton's nephew
George Luxton (1802-1891) stonemason of Morebath, it made an area
of 11 acres 3 rods and 0 poles, paying a rent charge of twelve shillings
and eleven pence.

No 1518 is marked as a "Courtlage (sic) and Garden" measuring one
rod 38 poles. A courtledge was a West Country term for the yard and
outbuildings of a house. The house shown adjoining the plot was
Robert's home, Box Hedge, which in the mid nineteenth century was
used by his daughters as a Dame School. The rest of the property

comprised No 1521 Call's Orchard, No 1522 Cottage and Garden, No 1516 Bottom Close, No 1517 Home Mead, No 1519 Higher Field, No 1520 Call's Mead, No 1523 Long Mead, No 1524 Western Close, No 1525 North Field and No 1526 Higher Orchard. This was a mixture of orchards, meadow pasture and arable land in the occupation of Denis Baker.

Robert's only son, John Luxton, died aged 30 on 20th January 1829 and he was buried at St Petrock's Church on 31st January 1829. Mary, his eldest daughter, married James Munden at Cornworthy, in South Devon on the 9th December 1822. James Munden, was a flax spinner, and the couple moved about the West Country before settling by 1861 at Church Lane in Yetminster, Dorset, where James was a manufacturer of rope and twine. Mary died aged 72 at Stoford Barwick, Somerset on the 15th January 1867. Robert's daughter, Martha, married Roger Brimicombe, a baker, in the parish church of St James, Taunton, on 4th August 1839. The couple settled at Box Hedge, Petton where the 1841 census describes Robert Brimicombe as a baker, aged 30. Jane (1796-1867) and Ann (1804-1868), the two remaining daughters, were schoolmistresses at the family home Box Hedge where they conducted a "Dame School". A "Dame School" was an elementary school run by women, the usual fee being 3d or 4d per week. They were very common up to the time of the 1870 Education Act. William Squire of Hookway near Crediton bequeathed the little school charitable donations of £5 in 1843 and again in 1846.

Jane and Ann are listed as schoolmistresses in the 1851 census and in 1856 a new school was erected at Box Hedge. Billings Directory for Devon published in 1857 lists Ann as the schoolmistress at Petton but she was assisted by her sister Jane and both are listed as schoolmistresses there in the 1861 census. Jane who suffered for some years with heart disease died aged 70 on the 28th January 1867 while Ann died aged 63 from "natural decay" on the 27th July 1868. Both are interred in their parent's grave at Petton. Martha Brimicombe, their married sister, returned to teach in the school where the 1871 census lists her as a 69 year old schoolmistress at Box Hedge. The school was replaced by another at Shillingford which opened on the 1st July 1878.

William Fisher Luxton (1843-1907), a kinsman to these sisters, was living with his uncle Thomas Luxton at Hutchings Farm in the early

1850s. It is tempting to think he received his elementary education at Box Hedge before emigrating to Canada in 1855. There he became a noted pioneer in the Canadian West, being the first school teacher in Winnipeg and the founding editor of its famous newspaper, The Manitoba Free Press. (It was later named the Winnipeg Free Press).

A mystery which continues to intrigue me is what became of Robert's family Bible which he bequeathed to his daughter Jane. Jane died unmarried in 1867 but my attempts to locate the whereabouts of the Bible have so far failed. If it is still extant it may contain record of Robert's baptism and other valuable genealogical details on the origins of the Luxton family who resided at Frogpit Moor, Petton, Bampton. When Jane died the Bible must have passed to her spinster sister Ann. When Ann died too in 1868 her married sister Martha returned to teach in the same school where the 1871 census has Martha Brimicombe aged 69 school mistress at Box Hedge. Given her age Martha must have been soon retired and she moved to Dorset to live with the family of her late elder sister Mary Munden (1794-1867). Martha aged 77, the widow of Robert Brimicombe, baker, died of bronchitis at Yetminster, Dorset, on the 27th February 1879. Her neice, Mary Chapman (1823-1904), the eldest daughter of Mary Munden, was present at the death and it seems likely that she had the family Bible. When she died in 1904 the Bible perhaps passed to her sister Jane Luxton Munden (1826-1913), who was a retired seamstress, the widow of John Swaffield, a clerk and storekeeper, when she died aged 85 at 30 St Paul Street, East Stonehouse, Devon in 1913. The grand-daughter of Robert Luxton the gunstock maker she was the last of the family I have traced in his line.

This is the full record of Robert's work on the Bampton highways, extracted from the surveyors of Highways Rates and Accounts books:-

1799 Sept 28th Paid "Mr Robert Luxon for repairing Cly (Clayhanger?) bridge 2 sh 0d
1809 August 26th Paid "Robert Luxons bill" £3..1s..6d
1810 Paid "Robert Luxon cleaning drains: 15s 6d"
1810 Paid "Robert Luxon as per bill: £1 5sh 10d"
1810 Paid "ditto repairing Tiller Bridge: 1sh 0d"
1813 Paid "Mr Luxton as per bill: £1 8 sh 9d".
1815 Paid "Robert Luxton for cleaning water tables: 2sh 11d".

7

ISAAC (LUXON) LUXTON (1751-1834) YEOMAN OF HUTCHINGS FARM, PETTON, BAMPTON, DEVON.

See tree 3

Isaac Luxton, the third son of Jacob Luxton (1715?-1759), husbandman of Hutchings Farm, Petton, Bampton and his wife Susannah Lake, was baptised in the neighbouring parish of Clayhanger, on the 14th October 1751.The Clayhanger register quaintly spells his name Isaack Luxon. An Isaac Luxon who was buried at Petton on the 8th October 1750 was probably an elder brother. His parents who married in 1747 had conceivably begun their married lives as tenant farmers or farm labourers at Clayhanger, for William Luxon, an elder brother, was baptised there on the 23rd July 1749. I can find no further reference to this William who may have died in infancy.

The family's movements can be traced through the baptism of their children. Jenny (1754-1775) was baptised at Bampton on the 1st February 1754 while Thomas (1756-1817) was baptised at Petton on the 5th September 1756. Jacob was a comparatively young man of perhaps 45 when he died and was buried at Petton on the 27th May 1759. His widow, Susannah, was left with three young children, Isaac 8, Jenny 5 and Thomas aged about three. John baptised at Petton on the 3rd February 1759 barely more than three months before Jacob's death almost certainly died in infancy as no more is heard of him.

Susannah Luxon, widow, signed the Bampton marriage register with her mark when she married for a second time to John Merson (sometimes spelt Mason) on the 4th September 1763. The family continued to reside at Petton where a further five Merson children were born. Susannah Merson was buried at Petton on the 19th July 1789, five days after the storming of the Bastille in Paris. Her second husband John Merson, aged about 80, was buried at Petton on the 14th December 1800.

I do not know if any provision was made for Isaac's upbringing. Diocesan Consistory Court papers for Exeter may provide details for the supervision of his welfare, perhaps undertaken by Abraham or Joseph Luxton his uncles. That Isaac inherited Hutchings, his father's small holding at Petton, is proven by property deeds.

Isaac Luxon of the parish of Bampton, husbandman, and Mary North of Morebath were married after the reading of banns by John Bere, the vicar, at the parish church of St. George, Morebath on Monday the 24th July 1780. Isaac signs his name Isaac Luxon in a bold and clear but erratic hand, suggesting he had little need to do much writing. His bride, Mary North, makes her mark as does a witness Elizabeth North who was her sister. George Morris was the other witness. Morebath is an upland parish situated on the southern edge of Exmoor and is mostly given over to sheep farming.

The North family who were resident in Uffculme earlier in the century were living in Morebath from at least the late eighteenth century. Mary's brother Thomas North, the younger, bachelor of Morebath, in his will dated 3rd March 1804, bequeathed "unto his sister Mary Luxon ffive pounds." They were two of five children born to Thomas North (1723-1804), and his wife Mary Stone of Morebath, who were married at Uffculme on 5th November 1746. It's interesting to note that Thomas North and his wife Mary were both adults when baptised at Morebath on Christmas Day 1772. The adult baptisms of their children, John and Anne, at Morebath took place on Christmas Day two years later. The family were probably Baptists and Title deeds dating 1767 & 1768, held in the Devon Record Office reveal the Stone family of Bampton and Morebath had close connections with Tiverton Baptist Church. Thomas North, senior, the third of four sons of John and Emlin North, was baptised at Uffculme, Devon on the 29th March 1723, while his wife Mary Stone the daughter of Thomas Stone and his wife Prudence was baptised at Uffculme on 6th March 1721. Her parents Thomas Stone and Prudence Kitchell, both of Uffculme, were married there earlier that year on 22nd July 1721.[52] The photograph on the next page shows St. George's Church, Morebath, with its saddleback tower.

Isaac Luxton and his wife Mary North had seven children. Ann, their eldest child, baptised at Petton on the 27th May 1781 moved to Bristol, possibly to be a domestic servant. There in the parish of St. Augustine the Less, she married Richard Hawks Twiggs, by banns, on the 2nd December 1807[53]. Thomas, (1783-1840), her brother, baptised at Bampton on the 9th November 1783, married Jenny Palmer at Raddington, Somerset on the 26th April 1816. Thomas, a stonemason and yeoman, was to succeed his father at Hutchings. Jacob, a second son, baptised at Bampton on the 4th June 1786, died aged eleven and was buried at Petton on the 25th September 1797. Isaac, a third son, baptised at Petton on the 1st February 1789, married Judith Skinner by banns at Skilgate on the 10th June 1812. Isaac, a stonemason settled at Kymmen Moor, Skilgate where his descendants continued to dwell until the close of the nineteenth century. Jenny Luxon, a fifth child, baptised at Bampton on the 1st January 1792, probably died in infancy. Jane her sister, baptised at Petton on the 3rd January 1796, married John Gamblin, a yeoman of Clayhanger at Bampton on the 14th May 1830. They moved to Hockworthy where they had a family. Jane Gamlin died, aged 43, of breast cancer, at Hockworthy, on the 14th June 1839 and was buried at Petton on the 21st June 1839. Jacob, the seventh and youngest child, was baptised at Petton on the 15th January 1800. A stonemason like his brothers, he married Harriet Greenway, at Milverton, Somerset on the 24th February 1826. The couple settled at Paradise in Chipstable where they reared a large family. They are my great-great-grandparents.

---

[52] At this date the year ended on 25th March.
[53] Richard Hawks Twiggs, son of Edward & Sarah was baptised at St Mary's Steps Exeter on the 16th April 1770.I have found three daughters on the I.G.I., Mary Ann 1810, Sarah 1815 & Mary Ann 1819 so the first Mary Ann must have died an infant.

It was in Isaac's lifetime that the earliest map to show the site of his farm at Hutchings was produced. The first edition O.S. one inch map of 1809 clearly marks and names Frog Pit Moor. Hutchings Farm is indicated but the house is not named and its field boundaries are not shown.

Isaac was one of 8000 freeholders in Devon who had the vote before the Great Reform Act of 1832. The Bampton Poll Books list Isaac's name for the parliamentary elections of 1816, 1818, 1820 and 1830.[54] The nature of his freehold was described as house and land occupied by him. In 1820 land only is listed while in 1818 he suffered the humiliation of having his vote rejected presumably because he did not possess the necessary freehold to qualify.

Annual Land Tax Assessments for Bampton in the years 1780-1832 reveal the Luxtons paid £1..16shillings for Frogpit Moor. It was not until 1819 however that the individual names of Robert, John[55] and

---

[54] D.R.O.Bampton Poll Books 1816,1818,1820 &1830
[55] John Luxton(1747-1818), yeoman at Corner House, son of Joseph (1719-1791)

Isaac Luxton are given and not until 1830 do we discover how much each one pays – Robert 18 shillings, Isaac 6 shillings and John 12 shillings. In the years 1818 to 1825 Isaac paid a further 6 shillings for Hedgemead Close (Hedgemead End Close in 1824) which was owned by Francis Mead.

The 1842 Bampton Tithe map and apportionment identify Isaac's house and land on Frogpit Moor in greater detail. Isaac's grandson, Thomas Luxton (1824-1893), paid a rent charge of two shillings on the house and land measuring 3 acres 1 rod and 33 poles. Hutchings, an L shaped house, lies in the corner of No 1527 on the map and is described as a 'Cottage, Garden, Orchard and Nursery'. Field No 1528 Home Field and Nursery was used for pasture and Field No 1529 "Mead" was a meadow. The property is marked on the 1889 six inch to one mile O.S.M. where the house name is incorrectly spelt as 'Hutchin's House'.

The basic diet in north Devon during Isaac's lifetime was wheat or barley bread and potatoes with cider or a light malt beverage, one to three pints a day. The food was supplemented with pickled pork, bacon or mutton with leeks and onions. The sunny aspect of Hutchings Farm on its south facing side was blessed with a quarter acre garden, enclosed by a substantial stone and turf embankment about three feet high. Here Isaac and his family must have spent many hours tending their kitchen garden. Indeed Charles Vancouver[56] in his General View of the Agriculture of the county of Devon (1808), considered that the culinary gardens of Devon were amongst the best in England. Highly flavoured wall fruit was grown and farmers and peasants alike grew excellent vegetables, especially leeks. On the north side of the house Isaac's apple orchard was sufficient to produce one or two hogshead of cider and a good sufficiency of winter storing apples. The pigs that provided the family with their pork, ham and bacon were housed in the single storey stone outbuilding that lay on the west side of the farm. There was a sheltered "pig run" on its west side.

The Bampton Surveyors of Highways Rates and Account Books reveal that Isaac Luxton paid his share to the maintenance of the highways.

---

[56] General View of the Agriculture of the County of Devon by Charles Vancouver (1808) David & Charles Reprint.

He paid 1sh..6d in 1781 and in 1782; one shilling in 1794, 1795 and 1798; 2 shillings in 1791, 1792, 1797, 1799, 1800, 1802, 1803, 1804; 6 shillings in 1807, 8 shillings in 1805, 1810, 11 shillings in 1811; 12 shillings in 1812 and 16 shillings in 1814.

To supplement his income from Hutchings it is likely that Isaac worked as a casual labourer on surrounding farms. Perhaps too, he held a farm tenancy or two, but I have no details of any arrangements. There was extra money to be earned on road work and Isaac was employed by the surveyors of the Bampton highways for which he was usually paid at the rate of 1 shilling and 2d a day. The Tiverton Turnpike Trust began in 1757 and the road from Tiverton to Wiveliscombe passed close by his home at Frogpit Moor. Isaac's earliest payment was dated 1784 when he received 2 shillings and 6 pence for 2 days work repairing the Tiverton Turnpike Road. His last payment was 31 years later in 1815 when he received 12 shillings and 4 pence for his "labour as per bill". It's frustrating that in these later accounts the location is often omitted. On the 27th September 1798, for instance, Isaac was paid 8 shillings and 6 pence for "cleaning 34 yds road at 3d per yd" and he received 3d for "20 faggots of browse". More illuminating was a payment made in 1804 when he received 7 shillings and 1$^{1}/_{2}$d for "Cleaning ditches Frogpit Moor 57 yards at 1$^{1}/_{2}$d per yard"; 6 shillings and 9 pence for "cleaning 27 yards at 3d per yard in Petton Lane" but only 3 shillings and 4 pence "at 1d per yard for cleaning 40 yards in Dryclose Lane".

It's the mundane details of everyday life which help us see family history in its true perspective. On the 16th October 1805, just five days before the Battle of Trafalgar, Isaac was paid 8 shillings for six days work "cleaning troughs in Petton Lane". Among other payments Isaac received £2..1shilling and 4d on the 23rd May 1807 for 31 days work "widening the road and placing stones at Frogpit Moor". Isaac was paid £5..7shillings and 5 pence on the 19th July 1807 "for digging 1289 seams stones" and for three days "plaining the same" he received a further 4 shillings 0 pence. He had been a very busy man because one seam was equal to a pack horse load. However, his biggest payment was in 1810 when he received £12..17shillings and 10d for "digging 3438 seams stones"This is a staggering amount of stone especially for a man who in 1810 was already 59 years old. Isaac is to be admired for his tremendous stamina and his capacity for hard physical work. His experience of work with stone on the Bampton highways helps explain too how three of his sons, Thomas, Isaac and Jacob became stone masons.

This is the full record of Isaac's work on the Bampton highways, extracted from the Surveyors of Highways Rates & Account books:-

1784 June 26th: "Paid "Isaac Luxon 2 days: to repair Tiverton turnpike": 2sh..6d.

1785 Mar 31st : "Paid "Isaac Luxon 1 day": 1sh..2d.

1789 Aug 21st : "Paid "Isaac Luxon 2 days: to repair near Shillingford": 2sh..4d.

1791 June 9th: "Paid "Isaac Luxon 2 days: to repair between Wey and Cleyhanger Wood": 2sh..4d.

1794 July 15th: "Paid "Isaac Luxon 1 day: to repair at Cornwood Hill": 1sh..2d.

1794 July 23rd: "Paid "Isaac Luxon 1 day: to repair at Cornwood Hill": 1sh..2d.

1794 Aug 21st: "Paid "Isaac Luxon 2 days: to repair at Cornwood Hill": 2sh..4d

1794 Sep 11th: "Paid "Isaac Luxon 2 days: to repair at Cornwood Hill": 2sh..4d.

1794 Sep 15th: "Paid "Isaac Luxon 3 days: to repair at Cornwood Hill": 3sh..6d.

1797 July 4th: Paid "Isaac Luxon 5 days": 6sh..3d.

1797 July 16th: Paid "Isaac Luxon 3 days": 3sh..9d.

1797 Aug 6th: Paid "Isaac Luxon 1 day": 1sh..3d.

1797 Aug 21st: Paid "Thomas Luxon and Isaac Luxon for 25 days": £1..11sh..3d.

1797 Oct 2nd: Paid "Isaac Luxon": 8sh..9d

1798 Sep 27th : Paid "Isaac Luxon for cleaning 34 yds road at 3d p yd: 8sh..6d".

1798 Sep 27th : Paid "Isaac Luxon for 20 fagots of browse: 3d".

1801 : Paid "Isaac Luxon for labour: 8sh..0d".

1802 : Paid "Isaac Luxon for labour: £1..18sh..0d".

1803 : Paid "Isaac Luxon bill for labour: £8..6sh..8d".

1804 : Paid "Cleaning ditches Frogpit Moor 57 yards at $1^1/_2$d p yard to Isaac Luxon: 7sh..$1^1/_2$d".

1804 : "ditto in Petton Lane 27 yards at 3d p yard: 6sh..9d".

1804 : "ditto in Dryclose Lane 40 yards at 1d p yard: 3sh..4d".

1804 : "ditto six days work: 8sh..0d".

1805 Oct 16th: "Paid "Isaac Luxon 6 days cleaning troughs Petton Lane: 8sh.".

1806 Feb 3rd : "Paid "Isaac Luxon for cleansing 90 P (perches) ditches in Petton Lane: 11sh..3d.".

1806 Feb 3rd : "Paid "ditto 11 days work Cleeve's Lane: 14sh..8d.".

1807 Jan 23rd : "Paid "Isaac Luxon for cleansing 134 Perches of Ditches between Rull and Petton Cross at 3d: £1..13sh..6d.".

1807 Jan 23rd : "Paid "ditto digging 90 seams of stones Petton Quarry: 7sh..6d.".

1807 Jan 23rd : "Paid "ditto 6 days work: 8sh..0d.".

1807 May 23rd: "Paid "Isaac Luxon for widening the road and placing the stones at Frogpit Moor 31 days: £2..1sh..4d.".

1807 July 19th: "Paid "Isaac Luxon for digging 1289 seams stones: £5..7sh..5d.".

1807 July 19th : "Paid "ditto 3 days plaining the same: 4sh..0d.".

1807 Oct 8th: "Paid "Isaac Luxon for digging 279 seams stones: £1..3sh..3d.".

1807 Oct 8th : "Paid "ditto cleansing 63 perches of ditches at 3d: 15sh..9d.".

1807 Oct 8th : "Paid "ditto 10 and a half days work: 14sh..0d.".

1807 - 1808 : Paid "Isaac Luxton 30 days work: £2..0sh..0d".

1807 - 1808 : Paid "ditto drawing 369 seams stones at 1d per seam: £1..10sh..9d".

1807 - 1808 : "Paid "ditto cleaning 86 perch of ditch at 3d per perch: £1..1sh..6d.".

1807 - 1808 :	Paid "Isaac Luxton for opening 17 perch of roads: £3..8sh..0d".
1807 - 1808 :	Paid "Isaac Luxton 189 seams stones: 15sh..9d".
1807 - 1808 :	"Paid "ditto 15 days work: £1..0sh..0d.".
1809 Mar 12th:	"Paid "Isaac Luxon 24 and a half days: £1..12sh..4d.".
1809 Mar 12th:	"Paid "ditto drawing 986 seams stones: £4..1sh..11d".
1809 Mar 12th:	"Paid "ditto drawing 701 seams: £1..8sh..4d".
1809 Aug 26th:	"Paid "Isaac Luxon drawing 433 seams stones: £1..16sh..0d".
1809 Aug 26th:	"Paid "Isaac and Thomas Luxon drawing 402 seams: £1..13sh..6d".
1809 Aug 26th:	"Paid "ditto for drawing 64 seams stones: 2sh..8d".
1809 Aug 26th:	"Paid "Isaac Luxon 20 and a half days work: £1..10sh..9d".
1809 Aug 26th:	"Paid "ditto cleaning 60 yards ditches: 15sh..0d".
1810 :	Paid "Isaac Luxon 66 days: £4..19sh..9d".
1810 :	Paid "ditto digging 3438 seams stones: £12..17sh..10d".
1811 :	Paid "Isaac Luxon 41 days: £3..1sh..6d".
1812 :	Paid "Isaac Luxon: £2..3sh..6d".
1812 :	Paid "Isaac Luxon: £2..12sh..2d".
1815 :	Paid "Isaac Luxon for labour as per bill: 12sh..4d".

Isaac's wife Mary died aged 77 and was buried at St Petrock's Church, Petton on the 24th March 1826. The ancient Celtic church dedicated to a sixth century British saint, Petrock, is sited on a hill overlooking Mary's home at Hutchings on Frogpit Moor. In his final years Isaac was cared for by his daughter Jane, and her husband John Gamlin, who lived with him at Hutchings Farm. However, according to the Index to death duty registers Isaac was residing with his son at Upton, Somerset when he died in 1834.

Isaac Luxton, senior, of the Parish of Bampton, Devon, yeoman, made his will on the 2nd July 1831. His daughter Jane Gamlin was to receive

£60, to be paid to her within a year of her father's decease. Jane was to further receive "all my Household Goods" provided she and her husband "give up quiet possession of all my House Lands and Premises to my son Thomas Luxton within one month after my decease or to have no Legacy". His son Isaac and daughter Ann Twiggs, were to have "the note of hand that I have against John Capron for sixty pounds with Interest due thereon". John P. Capron was a whitesmith (i. e. tinsmith) in Bampton according to White's Devon Directory 1850, page 323.

Isaac gave his son Jacob, "all my nursery of young apple trees for his own use". His "grand son Isaac Luxton son of my son Isaac Luxton" was to receive £5 when he was 21. The rest of his "worldly Goods Chattels and Effects whatsoever and wheresoever" Isaac bequeathed to his son Thomas whom he appointed sole executor of the will. Isaac signed the will which was witnessed by John and Thomas Hill.

Isaac died, aged 83, on the 26th October 1834 and his will was proved in the Archdeacon's Court at Exeter on the 19th December 1834 by his eldest son, Thomas Luxton, yeoman, of Upton, Somerset, the executor.

Isaac Luxton was buried at St. Petrock's Petton on the 2nd November 1834. There was no monumental inscription to Isaac's memory when my brother Ian and I visited Petton in April 1971. But the orchard of apple trees which Isaac left to his son Jacob, our great great grandfather, was still growing at Hutchings Farm.

8

THOMAS LUXTON (1756-1817) BULLOCK JOBBER OF NEW HOUSE TENEMENT, PETTON, BAMPTON

See tree 1

Thomas Luxen, the fifth child of Jacob Luxton (1715? –1759), husbandman, and his wife Susannah Lake, was baptised at St. Petrock's Church, Petton, Bampton on the 5th September 1756.

Thomas was about three years old when his father Jacob died and was buried at Petton on the 27th May 1759. His widowed mother Susannah was to marry again, this time to John Merson at Bampton on the 4th September 1763 and she was to have a further five children. Details of Thomas's upbringing are unknown but he did remain illiterate. He signed the Bampton marriage register with a mark when, as Thomas Luxen, he married Joan Morris of Bampton in the parish church of St. Michael on the 16th April 1792. There is no record of any children being born of this marriage. Joan Luxon was buried at Petton on the 14th January 1797.

Thomas Luxon married Ann Jenkins of Bampton, his second wife, at Bampton on the 10th December 1797. Ann, ten years younger than Thomas, was baptised at Carhampton, Somerset on the 29th June 1766, the daughter of Richard Jenkins, husbandman, and his wife Ann Towell. She appears to have done a little nursing. The Bampton Workhouse Monthly Account Book (1807-1812)[57] contains a solitary reference in March 1809 to "Thomas Luxton's wife" being paid two shillings for "attending" Richard Govier who was presumably a sick pauper living within Bampton parish.

The couple had at least four children. Jenny Luxon, a daughter, baptised at Bampton on the 20th January 1799, died at the age of seven and was

---

[57] Bampton Workhouse Monthly Account Book 1807-1812(1269A/PO11)

buried at Petton on the 7th October 1806. Thomas Luxton (c.1797-1885), their eldest son, baptised at Petton on the 1st May 1803, settled in Aller, Somerset where he became a successful farmer. He had two wives and sixteen children and was the ancestor of the family branches established at Aller and Bridgewater in Somerset. William (c1807/10-1845), a second son, a bachelor, was a labourer who suffered with consumption for five months before he died, aged 38, at Bampton on the 4th November 1845. The identity of an Elizabeth Thomas of Bampton who was present at his death is unknown. The Petton register gives William's age as 35 and records that he resided in Shillingford, Bampton before his burial on the 9th November 1845. The fourth child, Elizabeth Luxon, was baptised at Petton on the 6th March 1808 but no more is known of her unless she was the Elizabeth Thomas present at William's death.

North Devon cattle were greatly prized for their value as working oxen and they were reared for meat rather than milk[58].Thomas, according to his eldest son's marriage certificate, earned his living as a bullock jobber. His home at the west end of New House Tenement, Petton must have been the base from which he conducted his business of buying and selling cattle. It is marked as Plot No. 1513 on the 1842 Bampton tithe map and apportionment and it lay on the south side of the turnpike road between Bampton and Wiveliscombe.

The property originally belonged to his grandfather, Robert Luxton (circa 1664/69-1751), who most certainly had New House Tenement built. How the west end of the property came into Thomas's ownership is uncertain because the will of his grandfather Robert was destroyed in the Exeter blitz. Thomas may have inherited it from his father Jacob. We know that his brother, Isaac, inherited Jacob's smallholding at Hutchings Farm on Frogpit Moor. It may have been similarly agreed that Thomas would inherit the West End of New House Tenement. However, the property may have come into Thomas's ownership as a result of a business transaction in the family but, if so, the details have not survived. The adjoining East End of New House Tenement had been sold by his uncle, Abraham Luxton, to Joseph, another uncle, in 1770. Thomas Luxon was listed, along with his cousin Robert Luxon (1744-1831), in the Freeholders Register for 1807.

---

[58] General View of the Agriculture of the County of Devon by Charles Vancouver (1808). David & Charles Reprint.

The Bampton Surveyors of Highways Rates and Account Books reveal that Thomas Luxton paid in only four years towards the cost of road maintenance. He paid the surveyor 9d in 1791, 1 shilling and 6 pence in 1792 and 1 shilling in 1794 and 1795. It's not clear how he avoided paying the rate in other years, perhaps he lacked the necessary status to qualify. To supplement his income Thomas was employed as a casual labourer by the surveyors of the Bampton highways on road works in the sixteen years 1797 to 1812. His first payment was on the 16th July 1797 when he earned 15 shillings for 12 days work and his last payment was £2..12sh..8d in 1812 but the nature of his work is not specified. The rate of pay varied, but he was normally paid 1 shilling and 3 pence a day[59]. We find him being paid 2 shillings and 6d for two days work on the 6th August 1797 and 6 shillings and 3 pence for 5 days work on the 6th October that year. For working 25 days Thomas and his brother, Isaac, shared £1..11shillings and 3d on the 21st August 1797. In 1802 he was paid 4shillings for collecting 56 seams of stones. Too often, however, payments are made for his labour and no details are provided of the work undertaken. In 1803, for instance, the bill for his labour came to £1..9shillings and 8d. More interesting are references to him collecting stones out of the river Batherm. On the 8th October 1807 he was paid 11 shillings 0d which came to 1d per seam for collecting "132 seams of stones out of the River" and the same day he received a further 6shillings and 8d for "5 days work" which was the time he spent collecting the stones. Payments in the years 1807- 1808 included 16shillings and 8d for opening "50 perch of road at 4d per perch" and £4..4shillings "for opening 21 perch of roads". The 12th March 1809 was another good pay day when he received 7shillings and 0 pence for "drawing posts" and £3..3shillings..0d for"drawing stones". In 1810 Thomas was paid 5 shillings for "cleaning water tables" and the princely sum of £7..18shillings for

---

[59] In his General View of the Agriculture of the County of Devon (1808) the author remarked that wages had not kept pace with the depreciation of money during the Napoleonic Wars. He noted a casual labourer received 1s..4d a day with a quart or three pints of drink, probably cider.

"widening Bowden's Lane". The photograph on the last page shows Bowden's Lane with view of Quartley Hill in distance. There was a back payment due of £1..7sh..2d "due from last surveyor". Other payments that year included £1..2sh..4d for "cleaning water tables 67 perches at 4d a perch", 1shilling "for pitchers" and 9 shillings for "150 faggots wallet". For undertaking 113 days work in 1810 Thomas received £8..9sh..6d and in 1811 for 189 days work he was paid £14..3sh..6d and he earned a further £6..11shillings and 8d that year for "breaking and spreading 632 load of stones". Perhaps the most interesting payment made in 1811 was £1..13sh..6d paid to Thomas' wife "Ann Luxon for picking 400 seams of stones" presumably out of the River Batherm.

This is the full record of Thomas' work in the Bampton highways, extracted from the Surveyors of Highways Rates and Account books:-

1797 July 16th: Paid "Thomas Luxon 12 days": 15sh..0d.

1797 Aug 6th: Paid "Thomas Luxon 2 days": 2sh..6d.

1797 Aug 21st: Paid "Thomas Luxon and Isaac Luxon 25 days": £1..11sh..3d.

1797 Oct 6th : Paid "Thomas Luxon 5 days": 6sh.3d.

1802 : Paid "Thomas Luxon 56 seams of stones: 4sh..0d".

1803 : Paid "Thomas Luxon's bill for labour: £1..9sh..8d".

1807 Oct 8th: Paid "Thomas Luxon 132 seams of stones out of the River: 11sh..0d".

1807 Oct 8th: Paid "ditto for 5 days work: 6sh..8d".

1807 - 1808 : Paid "Thomas Luxton 50 perch at 4d per perch: 16sh..8d".

1807 - 1808 : Paid "Luxton 8 days work: 10sh..8d".

1807 - 1808 : Paid "Thomas Luxton for opening 21 perch of roads: £4..4sh..0d".

1807 - 1808 : Paid "Thomas Luxton 130 seams stones: 10sh..10d".

1807 - 1808: Paid "ditto 5 days work: 6sh..8d".

1809 Mar 12th : Paid "Thomas Luxon drawing stones: £3..3sh..10d".

1809 Mar 12th: Paid "ditto drawing posts: 7sh..0d".

1809 Aug 26th : Paid "Thomas Luxon's bill: £1..11sh..6d".

1809 Aug 26th : Paid "Isaac and Thomas Luxon drawing 402 seams: £1..13sh..6d".

1809 Aug 26th : Paid "ditto for drawing 64 seams stones: 2sh..8d".

1810 : Paid "Thomas Luxon cleaning water tables: 5sh..0d".

1810 : Paid "ditto widening Bowdens Lane: £7..18sh..0d".

1810 : Paid "ditto another bill due from last surveyor: £1..7sh..2d".

1810 : Paid "Thomas Luxon cleaning water tables 67 perches at 4d: £1..2sh..4d".

1810 : Paid "ditto for pitchers: 1sh..0d".

1810 : Paid "ditto for 150 faggots wallet: 9sh..0d"[60].

1810 : Paid "Thomas Luxon 113 days: £8..9sh..6d".

1811 : Paid "Thomas Luxon 189 days: £14..3sh..6d".

1811 : Paid "Thomas Luxon for breaking and spreading 632 load of stones: £6..11sh..8d".

1811 : Paid "Ann Luxon for picking 400 seams of stones: £1..13sh..6d".

1812 : Paid "Thomas Luxon: £2..10sh..7d".

1812 : Paid "Thomas Luxon: £2..12sh..8d".

Thomas Luxton, yeoman of Petton, in his Will, made on the 23rd May 1817, left "William Luxton my youngest son all my cottage dwelling house called Newhouse Gardens Orchards with the appurtenances thereunto belonging situated in the parish of Clayhanger......... Devon.....now in the possession of James Davey carpenter. To hold to him the said William Luxton his heirs and assigns for ever".

To Ann, his wife, if she remained a widow, he bequeathed, "the dwelling house orchards and gardens now in my own possession being part of ffrogpitts Moor known by the name of the west end of Newhouse during her natural life and immediately after her decease to Thomas Luxton my eldest son". When Thomas attained the age of 21 he was to pay his mother Ann one shilling per week "if the mother and son agree to live together". Also provided that Ann remained a widow she was to receive "the use of my household goods during her natural life money and monies worth that I shall die possessed of for her cloathing my children, repairing the said houses and premises". If Ann married again "my express will is that my oldest son Thomas Luxton have immediate possession of the aforesaid premises, and household goods to be equally parted between my two sons Thomas Luxton and William Luxton."

---

[60] Trees or shrubs encroaching on the roadside verge were cut in bundles of sticks & bound together as faggots for fuel, and packed into a large bag called a wallet.

Thomas appointed his eldest son, Thomas, as sole executor of his will signed with his mark on the 23rd May 1817. It was witnessed by his kinsman, Robert Luxton (1744-1831) gunstock maker of Box Hedge, Petton, Robt. Cottrell and John Hill.

Thomas Luxton died within a week of making his Will. He was aged 61 and was buried at Petton on the 1st June 1817. The administration of the Will was granted in the Prerogative Court of Canterbury[61] on the 23rd August 1817 to his widow Ann Luxton, the natural and lawful mother and Guardian to his son Thomas Luxton who was still a minor.

Ann Luxton, Thomas's widow was to live another forty years before she died aged 96 and was buried at Petton on the 30th November 1857.

---

[61] To use the Prerogative Court of Canterbury appears to be pretentious of Thomas as it was a higher court than was strictly necessary. However, Thomas was mindful that his sons were still minors and his use of a higher court probably made him feel more confident that his will would be implemented. The will of Thomas Luxton, yeoman, Public Record Office PROB 11/1595.

9

THOMAS LUXTON (1783-1840) MASON AND YEOMAN OF HUTCHINGS, PETTON, BAMPTON.

See tree 4

Isaac Luxton (1751-1834), yeoman at Hutchings, Petton, Bampton and his wife Mary North of Morebath, had three sons who reared families of their own. Thomas (1783-1840), their eldest son, a yeoman and mason, who succeeded his father at Hutchings had two adult brothers, Isaac (1789-1838), a mason at Kymmen Moor, Skilgate, and Jacob (1800-1868), a mason who lived at Paradise in Chipstable. The Bampton area was long known for its limestone quarries so with good building stone readily available it is scarcely surprising the three brothers became masons.

I am focusing on the life of Thomas and his family in this chapter. In the eighteenth century and later, Luxton was often written phonetically in Devon dialect, so that Thomas was baptised as Thomas Luxen at Bampton on the 9th November 1783. Christmas Day that year there was a heavy fall of snow in Devon and there was a severe frost which remained on and in the ground until the middle of March 1784. Roads were almost impassable with the snow and it was one of the most severe winters of the eighteenth century. Fortunately the infant survived but we know nothing else of Thomas's childhood although he evidently received a little schooling.

There was intense military activity in England in the opening years of the nineteenth century because of the threat from Napoleon's France and Thomas was one of the young men drawn in the ballot to be enrolled in the Militia. The Bampton Workhouse Monthly Account Book 1801-1806 lists payments made to him[62]:-

---

[62] Bampton Workhouse Monthly Account Book 1801-1806(1269A/PO11)

1803 Aug 28th – Sep 25th: "Paid Luxon drawn in the Militia as per order of the Colonel: £2..10sh".

and again

1804 Apr 1st – Apr 28th: "Paid Thomas Luxon drawn in the Army of Reserve: £2..10sh".

These two years before the Battle of Trafalgar were crucial in terms of the defence of England against an expected French invasion. Thomas appeared, however, to have remained in the Militia for only a short period while the emergency lasted. He did not enlist in the regular army. The next reference to him is in 1812 when he signs his name Thomas Luxon, as a witness to the marriage of his brother, Isaac, to Judith Skinner at Skilgate. Four years later Thomas Luxon of Bampton married Jenny Palmer at St. Michael's parish church, Raddington on the 26th April 1816. His wife, Jenny Palmer, who was living in Raddington at the time of their marriage was born in Ashbrittle, Somerset where the parish register records the baptism of Jenny and Betty base children of Grace Palmer on the 5th of August 1790[63]

St. Michael's, Raddington, in the photograph below, is balanced on top of a small round hill, looking over farming country. It is likely to have been an early pagan site as St. Michael is believed to have been the angel who threw the Devil out of Heaven and the Anglo- Saxons called on him when consecrating pagan sites for Christianity. The tower is thirteenth century, restored in 1695, roughcast rendered in the 20th century. Two of the four bells which hung in the tower until 1971 were cast in 1370 and the carved bosses in the roof contain the image of the green man. The main door is fourteenth century and well preserved with beautiful iron hinges and back-plates. One of the churches gems is its rood screen which bears on it some of the very finest naturalistic foliage carving. The windows are fourteenth and fifteenth century.

---

[63] The Palmer family farmed in the Ashbrittle/Stawley area of west Somerset in the 18th & 19th centuries.Successive generations of their male children were named Peregrine which means "a wanderer." The family may be related to the Palmer family of Fairfield near Stogursey, Somerset who also gave that name to male children following their move around 1600 from Parham in Sussex.

In the decade following their marriage the couple had five children. The baptismal records of their offspring furnish vital clues on Thomas's changing status and the family's movement between parishes. When Mary Luxon, their eldest child was born and baptised at Raddington in April 1817,  Thomas was a mason residing in the parish. By February 1819 when their second child, Jane Palmer Luxon, born in Bampton, was baptised at Raddington, Thomas was a mason living in Bampton. Thomas was a labourer at Petton when a third daughter, Elizabeth Luxton, was baptised at St. Petrock's in May 1821. He was in all probability labouring on his father's farm at Hutchings. In 1824 and again in 1827 when their sons, Thomas and John, were baptised at Petton, Thomas was a yeoman of Petton. His father, Isaac, was 73 in 1824 so it is feasible that Thomas had taken over the day to day management of the farm.

On his father's death in 1834, Thomas inherited the house and land at Hutchings. The property was a small holding of approximately four acres, and in order to eke out a satisfactory existence Thomas found it necessary to become a tenant farmer too. He was involved in farming activities in the parish of Upton, for as executor of his father's will, proved on the 19th December 1834 he signs his name as Thomas Luxton, Upton, Somerset, yeoman. The Land Tax Assessments for Upton in 1831 and 1832 reveal Thomas occupied land called "Priest Close" which he rented from Isett Phillip. The tax of four shillings a year had not been paid.

Thomas was dying by early 1840. His sons, Thomas and John, were masons aged 16 and 13 respectively, so it was necessary to take out a loan to pull the family through a difficult financial period. Hutchings Farm was used as security for the loan. By an indenture made the 18th February 1840, Thomas and Jane (Jenny), his wife, secured a mortgage on Hutchings with Robert Rickards of Taunton, gentleman. It was for the sum of "Eighty pounds sterling with interest for the same at the rate of Four Pounds and ten shillings per centum per annum". Banks and

Building Societies were not as available then as they are today of course and personal borrowing of money was a more common method of acquiring credit. It was also a profitable proposition for the lender, as 4 ½ per cent or so of interest was often charged, as in this case.

Thomas was dead and buried within a month of signing the indenture. He died at Bampton from consumption on the 5th March 1840 and his death certificate states he was a mason aged 55. Eight days later on the 13th March 1840 he was buried at St. Petrock's, Petton. The burial register records Thomas Luxton aged 56 of Hutchings.

The dying Thomas was mindful of his link in a family line which had occupied Hutchings from the middle of the 18th century. To the genealogist's delight the details are recorded in the 1840 indenture :-

"All that Cottage-house with the Gardens Orchard and two Closes of land thereto belonging……..formerly in the possession of Robert Luxton then of Jacob Luxton his Son afterwards of Isaac Luxton Son of the said Jacob Luxton and now in the possession of the said Thomas Luxton eldest Son and Heir at Law of the said Isaac Luxton deceased". Jane, Thomas's wife, released "all Dower right" on Hutchings so that it would be easier for their son, Thomas, to take over the property when he came of age.

At the time of the 1841 census Jane (Jenny), aged 50, widow, agricultural labourer, was living at Hutchings with three children, Elizabeth 20, Thomas 17, mason and John 14, mason. The eighty pounds was still owing to Robert Rickards together with the interest of one pound five shillings at 4 ½ per centum per annum. On the reverse of the 1840 indenture is a second indenture made on the 26th June 1841. Robert Rickards "having occasion" for his money "transferred the mortgage to the Revd. Robert Smith Bower of Wilton, Somerset for the sum of £81…5 shillings which is the principle sum of Eighty Pounds plus £1…5 shillings interest on the same for a year". The day to day management of the farm rested with Jane Luxton until 1845 when her son Thomas came of age. The Bampton poor Rate Book for 1843 lists – "The Widow Luxton, owner of part of Frogpitt Moor, 4 acres gross value of £7..2sh..6d, rated at 6sh..4d".

1844: "Jane Luxton, owner of Part of Frogpitt Moor, 4 acres, gross value of £7..2sh..6d, rated at 7sh..1d".

Ten years later in 1851 the head of the household at Hutchings was Jane's son, Thomas, aged 26, mason. Jane now aged 60 is called "Fanny"[64] which must have been the name by which she was known in the family. Two of her grandchildren were living at the farm. These were two seven year old boys, William Luxton, the illegitimate son of her unmarried daughter Mary, who was born at Bampton on the 10th October 1843 (baptised at Petton on 29th October) and his cousin, William Fisher Luxton, the illegitimate son of another daughter, Jane Palmer Luxton, who was baptised at Skilgate, Somerset on the 12th December 1843. 1843 must have been a year of much anguish and upset in the Luxton household at Hutchings.

The mid nineteenth century was a time of expanding opportunity in the new colonies and by the 29th January 1853, Thomas (1824-1893), the eldest son, had left Hutchings to settle near Palmyra, Orford Township, Canada. He proved a successful pioneer and by an indenture dated 11th May 1861 sold Hutchings for £180 to his younger brother John (1827-1906). In 1855 William Fisher Luxton, his nephew, aged twelve, also emigrated to Canada where he became a distinguished pioneer and leading citizen in Manitoba.

These changes at Hutchings are reflected in the 1861 census. The head of the household was John Luxton, 34, his wife, Eleanor, 34, and their sons Thomas G. Luxton, aged 10, and John, aged 6. John's widowed mother, Fanny,[65] now aged 71, and deaf, was living with them. John was a mason employing two men and two boys. The two boys were relatives living at the farm. They were his nephew, 16 year old William Luxton, a mason, who was the illegitimate son of Mary Luxton. Tragically William died at the early age of 24 on the 8th November 1867 as the result of a building accident in Bampton. He was buried at Petton on the 14th November. His death certificate states he collapsed six hours after receiving severe contusions to the legs from a wall falling on him. The other William Luxton (1849-1918), was a twelve year old servant, the son of John's cousin James Luxton (1813-1861), a mason in Skilgate. William who is described in the census as a "mason

---

[64] Her baptismal name was Jenny.
[65] The fact that both the 1851 and 1861 census gives Jenny the name "Fanny" suggests that was the name she was known by in her later life.

lender" born in Skilgate was to later establish his own successful building business in Bristol.

This chapter on Thomas Luxton and family at Hutchings Farm must end with the death of his widow, Jenny Luxton of Thorne House,[66] Petton. She died aged 79 on the 3rd February 1870 from "bronchitis and gradual decay" and was buried at St. Petrock's Petton on the 10th February 1870. The Return of Owners of Land for Devon (published in 1873) lists Jane Luxton, Bampton, owning 3 acres 1 rod and 31 poles, valued at £9...10s. By the date of publication Jane had been dead three years.

The interior of St Michael's, Raddington where Thomas and Jenny were married.

---

[66] There was no Thorne House listed in the fourteen pages for District 3(Petton) in the 1871 census. The house may have been part of "Frog Pitt Moor" which consisted of five dwellings.

10

THOMAS LUXTON (1824-1893) OF PETTON, DEVON AND PALMYRA, ONTARIO.

See tree 4

There was a large Devon migration to North America in the late 1840s and early 1850s. Thomas Luxton (1824-1893), mason and farmer at Hutchings Farm, Petton, Bampton, was one of the pioneers who joined in this migration to Canada.

Thomas was baptised at Petton on the 2nd May 1824, the eldest son of Thomas Luxton (1783-1840), mason and yeoman, and his wife Jenny Palmer. He was 16 when his father died from consumption in March 1840. The 1841 census reveals that his widowed mother, Jane (Jenny), aged 50, an agricultural labourer, managed the farm. Three of her children, Elizabeth aged 20, Thomas aged 17, and John aged 14, were still at home. Thomas and John were described as masons but they must have helped out on the farm too.

Hutchings was a small holding, and the earliest detailed map and description of the farm is contained in the Bampton Tithe map and apportionment, dated the 22nd August 1842.(See map below) Thomas, aged 18, owned Field No 1527 consisting of a cottage (i.e. Hutchings) Garden, Orchard and Nursery comprising three rods and twenty perches, Field No 1528 called "Home Field and Nursery" comprising one acre and twenty five perches which was used for pasture, and Field No 1529 called the "Mead" comprising one acre and one rod and twenty eight perches which was used as a meadow. The whole comprising three acres one rod and thirty-three perches was in effect the land that had descended to Thomas from his father, Thomas, his grandfather Isaac, his great-grandfather, Jacob, and his great-great-grandfather, Robert Luxton.

Some notion of the diversity of Thomas's activities at Hutchings is gleaned from a reading of the Journal that was kept by his first cousin,

Isaac Luxton (1815-1876) shoemaker, of Skilgate in Somerset. The journal records the following purchases from Thomas.

1848 Thomas Luxton
Petton   s   d
June 6   A Pig 6 weeks
2 days old   12 .. 0
March 9   6 lbs of cheese
-------------   2 .. 0

1850 Octr.   2lbs ¼ Honey
-------------   1 .. 2 ½
and again
1840 of Thomas Luxton
Sep 11   Bought a Watch
    £1 .. 15s
Given an old Watch an   £1 ..   0 paid

This last entry suggests that Thomas may have been a watch dealer and repairer too. Both Thomas and his cousin, Isaac, kept hives of bees. The straw hackles (i.e. straw coverings or roofings) were made of straw wound in a series of circles, open at the base, and possibly with a removable top. Bee keeping required skill and knowledge and many country folk in the 19th century would have kept hives.

In 1851 Thomas, a 26 year old master mason, was head of household at Hutchings. His widowed mother, Fanny, aged 60 and two illegitimate nephews, William, aged seven, born in Bampton, and William F. Luxton, also aged seven, born in Skilgate, were living at the farm. This was Thomas's last census in England before emigrating to Canada.

He was not alone in his desire to seek a better life in the colonies. Between 1851 and 1901 about 371,000 people left Devon to seek their future in places like Australia, America, Canada and South Africa. Thomas was settled by the 29th January 1853 on Lot 72, Talbot Road South, near the village of Palmyra, Orford Township, Kent County, Ontario[67]. His farm, located on the southern half of Lot 72, bordered on the shore of Lake Erie.

---

[67] Ontario Land Registry Office, Orford Township, Lot 72, Talbot Road South Folio 72-1,72-2,72-3 (Recopied from Book D folio's 41 and 180 and Book A2 folios 226 & 286.

In the early 1850s this southwest part of Ontario was opening up to settlement and Thomas joined many people from rural Devon and other parts of Britain who were moving into the province, purchasing land at a cheap rate. It was backbreaking work for the pioneers. They had to hack their farms and homes out of the primeval hardwood forest of oak, elm, maple and beech. The ground was cleared by burning the felled timber in big bonfires. Quick cash crops of potash and soft soap were made by leaching the ashes.

It didn't take Thomas long to settle in his chosen new land. He married Elizabeth McGugan, of Dunwich, by licence at St. Thomas Church, Ontario on the 22nd December 1853. Dunwich lies west of St. Thomas, not far from the Duart and Palmyra area where Thomas settled. His wife,  born in Ontario on the 10th April 1825, was a Baptist of Scottish descent. Thomas was now committed to his new country and by an indenture dated the 11th May 1861, "Thomas Luxton of Orford in the County of Kent in Upper Canada, Farmer", sold Hutchings for £180 to his brother John Luxton, mason.

Thomas built a house made of brick on his new farm that is still in existence today. He continued to employ his skills as a mason in Canada. The 1861 census for Orford Township, Kent County, Ontario, lists Thos. Luxton mason, 36, wife, Elizabeth 35, and their daughters Jane 6 and Mary 3. The 'Kent Gazetteer and General Business Directory' for 1864-5 advertises Thomas Lexton (sic), mason, Talbot Road South, Lot 72, Orford Township.

Thomas Luxton 42(sic), farmer, his wife, Elizabeth, 42, and their three daughters, Jane 15, Mary 12 and Elizabeth 8 were resident in Orford Township, Kent County for the 1871 census. The Kent County Directory 1880 registers Thomas Luxton farmer at Lot 72 South Talbot Road, Palmyra P.O. The Luxtons were a very well respected family in the community and Thomas's great-grand-daughter, Jean Kerr, said that even in her time people recalled, "what a fine man her grandpa Luxton was".

The 1891 census for Orford Township, Kent County, reveals that Thomas and Elizabeth Luxton were both aged 67 and they were Baptists. They were assisted in running the farm by Jane 32, their married daughter, and her Irish husband, Mathew Driver 35 who were Methodists with three children, Thomas 3, Sarah 2 and John S aged 1. Thomas Luxton died aged 69 on the 19th June 1893 and lies buried in a cemetery at Duart, a little village in Orford Township, Kent County with his wife Elizabeth who died aged 86 on the 31st December 1910. The pioneer couple are interred beneath a large brown granite headstone. Every year in August there is a decoration day in the cemetery. Thomas's daughter's grandchildren and his great granddaughter, Jean Kerr, always put flowers on the family grave.

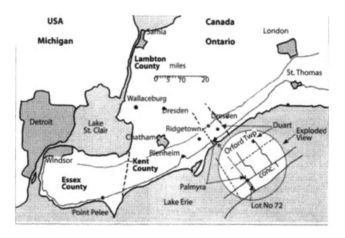

The epitaph reads: (side 1)
In memory of
Thomas Luxton
Died June 19, 1893
Aged 69 years.
Elizabeth McGugan
Wife of Thomas Luxton
Died Dec. 31, 1910. Aged 86 yrs
Gone but not forgotten
Luxton

(side 2)

Susannah Jane Driver
September 21, 1892-March 31, 1980.

Following Thomas Luxton's death in 1893 his widow, Elizabeth, and her eldest daughter Jane, born on the 5th January 1855, with her husband, Matthew Driver (1854-1928), continued to work the 115 acre farm. Jane died at the age of 74 on the 19th February 1929 and she lies buried at Trinity Anglican Church Cemetery, Howard Township. Her son Jack Driver operated a commercial fishery in Lake Erie, just off shore from the farm. When Jack died in 1938 the farm was sold to Mr Joseph Sedlac[68].

Thomas and Elizabeth Luxton had two other daughters who married and had their own families. Mary, the second daughter, born on the 13th March 1858, married Peter McPhail (1843-1922), Storekeeper and Postmaster at Palmyra, on the 4th June 1878. Mary died aged 76 in 1934 and she lies buried at Trinity Anglican Church Cemetery. Margaret Elizabeth Luxton, the youngest daughter, born at Palmyra on the 18th February 1862, was educated at Palmyra and was fond of recalling her school days at the little one-room school where there were no desks or chairs. Students sat around the walls on long benches to learn their lessons. All other living conditions were equally primitive. She married William Charles Sifton (1851-1923) at Trinity Anglican Church, Palmyra, on the 13th October 1880. Lizzie and her husband farmed in sight of her birthplace until 1920 when they moved to nearby Ridgetown, Ontario. She is known to have visited Petton and St. Petrock's Church, Devon, during the inter-war years. Mrs Sifton who died at Parkwood Hospital, London, Ontario on Monday 23rd November 1964 is buried like her sisters at Trinity Cemetery. Lizzie died at the advanced age of 102 and has the distinction of being the longest living member of our Luxton family.

What a treasure-house of stories she must have been on the Luxton family and their settlement in Canada. Her grandson, William C. Sifton, was the World Champion Soya-bean Grower at the Royal Winter Fair in Toronto in 1961.

---

[68] See letter of 16th December 1982 from Mr W.R.Sifton, R.R.1, Ridgetown, Ontario.

11

WILLIAM FISHER LUXTON (1843-1907) PIONEER TEACHER AND JOURNALIST IN MANITOBA, CANADA

See tree 6

William Fisher Luxton's family Bible in the possession of the Eleanor Luxton Archive at the Whyte Museum Banff, Alberta, records he was

born on the 12th December 1844 in Bampton, Devon. This too is the date and place given in published articles on his life. However, his birth certificate reveals that he was born a year earlier, on the 12th December 1843, in the neighbouring parish of Skilgate in Somerset. He was the illegitimate son of Jane Palmer Luxton who signed his birth certificate with a mark. Jane, a pauper when her son was baptised at Skilgate on Boxing Day 1843, was born in Bampton and baptised at Raddington, Somerset on the 28th February 1819. Her parents were Thomas Luxton (1783-1840), mason and yeoman, and his wife Jenny Palmer who lived at Hutchings, Petton, Bampton.

Jane was a twenty year old servant at North Hayne, a farm in Bampton in 1841. We do not know the identity of the child's natural father but there were two likely candidates living close by in the 1841 census. One was William Fisher, aged 20, a house servant to Robert Williams, a farmer and family at Upcott, Skilgate. He was not born in Somerset and perhaps came from Devon which borders Skilgate. However my hunch favours a second William Fisher (c.1811-1859) who was a 25 year old mason living with his parents by the churchyard in Bampton. Jane's father and brothers were masons so he would have been known to the family and perhaps worked with them at times. He was 48 when he died at Bampton on the 7th September 1859 from "Phthisis four months certified." Jane's father died of consumption and her own premature death was almost certainly the result of this infectious disease. There is no way we can now know the truth. No more is known of the father but family folklore, related by his granddaughter, Eleanor Luxton, has it that he belonged to a prominent entitled family and was accidentally killed. The story goes that for many years Jane refused to marry another man, preferring to bring up her child on her own.

The Victorian strict censure of illegitimacy meant that 1843 was a year of special anguish and shame for the Luxtons of Bampton. Jane's elder sister, Mary, gave birth to William, an illegitimate son, at Bampton on the 10th October 1843. This was just two months before Jane herself gave birth to her own illegitimate son, William Fisher Luxton. It's a paradox that although the Victorian's especially disliked and condemned the begetting of bastards as a public disgrace, more illegitimate children were born in Victoria's reign than in any other time in our past for which details are known[69].

The two unmarried mothers in 1851 were living apart from their children. Jane, aged 32, and Mary, 34, were assistants in a linen draper's shop in Fore Street, North Petherton, Somerset. Their seven year old children, William Fisher Luxton and his cousin William, were living at Hutchings, Petton with their widowed grandmother Jane Luxton, aged 60, and Uncle Thomas Luxton (1824-1893). Both boys probably received an elementary education at the Dame School, Box Hedge, Petton where the school mistresses, in 1851, were their kinswomen, Jane Luxton (1796-1867) and her sister Ann (1804-1868).

Jane Palmer Luxton married William Burnett, son of John Burnett, labourer, in the Independent Chapel, North Petherton on the 29th March 1852. Her husband, William Burnett, who had also been an assistant in the linen drapers shop in Fore Street, signed the register, while Jane made her mark in the presence of her sister, Mary, who also signed with a mark. William Burnett was a warehouseman when Jane gave birth to a daughter, Elizabeth Burnett, at their home in Tapper's Lane, North Petherton on the 14th April 1854.

---

[69] See Peter Laslett's "The World we have lost", Second Edition, 1970 Methuen and company Limited, Page 138.

Canadian biographies state that William Fisher Luxton emigrated to Canada with his parents in 1855. The success of his uncle Thomas Luxton (1824-1893) who had emigrated by January 1853 to Palmyra Ontario, must have been the spur for William, his parents' and Aunt Mary Luxton to emigrate too. They settled in St. Thomas Ontario[70] but the family were soon struck by tragedy. Mary Luxton, William's aunt, died aged 38 on the 5th October 1855 followed by his mother Jane who died aged 37 on the 29th July 1856, and Bessie Burnett, his half-sister died aged 8 on the 9th July 1862. There were no death certificates and we can only speculate that his mother Jane and her sister

succumbed to consumption like their father before them. According to a note William scribbled many years later on the end paper at the back of his wife's prayer book, the three were buried in the Church of England cemetery in St. Thomas. Today there is no headstone marking the site of their grave.

I do not know what provision was made for William's upbringing. He was still only twelve when his mother died in July 1856. His marriage certificate of 1866 records his parents' names as William and Elizabeth Luxton[71] but I think that this was to spare blushes regarding his illegitimate birth. The 1861 census records his step-father, William

---

[70] Before 1867 Ontario was known as Canada West.
[71] History of the County of Middlesex Canada originally published in 1889 by W.A. & C.L. Goodspeed, Publishers, Toronto and London. See page 430 of new edition by Daniel Brock (1972) which also states that William Fisher Luxton married Sarah Jane Edwards at Komoko, Ontario but a copy of the marriage certificate held by Gail Mesplay reveals the wedding took place in Strathroy.

Burnett, widower, and his half sister, Elizabeth, aged 6, living in Dunwich, Ontario, which is in the St. Thomas area. William Fisher Luxton was not living with them and he does not appear anywhere in a search of the 1861 census. This facet of William's early life in Canada remains a mystery and I am still searching for documentary evidence to establish where he was living in these early years following the death of his mother.

Family memory recalls that when he was living in Ontario, William, visited his uncle Thomas Luxton and family in Palmyra on a number of occasions. Tom's daughter, Mary, was aged 8, when William came to visit for the first time. This was in 1866 the year William married and he was still in his early twenties. He gave Mary a beautiful hand painted set of china doll dishes which are still in the possession of the family and in 1981 his school medals belonged to Tom's great-grand daughter, Jean Kerr. His uncle Thomas thought the world of William and was very proud of his success. When William became the editor of the Manitoba Free Press he sent a copy of the paper every week to his uncle Thomas in Palmyra.

William received his education in the common and grammar schools at St. Thomas and Lobo, paying his way as "a farmer's chore boy". An old school friend of William at Lobo later recollected that he came to school in his farmer's clothes and that he was extremely persistent and industrious. He would ferret out a problem until he got to the bottom of it. This was to remain a characteristic all through his life. His last teacher at Lobo was G.W. Ross, a future business partner.

William was very successful in his examinations and he became a schoolteacher at Adelaide Township, near Strathroy, Ontario. When Strathroy, or St. John's, was detached from Adelaide in 1865, to form a new parish with Katesville, W. F. Luxton was listed as one of the contributors to the new school. The Mitchell & Co.

101

Canada Classified Directory for 1865-6 reveals that William F. Luxton was a bookseller and stationer in Strathroy at the time of his marriage. His marriage certificate states that Mr. William F. Luxton of the village of Strathroy in the County of Middlesex and Province of Canada and Miss Sarah Jane Edwards (in photo) of the Township of Lobo in the County of Middlesex and Province aforesaid were duly and legally married by me, Rev. George Richardson, Pastor of the Regular Baptist Church in Strathroy C. W.(i.e. Canada West) on the 4th day of April in the year of our Lord one thousand eight hundred and sixty-six by virtue of a Special License, and the authority invested in me by the laws of the Province of Canada.

As witness my hand the day and year herein before written
Witnesses: Henry Edwards} George Richardson
Alex Girdwood} Baptist Minister

Sarah's family had a Loyalist background. Her ancestor, George Edwards fled New York City (his farm was really in what is now lower Manhattan) and went to Canada at the start of the American Revolutionary War. Her great grand father George was a brother of Jonathan Edwards, a prominent preacher and author of the day.

The young couple dwelt awhile in Strathroy where the assessment rolls for 1866 list Wm F. Luxton Bookstore, householder. William is described as an editor in the Strathroy rolls for the following two years. In 1867, a son, William Franklin Luxton, born in that year was also listed. He was the eldest of eight children, six boys and two girls. Curiously the 1867 roll also lists a dog which is the earliest recorded pet in the Luxton family. William is listed in the 1868 Second Class Militia Roll for Strathroy.

A booklet published by Wm F. Luxton is preserved in Weldon Library, University of Western Ontario. It is an almanac with space for notes beside each day.

The front reads:-
Luxton's Canadian Farmer's Almanac
for 1867
Published by Wm F. Luxton
Strathroy, C.W.
Printed by Robert Miller, Montreal.

The back reads:-

Wm F. Luxton
Bookseller & Stationer
Dealer in all kinds of
School, Miscellaneous & Blank Books
English, French and American Stationery,
Wall Paper & Windsor Shades
Portemonnaires, Writing Desks, etc, etc.
Agent
for
Pianos, Organs & Melodeans
of the Best Makers.
A large assortment of family Goods always on hand
Orders for all goods in the line strictly attended to.
"As good as the best, and as cheap as the cheapest"
at
Luxton's Bookstore
Union Block, Front Street, Strathroy C.W.

William displayed an inclination for journalism at an early age and he became a pioneer newspaperman in Canada. He was still in his early twenties when he established the Strathroy Age in 1866 in partnership with G.W. Ross, his former teacher, who subsequently became Sir George W. Ross, the Liberal Premier of Ontario from 1899 to 1905. In 1867 the paper was purchased by Ross who conducted it briefly until April 1868 when it was bought back by W. F. Luxton. He continued in charge only until the 1st August when Hugh McColl took over. Luxton moved to Seaforth, Huron County, where with Ross he purchased the village's weekly newspaper, the Seaforth Expositor, in 1869. It was also a success.

William F. Luxton was also the first librarian of the Seaforth Mechanics Institute and Library association which was incorporated in 1869 with a membership of two hundred. Later renamed the Seaforth Public Library, it was situated above Thomas Kidd's south store at the corner of Main and Market Street. In December 1870 Luxton and Ross sold the Seaforth Expositor to the brothers Alan and Murdo Mclean whose family were to run the newspaper until 1982.Lowell's Province of Ontario Directory for 1871 lists William as living in Seaforth which is confirmed by the 1871 census which records William, Jane his wife, and their sons living in the town. W.F. Luxton was editor too of the short lived Daily Home Journal, at Goderich, which was published from March to May 1871 but it proved an unprofitable venture.

In 1871 Luxton was sent by George Brown, proprietor of the Toronto Globe, to Upper Fort Gary (now Winnipeg, Manitoba) as the special correspondent in the North West Territories. He was to write about what was then a comparatively unknown land. For several years his letters to the Globe aroused considerable interest in the older parts of Canada.

Luxton, an early settler in the rapidly growing city of Winnipeg, was a pioneer in education and journalism in the Canadian West. He did not get off to a favourable start, however, because for a few weeks in that first year he suffered from an attack of typhoid fever. He was taken to the city hospital in Winnipeg, a private institution, situated on Albert Street, in a building at the rear of McArthur's Store. On his recovery he was deciding on whether or not to return to Ontario when the Protestant School Trustees persuaded him to remain in the city. They hired him at 500 dollars a year to instruct some thirty pupils in the first school established under the provisions of the Manitoba Schools Act of 1871.

The school was held in a one-room log house measuring twenty feet by eighteen feet on Point Douglas (The River Heights of pioneer Winnipeg). It was furnished with a teacher's lectern and a couple of rows of neatly painted desks with ink-wells for the pupils. In severe winter weather a stove pipe chimney served to keep the thirty hardy pupils warm. William Fisher Luxton became the first school teacher in Manitoba when this school opened on the 31st October 1871.

The Rev. Cyprian Pinkham, the Superintendent of Schools, visited the school on the 5th December 1871. He was "pleased with the admirable manner with which Mr Luxton imparts knowledge to the children.

He certainly does not spare himself and the children attending his school will make rapid progress. They are fortunate in having such a teacher".

His pupils were impressed too. Years later one of them recalled, "Yes, we all liked him, but you must not get the impression from that fact that he let us do as we liked. The reason we liked him was because he made education interesting".

However, W.F. Luxton had initially come to Winnipeg with the intention of giving the young town a newspaper of its own, and he had only consented to teach to start the Winnipeg public school on its course.

A few years before he arrived in Winnipeg the settlement had several newspapers –the Liberal, the Gazette, and the Manitoban. But these newspapers had made comments which upset Louis Riel and one night, during an election riot, Riel and his supporters wrecked every press and case of type they could lay their hands on.

Luxton's friend named Banning, who had been doing well in the lumber business came to him and said, "Now is the time to start your paper; you have a clear field".

To the 28 year old journalist who had founded Winnipeg's first school the year before here was an opportunity crying out for his particular talents. He resigned his teaching post and formed a partnership with John A. Kenny, a retired Ontario farmer. With his own savings and a 4000 dollar loan from Kenny, Luxton started a pro- liberal weekly newspaper, the Manitoba Free Press (renamed the Winnipeg Free Press in 1931). They bought a Washington hand press at the cost of over half their bank roll and on the 25th October, two weeks after the paddle-wheel steamer chugged up the Red River with the press they were in business. It was the first cylinder press north of St. Paul, Minnesota, and was run by human muscle power supplied mainly by the huge and powerful Kenny, who, among others turned the handle.

W.F. Luxton began producing his Manitoba Free Press in a decrepit little two storey tar-paper shack at 555 Main Street, Winnipeg. Situated near the

present Main and James Street corner, its north wall was so rickety Luxton
feared it would cave in and bury him with the press, prose and all. The rear
of the building was occupied by the presses and a big box stove. Luxton
who was editor lived with his wife and family upstairs while John A.
Kenny the publisher, who was a bachelor, lived in the garret. The staff,
John R. Cameron, reporter and humorist, and Justus A. Griffon, printer,
had a bunk downstairs in a cubby hole next to the front office and shared
meals with the Luxtons. The Manitoba Free Press began as a four page
weekly. A Prospectus edition to acquaint potential subscribers with the
nature of the new journal appeared in November and the first regular
edition was launched the 30th November 1872 although a few copies
distributed free appeared on the 9th November.

Liberal in philosophy, the Free Press was a leader among newspapers in
Canada. It became a leading daily and its sister weekly, the Prairie
Farmer, became the most widely circulated farm weekly in Canada. Of
twenty newspapers that started in Manitoba between 1859 and 1890,
only the Free Press survived.

The eight page first edition contained a variety of material, including a story, a poor man's news, telegraphic dispatches, editorials, local news, and classified adds. The first main story was the re-election of General Ulysses S. Grant as President of the United States of America. It was the only daily west of Toronto on 6th July, 1874. It cost 25 cents per week on subscription and there were 900 subscribers. In those early years, putting together a newspaper was a formidable task. All copy was written by hand and type was set by hand, one letter at a time. In very cold weather, even the red-hot box stove in the press room could not keep the ink and rollers warm and a row of 32 coal oil lamps was placed around the press.

Many other problems surfaced in those early years-failure of telegraphic services via Montreal and the U. S. A. due to adverse weather-storms, frost and prairie fire, unreliable paper supply that had to come by rail, steamboat or ox cart. For example paper shortage coincided with the hot story of the downfall in 1873 of Prime Minister John A. Macdonald's government. There was just enough paper for the Free Press to produce a hand bill –sized sheet carrying the news from Ottawa and apologies to readers[72].

The shack held out until 1874. That year as the Free Press had repeatedly urged it to do, Winnipeg became a city. The paper was by this time well established and had promoted itself from the shanty to a few blocks down the street to a new building on Main, opposite St. Mary Avenue. On the 6th July 1874 it became a daily as well as a weekly.

The Free Press continued to gather news and scrutinize editorially affairs in Winnipeg and the country at large. A great deal of its energy during the middle 1870s was directed at the progress, or lack of it, of the railway being built to Winnipeg. But finally, in 1877, the railway became a reality.

With the coming of the railway came the real estate boom. Winnipeg, almost overnight, became one huge auction block. Bars and gambling houses made fortunes and flamboyance was the keynote of

---

[72] I have researched William F. Luxton's life in the U. K. and for his private life in Canada much of my information is derived from his family especially Susan Freeborn and Gail Mesplay. For his newspaper career I have relied heavily on the Manitoba Historical Society and numerous other Canadian articles.

every operation. J.S. Coolican, the "King of the Auctioneers", celebrated his real estate "killings" one night at the Queen's Hotel by taking a bath in wine.

As the community boomed the Free Press grew apace. It became a morning edition in 1882and moved into "an imposing two storey edifice" on McDermot, the street which within the next twenty years was to become famous in Winnipeg and to the west as "Newspaper Row".

By 1885 the Free Press was deeply involved in a battle over the railway monopoly issue and it accumulated an impressive array of libel suits, criminal and civil. The criminal complaints were never prosecuted, however, and the civil suits were eventually lost in the courts.

In 1889 an evening edition of the paper was added to the morning issue. Luxton's original five-man operation had expanded to one with sixty people on the payroll. His partner Kenny had retired. Luxton himself was still writing his biting editorials in precise longhand and collecting talented writers the way he collected subscribers. The Free Press was the child of William F. Luxton's genius and love. He was offered the Premiership of Manitoba on one occasion but refused it because of his love and devotion to the Free Press. He was the first editor and remained in control for twenty one years.

Indeed, W.F. Luxton became a legend in his lifetime. He was slim and bearded in appearance and possessed a steady gaze. Endowed with a sharp wit he was inclined to puns. Though fiery by nature and impulsive by temperament he was considered just and generous in his treatment of people. His fearless editorials and straightforward policies did much to shape the future of the new city of Winnipeg and he saw his paper grow into one of the foremost publications in Canada.

The Free Press exemplified his good old-fashioned ideas about journalism. He was a great believer in printing the news, regardless of whom it helped or hurt but it had to be real news to be printed in his paper. He was intolerant of fakes and wild rumours and he gave the Free Press its reputation for accuracy in its facts and sobriety in its treatment of them. For example during the second Louis Riel rebellion in 1885 the Canadian newspapers were filled with alarmist reports from the west which were largely the figments of disordered imaginations but the Free Press announced that "when nothing occurs, nothing will be reported". It systematically lived up to this maxim. He strove to print only reliable news. Once a lawyer reported a meeting for him before it happened, arguing that it was only a small matter. Luxton replied that it did matter because the people of that small place knew that the item was not strictly true and they would naturally give no greater credence to other news. "I want only the truth in the Free Press", said Luxton.

W.F. Luxton was a born editor. His editorials were always crisp and dealt with the matters of the day without fear or favour. He fought for his political beliefs through the paper and was renowned as a great news-getter and an equally great editor. He taxed the resources of his establishment to secure telegraph news from the outside world and the Free Press gave a surprising amount of general information.

Luxton had an absolute devotion to the West and its interests as he perceived them. Through his paper he did much to inspire others with his buoyant optimism about the territory and its future. His belief that

the West should have its chance to develop was the root inspiration of his editorial policy and he fought for its rights with a passion and determination which made his name a household word in Manitoba and beyond. He strove to remove conditions which checked the development of the West such as short sighted laws, high tariffs and railway monopoly. Many of the most distinctive and praiseworthy traits of Liberalism in western Canada at the turn of the nineteenth century found their origins in the militant western policy pursued by the Free Press during the years W.F. Luxton's powerful individuality impressed itself upon the community. Luxton was described by one historian as "the dean of newspaperdom in the west" and he served as a mentor to countless frontier newsmen who themselves became legends in the history of Canadian journalism.

W.F. Luxton prospered in Winnipeg's boom years and he moved into a new home, a large white painted wooden structure named Armstrong's Point. He was at the height of his success when the Winnipeg census was taken on the 1st May 1891. The household comprised William Fisher Luxton, 46, newspaper editor, his wife Sarah Jane, 43, and their children, William Franklin, 23, brakesman Canadian Pacific Railway, Harry Addison, 20, medical student, Nellie 14, Norman K. 15, Louis P. 12, Olive 10, George E.8, Malloch H. 7, and two housemaids, a cook and a groom. The family including William are listed as Baptists.

The establishment of the Free Press had made him a leading figure in Winnipeg and he was active in many civic causes. He took a prominent part in securing the incorporation of Winnipeg as a city and in the first election for mayor in 1874 he was an unsuccessful candidate against a redoubtable opponent. W.F. sat on the Protestant section of the Manitoba Board of Education and was chairman of the Winnipeg School Board from 1885 to 1887. He was a charter member of the Winnipeg Board of Trade and was a very active member for many years. One of the founders of the Winnipeg General Hospital, he was a life governor. He was president of the Agricultural Society in 1878 and its director for ten years. In addition he was a founder of the Winnipeg Humane Society.

It was inevitable that Luxton with his high public spirit and reforming zeal should enter politics. His main goals were prohibition, the establishment of a secular school system, and the abolishment of French as an official language in Manitoba. He was very strongly opposed to the Canadian Pacific Railway and he strongly criticised its ally the Conservative government of Manitoba. He served in the Legislative Assembly for Rockwood in the years 1874-1878. He retired from provincial politics in 1878 but entered the national political field when he was elected for Winnipeg South, 1886-88. His defeat in 1892 ended his political career.

W.F.'s pronounced individuality and ardent temperament and his fearless and pointed editorials made him powerful enemies in the Manitoba government and the Canadian Pacific Railway. Following the collapse of Winnipeg's boom, Luxton unwisely accepted a loan from the unscrupulous and devious Scots born financier Donald Alexander Smith. When Luxton missed the crucial repayment deadline of September 1893 his opponents had their revenge. Smith and his associates in the Canadian Pacific Railway obtained control of the troublesome Free Press. They appointed a new editor and Luxton, according to his letter to the Winnipeg

William Fisher Luxton

Tribune was 'turned penniless onto the street without an hours warning'. His granddaughter the late Pat J. Luxton in Minneapolis in a letter of the 6th February 1983 commented that W.F. 'lost everything and all his sons had to go to work'.

When her husband was ousted as editor of the Manitoba Free Press his wife Sarah, moved back to London, Ontario where she lived from 1893 to 1896.She was joined there by their daughter, Olive and sons Louis, George and Malloch. William Franklin, the eldest son, also visited while they were in Ontario but William F. Luxton seldom made the journey there.

Undaunted Luxton launched another paper in Manitoba, the Daily Nor'wester, the prospectus for which appeared in late December 1893, with the motto, "Independant not neutral." He sold the paper in 1896.In

August 1897 the general manager of the Manitoba Free Press made a proposal that he rejoin his old paper. In reply W. F. freely admitted that the offered income of 30 dollars a week would mean a "transition to comparative comfort from very uncomfortable poverty, from which my family and myself have been more or less suffering.....since I was ejected from the Free Press almost without a dollar". However, because of the managers "base ingratitude, black hearted treachery and cunning duplicity to me in the past" he declined the offer.

Fortunately, his old friend J.J. Hill offered William a position with the St. Paul Globe in Minnesota, and that is where he ended his journalistic career. The family settled in St. Paul in 1899 where William F. began as business manager and subsequently became the editor and general manager of the paper. The U. S. census for the 5th June 1900 shows the family headed by William F. Luxton, newspaper editor, living in St. Paul, minus Eleanor (Nellie) and son William Franklin.

Their son Norman, a reporter, was living in the next household, and he gave his year of immigration to the U. S. A. as 1898.Another son Harry, who had entered the U. S. A. in 1894, and his wife Pearl, were living with his in-laws the Taylors in Minneapolis.

William's wife, Sarah Jane, was a small woman and a semi-invalid in her later years. Like all the family she enjoyed reading. She wrote

poetry and her son "Norm" had some of her poems bound in book form. The family photograph is of a gathering in St Paul, perhaps on Independence Day 4th July 1910.It may have been a double celebration. Ada Livingstone, who has the stars and stripe flag on her lap, and George E Luxton who has the Union Jack, were married in Minneapolis on 30th June. In front next to Olive, with the dog, is Nell's husband, Fred Foster. Malloch and Eleanor (Nell) are at the back with Louis, Harry, Sarah Jane and Norman in the middle row.

His years in Minnesota, however, were unhappy ones for W.F. Luxton who had problems with drinking and was prone to startling contrasts of elation and depression. William and his wife separated and while Sarah stayed with the family in St. Paul, Minnesota, William returned to Winnipeg in 1901.His colleagues at the St. Paul Globe banded together and gave him a going away gift of an 150 dollar ring.

In Winnipeg he became inspector of public buildings for the Province of Manitoba. The 1906 census lists him as a 62 year old "roomer" residing at 262 Graham Street, Winnipeg.

After his absence for several years his old friends were glad to see him return. Now however he was broken in health and occupied a quiet position suited to his failing condition. He was one of the best known figures in Manitoba but in these later years he lived a more retired life and was never to be seen in public gatherings. He was, however, a familiar figure

William Fisher Luxton + Louis Luxton (Winnepeg)

in the city streets where he daily received the friendly greetings of his countless friends. The photo shows W.F. with son Louis in Winnipeg.

Death came suddenly to W. F. Luxton who was seized with a fatal apoplectic stroke on a Saturday evening while taking a bath at the

Commercial Club in Winnipeg. He was at once removed to the General Hospital which he had helped to found but because of the enfeebled condition of his health and the severity of the attack he never rallied. His son Harry who arrived from Minneapolis on the Friday morning was at William Fisher Luxton's bedside when he died at 11pm on Monday 20th May 1907[73].

He was buried on Friday 24th May at St. John's Cathedral Cemetery in Winnipeg on a plot provided by the Masonic Fraternity. His funeral procession which included a guard of honour provided by the Winnipeg Typographical Union, was one of the largest in the city's history. Both friends and opponents praised his reputation for accuracy and fearless investigation. Typical of many tributes was that of the Reverend George Bryce of Manitoba College, who noted simply that Luxton never betrayed the truth.

His burial place in St. John's Cathedral Cemetery is the oldest established cemetery in Western Canada where many of the pioneers associated with the growth of the west are buried. William's grave is marked on Historic Guides to St. John's Cathedral Cemetery and Churchyard. A pink granite tomb it reads:-

Pioneer and Patriot
William Fisher Luxton
Born Bampton, Devon, England
December 12, 1844,
Died at Winnipeg, Manitoba
May 20, 1907

Erected by friends to testify their appreciation
of a leading journalist and useful citizen
LUXTON

A plaque on the side of William's tombstone reads:-

Sara Jane
His wife
1846-1927

---

[73] William Fisher Luxton's death record states he was a journalist aged 62 years 5 months and a member of the Church of England.It gives his cause of death at Winnipeg General Hospital as Hemiplegia cerebral haemorrhage,3 days.

William Fisher Luxton was highly esteemed in Winnipeg where his name is still commemorated in Luxton Avenue, a street five blocks north of the Cathedral. In the autumn of 1907 Winnipeg honoured its first teacher by naming a large new school, Luxton School. Located at 11 Polsen Avenue it was still serving its community at the end of the twentieth century. The telephone directory also lists Luxton Community Centre and Luxton Grocery.

William Fisher Luxton was not the most tactful or prudent of men but he was a courageous and influential journalist with a keen sense of justice. Born into humble circumstances in the West Country of England he was to leave his imprint in the distant prairies of the American West.

William and his wife Sarah Jane had eight children and one of these Norman Kenny Luxton (1875-1962), a real character and pioneer in his own right, is the topic of a future chapter.

See tree 6

12

HARRY ADDISON LUXTON (1870-1910) A SOLDIER IN THE SPANISH AMERICAN WAR OF 1898

See tree 6

Harry Addison Luxton is best remembered within the family for being a soldier in the Spanish American War of 1898, and a graphic letter he wrote following the capture of Manila in the Philippines. Harry, the second son of William F. Luxton, and his wife Sarah Jane Edwards, was born in Seaforth, Ontario on the 27th July 1870. His mother, Sarah, had a loyalist background. George Edwards her ancestor fled New York City (his farm is really in what is now lower Manhattan) and went to Canada at the start of the American Revolutionary War.

Harry was still an infant when his family moved to Winnipeg, Manitoba, where his father was prominent in newspaper work as proprietor and editor of the Manitoba Free Press. When he was old enough he worked at the paper, starting as a proof reader and later as a police reporter and a member of the city news gathering staff. His general cheery disposition made him popular with the many whom he met in his daily rounds. In his spare time Harry enjoyed singing, and a review in the Daily Nor'Wester, in February 1894, says that H.A. Luxton was "most efficient" in his role in the comic opera, "The Mountebanks," presented by the Winnipeg Opera Company. But when his father lost control of the Manitoba Free Press in 1893 the family moved to the twin cities of St. Paul and Minneapolis in Minnesota, U.S.A. The last mention of Harry still working with the Free Press is in March 1894 and that is confirmed by the 1900 U.S. census as his date of immigration.

In the twin cities Harry, in the photograph below, was an assistant health inspector, while his father became general manager of the St. Paul Globe before returning to Winnipeg where he died in 1907.

116

The Spanish American War, in which Harry was involved, was fought to clear Spanish Imperialism out of the American continent which the Americans believed belonged to them. When the U.S.A. declared War for Cuban Independence on the 25th April 1898 hostilities began in Cuba but there was fighting in other parts of the world including the Philippines. Two days after War was declared, Commodore George Dewey sailed with the American Pacific Squadron from Hong Kong for Manila, the capital of the Philippines which was then a Spanish possession. Early in the morning of 1st May he penetrated Manila Bay and within a few hours destroyed the inferior Spanish fleet.

There was wild rejoicing when news of the victory reached the U.S.A. "Yellow" journalism played a huge role in getting everyone riled up so that volunteers couldn't wait to sign up and wave the patriotic flag for 62 dollars 40 cents a month.

Harry resigned as an assistant health inspector to serve as an enlisted soldier in Company F of the Thirteenth Minnesota Volunteers at Camp Ramsey, Minnesota, on the 7th May 1898[74].The soldiers wore wide brimmed hats, white pants with knee high boots and a khaki top. Like all the other volunteers he was ready and eager to show patriotic pride and see the world and free the Filipinos from cruel Spanish rule. He was 25 years old, five foot nine and three quarter inches tall with fair complexion, grey eyes and brown hair. Harry must be somewhere in this photograph of Company F First Battalion of the Thirteenth Minnesota Volunteers in July 1898.

---

[74] Information obtained from Harry's army papers in National Archives Washington D.C.

He had many friends in Canada and the U.S.A. and the newspapers in Winnipeg and Minnesota reported that he had enlisted. The following report in the Manitoba Free Press, dated May 1898, makes it evident that Harry was a prankster but a very well liked one.

"Harry Luxton, formerly of Winnipeg, has enlisted with the Minnesota infantry for service in Cuba, if required. The Minneapolis Journal relates the following incident in connection therewith. Among the members of Company F, in which Assistant Health Inspector Harry Luxton has cast his lot is a German, who claims to have seen service in the German army, and goes under the euphoalus of "Dutchy." He is a stalwart fellow, the very incarnation of good nature, and, as might perhaps be expected, he has been made the butt of a lot of good natured jesting. Those who know Luxton will not need to be told that he had had a prominent part in the badinage that has greeted the erstwhile subject of King William, and his sallies at Dutchy's expense. The Teuton has now turned the tables, and the laugh is on Luxton. This morning when he came out of the stall in which he has established his boudoir, he caught sight of a sheet of paper pinned up on one of the posts, on which the Dutchman had written the following stanzas-

Hung be the skies with solemn black,
Put out the smiling sun;
For trouble waits for all the world
Since Luxton got a gun.

With air quite military, he
Struts round from sun to sun;
The warmest thing that ever happed
Is Luxton and his gun.

When first he grasped it in his hand,
Tears from his blue eyes spun;
His rapture he could not conceal,
When he, too, got a gun.

And just as soon as he has learned
Which end is the front one,
He'll mow the Spaniards down like
Grass------
Will Luxton with his gun.

For forty cents and three square meals
Each day his duty's done,
"But then, that beats the Penny
Press,"
Says Luxton to his gun.

Give o'er, all ye who desolate,
Mourn husband now or son;
No harm can come to those you love,
For Luxton has a gun.

And you, my country, you're o.k.,
And all your foes will run,
As soon as in the battle's van
Go Luxton and his gun.

Training was brief for on the 25th June Harry was on the ship "City of Para" sailing out of San Francisco to Manila, arriving there on the 25th July. They arrived during a monsoon season so they had to spend an extra week just sitting on the ship in the harbour before the weather cleared enough for local boats to be able to ferry all the troops ashore. In what sounds like a chapter out of a fiction novel it turns out that the Americans had cut the cable connection between Manila and Hong Kong so there could be no communication from the Spaniards in Manila and Spain but it also made it impossible for the Americans to have contact with the outside world. As a result they never realised that there was a peace treaty negotiated between the U.S. and Spain the day before the Battle of Manila happened[75].

Harry's Company F was never involved in the intense battles but was usually left in charge of trenches as they were cleared and to take care of any skirmishes that might arise. Manila was captured on the 13th August 1898, a few hours after Spain agreed to a truce. The Treaty of Paris signed in December 1898 led to Spain evacuating Cuba and ceding Puerto Rico to the U.S.A. which now dominated the Caribbean. The Americans also paid Spain twenty million dollars for the Philippines which gave the U.S.A. a stake in the Far East.

When Manila was taken the Thirteenth Minnesota Volunteers became the Provost Guard of Manila and were charged with cleaning up the city and keeping the peace as well as keeping the Filipino rebels from trying to take over Manila. They had new uniforms of white pants and shirts with straw hats. The Americans had gone into Manila to free the people but they ended up being policemen with the Filipinos eventually turning on them when the Americans didn't leave as promised. The result was the Philippine – American War of 1899-1902.

The Americans did not have an easy time in the islands. Emilio Aguinalda, the able guerilla chieftain, led a rebellion which required over sixty thousand troops and two years of fighting to suppress. The first hint of Harry's later serious health troubles dates from this campaign in which he suffered sunstroke and other privations. On the 23rd August 1898, just ten

---

[75] The book, "In the Shadow of Glory" by Kyle Roy Ward has provided great insight into what Harry went through during his time in the Philippines.

days following the capture of Manila he was being treated for tonsillitis in French Hospital (Civil), San Francisco. Harry was returned to Manilla and he was performing his military duty on the 4th October 1898 when he was overcome by the heat of the sun. He suffered sunstroke and was unconscious for twenty minutes. He never really recovered from the initial attack and afterwards suffered from recurrent headaches, nervousness and an inability to stand exposure to the sun.

On the 3rd December 1898 he was admitted to the Regimental Convalescent Hospital in Manila. Doctors who observed his case for 65 days diagnosed that he was suffering from subacute meningitis due to disolation. This was accompanied by intense headaches exaggerated reflexes and a general weakness which had "unfitted him for duty since 1st attack". They concluded that he was disabled from earning his subsistence by one half. Consequently he was discharged from the army on the 12th January 1899 and was sent home. The rest of the Thirteenth Minnesota Volunteers returned home in August that year.

Harry remained popular in Winnipeg even after he had left the city and a number of his articles appeared in the Manitoba Free Press. When he fell ill in Manila a number of his Winnipeg friends lobbied the military in January 1899 to have him sent home. Then on the 24th February 1899 there was the following notice in the paper that he was alright and had been discharged.

Mr. Harry Luxton returned to Minneapolis on Wednesday with several discharged members of the 13th Minnesota Rifles. He is reported by one of the papers as follows, "This is the only country on earth, right here," said Luxton, as he grasped the hands of his old time friends, and laughed a real, genuine laugh, an American laugh, not one of those Philippine kind. "You all know this is the best corner of the earth, but not so well as I do. Why Manila is not fit for a white man's dog to live in. Go back there? Well, I guess not, never. My advice is, never go there even on a visit, for it is not worthwhile. It will be so much time lost out of your life."

Harry then made a couple of appearances at benefits, giving speeches and lectures in March 1899 about his experiences in Manila.

On his return to the twin cities, Harry married to Pearl M. Taylor in Gethsemane Church, Minneapolis on Saturday the 8th July 1899. Pearl was not popular with his family and there were no children. Harry, a health inspector, and his wife Pearl are listed in two census records for 1900.The first dated 6th June 1900 shows them living with Pearl's family in ward 5 Minneapolis and the second is dated 14 June 1900 in ward 8, Minneapolis and shows Harry and Pearl living on their own. Perhaps they were in the middle of moving and someone in Pearl's family answered the census questions as though they were still living with them. The City of Minneapolis census taken on the 14th June 1900, lists Harry Luxton, 28, born July 1871[76] in Canada, Health Inspector, and that he had immigrated to the U.S.A. in 1894.His wife Pearl, 22, was born November 1877 in Iowa, U. S.A. and her father was born in Scotland.

Harry later found employment in the District Court Offices where he became Chief Deputy District Court Clerk. He had lost none of his sense of fun as the following report in the Minneapolis Times for 17th August 1905 relates~

> Harry Luxton, one of the most popular deputies in the office of A.E. Allen, clerk of courts is looking for the man-or rather men-who persuaded him to play baseball at the Tenka Bay picnic Saturday. Incidentally Luxton is keeping himself in close proximity to a large stuffed club, for he now feels that he is much wiser than he was Saturday.

All of Sunday Luxton was in bed. It was because he couldn't move enough to get out. The game had been altogether too strenuous for him. When he slid bases the earth trembled, and when he hit the ball the fans used their telescopes to follow its train. Luxton was "great" during the game. He was so "great" that he knocked a man clean off third base and his friends had to dig him out of the sand. Luxton during the game weighed 230.That's why there was nothing small about the way he did things, even though he did weigh but 220 after the game.

At the time of his death he was living temporarily with his brother George E. Luxton at 138 Arthur Avenue S. E. Minneapolis because his wife Pearl was in Milwaukee where her mother was ill. Harry was

[76] 1870 is the date of his birth given in the family Bible.

unwell and had been complaining of his heart for sometime. At 10.30 pm on Thursday the 15th December 1910, while waiting for a jury to report at the Court House, he had a fainting spell but was revived by fresh air and was apparently himself again shortly after. At 10.40pm, he left the Courthouse. He was returning to his brother George's residence when he died.

The brothers were accustomed to use the short cut path on which his body was found by a passer-by shortly after 7am the next morning. It lay on a vacant lot off University Avenue S.E. near Arthur Avenue, at the top of a hill, the ascent of which evidently had brought on the fatal attack. His brother George was one of the first to arrive on the scene after his body was found. The condition of the corpse indicated he had been dead several hours. The police were notified and the body was taken to the offices of Hume and Davis undertakers. Death was pronounced by Gilbert Seashore, the coroner, to have been the result of heart failure.

The private funeral took place at 1.30pm on Saturday 17th December 1910 from Davis' undertaking rooms at 19 Eighth Street S. with interment in Lakewood Cemetery.

Harry was not forgotten in Canada where his obituary in the Manitoba Free Press says that there was no more popular resident of Winnipeg than Harry Luxton. He was renowned for a great sense of humour and was not past playing jokes on his friends.

Harry was a soldier, stationed in Manila, when he wrote to his father W.F. Luxton, the following graphic account of his small part in the capture of the city and the problems faced there by the occupying army.

Manila Nov 11/98

Dear Father,

I judge from the letter I received from mother the mail before this that you have not received all the mail I sent. Of course it takes a long time for letters to reach their destination and I understand from some of the ships captains lately in from Hong Kong that there are several hundred sacks of mail piled up on the wharf at the point awaiting transportation to the states. A considerable portion of our mail has gone direct to the States on government transports but much has gone via Hong Kong and it has grown to such dimensions that the post office authorities have had more to do than they could cope with. I know two letters sent the Mpls Trib (i.e. Minneapolis Tribune) have not yet appeared and they were mailed several days ...... (a few words are unreadable) that have been published. I have made an effort to write a couple of times a month and if you have not received all it is due to the crush of general matter at Hong Kong and they will doubtless be along sometime.

I suppose you have seen my stuff from time to time in the M'polis Tribune. Mr Hamblin, the managing editor, was kind enough to write to me on two or three occasions to the effect that he was very much pleased with the articles and that they had made a hit. When I wrote the "scrap stuff" it was Monday night and I had had only few hours sleep and that in a street gutter in a regular torrent of rain. On Saturday Aug 13 we started on the march to the front at 5:30 and made about 16 miles through mud and water at times up to our waists and were in Manila at 5 that afternoon with only 4 hard tack to eat all day. We had to go on guard in the streets immediately and were not relieved till five o'clock Sunday afternoon, when we were sent to the barracks for grub. I was too tired to eat as were 95% of all the boys and laid down to get some rest but had not been on my back over 15 minutes when an alarm came in and we were all "kicked" to the outskirts of Malatta, a suburb of Manila to prevent the insurgents making a raid into the city. It began to rain and the water came down on us in tubfulls. I never saw such rain in my life. I stood guard with one of the others at a cross road till 10 p.m. and then our relief came. There was no place to go so I just laid down in the street and went off to sleep in the most enjoyable dreamless sleep I ever had. I was awakened at three o'clock to go on guard again and it was then I discovered that I had rolled into the street gutter and had succeeded in converting myself into a first class dam until the water rose higher and higher to flow over my hips. That was the last and only sleep I had until late that Monday night. I was turning in when I heard one of the officers say that mail was leaving for the States next day. I kicked up the correspondent of the Times who is the same mess as myself and we began to grind. What I wrote I had not the slightest idea when I was through and I was so tired that to tell you the truth I didn't much care. Later however I began to worry and looked for the paper with considerable anxiety. When it came it was almost like new stuff and pretty bum stuff at that. The Trib. evidently thought it was all right but I guess that anything almost would have been acceptable from the front.

Our life here is monotonous in the extreme and we are all sick and tired of being policemen. There is no particular fun in arresting drunken Chinamen and Philippinos. As long as the country needed us for actual field service we were anxious to do our small part but playing at soldiers is not agreeing with our digestions and we want to get out of this regular hell hole. It seems to be pretty well conceded that this is one of the suburbs of hades. It is filthy and there is a great deal of sickness. Smallpox is spreading and typhoid fever is rampant. The heat is intense and this is the cool season. God knows how we boys will ever get through April May and June but perhaps by that time we will be away from here. If we are not then the blood of half the regiments stationed at Manila will be on the heads of the administration. For myself I hav'nt the slightest fear but many of the boys are in poor health now and out of our company alone 12 are in the hospital and twice as many more confined to quarters.

I send a photograph taken in the uniform we wore the day of the "scrape". We carried 150 rounds of ammunition and when we got to Manila my gun, bayonet and cartridges weighed as much as a ton of hay.

    With all my love to the dear ones at home I am
       Your affectionate son
        H.A. Luxton[77]

---

[77] I am very grateful to my cousins Gail Mesplay in Golden, Colorado and Susan Freeborn in Calgary for supplying me with a vast body of information on the family in Canada and the U.S.A.

13

NORMAN KENNY LUXTON (1875-1962), ADVENTURER, TRADER, RED INDIAN CHIEF, AND FOUNDER OF THE LUXTON MUSEUM IN BANFF, ALBERTA.

See tree 6

Norman Kenny Luxton, the third son of the prominent Winnipeg pioneer William Fisher Luxton (1843-1907) and his wife Sarah Jane Edwards, was born at Upper Fort Gary, Red River, Manitoba on the 2nd November 1875[78]. The name Kenny was bestowed on him in honour of John A. Kenny, a retired Ontario farmer who was his father's friend and business partner. Norman attended school in Winnipeg but when he should have been doing arithmetic, "he was digging in Indian mounds" or hunting along the River Assiniboine.[79]Childhood summers were spent on canoe trips in Manitoba where he learnt to be a good shot. He won many championships including the championship of Western Canada where he was up against some of the finest shots from Minnesota and the Dakotas.

His father, the owner and editor of the Manitoba Free Press, considered it a foregone conclusion that his son would grow up to work in the newspaper. For a short period in his mid teens Norman was employed on his father's newspaper but at the age of 16, he was on his own, as an apprentice clerk with the Indian Department at Rat Portage (now Kenora, Ontario) and had embarked on what the Toronto Star in 1934 colourfully described as a "rainbow painted career".

---

[78] The family Bible records Norman's year of birth as 1875 which is confirmed by his birth announcement in the Manitoba Free Press as November 2, 1875. Norman's tombstone records 1874 and the biographies about him, including what he wrote in the book Tilikum gives the date as 1876.

[79] See Chapter XXIV, Luxton of Banff in Fifty Might Men by Grant MacEwan, Western Producer Prairie Books, Saskatoon, Saskatchewan (1975) which is an excellent write up on Norman.

He found the work dreary and humdrum. The virgin country further west was beckoning and in 1896, Norman was in Calgary, working for the Calgary Herald. Duties embraced a little of everything from business manager to delivery boy and when cash reserves dropped alarmingly, he went out and sold brand books which the Herald was printing at the time. Then he became involved in the Kootenay gold rush of the mid 1890s. When the excitement in the Kootenays began to fade he was still restless so in

1898 he moved west to Vancouver. There with two partners he issued a weekly gossip sheet called "Town Topics" which was printed by hand. The newspaper was a success until it upset local churchmen. Norman then had a job on the Vancouver Sun. He also bought a canoe and made long treks through the little known waterways of the North West, travelling along miles of Indian game trails. His love of adventure was developed on these journeys and his restless spirit found some purpose in life.

During 1898 he migrated to the U.S.A. and the 1st June 1900 census lists Norman, 24, a reporter, dwelling in the household next door to the rest of his Luxton family in St. Paul, Minnesota. The St. Paul daily that employed him was, he thought "a paper run by an outfit that owned blackmailing sheets from New York to San Francisco." He disliked the dirty work and the city life so late in 1900 he was back in Vancouver where the 1901 census lists him as a publisher and business manager. He opened a stock-broker's office but the crash of 1900 put him out of the brokerage business. "I sold the furnishings," he relates, "for a good price. I got nothing at all for the good will; there wasn't any."

At this point the great adventure of his life began when he sailed the Pacific in an Indian war canoe. The voyage originated as a result of a dinner in Minnesota U.S.A. at which there were a number of Canadians and Americans present. The Americans were praising Captain Slocum who had recently sailed around the world in a small boat, when Norman declared that the Canadians could go one better.[80] A wager of 5000 dollars was made, the conditions being that the boat was to be smaller than Slocum's "Spray" and that after once leaving Vancouver the voyagers were not to draw on home for supplies but were to make their own way.

Luxton persuaded Jack Voss, an old Danish sea captain, to undertake the navigation of the craft in this perilous around the world voyage. Norman then purchased a forty three year old Nootka dugout canoe which he found on a beach near an Indian village on the east coast of Vancouver Island. Its Indian owner claimed it had been in many Indian battles on the west coast of British Columbia. It was built from a single red cedar log, thirty-seven feet in length and five ft 8 inch in the beam, and was made for paddling around the North American shores. It was never intended for ocean voyages. Luxton and Voss strengthened the dugout with oak frames, fastened with galvanised iron nails, raised her gunwales, planked in the deck, constructed a small cabin and storage areas for food and water and rigged her as a three sail schooner. Three hundred pound of lead was fastened to the keel. They gave their ship the name Tilikum, a Chinook word meaning "friend" and they set sail from Oak Bay, Victoria, British Columbia on the 20th May 1901[81].

Nobody could say the little boat was over loaded with modern nautical equipment. There was a small sextant with a cracked mirror, a pocket compass, a watch for a chronometer and a chart showing the approximate locations of South Sea Islands. For fire-arms, they had a rifle, shotgun, pistol and an ancient, small-bore Spanish cannon that Luxton uncovered when digging sand for boat ballast. The cannon was to prove its value. There was world wide interest in their forth coming voyage-"Messrs Voss and Luxton, are about to undertake a curious and somewhat novel voyage. On Tuesday they set sail from Vancouver for Australia in an Indian war canoe, some forty feet long. From Australia they proceed to the Pacific Islands, Thence to S. Africa and finally to

---

[80] Aberdeen Journal, Saturday 27 February 1904. Norman disowned the bet story which he attributed to Voss who appears to have made it up to seek publicity. See letter at end of chapter.
[81] There survive a number of letters from Norman to his family in Minniapolis in 1901 before he set sail on the Tilikum and also a couple that were sent home during the trip. Two of these letters are printed at the end of this chapter.

England. Mr. Luxton is a journalist and will embody his experiences in book form"[82].

The crew experienced many exhilarating and extra-ordinary incidents during their long voyage. When they were some twenty-five miles past Beal Light off the Canadian coast, the Tilikum ran into a school of whales which stretched for miles. To Luxton's consternation the dugout was nearly crushed by a whale which leapt out of the water to avoid the deadly pursuit of thresher sharks. Norman knew that the Tilikum was lucky to survive the incident.

The sleepy doldrums brought the first trouble between Voss and Luxton. The two men glared at each other while the vessel lay dormant. Their water gave out and the food went bad. They were ready to cut each other's throat at the end of seventeen days but fortunately a breeze came up and friendship was restored.

The Tilikum made it to Penrhyn Island. There a chief offered Norman a choice of one of his three daughters in marriage and the ownership of hundreds of coconut trees if he would stay on the island. Norman only

---

[82] Cheshire Observer, 25th May 1901

got away by persuasive talking. The dugout reached Manihiki Island where the crew received a friendly welcome before sailing on to Samoa where the famous author Robert Louis Stevenson had lived and died less than a decade earlier.

At Niuafo'ou, part of the Tonga group the island cannibals prodded Norman and sighed for a human steak. Norman managed to return to the Tilikum where he sprinkled the roof of the cabin and foredeck with carpet tacks while Voss loaded the tiny brass canon. The next day the tribe attacked in their catamarans. Voss waited for them to get in mass formation and close enough. Then he trained the canon on them and fired. The tribesmen tumbled out of their canoes and swam ashore. They left a score of hand-carved paddles and other weapons which Norman collected out of their canoes.

The Tilikum continued on her voyage. Things went better for a time and then worse. Away to the west a tropical storm dashed the Tilikum on a coral reef and tossed Luxton on jagged rocks where he lay semi-conscious all night. When Voss took him off in the following morning he believed him dead. Norman's body was a mass of cuts and bruises from the pounding he had taken on the coral. He was tough though and had the grim pleasure of sitting up while his grave was being dug. Norman is pictured in Banff in 1923 with a model of the Tilikum and one of his dogs.(Either Larry or Barney)

By the time the Tilikum reached Suva, Fiji on the 18th October 1901, Luxton was hideously swollen – a victim of coral poisoning and was sick for a long time after the swelling went down. Norman stayed behind in Samoa because of the coral fever. By now Voss and he hated each other and Norman was certain that Voss meant to do him harm. Voss continued on with a new mate to New Zealand, Australia, Cape Town, Azores and finally arrived in London on 2nd September 1904.[83]

---

[83] The Venturesome Voyages of Captain Voss, Martin Hopkinson, second edition 1926.

In 1930 William A. McAdam, the agent general for British Columbia in London, found the boat lying in the mud of the Thames off Greenwich. She was owned by two members of the Greenwich Yacht Club who readily agreed to present the yacht to Canada. Through the courtesy of the Furness Withy Line she was crated and shipped to Victoria. The Tilikum, restored to her appearance when she set out from Victoria on that May morning in 1901, is preserved in Victoria in the Maritime Museum of British Columbia.

Norman meanwhile left Suva, in Fiji, in late October 1901 aboard the steamer Berksgate bound for Sydney, Australia. When he was sufficiently recuperated he returned to Vancouver in 1902, working his way as an able bodied seaman aboard the passenger ship "Aorangi" which belonged to the Canadian-Australian Steamship Company. He applied for a job with the Calgary Herald but was turned down so moved to Banff where he hoped to regain his health. There he began his long business career when he opened a branch haberdashery, representing a Calgary merchant.

Soon old Indian friends began to turn up with game heads and bead and leather work which they wanted to sell. That gave him the idea of establishing an Indian Trading Post and in 1903 he opened, "The Sign of the Goat Trading Post" where he sold beadwork and quilts made by natives from the nearby Stony Reserve. He was a skilled taxidermist and shipped big game heads, furs, Indian beadwork and buckskin goods of all kinds everywhere in the world to royalty, millionaires, hunters and tourists. Norman wearing one of his specially made Stetson hats is pictured at his Indian Trading Post, Banff with his Irish setters Larry and Barney O'Toole, flanked by brothers George (left) and Louis. Louis, a fur expert, was 5ft 5inches tall with hazel eyes. He was aged 47, a merchant, when he landed at Eastport, Idaho on 27th October 1927 with his wife Elsie and their three children from Banff, destined for Vancouver. He made a second trip to Eastport in 1935.

The photograph next page shows Norman feeding his pet bear outside the Sign of the Goat Store about 1907.Once his business was established Norman married Georgia Elizabeth McDougall, the daughter of David McDougall, a noted trader and rancher, in Banff on the 2nd November 1904. Georgia was born in Morley in 1871 and was the first white child born in what is now Alberta, then part of the North West territories. She grew up with the Indians, spoke fluent Cree, and

was an accomplished musician who played the organ in the Morleyville MacDougall Mission Church for many years. The 1906 Canada census for N.W. Provinces gives their address as Block 3 Lot 8 Banff. The couples only child, Eleanor Georgina Luxton (1908-1995), born in Banff, Alberta on the 31st July 1908 was the author of two books, "Luxton's Pacific Crossing" (1971) and "Banff, Canada's First National Park" (1975) which I have freely used in compiling this account.

When Banff's first newspaper failed, Norman bought the little Gordon Press along with the boxes of type stored in cigar boxes and coffee tins, and published the magnificently named 'Crag and Canyon' newspaper from 1902 to 1951. Because Banff needed a hotel which would remain open the year around, he celebrated the official opening of his King Edward Hotel in 1904 by publicly throwing the keys away in the bush. N.K. Luxton like all good business men advertised what was on offer as far away as London, at the heart of the Empire:-Hotel King Edward (Canadian National Park) First-class, central to all the hot springs. Special attention given to guests to see the sights. Rates 2dollars per day. Hunters and sportsmen will do well to correspond with us[84].

When the hotel was destroyed in a fire on the 7th February 1914, and the livery shortly afterwards, he promptly constructed the Lux Block, containing a new hotel, several stores and a moving picture theatre called The Lux. In 1915 he purchased the Morley Trading Company on the Stony Indian Reserve and the following year it advertised "Ice Cold Coco-Cola" and Everyday Orange Crush – Good for Thirst." He also owned the town morgue and was part owner of an airline he started with Freddy McCall.

Norman was a strong advocate of Banff as "The Playground of the Canadian Rockies". As early as 1906 he published a booklet entitled, "Fifty Switzerlands in One – Banff the Beautiful" which was sent all over the world. On the north shore of Lake Minnewanka, nine miles outside of Banff, he operated a woodburning steam boat and a chalet and ran a livery and sight seeing tours, first with horses and then with cars. His Lake Minnewanka Chalet advertised fish dinners, "A Beautiful Lake, a sunset view, a dandy fish dinner, built for two."

---

[84] London Evening Standard, Friday, 4th June 1909.

For years, it seemed that Norman Luxton was the man behind every Banff project. He became known as "Mr Banff" for all he did to develop the place and was a leading citizen in its affairs. He helped organise the Banff Advisory Council and the old Banff Board of Trade. The Winter Carnival was conceived when he and B.W. Collison played cards with their friends one night in 1909 and from that year until 1950, Luxton conducted the Annual Indian Days, a feature of the Banff holiday season, presented in the best Stony traditions. From the reservations came the Stony Indians and the Blackfoot Indians to spend a week as the guests of the people of Banff who arranged all manner of ancient Indian sports and awarded substantial prizes. In 1912 Norman attended the first Calgary Stampede and for the next twenty five years he was the judge of all its Indian events. He knew the Indians as few other white people did – celebrated with them, hunted with them. Norman used films too to promote Banff and he appeared in two movies. One was a 1916 promotional film about Banff Indian Days and in one scene Norman plays himself. The other was the 1941 Hollywood movie, 49th Parallel, which was about German soldiers escaping from the Canadian authorities.

Norman's greatest achievement was the Luxton Museum in Banff which depicts the life of the Prairie Indians. He was a friend of the Indians from his boyhood days when with his father he had met the Canadian rebel, Louis Riel (1844-1885) in the United States and admired Riel's determination to improve the lot of his half-breeds. His apprenticeship at the Indian Agency at Rat Portage had reinforced his natural empathy with the Indians. In 1918 when the influenza epidemic devastated the Stony Indian Reserve at Morley, Norman organised burial parties. He took food and supplies from his store in Morley and drove hundreds of miles over the Reserve visiting and re-visiting the sick and giving them whisky and aspirin which were the only two medicines available. It was scarcely surprising that Norman himself was taken ill with influenza.

For these endeavours and for his support of the Indian Association of Alberta in its struggle to obtain more land for the Stony's, Luxton was taken into the Stony Tribe as an honorary chief with the name Ya-Ha-Chunga-Choon (which translated means 'Chief White Shield'.) Because of Mrs Luxton's interest in the Indians she too was taken into the Stony Tribe as Princess and Blood Sister. The Indians bestowed upon her the name of "Rainbow Woman", because, they explained, she always brought peace after the storm. The Blackfoot too honoured Norman with the rank and title of "Chief White Eagle".

Norman was the founder of the Luxton Museum which developed from the Indian Trading Post he opened shortly after his arrival in Banff in 1903. He collected Indian artefacts, mostly from the Blackfoot, Sarcee and Stony tribes of Southern Alberta who participated in Banff Indian Days. In 1951 he built the first log building to start the now famous Luxton Museum. It displayed his collection of weapons, buckskins, beadwork and conveyances, depicting the life of the Prairie Indians. Then he moved the old Banff Gun Club building which he had built himself to adjoin the museum as a caretaker's residence. In 1955, the second larger addition, was added. Then Mr Eric Harvie, a Calgary lawyer and philanthropist, became interested and in 1957 the fort-like structure, the largest room of all was constructed. The final addition in 1960 was the rounded room on the east end. Life size mannequins of Indians with faces modelled from live subjects were used to show types of dress and depict how the Indians worked, played, danced and travelled. Artists, designers, researchers and visitors came by the thousands to see the museum. Norman's life long project had a permanent home.

Nobody knew the West, the mountains and the pioneers better than Norman Luxton and he was president one year of the Southern Alberta Old Timers' Association. In his later life he became especially interested in the conservation of wild animals and as a member of Ducks Unlimited he took a count of the wild animals and wild fowl he saw on his paddling journeys. He canoed from Jasper in Alberta right through to Rainy Lake in Ontario and knew all the connecting streams. Indeed, it was through Norman's foresight and imagination that the buffalo were re-introduced into Canada. In the fifty years 1830 to 1880 it has been estimated that no fewer than forty million buffalo were slaughtered on the North American Prairie. Buffalo hunts in the frontier days were, from all reports, rather tame affairs, less sporting some said, than potting a rabbit. Buffalo Bill once boasted of shooting 200 in one day. By the 1870s the buffalo was in real danger of extinction. In 1873, Walking Coyote, an Indian, saved four Prairie Buffalo calves from slaughter in S.W. Alberta and drove them to the St. Ignatius Mission Alberta. By 1884 the number had increased to 13. In that year Michael

Pablo bought ten of the Buffalo to roam on the Flathead Indian Reserve in Montana. His herd had increased to 631 by 1907 but disaster struck when the U. S. government threw open for homesteading what had been the property of the Flathead Indians. To save the herd Pablo offered it to the U. S. government for 150,000 dollars but congress looked upon the expenditure as absurd. At this point Norman stepped in to save them. He set up a deal with the U.S.A. federal government in 1910 to purchase one thousand buffalo at ninety dollars per head from the herd belonging to Michael Pablo at Flat Head Lake in Montana. Norman saw that the purchased animals were shipped to Wainwright National Park in Canada.

Like the rest of us Norman had his imperfections too. He was an expert canoeist but was dangerously wreckless on the highway. He thought the laws of the road were made for other people, not himself. He was frequently stopped by the police for driving the wrong way on oneway streets, for driving through traffic lights, and for ignoring speed limits.

His daughter Eleanor has written a vivid pen portrait of Norman in his mature years:-

"A slight man, five foot seven, Norman remained through his life wiry and resilient. His step was springy, his reactions quick, his temper uncertain, his blue eyes piercing yet always with laughter in them. His two-inch-brimmed round Stetson hats, specially made for him, were so much part of him they became symbolic. He was a steadfast friend to young and old alike and generous to anyone in need. For a man of action he was an omnivorous reader of history, travel and Indians".[85]

The late William John Luxton (1909-1992) of Guildford, during a visit to Canada, observed for himself Luxton's uncertain temper. When he asked Norman about his Devon roots, he yelled "Get out of here! I'm not interested. I don't want to know about my family." Perhaps this outburst was because Norman felt shame and bitterness about his father's illegitimate origins.[86]

---

[85] See page 19 "Luxton's Pacific Crossing" (1971) by Eleanor Georgina Luxton
[86] See John Cornwells "Earth to Earth" published by Allen Lane Penguin Books Ltd (1982). On page 92 the author incorrectly attributed this encounter as taking place in

An amusing article written by Larry Gough in Liberty Profile on 30th March 1946 illustrates how Norman became a legend in his lifetime:-

"Luxton, even when seen in the framework of his Indian Trading Post being coolly charming to the tourists who come to buy big-game heads or Indian beadwork, has the appearance that is demanded of the hero of any action story. He is tall, erect, and at seventy, still as lean and compact as a hickory wagon tongue.

Luxton spent most of his youth involved either with gold hungry prospectors or Western Indians, visited the South Seas as a partner in a screwball expedition that is known to every yachtsman who can read, passed up one chance to marry a princess only to take advantage of a second such romantic opportunity, and made and lost at least one considerable fortune before he settled down to a comparatively normal life.

Two of the three rooms of the Indian Trading Post are known to almost every visitor to Banff. They contain examples of Indian craftsmanship, big game trophies, and an assortment of Western souvenirs. The third room is even more closely packed with fascinating curios and mementoes of the past but is distinctly not in the public domain. It is the refuge of Luxton and his one constant companion, an Irish setter pup named Larry O'Toole.

The dog serves as a link with the past and as an illustration of the sentimental streak that occasionally shows through Luxton's appearance of competent hardness. When he was sixteen Luxton acquired his first Irish setter. For more than fifty years he owned, successively, the son, grandson, and further direct descendants of the original Larry O'Toole. The last of the line died three years ago. The present Larry is not directly descended from the original. Nevertheless the dog is a beloved shadow of his master, following him whenever he moves, curling up at his feet whenever he sits talking on his buffalo robed couch or works at his gigantic cluttered roll top-desk.

1963, a year after Norman's death. Among a multitude of errors in his very readable book, Cornwell states that Norman Luxton left Winkleigh in the 1890s and that he had lived at first by bartering pelts for tobacco.

At sixteen Norman was clerk to the Indian agent at Rat Portage, a community now known as Kenora. There his lifelong interest in Indians really began. His constant sidekick was an Indian boy and his work kept him continuously among the tribes for a year.

When the agent travelled among the Indians to deliver their cash grants from the Crown, Norman would sit in the big eight-man canoe with the strap of the heavy cash box tied around his neck. The agent felt that if the canoe should founder while shooting a rapid, the cashbox would be easier to find if it were attached to a floating body....".

Norman Kenny Luxton, Banff's most celebrated citizen, died aged 85, at the Holy Cross Hospital, Calgary, on the 22nd October 1962 and was laid to rest in his beloved Banff. The Indians, dressed in full ceremonial beaded costumes, held a special service at the graveside, and hymns were sung in both English and Cree. Georgia, his widow, died, aged 95, in her home in Banff on the 27th March 1965 and lies buried with her husband in Banff Cemetery.

The Luxton Museum, following its founder's death, operated as a division of the Glenbow Museum. In early 1991, the Glenbow announced plans to close the museum, citing a shortage of finances and the need for major repairs to the log structure in which the Luxton artefacts are housed. Several groups expressed an interest in taking over the Luxton, and in March 1992 the Luxton Museum of the Plains Indians was sold to a predominantly native group, the Buffalo Nations Cultural Society. The museum officially reopened on Saturday the 29th August 1992. To mark the occasion there was a parade and the re-launching of Banff Indian Days as the Buffalo Nations Festival.

The Buffalo Nations Cultural Society is made up of nations from the five tribes which signed   Treaty Seven in 1887 and other Canadians. It is established to promote a better understanding of aboriginal cultures. The initial focus is on the plains cultures of Western Canada. Norman Kenny Luxton would have approved of these aims.

Norman's daughter, Eleanor, after a brilliant academic career, graduated in mechanical engineering and for several years worked on locomotive design for the Canadian Pacific Railway in Montreal. She was also a lecturer at McGill University and the technician in charge of a medical laboratory. Eleanor lived in her parents old home at 206 Beaver Street, Banff, where she died of liver cancer in her 88th year on the 22nd June 1995. Her ashes were interred in the family plot in the old Banff Cemetery. In the photograph Eleanor is wearing an Indian dress c.1928.

She left her estate to set up the Eleanor Luxton Historical Foundation which retains her family home at 206 Beaver Street, Banff as a museum open to the public. It is dedicated to the history of Banff and all of western Canada and opened its doors to the public on Saturday 1st August 1998. Norman built the house in 1909 for his bride. The museum shows how a pioneer family in Banff lived during the approximately ninety years that Eleanor's family occupied the property. The home features fine collections of native artefacts, rare books and memorabilia, trophy heads and period furniture reflecting the development of western Canada from the 1890s to the 1990s. An extensive collection of archival

materials is available to researchers in the Eleanor Luxton Reading Room of the Whyte Museum in Banff. An outstanding period costume collection is another feature of the Luxton Legacy.

I close this chapter with two letters Norman wrote to his parents in Minneapolis about his trip in the Tilikum. They make interesting reading as Norman is still bubbling with the excitement of his adventure:-

International Hotel R. Easthope, Proprietor Apia, Samoa Oct 3rd 1901

My Dear Father& Mother-I suppose before this reaches you the Tilikum will have been heard of since crossing the Pacific Ocean. I am not going to try to tell you all that has happened since we left the B. C. coast, in fact I doubt if there would be enough paper in Samoa to do that. We have had some very queer times and I may say some very thrilling adventures all that will tell better when I am once more in America.

The reason I have not written before was because this the first place we have had of sending any mail. Not even a vessel did we pass at sea by which we could send a note. The first boat we passed was after we had been out two days. The next –six days & after that for 58 days we saw no boat or land until we reached Penrhyn Island about 800 miles NE of this place. We were in a pretty sorry condition when we got to that place: our provisions had nearly all gone over board having got bad. Our water was about out and I tell you I felt as if sailing a canoe across the Pacific was no summer dream. However all this was over looked and forgotten at Penrhyn where we stayed two weeks. As long as I live I will never forget the good days and rest I got there. A couple of traders by the name of Captains Dexter and Winchester treated us like long lost brothers repainting our canoe, re-provisioning her throughout and loading us with kindness until I felt embarrassed beyond telling. Outside of these people all are natives and even they tried to surpass each other in giving us coconuts, mats, hats and goodness knows what all. We then called at Humphrey Islands and also Danger Islands landing at Samoa last night. We leave here tomorrow for Fiji Islands and from there to Sydney.

In crossing the Pacific the canoe proved more than I ever expected she could do. At the equator or in about lat. 8N to lat. 3S for 15 days we had nothing but bad weather and rain. Also our adventures with a school of whales which we ran through for a day and a half was very exciting, as I was in continual fear of running down a sleeping whale. Flying fish, turtles and sword fish, all come under the same head excitement. Taking it all through I would not have missed seeing what I have these South Sea Islands for anything yet again I would not go through what I did for the whole world. The reason we did not make Tahiti was because we were blown out of our track to the south which was in long. 120 to 124 to as far as lat.8N when we shaped our course S. W. to Penrhyn. I was sorry to miss seeing this French colony as it must be a very interesting place. The distance we have gone is now is 6490 miles averaging 102 miles each day of sailing, sometimes going 180 miles a day, sometimes going back in one day in what we made in two. From now out we get good weather. In fact we have had no bad weather since leaving L. 2 south. It will be about the middle of November before we are in Sydney as we intend fixing up in Fiji Islands.

Often I have thought of all of you at home and wondered how everything was, and I suppose you have often wondered where I was. I have made up my mind that when I get to Sydney that will be the last time I get into that canoe to cross any open sea. If we can push through to England I go by liner and ship a man in my place but no more small boats for me. When I got on Penrhyn Island I could not walk for two days without falling all over the street. The roll of the boat still brings in my legs. I wish I could describe these islands to you the way I saw them. At each island & village we were feasted like kings. I have eaten as many as 6 to 20 dinners in one day given to us by different heads of the large families of the villages. All the food was of native make cooked in ovens in the ground. Our Bill-of Fare was something like this. A roasted pig -raw fish with limes-coconuts in a dozen different ways, yams, native wines and fruit in loads. We would hardly get through one dinner when we would be marched off to another until I could hardly walk, now I am no glutton but tasting soon fills you up and taste we had to or else insult our host. The funny part about these dinners were that the Captain and I were the only ones who sat down to them always on the ground on a large mat. Our host and his friends squatting all around us and the more we ate the more we were admired by our spectators. In the evenings and as late as 2am we were always entertained by singing and dancing and such singing and dancing the wild native music was music indeed of which I never tired of listening to. During these entertainments we rested on mats with a continual string of green coconuts being handed to us. It is astonishing the number of these nuts you can eat, 20 to 30 was an ordinary number to drink in an evening. These are a few of the pleasures that we saw the natives had. There is the other side such as from a commercial point, pearl shell fishing & diving, cobra making and so on. How the natives lived their troubles & court-houses, fines imposed on evil doers & law breakers was all very interesting. I wish I had room to tell you all about it, but as I said before I could fill a book and then only tell half. I guess you will have to pass this letter around as the mail boat goes in about two hours and as I have to go out to the canoe to get some letters given to us to post by the traders from the islands I will not have time to write Harry or the family. I will make up for it in Fiji which will be in about a week's time. So good bye for the present dear folks with best love to all. From Norm

Heard of the death of McKinley, quite excited over it here though it is a German Colony

Australasian United Steam Navigation Co. Ltd.
S.S. Berksgate
From Port Suva Fiji to Sydney Oct 26 1901

My Dear Father & Mother-

I suppose you will be glad to hear that I have run away from the canoe and at present am on the road to Sydney in an ocean liner. Well to tell you the truth, when I got to Suva, Fiji from Samoa the last place I wrote you I discovered I was none too well, the trip had been harder on me than I had supposed. So I worked a deal with the Suva newspaper & got me a pass to Sydney.

It seemed kind of mean to leave the old boat & honest I would much rather be on her than on this rolling old tub. She does roll & no mistake so if this writing is worse than usual you understand why.

Do not think I am sick far from it. I got some coral poisoning at Penrhyn Island in my feet which gave me a good deal of bother and as the doctor said nothing but rest would cure them I decided to let Cap Voss to go on to Sydney. I shipped a sailor in my place to that Port.

You do not know how I am looking forward to getting my mail in Sydney. Almost four months is a long time to go by without hearing from home, and it seems like years since I saw the shore of Van Island. After we left Samoa we headed for Fiji Island & made it in 8 days, after one of the worst trips we experienced yet. We all but got ship wrecked on a coral reef. It was like this. It happened about 2 o'clock in the morning. I was on watch, I thought something had gone wrong with the rudder, so I crawled aft to examine it & when I got back to my seat the boat was going before the half gale of wind, that was blowing, like a wild thing. It was as dark as pitch, but suddenly I heard breakers ahead then I saw them, I turned the boat as quick as possible, she was only half way around when a big wave came along carrying her right on to the reef. Luckily the canoe only draws about 18 inches of water and as the reef had about 15 inches of water we did not get hurt. The next wave came along, washing right over everything carrying the boat in the sheltered side of the reef. Banged me to the other end of the cockpit & the Captain who felt the boat strike, had his head out of the hatch, was forced back into the cabin. I got a good black eye where I struck the compass box. It all happened in half a minute. On the far side of the reef we stayed until morning & then made an uninhabited coconut island where we dried out. Two days after we made Suva harbour, the capital of Fiji Islands. Here we stayed six days & glad I was to get on British soil once more.

Now I am sending you a newspaper clipping. Part of it is true & part is not where the editor got all his information is a puzzle to me, he is an American so perhaps that explains it. The bet is a story of the Captain Voss's as he says.[87] It gives some reason for our trip and perhaps it will help us in business though honest I am not very much struck with it myself. Well dear folks I will write again when I get to Sydney, as on this boat I am almost standing on my head she is rolling so & the bunk is the only comfortable place to be. Goodby with love to you & all from

Norm

---

[87] Norman disowns the bet aspect of the story for his voyage which he is attributing to Captain Voss.

14

GEORGE EDWARDS LUXTON (1881-1962) MOVIE HOUSE PROJECTIONIST, NEWSPAPER PHOTOGRAPHER AND AUTHOR

See tree 6

George Edwards Luxton, the fifth son of the newspaper pioneer William Fisher Luxton (1843-1907) and his wife Sarah Jane Edwards, was born in Winnipeg, Manitoba, on Tuesday 25th October 1881.He moved with his parents and siblings in 1899 to St. Paul, Minnesota, where he is listed as an 18 year old clerk in the U S census of 5th June 1900.

Later that year George was working in Victoria, British Columbia, at Oliver B Ormond, Bookseller and Stationer, at 92 Government Street. His employer Mr Ormond, was a good friend of George and his elder brother Norman (who nicknamed him Lobster).The 1901 Victoria census lists George as a 19 year old clerk in a bookstore, lodging with his brother Norman. George quit, however, and moved to St Paul, Minnesota in the U.S.A. to be with the rest of the Luxton family. This was around 1905 when he began his newspaper career. He continued to serve as his brother Norman's "PR" man, supplying stories of the Tilikum's voyage and pictures to papers around the world.

George married Ada E Livingstone in Minneapolis on Thursday 30th June 1910 and after their wedding the couple moved to Banff in Alberta where George ran the Lux Theatre for his brother "Norm" for a while. The Lux Theatre which opened on 17th May 1913 had a complete stage and setting. It had a short life however, as the next year, following a disastrous fire Norman built the Lux Block containing a new hotel, several stores and a moving picture theatre, The Lux, which George also ran.

His wife Ada couldn't settle in Banff so the couple returned to Minneapolis where George worked at a movie house, the Rialto Theatre, as a projectionist. His World War 1 Draft registration card for

The First George Luxton (right), garden editor of the Minneapolis Morning Tribune, was presented with the first of a new type of the gloxinia, named for him and created in his honor, at the Builders' Show in the Minneapolis auditorium Wednesday. Ralph Bachmann (center), of Bachmann's, Inc., city florists, made the presentation. The new gloxinia, rated by experts at the flower show as the finest in the United States, was produced by Dick Miller (left), a hybridist employed by Bachmann's, who worked two years on the project.

1917-18 lists George 36 and Ada residing at 138 Arthur Avenue in S.E. Minneapolis. He is a manager of the Rialto Theatre Supply Company at 731-3 Hennepin Avenue.

The 1940 U.S. census for Minneapolis Hennepin County, Minnesota lists George Luxton, 59 newspaper photographer, Ada his wife 56 and their daughter Patricia, 20. We learn more from his 1942 World War Two draft registration card. George is 60 and he and Ada continue to live at 138 Arthur Avenue. He is 5ft 8 inch and has a light complexion, weighs 133 lbs and has blue eyes and light brown hair. He is employed by the Minneapolis Star Tribune

A keen photographer, George, became in time, the number one photographer for the Minneapolis Star Tribune. He was also known to be an enthusiastic gardener, and when the newspaper's gardening correspondent became sick, George was taken on to write the gardening column, and ended his career as the paper's garden editor. He retired in 1946.

George wrote a best selling gardening book "Flower Growing in the North" (1956), published by the University of Minnesota Press. The book was a popular spin off of his Sunday Edition Garden Column in the newspaper. His mother, Sarah Jane Edwards (1846-1927), was the "Grandma" who features so prominently with gardening hints in the book.

As one of the most popular columnists in Minneapolis, George was much called on as a guest speaker. He had a gloxinia[88] named after him

---

[88] A newspaper clipping dated April 1951 features a photograph of George being presented with a new gloxinia named after him.

as well as Luxton Park in Minneapolis. George was 81 when he died on 1st November and was buried at Sunset Memorial Park, Minneapolis, on 3rd November 1962.

The couple's only child, Patricia Jane Luxton (1919-1988), was born in Minneapolis on 17th May 1919[89]. Pat who worked as an accountant and was at one time the Secretary to Liberace lived in the family home on Arthur Avenue, Prospect Park, Minneapolis all her life, except for a time in the mid 1940s when she was employed in Canada. A violent fall at the age of ten on the ice rink now named Luxton Park, left Pat with a freakish physical handicap which she carried all her life.

She had MS for many years and towards the end of her life was in much pain. A big tea drinker she wrote lovely letters and when in pain would watch old films shown on TV in the early hours of the night. Pat died in Minneapolis on 11th January 1988 in her parents old home, where she much enjoyed being able to overlook the Park named in honour of her father.

---

[89] Pat believed she was born on the 19th May but the family Bible records she was born on the 17th May 1919.

15

HAROLD MALLOCH LUXTON (1884-1915)
A SOLDIER IN THE GREAT WAR

See tree 6

Harold Malloch Luxton, the youngest son of W.F. Luxton, editor of the Manitoba Free Press, was born in London, Ontario on Saturday the 2nd February 1884. He began his education in Winnipeg, but when his parents and siblings moved to St. Paul Minnesota in 1899 he attended school there. The U. S. census on 5th June 1900 for Minnesota lists him as a 16 year old clerk, residing with his parents in St. Paul. Malloch, the name by which he was popularly known, was bestowed in honour of a Mrs Malloch, a family friend in London, Ontario[90].

He left St. Paul in 1905 to settle in Banff, Alberta, where his elder brothers, Norman and Louis, were already engaged in business. Ten years later the Great War in Europe led to a change in plan. Pte. H. M. Luxton (No 467056) enlisted in Calgary, on the 23rd July 1915, in the Canadian Overseas Expeditionary Force which was being sent to France.

Further details of Malloch are gleaned from his enlistment papers, preserved in the National Archives of Canada in Ottowa. He was a single man, aged 31 years 5 months, and while in Banff had been employed as a Time keeper. In stature he was 5ft. 8 inches with a chest girth of $35^1/_2$ inches when fully expanded. He had blue eyes and brown hair and his complexion was fair. His religious denomination was Presbyterian.

---

[90] Malloch's late neice, Mary Graeber in San Diego, insisted that Mrs Malloch was William Fisher Luxton's mistress.His name is spelt Malloch in the family Bible but Harold's correspondence reveals he preferred to spell it Mallock which is the spelling recorded in his military papers and on his headstone.I spell his name Malloch in my account but where he spells it Mallock and where it is spelt that way in army letters and on his headstone I too spell it Mallock.

Malloch was taken on the strength of the 17th Canadian Battalion when he arrived in England on the 24th September 1915. The pressure of events must have been very stressful, as on the 27th October, Malloch was fined £2 and his pay was withheld 15 days for being drunk in Hythe, a town in Kent. Then on the 30th November he was transferred to the 31st Canadian battalion, 2nd Division, 6th Brigade. He arrived at the Canadian Base Depot, Havre, France on the 1st December 1915. Ten days later on the 11th December he was taken on the strength of the 31st

Battalion Canadian Infantry in the field. He was now on the Western Front and had a week to live.

He was "killed in action in the field" on the 18th December 1915. His body was interred the following day, 19th December, at Kemmel Chateau Military Cemetery, Heuvelland, West-Vlaanderen, Belgium. The cemetery is located eight kilometres south of Ieper (better known by its First World War name of Ypres) on a road leading from Kemmelseweg, connecting Ieper to Kemmel. Mont Kemmel, on the other side of the village of Kemmel, is the eastern-most of a range of low hills running between Bailleul and Popinghe. The village and hill was the scene of fierce fighting on the southern sector of the Belgium Front. There are over 1000 1914-1918 casualties commemorated on the site. The cemetery is enclosed by a brickwall and Malloch's grave reference is K.71. His headstone reads:-

In Memory of
HAROLD MALLOCK LUXTON
Private
467056
31st Bri, Canadian Infantry (Alberta Regt.)
who died on
Saturday, 18th December 1915. Age 31.

A postcard which Malloch sent to his mother shortly before he was killed reads:-

My dear mother,

Your loving letter just reached me today in sunny France where I am now located. As great restriction is placed on correspondence I will have to curtail details. Am perfectly well and free from danger. Mother dear keep a brave heart. I will see you soon again. This will soon be over and the sun will shine once more for us all. With best love to all and many thanks for all kind favors. I am your son Mallock

The postcard was quickly followed by Malloch's last letter:-
"Somewhere in France"

December 14th 1915
My dear mother,

No doubt by the time this little note reaches you, you will have received an abbreviated Post Card from me which states all is well with me.

I received a few minutes ago a P.C. from Nellie (sister Eleanor Luxton Foster) in which she advises me that a cake from you dear and little luxuries from the other dear ones at home, were on the way to me and I am sure to receive everything in goodtime as the post system is perfection here.

How kind of you all to remember me with these good things goes without saying but I deeply appreciate and thank you all for your thoughtfulness of me.

Now my little Mother mine I do not want you to worry a bit about me. I am going to come through this all right. I feel it, and firmly believe the <u>Great Guiding Power</u> will bring those that do the right thing to a safe heaven. <u>Though the voyage may be very rough at times</u> and the temptation to give up now and then is strong within you. Nevertheless at a critical time like this God proves himself to be the only Master of men and one only has to believe this fact and all is well.

I am so sorry I cannot tell you about my personal experiences while travelling through these strange lands but it is absolutely forbidden but someday I will tell you all about this wonderful trip.

Christmas will soon be here and a very strange one it will be for most of us here as there is no snow and no frost as yet to make it seem more natural, however no doubt my next Christmas will be spent with my own folk at home.

Remember Mother mine your boy is always thinking of you and keeping a brave heart for his little hero of a Mother who has suffered so long without complaint. God bless and keep you.

Give my very best love and thanks to all the dear ones at home. I wish them all a very very Happy Christmas.

Tell the little one that I received his little letter with all the brave words and thousand kisses which I heartily return tenfold. Also your little letter with enclosure of clipping (which I read with interest and the picture of a dear little baby girl (Mary Hosking Graeber) all of which gladdened the weary hours.

As I close this letter I can feel your presence with me and your dear face very close to mine.

Your own boy

Mallock

B.E.F. c/o C Company Thirty First Batt. Army Post Office, London, England2nd Division, 6th Brigade.

I am perfectly well and comfortable.

A second letter, dated the same day, 14th December 1915, which Malloch posted to his married sister, Mrs F. K. Foster in Winnipeg, reached her on the 5th January 1916. The following day, the 6th January, a casualty list published in Calgary by the Canadian government recorded that Pte. H. M. Luxton aged 30 of the 31st Canadian Battalion had been killed in action "somewhere in France".

Malloch was the first man from Hennepin County Minnesota U.S.A. to fall in battle in World War 1. He had joined the Canadian Forces and had been killed in Belgium on the 18th December 1915 before the United States joined the allies.

His widowed mother, Mrs W. F. Luxton of 596 Cherokee Avenue, St. Paul, Minnesota received a letter from Captain William R. Walker, the chaplain to Malloch's company, explaining the circumstances of Malloch's death. It reads:-Headquarters,

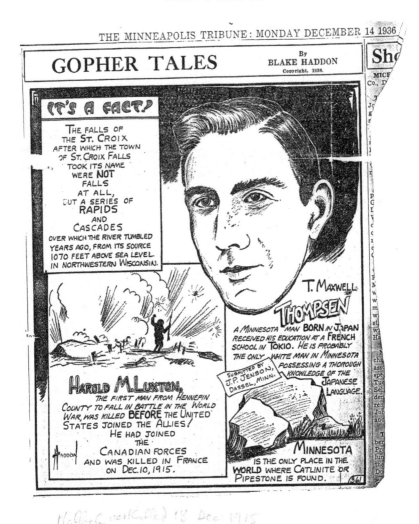

THE MINNEAPOLIS TRIBUNE: MONDAY DECEMBER 14 1936

4th Can. Fld hut
B.E.F.
Dec 20/15

Dear Mrs Luxton,

It is with heartfelt sorry & sympathy for you that I write to you about the death of Pte Harold Mallock Luxton of the 31st Batt C.E.F.

On Saturday the 18th December your son was with his comrades in the trenches. As he was passing along the front line where the parapet had fallen a little he was shot by a sniper through the lungs. How inadequate are my words to express how deep is my sympathy for you in this sad loss. Mingled with your sorrow is the sorrow &sympathy of his comrades. They grieve with you as they mourn the loss of a good comrade. He had left them to go for his dinner & while he & another comrade were passing, which prevented their stooping at the dangerous part of the parapet, the bullet from the enemy's rifle ushered both into Eternity.

He had finished his work & done his duty & at the Saviour's call "Well done good & faithful servant enter into the joy of thy Lord", passed into his rest.

As his chaplain I spent sometime the previous day with his company & he was with them. They all love me to be with in the trenches & shelters & from this attitude which is more expressive than words I know that all of them are prepared for any sacrifice their duty demands of them.

I buried Harold in a cemetery at KEMMEL along with his comrade where many soldiers are already laid to rest. A cross will be placed at his head with his name & regiment stamped on metal upon it. All the graves there are neatly kept by the soldiers.

His personal effects & money will be sent to you through the proper channels.

Any further particulars which you may care to have I shall be pleased to forward to you.

Once more expressing my sorrow for you & trusting that God will give you Grace to stand the loss of Harold.

I have pleasure in remaining

Yours sincerely

Wm R Walker

Captain

In his enlistment papers Malloch names his mother Jane as his next of kin and her address as in Banff so that is why a next of kin memorial plaque ended up at his brother Normans house in 1922.The memorial plaque or "Death Plaque" or "Widows Penny" as it was colloquially called was awarded to the next of kin of the men or women who died during the First World War.

The selected design was a 12 centimetre disk cast in bronze gunmetal, which incorporated the following, an image of Britannia holding an oak spray with leaves and acorns, an imperial lion, two dolfins representing Britains sea power, the emblem of Imperial Germany's eagle being torn to pieces by another lion, a rectangular tablet where in this case his name Harold Mallock Luxton was cast into the plaque.

No rank was given as it was intended to show equality in their sacrifice and the words. "He died for freedom and honour."

The memorial plaque would be accompanied by a memorial scroll in the form of a letter from Buckinghham Palace. They would not usually arrive as a single package but as a series of separate mailings.

154

16

JOHN LUXTON (1827-1906), FARMER AND MASON, HUTCHINGS FARM, PETTON, BAMPTON

See tree 5

John Luxton, the youngest of five children born to Thomas Luxton (1783-1840), mason and yeoman, and his wife Jenny Palmer at Hutchings Farm, was baptised at Petton on the 7th January 1827. His father Thomas died of consumption in March 1840 and the 1841 census lists John aged 14, a mason, his sister Elizabeth 20, and elder brother Thomas 17, also a mason, living at Hutchings Farm with their widowed mother, Jane, an agricultural labourer. John was working as a mason in Wellington, Somerset, when he married Eleanor Greenslade, spinster in the parish church Wellington on the 3rd October 1850. William Burnett, one of the witnesses, was to marry John's sister, Jane Palmer Luxton in 1852.

Eleanor (1826-1900), the daughter of Thomas and Ann Greenslade, yeoman, was born in Petton and when the 1851 census was taken her husband, John, a 24 year old master mason, and Eleanor were living at Harris Cottage, Petton, the home of her father, Thomas Greenslade, a 63 year old widower and farm labourer, and her 25 year old brother William, also a farm labourer. In Billings Devon Directory for 1857, John Luxton was listed as a mason and bricklayer. residing in Petton, Bampton. Their eldest child, Thomas Greenslade Luxton (1851-1926) was baptised at Petton on the 18th April 1851. John (1854-1932), a second son, born on the 31st August 1854, was baptised there on the 24th September 1854 while a daughter, Elizabeth Ellen Luxton (1864-1947), known as "Bessie" was baptised on the 3rd July 1864.

John was standing outside Mr. Heywood's "beer-house" at Boxen Hedge, conversing with a Mr. Deer on the 3rd October 1853 when he was violently assaulted. Francis Greenslade of Chipstable approached, in a belligerent mood, accusing John of taking away a ladder from scaffolding on which he and his brother John Greenslade were at work.

"Now" he said "I'll bang your head off" and immediately struck John several violent blows in his face with his fists. John Greenslade then joined in the attack and they struck and kicked John Luxton severely. At the Bampton Petty Sessions, when the Bench heard the case in late November, Francis Greenslade was fined £1 and costs and his brother John was fined 10shillings and costs for assisting in the assault[91].

There was a full house at Hutchings Farm in 1861. John, aged 34, a mason employing two men and two boys, was head of household. His wife Eleanor, aged 34, and their sons, Thomas G. aged 10, and John aged 6, lived with John and his widowed mother "Fanny" aged 71 who is described as deaf. The two boys John employed were relatives who also resided at the farm. William Luxton (1843-1867) aged 16, mason, was his sister Mary's illegitimate son, while a second William Luxton (1849-1918) aged 12, a 'mason's lender' was the son of James Luxton (1813-1861), mason of Skilgate, who was a cousin to John.

John Luxton, later in that same year, by an indenture dated 11th May 1861, purchased Hutchings for £180 from his elder brother Thomas, who in the early 1850s had emigrated to "Orford in the County of Kent in Upper Canada".

The census returns are helpful in tracking John's activities. In 1871 John Luxton, aged 44, mason and farmer, his wife Eleanor aged 44, their children, Thomas G., aged 20, mason, and Elizabeth E., aged 6, scholar, and Thomas Greed, aged 13, servant, mason's labourer, were living at Hutchings, Frogpit Moor. John owned three acres at Hutchings and employed one man at the masonry. Their son John who was aged about 16 was living away from home.

The situation had been transformed by 1881. John and Eleanor, both aged 55 inhabited the Parsonage House at Raddington, Somerset, a few miles away where John was a farmer of sixty two acres. Two servants lived with them at the Parsonage. Kelly's Directory of Somerset and Bristol 1883 also lists John Luxton as the farmer at Parsonage. In April 1887 John was appointed one of the overseers for the parish of Raddington.[92]The couples eldest son, Thomas G. Luxton was married

[91] Western Times, Saturday 3rd December 1853.
[92] Taunton Courier, Wednesday 6th April 1887.

and living at Brembridge, Petton where he farmed one hundred and fifty six acres. Hutchings was occupied by their son John, aged 26, a tailor and grocer, while his sister Elizabeth Ellen, aged 16, was the house keeper.

John was in his early 60s when he retired from farming in the summer of 1889. The Parsonage House, Raddington was held on a lease and in June the Tiverton Gazette[93] invited tenders to be sent on or before the 6th July 1889 by anyone interested in renting the farmhouse and premises and some 61 acres 2r 39p of Glebe lands from Michaelmas next. More interesting is an advert in the same paper, dated 16th April 1889. Auctioneers, Knowlman and Wood, were instructed by Mr. Luxton "who is retiring from business, to sell by auction on Wednesday, April 17th 1889, at two o'clock, the whole of his livestock, implements and grass of the farm until Michaelmas next, comprising:- 25 double and single couples, 12 ewe hogs, 1 ram, 2 heifers in milk and a calf, 1 cow in full milk, 2 two year old heifers in calf, 4 two year old steers, 8 steer yearlings, 2 heifer yearlings, 4 steer calves, cart horse, 4 years old; capital mare with foal at foot, "Damsel" cart mare, 8 years old, an extraordinary good cart colt, coming three years old, implements, &c. Also the grass of the farm, nearly all to be mown and carried off." The auctioneers were impressed by what was on offer and "can with confidence thoroughly recommend the above sheep and cattle. The horses are well shaped, strong in all kinds of work; the implements much above the average, & the fertility of the grass land is well known in the neighbourhood. There is a good supply of water. The whole will be sold without reserve.[94]

John, a member of the Ancient Order of Forresters Court Huntsham Lodge, attended the annual fete and sports day in July 1889. Members dined at the Tiverton Hotel before the company led by the Bampton Band marched to a field where sports were held.[95]The Order was formed in 1834 to provide financial and social support to members, paying a few pence a week into a common fund; they would be able to offer sick pay and funeral grants when needed.

---

[93] Tiverton Gazette, Tuesday 25th June 1889
[94] Tiverton Gazette Tuesday 16th April 1889
[95] Western Times, Tuesday 16th July 1889.

In March 1890 John brought another case when at the Wellington County Court he claimed that the Rev. John Popham Hayne owed him £11.. 18s..3d for work which he had done. However when the Rev. Popham Hayne made a counter claim that John owed him £20..15s. the court adjoined the case and a hearing was fixed for the April sitting of the Tiverton Court. I have found nothing more in the newspapers and further research is needed in court records[96].

In 1891 John and Eleanor, both aged 64, were back in residence at Hutchings where John was described as a mason but he was a retired farmer when his daughter Bessie married in December that year. His older married sister, Elizabeth Incledon, aged 69, the wife of William Incledon, coachman, was staying with them. She died of senile decay at Hutchings on the 30th March 1899. In the 1851 census Elizabeth, 31, had been one of four house servants to Richard Bere, 58, rector of Skilgate, living at East Timewell, Morebath.

I possess a 'cabinet print' of John, his wife Eleanor, and their daughter Elizabeth Ellen Luxton, which was probably taken just before "Bessie" married James Chibbett, a cabinet maker, at the Bible Christian Chapel in Tiverton, on the 31st December 1891. The photograph executed by Herbert H. Hole, (1838-1900) "portrait and landscape photographer of Williton Watchet and Minehead" was taken in Williton where Bessie's husband James Chibbett lived and where the couple settled following their marriage. On the reverse side Hole advertises that he won First prize at the Minehead Fine Art Exhibition. The local newspaper accounts for this Exhibition together with electoral registers and Trade directories may help date the photograph more precisely.

In the photograph John, erect and slightly built, stands between his seated wife Eleanor and daughter Bessie. He is dressed in a three quarter length

---

[96] Western Times, 10th March 1890.

woollen coat, trousers, a single breasted waistcoat and chequered cravat. He appears to be in his early sixties with his thinning hair "brushed over" and is sporting greying side whiskers with a "Newgate fringe" under his chin. Eleanor, seated on his left, is wearing a black dress with a button fronted top decorated with embroidered black lace and is holding an open book on her lap. Bessie, their daughter, a "modern" young woman is wearing a plain tailored woollen suit or "tailor made" which was becoming increasingly popular for everyday wear during the early 1890s and she is wearing it with a masculine looking shirt and chequered tie. Her hair, in the prevailing neat chignon, is dressed fairly high on her head. John and Eleanor gaze with a steady thoughtful pose while young Bessie has a slightly haughty look.

Their home, Hutchings Farm is named "Hutchins's House" on the ordnance survey six inch to one mile map published in 1889. The field boundaries at Frogpit Moor are the same as in the 1842 Bampton Tithe Map but there has been a great change in the landscape. The Devon and Somerset branch line of the G.W.R.[97] cuts in an east west line across the moor, right through the middle of the fields held by the Luxton family at the time of the 1842 tithe map. Hutchings and its fields which belonged to John's brother Thomas in 1842, lie undisturbed to the north of the new line. This branch line is interesting because it was part of the first steam railway to reach Devon. Constructed at the instigation of Bristol merchants who formed the Bristol and Exeter Railway, it lay on the line from Taunton to Exeter and was opened for traffic on 1st May 1844. The G.W.R. took over its management in 1876 when it acquired the Bristol and Exeter Railway.

The Luxtons at Hutchings were Bible Christians and John Luxton, farmer, was one of eleven trustees for the denomination when his kinswoman, Miss Mary Ann Luxton, conveyed them a plot of land beside the old A361 at Petton on the 11th August 1892. The land was the proposed site of a chapel and for a number of years a converted railway carriage from the Lynton and Barnstaple Railway placed on the plot was used as a place of worship. Meanwhile a Bible Christian Chapel was built in 1901 about two hundred yards up the road at Frogpit Moor on land given by H. Acland Troyte J.P. and the original site was sold in 1904 to Mr William Hawkins for his traction engine repair shed.

---

[97] Great Western Railway.

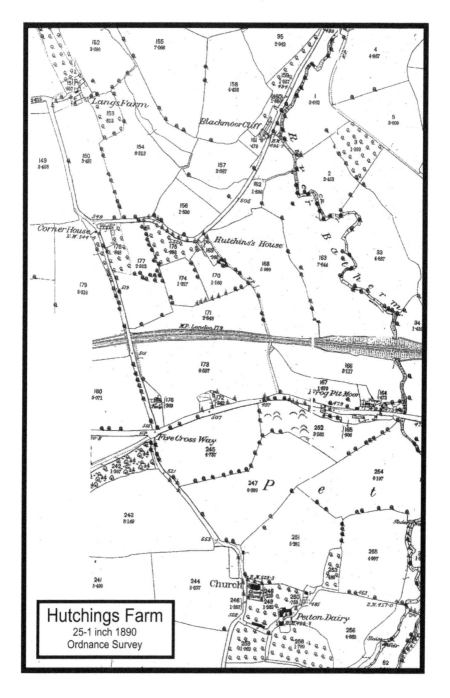

Hutchings Farm
25-1 inch 1890
Ordnance Survey

Hutchings was mortgaged to repay the £180 which John had paid his brother for it in 1861. By an indenture, dated the 13th July 1861, the farm was mortgaged to George Pitt of No 248 High Street, Exeter, Grocer, and Thomas Row Densham of Bampton, gentleman, for £160 with interest at the rate of five per cent a year. Twenty nine years later Pitt and Densham were dead and their executors, Richard Densham and Thomas Row, gentlemen of Bampton, desired repayment of the £160 to which they were entitled. The mortgage was transferred to John Moore, a tailor and draper, of Dulverton, Somerset, by an indenture, dated the 27th October 1890. Moore paid Densham and Row the £160 due to them and John Luxton covenanted to pay John Moore, his new mortgagee, the sum of £250 with interest at the rate of four per cent a year. John settled his debt by an indenture dated the 27th October 1902 which is made on the reverse of the 1890 indenture. John Moore, "in consideration of all principal money and interest secured by the within written Indenture having been paid" reconveyed Hutchings to John Luxton to hold, "in fee simple Freed and discharged from all principal money and interest secured by and all claims and demands under the within written Indenture".

Following the death of his wife, Eleanor, aged 73, on the 28th March 1900, John instructed James Phillips & Sons to sell the livestock and furniture at Hutchings by auction on Monday 14th May 1900, commencing at three o'clock in the afternoon. The farm was described as lying about halfway between Venn Cross and Morebath stations on the Devon and Somerset Railway.[98]

Live Stock-Cow, in full milk (barren), cow in calf (time up the latter part of May) heifer, coming two years old; heifer calf (off the bucket), large size sow, 8 capital slip pigs, 18 fowls.

Out –door Effects-chaff cutter, several empty casks; pipes, about 6 hogsheads cider, to be sold with casks, tubs, vats, funnels, pigs' troughs, ladders, hay knife, wheel barrow, 20 hurdles, nearly new pulper, cider-press, apple mill, garden tools, mason's tools, hampers, tubs, sieves.

Furniture-Three wood bedsteads, iron single ditto, 4 feather beds, bolsters and pillows, bedding, mattresses, 3 washstands, 3 sets ware, 3 towel rails, table, 4 swing glasses, 2 chests drawers, carved oak box,

---

[98] West Somerset Free Press 28th April 1900.

carpet, 3 cane-seat chairs, American clock, night commode, pier glass, large bath, oak writing desk and cupboard combined, mahogany Chippendale arm-chair, matting, heath-rug, birch table, deal table, glass cupboard, round table, several pictures, ornaments, china and glass, coal scuttle, long kitchen table and form, sofa, 6 kitchen chairs, 3 easy chairs, dresser and shelves, grandfather's clock, barometer, 3 lap screen, fender and fire irons, jibs, 6 milk pans, 6 brass pans, 2 butter tubs, 2 safes, scales and weights, boilers, tea-kettles, pots etc.

The above mentioned cows are splendid quality Devons and good milkers and as Mr Luxton is retiring, the whole will be unreservedly sold. Note Hutchings Farm, comprising a nice convenient dwelling house, out-buildings, orchard, and meadow, the whole being just over 4 acres, will be offered by auction in July next, full particulars will be shortly issued. Dated, Bridgtown Mills, Dulverton, and Town Mills, Minehead, April 24th 1900. (The Devon is an ancient breed of cattle from North Devon. It is a rich red or tawny colour and this gives rise to its nickname Devon Ruby or Red Ruby).

John decided to let Hutchings. Among the Hutchings muniments there survives a fascinating "Memorandum of an Agreement" for the leasing of Hutchings on an annual basis. In the agreement made on the 27th October 1900, John Luxton farmer of Petton, agreed to let Hutchings to John Broom of Brembridge, Petton, farmer. It was let "From the twenty fifth day of March last from year to year determinable at the end of any year by twelve calendar months notice in writing given by either party". The yearly rental of £17 was to be paid "by equal quarterly payments on Midsummer Day Michaelmas Day Christmas Day and Lady Day in each year". The first payment was due and payable on Midsummer Day 1900. A further yearly rental of fifty pounds was to be paid for every acre and a proportionately less amount for every quantity less than an acre which was broken up or converted to tillage. Such further rent was to be payable quarterly on the above mentioned days.

John reserved to himself "all timber and other trees mines minerals and quarries and the right to enter on the premises to fell or work and carry away the same and for all other reasonable purposes".

Among other things the tenant agreed "To use and occupy the said house and premises in a fair and tenantable manner.

To keep in repair the glass of the windows the bolts locks and fastenings of the windows and doors and the interior of the dwelling house and buildings, the cider-press and Screw, and the gates bars and fences of and belonging to the premises. And not to cut any hedgewood in the last year of the tenancy.

To keep the orchard well filled with good thriving apple trees.[99] Not to break up or convert to tillage any part of the premises except the garden. Not to sell remove or carry off the premises any grass hay or other produce to arise or be made thereon. But to consume the same on the premises and properly use and spread the dung arising therefrom on the land.

Not to assign or underlet the premises or any part thereof without the written consent of the Landlord.

And generally to use manure and manage the premises in a good husbandlike manner and not to commit or permit any act of waste or spoil thereon And at the end of the tenancy to deliver up possession of the premises with the cider press and Screw, wardrobe or hanging press in the dwelling house (upstairs) furnaces ranges and other landlords fixtures in fair and proper order and condition". The landlord for his part agreed to "keep the walls and roofs and outside of the premises in repair during the tenancy."[100]

John was still grieving the loss of his wife Eleanor, when he and his married daughter Bessie on Thursday 12th April 1900 had the distressing experience of finding 16 year old William Flew, a farmer's son from Raddington, lying fatally injured. The boy's horse and cart had over turned while he was returning home from Venn Cross. In an inquest held at Hutchings Farm, John, described as a dairyman, said that about 10AM

---

[99] Most farms in the Bampton area had an orchard. John made his own scrumpy cider, as many farmers did. It was powerful stuff. Drunk in excessive quantities it was either mind blowing or a powerful laxative. A form of colic was diagnosed as having its origins in the cider, and was known as Colica Damnoniensis – the Devonshire Colic.

[100] Hutchings was farmed in 1901 by John Broom, a 63 year old widower, and his sons Charles and Thomas with his daughter Mary as housekeeper. Ten years earlier in 1891 John Broom had farmed the 156 acres of Bremridge, Petton which had been farmed by Thomas Greenslade Luxton in 1881. Bremridge was unoccupied at time of 1901 census.

on Thursday morning he was in his (grocer's) shop when he heard a horse and cart coming down the road. It stopped suddenly and his daughter Bessie looking out of the window called out that a horse had fallen down. They hurried out and saw that a cart containing some bags of manure had turned over and the boy was under it. With the assistance of Bessie he lifted the cart and got the boy out. The boy managed to walk into the house unaided and sat on a chair near the fire where Bessie gave him some brandy. His condition rapidly worsened and John laid him on the sofa where he died about fifteen minutes later[101].

In 1900 John went to live with Bessie Chibbett, his married daughter in High Street Williton, but he was staying with his son, Thomas Greenslade Luxton at Forde Farm, Cheriton Fitzpaine, when he died in his eightieth year on the 10th August 1906. He was buried on the north side of Petton churchyard on the 15th August 1906. His headstone reads:-

Thy will be done
In Loving Memory
of
Eleanor Luxton
who died March 28th 1900
aged 73 years
Also John Luxton
her beloved husband
who died Aug. 10th 1906
In his 80th year.
Peace, Perfect Peace.

John Luxton of Hutchings, Bampton, Devon, farmer, made his Will on the 28th April 1899. "All my estate and effects of every description and wheresoever situate", he left to his daughter, Elizabeth Ellen Chibbett upon trust to pay his debts and funeral and testamentary expenses. His son Thomas Greenslade Luxton was to receive the sum of fifty pounds while his grandson

---

[101] Exeter and Plymouth Gazette, Saturday 14th April 1900 and Tiverton Gazette Tuesday 17th April 1900.

Victor John Luxton born in 1889 was to receive £10 when he reached the age of 21. Elizabeth Ellen Chibbett, his daughter, was to hold and retain the residue of his estate and effects for her own use and benefit. She was appointed sole executor. Bessie Chibbett was granted probate of the Will on the 28th August 1906 when her father's effects were valued at £416—16shillings.

Hutchings Farm was in Bessie Chibbett's possession in April 1912 when she leased it on a yearly lease. The farm which had been bought by Jacob Luxton from Robert his father in 1745 for £30 was held by six generations of the family before Bessie sold it for £670 by an indenture dated 9th February 1923 to Charles Elworthy of Kingston Farm, Raddington[102].

Bessie's husband, James Chibbett died aged 65 on the 27th September1928. In his Will made on the 30th April 1928 he left his share in James Chibbett & Sons, Builders and House Decorators, to his wife Bessie who proved the Will on the 27th August 1929.

Bessie Chibbett died aged 82 on the 30th March 1947. The Will of E.E. Chibbett of Catwell, Williton, widow, made on the 17th September 1936 with codicil of 19th March 1946 bequeathed the house, shop etc in High Street, Williton to her nephew Henry James Chibbett. Bessie bequeathed £300 to her companion, Henrietta Brown and made bequests to her nephews William Henry Luxton, Ernest Edgar Luxton and niece Olive May Adams who were the children of her brother John Luxton (1854-1932).

Bessie and her husband Jim had no children so they 'adopted' her niece, Eva Ellen Luxton, who tragically died aged 14 of meningitis on the 21st July 1900. "Nellie" as she was known in the family lies buried with her uncle and aunt at St. Decuman's Watchet[103] where in the south east corner of the churchyard a black granite gravestone consisting of three steps, surmounted by a chamfered cross, carries the following inscription in lead lettering:-

---

[102] Mrs. J. Gathercole, Hutchings Farm, Petton Cross, kindly supplied me with a photocopy of the deed on28 February 1990.
[103] St. Decuman's was the actual name of the parish covering Watchet and the village of Williton.

In
loving memory
of James,
Beloved husband
of E.E. Chibbett
at rest Sep. 27th 1928,
aged 65 years.
Thy will be done.
Also Elizabeth Ellen
wife of the above
died March 30th 1947
aged 82 years.
In
loving memory
of
Eva Ellen Luxton
Their niece
at rest July 21st 1900
aged 14 years.

17

THOMAS GREENSLADE LUXTON (1851-1926)
"THE PREACHER".

See tree 5

On visits I made to the West Country in the 1970s, relatives said I reminded them of a kinsman, Thomas Greenslade Luxton (1851-1926), "the Preacher". His name kept turning up and little by little I  have put together notes about his life. Thomas Greenslade Luxton, son of John and Eleanor Luxton, mason, was baptised at St. Petrock's Church, Petton on the 18th April 1851. Petton, a hamlet in the parish of Bampton, on Devon's border with Somerset, had been the home of his Luxton forebears since the early 1700s. John Luxton and Eleanor Greenslade, his parents, were married in Wellington, Somerset on the 3rd October 1850 and Thomas was the eldest of their three children. They settled in Petton where John (1827-1906), a mason and farmer, in 1861, purchased the old family home Hutchings Farm from his brother Thomas who had emigrated to Palmyra, Ontario, Canada.

Thomas Greenslade Luxton, aged 24, builder[104], of Petton, Bampton the son of John Luxton, builder, married Eliza Jane Mantle aged 20 of Great Rill Farm, Bampton, daughter of William Mantle, farmer, at the Wesleyan Methodist Chapel Tiverton on the 24th October 1876. I possess a much handled and battered photograph of the wedding group which was taken by W. Mudford, Fore Street, Tiverton. The groom is wearing a frock coat,

---

[104] Whites Directory (1878) P124, Thomas Greenslade Luxton, builder, Petton.

identifiable by its double-breasted fastening. His bride, dressed in white, has her face covered by a veil and the young girl with her arm resting on Thomas's knee was his twelve year old sister Elizabeth Ellen Luxton who is wearing a stylish hat and has a profusion of ornamental frills and bows on her bodice and skirt. The clean shaven young man in the back row was Eliza's brother, Thomas Mantle, who was best man. Elizabeth Tarr, who was one of the witnesses at the wedding, is probably the bridesmaid standing to his right.

I have too a head and shoulder photograph of T.G. Luxton, framed within a medallion, which was taken on his honeymoon by M. Gutenberg, 12 Royal Promenade, Clifton, Bristol. His hair is parted on the side and the front has been combed back over the top of the head. He has a moustache with side whiskers and is sporting a rose in the button hole of his morning coat. It has deep lapels which were characteristic of men's fashion in the mid 1870s. So too were the high collar and cravat he is wearing. Taken at the same time is a head and shoulder medallion portrait of Eliza Jane Mantle. Her hair is dressed close to the head with a neat coil down the back which was fashionable among young women and her high neckline is set off with white lace and a brooch and pendant.

In 1992 T.G. Luxton's family Bible came into my safe keeping. It is inscribed on the fly leaf, "T.G. Luxton, Petton, 1876", the year of his marriage to Eliza Jane Mantle. Printed by W.R. Mcphun & Son, Glasgow and London, in 1875, "The National Illustrated Family Bible" is a large blackbound volume with gold decoration on the spine and covers. It incorporates the commentaries of Scott and Henry with thousands of critical and explanatory notes and was edited by the Rev John Eadie, Professor of Biblical Literature to the United Presbyterian Church. It contains a four page family register which is placed

between the Old and New Testament. Sadly this register contains no entries as Thomas and Eliza had no children of their own.

In 1881 Thomas, aged 30, was a sheep farmer of one hundred and fifty six acres, employing one labourer and two boys at Bremridge, Petton, Bampton and his wife Eliza aged 25 was born in Cutcombe, Somerset. T.G. Luxton was to become a noted Bible Christian lay preacher. The Bible Christians were particularly strong in Devon and the West Country. They had begun with a small class of twenty two members, started by William O'Bryan a Cornish farmer in 1815 in Lake Farm the home of Mr John Thorne at Shebbear in north Devon. Originally called Bryanites they received the name Bible

Christians as a nickname given because of the extraordinary familiarity which their early preachers shared with the contents of the Bible. Their founder was a Wesleyan lay preacher and the Bible Christians were a branch of the Methodists.

The Bible Christians took root in the early nineteenth century because in many ways the Anglican Church was failing to meet the needs of the people. Throughout the rural countryside the clergy were unpopular because they exacted tithes from the farming community. Incumbents too were frequently absentee priests who hired a succession of poorly paid curates to do their work for them. Church buildings were neglected and too many clergy were noted for their drinking habits and riding to hounds than for their sermons or the faithful discharge of their pastoral duties. From their early days the Bible Christians relied heavily on men like T. G. Luxton with some standing in the local community who could help meet the cost of building chapels. Always short of money the Bible Christians only had a limited number of full time preachers and relied on farmers like T.G. Luxton to become local lay preachers. Driven by a strong missionary zeal Bible Christians were almost as committed to education as to preaching the Gospel and realised the importance of a good education without which they could not develop their potential to the full nor would they be able to be active or influential members of society.

It was Eliza Mantle who first introduced T. G. Luxton to the Bible Christians. He joined the church at Bampton where he was a valued member. The Bible Christians at Petton had initially met for worship in member's houses but as the cause grew in number a permanent place of worship became necessary. It may have been T. G. Luxton's influence which persuaded his relative Miss Mary Ann Luxton, the matron of the Midland Institution of the Blind in Nottingham, to convey a plot of land at Petton Cross for the erection of a Bible Christian chapel. The deed is dated the 11th August 1892 and the necessary land was sold for a mere £2. Two of the eleven trustees for the proposed Bible Christian chapel

on this site were Thomas's father John Luxton (1827-1906) and Thomas Mantle, his brother in law. Worship began in a converted railway carriage, measuring 9 feet 6 inches wide and 25 feet long. It was fitted with a rostrum and a harmonium and was capable of seating sixty worshippers.

The Petton chapel was finally built, however, in 1901 about 200 yards up the road on land given by H. Acland Troyte J.P. Thomas G. Luxton was listed as one of the trustees of the chapel and when the foundation ceremony took place on the 18th July 1901 he paid £3..3shillings to lay one of its foundation stones inscribed – Mr Luxton Cheriton.

In the mid 1880s Thomas and Elizabeth moved to Forde Farm, Cheriton Fitzpaine, which he rented before purchasing. As a member of the Bible Christian Methodist Connection on the Tiverton and Bampton Circuit, he may have been acquainted with his old kinsman, Charles Luxton (1813-1885), a lace worker at Taunton and Tiverton, who was also a staunch Bible Christian.

Thomas was closely involved with the Cheriton Fitzpaine Dairy Company, founded in1896, which prospered and in 1899 he was the company chairman[105]. The 1901 census lists Thomas G Luxton, 50, farmer at Forde, with his wife, Eliza Jane, aged 46, born in Cutcombe. Her 84 year old widowed mother, Eliza Mantle, born in Upton, Somerset and their thirteen year old niece, Henrietta Mantle, lived with them. Emma Iles, a fifteen year old domestic servant, and James Yeo, 18, a cattleman, completed the household. When Cheriton Fitzpaine celebrated the Coronation of Edward VII in 1902 young Hettie Mantle helped light the large bonfire in a field on the farm. Bertie Sanders, a local schoolboy, described the event in a letter to the press"...Oh my, didn't it make a blaze! We couldn't stand very near to it, or we should have been scorched. We stayed there...watching it burn...and seeing a lot of fireworks going up".[106]

T.G. Luxton advertised in the Tiverton Gazette on Tuesday 26th February 1889-To let Dairy of 8 cows, taker find his own. Good opening for poultry & butter trade. On Friday, 17th October 1902 Thomas placed the following advert in the Western Times-For sale Phaeton: good condition: suit elderly lady or gentleman-Luxton, Forde, Cheriton Fitzpaine.

In a sale of rams at Exeter Cattle Market on 30th July 1915 he sold a prize ram; Torweston, good neck for 17 and a half guineas. Like his father, John, he had a good eye for Devon cattle. In October 1917 at the 35th show and sale of pure bred Devon cattle, under the auspices of the Devon

---

[105] Western Times, Wednesday 1st March 1899.
[106] Western Times, Friday 5th September 1902

Cattle Breeders' Society held in Taunton, he paid 48 gns for Mr. Tom
Tarr's "Bonnie Handy Boy."[107]

T.G. Luxton also had close connections from their beginning
with the Bible Christians at Upton, Somerset. In January 1878 he put in
a successful tender to build their new chapel at Rainsbury for the sum
of £245. It was to be 25ft long, 17ft wide and about 12ft high, with
seating for about 90 persons. The work was to commence by the end of
June. Tom had laid the memorial stones of the new chapel by early
March that year when despite bad weather many were present for the
ceremony. His wife, assisted by his young sister, Bessie, provided tea
afterwards in the school-room.[108]Their chapel was built in 1878 and the
centenary programme of Upton Methodist Chapel for the 21st to 23rd
July 1978 lists Thomas Greenslade Luxton (builder) as one of the
families sustaining the Upton Church. He was also one of the original
trustees of Upham Bible Christian Chapel, Cheriton Fitzpaine. It was
built in 1895 and its records reveal he was paid £1..15s..0d for carrying
stones used in building the chapel[109].

T.G. Luxton was very interested in missionary work. When he was a lad
he visited a gypsy encampment where he preached the Gospel which was
well received and attended with success. The Gospel was a very real
thing to him and he held his belief in the Christian faith intelligently. His
friends considered him thoughtful, kind and always considerate and
attributed these qualities to his conviction in the principles of Christianity.

T.G. Luxton's home at Forde was "open to all believers" said his friend
"Gypsy" Smith, and for nearly forty years Forde, was always an open
house for circuit ministers, deputations to the circuit and local preachers
and evangelists. The church people on the occasion of the couples
Golden Wedding celebrations in 1926, as tokens of their esteem,
presented T.G. Luxton with a gold mounted walking stick and his wife
Eliza with a gold mounted umbrella.

I possess "A Little Book of Cheer" by the Rev. Albert E. Sims.
It belonged to Luxton and has his signature "Thos. G. Luxton" on the

---

[107] North Devon Journal, Thursday 18th October 1917.
[108] West Somerset Free Press, Saturday 5th January & 9th March 1878
[109] See Upham Methodist Chapel, 100 years 1895 to 1995.

flyleaf. It is packed with inspiring quotations useful for a preacher. Surviving Methodist Preaching Plans for the United Methodist Tiverton and Bampton Circuit, reveal that in 1904 T.G. Luxton was due to preach at Templeton on the 14th August, Upham on the 4th September, Clayhanger on the 11th September, Cadeleigh on the 25th September and Halberton on the 2nd October. In 1910 he was due to preach at Cadeleigh on the 21st July, Stockley Pomeroy on the 18th August and Upham on the 6th October.

T.G. Luxton was one of the most valued laymen in the Tiverton Circuit and for nearly twenty years he held the office of circuit steward. His death was sudden. He attended the Circuit Quarterly meeting on the 16th December 1926 when he appeared to be in his usual health. The following Sunday, however, he felt unwell and was unable to attend chapel. On the Monday evening he was taken worse and became unconscious and died in the evening of the following day, the 21st December 1926[110]. He was buried two days after Christmas in the little burial ground in front of the Bible Christian chapel at Cheriton Fitzpaine where for so many years he had preached the Gospel. A very large number of people and sympathetic friends gathered from the countryside for the service.

A graphic account of the funeral is provided by a local newspaper cutting. "Six local preachers of the circuit acted as bearers, and in the presence of a large number of relations the mournful cortege left "Forde" where the deceased had resided for nearly forty years and where he had graciously played the part of host to a long line of ministers, missionaries and evangelists. Rev. T. L. Rogers officiated, the lessons were read by Revs. J.F. Luke (Crewkerne) and W.H. Arundell (rector). Rev. W. Bennett, in his address, stated that he had known the deceased for more than forty years, and like many others, he had learned to love and admire him. He was always kind, thoughtful and sympathetic; he was in the finest sense a minister's friend....... His Christian life was a daily walk with God; he practised the Divine presence, religion with him was a joyous reality and he was a man of unfailing courtesy".

His widow, Eliza Jane, died on the 10th December 1929 at the home of her adopted daughter, Mrs. A.J.D. Budge in Crediton. "Held in high

---

[110] His headstone records he died on the 20th December 1926

esteem by reason of her noble character and amiable disposition she was a loyal supporter and active worker, especially in the missionary cause at the United Methodist Church."[111] She lies with "Unkie" as she affectionately called T.G.L. in the little burial ground in the front of the Bible Christian Chapel (built 1887), Cheriton Fitzpaine. Their slate headstone, decorated with carved ivy leaves on the border, has a surrounding kerb of white and black grained granite enclosing a bed of loose granite chippings. The incised epitaph reads:-

In Loving memory
of
Thomas G. Luxton
Died Dec. 20th 1926
aged 75 years
also
Eliza Jane
wife of the above
Died Dec. 10th 1929
aged 73 years.

The couple had no children but adopted Eliza's niece, Henrietta, the two year old daughter of her brother, Thomas Mantle. Henrietta married Mr J.A.D. Budge. They too are now dead and lie buried with the Luxtons at Cheriton Fitzpaine. Their son, Mr Ralph Budge, gave me T.G. Luxton's family Bible and much other valuable information. His elder brother, Mr T.J. Budge, kindly provided me with a valuable collection of family photographs. In a most evocative letter, dated the 2nd March 1976, he recalled T.G.L. and life at Forde Farm. I will close this account of the "Preacher's" life by quoting Mr Budge's eloquent and poignant letter on life at Forde in the years just after the Great War:-

Thomas Greenslade Luxton was in his 60s when I was born and I cannot remember him until he was in his 70s. Stature-wise my recollection of him is that he was of medium height of about 5ft.8 or 9 inches (not more) and of slim build. His full beard had by then been clipped to about 1 inch long. He was a little deaf at his death. I can also recollect that he wore a "boater" in the summer months

---

[111] Western Times, Friday 20th December 1929.

174

and a bowler in the winter, and when he died his hair and beard were not white or particularly grey but had maintained colour very well. His death came rather suddenly – he had a carbuncle on his temple and retired to bed and was found unconscious and died within a day if not immediately. I was in my very early teens and death at that age is rather incomprehensible and remote and I do not remember the details, though I can remember running about 2 miles on a dark winter's night

to summon the Doctor (no telephone then) and it could well be that he was pronounced dead later that night. I can however remember most vividly his wife coming down from their bedroom into the sitting room where we were at the time and saying, "Well my dears I am a widow".

His funeral was perhaps the largest in the little Bible Christian Chapel at Cheriton Fitzpaine. The little chapel was packed to overflowing and sympathisers sat in the adjoining Sunday school. The service seemed interminable as his virtues were eulogised at great length. A particularly noteworthy thing about the service was the large pulpit was occupied not only by two Methodist Ministers but also by the local C. of E. Rector. It was the first time the Rector had ever darkened the doors of the Chapel and his presence and participation in the funeral service was a nine – day wonder. This may lead you to wonder why T.G.L. was given such a farewell.

He was extremely well-known for many miles around. He was (a) one of the village school managers (b) a member of the Board of Guardians (c) for a great many years a rural district councillor and always his loyalty was to his Chapel. Remember that in those days (and largely still is) Methodism was very strong in the S.W. (d) he was a local preacher for 50 years and (e) Circuit Steward.

The Methodist Circuit to which the little chapel at Cheriton Fitzpaine belonged was very large, with Cheriton at one extreme and Petton at the other – some 20 miles apart. He would leave at a very early hour on Sunday mornings in his pony and trap and drive off to preach and return late on Sunday night. The burning religious enthusiasm of the day made light of winter's cold and summer heat. West Forde was at all times an open house for all Methodist Ministers – their pony provided with a stable and fodder, the Minister with food, bed and religious discussion. My impression as I look back over 50 years to those days is one of narrow minded bigotry – where everything connected with the world was evil. The narrow mindedness of some of T.G.L.'s contemporaries amazes me now; it was an age of "do nots". My mother in those days had her hair bobbed and I am sure that it was with apprehension and some trepidation she viewed what the local chapel people would think or say. Nevertheless, perhaps it is wrong for me to be too critical – who am I to judge – these old people lived their lives as they thought they should be lived – perhaps with not much imagination, except the reality of hell fire. They possessed a fervour for their religion equalled only today by certain soccer fans for their teams. The difference being that when the Last Trumpet sounds they will not be found wanting: if they were there would be no justice in this world or the next.

T.G.L. however was a slightly different mould – on the farm he made cider and every day his home–made cider was brought to the dinner table for him. I remember the jug – of the type you can buy at Widecombe in the Moor with a verse in Devonshire dialect (what the verse or phrase was I have entirely forgotten). When not at table the jug stood on a bagatelle board covered with a piece of paper or material. Certainly it was this jug that first introduced my young brothers and myself to Devonshire Cider – T.G.L. never seemed to realise that any had disappeared – this lack of observation I feel saved us from a hiding or two. The taste for Devonshire Cider has long since left me!

He also liked a tot of whisky, and also liked to listen to the wireless though he had some difficulty because of his deafness. In winter, I think it was on Boxing Day, friends and neighbours arrived at the farm for a "rabbiting party" and after the shoot the long, long dining table resounded to excuses as to why someone had missed shooting a rabbit or alternatively how another had shot one with an excellent shot. Thus you will see he was somewhat enlightened for the age and environment in which he lived. My mother, dear soul as she is, has never lost this atmosphere in which she was reared. My father, however, "mellowed" in his later years very considerably. My brother (one brother died $2^{1/}_2$ years ago), my sister and myself do not belong to the Methodist connection but are members of the C. of E.

Had T.G.L. lived today he would have been very amenity conscious. He loved trees and would not cut down the trees in the farm hedges. The lane to West Forde, some 150 yards long, had roses planted along the top of its hedges. In fact the Copper Beech tree my father planted in the 20s still grows in his memory, though it has been sadly mutilated by the P.O. whose wires its branches impeded. With the exception of the beech, the trees, the roses, the flowering May tree etc., have all disappeared in the wake of progress.

West Forde farm house was quite a superior style of Devonshire farmhouse – T.G.L. tended the ornamental box hedges with great care; we played croquet on the lawn and had tea parties on the lawn under the many tall trees. In July and August and at Christmas the farmhouse always seemed full of relations and visitors. Peaches, pears and plums grew on the wall of the garden; a huge asparagus bed thrived nearby as did a huge bed of lilies of the valley, a little stream flowed lazily at the bottom of the lawn beyond the pampas grass; and the blackbirds always seemed to get into the fruit cage after the strawberries, raspberries, gooseberries and currants. The "War to end Wars" was over, the motor car had barely arrived; my brothers and myself were sent off to the local Grammar School some miles away; we helped with the harvest in the long summer holidays, "Darling" and "Prince" plus another the name now forgotten, were the Shires that pulled the plough and wagons, Jack was the horseman and Will and Reg (Jack's son) were the general farm workers. Then came the depression in the agricultural industry, the farm barely paid. My brother and myself decided farming with no profits was not for us (my young brother was too young to have any views), so West Forde was sold and we moved to Crediton[112] where Eliza Jane Luxton, after having had one operation, died of cancer.

---

[112] The family set up a Dairy &shop at 36 Mill Street.

Both T.G.L. and his wife were kindly, gentle folk, but I doubt if he was much of a business man. Certainly over the many years he farmed he made no money, a fact his will showed. He owned West Forde but when he died he had not paid off the mortgage he had on it. I have never been able to establish any clues as to his finances. I was too young to consider these things at the time and now I no longer care and doubt I could do anything if I did. To be fair the Christianity he preached he also practised. Just one example – the daughter of a farm worker of E.J.L.'s father entered the domestic service of Mrs E.J.L.'s father as a young girl. She never married but T.G.L. gave a home to this servant and so did my father when we moved to Crediton where she died at the age of 80. It was either that or the workhouse, but a real example of the Good Samaritan.

His wife called T.G.L. by the name of "Unkie" I think, though it has not been confirmed, that this may have perhaps originated as baby talk when my Mother was a child, for Mother always referred to them as Uncle and Auntie. As far as Eliza Jane was concerned this name persisted until her death. I know too a very few friends referred to him by this name behind his back. But to my Father, Mother, my brothers, my sister and myself he was Uncle – only to Eliza Jane was he "Unkie".

As you realise, I have no Luxton blood and am able to give you this information simply because they "adopted" my Mother who was T.G.L.'s niece, being the daughter of E.J.L.'s brother, Thomas Mantle.

The marriage certificate I am sending you shows T.G.L. to have been a builder when he married. This is interesting and something I did not know – as far as I can recollect he did no building repairs at West Forde but a local jobbing carpenter was always employed for necessary small building jobs and for any repairs to buildings and farm gates. I wonder why T.G.L. never turned his hand back to his original occupation when necessary.

So T.G.L. and E.J.L. rest closely by their old cronies and E.J.L.'s parents at Cheriton Fitzpaine. My Father's ashes are in the same grave and there one day my Mother's will join them.

I have written too much – if some does not interest you then forget it. I hope though that some of my meanderings into my childhood will be helpful to your project for my early days were very much bound up with T.G.L. and E.J.L.

T. G. L. is wearing a bowler hat in this photograph at West Forde. His wife Eliza is standing next to her seated mother, Martha, and the girl is Hettie Mantle.

18

JOHN LUXTON (1854 – 1932) TAILOR OF WELLINGTON SOMERSET AND HIS FAMILY

See tree 5

John, the second son of John Luxton (1827-1906), and his wife Eleanor Greenslade of Hutchings Farm, was born at Petton on the 31st August 1854 and was baptised at St. Petrock's Church on the 24th September that year. At the age of 16 in 1871, John was the youngest of four tailors, working at Lower Croft, Skilgate, the home of William Melhuish, a 38 year old tailor[113]. In 1881 his parents were farming the sixty two acres at Parsonage Farm, Raddington, while John, aged 26, was a tailor and grocer, living at the family home Hutchings, Frogpit Moor, Petton, where he was assisted by his sister Ellen, aged 16, who was his housekeeper.

John was a tailor in Tiverton when he married Eliza, the daughter of James Bradford, Dairyman, at St. Peter's Church, Tiverton on the 3rd October 1884. In 1891 John, 36, tailor, and his wife Eliza, 26, lived at Venn, Chipstable with their three children Ellen 4, Victor John one and Alice aged six months. He was a tailor in the Market Place, Wiveliscombe, in 1892 but he also dabbled in the butter trade and by November that year he had lost the considerable sum of £200 in that business. His debt resulted in an appearance before Judge Paterson at the Tiverton County Court who ordered an administration of John's estate and he was ordered to pay 6s..8d in the £1 of his debt by instalments of 10s. a month. By February 1893 John had paid nothing to settle his debt and in a second appearance before Judge Paterson, under Order 15, Rule 1, of the Small Bankruptcies Act the Judge set aside the order, leaving the creditor's free to act as they chose[114].

---

[113] The Melhuish and Luxton families were related by the marriage of James Luxton (1813-1861) mason of Kymmen Moor, Skilgate to Molly Melhuish, the daughter of John Melhuish, butcher, at St. John the Baptist Church Skilgate on 8th November 1844.
[114] Western Times, Saturday 25 November 1892 and 14th February 1893.

He then went to work for Eggerton Burnett's, a tailoring establishment in Wellington Somerset[115]. The family had grown by 1901 and was settled in Springfield, Wellington where John, 46, tailor was head of household with his wife Eliza, 34 and six children-Thomas13, Victor11, Alice10, William8, Ernest6, and Olive who was just two months old. By 1911 the family, living at 25 Hollyoak Street, Wellington were John 55, tailor, Eliza, his wife, 45, Thomas James 23, textile pattern maker to a woollen manufacturer, Alice Maud 20, tailoress in a serge warehouse, William Henry, 18, assistant ironmonger, Ernest Edgar, 15, assistant baker, and Olive May 10.

The first four of the couple's seven children died tragically young. Their eldest child, Eva Ellen "Nellie", was born on the 24th May 1886 and baptised at Petton on the 20th June 1886. "Nellie" adopted by her aunt Bessie Chibbett in Williton, Somerset was fourteen when she died of meningitis on the 21st July 1900 and lies buried with her uncle and aunt Jim and Bessie Chibbett at St. Decuman's, Watchet, Somerset. Her sister Alice Maud, the fourth child of John and Eliza Luxton, was born on the 30th October 1890 and was baptised at Ashbrittle, Somerset. Alice, a tailoress at Eggerton Burnett's, Wellington, who suffered with kidney disease and acute bronchitis died aged 24, on the 16th October 1915. She is buried with her parents at Rockwell Green near Wellington. The death of the two girls did not mark the end of tragedy for the two oldest sons, Tom and Vic, died in the Great War.

Thomas James Luxton, born on the 15th January 1888, was baptised at Petton on the 4th March 1888, and his brother, Victor John Luxton, was born in Ashbrittle, Somerset on the 6th August 1889. Prior to the Great War, Tom served three years and Victor two and a half years, in the Somerset Light Infantry, before emigrating to Winnipeg, Manitoba. Tom, aged 24, labourer, lists Winnipeg in Manitoba, as his destination when he sailed from Bristol to Nova Scotia, arriving in Canada on the 10th April 1912.The passenger list does not name Victor, who must have sailed to Canada in another ship[116].Victor was not at home in the 1911 census so may have already emigrated.

---

[115] See letters of 3rd March & 26th May 1976 from Willie H. Luxton of Wellington. Somerset who gave me valuable help in compiling this chapter.

[116] Library and archives Canada. Passenger lists, 1865-1935, Ottawa, Ontario, Canada RollT-4743.

I have a postcard photograph of Tom, (on left) and Vic, (on right) with a friend which they sent to their uncle Thomas G. Luxton and his wife Eliza Jane at Forde Farm, Cheriton Fitzpaine. Tom the eldest brother wrote the card sent for Christmas c.1914.

777 Mc Dermott
Winnipeg
Manitoba
Canada

Dear Aunt & Uncle
    Just a card to let you know we are both quite well, we would like to hear of you at times, has (sic) we have a little spare time between the love letters to answer, it his (sic) now winter, today we had it very cold it where (sic) 27% Below Zero & have two to Three foot of snow on the ground, we may be able to send you a winter view soon, we have an Album of ones we have taken, so do not forget us with a photo,

Yours Ever Nephew Tom

P.S. May you have every Prosperity & Happiness in the Coming year

The brothers were employed as 'railroaders' when on the 8th April 1916, they enlisted for the duration of the war in the 144th Battalion of the Winnipeg Rifles, which formed part of the Canadian Over-Seas Expeditionary Force. On the day of their enlistment, Tom, (Regimental Number 829003) was aged 26 years 3 months[117]. He was 5 ft 9 inches tall with a ruddy complexion, blue eyes and brown hair and weighed 130 lbs with a chest measurement when fully expanded of 34 inches. Victor (Regimental Number 829002) was aged 24 years 7 months, 6 foot tall and weighing 150 lbs with a maximum chest measurement of 36 inches[118]. He too had a ruddy complexion, blue eyes and brown hair. Their religious denomination was Baptist.

The brothers embarked for Europe on the four funnel luxury liner the S.S. Olympic, a sister ship to the ill-fated Titanic, which sailed from

---

[117] Thomas Luxton-Regimental No829003, File5802-36 National Archives of Canada.
[118] Victor John Luxton-Regimental NO.829002, File5802-38 National Archives of Canada.

Halifax in Nova Scotia on the 18th September 1916, and disembarked at Liverpool on the 25th September 1916[119].

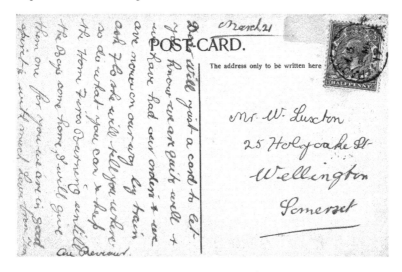

The brothers in their wills, made on the 5th January 1917, left their property to each other but in the event of both their deaths their possessions were to go to their mother Eliza Luxton, of 25 Holyoake Street, Wellington in Somerset. Seven days later on the 12th January 1917, they were transferred to the 18th reserve Battalion at Seaford. They arrived in Dibyate, France, on the 21st March and were taken on the strength of the 44th Battalion Canadian Infantry (New Brunswick Regiment). That day, the eve of their first day in action, Tom sent a coloured postcard view of the Marine Walk Folkestone, to his younger brother, Will, at 25 Holyoake Road, Wellington. The poignant message informing Will that the brothers were heading for the Western Front, reads:-

21st March 1917

Dear Will just a card to let you know we are quite well & we have had our orders & we are now on our way by train ask Flo[120] she will tell you

---

[119] I have a photograph of the S.S. Olympic, taken in March 1917, when she was crossing the Atlantic in full steam. It was taken by my maternal grandfather J.R.Campbell, a Lieutenant Engineer on H.M.Y.Beryl during the Great War.

[120] Flo may have been Tom's girl friend. I possess a card she wrote to him in 1911.

where so do what you can & keep the Home Fires Burning untill the Boys come home[121], I will give them one for you we are in good spirits with much Love from Tom

Au Reviour

'The average life expectancy for a soldier on the Western Front was three months and within three months both Tom and Vic were dead.

The 22nd March 1917 the day after Tom wrote his postcard to Will, the brothers went into action with the 44th Canadian Division. It was involved in the "flanking operation towards Lens" including the "affairs south of the Souchez River" from the 3rd to the 25th June 1917.This was a part of the battle for Vimy Ridge. On the 7th May Victor was concussed and received a slight wound on his right hand. He had shell shock and was evacuated from the front line. Four days later on the 11th May he rejoined his unit. Then on Sunday 3rd June 1917, he was fighting in trenches north east of Givenchy-en-Gohelle when he was reported missing after action and was struck off the strength of the regiment. This was later confirmed as killed in action. Victor (above in Folkstone) was temporarily buried at Avion Cemetery (or The Sandpits), in the woods west of Avion near Lens, but by April 1920 he was re-interred at La Chaudiere Military Cemetery which is at the foot of Vimy Ridge, Pas de Calais, France. Pte. V. J. Luxton, Grave Reference Plot V. Row C. Grave 8.

Three days later on Wednesday 6th June 1917, Tom (on next page, in Folkestone) died "of wounds received in action in the Field" at no. 13 Canadian Field Ambulance. He was buried the same day at Villers Station Cemetery, Villers – Au – Bois, France, a village in the Pas-de-Calais, seven miles north west of Arras. The Canadian Corps headquarter were sometime near the cemetery and many of the graves in Plots V to X are associated with the Battle of Vimy Ridge. Pte. T.

---

[121] Keep the home fires burning is the first line of a popular 1914 song, ending "till the boys come home" words by Lena Guilbert Ford, music by Ivor Novello(1898-1951)

Luxton, Grave Reference Plot IX Row C Grave 12.[122] The parents never recovered from these tragic events especially the loss of their sons Thomas and Victor at Vimy Ridge.

William Henry Luxton (1893-1986), their fifth child, born in Wiveliscombe on the 1st April 1893, was a 24 year old ironmonger's assistant in January 1918 when an Urban Tribunal granted him three months exemption from service.[123]He married Phyllis Annie Ashton Richards, an office clerk, at Wellington, Somerset on the 27th June 1927. When I met Willie and Phyllis in 1976, he was a retired ironmonger living at No 2 Victoria Street, Wellington. The couple introduced me to their son Beverley Thomas Luxton who was born on the 2nd May 1931. His father's ironmongery was located at 24 High Street and in March 1949 in order that he might assist his father in the business Beverley made a successful application at Wellington Magistrates Court for the removal of a two year driving ban imposed on him in February 1948 when he was 16 for riding an unlicensed motor-cycle.[124] In June 1937 an unemployed clerk was sentenced to a month's imprisonment with hard labour for stealing 12 door knockers worth 18 shillings from the premises[125].

Beverley, who was a car sales manager when we met, resided in Wellington where he married Patricia Rose Betty Phillips, on the 26th December 1953. He died on 7th November 2017 following a massive stroke.

They had two children, Deborah Jane Luxton, born on the 27th April 1955, who was a student nurse at Musgrave Hospital, Taunton and David John Luxton, born on the 2nd January 1964. Deborah married William John

---

[122] Tom's date of death was the 6th June 1917. This is the date on his death certificate issued by the Canadian Expeditionary Force Militia Headquarters Ottawa on the 20th June 1919. The Imperial War Graves Commission erroneously copied the date as the 4th June 1917 and this error was on his temporary wooden cross and was the date his parent's put on their memorial at Rockwell Green.
[123] Taunton Courier, Wednesday 30th January 1918.
[124] Taunton Courier, Saturday 12th March 1949.
[125] Taunton Courier, Saturday, 12th June 1937.

White at All Saints, the parish church of Wellington, Somerset 30th July 1983 and they have two daughters, Charlotte and Catherine. Her brother David, married Angela Mary French at Paralimni, Cyprus on the 18th September 2002. They live in Taunton and have two offspring by Angela's previous marriage.

Willie and family are in photo taken in front of 2 Victoria Street when I visited them in 1976. Beverley Thomas, on left, is next to his son David. Willie stands by his wife Phyllis.

John and Eliza had two more children. Ernest Edgar Luxton (1894-1968), born on the 14th October 1894, baker and confectioner, was 5ft 6 inches with fair hair, blue eyes and a fresh complexion when he enlisted in the Royal Navy on the 30th September 1916. He served as a cook's mate on H.M.S. Vivid 1 which was the name of the naval barracks at Plymouth and then the battle cruiser HMS Tiger, on patrol in the North Sea. Ernest was paid a war gratuity when he was demobbed on 15th July 1919. He married in 1924 to Olive Victoria Churchill (1904-1974) who was a tailoress at Fox Brothers in Wellington[126]. There were no children.

---

[126] The Fox Brothers were enlightened employers. See The early years of Fox Brothers & Co. Ltd Woollen Manufacturers, pages100-101, The Greenwood Tree in The Somerset and Dorset Family History Society Journal November 2011, vol.36, no.4.

A baker of 12 Rookery Terrace, Wellington, Somerset, Ernest died on the 15th December 1968. Probate was issued in London when his personal estate was valued at £2385. Olive May Luxton, their last and seventh child, was born on the 6th January 1901. Olive, an office clerk, married Alan William George Adams (1889-1973), a tailor from Uffculme in Devon, in the Baptist Chapel South Street, Uffculme, on the 22nd August 1921. A widow of 17 Bulford, Wellington she died at Tidcombe Hall, Tiverton on 15th July 1939.

John and Eliza Luxton lived at 25 Holyoak Street, Wellington where Eliza died aged 61 on the 10th October 1927. Her will, made on the 24th September 1927, was proved in London on the 8th November by her son William Henry Luxton, ironmonger of 2 Victoria Street, Wellington, the sole executrix. Eliza's personal estate was valued at £1034 ..16 ..3. She left her house at 25 Holyoak Street to William and gave £300 each to her son Ernest Edgar Luxton and daughter Olive May Adams. Olive was also to have "my piano, tea set and feather bed". The remaining furniture and any surplus money were to be divided among her three children.

John Luxton died aged 77, on the 15th January 1932 and is buried with his wife Eliza at Rockwell Green, Wellington. The grave is marked by three white carrara marble steps surmounted by a marble cross. The epitaph in lead lettering reads:-

In Loving
Memory of
Eliza wife of
John Luxton
Who entered into rest
Oct. 10th 1927 aged 61
Also the above
John Luxton,
Who passed away Jany 15th 1932

Aged 77
Also of
her sons

Thomas James
Died of wounds in
France June 4[127] 1917,
Aged 29
and Victor John
killed in France
June 3rd 1917
aged 28
Also of
her daughter
Alice Maud
Who died Oct 16th 1915
Aged 25
To live in the hearts of those we leave
Behind is not to die.

---

[127] Tom died on the 6th June 1917.

19

ISAAC LUXTON (1789-1838), MASON OF KYMMEN MOOR, SKILGATE, SOMERSET AND HIS FAMILY

See tree 7

Isaac Luxton (1751-1834) yeoman farmer at Hutchings, Petton, Bampton and his wife Mary North of Morebath, Devon had three sons who married and reared their own families. The eldest, Thomas (1783-1840), yeoman and mason, succeeded his father at Hutchings. The second, Isaac (1789-1838), the subject of this chapter, was a mason residing at Kymmen Moor Skilgate, and the youngest, Jacob (1800-1868), was a mason who lived at Paradise in Chipstable.

We have only the bare details of Isaac's life. There survives no physical description or interesting biographical minutiae, although tucked away in County or National Archives there may be riveting facts awaiting discovery. He was baptised Isaac Luxon at Petton on the 1st February 1789, the year of the French Revolution, but was to live his life quietly and peacefully in his native parish and the adjoining parish of Skilgate, across the border in Somerset. It was at St. John the Baptist, the parish church, Skilgate, that Isaac married Judith Skinner on the 10th June 1812. Isaac, who was twenty three, was to reside the rest of his life in Skilgate. Judith, his bride and nearly six years his senior, baptised at Skilgate on the 15th June 1783, spent her whole life in the parish. Her parents, James and Phillis Skinner, came from the neighbouring parish of Upton in Somerset.

Isaac and Judith had eight children baptised at St. John's Skilgate. One son, William, died in 1825, aged 2 and two more sons died comparatively young. John (1817-1845), aged 28, died on the 11th March 1845 from "Phthisis Pulmonalis" which is more commonly called consumption. John was probably a victim of silicosis caused by the stone dust in his work as a mason. His younger brother, Thomas Luxton (1825-1849) who died aged 24 at Skilgate on the 17th November 1849, was also likely a victim of the dust related work. His death certificate describes him as a baker, but the Skilgate burial register

states he was a mason. The cause of death is given as "contraction of the trachea 18 months& bronchitis 13 weeks". Isaac and Judith had two other sons, James (1813-1861), the eldest was a mason and Isaac (1815-1876), named after his father and grandfather, was a shoemaker. Both married and raised families.

There were three daughters. Phillis (1818-1869), the eldest daughter, married in 1843 in Westminster, London to Charles Ash, bricklayer. The couple with their young children lived in 1851 and 1861 in Bridgewater, Somerset. Phillis died on the 3rd December 1869. Her sisters, Sarah Skinner (1820-1878), and Mary Anna (1821-1891), never married and spent their lives in domestic service. In 1851 Sarah was the domestic servant to her older sister Phillis Ash and her young family in Bridgwater, Somerset. By 1861 she was a servant to the Revd. Joseph Stephenson in Lympsham, Somerset.

Meanwhile in 1851 Mary Anna, was a servant to Eliza Murray, widow, an annuitant of Bulick Colony, Jamaica, at Kensington Villa, Torquay. 1861 finds her a house maid to Vice Admiral Fanshaw and family in Stone Hall, East Stonehouse. She was the 49 year old house keeper in 1871 to a 53 year old widower, John Gamble, woodman, and his eight year old son at Holt Cottages in Adel Cum Eccup, near Cookridge in Yorkshire. Her sister Sarah, 57, formerly a servant, was boarding with her. In 1881 Mary Anna, herself now a retired servant, aged 59 was living at Kymmen Moor with her widowed 62 year old sister in law, Florence Luxton. By 1891, aged 69, on a pension, she lived alone at No 2 Royal Oak Cottages, Skilgate. When she died at Petton her cousin, Thomas Greenslade Luxton of Forde Farm, Cheriton Fitzpaine, was in attendance. Like her elder sister Sarah she was buried at Skilgate.

Isaac Luxton (1789-1838), mason, and his family lived at Kymmen Moor, Skilgate, and in Somerset Record Office, Taunton are preserved various deeds relating to this property[128]. From other sources the name is variously spelt Kymmen, Kymen, Kimins, Kimmis, Chippen Moor, Keeping Moor etc but throughout this collection of deeds it is uniformly spelt as Kymmen Moor.

The deeds shed intriguing light on Isaac's business ventures. In the earliest, dated 14th November 1810, Elizabeth Blake widow of Honiton, Devon, only child and heiress of William Smith late of Honiton, labourer, deceased, sold the ruinous property for £10 to James Welsh, gentleman of Skilgate. This was for a term of 1000 years and the payment every Michaelmas of 1 penny "if the same shall be lawfully demanded". Welsh profited when he sold Kymmen Moor to Isaac Luxton mason, for £14 on the 30th April 1817. It was agreed that Isaac could immediately enter "peacefully and quietly" into the premises during the residue of the term of 1000 years. The property was described as "All that toft or plot of ground whereon lately stood a Cottage or Dwelling house now fallen into ruins. And also all that garden ....adjoining and belonging situate....in a certain common within.... Skilgate commonly called or known by the name Kymmen Moor which said Cottage or Dwelling house and garden were formerly in the possession of William Baldrop late of Skilgate, yeoman deceased, since of the said Elizabeth Blake but now of the said James Welsh....".

During the next ten years Isaac built a new cottage, with workshop and other buildings on the Kymmen site. The work was completed by the 16th August 1826 when he took out an insurance policy No 47819 with the West of England Insurance Company insuring the premises at

---

[128] There are five documents in the bundle, reference DD/BR/dhb 21 which refer to the property at Kymmen Moor Skilgate. These are dated1810 (2)1817, 1826 and 1833.

Kymmen Moor from loss or damage by fire in the sum of £100. Within a fortnight, Isaac sold the property on the 29th August 1826 for £100 to Mary North, spinster of Wiveliscombe. I believe she was the daughter of Mary North, aged 72, of independent means, who in 1841lived at Golden Hill, Wiveliscombe. Mary was perhaps a kinswoman, possibly a first cousin to Isaac, whose mother Mary North of Morebath, Devon, married Isaac Luxton senior in 1780. By this 1826 indenture, Mary bought "All that new built cottage or Dwelling house, workshop and other buildings thereto belonging, lately erected by the said Isaac Luxton on All that Toft or Plot of Ground whereon stood a cottage or Dwelling house which had fallen into ruins".

Isaac, it seems, planned to buy back the property, for an "express condition" was agreed that if he paid Mary North the full sum of £100 with lawful interest by the 29th February 1827 the sale would be "utterly void and of none effect". It was agreed too that if Isaac failed to pay the money due by the deadline date Mary would be entitled to "sell and absolutely dispose of the property… and every part thereof either by public auction or private contract…".

Isaac failed to repay by the agreed deadline and Kymmen Moor was sold by public auction on the 5th February 1833. Conceivably the most fascinating of the seventeen conditions of sale was the final one. "That there are about eighty young apple Trees and Gribbles standing on the said premises which were planted in the Spring of 1832 which are not to be sold therewith and the same shall be allowed to remain thereon until the month of December next and the vendor is to be at liberty to enter on the premises at any time before the month of December next and remove the same…". The purchaser was given the option to buy the trees for £2 – 10 shillings.

Gribbles were young apple trees raised from seed or the young stock of a tree on which a graft was to be inserted. A duty of ten shillings a barrel imposed on the making of cider was repealed in 1830 and it was probably the repeal of this duty which accounts for Isaac planting his apple trees at Kymmen Moor in the spring of 1832. His father, Isaac Luxton, yeoman at Hutchings Farm, Petton, Bampton just across the border in Devon also took the opportunity offered by the repeal of the duty on cider to plant an apple orchard. In his will made on the 2nd July

1831 he left his youngest son Jacob, "all my nursery of young apple trees for his own use".

The reverend Richard Bere of Morebath was the highest bidder for Kymmen Moor at the public auction conducted by William Collard, auctioneer, in Wiveliscombe on the 5th February 1833.Through his representative, Henry Dawbrey Harvey of Wiveliscombe, gent, the Revd. Bere paid a deposit of £14 – 16 shillings into the hand of Mr Benjamin Boucher, solicitor, Wiveliscombe, the agent of the vendor, Isaac Luxton. The remaining money due was to be paid at the office of Mr Boucher in Wiveliscombe on the 25th March 1833 "by eleven o'clock in the forenoon".

This is the date of the final deed in the collection at Taunton Record Office. On the day appointed the Revd. Bere settled his outstanding debt. He paid £112 – 16 shillings to Mary North who was the new wife of James Govier of Ilminster, waiter. It was her due on the principal money and interest on the mortgaged premises.[129] The Revd. Bere also paid Isaac Luxton a further sum of £20 – 17 – 6d which was the residue of the purchase money of £148. Isaac and his family now became tenants to the Revd. Bere and they continued to dwell at Kymmen Moor.

The marriage certificate of Phillis, his daughter, states that Isaac made his living as a plasterer. He died aged 49, on the 2nd February 1838, from what his death certificate describes as "Inflammatory fever" and was buried at Skilgate on the 9th February 1838. Judith, his widow, died aged 67 from consumption and dropsy on the 23rd of May and was buried at Skilgate on the 1st June 1850. The couple's two married sons, James and Isaac, continued to live at Kymmen Moor with their families until Isaac's widow Florence died in 1893. Today Kymmen Moor, in photograph below, has a tin roof. It must have had a thatch when the Luxtons lived there. The orchards have all gone and the place is owned by someone involved in agricultural transport.

---

[129] In 1851 Mary aged 56 and her husband James Govier 58 Fund Holder lived at Golden Hill, Wiveliscombe. I believe her mother was the Mary aged 72 who lived at Golden Hill in 1841.

20

JAMES LUXTON (1813-1861), MASON OF KYMMEN MOOR, SKILGATE SOMERSET AND HIS FAMILY

See tree 8

James Luxton (1813-1861), the eldest of eight children born to Isaac Luxton (1789-1838) mason of Kymmen Moor, Skilgate, and his wife Judith Skinner, was baptised James Luxon at Skilgate on the 29th December 1813. He was qualified as a mason by the time he married Mary (known as Molly) the daughter of John Melhuish, butcher, at St. John the Baptist, Skilgate on the 8th November 1844. The couple settled at Kymmen Moor in a cottage which had been rebuilt from a ruin by his father Isaac.

In 1851 James, 37 mason, Molly 35, and two infant sons lived at what the census called Higher Chippenmoor. There they had five children, two boys and three girls. James, their eldest son, born on the 23rd October 1846 was baptised at Skilgate on the 24th January 1847. He was followed by the baptisms of William (1849-1918) on the 19th April 1849, Sarah Skinner on the 12th September 1852, Phillis on the 29th July 1855 and Mary Ann on the 22nd August 1858. In 1851 the population of Skilgate was 266 and there was a small day school for boys and girls.

The family at Keeping Moor in 1861 were James 47, Mary 45, and their children James 14, Sarah 8, and Phillis 6. James Luxton, mason, was to suffer for two years with phthisis, more commonly called consumption, before his death at Skilgate on the 2nd December 1861. He was aged 48 and his younger brother Isaac who lived in an adjoining cottage was present when he died. His widow Molly moved to nearby

Bowtown House, Skilgate where in 1871 census aged 55 she lived with sons James 24 William 22, daughter Sarah 18 and Mary Hill 68, boarder. Molly Luxton died at the age of 57 and was buried at Skilgate on the 20th April 1873.

James Luxton (1813-1861) and his wife Molly Melhuish had three daughters. Mary Ann, the youngest, born in 1858, died aged nine months from asthenia (i.e. loss of strength debility) on the 12th April 1859 and was buried at Skilgate on the 17th April. Sarah Skinner, the eldest, born in 1852, married William Blew, a farm labourer in St. Gabriel's Church, parish of St. Philip & Jacob without, Bristol, on the 16th August 1881. Ten years later the couple were living in Penfield Street, Bristol where William was a mason's labourer. The year 1901 finds Sarah a widow living at 40 Claremont Street. Sarah who had no children, lived most of her later life in 15 Armoury Square, (no thoroughfare) off Stapleton Road, Bristol where she died aged 83 on the 16th January 1936. Her sister, Phillis, born in 1855, went to live with Sarah in Bristol where she worked as a housekeeper for a man whose wife was in an asylum. Her employer gave her a son out of wedlock, Francis William Luxton (1884-1948) who was brought up by his aunt Sarah Blew. She was present at his birth in New Town Llantarnam, Monmouthshire on the 21st February 1884. Phillis later married Richard Johnson, a divorced farmer, at St. Gabriel's Bristol on the 4th October 1897. In 1901 they lived in Gloucester Road, Malmesbury, where Richard was a potato merchant. Phillis, widow of Richard Johnson, market gardener, died aged 65 at 15 Armoury Square, Bristol on the 10th August 1920.

Francis William Luxton was a 19 year old general labourer, when he enlisted in the 4th battalion of the Somerset Light Infantry on the 27th February 1903. He gave his place of birth as Bedminster, Bristol where he resided at 2 Boot Lane and was a member of the Church of England. There was a tattoo anchor on his left forearm and he was just over five foot six inches tall with grey eyes and brown hair. Phillis Johnson, his mother of Gloucester Road, Malmesbury, Wilts was his next of kin. He purchased himself out of the army at Taunton on the 16th April 1904 and worked in the building trade. In 1911 he was living at 15 Armoury Square with Aunt Sarah Blew who raised him. He married Beatrice Ethel Major, a 33 year old spinster and show card finisher, at Holy Trinity, Bristol on the 31st May 1914. The couple were unable to have children so adopted a daughter. In the First World War he was in the Royal Army Service Corps and was awarded the British War Medal and the Victory Medal. Francis of 151 Mina Road, St. Werburgh's Bristol died aged 64 on the 12th December 1948 and the administration of his personal estate valued at £798..10shillings was granted to Doris Ethel Stone (wife of John Stone) in Bristol on the 16th February 1949.

James Luxton (1846-1912), the eldest son of James Luxton (1813-1861) and Molly Melhuish, trained as a mason and was aged 14 in 1861 when he was living with his parents at Kymmen Moor. He was aged 27 when he married Alice Pugsley, 22 of Kenilworth Terrace, Newtown, daughter of James Pugsley, cooper, at the Register Office, Clifton, Gloucestershire on the 27th September 1874. The newly weds signed the register with their names. He worked for Poultenay Potteries, Fishponds, Clifton. The pair settled in Bristol where in the 1881 census James 34 mason and his 29 year old wife Alice and five children lived at 4 Albany Crescent. Ten years later James and Alice with five of their children were living at 56 Regent Street in the city. In the 1901 census, James a 54 year old mason lived at 18 Plummer Street, St Gabriell, Bristol with his wife Alice 49, born in Cutcombe, Somerset and their children Lucy Maud 24 dressmaker, Alice Louise 23 dressmaker, Walter 20 a cigar box maker, Charles Leonard 18 a woodcarver, and Daisy 16 an assistant in a draper's shop. James a journeyman mason, died aged 65 from stomach cancer at his home Beech House, Conham Hill, Hanham Kingswood in Keynsham, Bristol on the 23rd January 1912. Alice, his widow, died aged 89 at 4 St Lukes Street, Barton Hill, Bristol on the 26th August 1941.

They had seven children, four boys and three girls. Lucy Maud (1876-1954) baptised 31stMay 1876 at Newtown United Methodist Church Bristol, and her sister Alice Louise (1877- 1955) were spinsters and dress makers who lived at 4 St Lukes Street Barton Hill, Bristol where they died in the 1950s. Their sister Daisy born in 1884, a drapery worker in St. Ebbes Street, Oxford in 1911, married Thomas Plumb in Pima, Arizona about 1912 and they settled in Los Angeles California where they had two sons and a daughter. The first two boys born to James and Molly Luxton died in infancy. Francis James, aged 5 years 3 months, died of rickets on 4th February 1884 and his brother Charles Leonard, aged 18 months, died of bronchitis on the 18th May 1881. The eldest surviving son, Walter (1881-1916), a Primitive Methodist

Minister[130] aged 30 and single, was a "Pastor Evangelist" at the Smitham Mission Hall in Coulsdon, Surrey in 1911 where he lodged with Albert Arnold and family at 40 Edward Road. He answered the call to become the minister at Goadhurst, Horsmonden and Marler in Essex in November 1913[131] but had moved to Brentwood by 1916. Walter aged 36 of Morescot Road, Brentwood, Essex, was found dead at the Primitive Methodist Chapel, Warley Road, Great Warley, Hornchurch, Essex on the 28th October 1916.

The coroner's inquest,[132] held on the 30th October, revealed that the dead pastor had gone to the church on Friday 27th to do repairs to a door. When he did not return home his wife sent her son to look for him but as the son found the church door locked it was assumed that the deceased had proceeded to Chelmsford to keep an appointment. He did not return home that night and when the doors of the church were opened the next morning his 13 year old son Frank Luxton[133] found the body of his father lying near a gas bracket in which he apparently had been fixing a screw. The body was lying with one arm around a portable boiler and his face near a gas ring, the tap of which was turned on full. He had a pair of pliers in one hand and with these the son turned off the gas. The jury decided that he was "found dead having first been overcome by faintness and subsequently dying from coma owing to his inhaling coal gas." The family think he committed suicide and the Rev. Luxton's strange death was widely reported in the Press. His funeral took place on Thursday 2nd November, the remains being laid to rest in Christchurch Cemetery, Warley. The mourners included his wife and son and Mr. H. Inchcomb of Croydon with whom Walter did missionary work for five years.

His brother Charles Leonard Luxton (1882-1935), married Florence Amesbury (1878-1965) at St. James Mary Oldfield Bristol on the

---

[130] The Primitive Methodists, vulgarly called "Ranters," were founded between 1808 and 1811 and were an offshoot from Wesleyan Methodism. In 1932 they joined with the Wesleyan Methodists and other Methodists to form the modern Methodist Church of Great Britain. Primitive Methodism was the plainest & most austere form of Methodism favoured by those towards lower end of the social scale.
[131] Kent & Sussex Courier, Friday 21st November 1913.
[132] Essex Newsman, 4th November 1916.
[133] Walter was single in 1911 census so Frank must have been a stepson.

11th March 1907. Deaf from birth, he trained as a cabinet maker, and was a wood carver and wooden box maker, lodging at 11 Princes Street St. Paul in 1911. The same census reveals his wife Florence 32, a tailor, with two infant children, Daisy Violet 3 and Mervyn 1 were living in three rooms at Windsor Place, Mangotsfield. He was an upholsterer when Fanny Lilian, the youngest was born in 1917. Both daughters married. Charles of 4 St. Lukes Street, Barton Hill, Bristol died aged 53 of T.B. on the 13th October 1935. His son Mervyn Luxton (1909-2002) of Blackhorse, Bristol, who served in the R.A.F. was an ambulance driver when he married Irene May Heames at the Register Office, Kingswood on the 16th November 1947. Mervyn of 34 Elm Tree Avenue, Mangotsfield, a retired maintenance operative and handyman, died 25th December 2002 at Southmead Hospital, Bristol.

James and Molly's second son William (1849-1918), was a twelve year old 'mason's lender' in 1861 when he was living at Hutchings, Petton, Bampton, where he was working for John Luxton (1827-1906), a mason, his father's cousin, employing two men and two boys. William was a 26 year old stonemason living in Glyntaff, Glamorganshire when he married Selina James, at Christchurch, Clifton on the 24th November 1874. Both sign the register. Selina, the daughter of John and Harriet James, shoemaker, was born in Skilgate on 26th December 1847. In 1871 she was a 23 year old dress maker, residing with her uncle Robert Melhuish, a 57 year old butcher and farmer of seven acres at Higher Croft Skilgate. The couple's first child, Harriet Ann ("Auntie Hetty") was born in Glyntaff Street, Pontypridd on the 15th October 1875.

William became a mason and builder in Bristol, and the family were settled at 8 Stanley Terrace, Woolcott Park, Redland, Westbury when a son William James Luxton (1877-1907) was born there on the 16th November 1877. The photo next page shows Selina with her children Harriet Ann and William James c.1878. Francis Charles Luxton (1879-1954), a second son was born at 8 Victoria Street Stapleton Road, Bristol on the 3rd August 1879.

The 1881 census lists William Luxton 32 mason, his wife Selina and their three children dwelling at 8 Victoria Street, Stapleton Road, Bristol. The family had moved by 1891 to 7 Victoria Street where William 42 stone mason, Selina 43 dress maker, Harriet 15, living at home, William James 15, Post Office Boy, and Francis 11.

He advertised for work in the Western Daily Press, Wednesday 30th March 1898-Good Jobbing Mason, at once,- W. Luxton, Victoria Street, Stapleton Road.

William Luxton mason was still there in 1900 and 1910 when he is described as William Luxton, builder. His wife Selina suffered with "jaundice 3 months and softening of the brain 14 days" before she died aged 63 at home in 7 Victoria Street Stapleton Road on the 22nd September 1911. Her pink lustre jugs are in the possession of her late granddaughter Gladys Louisa's family. The Bristol Directory for 1919 lists William Luxton & Son builders 7 Victoria Street, Stapleton Road but William had died on the 2nd October 1918.

William Luxton of 7 Victoria Street, Stapleton Road, Bristol, retired builder and contractor, had prospered in the building trade and was comfortably off when he died. His will made on the 7th December 1916, was proved on the 13th May 1919 when probate was granted to his children, Francis Charles Luxton, builder and Harriet Ann Luxton, spinster, the executors. Harriet who had been his house keeper received all his "household furniture, plate, plated articles, jewellery, linen, wearing apparel, china, glass, books, prints, pictures, ornaments and other household articles". Hetty was also bequeathed his freehold house Number 1, Hamilton Road, Stapleton Road together with his freehold dwelling house known as "Higher Croft" Skilgate near Wiveliscombe. This property had been the home of John and Harriet Melhuish, his maternal grand parents. His freehold dwelling house, Number 7 Victoria Street, Stapleton Road was left to his son, Francis Charles Luxton. His grandchildren, Gladys and William Luxton, the children of his late son William James were left a legacy or sum of £10 each.

Harriet Ann Luxton, his daughter, married Edwin Huntley at Bristol Registry Office on the 3rd September 1919. There were no children and

"Hettie" died in 1960 aged 85. William James Luxton, his eldest son, married Louisa Bryant at St. Michael's, Two Miles Hill, Kingswood, Bristol on the 22nd September 1900. In 1901 William, 23, clerk in a boot factory, and his wife, a boot machinist, lived with her widowed mother at 7 Hudds Hill, St. George, Bristol. William became chief clerk to Thomas Cox, a General Builders Merchant with a head office at Whiteladies Gate and Cement and Sand Stores at 8 The Grove, Queen Square, Bristol. He was only aged 29 when he died at 1 Hamilton Road, Stapleton Road, on the 25th August 1907. His death certificate describes him as a Commercial Clerk and gives the cause of death as "Cerebral haemorrhage 2 days".

Gladys Louisa Luxton (1901-1983), his daughter, (with parents in photo c. 1904) who became Mrs Reginald Siddorn, wrote that her father died as a result of a cycling accident. He is said to have run into a stationary refuse truck. His widow Louisa was a 30 year old boot maker machinist in 1911 with children Gladys 9, William 3 and her 66 year old widowed mother at 1 Hamilton Road.

Louisa's son William Henry Luxton (1907-1981), a builder, retired about 1975, to live in Appledore north Devon. He enjoyed relating a story about his sister Gladys (on Right) who had a brief moment of radio fame. Apparently hers was the first singing voice aired over "crystal radio" from Bristol Radio Station. As a member of "Bristol Operatic" she recorded "Madam Butterfly", to find out if a singing voice would come across on radio. The fun side of the tale was that while 'prim and proper' Gladys was practising her musical scales, her brother Willy was mimicking her, from the garden, with "Ah-sol, ar-sole". Then he shot a pea from his 'shooter' which lodged in Gladys' throat almost choking her. Bill's tyrant Grandmother Bryant almost pulled his ear off. Years later when Bill was 'telling the tale', he would say, "You should'ave 'eard our Gladys singing "Walla walla catsmeat on the wireless"[134].

Francis Charles Luxton (1879-1954), William and Selina's second son, was a successful house decorator and builder in Bristol, living at 26 Victoria Street in 1911 and then 7 Little Victoria Street before finally settling at 147 Stapleton Road. He was married to Susie Emma Hall, born in Lambeth, and died on the 14th January 1954 leaving a personal estate valued at £1018 – 14 – 9d to their children, Francis Albert Luxton (1907 – 1972), carpenter and shopfitter and Daisy Kathleen Luxton (1910-1965).

The photograph shows Francis, his wife Susie and children c.1925. Daisy, a keen dancer, gave her interpretation of a sailor's hornpipe at a Y.M.C.A. children's party in 1926 and her pupils gave a delightful display at a British Legion Benevolent function at Wootton-Under Edge in 1935[135]. Her Daisy Luxton Dancing Academy was based in Stapleton Road, Bristol and she did a great deal of charity work with her troupe of tiny tap dancers. In December 1936, for instance, her dancing displays raised £22..10s ..4dfor the Bristol Blind Fund. She was a talented pianist too[136].

---

[134] See letter of 12th September 2003 from Ian and Cynthia Green 22 St. Merryn Holiday Village, Padstow, Cornwall.
[135] Western Daily Press, 5th January 1925 &Gloucester Journal 7th December 1935.
[136] Western Daily Press, 3rd December 1936.

This branch of the family is represented today by the children of the late William Henry Luxton (1907-1981) carpenter and joiner, who married Rosa Grace Hope Gourd at St. Mark's Church, Easton, Bristol on 27th August 1932 (wedding photo below). In 1944 they lived at 41 Stanley Park Road, Staple Hill, Bristol. Their son Keith Charles Luxton (1944-), warden at the Camping and Caravan Club Site in Lynton, north Devon, and his wife Jean Lovell, have two adult children, Gary Keith Luxton (1966-) and Deborah Jean Luxton (1969) who themselves are married with children and live in Northam, Bideford. Keith's sister, Cynthia Pamela Luxton, the widow of Ian Michael Green, lives in St. Merryn near Padstow, Cornwall and has a daughter and two sons. I am grateful to them for their help compiling this chapter.

21

THE JOURNAL OF ISAAC LUXTON (1815-1876) SHOEMAKER AND PARISH CLERK SKILGATE SOMERSET

See tree 9

Isaac Luxton, a shoemaker and Parish Clerk, who lived at Kymmen Moor in the sequestered sylvan village of Skilgate on the southern slope of Haddon Hill in north west Somerset is noteworthy for having kept a journal which has survived to the present era.

St John the Baptist Skilgate

Judith, his mother, the daughter of James and Phillis Skinner from the nearby parish of Upton, lived all her life in Skilgate where she was baptised in 1783, married in 1812, and buried in 1850. Isaac Luxton (1789-1838) senior, his father, was a stone mason, born a few miles away across the Devon border in the hamlet of Petton, Bampton where his family had farmed at Hutchings since the early eighteenth century.

204

Upon his marriage in 1812 Isaac senior set up home in Skilgate where on the 30th April 1817 he purchased the site of a ruined cottage at Kymmen Moor. During the next ten years he built a new cottage on the Kymmen Moor site with a workshop and other buildings. Although it was sold by public auction on the 5th February 1833 the Luxtons continued to reside there as tenants.

Isaac senior died, aged 49, at Skilgate on the 2nd February 1838 from what his death certificate describes as "Inflamatory fever". Two years later, in 1841 the Skilgate census lists his widow, Judith, residing at "Keeming Moor" with their sons James, Isaac, John and Thomas. Judith who died, aged 67, on the 23rd of May was buried at Skilgate on the 1st June 1850. Her son Isaac was present at her death. An old photograph of Kymmen Moor is below.

The subject of this chapter, Isaac Luxton, the shoemaker, the second of eight children born to Isaac and Judith Luxton, was baptised at St John the Baptist, Skilgate on the 9th July 1815. Details of his childhood are wanting but he received an elementary education and the family tradition is that apart from the parson and the school mistress at Skilgate he was the only person sufficiently literate to act as parish clerk. His late great grandson, Geoffrey W. Luxton, in Worsley,

Lancashire possessed a copy of Walker's Dictionary (1836). It is beautifully written and embellished on the fly leaf, "Isaac Luxton his book June the 6th 1838."Geoffrey was given the book by his aunt Mabel Luxton who lived in South Street Wiveliscombe.[137]

Isaac's three brothers and all his Luxton cousins were stone masons so why he chose to be a shoemaker is not clear. His grandfather Isaac Luxton (1751-1834), yeoman of Hutchings, Petton, bequeathed £5 to be paid to him when he was twenty one and the bequest may have helped pay the cost of his apprenticeship. Perhaps too, he was a favourite for he was the only one of fourteen grandchildren to receive a personal bequest in the will.

Isaac, a 30 year old bachelor and shoemaker, married Florence Martin (nee Tout), a 27 year old widow, at St. Mary, King's Brompton, Somerset on the 19th March 1846. Florence was the daughter of Thomas Tout, a thatcher of Bury village. The newly wed couple signed the register in the presence of George Tout and Charlotte Vicary who witness with their mark. The 1859 Bristol Post Office Directory and Gazette lists Isaac Luxton Skilgate, Boot& Shoemaker.

Kymmen Moor where Isaac took his bride to live, is indicated as two cottages and a garden lying to the north of the parish church on the plan of Skilgate parish surveyed in 1844 by Robert Newton of Croford, Wiveliscombe, for the tithe map and apportionment. It is marked on the parish map as No. 308, 309, 310 and 311 and is occupied by James, Isaac's elder brother, as a tenant to the owner, the Revd. Richard Bere of Morebath.[138] While the property is listed in James name it is evident from census details that Isaac and his family resided in one of the two cottages. An area of one rod was tenanted and in No 309 on the tithe map is marked the apple orchard planted by Isaac Luxton senior in 1832.

In 1851 Isaac and Florence with their children, Levi, aged 2, and Isaac Abel, aged 8 months, continued to reside in one of the two cottages at

---

[137] John Walker (1732-1807) who is buried in St Pancras Churchyard in London was an actor, philogist and lexicographer. His Critical Pronouncing Dictionary and Expositor of the English language, first appeared in 1791. Isaac's copy dated 1836 is the 32nd edition.
[138] The 1844 Skilgate Surveyors Report in possession of Dixon Luxton. See his letter dated 16th December 1992.

"Higher Chippenmoor". His elder brother James Luxton (1813-1861) mason, his wife Mary, the daughter of John Melhuish, butcher, and their family lived in the other cottage. The family were still residing at "Keeping Moor" in 1861 when Mary Hill who had been lodging with Isaac since 1855 was described as a 58 year old blind spinster. James, aged 48, and his family continued to reside in the adjoining cottage but he was already desperately ill with consumption and suffered from the disease for two years before his death on the 2nd December 1861. The "Phthisis" recorded on his death certificate was most likely silicosis caused by inhaling stone dust in his occupation as a mason. Isaac was present at the death and James was buried at Skilgate on the 7th December 1861. Molly, James widow, who died aged 57, was buried at Skilgate on the 20th April 1873.

Isaac, the shoemaker, was now the sole surviving brother. John had died aged 28 in 1845 to be followed by Thomas aged 24 in 1849 and finally James aged 48 in 1861. The stone dust inhaled by them in the course of their work as masons must have contributed to their early deaths. Perhaps being a shoemaker was a healthier occupation.

On the 24th March 1865 Isaac moved into Robert Melhuish's house in Skilgate for which he paid Robert a rental of seventeen shillings and sixpence a quarter year. However, his stay there was of short duration for misfortune struck abruptly on the 12th December 1865. "Our house burnt down" is the stark record of the disaster in Isaac's journal. Tantalisingly he provides no further details of what must have been a traumatic experience. Robert Melhuish's house called "Higher Croft" was marked No 39 on the Skilgate tithe map of 1844. The house was later rebuilt and it is in a good state of repair today.

By 1867 Isaac was once again in residence at Kymmen Moor where he was paying Mrs Bere, the widow of the late Rev. Bere, a rental of £1..15shillings a quarter year, payable at Lady Day, Midsummer, Michaelmas and Christmas. Isaac continued to reside at Kymmen Moor until his death at the age of 60 on the 27th February 1876 from "a chill Broncho-pneumonia 8 days". Florence his widow was still resident at "Chipping Moor" in 1881 when her sister-in-law, Mary Anna Luxton (1821-1891) aged 59, a retired servant, was living with her. Ten years later Florence, 72 a widow living on her own means, resided at Chipping Moor with her relative Elizabeth Tout, an 80 year old widow annuitant. Florence, who died aged 74 and was buried at Skilgate on the 9th May 1893, is thought to be the last of the family to occupy Kymmen Moor. Her grandson, Clement Henry Luxton (1882-1957) of Wiveliscombe, visited Kymmen Moor when he was a small boy. His grandfather, Isaac, was dead but he heard stories about the old shoemaker and his wife Florence who were regarded as a, "very formidable and strict pair".[139]

This assessment seems to be borne out by surviving photographs. On the 4th October 1870 Isaac Luxton travelled from his home at Kymmen Moor in the village of Skilgate to the market town of Tiverton to have a "little likeness" made. He was aged 55 and the photograph betrays a severe and strict demeanour[140] with side whiskers and an under chin beard, the "Newgate fringe" which became fashionable after the Crimean War. He is dressed in a check pattern shirt or muffler beneath a double breasted high  waisted waistcoat with a parallel row of horn buttons and a high round neck turned over collar. Over the waistcoat he is wearing a loose fitting hip length lounge type jacket, perhaps made of velvet or corduroy which was the most usual material for country work clothes. The hat is a low crowned bowler with a fairly broad brim, turned down. His hands, long and sinewy, are the hands of a cobbler.

A second photograph, a carte de visite, was taken perhaps in the mid 1860s or early 1870s by F. H. Brent 449 Southwark Park Road, London. Isaac Luxton (1815-1876), the parish clerk of Skilgate, is the

---

[139] See letter of 16th December 1992 from Dixon H. Luxton.

[140] In mid Victorian times people posing for photographs often appear stiff and unsmiling because they were required to sit perfectly still, helped perhaps by a head clamp or brace, for one or two minutes.

full length standing figure using a chair as a hand rest. He is wearing a lounge suit and has a watch and chain in his waistcoat. His wife Florence (c.1819-1893) is the full length seated figure wearing a crinoline with black velvet braid bands and edging on the cuffs of her sleeves. Her buttoned up bodice above the crinoline is cut to mould her figure. Florence's plain hair style is smoothed back into a bun from a central parting and her ears are exposed which became the fashion in the mid 1860s. Isaac's heavy silver pocket watch was in the possession of his great grandson, Dixon Luxton, when I visited in 1974.

Inside the watch were bills for its repair, the earliest of which is dated 1855.

We learn much more of Isaac and life in Skilgate from the journal which he kept from c.1847 until his death in 1876. A small unpretentious volume, it is mostly an account book concerned with Isaac's craft as a shoemaker, but there are brief jottings which evoke the flavour of country life in mid nineteenth century rural Somerset.

The brevity of Isaac's Journal[141] and the cryptic nature of the commentary are to be regretted. More seriously, perhaps, is the omission of family events which must have been well known to Isaac. There is no mention for instance to his cousin Thomas Luxton (1824-1893) of Hutchings Farm, Petton, emigrating to Ontario about 1853 or of Thomas's nephew, William Fisher Luxton (1843-1907), who emigrated at the age of ten in 1855. There is no reference either to his uncle Jacob Luxton (1800-1868) who died in Chipstable the neighbouring parish in 1868 or of Jacob's sons George and John migrating to Clevedon near Bristol in 1863. We may infer that Isaac's failure to mention these and other events suggests that the extended family were not close knit but in truth we really expect too much.

---

[141] The Journal is in the safe keeping of the family of his late great grandson Dixon H. Luxton in Wiveliscombe.

Isaac was not writing for posterity or the genealogist and family historian. He was keeping little more than a memo pad. Even so we glean much of interest from it. In the quarter century 1850-1876 Isaac only once records leaving his home district[142]. This was in 1851 when he spent the week of 26th July to 2nd August in London at the Great Exhibition which must have been a memorable experience for Isaac and many more of his generation who rarely left their native hearths. He may have taken advantage of one of the exhibition savings clubs which were started by many Taunton inns. The Phoenix and the Fleur de Lis in particular enrolled 480 working men to spend a week in London at the Great Exhibition. They travelled on special cheap rate excursion trains and were packed in third class carriages open to the skies. At the exhibition they were amazed by Paxton's glass dome "Crystal Palace" and were stunned by the range of exhibits gathered from all over the world.

Most of his life Isaac spent in Skilgate with occasional trips to towns and villages such as Wiveliscombe, Dulverton, Watchet, Wellington,

---

[142] However the carte de visite of Isaac & Florence taken by F. H. Brent 449 Southwark Park Road in the mid 1860s or early 1870s reveals that Isaac and his wife must have made at least one more trip to the metropolis.

Taunton and Bridgwater in West Somerset and Morebath and Tiverton in East Devon. There were a few pleasures – half lb of tobacco and pouch from his son Isaac Abel, singing at Morebath, a new hat, a likeness taken in Tiverton – little more. Isaac is mostly concerned with paying his debts and collecting his dues, in planting and harvesting food to eke out his existence as a country shoemaker. The rhythm of country life flows through its pages with only the odd acknowledgement of the outside world; Robert Sadley, a native of Skilgate, drowned in America in 1867, peace celebrations at Morebath to mark the end of hostilities in the Crimean War, mention of the first day of the "Indian War" (i.e. Indian Mutiny), the Great Exhibition of 1851 but these entries are very much the exceptions.

Much of Isaac's Journal consists of accounts, giving itemised details of bills. Cordwainers needed to keep material in stock so we find Isaac purchasing different types of leather – cordovan[143], patent, kip, kid etc. He buys items such as vamp, welt, butt, sprigs, hemp, flax, galloon together with trade tools like an awl. He sold supplies to other shoemakers. Isaac Collard, a shoemaker in Taunton for instance, purchased leather, shoe nails; awl blades etc from Isaac and on the 7th June 1851 the bill included 11 eggs at $5^1/_2{}^d$ and 3 pints of goose berries at 3^d.

Thomas Atkins, a Skilgate blacksmith, supplied Isaac with many of the metal items he needed in his trade. Typical items included in a bill of the 28th May 1856 were '1 pair tips 4^d' '200 nails $1^s...4^d$'.

There are lists of customers who have settled with Isaac for the making of boots and shoes ; For instance on the 12th July 1850

Hariot Patterson	Boots	1s...0^d
Ann Blew	Boots	1s...0
Wm Pugsley	Boots	0 -- 8

and on Christmas that year

George Tout	Slippers	1 – 2

Repairs are also recorded and typical were the following items extracted from Mr Follett's bill for 1864:-

---

[143] Cordovan is a fine goatskin leather originally from Spain

May 24 Mr Chas p straps for Trousers	0 – 2[d]
--- 30 Mr. one Boot righted	0 – 4
June 1 Miss Verna Boots revampt[144]	1 – 6
Sept 12 Mr Edwin p leggings rd	0...4
On December 11th, 1865 he repaired the bellows for	
John Atkins the blacksmith	1[s] .. 4[d]

The Revd. John Bere often called on Isaac as part of his bill of 1869 reveals

Octr 26 Harness rd	0 – 3[d]
Decr 2 p Laces	0 – 2
Aug 23 portmanteau rd	0 – 4

Isaac and his donkey and cart must have been a familiar sight in the village where he worked as a tranter or irregular carrier. He frequently carried out work for various people and this bill for work he undertook in 1851 for Farmer Luxton of Townsend Farm, Skilgate is typical.

	s ... d
One day work in church hill	1 ... 8
Horse & Waggon Drawing work	3 ... 6
Drawing Turf 3 load	3 ... 0
Drawing ferns 2 load	3 ... 0
Drawing 10 Bushels genins[145]	2 ... 6
Drawing Potatos from Paddick	2 ... 6
Drawing Dung in church hill	3 ... 0

Isaac in his strive to be self sufficient kept donkeys, pigs, hens, ducks, and bees and grew crops of potatoes and broccoli etc. Apart from 'Cyder' which he sometimes bought or made himself, Isaac purchased ale and occasionally beer, usually by the quart. For example he paid Thomas Tout £19 .. 9[s] in settlement of a bill which began on the 30th March 1848 & was settled on the 19th February 1849. The items included 2 pecks of ale, 58 quarts of ale, 3 quarts of beer, 1 peck of potatoes 2s ..0d.

---

[144] The vamp was the front part of the boot.
[145] Genins were some sort of plant perhaps digitalis(foxgloves)

When Isaac was appointed Parish Clerk[146] of Skilgate in 1864, one of his tasks was to purchase bread for the sacrament as is revealed in this bill of 1875

Mr Morse Churchwarden
To I Luxton Bread for
Sacrament

April 4	½ loaf	0 - 2 ¾
May 16	½ loaf	0 - 2 ¾
June 27	½ loaf	0 - 2 ¾
July 25	½ loaf	0 - 3 ¼
Septr 5	½ loaf	0 - 3 ¼
Octr 3	½ loaf	0 - 3 ¼
Novr 14	½ loaf	0 - 3 ¼
Decr 26	½ loaf	0 - 3 ¼
1876		
Feby 6	½ loaf	0 - 3 ¼
		2 - 3 - ¾

The exact job of the Parish Clerk varied parish by parish. His usual function was to act as the vicar's secretary and accounts clerk. He would have to collect fees and write a list of banns for future marriages. Parishioners would approach him too as an intermediary to inform the vicar to visit the sick and the dying. One of his functions was to lead the hymns and psalms in the services and carry out all sorts of jobs which helped the vicar, such as supervising the work of the sexton. He also signed the marriage register in some cases as a witness.

His wife Florence received payment from the Revd John Bere for washing his surplus & clothes. This bill is typical:-

1871. Mr Bere To F Luxton		s	d
Janry 1	washing surplus	0	10
March 12	washing surplus & Cloths	1	0
June 4	washing surplus	0	10
Aug 13	washing surplus & Cloths	1	0
Aug 26	washing surplus	0	10
Novr 5	washing Surplus & Cloths	1	0
		5	6

---

[146] For an excellent account of a parish clerk's duties see Diana Summers article on George Chivers(1774-1844), Parish Clerk, pages 161 to167 in volume 30 number 5 March 2012 issue of the Genealogists Magazine.

Isaac itemises the cost of keeping his donkey and cart for the year 1852

Dunkey Expenses	£	s		d
Dunkey		12	+	0
Cart & Harness	1	4		0
keep -		15	+	0
Drench[147] -		1		0
Chair		5		0
Linney[148]	1	0		0
Wheels	1	2		0
Cart		9	+	0
Iron		10		0
hay		1		0
Oats		2		0
shoeing		4		0
	£6	5		0

July 30. 1852.

The Journal contains the draft for the meeting of the Inhabitants of the Parish of Skilgate assembled at a vestry at the usual Place on the 2nd May 1851. It was "Unanimously agreed that no Ashes should be sold to be Carried out of the Parish by any that cut Turf[149] – on the Poor Lotment". It was agreed among other details that in future those cutting turf had to produce a certificate or they would be excluded from cutting the turf. Isaac and his brother James were among those included in a list of twenty five people who had the right to cut turf on Haddon Hill.

At the back of Isaac's Journal there are several pages of addresses, mostly referring to members of his family. Two of his spinster sisters who were in service are listed. Sarah (1820 – 1878), has three addresses in Yorkshire at Leeds, Sheffield (on July 17, 1866) and Cookridge near Leeds in 1868[150]. She was residing in the parish of Upton Somerset, at the time of her death and was buried in Skilgate. Another sister Mary

---

[147] A draught or dose administered to an animal.

[148] Linney(or linhay) farm shed or outbuilding open along the front.

[149] Turf was used as a domestic fuel. Ancient turbary privileges gave the twenty five people named the right to dig turf which kept them in 'firing' for their domestic fires.

[150] In 1871 Sarah aged 51 was a boarder, formerly servant, in the employ of John Gamble & his son Albert at Holt Cottages, Adelcum Eccup, Cookbridge, Yorkshire, Mary Anna, aged 49, her sister was a servant there too.

Anna Luxton (baptised in 1821), gave her address on August 5, 1875, the Revd. Baring Gould's, Oakland, Sidmouth, Devon[151]. Isaac's nephew, John Luxton (1843 – 1928), the son of his brother John, moved to London where his address on August 1st 1870 is given as Mr John Luxton, 64, Stainsby Road, Poplar, London. By 1875 he was living at No 4, Glaston Terrace, Glaston Road, Croydon, Surrey. John set up in the milk business before buying Luxton's Farm, Sanderstead Road, South Croydon where he prospered as a cattle dealer.

Isaac had a fierce temper and his sons Levi (1848 – 1905) and Isaac Abel (1850 – 1918) left home for Wiveliscombe, where they became Methodists. Levi enlisted in the Coldstream Guards and five addresses are given for Private Levi Luxton, including Brentwood, Essex, Dublin, Tower of London and Windsor. His brother Isaac Abel, became a Sergeant in the Metropolitan Police and eight addresses are listed for him including one when he had a spell working as a sergeant at the naval dockyard in Devonport. There are three addresses in London for his in laws, the Tout family. The addresses of other friends in Bridgwater, Bath and London are recorded. The world was a rapidly expanding place and two addresses are for Skilgate emigrants:-

Mr Samuel Tout, Calabash Station, Marengo, New South Wales, Australia and Mr Wm Boucher, Oregon Township, Wine County, State of Pennsylvania, America.

One of the most fascinating items in Isaac's Journal is the recipes in the front and more particularly the back of the volume. Some are for items that today we would not make ourselves or even use. There are recipes for Blacking, for making ink, to buff. The recipe for Razor strap simply reads:-

    A flower of Crokus
    Best Olive oil
    For Razor strap

There are nine recipes for food and drink. They include sauce, "Chutnee", with a second chutney recipe from Maria Palmer, "Rubarb

---

[151] The celebrated Sabine Baring-Gould(1834-1924) wrote hymns including Onward Christian Soldiers and was the author of the classic "Lives of the British Saints" and many other notable works.

Wine", Marrow Pickle, To cure a ham, Lemonade, Fruit Syrup and "To Make Parsnip Wine".

There are eight recipes for treating sick horses including "A Receipt for breast ill in Cattle or human beings". However, the greatest number of recipes are for the cure of human ills. An 1851 recipe for treating toothache was "Kreosote" while another recipe was "Tincture of Myrrh mixed with water". There are recipes for Cough Mixture, pain in the Back, Lumbago, A Receipt to get out fire, for Erysipilsis (i.e. erysipelas), Receipt for Curing Skins from the Budget, A Valuable Receipt for inflammation to & pilk swelling, For Cholera of Diorea, Dr Sully[152] receipt for Diorea, for a Burn, Plaster for preventing or (if to far gone to prevent) relieving a broken breast, Eyewash, Effervesence Salts, Quinsay Sore Throat, For A Sprain, For bad leg of long standing, A Stimulant, A Tonic, A Receipt for Rhewmatick and two Receipt for Cancer.

Finally there is a group of recipes which consist of spell words used as desperate prayers or incantations to ward off ill.

Incantations have been used by civilised man since the dawn of history. Here they have taken on a Christian garb which coincides with the arrival of Christianity in this country:-

> A Receipt for St antonys fire
> there was three Virgins came
> from divers lands to cure thee - - -
> of this barren gun this black
> barren gun the Red barren
> gun the firey barren and
> the St. Anthony fire among
> in the name of Father and of
> the son and of the holy ghost
> Amen.

Charms for healing and other purposes and spells of various kinds were popular in rural areas until well into the 19th century. Doctors of the old

---

[152] Henry Sully was a surgeon living at Wiveliscombe Somerset in 1830. See will of Robert Luxton, Gun Stock Maker, Bampton, Devon, proved 26th September 1837.

school who failed to cure the complaints from which their patients suffered, invariably recommended the persons to a noted "healer", by which they meant a charmer. Some of these men – and women, too – had almost miracle – working powers, and they were much sort after by people of all classes.

The power to heal by charms or other mysterious or secret agency was inherited. The gift was passed from father to son, or mother to daughter, and was said never to leave the family. Then, again, the healing charm had to be gratuitously done, or the virtue would leave the charmer. Money was never taken for the work, but the person who had received temporary relief or cure was expected to send a gift in kind. In some instances a money gift was accepted, but never a fee. The secrets of the art were seldom divulged.

Isaac, it seems, was what in some parts of the country they called a conjuror or "cunning man" who dealt with benevolent magic – the male equivalent of a "white witch". It's fascinating to consider the possibility that the incantations used by Isaac may have been passed to him by his Luxton forebears. The will of his grandfather Isaac Luxton, yeoman at Hutchings, Petton suggests he was a favourite grandson. Elsewhere I have published an article "William Jenkin, The Wizard of Cadoxton – Juxta – Barry"[153] which relates how the power of witchcraft, like the apostolic succession, descended through the male and female lines of his family for more than two hundred years. Isaac's Journal seems to be providing us with a fragmentary glimpse at a strange and mysterious aspect of our family's life which perhaps had been practised for generations and was to die with Isaac.

Here are three more incantations used by Isaac.
> A prayer for Thorne
> Our Saviour came
> down from heaven
> with a thorne in
> his flesh he neither
> cankerest nor
> neither

---

[153] See Morgannwg, volume XX1V 1980, pp's 31-60, The Journal of the Glamorgan History Society.

shall thine in
the name of the
father & of the son
& of the holy ghost

The Lords prayer after
stoping blood ----------------
Jesus Christ was born
in Bethlehem christened
in the river Jordan
& the river being wild &
rude the child being
mild & good & why shouldn
this blood stop

A Receipt for A scald
there was two Angels
came from the west
the one brought fire
and the other brought
frost out fire and
in frost in the name
of the father and of the
son and of the Holy Ghost

S. Baring-Gould knew a late nineteenth century white witch, Mariann
Voaden of Bratton Devon. Her charm for Burns and Scolds which had a
slightly different wording to Isaac's was to be recited over the place of
injury while her charm for Staunching Blood had to be repeated
thrice.[154]

It's unfortunate that Isaac fails to record what physical movement (if
any) was needed when reciting these charms. In Wales the following
similar charm was recited as a cure for burns and scalds: "Three little
angels came from East and West. Each one tried the fire and ice to test.
In frost, out fire! In the name of the Father, the Son, and the Holy

---

[154] See Baring-Gould, Devonshire Characters and Strange Events (1908) by Bodley
Head.

Ghost". While repeating this the reciter described a circle with the index-finger of the right hand. Three circles were made from right to left, going "wildershins", or contrary to the sun's motion. Nine circles in all were made, and then the reciter would blow three times on the affected part.[155]

The Luxton family have continued their association with Skilgate and district until the present day. In 1872 Isaac, as Parish Clerk, witnessed the laying of the re-built church's foundation stone and in 1972 his great grandson, Dixon Henry Luxton of Wiveliscombe, secretary of the Deanery Synod, attended the centenary celebrations to mark the rebuilding of the church.

Today Isaac's descendants continue to live in the West Country at Wiveliscombe and Winterbourne, near Bristol. The last hundred years, however, have seen families split up and move away so that Isaac has descendants living further afield in Manchester, Folkestone and New Zealand.

Isaac's Journal provides us with a rare glimpse at a way of life which with the coming of the railways was rapidly changing in his own time. He chose to stay in his native Skilgate and his Journal details a way of existence which had been lived for centuries by hard working and skilled artisans, eking out their livelihood by growing their own potatoes, beans "brocklows", pigs and bees. Their way of life was not a hobby indulged in by a modern allotment holder but a serious necessity to sustain their livelihood.

---

[155] See Folk-Lore and Folk-Stories of Wales, page 227.

22

LEVI LUXTON (1848-1905) COLDSTREAM GUARDSMAN AND POSTMAN OF WIVELISCOMBE SOMERSET

See tree 9

Levi, the eldest son of Isaac Luxton (1815-1876) and his wife Florence Tout, was born in Skilgate on the 10th June 1848. References to the growing Levi and his younger brother Isaac Abel (1850-1918), are contained in his father Isaac's Journal. The children were "Bad in Measles" on the 6th October 1852 but were better by the 21st October when there was a children's tea at the parsonage.

Many references concern the education of Levi and Isaac Abel. Levi was nearly five when the two brothers began their schooling on the 23rd May 1853 at Miss Hill's School. Isaac paid Miss Hill four pence a week for teaching his two sons. They had a four week break at mid summer and another break at Christmas. Both boys also "staid home from skool bad in Cold" on the 12th January 1855. They were taken from Miss Hill's school on the 23rd February 1856 when Levi was sent to Mr Uzzell's school in Morebath,[156] while Isaac Abel attended Miss Mary Merson's[157] school.

---

[156] In 1688 John Brook gave £100 for building an almshouse in Morebath for two poor persons and a school house over it. He charged his estate with twelve shillings a month for the almshouse and £10 per annum to the schoolmaster for the parishes of Morebath in Devon and Skilgate in Somersetshire. See Daniel Lysons "Devon"(1822) Page 356.
[157] Mary Merson (1830-1894) second daughter of Francis and Sarah Merson of Skilgate married John Darby in 1864. She died on the 28th October 1894 and is buried in Skilgate.

In February 1858 Levi too, attended Miss Mary Merson's school but a Mr Aldred was his teacher in 1859 and 1861. Isaac paid Mr Aldred on the 25th February 1861 4s…9d for Levi's schooling and 3d for books.

Levi finished schooling when he was thirteen. He went to work for Mr George Follett, Shute Farm, Skilgate who on the 11th July 1862 paid Levi's wages amounting to 13shillings up to Midsummer. Levi was still working for Mr Follett on the 31st March 1864 when £1..10s..8d was paid for wages due at Lady Day[158]. Other references to Levi in his father's Journal include the purchase of clothes. On the 18th March 1857, for instance, Isaac bought Levi a new jacket and velvet waistcoat.

Levi learnt his father's trade as a shoemaker but did not get on well with Isaac who had a fierce temper. It was probably this and the thought of adventure which led him at the age of eighteen to join the army. He went to Taunton where on the 16th July 1866 he enlisted with Regimental No.1790 in the First Battalion of the Coldstream Guards, the famous regiment formed in 1659 by General Monk.

Isaac's Journal provides further details:-

1866   July 13 – Levi gone A soldier Inslisted in the Coldstream Guards

July 30 – Went to Taunton to see Levi

Aug 1 – Florence & Isaac gone to Wellington to see Levi

Aug 15 – Levi gone to London to join the Rigment

The Journal contains five addresses for Private Levi Luxton including Brentwood, Essex, Dublin, Tower of London & Windsor.

Army records reveal that Levi was 5ft..11inches with fair complexion, light brown hair and hazel eyes. He served in the Coldstream Guards for just two years and 97 days. His army career was cut short because he became infected with "syphilis constitutional" which occurred

---

[158] George Follett was a 57 year old farmer of 250 acres at Shute Farm in Skilgate in1861, employing three labourers and two boys. The method adopted for paying wages in those days was almost unbelievable! Wages were paid quarterly and a quarters pay was kept in hand so that new workers had to wait six months for their first pay packet!

during his spell in the service. He was discharged on the 20th October 1868, unfit for further service. Levi suffered with imperfect vision in his right eye and "syphilis erupting on his face and body". He was thought capable of contributing towards a "modified livelihood"[159]. If an invalidated soldier was desirous of Post Office employment his commanding officer would, provided he was trustworthy, write out a handwritten certificate, worded as follows- I believe (name of applicant) is thoroughly trustworthy and to the best of my belief he has never been under the influence of liquor within the last three years.

Levi took up this offer and the 1871 census records the 22 year old Levi as a rural postman, lodging with James Dudderidge, a butcher at Golden Hill, Skilgate. His father's Journal has a few tantalisingly vague references to his business activities.

1870	28 September – Levi Bought sack of Barley Meal 17s – 0d
1873	20 January - Levi Bought 2 Pigs of Mr Bicknell
1873	December – Reconed with Levi up to Decr 8 Paid
1874	10 Aug – Reconed with Levi and now due to me 19s – 6d
1875	17 February – Levi bought 4 fowls of J. Perrot Golden spangles[160]
1875	31 May – Settled with Levi.

He also continued to work as a shoemaker and he is listed in Kelly's Somerset Directory for 1889, 1897 and 1902. Levi was fined 2s..6d and costs at the Somerton Petty Sessions for allowing a mare and a colt to stray in Little Hook Drove, Skilgate on the 14th June 1875.[161]

He married at Wiveliscombe on the 10th April 1879. His bride Lucy Kemp the daughter of E & S. Kemp was born at Ryde, Isle of Wight, on the 11th December 1843. In 1881 Levi was a 32 year old postman, living at Abbotsfield Cottages, North Haydon, Wiveliscombe with his wife Lucy, aged 37, and their daughter, Florence Hilda, aged one.

---

[159] See Private Levi Luxton's(no.1790) discharge proceedings from Coldstream Guards 20 October 1868 WO 97/1273 99852
[160] A type of bantam. The full title is Golden Spangled Hamburg, described as a beautiful golden mahogany red with greenish black spangles.
[161] The Western Gazette, Friday 25th June 1875.

The family had moved by 1891 to West Road, Wiveliscombe where lived Levi, 42, rural postman, Lucy, 47, and their children Florence 11 and Clement 8 who both attended school. Levi, a 52 year old rural postman, his wife Lucy 57 and their daughter Florence 21 and son Clement 18, a cabinet maker's apprentice, dwelt in South Street, Wiveliscombe when the 1901 census was taken.

Levi, a Sunday school teacher in the Wesleyan Methodist Church, Wiveliscombe, was one of the adults who accompanied the children on their annual outing on a Thursday in late July 1890 to Burnham on Sea. They set out by train at 9 A.M. and on arrival at the destination they had refreshments at the Press Puzzle Gardens before play on the beach. Further refreshments at 3 P.M. were heartily enjoyed before setting home.

Levi Luxton, aged 56, rural postman, died at Wiveliscombe on the 11th January 1905. The cause of death was given as syncope and his son Clement Henry Luxton, a cabinet maker, was present at his death. Clement of 15 Berkeley Terrace, Newbury, Berkshire was granted probate of his father's estate valued at £261 .. 3s .. 4d.

Levi's brief but informative obituary appeared in the West Somerset Free Press, Saturday 21st January 1905:-Wiveliscombe. The death is regretfully announced of Mr Levi Luxton an old inhabitant of this town, which took place on Wednesday. For many years he worked the Upton and Raddington district as rural postman. He was connected with the local Wesleyan Chapel, in which he performed, in a quiet and unostentatious manner, many good services.

Levi's widow, Lucy, aged 67, lived in their five room house at Lambrook Cottage, South Street, Wiveliscombe in 1911 with their 31 year old daughter Florence, a shirt maker at home, and their son Clement 28, a building carpenter. Lucy died aged 74 on the 17th February 1918.

Levi's late grandson, Dixon Henry Luxton, had a family photograph album which belonged to his great-grandfather, Isaac Luxton. One of the most interesting photographs is of Levi and his brother Isaac Abel. (in photo at head of chapter). A dark jacket worn with light trousers had gone out of fashion in London by the mid 1860s when matching clothes for men had become the rage. The London fashion, however, had not caught on in the provinces when Levi (1848-1905) standing, and his brother Isaac Abel (1850-1918) who is seated, posed for this portrait in the late 1870s. Both men are smartly dressed in dark narrow cut jackets and light trousers. Levi's jacket has a deep lapel with a velvet collar. He is holding a walking cane and his low crowned top hat has a noticeably curved line of brim. Facial hair had also become popular and both men display moustaches and "dundrearies"[162], extra long and exaggerated side whiskers, worn without a beard. Their wing collars are accompanied by the long knotted "four-in-hand tie." Levi has a striped tie while Isaac Abel's tie has a polka dot pattern. Their light narrow cut trousers have raised or braided side seams and the toes of their shoes are relatively pointed in the fashion of the time.

The couple had three children, Florence Hilda (1880-1938), their eldest child, was born according to an entry in the Family Bible at 10 – A.M. on the 12th January 1880. Florence who remained a spinster became a housekeeper to her kinswoman, Bessie Chibbett, in Williton. She was living at the Hayes, South Street, Wiveliscombe Somerset when she died on the 5th September 1938 at Holmoor House, Trinity Street, Taunton, after a long illness at the age of 58. "Of a rather retiring disposition, Miss Luxton was much liked and respected. She was for many years associated with the Wiveliscombe Wesleyan Methodist Church."[163] Administration of her estate valued at £269 ..12s .. 9d was granted on the 20th October to her brother Clement Henry Luxton, cabinet maker.

Their second child, Clement Henry Luxton (1882 – 1957), born at noon on Tuesday 10th October 1882, as a youngster was a member of the Wesleyan Band of Hope in the village, performing a "stump speech" "The New Woman" and a

---

[162] Named from the character Lord Dundreary, a brainless peer in T. Taylor's comedy "Our American Cousin" (1858).
[163] Taunton Courier, Saturday 10th September 1938.

recitation "I'd rather not go."[164] He became a cabinet maker in Newbury, Berkshire before returning to his native Wiveliscombe.

Clement was a carpenter and joiner, aged 33 years and 3 months, of South Street, Wiveliscombe when as Private Clement H. Luxton (Reg. No. 26180) he enlisted on the 10th January 1916 in the Duke of Cornwall Light Infantry. He was 5 foot 10 ¾ inches tall with a chest girth of 37 inches when fully expanded. His unit was posted to France on the on the 7th of May 1916 and he was appointed a Lance Corporal in the 12th Battalion D.C.L.I. on the 15th June 1916 and promoted to Corporal on the 4th December 1916.

The fine head and shoulder photograph (above) of him as a Corporal in the Duke of Cornwall Light Infantry, must date to this time. In May 1917 he was transferred to the Labour Corps and by the time he was demobbed he had served two years and 330 days in the army. He was awarded the British War Medal and the Victory Medal. He had suffered thirty per cent disablement in the service and in consequence his army pension was increased by a bonus of twenty per cent to six shillings a week from 1st March 1919.

He married Mabel Elizabeth Harvey at Dulverton Congregational Church on the 12th June 1919. The couple settled at the Hayes, (in photo above) South Street, Wiveliscombe, where Clement died on the 5th June 1957. A keen gardener he won second prize for his currants at the Wiviliscombe Horticultural show in August 1934.[165] He was an active member of the Ancient Order of Forresters and represented Wiveliscombe at a district meeting at 49 East Street Taunton on 16th April 1941[166]. His wife Mabel Elizabeth, died aged 90, on the

---

[164] Taunton Courier, Wednesday 11th April 1894 & 23rd March 1898.
[165] Taunton Courier, Wednesday 15th August 1934.
[166] Taunton Courier, Wednesday 26 April 1941.

28th April 1973. They had two sons, Edward Harvey Luxton (1920 -2010), an architect, and Dixon Henry Luxton (1925 -2013), a civil servant, who obtained probate of their father's personal estate valued at £3982 .. 5s .. 3d.

Walter Kemp Luxton, Levi and Lucy's youngest son, born at 2 p.m. on the 19th December 1884, died aged 11 months and eight days on the 27th November 1885.

Two of Levi's grandsons, the children of his son Clement Henry Luxton, helped me with information for this branch of the family. Edward Harvey Luxton, born at 11 A.M. on the 30th March 1920, an architect, married Gladys Daisy Grandfield, daughter of the late Mr. and Mrs. S. Grandfield of Halsbeer Farm, Kentisbeare, at St. Andrew's, Cullompton, Devon on the 12th February 1944. They had issue two daughters, Cecilia Ann and Elizabeth Joan and lived at 66 Station Road, Winterbourne, Bristol. Before joining the forces he was articled to a firm of ecclesiastical architects. Edward, commissioned as a Second Lieutenant in the Royal Armoured Corps on 3rd July 1942, had recently returned home from foreign service when he married and his brother, Dixon (standing to his right), the best man was a Private in the R.A.S.C. Their father Clement Luxton is the tall man standing in the back row. Edward (1920-2010) of Winterbourne, near Bristol, owned a Grandfather clock made in Skilgate.

Dixon Henry Luxton, born at 12.45 A.M. on the 7th September 1925, was a civil servant in Exeter. He married Hannelore Emma Augusta Warttman at the Garrison Church British Army of the Rhine at Bad Beynhausen, Westphalia, Germany on the 2nd June 1947. They lived at the Hayes, South Street, Wiveliscombe but moved in December 1986 to "East Stoweys", Lower Langley, Wiveliscombe. Dixon was elected Churchwarden at Wiveliscombe at Easter 1976. Both brothers, like their father before them, enjoyed recitation in the Methodist Church, Eddie reciting, "The Other Way Round" and Dixon reciting "Grandpa's Spectacles."[167] Lore and Dixon were members of the Wiveliscombe Choral Society[168] while Dixon presided over a meeting of the Wiveliscombe Young Conservatives in July 1950

Hannelore (Lore) Luxton, died peacefully in her sleep on Thursday the 9th March 2000 at Frethey House Nursing Home after a long illness. Dixon too died peacefully in hospital about 11 P.M. on 19th January 2013 and they leave an adopted daughter Victoria Emma Luxton, born on the 7th August 1962, who is married with two daughters, and lives in Lille, France. The photograph below of Dixon and Hannelorre was taken by the author at the Hayes, Wiveliscombe in 1976.

The Somerset County Gazette for 31st January 2013 carried the following tribute from Dixon's friends:

-Friends of a community stalwart in Wiveliscombe who died following a battle with cancer say he epitomised everything good about the town.

Dixon Luxton served 40 years on the parish council and oversaw wholesale changes, as well as being churchwarden at St. Andrew's Church from 1976 before dying this month aged 87.

On Friday, dozens packed into the church to pay their respects at a funeral service. Parish council vice-chairman Brian Collingridge described Mr Luxton as "a true Wiveliscombe man." He added:

---

[167] Taunton Courier, Wednesday, 7th February 1934.
[168] Taunton Courier, 1st March 1958 & 29 July 1950.

"He lived here all his life and played a prominent part in many aspects of the town's life. He and I got on well and he is one of the church's longest serving wardens but, above all else, he was a Wivey man. He used to say: "If it's for the benefit of Wiveliscombe, I am for it.""

Mr Luxton grew up in South Street and attended the primary school before being called up to the army on his 18th birthday, later taking part in the D-Day landings. While setting up admin units in the Rhine a year on, he met his late wife, Hannelore, after choosing her out of four English speaking women offered by the labour exchange.

The couple returned to Wiveliscombe in 1946, with Mr Luxton later taking up several posts within the parish council, including chairman until 2011.

Rev David Widdows, of St. Andrew's Church, said: "He loved the town and church where he was involved at every level of church life. Through his various activities, he gained an encyclopaedic knowledge of the people and families of Wiveliscombe and their history and earned much respect and affection."

23

ISAAC ABEL LUXTON (1850-1918) OF SKILGATE SOMERSET, DETECTIVE SERGEANT IN THE METROPOLITAN POLICE

See tree 10

Isaac Abel was born at Skilgate on the 29th July 1850, the son of Isaac Luxton (1815-1876), shoemaker and Parish Clerk, and his wife Florence, the daughter of Thomas Tout, thatcher. A few details of Isaac Abel's life are to be found in his father's Journal:-

1852   25 Octr.   Weaned Isaac Able[169]

There are numerous references to his education and his father's payments for his schooling. Isaac Abel was aged 2 years 10 months when the two brothers began their schooling on the 23rd May 1853 at Miss Hill's school. On the 23rd February 1856 both boys were taken away from Miss Hill's school.

1856   25 February – Isaac gone to Miss Mareys
              This is a reference to Miss Mary Merson, Isaac Abel's
              new teacher.
1856   25 June – Paid Miss M. Merson Isaac's schooling 1s .. 4d
              settled up to 23rd.

Similar such payments follows.
1861   21 October – put Isaac Abel to Skilgate school.
1862   6 January – paid Miss Es Townsend Isaac's schooling up
              to   Christmas.
1863   27 April – Isaac Abel at Mr Aldred's school.
1863   1 June – Left school I. Abel.

---

[169] Isaac Abel was nearly 2 years 3 months old.

There are other references too. On the 21st May 1856 "Isaac Abel's best cloths" were burnt in the fire which burnt Betty Sadley's house to the ground at one o'clock in the morning[170].

1856	10 July – Florence & two boys to Dulverton Fair
1865	24 April – I Abel work for John How[171].
1866	15 August – I Abel to Tiverton Races.

It was the same day his elder brother Levi went to London to join the Coldstream Guards.

The lure of London was soon to attract Isaac Abel:-

| 1869 | Febry 6 – Isaac gone to London |

On the 25th March 1869 he was staying at the Buck's Head, 202 High Street, Camden Town, London.

| 1869 | Septr 6 – I.A. sent me ½ lb of tobacco and a Pouch. |

| 1870 | July 23 – Isaac came home from London. |
| 1870 | August 1 – Isaac returned to London |

His address on the 18th November 1870 was 10 Dartmouth Street, Westminster. This was shortly before he joined the Metropolitan Police.

The police were established by Sir Robert Peel, the Home Secretary, in 1829 and the Metropolitan Police attracted recruits from all regions of the country. Isaac Abel Luxton who served in the force during Queen Victoria's reign was the first policeman in my family. The Metropolitan force which he joined was organised into divisions. Each division was in the charge of a superintendent, under whom were four inspectors and sixteen sergeants. Recruits were expected to be under thirty-five, well built, at least five feet seven in height, literate and of good character. The minimum age was usually considered to be twenty years but the

---

[170] The Sadleys were living at Chipping Moor Skilgate in 1841 census. Betty Sadley married William Heywood on the 9 July 1856 according to Isaac Luxton's Journal.

[171] There was a John How, 36, carpenter employing 4 men at Higher Rock, Brompton Regis, the parish adjoining Skilgate in 1871. But this refers to John How, a farmer of 300 acres at Kendale Farm in Exton, west Somerset. In 1861 he employed two men and two boys, including John Luxton, 18, carter, a first cousin to Isaac Abel who almost certainly took over the job when John left for London.

certificates of service include recruits as young as eighteen. London was divided into fifteen minute segments, meaning that every beat constable was fifteen minutes run from every possible spot in the territory he patrolled. Isaac on the beat, was supplied with a bull's eye lamp, and a rattle[172] and he drew out his billy club from the loop on his belt when trouble loomed.

Isaac Abel was twenty when he joined the Metropolitan Police at Great Scotland Yard on the 5th December 1870[173]. His service began in the S or Hampstead Division but on his promotion to Sergeant he was transferred to Devonport on the 15th November 1875. The 1881census lists Police Sergeant Isaac Luxton, aged 30, in charge of eight constables, residing at the Metropolitan Police Station H.M.S. Dockyard, Stoke Damerel, Devon. From Devonport he returned to London on the 12th December 1882 to serve in the N. or Southwark Division. His posting to new stations can be tracked in his father Isaac's Journal. Six addresses with dates are supplied:-

23 December 1870 the Police Station, Albany Street, Regent's Park

12 August 1871 the Police Station, New Street, Portland Town, London.

17 August 1871, Police Station, Barnet, Herts.

19 August 1873 the Police Station. Whetstone, Middlesex.

23 November 1875 Police Quarters H.M. Dockyard Devonport

The final address provided in the Journal is:- Mr. I. Luxton Police Sergeant R^L W^n Victualing Yard Stonehouse Devon. A fine photograph

---

[172] The Metropolitan Police replaced rattles with whistles in 1884. Peel's first policemen were issued with a small and usually folding rattle which fitted neatly into pockets in the swallow tails of their coats.

[173] For Metropolitan Police career of Isaac Abel Luxton, joined 5th December 1870, resigned 11th September 1886, I consulted his pension papers MEPO 21/17 in the Public Record Office.

of Sergeant Isaac Abel Luxton resplendent in his uniform with its Sergeant's stripes was in the possession of Mr. Dixon H. Luxton of Wiveliscombe, who was a grandson of Isaac's brother Levi. The portrait taken by T. Grey, 60 Union Street, Stonehouse, Devon must date sometime between 1875 and 1882 when Isaac was a Sergeant stationed in Devonport.

Isaac, aged 27, a Police Sergeant was initiated on 21st March 1877 a member of the "Carew" lodge of Freemasons, Freemason's Hall, Torpoint, Cornwall. Before he left Devonport he received a certificate, dated the 20th December 1882, which recorded that he had 'faithfully met all fraternal obligations and fully discharged all Masonic Dues and Contributions required of him during his sojourn among us'.

Family tradition is that Isaac retired prematurely on medical grounds but no reference is made to this in police records. These reveal that Isaac Luxton, late a Police Sergeant, was residing at 42 Falmouth Road London S.E. when he resigned from the N. or Southwark Division on the 11th September 1886.

Isaac who is described as single was fortunate to have suffered no injuries during his service. He received his pay to the 7th September 1886 and his pension of £29 .. 12s .. 10d per annum commenced the following day the 8th September 1886. His next of kin was his widowed mother, Florence. He was described as aged 36, 5ft 8³/₄ inches tall with fair hair, blue eyes and a fresh complexion with no particular mark, defect or infirmity by which he could be identified. He intended to reside in Skilgate and draw his pension there.

Isaac Abel, like his father before him, took a widow for his wife when he married Elizabeth Rawle,[174] aged 32, daughter of Richard Hobbs,

---

[174] Elizabeth's mother, Eliza Ann Rawle (1824-died March1896) married Richard Hobbs (1821-died 15 February1895) stonemason of Withecoombe. See letter of 6th October 1975 from Geoffrey Luxton, Laneswood 2 Rutland Road, Worsley, Lancashire.

His brother, Harold James Luxton, in a letter of the 27th October 2013 adds that Eliza Ann Rawle was born at Hoe Farm, Winsford. The family legend says that R D Blackmore stayed with Eliza Ann whilst gathering material for his celebrated novel "Lorna Doone(1869) set in the later 17th century on Exmoor where an outlaw family, the Doones, terrorize the surrounding countryside. His story is based on fact as the mason, at the Independent Chapel, Dulverton on the 23rd August 1888. James Sully Rawle, Elizabeth's first husband had died aged 35 at Bury village, Kingsbrompton, Somerset on the 1st January 1886.

Elizabeth was the shopkeeper at Bury and that is where the newly wed couple settled. She owned meadowland around Bury and they bred horses there. They also kept sheep and in February 1889 Isaac was fined 18shillings at Dulverton Petty Sessions for allowing thirteen sheep to stray on the highway on the 7th January that year.[175] Isaac Luxton, Bury, Brompton Regis, Dulverton is listed in Kelly's 1889 Directory of Somerset and as a shopkeeper at Bury. The 1891 census has Isaac, 40, grocer, his wife Elizabeth, 36, and Mabel, aged 10 months, living at Hurmans, Brompton Regis.

Isaac Abel and his wife Elizabeth Ann, are pictured for the christening of their eldest son Isaac Hubert in 1891. Mabel their first child is in the pram and the family pet dog is in the picture. Isaac is dressed in a morning coat, identifiable by its sloping front edges. His exposed waistcoat features a watch chain, the watch tucked into the waistcoat pocket. His medium-crowned bowler with a curved brim was fashionable in the closing decades of the nineteenth century. Elizabeth's short thick gold chain is probably suspending a gold medallion.

Doones were indeed a notorious family in 17th century Exmoor. He was interested in Eliza Ann's Rawle ancestors who came from Oare, where throughout the 17th century they lived at Yenworthy Farm. This puts them firmly in the right place at the right time for a connection with the Lorna Doone story. There are various accounts of a Doone raid on Yenworthy Farm, during which, the Doones were chased off by a woman firing at them with a long duck gun, killing one and injuring others-the stories vary slightly. This victory was supposed to have given the local people the confidence to unite and launch a full scale attack.

RDB tells a version of the story in Lorna Doone-ch.48, but the earliest printed account we know of is in Thomas Henry Cooper's "A Guide to Lynton" published in1853, predating Lorna Doone by 16 years. We cannot know what Eliza Ann was able to tell RDB, but we do wonder if maybe the "Ridds" of the novel were modelled on her Rawle ancestors, which would mean she was a descendant of the family the "Ridd" family was based on.

There are similarities:-Her ancestors like the "Ridds" had been sheep farmers at Oare for many generations. She had two relatives-an uncle and anephew-both called John Rawle, who like the hero of the story "Girt Jan Ridd"himself were renowned for their great size, strength and wrestling skills...coincidence?

[175] Tiverton Gazette, Tuesday 5th February 1889.

Four children, three boys and a girl, were born and Harold the youngest was only fifteen months old when Elizabeth died from "Heart Disease" and "Syncope" at the age of 42 at Bury in the parish of Kingsbrompton on the 28th November 1898. The administration of her estate valued at £107 16 0 was granted to Isaac Abel in Taunton on the 9th January 1899. In this document it is noteworthy that Isaac is described as a "Farmer," when he is usually described as a shopkeeper. The family had some meadow land around Bury where he kept sheep and owned a stud farm.

Mindful of his own mortality Isaac Abel Luxton of Bury in the parish of Kingsbrompton Somerset, ex-Sergeant of the Metropolitan Police, made his Will on the 30th December 1899. His brother Levi Luxton of Wiveliscombe, Postman, and his friend, Henry Charles Harvey of Dulverton, coachman, were appointed executors and trustees. He left his money and "my household furniture, linen and wearing apparel, books, plate, pictures, china, horses, carts, live stock and carriages .... for the maintenance and education or advancement in life of my children".

Isaac was one of the dealers selling at the annual horse sale held at the Carnarvon Arms Hotel, Dulverton, in October 1896 at the close of the stag hunting season.[176] At an auction held at Withywine Farm, Morebath, on Thursday 24th March 1898, Isaac of Bury, Dulverton auctioned his "Bay mare pony, aged, good in any harness; a black mare pony, three years old, unbroken; a bay mare pony two years old, unbroken; a new heavy dog-cart, suitable for a butcher or baker with set of trap harness.[177] On a depressingly wet Wednesday in August 1901 he won the 10 shillings third prize at the Exford Horse Show in class 12

---

[176] West Somerset Free Press, 31st October 1896.
[177] West Somerset Free Press, Saturday 12th March 1898

for two year old geldings or fillies, calculated for riding or driving with his two year old sire Secundus which he had bred.[178]

At the prize day held in the National school Bury in April 1900 Isaac's daughter Mabel in standard 4 was awarded a needle-work prize given by the Lady Dowager Lady Carnarvon. The master also awarded gloves, prayer books, magazines, writing cases etc. for general subjects and regular attendance to Hubert, Thomas and Mabel.[179]

In 1901 Isaac, a 50 year old widower, was the grocer in charge of "The Shop" Bury, Brompton Regis, with his four children, Mabel aged 10, Isaac Hubert 9, Thomas George 8 and Harold aged 3. He was assisted by 49 year old Zillah Venn, his unmarried housekeeper. The early death of his wife, leaving Isaac with four young children to raise placed extra stress on his fragile mental health. He comes across as quite a belligerent character in a number of court cases reported in the local press. The Exeter & Plymouth Gazette of 31st August 1899 reported a case in which Isaac summoned a neighbour John Brewer, a farmer, before Dulverton Petty Sessions for using "profane language" but the case was struck out when Isaac failed to appear in court. On the 31st July 1901[180] he applied to the Bench at the Dulverton Sessions for the withdrawal of a case in which he had summoned his former housekeeper, Zillah Venn of Bury, for assaulting him on the 17th July. The Bench consented to his appeal on his paying the costs.

Then on the 29th August 1901[181] he summoned John Bristow of Bury, a farmer, at Dulverton Sessions, for obtaining two glasses of bitter ale from him by false pretences. He said on the defendant agreeing to lend him a pony and trap to go to the Exford Show he gave Bristow two glasses of ale to "clinch the agreement." On his going for the pony and trap the defendant refused to lend it. The case was a very complicated one but on hearing Isaac's evidence the Bench dismissed the case with costs, stating that there was no false pretence whatsoever. Luxton then appeared as the defendant to a summons taken out against him by

---

[178] West Somerset Free Press, Saturday 17th August 1901
[179] West Somerset Free Press, Saturday 28th April 1900
[180] Western Times, Thursday 1st August 1901. See Round the Courts.
[181] Western Times, Friday 30th August 1901 & West Somerset Free Press, 31st August 1901

Mr William A. Hawkins, a solicitor's clerk of Dulverton, for assault, and as a complainant in a cross-summons issued against Hawkins. This case arose out of the previous case. Hawkins was playing cricket when at between six and seven in the evening Isaac approached him "in a very abusive manner ordering Hawkins home. Hawkins put on his coat to go but Luxton caught him by his collar, pushed him up through the field and tried to knock him through the gate. A scuffle ensued and Hawkins managed to get Luxton by the neck where he held him until he promised to be quiet." After hearing the charges the Bench fined Luxton 10shillings inclusive, but dismissed the case against Hawkins whose costs were ordered to be paid by Luxton.

In October 1903[182] Isaac, described as a retired Sergeant of police, sued Sydney Wood, a general dealer of Bampton for £12 which was the balance of the purchase money in respect of a pony sale on 26th March that year. The pony had taken a prize at the Exford Horse Show so it may have been Secundus. The solicitor representing Wood, claimed the pony was a very poor one describing it as absolutely a "jibber." This time, however, the Bench gave judgment in favour of Luxton.

At the Tiverton County Court in September 1904,[183] Isaac sued Mrs M. L. Durnford of 76 Chesterfield Road, Bristol for £5..10shillings for breach of contract concerning the letting of a house at no19 Fore Street, Bampton. Prior to the house being let to Isaac by Mrs Durnford, her agent had let the property to another person. Isaac claimed that he had no knowledge that the house had been let to another person when he moved his furniture there and his claim of £5..10shillings was for expenses incurred in packing and removing the furniture etc. The judge however decided that Isaac should not have been in such a hurry to remove his furniture until an agreement had been drawn up and he non-suited him with costs.

Although he engaged two or three women to look after the house and children it is clear that the years following the death of his wife were dark and distressing times for the family. There was a deterioration in Isaac Abel's mental state which rendered him incapable of properly

---

[182] Western Times, Friday 30th October 1903
[183] Exeter & Plymouth Gazette, Monday 26th September 1904

caring for his young children. This was compounded by the cruelty of his hot-tempered housekeeper Zillah Venn. At the Dulverton Petty Sessions on the 26th March 1902 the NSPCC preferred a charge against Venn of wilfully ill-treating two of the children, Thomas, aged 9, and Harold, aged 4 years.

P. C. Bishop gave evidence that on the 5th February he visited the defendant who admitted that she had put the boy Harold, naked, into a pump-trough and pumped water over him; further that she had stood him in a bucket of water, and afterwards laid him on some straw. This took place in a shed outside the house on a very frosty morning.

The defendant also beat the lad about the body with a stick (produced). Inspector Simpson, officer of the prosecuting Society from Taunton, said on examination, the boy Harold was covered with old bruises, of a yellowish-green tinge. There were also bruises which had evidently recently been inflicted. The defendant, in reply to the witness, said she put the boy in the pump –trough and the bucket to "cool him down, as he was so hot-tempered." The witness examined the other lad Thomas, who was bearing the marks of a wound (above the ear) 1 ½ inches long, from which matter was oozing. Asked the reason for this, the defendant said the boy had allowed some potatoes to burn, and in trying to strike him with the wooden part of a potato-chopper, she accidentally struck him with the sharp portion of the instrument.

Albert Greenhouse, schoolmaster of Bury, said the children attended his school, and frequently had cuts and bruises about their bodies. He had noticed Harold frequently eating food which other children had given him.

The Bench heavily fined Venn £5 including costs and censured Isaac Abel for allowing his children to be so ill-treated[184]. In a second appearance before the Dulverton Petty Sessions in January 1903 Venn was summoned by the NSPPC for ill-treating Mabel another of the children. On the 31st December 1902 Mabel took some boots to Venn who in a fit of temper hit her on the eye with one of them causing the eye to be black for a week. This time the brutal housekeeper was sent to goal for two months[185].

---

[184] See The Western Times, Thursday 27th March 1902.
[185] See The Western Times, Thursday 29th January 1903.

Sometime after this the family moved to Morebath, across the border in Devon. There Inspector Thompson of the NSPCC with Police Sergeant Parnell visited Isaac Abel's house on the 13th December 1904. Mabel was ordered to bring a candle as it was getting dark. She was wearing a black sailor hat, and the Inspector noticed that a portion of her hair had been singed, a sure sign that the child's head was verminous. Hubert was working at Mr. Chattey's farm while George was out picking watercress for tea. The youngest, Harold, who was in the house was in a filthy state, and later when Hubert was questioned he said he often went to bed with his clothes and boots on as it was easier to get up in the morning at quarter to seven to go to work[186]. The condition of the place was so bad the police sent for a doctor who ordered the removal of the children to the Tiverton Workhouse.

For a time, during the visit, Isaac Abel, who wore a Christian Endeavour badge, appeared quite rational, but later talked about religion and started to sing, "I do believe; I will believe" and to their annoyance he dinned into their ears for nearly an hour. Isaac Abel was subject to fits and it was suggested in the subsequent court case that his mental condition was not what it should be. On the 27th December 1904 he was fined £5 and costs at the Tiverton Petty Sessions for having during the last six months neglected his four children Mabel 14, Isaac Hubert 13, Thomas George 12, and Harold 7, in a manner likely to cause them unnecessary suffering and injury to health. The children's rooms and the children themselves were dirty and verminous and some of their bedding was rotten by reason of neglect. It was admitted, however, that the children were fairly well nourished and there was no suggestion that they had been ill-treated by punishment[187]. The boys in the Tiverton Workhouse were registered to attend Elmore School in Tiverton, on the 15th December 1904, for Thomas and Harold, and for Hubert on the 16th December. Not a whisper of these sad events or the removal of the children to the Workhouse was passed down to future generations!

---

[186] See the Tiverton Gazette & East Devon Herald 3rd January 1905 for a detailed report of this case.
[187] See Exeter & Plymouth Gazette, Thursday 29th December 1904 and The Devon & Exeter Gazette, Friday 30th December 1904.

Isaac's mental health was very fragile and his religious mania showed no sign of abating. His erratic behaviour became known to W. H. White J.P. who called on the assistance of Dr. Henry Paine, Castle Street, Bampton to examine him. This took place on the night of 14th February 1908 in the street in Morebath. The doctor's observations reveal Isaac's pitiful state:-

> He talked to me in the street at night in a rambling manner on religious subjects without any encouragement from me to do so. He said he hoped that last night would be his last night in this world, and that he was likely to be in Heaven next morning. When I enquired about his daughter's absence, he told me he is going to write to the Secretary of State about her, and thinks that his letter will have great influence.

Mr. John Gooding, junior, a farmer at Higher Trickey's Farm, Morebath, told the doctor that Isaac had threatened to throw his daughter Mabel out of a window. The doctor concluded that Isaac was suffering from a dangerous religious mania and cited epilepsy as a contributing factor.

The following day 15th February 1908 Isaac was admitted to the Devon County Mental Asylum, Exe Vale, Exminster situated about four miles outside the city of Exeter. He was to remain in the asylum until his death on 7th January 1918. On admission he was described as a 59 year old fairly well nourished man of average height with grey hair, bald on crown. He had a grey close cut beard, moustache and whiskers. His weight was 12 stone 7lb. He was subject to epilepsy and was suicidal and was considered dangerous to others as he had attempted to push his daughter out of a window.

Mabel, near 18years of age at the time of the incident, was residing in Morebath. It is likely she had tried to help her father before his attempt to defenestrate her and she must have fled the house to raise the alarm. Isaac in a pitiful state had gone into the street that night, ranting religion where he was examined by Dr. Paine who committed him to the asylum. Isaac was a Bible Christian so he was well versed in scripture to fuel his ranting. His father's cousin John Luxton (1827-1906) at Hutchings Farm, Petton was also a Bible Christian who gave land for a Bible Christian Chapel at Petton and became a trustee of the cause there. His son Thomas (1851-1926), farmer at West Forde, Cheriton

Fitzpaine, a contemporary of Isaac, was a noted popular lay preacher on the Tiverton circuit.

Isaac's asylum records reveal that he had suffered, "a blow on the head while in the Metropolitan Police, since then he has been subject to fits and was pensioned." There is no reference to this incident in his Metropolitan Police records but it does go someway to confirm a family oral tradition that he received a savage kick to the head inflicted by a horse and died in a pitiful mental condition. The asylum medical casebook from his admission to 24th November 1909 says that he repeatedly made requests for a pair of scissors to trim his beard and demands to be taken to church. He is full of complaints about the asylum attendants. His mental state does not improve. In October 1910 we read he is "very mad on religion, singing to convert all the patients." By October 1911 he "seems to enjoy his life, full of accusations against his attendants." On 10th January 1912 there was "no material change in his mental state; has a large number of small fits; physical health is good." Other reports refer to him as "very noisy and full of religious ideas" (16th October 1912) "always making unfounded charges against the attendants, querulous and noisy"(14th February 1913). "Delusions of being robbed of parcels, which are being sent to him every day" (14th November 1913) are just a few samples. The register continues to log his epileptic fits and his health continues to fail over the next few years. During the last nine months of his life he suffered from "tuberculosis of the lung" but a cerebral haemorrhage was the immediate cause of death at the Asylum[188]on the 7th January 1918. Probate of his estate valued at £190..8s..8d was granted at Exminster on the 21st August 1918 to Henry Charles Harvey retired coachman, the surviving executor.

Isaac and Elizabeth's eldest child, Mabel Luxton, born on the 20th May 1890, went to work for Mr. James Palfrey at Whitehall Farm, Morebath. We have no dates but the Palfrey family took over the farm about 1906/7. This postcard photograph of Mabel standing on the steps of Whitehall Farm is dated 17th January 1909. She sent it to her cousin

---

[188] I am grateful to Gill Luxton Isaac's great granddaughter for providing copies of relevant documents from the Admission and Medical Registers of Devon County Hospital. See Admission Papers, 1908 3769/A/H2/62a/11328. Medical Case Book May 1907 to January 1909 3769A/H9/16 and Case Book of male deaths January 1916 to March 1919 3769A/H22/2. Devon Record Office.

Florrie Luxton at Lambrook Cottage, Wiveliscombe, wishing her a happy birthday. Mabel remained friends of the Palfrey family for the rest of her life. She also worked for a time at the Dragon Hotel on the A39, opposite the turning to old Cleeve. In 1911 census Mabel was a domestic under-housemaid for retired army captain Alexander Luttrell at the Court House, East Quantoxhead. Eventually she went to London to work as a cook for Lord Ranfinley and here she met parlour-maid Janie Lang from Devon. When Mabel and Janie left service in London, they bought a farmhouse in Teignmouth, Devon where they took

in foster children. On retiring, they moved to Wiveliscombe, taking Levi's old house, Lambrook Cottage in South Street, but they changed the name to Little Buddleford, after their farmhouse in Teignmouth. Mabel died at 11 South Street, Wiveliscombe on the 24th January 1967. Probate of her personal estate valued at £2519 was granted to her surviving brothers, Thomas George Luxton, retired hotel proprietor and Harold Luxton, retired Imperial War Graves employee.

Isaac Hubert Luxton (1891-1934), the oldest son, born on the 23rd May 1891, was the fifth generation in the family to be christened Isaac, but preferred to be called Hubert. While still at school he worked at Whitehall Farm, Morebath when Mr. Chattey was the farmer and he had most of his meals there. He and his brother, Tom, went to work in Wales. Tom worked in the mines for a while and Hubert had a milk-round with a pony and cart. Both worked on the Taff Vale Railway where at the age of 17, Hubert was a lampman at Tonypandy, in the Rhondda, between November and

March 1909, before going to London to work for a Tout relative who had two licensed houses.

His daughter "Marie" remembers him as a very kind and loving man although he was a very sick one due to his experiences in the Great War where he served as a private Reg. No.2329 in the 9th Battalion Royal Fusiliers (City of London Regiment). Hubert was a barman, aged 23 years 2 months, when he attested at Kingston on Thames on the 2nd September 1914. At 5 ft.6 inches he weighed 130lb, had grey eyes, fair hair, a fresh complexion and a maximum chest expansion of 36 inches. He first saw action in France on the 1st June 1915 and was awarded the 1914 Star, the British War Medal and the Victory Medal. The Germans gassed and wounded him before taking him prisoner and when he came back to civilian life he was quite a broken man in health[189].

Hubert was a 28 year old licensed victualler's barman when he met 32 year old Jessie Maud Stanynought, who had two children she was rearing as a single parent, and they were married at Wandsworth Registry Office, on the 27th February 1920. The marriage did not go down well with some members of the Luxton family but the couple were happy and their only child Maria Stella (known as Marie) was born in St. Thomas's Hospital London on the 5th June 1926. Hubert developed T.B. which was rife in those days and Jessie his wife soon caught it too. He was now only able to work in short spells as a barman and the couple spent spells in convalescent homes or sanatoriums.

Sadly, Jessie of Bowes Road, Barking died aged 47 from chronic pulmonary tuberculosis at 1 Old Church Road, Romford on the 16th February 1934. Her husband, Hubert, an army pensioner and barman of 12 Bowes Road Dagenham, died aged 43 also from pulmonary tuberculosis at 46 Ouseley Road Balham in south London on the 12th November 1934. His war experiences and wounds had contributed to his premature death. Their daughter Marie who was 6 or 7 years old when her parents' died was brought up at the Fox and Hounds, Old Carshalton, Surrey by her uncle Thomas George Luxton and his wife Frances, but says her two half sisters were good to her and remained so till they died. Marie married Charles Robert Speirs and they had four

---

[189] See his daughter Marie Ronald's letter of 13th April 2002.

lovely daughters but the marriage was not a success and eventually she married a Scot, Ian Gould Ronald in St. Alban's Registry Office on the 1st March 1975.

Thomas George Luxton (1892-1978), the second son of Isaac Abel and his wife Elizabeth, was born on the 29th July 1892 at Bury near Dulverton in west Somerset. In 1911 Tom was a 19 year old barman in the Lord Hill Hotel at 83 Waterloo Road, Lambeth. During the Great War he served as a driver No 41560 in the Royal Army Service Corps and was serving on the Western Front on the 19th August 1914. As one of the Old Contemptibles he was awarded the 1914 Star, the British War Medal and the Victory Medal. Tom, who became an hotelier, married a widow Frances Mary Howard (nee Denteth) at Tooting parish church south London on the 19th September 1920. His three siblings are in this wedding photograph. Mabel is seated on the far left while Harold is standing behind Frances. Hubert and his wife Jessie are standing back row, left.

For many years he worked as a barman until on the 17th December 1934 he took over the management of the Fox and Hounds in High Street, Carshalton, Surrey. The photograph of Tom on next page behind the bar was taken on 17th December 1955 to celebrate his 21st  anniversary as manager. He remained the manager there until his retirement in September 1961 when with his wife Frances he moved to 11B King Edward Road, Minehead, in Somerset. Frances had a stroke the following year and was taken into hospital where she died on the 14th January 1965. Tom remained in Somerset until 1974 when he went to live with his married daughter, Frances M. Franklin and family, in Swindon village near Cheltenham. There he enjoyed his remaining years and joined in village life, playing cards, visiting the betting shop and local village hall. He died on the 20th February 1978.

Harold Luxton (1897-1989) O.B.E. B.E.M., the youngest son of Isaac and Elizabeth, was born on the 30th August 1897 in Bury near

Dulverton, Somerset. He was nearly fifteen months old when his mother died and he was brought up from when he was about 9 years old by his aunt Sally Eames, (his mother's sister) who owned the village shop in Withycombe. He is listed there as a 13 year old scholar in 1911 living with his uncle William George Eames, 54, grocer and his wife Sarah Jane Eames, 48.

His schooldays over, he found employment in the nursery and gardens of a large house in Williton, and on the day war was declared he won first prize for his display of Golden Wonder potatoes at the Dunster Show.

HAROLD LUXTON   SOMERSET LIGHT INFANTRY
1897 - 1989   No 25657 7-2-1916 — 7-1-1918.

On 7th February 1916 Harold Luxton enlisted in the Somerset Light Infantry, 1st Battalion, and with the 4th Division embarked for France in September of that year. At Easter 1917, during the first battle of Arras, he was seriously wounded by machine gun fire, and he completed his recovery in a military hospital in Manchester. Visits to the wounded soldiers were made by the church parishioners in the area, one of whom, Maud Woosnam, the only daughter of Richard Woosnam from Monmouthshire and Louisa Barrett-Holt, married Harold, Foreman gardener, of 33 Mellison Road Tooting at the Register Office, Wandsworth on the 7th June 1923. His sister Mabel and brother Hubert witnessed the marriage.

In this studio photograph Private Harold Luxton (1897-1989) No. 254557 of the Somerset Light Infantry is wearing a gold wound stripe on his left cuff, an indication that it was taken sometime after Easter 1917 when he was seriously wounded at Arras. He was discharged from the army as a result of his wounds on the 3rd January 1918.

In 1982 Harold compiled the following "short précis"[190] of his involvement in the 1914-18 War from records of the Somerset Light Infantry and his own memory of events:-

13th September 1916
Embarked for France via Folkestone/Boulogne, the new intake for 1st Battalion Somerset Light Infantry (SLI) in the Somme area, all our training completed on Salisbury Plain, further training until Christmas Eve.

26th December 1916
Posted to a works Battalion at Bray sur Somme, stores duties but chiefly making and placing "Facines" (wood and wire for trench sides) for the front.

22nd February 1917
Rejoined the Ist battalion at Le transley for further training.

4th March 1917
This morning we marched off late in the afternoon to spend the night at a place called Allonville.

5th March 1917
Another day's march to spend the night at Talmas.

6th March 1917
Weather very cold and stormy, another march to spend the night at Gazaincourt.

7th March 1917
A short march today to Noeux arriving at 1pm. We spent the next 14 days and nights practicing "open warfare" tactics, weather cold with some snow.

21st March 1917
We moved this morning in buses and lorries to a place called Dieval, for 10 days further training.

---

[190] Received on 15th November 2003 in a letter from his son Harold James Luxton of Folkestone.

2nd April 1917

We have been told that we shall soon be going to the front, and today a party of our officers went to the "forward" trenches North of Arras to reconnoitre the area. The next five days were spent in lectures and equipment checking.

7th April 1917

Today is "Jellalabad"[191] day celebrating the SLI's famous victory, we are told that in view of our approaching battle this is a "good omen". We marched to Hermaville, and billets in huts. A concert was laid on 5.30 to 8.30pm, plenty of beer and music from a piano. (From 9 to 11pm the officers entertained the NCO's to a musical evening).

8th April 1917

We moved today to a place near Maroeuil and into tents.

9th April 1917

We marched off at 6am to a field just south west of St Catherine (map reference G15A). Heavy rain fell, but it cleared up later. We stopped at the assembly area and breakfast rations were issued. At 10am the battalion moved in column of route to cross the railway line (H7D), a few stray shells fell without causing casualties. We reformed in the railway cutting then continued our march forward. From then on very little shelling was encountered, and we reached our place of assembly (H9C) ahead of the time table.

At 3pm we moved forward again, but now the Germans shelled us again and caused some casualties.

We continued our advance and reached a point below the crest of a hill (H9/H10) as planned. At this point we had crossed the old German 1st, 2nd and 3rd line trenches taken over the past few days, and as we approached the 4th line trench we encountered machine gun fire, and discovered that the wire had not been cut by our artillery fire! We dug in for the rest of the day, a heavy exchange of fire took place, and our artillery "got the range" resulting in the 4th line surrendering.

My company "C Company" was ordered to push forward through the 4th line to the "Sunken Road". We met some resistance including

---

[191] The Somerset Light Infantry had the honour of the name "Jellalabad" added to their cap badge for their acclaimed defence of that fort in 1842 during the First Afghan War.

machine gun fire, but this was speedily overcome, and we took several prisoners including 3 officers.

The German guns ranged onto our new positions and fired a considerable number of shells. At 6.30pm we were told that the Battalion HQ was going to withdraw, but "C Company" was told to hold the captured trenches. The night was miserably cold with rain and sleet, but the Germans did not counter attack.

10th April 1917
Preparations were made for the Battalion to attack the "Hyderabad Redoubt", a cavalry battalion would lead the charge and the SLI would send out patrols, give covering fire (machine gun) and when the Redoubt had been captured, secure the Redoubt.

By mid afternoon we learned that the cavalry would not participate, but the SLI would still attack at 6.30pm following artillery barrage, which would cover the advance. "C Company" would attack from the southern end of the Redoubt.

The artillery fire was not forthcoming but we still attacked as planned and ran into heavy machine gun fire. "C Company suffered exceedingly heavy casualties and practically ceased to exist. I was wounded in the right shoulder and with Fred Crocker wounded in the knee, spent most of the night in a shell crater. Somehow we made our way back through no mans land (snowing quite heavily) to our lines at dawn.

11th April 1917
Spent the day No. 12 SH Field hospital near Camiers.

12th April 1917
Transferred to 2nd Australian General hospital Boulogne.

13th April 1917
Left for UK and Manchester.

In August 1921 he joined the Imperial War Graves Commission serving in many districts of the Somme. He was Foreman Gardener of The Rue, Sainte Colette, Corbie, Somme, France when his daughter Sylvia Maude was born in Manchester on the 4th March 1930. In 1931 he was awarded the O.B.E. for meritorious service.

In May 1940, at the height of the German blitzkrieg, he managed, by keeping just one day ahead of the Germans, to return to England, joining his wife and children, who had proceeded him to Manchester. During the war he was employed by the Manchester Parks Department at Heaton Park on essential food production. He returned to France at the end of hostilities to continue his work and make good the damage caused by the Second World War, finally retiring in August 1962 as a senior horticulture superintendent. He was also made an A.H. of the Royal Horticultural Society.

On retirement Harold moved first to Wiveliscombe, then Dunster and Minehead until 1975, when he moved to Walkden in Lancashire to be nearer his youngest son. His wife Maud died in December 1982, and he continued living in Walkden, retaining his independence, and looking after himself in spite of many disabilities until his death on the 1st April 1989.

He left a married daughter, Sylvia Maud Godsell (1930 -2006) and family in New Zealand and two sons, Harold James Luxton (1924-2016) and family in Folkestone, Kent and Geoffrey William Luxton (1931-2002), the director of a small electronic company in Manchester. I have a photograph of his eldest son Harold James Luxton(1924-2016) no. 14609053, Royal Electrical and Mechanical Engineers, taken in May 1943, when he joined the army. He is dressed in a 1940 pattern battledress blouse and has the cap badge of the R.E. M.E. on his side cap. Side caps were beginning to be phrased out in 1943 as the standard head-dress of most English and Welsh line infantry regiments and corps. Harold was demobbed in June 1947.

24

JOHN LUXTON (1817-1845), MASON OF SKILGATE AND HIS FAMILY

See tree 11

John Luxton (1817-1845), the third son of Isaac Luxton (1789-1838) and his wife Judith Skinner, was baptised at Skilgate on the 31st March 1817. He married Mary Ann Atkins, the daughter of John Atkins, a Skilgate blacksmith, in the parish church on the 8th March 1843. The marriage was of short duration, however, as John died at Skilgate on the 11th March 1845, just two years after the wedding. Mary Ann was present at her husband's death and for some reason there was a delay of eleven days before his burial at Skilgate on the 22nd March. He was aged 28 and his death certificate records that he died from phthisis pulmonalis which is more commonly called consumption. A modern doctor would probably diagnose his fatal illness as silicosis induced by the stone dust in his trade as a mason. His brother James also a mason, who died aged 48 in 1861 was another likely victim of this disease.

John's widow, Mary Ann, was left with an infant son John (1843-1928), born at Skilgate on the 12th May 1843. She married at Skilgate for a second time on the 26th June 1851, to John Greenslade, a servant at Kingston St. Mary, the son of William Greenslade, a dairyman. By her second husband Mary Ann had, "four flaxen haired very pretty daughters"[192]. John Luxton, junior, however, was not happy with the new family arrangement and in 1851 when he was aged six he was living with his uncle James Atkins, a veterinary surgeon and family at Red Croft, Skilgate. John, aged 18, was living in 1861 at Kendale Farm, Exton, in west Somerset where he was employed as a carter for John How a 57 year old farmer of 300 acres, employing two men and two boys.

---

[192] See letter from Mrs Marjorie Shaw, dated 29th November 1976.

In the mid-nineteenth century steam power was responsible for a huge transformation in people's lives. Railways were stretching over the country, rendering a transport and interchange of commodities possible with a quickness and at prices that earlier generations could never have dreamt of. Gas was becoming quite a common illuminent, while oil lamps replaced the rushlight and tallow flares of an earlier age. John was one of many rural dwellers who took the opportunity offered by the new railway network to seek a better life in London.

He left Somerset at an early age and for a time he lived with his cousin Edgar and Millie Atkins who bred shire horses on a farm at Toot's Mill in Ongar, Essex. He soon moved on to London where he set up his own milk delivery business in Limehouse and Paddington, The Royal Shorthorn Dairy at Paddington Green[193]. In London he met Eliza Reeves who was born in Wisborough Green in West Sussex, a place noted for its annual marbles contest. Eliza had travelled to London in one of the first trains of the new London to Brighton Railway. A man carrying a red flag had ridden on horseback in front of the train and the journey in an open top carriage had taken five hours! John and Eliza were married in Kensington parish church on the 4th December 1865. John who was illiterate signed the marriage register with his mark. By April 1870 the couple were settled at 64 Stainsby Road, Limehouse where the 1871 census lists John a 27 year old dairyman, his wife Eliza 30 and their children Eliza 4 and John 3 and Mary A aged eleven months. John and family later moved to Selhurst north of Croydon where again he ran a milk business.

He was impressed by the opening of the London to Brighton Railway which coincided with the opening of the Croydon Cattle Market in this wood engraved print of 1851. This was adjacent to the railway line at South Croydon and he moved there by 1875, first working as a general labourer before farming at Luxton's Farm, 26, Sanderstead Road, South Croydon where he was the manager for a cattle dealer. When the census was taken on 3rd April 1881 John Luxton, aged 37, general labourer, his wife Eliza, aged 40, with their six children Eliza14, John

---

[193] See letters of 7th July 1983 and 6th February 2001 and other correspondence from Cyril Luxton(1920-2009) of Hove a grandson of Johnnie Dear who supplied me much of these personal details of the family.

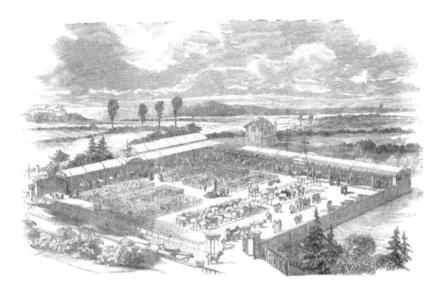

J.13, Mary A.10, William A.8, George 6, and Walter aged 2 were living at 6 Elm Cots, Sanderstead Road, Croydon, Surrey.

Ten years later in 1891 John Luxton, 49, was a "cattle labourer drover" at 26, Sanderstead Road, his wife Eliza was 53 and their children at home were John James Luxton 23 "Driver Drover", Mary 20, domestic servant, William18, gardener, George16, porter, and Walter12, scholar. They were still at 26 Sanderstead Road in 1901 when John 59 was the foreman for a cattle dealer, Eliza 64, Mary30, William 28, jobbing gardener, George 26, bricklayer and Walter22, was a milkman. Elm Cottage, 26, Sanderstead Road was where John, cattle dealer, was living in 1911, aged 69, and wife Eliza, 74, with daughter Mary, 40, single domestic and 15 year old grand daughter, Lottie Parfitt, shop assistant. In June 1913 when a herd of pure bred Sussex belonging to Sir Henry Bell were auctioned, Mr. Luxton of Croydon, paid 18 gns for one of the cattle and also bought a Guernsey bull for 13 guineas.[194]. He prospered well but the land at Sanderstead Road was eventually taken over as a recreation ground by the local authority.

John then obtained what was to become known as Luxton's Yards, South Croydon, adjacent to Croydon Cattle Market. He prospered here

---

[194] Surrey Mirror, Friday 6th June 1913.

too and was one of the biggest horse and cattle dealers in the south of England but preferred horses to cattle. He had dealings with the Chartwell Estate in Westerham, Kent which Churchill bought in September 1922 and knew Winston Churchill who gave him one of his cigars. Churchill, a great swearer and curser, had a cinema in the basement and qualified as a veterinary surgeon before he died.

John who had keen blue eyes was known affectionately by his wife and children as "Johnnie Dear" and I possess a photograph of him taken c.1916. He is standing with his horse and trap outside the White Lion, Warlingham, one of his favourite haunts. A large robust man, weighing about 18 stone, with a neatly clipped Van Dyke beard and moustache, he is wearing a heavy blue "Milton" coat, gloves, stout boots, and a curled brim bowler. Endowed with immense physical strength he once grappled with a bull which attacked him. He saved himself by poking the bull in the eye and holding it by the ring in its nose.

John spent the evening of 23rd June 1906 at the White Lion, Warlingham. He had met Robert Thompson, a farmer of Hamsey Green farm at Hammond & Hastings, the ironmongers in Croydon, earlier that day. They adjourned to the Greyhound Hotel where they had two whiskies. Thompson then drove them in his horse and cart to the Swan and Sugar Loaf, where they had a further glass of whisky. From there they went

to Mr. Thompson's meadow at Hamsey Green, where Luxton bought two cows. Their next stop was the White Lion to celebrate. They left there gone ten and drove to the top of Sanderstead Hill from where Luxton made his way home. Thompson continued on his way too. Two patrolling policemen were cycling along when they heard a horse and cart being driven furiously in their rear. To avoid a collision they moved to the side of the road. As the cart passed they could see the driver swaying from side to side while the horse and cart zig-zagged all over the road. They went cycling in pursuit and finally caught up with Thompson at Hamsey Green Pond. Thompson rolled out of the cart and they could see he was drunk. At the Oxted Petty Sessions Thompson was fined 30s. and 4s. costs.[195]

John enjoyed his gin and as a result of too much drink he had several serious accidents in his horse and trap. On one occasion he was thrown in the snow where he lay several hours with a broken arm, before being found. In his old age he was thrown head first from his trap, and he lost his eyesight after the end of the 1914-18 war. Walter, his youngest son, purchased the Brighton Road yards from John who spent the rest of his days in retirement at Florence Cottages, Brighton Road. His grandson Wilf Luxton visited him every Sunday morning and was with him the day he died. On that final day his grandfather was laid out on his great big bed breathing very heavily before he died in the early afternoon.

John Luxton of 26 Sanderstead Road, Croydon, cattle dealer, was in his prime when he made and signed his will with a mark on the 4th June 1909. He appointed his sons William and Walter Henry Luxton, as executors and trustees and they were to sell, call in and convert into money all his property both real and personal. The money produced was to pay his funeral and testamentary expenses and debts and the residue was to be invested in trust "to pay the income there of to my wife during her life and after her decease in trust for all my children ....in equal shares". In photograph on next page Johnnie Dear is in his garden at Florence Cottage in the mid 1920s with his daughter Lottie, and his grand-daughter Phyllis Parfitt and child.

Eliza Luxton died, aged 86, on the 16th March 1923 and John Luxton of 7 Florence Cottages, Brighton Road, Croydon, died, aged 86, on the

---

[195] Croydon Chronicle, Saturday, 14th July 1906.

15th January 1928. The couple lie buried at Queen's Road Cemetery, Croydon. Probate of his personal estate valued at £739..11s..3d was granted to his youngest son, Walter Henry Luxton, cattle dealer, on the 17th March 1928.

"Johnnie Dear" and Eliza had six children. Eliza, their eldest child, born on the 7th June 1866 at 16 Burgess Street, Limehouse was followed by John James (1868-1947), born at 14 Francis Street, Limehouse on the 4th February 1868, Mary Ann Charlotte born at 64 Stainsby Road, Limehouse on the 18th April 1870, William Arthur born at 14 Bridge Terrace, Paddington on the 1st October 1872, George born at 4 Gloucester Terrace, Gloucester Road, Croydon on the 13th March 1875 and Walter Henry born in Croydon on the 13th November 1878. Eliza (1866-1963), the eldest daughter, married William Parfitt, a labourer, at St. Augustine's Church, Croydon on the 3rd June 1895. In 1901 and 1911 they lived close to her parents at 16 Sanderstead Road. The couple who later lived at Waddon, on the west side of Croydon had four daughters before Eliza was widowed at an early age. In July 1945 she was granted administration of her sister Mary Ann Charlotte Luxton's will. Eliza of 124 Crawley Crescent, Waddon, widow of William Parfitt, labourer in Sanitary Department, died 11th January 1963.

The eldest son, John James Luxton (1868-1947), aged 27, and a carman of 26 Sanderstead Road, married Clara Dolding, aged 22, of 27 Sanderstead Road at St. Augustine's Church Croydon, on the 14th October 1895. Jim, as he was called, worked as a cattle drover for his father who was the manager for a cattle dealer but when his father refused to raise his salary he left to work for Yates the Corn and Seed Chandler at 35 High Street, South Croydon. Jim and his wife lived over the shop where their first three children, James, William and Lily were born.

The family moved to 74 Tanfield Road, Croydon, where Charles Henry Luxton (1907-1984), their youngest child was born. In 1911 the family, living at 1 Parker Road, South Croydon, were John James, 43, foreman to a corn merchant, Clara his wife, 37, born in Bexley Heath, John James, 14, left school, Clara Lilian 13, William Ralf 10 and Charles Henry 4. Some time later Jim Luxton was working as a labourer for Crowley's Brewery, High Street, Croydon and drove their horse drawn dray. He continued to work for Crowley's until his retirement. John J is listed in the 1939 register as an unemployed brewer's drayman, living at 23 A, Church Road, Croydon with his wife Clara and son William Ralf, unemployed postman. He then had a newspaper stand outside a well known local landmark, "The Swan and Sugar Loaf" at South Croydon which he ran for some years prior to his death. John James Luxton was living at 53 Church Road, Croydon when he died aged 79 of heart disease at Woodcroft Road, Croydon on the 18th November 1947. Clara, his widow, died aged 83 at Mayday Hospital, Mayday Road, Thornton Heath on the 17th February 1957.

The couple were living at 1 Parker Road, Croydon when their eldest son John James Luxton (1896-1917) enlisted in September 1914 in the Queen's Royal West Surrey Regiment at Bury St. Edmund's where he was residing. John served in France and Flanders with the Fourth Battalion from July 1916 and he was involved in the third battle for Ypres known as Passchendaele which lasted from 7th June until 6th November 1917. A Corporal in the Suffolk Regiment aged 21 he was killed fighting on Monday the 19th November 1917 when the main thrust was over.[196] He has no known grave but is commemorated on panel 40-41 on the Tyne Cot Memorial in Zonnebeke, West-Vlaanderen, Belgium. Further details on this branch of the family are contained in the family tree.

John and Eliza's second daughter, Mary Ann Charlotte Luxton (1870-1945), never married, and was known as Lot or Lottie. Lottie became governess to the daughters of a wealthy tea-grower who lived at Caterham-on-the-Hill. It is thought that she stayed with the family until her mother's illness and her father's blindness when she returned home to care for them. Lottie was 'a very dear and kind person' who kept in

---

[196] See letter dated 26th January 1985 from Queenie Luxton 111 St. Peters Street, South Croydon and the Croydon Advertiser for 15th December 1917 and the Croydon Roll of Honour.

touch with the various members of the family including her father's west country relatives. For a time at the height of the bombing in the 1939-1945 war she went to stay with a relative or friend at Barnstaple. When her brother George lost his wife during the war she went to stay and look after him at Rosedean, Findon Road, Worthing where George had his retirement home. She died there on the 29th April 1945, leaving a personal estate valued at £122..2..8 to her eldest sister Eliza Parfitt, widow. Lottie is buried at Queen's Road Cemetery, Croydon.

William Arthur Luxton (1872-1935), the second son of John and Eliza Luxton, was a jobbing gardener who lived at Florence Cottages, Purley, a few doors away from his parents. A Private in the 6th Battalion he was listed as a war casualty in November 1915.[197] As a result of horrendous experiences in the Great War he suffered badly with his nerves and was committed to Warlingham Park Hospital, Chelsham, Surrey, where he remained for the rest of his days. The hospital which opened in 1903 as the Croydon Mental Hospital was a pioneer psychiatric hospital. He died aged 62 on the 12th January 1935 and is buried in Queen's Road Cemetery, Croydon. William Arthur and his wife Winifred Corke, who he married at the Register Office, Camberwell, on the 19th September 1902, are listed in 1911 with daughters Vera 10 and Iris 2 living at 3 Salisbury Villas in Lower Road, Kenley, Coulsdon. Winifred, William's widow of 684 Brighton Road, Purley died aged 84 at Purley Cottage Hospital, Croydon on the 27th April 1953.

They had three children. Doris Gwendolene Vera, born 15th June 1900, before her parents' marriage, was baptised the 14th April 1912 at St. James in Coulsdon. Vera, of Florence Cottages, Brighton Road, a 23 year old typist, married George Leslie Ronald Ritchings in Christchurch, Purley, on 30th June 1923. Her address was in Homefield Road, Coulsdon, when she died on 22nd April 1987, leaving an estate valued £93,338. Her sister Iris Winifred Audrey, born on 9th May 1909, married George Charles Parkinson at Christchurch, Purley, on 4th July 1940. Iris died in 1997. Basil William Roy Luxton (1913-1992), the youngest sibling, born on the 15th November 1913 enlisted in the Royal Artillery in 1940. He became a prominent Labour member of

---

[197] Surrey Mirror, Friday 5th November 1915.

Purley Urban District Council and he died on 19th March 1992, leaving an estate valued at £341,388.

George Luxton (1875-1944), the third son of John and Eliza Luxton, was in the building trade for many years but when he married Annie Maud Collins in 1907 he became a dairyman, and assisted by his wife Annie, he was living at 76 Avenue Road, Beckenham, Kent in 1911. The couple had lost a child but had a six month old daughter, Marjorie, and lived in a five room property. They established Church Farm Dairy at Nutfield Road, Merstham, Surrey and made a great success of the business. His wife ran the dairy shop and he had a milk delivery business. He was a member of the Redhill & Reigate Daiyman's Association which increased the price of milk by one penny per quart on the 26th September 1915 because, as a result of the war, there was a serious scarcity of labour, an increased cost of cows, and high prices for cattle feeding stuffs.[198]

When the business was destroyed by a land mine in 1940, he decided it was too much to try to rebuild in view of his age, so he sold out to a national company. He and his wife Annie retired to live at Rosedean, Findon Road, Worthing. Annie Maud died at Charnwood Nursing Home, Farncombe Road, Worthing on the 26th September 1941 leaving a personal estate valued at £595..14s..6d to her husband George, a retired dairyman. She was buried at Durrington.

George had made and signed his will many years before on the 13th September 1924 when he was a dairyman at Church Farm Dairy, South Merstham, Surrey. He gave his sister Mary Ann Lottie Luxton "the fifty pounds £5 per cent War Loan 1927-1947 (Registered No 28137) in consideration of her devotion to my father and mother....". The rest of his estate he left to his wife Annie Maud whom he appointed sole executrix. When George died on the 19th June 1944 he left a personal estate valued at £8821..18s..1d to their married daughter, Marjorie Alice Shaw (1910-2000), the wife of John Shaw.

Walter Henry Luxton (1878-1937), John and Eliza's youngest son, was a 23 boiler riveter, visitor, in household of George Ward, in Croydon in 1901. He married Nellie Gadsdon at St. Lawrence Church, Catford, Lewisham on the 27th June 1907. In the 1911 census Walter, 32, a cattle

---

[198] Surrey Mirror, Friday 24th September 1915.

dealer employing two, lived in a five room property at 18 Uplands Road, Croydon with his wife Nellie, 24, and son John 2 and his mother in law. Walter, who as noted earlier, worked with his father and purchased the Brighton Road Yards from him, continued there as a cattle dealer until about 1927/28. Then because of the increase in road traffic he moved the business to Ballard's Farm in the Shirley/Addington area but resided at "Clovelly" 405 Brighton Road, South Croydon as he and his wife did not wish to live at Ballard's.

He was running the business in the Brighton Road Yards in June 1924 when an outbreak of foot and mouth disease destroyed his valuable herd of cattle. The Surrey Mirror, Friday 27th June, 1924, carried the following graphic account:-

Foot and Mouth Disease
Whole herd destroyed at Croydon

Within a few days of a farm sale of bullocks at Sutton on Friday, foot and mouth disease broke out, and one cow, three heifers and four calves were subsequently traced to Mr W. Luxton, of "The Fair"ground, Brighton Road, Croydon. A cow purchased from this herd fell ill from foot and mouth disease at the Mental Hospital Warlingham on Monday night, and later another cow, also purchased from Mr. Luxton, was found to be diseased, and had to be killed. It is hoped to save the remainder of the herd. On Tuesday the disease was traced to Mr. Luxton's valuable herd of 28 cattle. The whole of the herd was shot by the police on Wednesday morning, and burned late at night in the presence of hundreds of people. An order has been issued prohibiting movement within two miles of the infected field.

An old newspaper cutting[199] provides further details of the epidemic:-

Valuable Herd Shot
Foot and Mouth Disease in Croydon
Remarkable Scenes off Brighton Road
Huge Night Pyre

---

[199] Contained in correspondence from the late Cyril Luxton of Hove.

Foot and mouth disease has broken out in Croydon, and on Wednesday morning a valuable herd of cattle belonging to Messrs Luxton and Son in an enclosure known as the Fairfield, just below Purley Oaks Station, and a few yards from the main Brighton Road, was slaughtered with the humane killer. The Ministry of Agriculture insist on the use of this method.

Two cows were on Tuesday discovered to be infected with the disease, and to avoid the risk of further infection the whole herd of twenty-eight, many with calf, was expeditiously dispatched in the presence of an inspector of the Ministry of Agriculture.

During the day every precaution was taken to isolate the field, warning notices in heavy red type and buckets containing strong disinfectant were placed at the entrances, and a gang of men were got together to dig a huge pit in the centre of the field-a few yards from the pen where the cattle were slaughtered-into which tons of coal and wood and large quantities of straw with other highly inflammable material were thrown. Late at night the carcases were consumed in an enormous fire. The glow from which could be discerned from miles around, while the roasting flesh threw off a pungent and not altogether unsavoury odour. The carcases were principally those of healthy animals in fine bodily condition. They were all treated with disinfectants immediately after being shot.

Hundreds of people gathered on Castle Hill and in the approach to Purley Oaks Station to witness the gruesome sight of horses dragging the dead cattle to the edge of the pit.

Passenger traffic on the Brighton Road slowed up to get a view of the unusual spectacle, and many timorous passers-by instinctively held hankerchiefs to their mouths until well away from the field.

The burning of the carcases occupied many hours and during Thursday the pit was filled in on the black and smouldering heap—

--Messrs Luxton and son are well known cattle dealers, and the head of the firm is one of Croydon's oldest tradesmen.

We understand that compensation will be made by the Ministry of Agriculture in respect of the slaughtered herd, but this will partially cover the loss only. Many of the animals were of considerable value as milkers.

Walter set about rebuilding the herd when he moved the business to Ballard's Farm. In September 1928 he paid £33, purchasing stock at the auction of Mr C. V. Manwaring's dairy short horns and cross bred cows.[200] The following month he attended Mr. Leveson Gower's auction of his pedigree shorthorn cattle at Titsey Place where he paid 36 guineas, the top price of the sale, for "Titsey Fair Bird," a light roan calved in May 1926, and bred at Titsey. "Snowberry Second,"a non pedigree animal, born in 1922, and bred at Titsey was purchased for 23 guineas and "Gresham Snowball" bred at Titsey was bought for 18 guineas.[201]

I have a photograph of Walter Henry Luxton and his wife Nellie and two of their children, Wilfred George and Cyril in their Aldis motor car. Jack, the eldest son took the picture. The car has "artillery wheels" and Nellie is wearing a ladies bell-shaped "cloche" hat which was fashionable in the early 1920s.

Another intriguing photograph is of a cattle sale at Fox Farm, Sanderstead in September 1931. Arthur A. Brown of Fuller Moon and Fuller, is auctioning a cow in a straw strewn ring, surrounded by farmers and cattle dealers. Walter Henry Luxton, a stout man with a walking stick in his right hand, is standing eighth from the right in the front row in photograph below. He is wearing a peaked cap and has an unbuttoned overcoat over his suit.

---

[200] Kent and Sussex Courier, Friday 28th September 1928
[201] Surrey Mirror, Friday19th October1928

Walter, a farmer and cattle dealer of "Clovelly" 405 Brighton Road, Croydon made his Will on the 26th November 1936. He appointed his wife Nellie Luxton and two friends as trustees to be the executors of his estate. To his son Wilfred George Luxton he gave "the goodwill of my business of a cattle dealer at present carried on by me at 405 Brighton Road Surrey". The trustees were to sell the rest of his estate and invest the money and the income was to be paid to his widow and then divided equally between his sons, Wilfred George and Cyril Luxton. Walter died aged 58 on the 3rd January 1937, leaving a personal estate valued at £2555..0s..5d. He and his wife Nellie are buried at Queen's Road Cemetery, Croydon, a few graves along from his parents.

The report of Walter's funeral appeared in The Croydon Advertiser:-

Mr. W.H. LUXTON
DEATH OF WELL KNOWN
CATTLE SALESMAN

The death occurred on Sunday after a long illness of Mr. W. H. Luxton, aged 58, of 405, Brighton Road, Croydon, one of the best known cattle salesmen in the south of England,

He followed his father in the business at a time when Croydon was a good class suburb and at the same time had most of the characteristics of a market town. There was a Corn Exchange in Katharine Street and the cattle market was of considerable importance. Engaged in the cattle trade for nearly forty years, Mr Luxton travelled extensively and there is scarcely a market town throughout Surrey, Kent, Sussex and Hampshire where he was not known. He also had an extensive connection in Bucks and Bedfordshire and the Midlands. He bought extensively for hospitals and other institutions.

Although during his lifetime he saw the gradual decline of Croydon's interest in agriculture, until neither corn nor cattle market are now held here, his own business activities were pursued over a very wide area.

He belonged to an old Croydon family, was very popular among a wide circle of friends and in all his business transactions was looked upon as a man of the utmost integrity.

A keen lover of flowers, Mr Luxton was never seen without a buttonhole in his coat and he was an enthusiastic grower of roses. His health was good until fifteen months ago. The funeral took place at St. Augustine's Church, South Croydon, on Thursday.

The eldest son, Walter John Luxton (1908-1949), in his early years spent such a great deal of time with his grandfather John Luxton and his father Walter he became known as Jack, to prevent confusion. He began his working life as a cattle salesman but was an engineer officer in the merchant navy during the 1939-45 war.

The 1939 Register lists him as involved in armament transport, living with his wife Phyllis M, born 25th December 1907 at 200 Selhurst Road, Croydon. His home port was Barry in South Wales. Barry lost five hundred out of the 3500 to 4000 merchant seaman registered in the port during the war, which was more in proportion to her size than any other port in the country. Jack rented a bungalow in Whitchurch, a suburb of Cardiff, and his wife Mildred moved there from Croydon to be with him when he returned to base. Voyages were made to

Alexandria, in Egypt and to Australia and elsewhere. When Jack's ship was torpedoed in the South Seas it went down in two minutes and he was adrift in an open boat, dressed only in his shorts and singlet for twelve days[202]. He was rescued but invalided out of the navy. His health deteriorated due to the exposure he had suffered and he died in 1949. Jack's widow Mildred went to live in California where after two marriages she died in 1994.

Wilfred George Luxton (1911-1998), the second son, farmed with his father Walter Henry Luxton. He served in the RAF during the Second World War and when the war was over he lived and worked in Sheffield, Yorkshire but retired to live in Barry in 1977. His brother Cyril (1920-2009) joined the RAF in early 1940, and had four years service in the Middle East. He later lived in Maidstone before settling in the Brighton area. Towards the end of his life Cyril's eyesight worsened and it became necessary for him to go into St. Michael's Nursing Home in Hove where he died on the 16th February 2009. He is buried in Hove Cemetery. The photograph is of Wilfred George Luxton with his brother Cyril on right.

Wilf's daughter Christine lives in Hertfordshire and his son, Peter John Luxton, who was a flight engineer with Ward Airlines in Toronto now resides in Vancouver. This concludes my account of the descendants of John Luxton (1817-1845) of Skilgate in Somerset.

---

[202] In letter of 15th October 1976 his brother Cyril Luxton says, "he sank & was adrift in Carribean Sea for nine days which eventually caused his death." Also see his letter of 19thJanuary 2001 which gives conflicting information.

25

JACOB LUXTON (1800-1868) STONEMASON
AT PARADISE IN CHIPSTABLE

See tree 12

The parish of Chipstable, situated on the River Tone in the red soil hills of north west Somerset derives its name from the Anglo-Saxon Sceap – estaple i.e. sheep market although sheep markets have not been held there for centuries. Chipstable is bounded by the parishes of Wiveliscombe, Milverton, Huish Champflower, Raddington and Clayhanger which lies in Devon. Wiveliscombe the nearest town is about $2^3/_4$ miles from the church by the Bulland Road. Taunton is distant about 13 miles, Wellington nine miles.

Collinson in his History of Somerset describes Chipstable as "a romantic spot varied with hills, dales, woods and craggy rocks. The rocks are a kind of pale granite, full of red, blue and rust coloured veins. In the hedges are curious mosses and mountain ash grows spontaneously". Conan Doyle showed he had some acquaintance with it in his novel, Micah Clarke, and it was formerly a part of Exmoor when Exmoor covered a considerably wider district than it does now. It lies in stag and fox hunting country and one rector in the last century kept his own hounds. At no time in the nineteenth century save in 1871 did the population exceed 400, and the increased figures for that year, 420, were due to the influx of navvies for the tunnels and viaduct on the railway line constructed between Wiveliscombe and Venn Cross.

In 1969 I knew none of this. I had not even heard of Chipstable. I knew that my grandfather, E.A. Luxton, was baptised in All Saints Church, Clevedon, in 1875, the son of George Luxton, mason, but a search of the registers at Clevedon and Nailsea where the family later settled, indicated that George had arrived in the area in the 1860s. I needed to know where George came from. I wrote to the General Register Office, Somerset House where a search in the 1871 Clevedon census revealed George Luxton, 23, mason, was born in Chipstable. From Crockford's Clerical Directory I acquired the name and the address of the rector. I wrote and in return the rector kindly supplied details from the Chipstable parish registers. George Luxton, my great grandfather, born in 1847, was the last but one of eleven children born to Jacob Luxton, mason and master bricklayer and his wife, Harriet Greenway.

Jacob Luxton (1800-1868), fourth son of Isaac Luxton (1751-1834) and Mary North of Hutchings Farm, Petton, Bampton Devon, was baptised Jacob Luxon at Petton on Wednesday 15th January 1800. He qualified as a stone mason and was living in the neighbouring parish of Raddington, when he married Harriet Greenway, aged 18, at St. Michael's (in author's photo below) the parish church of Milverton, Somerset on Thursday 24th February 1826. Jacob's sister, Jane Luxton, was a witness to the marriage. Harriet, the daughter of Charles Greenway and his wife Elizabeth Cleeve, was baptised at Milverton, on the 28th February 1808. The young couple settled in Chipstable which was the home village of Harriet's parents who married there on the 25th November 1806. The 1846 Poll books for the Wiveliscombe Polling District which includes Chipstable, lists Jacob Luxton with freehold house and land at Paradise, Chipstable in 1832 and 1834. Paradise is described in the Poor Rate Book 1847-1856 for Chipstable as two cottages and a garden measuring 10 poles, ratable value £3. Jacob Luxton occupied one of these cottages and the other was occupied by

Amy Hart. In the years 1853-1856, Jacob Luxton and family were the sole occupants of Paradise.

My brother and I visited Taunton Record Office where we consulted the 1840 Chipstable Tithe map and the attached commutation document dated 16ᵗʰ April 1841. Paradise, occupied by Jacob Luxton and family, was listed as property No. 667, a cottage and garden measuring 13 poles. The rent charge payable to the rector was 3d. Paradise in the centre of the village, adjoined the churchyard wall of the ancient parish church of All Saints on its northern side. It overlooked the church and its graveyard and is probably the thatched cottage which is partially in the pre-1868 view below of All Saints, Chipstable.

This painting shows how the church looked before it was rebuilt in 1868.

In 1841 the Chipstable census lists Jacob, 40, mason, and his wife Harriet, 30, living in the village with their young family, Charles 10, Elizabeth 7, Mary 5 and Isaac 2. The 1851 census records that Jacob Luxton, 51, master bricklayer, his wife Harriet and six of their children were still living at Paradise Cottage, Chipstable. The eldest Charles, 21, was a journeyman bricklayer, Isaac, 12, was a bricklayer's labourer. Jane, 9, Ann, 6 and George 3, were scholars and John was a 5 months old baby.

Harriet, who suffered with valvular heart disease for four years, died, aged 46, at Chipstable on the 16ᵗʰ November 1854. Jacob was present at her death. Harriet was buried in the churchyard four days later on the 20ᵗʰ November and in the years ahead family members began to go their own way. Even at this distance in time one feels the tragedy of Harriet's early death, especially as her younger children were now motherless. The arrival of the Railway Age set people free to move more easily and within little more than a decade Jacob's large family had dispersed elsewhere. The 1861 census finds Jacob Luxton 61, widower, building mason, resident with the Parkman family at Daniel Cottage. This place is identified with Dinhill Cottage which in

1841 formed part of Chipstable farm. Jacob's home, Dinhill Cottage was a derelict out building at the farm when I took this photograph.

In the same census Jacob's son, Isaac, 23, a building mason, his wife Jane and their children Charley 2 and Mary aged 15 minutes were living at Larcombe's Cottage (in photo below). Isaac's younger brother George, aged 14, mason's labourer, my great grandfather was dwelling with the family.

Disaster struck the Luxton's for a second time in February 1863 when Isaac died at the early age of 24 from what his death certificate describes as phthisis. This was probably silicosis caused by the stone dust created by his work as a mason. The widow Jane remarried James Smith in

September 1864 and had a second family. Early in the 20th century the Smiths were recorded as having had a long and honourable connection with change ringing the peal of bells in the parish church.

My great grandfather, George (1847-1918), and brother John (1850-1925), upon the death of Isaac, moved to Clevedon in east Somerset where an elder sister, Jane married William Stock a labourer, on the 14th November 1864. Both brothers settled in the Clevedon and Nailsea area where they married in 1869 and produced large families.

His wife dead and his children dispersed, Jacob may have developed a drink problem in later life. The death of Isaac, his son in 1863, was a further depressing blow to Jacob who died at Chipstable on the 23rd February 1868, following two months paralysis. James Smith, who married Isaac's widow, Jane, was present at his death. Jacob Luxton, stone mason, aged 68 was buried at Chipstable on Sunday 1st March 1868, the fifth anniversary of his son Isaac's burial.

Jacob and Harriet had eleven children, six boys and five girls, who were baptised at All Saints the parish church of Chipstable. Two of the boys died in infancy. Jacob, a son baptised on the 10th August 1829, died aged eight months and was buried there on the 4th April 1830. Thomas baptised on the 12th November 1840, died of asthma aged five months on the 9th April and was buried on the 16th April 1841. The four remaining brothers, Charles (1831-1911), baptised 6th February 1831, Isaac (1838-1863), born on the 28th July 1838, George (1847-1918), baptised the 1st August 1847 and John (1850-1925), baptised on the 20th October 1850, married and raised families. The three eldest were stone masons but John, the youngest, who qualified as a cooper, made his living as a chimney sweep. They feature in future chapters.

Emma, the eldest girl and first born, baptised on the 13th August 1827, was a 16 year old servant, when she died of inflammatory fever on the 12th August 1843. She was buried at Chipstable on the 20th August 1843. Two of her closest siblings, Charles and Elizabeth, named their eldest daughters, Emma, in tribute to her memory. The four remaining daughters married and raised families. The three eldest emigrated to Canada where their cousin, Thomas Luxton (1826-1893), of Hutchings Farm had settled in the early 1850s, soon followed by his sisters Jane and Mary about 1855.

Elizabeth, baptised on the 11th August 1833, led the exodus. In 1851 she was a 19 year old house servant at the 350 acre Kittisford Farm, in Kittisford, Somerset which employed 20 labourers. She married William Yeandle, a 25 year old labourer, at Chipstable, on 9th October 1854. With a young family the couple were settled in Ontario by 1859 when their eldest daughter, Emma, was born. By 1861 William, 30, a farmer, and Elizabeth, 27, with three children were living in a log house in the township of Dunwich in Elgin County. Ten years later, in1871, with seven children they were farming in the township of Southwold.

Elizabeth, a 57 year old widow, was living in 1891 with her eldest son Samuel 35, a farmer, and his wife, Jennie, in Elgin East, Yarmouth. Elizabeth died in1898 and she is buried with her husband William (1830-1888) at St. Thomas, Elgin County, Ontario, where a grey granite headstone commemorates Elizabeth and other family members.

Her sister, Mary, born on the 12th October, and baptised on the 1st November 1835, emigrated to Canada in 1865. In 1871 she was a servant in London, Ontario to Lawrence Lawless, a postmaster and his family. At the age of 40 she married on the 6th January 1876 to a widower, George Johnston, a 50 year old herdsman, in North Street, London, Ontario. The census on 15th April 1901 lists George Johnston, 75 and Mary 65, living in retirement in Hullett, Huron County, Ontario. Their son Frederick (1876-1967) a painter, married Sarah Hill on 29th January 1902 and they had a son Harold who was born in January 1906. Mary, a 75 year old widow, was living on her own in Hullett in the 1911 census. She died aged 80 from chronic Bright's disease on 9th June 1916 and she lies buried with her family in Londesborough Cemetery, Hullett, Huron County, Ontario.

Jane baptised on the 20th March 1842 married William Stock, a labourer, at Clevedon parish church on the 14th November 1864. The couple emigrated to Canada in 1865, sailing on the SS. Peruvian from Liverpool to Quebec. They were living in Yarmouth near St. Thomas, Ontario when sons, Thomas William Stock was born in 1871, and Walter John Stock in 1874. They had moved to Port Stanley, a small port that was used from 1669 by French explorers and is still used today by boats fishing on Lake Erie when Jane died on 12th November 1878, due to complications in her sixth month of pregnancy. She was aged 36 and her religious denomination was Baptist. William Stock took a new wife in 1879. In 1881 he was a railroad labourer, living with his new wife, Maria Mckenzie, and family at Eckford near St. Thomas. Three more children were born and they may have moved to Ohio in U.S.A. by 1900.

Ann, the youngest daughter, baptised on the 8th April 1845 was 21 when she married Francis George Priest (1838-1926), a groom from Amersham, at Stratton Audley in Oxfordshire, on 4th June 1866. In 1871 they were living with a young family in Woburn, Buckinghamshire but had moved to live in the High Street, Amersham in the same county by

1881. They had issue six children in fifteen years. Ann died at home in High Street, Amersham, aged 66, from cirrhosis of the liver on 19th April 1911.

I first visited Chipstable at twilight in March 1970, and for a second time on a bright sunny day in April the following year. I took photographs of the church, the nave of which was rebuilt in 1869, and of cottages to the north of the churchyard. Paradise cottage, occupied by Jacob Luxton, no longer stood. Photographs were taken of Larcombe's Cottage and Dinhill Cottage which were also associated with the family. There were no Luxton monumental inscriptions and there were none in the church or churchyard in 1919, when the rector the Rev. A.T. Cameron transcribed the church and churchyard inscriptions.

I received a tangible link with my Chipstable past in March 1970, when my great uncle, Thomas John Luxton (1890-1972), gave me his father George Luxton's six inch boxwood and brass spirit level and a 24 inch brass folding rule. The spirit level had previously belonged to Isaac Luxton (d. 1863) and it has his initials scratched on it. A great aunt gave me George Luxton's framed certificate dated 26th March 1866, presented to him when he qualified as a mason.

A further link with Chipstable was forged in 1979 when I met Malcolm Luxton, a native of Cardiff and resident in Kent. Malcolm's great-grandfather, Charles Luxton (1859-1911), was the Charles aged 2 son of Isaac Luxton in the 1861 Chipstable census when the family lived at Larcombe's Cottage. Charles married at Wiveliscombe in 1880, and the newly married couple settled in Cardiff. Malcolm had independently traced his family to his three times great grandfather Jacob (1800-1868).

Malcolm drew my attention to a 38 page booklet, "Chipstable a Brief Sketch of the Parish and Church" (1919) by the rector of Chipstable, the Rev. A.T. Cameron. In 1980 I appealed to the Rev. M.J. Balchin, the incumbent, in the hope he could find me a copy. He replied that there appeared to be only one copy in the parish and that was not for sale. Malcolm and I decided to search for our own copies. When Malcolm informed me at Christmas 1991 he had acquired a copy in the Isle of Wight I redoubled my efforts, and in March 1992 was delighted to purchase a good copy from Ron Eastwood in Puriton, Bridgwater. It is a fascinating little read and supplies valuable local history knowledge vital to the family historian.

The book answered a number of questions such as where my great-grandfather George was educated. He had grown up in the mid 19th century before compulsory education was introduced by the 1870 Education Act. As a schoolteacher and former churchwarden, I was especially interested to read that it was through the untiring efforts of an Anglican clergyman, the Rev.Z. Edwards, Curate in Charge of Chipstable from about 1833-1842 that an elementary school was provided for the village. These were the years when Jacob and Harriet Luxton's young and growing family would be among the beneficiaries of schooling. The Rev. Edwards appealed to landowners and others interested in the parish and subscriptions were readily forthcoming. A bazaar held in aid of the school Building Fund was evidently a great success. In 1836 Henry Ball, a landowner, gave land at Easter – above – Church in Chipstable for the erection of a schoolhouse, "for the religious education and instruction of the children of the poor in the said Parish of Chipstable, in connection with the established church ....."

This first Schoolhouse was opposite the lynch gate where the building still is. It has been slightly extended but is basically the same as it was in the 1840s. It was built with an external staircase and had I think four rooms. There was a dwelling house on the ground floor and a schoolroom above. It was built free of debt, much of the labour being voluntary, especially the hauling of building materials. The playground was the adjoining lane and fields. The amount paid to the school mistress £10 per annum was probably supplemented by the scholars' fees. When Mr Nicholetts, a new incumbent, came as rector he placed the school on a new and flourishing basis, the number of scholars in 1856 being no less than 50. The school did a useful work and finally came to an end after the passing of the Education Act in 1870. It was replaced by a Board School built in 1876 and the old schoolroom was used for church religious and instruction purposes. I am proud to think that my great-grandfather George and his brothers and sisters received their schooling in this place.

The school accounts for 1838-1842 were interesting reading for me. Payments for 1838 include November 21st Jacob Luxton, for lime, 1/-; 12 cwt. Of coal 12/-; December 24th, two panes of Glass 1/2d.

In 1838 the young Queen Victoria was on the throne and Charles Dickens has left us an indelible image of an early Victorian Christmas which conjures up great poverty and social deprivation amid the bow front shop windows, top hats, snow and stage coaches. I like to imagine that my two times great-grandfather, Jacob, with money in his pocket that Christmas Eve of 1838, bought a goose and plum pudding so his family could celebrate the festive season. It is evident too that the census description of Jacob, as a mason and master bricklayer, fails to provide a full description of how he made his living. He almost certainly owned a horse and cart and was probably engaged as a tranter in conveying building materials and other supplies around Chipstable and its environs.[203] As he was a stonemason and bricklayer he probably had some part in the building of the schoolroom too.

When I had completed this article I sent a copy to the Rev. J.P. Bird, rector of Chipstable to enlist the help of residents with local knowledge. His churchwarden recalled that years ago when he worked for the Poole family who built early engines in Chipstable, old Mr Poole told him a story relating to Jacob Luxton and the Rev. Mr Nicholetts. It seems that Jacob was working on a barn at North Combe, a farm just to the north of the village with another man called John Venn on a Sunday. The rector was most put out and walked up to see the men at work. Finding them and not being satisfied as to their reasons for being at work he called out to them, "Luxton, you are a drunk and Venn a glutton". Strong stuff! I doubt the Rector won many friends. But the barn is still there and there are very similar barns at East Barn, Crooks and Dinhill. They are of an unusual design so the chances are Jacob had a hand in

---

[203] James Smith, born 1846, who married Jane Luxton(nee Vickery)(1838-1898) widow of Jacob's son Isaac(1838-1863) was a 16 year old carter in 1861 living at Lower Brown Farm, Huish Champflower. He was with Jacob when he died.

building them all.[204] The photographs are of the barn at North Combe in 2012.

There is a great deal more in the Rev. A.T. Cameron's booklet on Chipstable. The author observed that by 1919 the thatch on the old cottagers' dwellings had been replaced by slate or tiles. In the mid nineteenth century the parish tap had been supplied from what was an open well above the rectory. Through the efforts of Mr Nicholetts, rector 1857-1901, a pipe was run from this well to a point more convenient for the village to draw water, and the well was excavated and covered, the key being kept at the rectory. Mr Nicholetts also had an open watercourse to the village covered, the roadway widened, and the churchyard on the north side enlarged. An accumulation of earth against the north side of the church was taken away and deposited at the S.W. of the churchyard to level it. This work was occasioned by the rebuilding of the nave in 1869.

Jacob Luxton's old home Paradise Cottage, which abutted close to the church on this north side, was considered by Mr Nicholetts and the Vestry, as a detriment to the amenity of the church and churchyard. Its removal improved the northern approach to the church.

In 1919 the Church Chest contained other treasures for the family historian. These included the important Inclosure Award of 1836 and letters relating to the Old School-room Trust. The Vestry Minute Book in the rector's possession has the first entry in 1867. The Churchwarden's Accounts date from 1850. A survey of Chipstable made in 1840, discovered by the Rev H. F. Dunn, rector of Upton, was deposited with the rector. These and the Vestry Minute Book dating from early in 1800 and the Trust Deed of the Church Hall, Waterrow are documents I need to consult. I must journey again to Chipstable to see the parish records and Jacob's barns in the springtime when the hedge bank primroses are in flower.

---

[204] See letter dated 3rd July 1992 from Rev.J.P. Bird, The Rectory, Chipstable, Taunton, Somerset, TA4 2PZ. The story must date to sometime after 1857 when Nicholett's became incumbent but before the death of John Venn, a carpenter, in 1864. Thanks to Peter & Susannah Nurse for the barn photographs.

26

CHARLES LUXTON (1831-1911) MASON OF CHIPSTABLE SOMERSET AND LAMBETH, LONDON

See tree 12

Charles Luxton, the second son of Jacob Luxton (1800-1868) mason and his wife Harriet Greenway, was baptised at Chipstable on the 6th February 1831. When the census was taken on the 30th March 1851, he was a twenty year old unmarried bricklayer, living with his parents and family at Paradise in Chipstable.

Within a year or two he had moved to Taunton, and as Charles Luxton 22 year old mason of North Town Taunton, he married Louisa Byrd, 23 spinster, daughter of John Byrd, yarn spinner at the Register Office, Taunton on Christmas Day 1853. Both sign the register and the marriage was witnessed with the marks of John and Clara Byrd who were Louisa's father and sister.

The twosome settled in Louisa's home village of Uffculme, Devon where three children were born. Emma, daughter of Charles Luxton, journeyman mason and his wife Louisa Byrd, born on the 19th May 1856, was followed by a son Willie, born on the 5th October 1858, and Hannah born on the 19th November 1860.

In April 1859, Charles, a mason, summoned his employer Mr. Taylor at the Chard Petty Sessions, for a balance of wages, amounting to £2..19s..4½d. The Bench questioned Charles at some length and advised him that Mr. Taylor was liable to pay but as Mr. Taylor's residence was at Exeter the case must be heard there[205].

---

[205] Exeter and Plymouth Gazette, Saturday 9th April 1859.

Charles and Louisa separated on the 5th November 1860, because Louisa continued to live at home with her father, and Charles thought it much better to part than to be always living in animosity. He did not object to live with his wife but with his wife's family. He could never go back to live with her in Uffculme.

Charles moved into lodgings and in the census taken on the 7th April, 1861, Charles a 29 year old mason, was lodging with James Moore, a 55 year old lime burner and his family at Herbeds South in the nearby village of Hockworthy, Devon. Louisa, described as a 30 year old mason's wife, and her children, Emma 4, Willie 2 and Hannah 4 months were living at Myrtle Rose, Coldharbour, Uffculme (inset next page) with her widowed father, John Byrd, 57, who was an engine cleaner in a woollen mill. About the end of April Charles moved into lodgings with Mr. Thomas Broomfield in Hockworthy. Broomfield formed a good opinion of Charles who he said conducted himself in a, "Very proper manner; he was a very good workman, had plenty of work, was beloved by his employers, and those he worked with."

On Saturday night 21st July 1861 Charles, depressed by the failure of his marriage and rather the worse for liquor, came into his landlord's room at about half past ten and asked for a candle to go to bed with, and for some matches. He told Broomfield he was going to write a letter to his wife but the landlord tried to persuade him to leave it to the next day. Charles, having obtained the candle took a sort of inventory of his tools and then said to Broomfield, "Good night, old fellow, I shall not trouble you again!" The landlord replied, "Nonsense, Charley, go to bed like a good man, and don't trouble yourself like that." Charles then went upstairs to his room. Broomfield seeing his manner so altered went shortly afterwards to the door of his room, to see what he was about, and heard papers rustling within.

Thinking all was not right, after some hesitation, and consulting with others, he entered the room, and saw that Charles had an open razor in his hand. Without any hesitation he rushed forward and caught hold of him, saying, "My dear fellow, do you know what you are about?" He took the razor away from him and after some ado, restrained him from the rash act. Charles soon afterwards went to bed and another man stayed with him until the morning, when he was taken into custody.

P. C. Smith apprehended the prisoner about 6 o'clock on Sunday morning and found upon him a silver watch, knife, key, razor, etc.

At the Cullompton Divisional Petty Sessions on Monday 29th July 1861 Charles, "a tall, able-bodied man, 29 years of age, of Chipstable mason" was charged with having attempted to commit suicide, by cutting his throat with a razor, on Saturday night at his lodgings in Hockworthy.

Charles in his defence said that he was the worse for liquor or nothing of the sort would have occurred. He added that after retiring to his room he tried to open the door but found that someone was holding it and he could not pull it open. He then called out, "Just open the door, or I'll cut off your fingers." It was with the intention of doing this, he added, that he had the razor in his hand, but he would not have done it had he not been drunk. He told the court he had tried for seven years to live with his wife, who he said didn't want anything to do with him and whether he sent home money or sent home none, it was all the same. His wife had been sending him three or four letters a week to come home but he could never go back to live in Uffculme. Louisa had not come to see him, until last Tuesday, since Good Friday, and that he thought, was not showing a proper feeling for her husband. Charles told the court that he had no intention of destroying himself, that he was in liquor and hardly knew what he was about. The chairman, the Rev. John Huyshe observed but for drink, the prisoner then before the court would not have been there. The Bench dismissed the charge, exhorting the prisoner to give up drinking, except in moderation.

Louisa, his wife who had been in court, came forward with "a rather jaunty air" and said that she had a great desire to live with him, but he had no house for her. She was ready to leave her father at any time and go to live with him. Charles said that he had no means of procuring a home for them to live in. They were advised to become reconciled and to try to live together again comfortably. The Bench said that the whole affair had arisen in consequence of drink which was the foundation of all evil[206].

The couple do not appear to have lived together again. Louisa and the children continued to live in Uffculme. In 1871 they lodged at Sparkes Cottage with Louisa's father, John Byrd 67, a labourer in a woollen factory. Louisa 39, married, was a washer in the woollen factory. The youngest daughter, Hannah, aged 10, was still in school while Emma, 14, was a spinner in a woollen factory, and brother, Willie, aged 12, was a mill boy with John S. Spilsbury at the Mills, Uffculme. Actually William 12 appears again in the same census as a servant to George Southey at Kitwell Street, Uffulme! The family had moved to 1 Myrtle Cottage, Uffculme, by the 3rd April 1881 when Louisa, aged 48, and still said to be married, was the housekeeper to her father John Byrd, a 77 year old factory hand. Her adult children were unmarried and living at home. Emma, 24, was a worsted winder, Willie, 22, was a foreman in a flour mill and Hannah, 20, was a wool spinner. When the 1891 census was taken, Louisa, a widow, was living with her married daughter, Hannah and her husband William Henry Drew, a tailor and breeches maker, at 100 Wycliffe Road, Battersea, London.

The Tiverton Gazette for the 12th December 1899 records Louisa's death"-December 7at 36 Sunwell Street, Peckham, London, Louisa Luxton, late of Uffculme in her 70th year." On her death certificate she is described as 'widow of Charles Luxton, builder' but searches failed to locate an appropriate record of the death of Charles Luxton. This led me to speculate that Charles had changed his name and bigamously

---

[206] Western Times, 3rd August 1861 and Taunton Courier and Western Advertiser, Wednesday 7th August 1861.

married. There is growing evidence that bigamy was quite common in Victorian England, despite the penalties if caught, as divorce for the poorer classes was well nigh an impossibility.

It was relatively easy to "disappear" in the London of the nineteenth century and to "repackage" oneself-to an extent that would be impossible in the present day[207].I have concluded Charles Luxton deserted his wife Louisa Byrd in 1860 and sought to cover his tracks by changing his name. He turns up as Charles Whitbee, 36, mason, with a "wife" Jane, 30, and a son Frederick, aged 11, at 1 Combermere Road, Lambeth in the 1871 census. The family remained in Lambeth where their name is spelt Whillee in 1881 before settling as Whitby in 1891, 1901 and 1911. These subsequent census returns provide further details on Charles Whitby and family. He is a mason born in Tiverton, Devon, while Jane, his wife, is born in Yarcombe, in the same county, with two sons Frederick, born c 1860 in Ilchester, Somerset and Charles, born c 1874 in Stockwell, Lambeth.

Frederick had left home by the date of the 1891 census, and I have not picked up his trail, but in 1891 his brother, Charles, was a 17 year old porter, still at home in Lambeth. He was a 27 year old grocer, still living at 1 Combermere Road, Stockwell, Lambeth, when he married Louisa Webb, a 27 year old farrier's daughter at All Saints Church, Battersea, after banns on 10th June 1900. When the 1911 census was taken Louisa, 38, married 11 years, with one son, Harold Leslie Whitby, aged 3, was residing with her brother, an insurance clerk, and her parents at 6 Glenfield Road, Balham, Wandsworth. The son, Harold Leslie Vere Whitby (1908-1942), of 113 Barcombe Avenue, Streatham, Surrey died 11th April 1942. Administration of his estate valued at £994..15s..5d was granted to his widow, Laura Mabel Whitby.

I have been unable to find any G.R.O. registration for the marriage of Charles "Whitby" and Jane. The couple were certainly cohabiting as man and wife but Charles was still legally married to Louisa Byrd. He was no doubt aware that a legal union with Jane would have constituted

---

[207] See Christopher T. Husbands article, William Rawson Turner (1824-1894) and Thomas Hatfield Turner(1825-1901), pages 393-400 in Genealogists' Magazine, volume 30, number 10, June 2012.

the criminal offence of bigamy, carrying a sentence of up to seven years penal servitude under section 57 of the Offences Against the Person Act of 1861.

Confirmation that Charles changed his name and identity comes from the death certificate of a Charles Luxton or Whitby, aged 79, journeyman mason, of 1 Combermere Road, Stockwell, Lambeth, who died at Lambeth Infirmary, Brook Street, Kensington, London on the 26th June 1911. Charles Whitby's age and occupation match with Charles Luxton and I think it is too much of a coincidence that the death registrations, in the Lambeth register, for Charles Luxton and Charles Whitby are sequential:-

Charles Luxton died 1911 (2nd qtr) age 79 – Lambeth 1d/161
Charles Whitby died 1911 (2nd qtr) age 79 – Lambeth 1d/162

Mrs Louisa Whitby, his daughter-in-law, of Glenfield Road, Balham, was present at his death, and informed the registrar of his demise. She was clearly aware of his dual identity. Perhaps Charles made a death bed confession.

The foregoing account was written, when to my delight on a final trawl through records I found Charles Luxton, 79, widower, stone mason, born in Chipstable was living in one room at 1 Combermere Road, Stockwell in 1911. Charles had indeed confirmed his true identity in the 1911 census! He signs the census enumerator's record in a clear steady hand. Now an old man and widower, who was to die that summer, Charles knew there was no longer any need to hide his true identity. Last heard of at his trial in 1861, Charles Luxton had lived as Charles Whitby in London for half a century.

I know more of Charles Luxton's children. Hannah (1860-1939), a 21 year old spinster, of Uffculme, daughter of Charles Luxton stonemason, deceased, married William Henry Drew, 22, bachelor, Tailor of Kensington, son of Samuel Drew, joiner, at the Independent Chapel in Uffculme on the 15th August 1882. The bride and groom sign the register and the marriage is witnessed by Hannah's brother and sister. Her sister, Emma, 28, spinster, residing at Selgar Mills, Halberton, daughter of Charles Luxton builder (deceased) married Henry Moore Bailey, 26, bachelor, butcher of Penslade, Uffculme, son of Thomas Bailey, Farmer at the Independent Chapel, Uffculme on the 28th July

1887. Both sign, witnessed by Willie Luxton and Hannah Luxton, who for some reason signs under her maiden name. Their brother Willie Luxton, 28, bachelor, miller at Selgar Mills, Halberton, Devon, son of Charles Luxton builder (deceased), married Sarah Ann Trott Pine, 25, spinster, of Way Mill, Halberton at the Independent Chapel, Tiverton on the 18th August 1884. The marriage was witnessed by Willie's sister Hannah Drew and her husband, W. Henry Drew.

Willie Luxton's career as a miller was brought to an abrupt end by a devastating fire which destroyed Selgar's Mill early on Sunday morning the 3rd March 1889. Willie rented Selgar's Flour Mill, situated about one and a half miles from Uffculme, on the Tiverton Junction road to the village, from Mr. George Coombe of Mount Stephen and he lived in a house close to the mill. He had a large and thriving business and was very busy working his mill until late on Saturday night the 2nd March. When he shut the mill down about 10:30 everything appeared to be alright.

He was awakened about one o'clock on the Sunday morning, the 3rd March, by the strong smell of burning, and from his bed-room window which was right opposite, he could see his mill was on fire. He quickly dressed and aroused the people in the house, and on going into the yard he could see flames issuing from the roof of the mill. He found that one of the fenders which kept back the water had accidentally slipped down and this had started the mill wheel. It was the friction of the millstones that had caught the place on fire. Willie at once dispatched his assistant, George Curtis, on horseback to Cullompton for the fire-engines.

With the assistance of his wife and others he quickly got out the horses, bullocks and other livestock. Two policemen on night duty in nearby villages saw the illumination of the fire and they arrived to render help.

The heat had become so intense that the roof soon fell in. The West of England fire-engine arrived about half past two, soon followed by the Farmer's Society fire engine but they arrived too late to save the building and a large stock of corn which was consumed in the blaze. They were, however, able to save his dwelling house. Hundreds of people visited the scene that morning to see the smouldering ruins[208] and during the day one or two of the walls fell in. A hundred years later, in 1990, new arms (in photo) were fitted to the waterwheel, and in 1998 the three storey five bay mill with a large millpond, was up for sale.

By 1891 Willie, 32, and his wife Sarah, 28, were farming at Sampford Moor Farm, Sampford Arundel, in Somerset. Sarah's parents lived with the couple who employed Emma Palfry, 15, a general servant. Ten years later the couple were still farming at Sampford Moor. Sarah's parents were living with them and William's cousin, Willie White, aged 9, who was born in Burlescombe, Devon. Willie had established himself as a farmer, when a son, Willie, was born at Dykes Farm, Sampford Arundel, Somerset, on the 16th March 1905.

Willie Luxton, senior, moved from Dykes Farm soon after the birth of his son Willie for Kelly's Directory of Somersetshire, 1906, lists him under Farmers and Farm Bailiffs as William Luxton, Clavengers, Nynehead, Wellington. He was living in a nine room house at Clavengers in 1911. That is where Willie Luxton, farmer, died in 1916, at the age of 57, from bronchial asthma and emphysema, cardiac failure. His cousin, William White, also of Clavengers, was present at his death.

The will abstract records that Willie Luxton of Clavengers ·Farm, Nynehead, Somerset, yeoman, died on the 17th May 1916. The probate of his will was issued in Taunton on the 18th August to his widow, Sarah Ann Trott Luxton, when his personal estate was valued at £2530..18..2. In August 1917 an apple sale at the George Hotel, Taunton, made £23..5s. for Mrs Luxton from her one acre Clavengers Orchard[209]. Sarah retired in the spring of 1929, when she let Clavenger's Farm, and

---

[208] The Western Times, Monday 4th March 1889 and The Miller 1st April 1889 and the Exeter Flying Post Saturday, 9th March 1889 and Tiverton Gazette 5th March 1889.
[209] Taunton Courier, Wednesday 22nd August 1917.

the dairy cattle and young stock, horses and harness, pigs and implements on the farm were sold by auction.[210] Sarah Ann Trott Luxton, widow, aged 74, late of Clavengers Farm Nynehead, 38 Cheddon Road, Taunton died on the 30th June 1936. Probate was issued in London on the 23rd July 1936 to her son, Willie Luxton, insurance agent and Geoffrey Peard Clarke, solicitor, when her personal estate was valued at £115..11..11.

The son Willie Luxton, married Constance Lavinia Willey, at Gotham Parish Church in the County of Nottingham on the 11th April 1936. Willie, a clerical officer in the motor taxation department, lived at "Hawthorns", Lynford Lane, Taunton and he died, aged 64, at Musgrove Park Hospital, Taunton on the 16th February 1980. His widow, Constance, was born in Washingboro, Lincolnshire on the 24th December 1908. A retired nurse of "Hawthorns" Lynford Lane, Taunton, she was found to be dead on arrival at Musgrove Park Hospital, Taunton on the 15th February 1990. No children were born to this couple.

---

[210] Taunton Courier, Wednesday 1st May 1929.

27

ISAAC LUXTON (1838-1863) STONEMASON OF CHIPSTABLE, SOMERSET AND HIS FAMILY

See tree 13

Isaac(1838-1863), the third son of Jacob Luxton(1800-1868) and Harriet Greenway, was born in Chipstable, Somerset on the 9th June 1838. He qualified as a stone mason before marrying Jane Vickery at the parish church of All Saints, Chipstable on the 28th July 1858. Jane, one of eight children, the daughter of William Vickery(1795-1864) yeoman, and his wife Joany Ridler (1801-1863), was born at Shute Farm, Huish Champflower, on 4th November 1838. In their marriage,

which lasted less than five years, the couple had three children, baptised in the parish church at Chipstable, beginning with Charles on the 10th April1859, followed by Mary on 5th May 1861 and Frank on the 21st December 1862. The 15th century tower of All Saint's Church, Chipstable, stands high above the village in this old postcard view.

Isaac died in Chipstable, at the early age of 24 on the 22nd February 1863, and he was buried there on the 1st March 1863.

His death certificate records that he died from "phthisis," which was commonly called consumption. It is more familiarly known today as tuberculosis. In the 18th and 19th centuries it was a leading cause of death, and one early 19th century doctor estimated

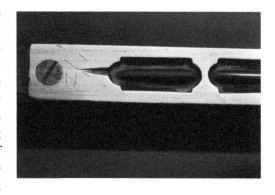

that it killed more than 55000 people a year in Great Britain. The disease was thought to be hereditary but in 1882 it was established that T. B. was an infectious disease. It commonly manifests itself as a disease of the lungs. In most cases it was caught as a result of the bacilli being inhaled from the droplets being released by a suffer's coughing or sneezing. However, given Isaac's occupation of stonemason, the dust disease silicosis (once called "stone cutter's phthisis") is the most likely cause of death. Two of Isaac's cousins, John Luxton (died 1845 aged 28) and James Luxton (died1861 aged 48) were also masons and their early deaths were probably from the same cause. Isaac's spirit level above, is scratched with his initials. I/L

Jane, Isaac's widow, married James Smith, aged 26, an agricultural labourer, at Chipstable on the 19th September 1864. James, born in Chipstable on 12th January 1845, was one of ten children born to William Smith and his wife Ann Wyatt. The family were living at Crooks, Chipstable in 1871 when the census described them as James Smith, aged 26, agricultural labourer, his wife, Jane, 32, and six children born in Chipstable-Charley Luxton aged 12, Mary Luxton aged 9, Frank Luxton aged 8, Elizabeth Smith aged 5, James Smith aged 3, William Smith aged 1. George Smith, a son, was born in Chipstable on 16th June 1871.

The family moved to Combe in Milverton which is quite isolated, just a cart track and one other house, where three more children, Jane 1873, Fred 1876, and Bessie 1878 were born. When James employer, Richard Chown of Hagley Bridge Farm, Milverton, moved to Mapledurham, a small village on the banks of the Thames in southern Oxfordshire in about 1879, all but Charles Luxton, the eldest step son went with him.

The move was probably a good idea as they had a pleasant thatched cottage at Gravel Hill Cottages, near the main road, and were only two miles from Caversham. They needed it as the family continued to grow with the birth of Ellen in 1880 and Albert in 1884. When Jane Smith (nee Vickery) died at Mapledurham on the 25th June 1898, she was the proud matriarch of the family. She had left her relatives and friends in Somerset but successfully established her large family in a new and prosperous part of the country.

Charles Luxton(1859-1911), the eldest son of Isaac Luxton and his wife Jane Vickery, was born on the 10th March 1859, and baptised a month later on the 10th April at All Saints Church, Chipstable. He married 19 year old Ellen Carpenter, the daughter of James and Sarah Carpenter, at Wiveliscombe, Somerset on the 26th July 1880. The newly wed couple moved to the boom coal port of Cardiff, in South Wales, where Charles was variously employed as a mason, coal tipper and labourer.

The 1881 Cardiff census lists Charles and Ellen with a baby daughter living with William Lane and family at 21 Kingarth Street, Roath. Four children were born to them in South Wales. The eldest, Bessie Ellen Luxton, born at 166, Bute Road, St. Mary's Parish, Cardiff on the 21st October 1880, was followed by Albert Charley (1882-1938), born at Kingarth Street, Roath on 24th May 1882, Sarah Jane, born at 70 Bedford Street, St. John's Parish, Cardiff, the daughter of Charles Luxton, coal tipper, on the 21st December 1886 and finally Arthur George (1889-1934), known as Bert, who was born at 32 Rose Street, Roath, son of Charles Luxton, coal tipper, on 11th May 1889. The 1891 Cardiff census reveals that Charles Luxton, General Dock's labourer aged 31, his wife Ellen and four children, Bessie, Albert, Sarah and Arthur lived at 32 Rose Street, Roath.

In 1900 Charles Luxton, coal tipper, was living at 140 Strathnairn Street, Roath but had moved to Eyre Street by 21st October 1901, when he was involved in a nasty accident which could have cost him his life. The bustling port of Cardiff was in its heyday at this time and the conditions for workers were often extremely dangerous. The accident was reported in the local press:-Charles Luxton, an employee of the Cardiff Railway Co., residing at 49 Eyre Street, Moors, whilst engaged in the vicinity of one of the tips at the Roath Dock, this morning, was caught between the buffers of two trucks and severely injured on the chest and left side. He was taken home[211].

He was living at 43 Eyre Street in 1903-4 but had moved to 127 Pearl Street by 1907. In 1911 Charles 51, lived at 127 Pearl Street with his wife Ellen aged 50, Sarah Jane 23, Arthur George 21, brakeman and his niece, Elizabeth Carpenter, a 20 year old domestic.

Charles Luxton, coaltipper, was living at 127 Pearl Street, Roath, Cardiff when he died, aged 51, on the 11th April 1911. His death certificate gives the cause of death as "Diabetes Mellitus Coma Exhaustion." Ellen his wife (photo on previous page) died, aged 66, at 151 Habershon Street, Splott, Cardiff on the 13th March 1928.

Albert Charles Luxton (1882-1938), their eldest son, was Chief Dock Foreman for the G. W. R. Cardiff Docks when he retired through ill health. He died, aged 56, on the 14th December 1938 and was buried in Western Cemetery, Cardiff. He married Violetta Elizabeth Brooks (1883-1973), at St. Catherine's Church, Kings Road, Canton, Cardiff, on the 26th December 1904. (photograph on right). The Western Mail Cardiff Directory lists Albert Charles Luxton living at 49 Wyndham Street, Canton in 1911. The census that year has Albert, 29, railway guard, living at 41 South Morgan Street with Violetta, 27, George 2 and Ivor 6months. The family moved to 147 Eldon Road which was later renamed Ninian Park Road.

---

[211] Evening Express, 21st October 1901

The couple had eight children, Albert William Charles Luxton (1906-1997), George Edward Luxton (1908-1989), Ivor James Luxton (1910-1964), Violetta Luxton (1912-2003), Frederick Walter Luxton (1914-1997), Queenie Luxton (1917-1999), Nancy Doreen Luxton (1919-), Bessie Joan Luxton (1922-2010). These offspring have produced extensive families living in Cardiff and elsewhere in the U.K.One of these Malcolm Warren Luxton (1944-), a teacher, examinations assessor, and Borough Councillor of Maidstone, Kent, son of George Edward Luxton, is an enthusiastic genealogist who has helped me link his branch into the greater Luxton of Petton, Bampton family tree.

Because of his job, Albert Charles, was able to obtain free railway travel and the family made good use of this privilege. Albert Charles, his wife Violetta are seen with the whole family on Tenby beach where they are dressed for the occasion. This photo of the family and another at Paignton beach date to the 1920s.

Charles and Ellen's youngest son, Arthur George Luxton (1889-1934), in photo below, known as Bert, a railway signalman at Cardiff Docks, married Daisy Hopkins who died on the 19th October 1978. Bert, who lost a leg in the course of his work as a railway coupler, died on the 2nd January 1934 and was buried at Cathays Cemetery, Cardiff.

This couple had three children born in Walker Road, Splott, beginning with Violet May Luxton, on the 16th March 1918, Bernard Luxton, on 12th June 1919 who died aged two from diphtheria in April 1922, and Mervyn Charles Luxton, born on the 30th September 1923.

The 1939 register lists Daisy, and her children, Violet, a filing clerk, and Mervyn; a lodge boy in a steel enamel works, living at 28 Walker Road, Splott. Mervyn married Annie Thompson, a Scot, at Martyrs and North Church, Greenock and in 1989 he married Doris Painter. A retired pipe-fitter of 155 Moorland Road, in Splott, Cardiff Mervyn died of prostate cancer at Llandough Hospital Penarth on the 31st May 2005. Mervyn and his first wife Annie have a son, Brynmor George Luxton born on the 8th August 1947. Brynmor married Janet Biggar, a Scot, in Trinity Church, Stanwell Road, Penarth. They live in St. Athan in the Vale of Glamorgan and have a family including a son Jonathan Charles Luxton.

Isaac Luxton and his wife Jane Vickery had two more children in their brief marriage. Their daughter Mary Luxton, (1861-1887) baptised at Chipstable on the 5th May 1861, was aged 9 and was living in Chipstable with her mother, stepfather and family in 1871. Ten years later the 1881 census for St. Mary Parish, Reading, lists Mary Luxton, 20, general servant, living and working in a shoe shop at 114/115 Broad Street, Reading. Mary moved to Bradfield, Berkshire where she describes herself as the daughter of Isaac Luxton, stonecutter, when she married John Wheeler, (1859-1919) labourer, of Upper Basildon, son of Thomas Wheeler, labourer, in St. Andrew's, the parish church at Bradfield on the 21st July 1883. A daughter, Alice Wheeler (1884-1972) was born the 23rd August 1884 in Upper Basildon, Pangbourne, Bradfield. Sadly Mary was only aged 26 when she died in Bradfield and she was buried at St Mary the Virgin, Purley, Berkshire on 12th November 1887.

Before her marriage she gave birth to an illegitimate daughter, Annie Luxton (1879-1956), who was born in the Union Workhouse, Bradfield, Berkshire on the 13th November 1879. Annie, aged 23, of Sacred Hill, Mapledurham, falsely describing herself as the daughter of John Luxton, labourer, married Arthur Tegg, 23, porter of Tidmarsh in St. Paul's Church, Mapledurham, Oxfordshire on the 29th September 1902. She later married Edmund Carter (1863-1931).

Frank Luxton, baptised at Chipstable on the 21st December 1862, was aged 8 when the 1871 Chipstable census was taken. Ten years later in 1881, Frank aged 18, an unmarried agricultural labourer, lived in the household of his stepfather James Smith in the village of Mapledurham,

Oxfordshire[212]. His illegitimate niece, Annie Luxton, aged one, born in Bradfield, Berkshire who was the daughter of his sister Mary, was living in the same household.

Frank, aged 25, a labourer residing at St. Mary's Maidenhead, Berkshire, married Sarah Jane Reeves, aged 20, daughter of Robert Reeves, carpenter at St. Luke's Church in the parish of St. Luke's, Maidenhead, Berkshire on the 8th September 1888. Both sign the register in front of witnesses. Frank, 28, general labourer and his wife, Sarah Jane, 21, were living in 1891, at 3 Cornwallis Road, Cookham, Maidenhead, Berkshire. Ten years later in 1901, Frank, a 38 year old, general labourer, and Sarah, 32, laundress, dwelt at 29 Garden Cottages, St. Luke's, Maidenhead, Berkshire. The couple had moved home again by 1911 when Frank, 48 general labourer, and his wife Sarah Jane, 42, lived in the four roomed 5 Gothic Cottages, Highway Estate, Bath Road, Maidenhead. There were no children born to the marriage.

Frank was found drowned in the Grand Junction Canal, Hayes, Middlesex on the 6th August 1921. The body was unidentified when an inquest was held on the 8th August. His death certificate was corrected by the coroner on the 27th August 1921 when he was described as Frank Luxton, aged about 59, a general labourer, married and living at 33 Regina Road, Southall. The Middlesex Advertiser and Gazette for 12th August 1921 contains a report, although it incorrectly names him "Frederick" Luxton. It reads:-

> "Southall Man's Fate
> Found drowned at Hayes

Walking along the towing path of the canal near the Iron Bridge, Hayes on Saturday afternoon, Mr. Harry George of Bull's Bridge, saw the body of a man in the water. With assistance he got it to the bank and Dr. Bendle, who was called, stated that the body had been in the water two or three days. In spite of every enquiry the police have been unable

---

[212] Five farmers and their employees, a total of 74 people, including James Smith and his family left the Milverton area of west Somerset in the years 1877-9 to settle in Mapledurham Oxfordshire. See West Somerset Exodus by E. G. Smith, page 85, volume 33, in August 2008 issue of the Somerset and Dorset Family History Journal.

to establish the identity of the man whose description is as follows: Age about forty-five to fifty; height, six feet; complexion, sallow; hair, brown; moustache, ginger; eyes, blue; good teeth. Dress-navy blue coat and vest, blue dungaree overall trousers, fleece lined pants and vest, blue striped cotton shirt, black laced boots; navy knitted tie, brown leather belt and flannel body belt. On the body was found a leather purse containing 1 ½ d; pair of yellow metal rimmed spectacles in black case; pocket knife, two keys, tobacco pouch, a piece of rope, and a copy of the "Daily Mirror" dated August 3rd, and a black enamelled metal badge bearing the words, "National Society, established 1920, B.L.W.C." (in monogram form). At the inquest on Monday Dr. J. S. Crone, the deputy coroner recorded a verdict found drowned. He examined the badge through a microscope in the hope of finding something on it by means of which the man might be identified. We learn that the man has since been identified as Frederick Luxton, of 33 Regina Road, Southall. Deceased was living there with a stepbrother. He left home last Wednesday, presumably to search for work."

The B.L.W.C. monogram on Frank's black enamel badge was the Basingstoke Lock Wrecker's Club. This was a 1920s protest group, opposed to the preservation of the Basingstoke Canal Waterway. Their opponents, the Surrey and Hampshire Canal Society, wanted to preserve the canal and referred to B.L.W.C. members as being akin to rodents! Did Frank slip or was he pushed into the canal, one wonders?

To conclude my account of the descendants of Isaac Luxton (1838-1863) stone mason, of Chipstable. Somerset are two wedding photographs. Albert William Charles Luxton (1906-1997), married Elsie Wicks at Mount Tabor Primitive Methodist Church, Moira Terrace, Cardiff, on the 11th April 1936. L to R Albert senior, Violetta, Albert, his brother George who was best man, Elsie, Mrs Wicks, Mr. Wicks, Queenie (seated) and an unknown lady.

His brother Ivor James Luxton (1910-1964), a carpenter, married Frances Desmond at St. Patrick's Roman Catholic Church, Grange Gardens,

Grangetown on the 11th August 1934. L to R. Frances' parents, Ivor, Albert, his father, Frances and Violetta, his mother.

I conclude this chapter with a photo of Frederick Walter Luxton (1914-1997). He joined the Royal Welsh Fusiliers in 1932, serving in Hong Kong, Shanghai and the Sudan pre-war. In World War Two he was in India where this photograph was taken and Burma. He wears a regimental badge on his side cap, along with a jungle green four pocket bush jacket. He was awarded the Burma Star and has a medal ribbon above his left pocket. He wears a regimental slip-on sergeant stripe upon his epaulette. Badges on these uniforms are often only pinned on because they would require regular laundering. The photo dates 1945/46. He was demobbed in 1946.

28

GEORGE EDWARD LUXTON(1908-1989) CHIEF INSPECTOR AT CARDIFF CITY CENTRAL POSTOFFICE ASSISTANT POSTAL CONTROLLER CORYTON CARDIFF

George Edward Luxton, the second son of Albert Charles Luxton (1882-1938), and his wife Violetta Elizabeth Brooks, who had eight children, was born at 47 Wyndham Street, Riverside, Cardiff on 16th September 1908 and was christened at St. Catherine's Church, Kings Road, Riverside. The 1911 census shows George, aged 2, with the family at 41 South Morgan Street, Cardiff. He attended school until the age of 14 at Kitchener Road School. Only one photograph survives of this time and this shows George working on a woodwork project in a classroom where a teacher appears to be instructing a variety of curriculum subjects at the same time! At 11 he joined the Boys Brigade, and his good attendance badges survive. He played football when time allowed, and his son Malcolm also has a number of badges he received when his team won the various leagues in which he played. Football was to be an interest which he played until damaging his knees, and he remained a lifelong fan of Cardiff City at their home games. See tree 13.

His elder brother, Albert, had followed his father with a career on the railways, but on leaving school at 14, George took a Post Office entrance examination and was one of a few successful boys. He started work as a Telegraph Boy but was very career minded, especially following his marriage in September 1938, when at the age of 30 he became a Head Postman at Cardiff's Head Post Office. He found the position of authority quite difficult to handle at times, as many of his friends were the postmen he had previously worked with. He was called up in the war (1023290) on the 27th September 1940, and is described as 5ft 8 inches, 34inch chest, dark brown hair, hazel eyes and with a sallow complexion. On the 29th September 1940, he was made Aircraftsman Second Class,

on the 1ˢᵗ July 1941, Aircraftsman First Class, on the 1ˢᵗ August 1942, Leading Aircraftsman, on the 1ˢᵗ March 1944 Temporary Acting Corporal and Substantive Corporal on the 31ˢᵗ December 1944. He received the First Good Conduct Badge (A) on the 11ᵗʰ November 1943.

During the war years he became qualified to work on various aircraft notably the Whitley bomber, Hudson bomber, Lancaster bomber, Halifax bomber, Wellington bomber, Beaufighter, Albermarle glider and Stirling bomber. He was stationed at Padgate near Warrington on the 27ᵗʰ September 1940, at Blackpool on the 13ᵗʰ November 1940, on the Isle of Man and at St Athan near Cardiff. He was released on the 15ᵗʰ October 1945, and discharged on the 11ᵗʰ December 1945.

I know from the numerous times he spoke about these years that he thoroughly enjoyed making new friends from around the country, especially Tate Grant from Scotland, and learning new skills as an RAF corporal, aircraft fitter, specialising in the new 'radar' technology. The family had their share of misfortune during the war with George's sister Bet losing her newly wed husband Percy Dibble and Iris, George's wife, losing her only brother Roy in a flying boat crash in Crete.

Following the war George's vocabulary was smattered with strange foreign words which he loved to use. Some are as follows and are spelt phonetically as he spoke them and no doubt would have spelt them if asked:- Mar-leesh and San-fairy-an[213] meaning "I don't mind", Im-she meaning "go away" and numerous others. His conversation was also often punctured with sayings he had either picked up in the war or in the Post Office. Some of these are as follows:-"Excuse my round shoulders" when meaning "I beg your pardon" "Suffering from a shortage of skin" when referring to someone breaking wind, etc. These strange sayings and 'Post office' stories were a source of constant amusement to the rest of the family.

His one personal regret from the war years was that on returning to the Post Office in Cardiff, he found that some workers who for various reasons had not been called up and were previously junior

---

[213] Burt Arthur Luxton (1913-2007), a fitter/ turner in Barry Graving Docks during the war, used the expression San-fairy-an when someone was irresponsible and careless.

to him, had gained promotion in his absence. However, this served to make him even more determined than ever to rise as far as he could. In this he was very successful, and despite turning down promotions in other towns, he stayed in Cardiff, became Chief Inspector and finally retired as Assistant Postal Controller at Regional Training School, Coryton, Cardiff. This determination to succeed made him a very serious person, careful with his money, without close friends, and very family orientated. He was devoted to his mother, following his father's death in 1938, and took it upon himself to cycle each week to 147 Ninian Park Road to help in any way that he could. He was very good with his hands and hence repaired all the family's shoes and did much of the decorating.

Socially, Great Britain was changing dramatically after the war, and a 'middle' class of people, who were not content with a meagre standard of living but wanted to buy their own house, and increase their possessions, was growing. To do this meant working hard, saving as much as possible and trying to ensure a prosperous future for themselves and their families. George wanted his sons to have all the opportunities he was denied himself as a child.

It was on the 3rd September 1938 that George Edward Luxton, 29, postman driver, married Iris Eileen Mabel Warren, 24, daughter of Herbert Warren, decorator, and Mabel Gladys Warren (nee Carne), at Victoria Park Methodist Church, following a courtship of about seven years. It was a quiet wedding, insisted by George, as his father was in a poor state of health. Iris would have preferred to have invited more of her friends and relations, but as was typical of that time, the husband had his way! The signing of the register was witnessed by Herbert Warren, father, and Albert William Charles Luxton, his eldest brother.

All their married life the couple lived at "Fairfield", 35 Bishops Walk, Llandaff, Cardiff. George was rarely off work through illness and lived his job. He did 'shift' work until the latter years of his working life, which he did not enjoy. He strove to do his best for his family and was very practical doing all the DIY around the house. If a job presented itself that he couldn't do himself he found one of his postmen, whose previous trade it was, to help him. In this way he was able to build his own garage, rebuild the garden wall, plumb in a new bathroom, etc. Harry Card, a postman, came to the house for many years to cut the families hair! George did not suffer fools gladly and anything less than perfect irritated him. He would often be seen staring at small imperfections in his wallpapering or speak derogatively about someone who was not up to the mark. The husband of a friend of theirs, preferred to pay a tradesman to rewire a plug rather than spend time doing it himself. and this George couldn't understand.

Family life in the Luxton household followed a similar pattern each week, and each year. Iris was expected to cook seven dinners a week at 12.30pm, often the same seven each week, and tea time at 5pm was sandwiches, cake and perhaps a pudding. Following the purchase of the car in 1953, KKG 843 a Morris Minor, Saturday trips to the seaside were a regular outing if George wasn't working. These were usually to Ogmore or another bay where you didn't have to pay to park! Malcolm often had a school friend with him, usually Michael Glover or Michael Wilson, who lived in the same neighbourhood. The Primus stove always accompanied these trips as a cup of tea was a necessity. Café's were few and far between in those days and of course far more expensive than making your own. Malcolm cannot remember the family ever eating out until he was in his late teens.

Iris had a few friends, with Mrs Williams, (Aunty Eadie) who lived next door at 37, being someone who could always be relied upon to help out in any time of trouble. Eadie's husband, Dan, was a grocer, with a shop in Mackintosh Place, Cardiff and Iris placed her order each week, before the supermarkets forced Dan to shut up shop. Malcolm was also very friendly with the Williams boys, Tim and Martin, and stayed in touch throughout their lives. Iris' closest friend was Edna Forde whom she met when working at Howells department store in Cardiff during the war. Edna lived with her husband, Jock, an Irishman, (real name George!) in Arosfa, Five Lanes, Llanfair Discoed, near Chepstow. For many years Edna and Jock were regular Saturday evening visitors as they came to Cardiff to see Edna's dad. Whilst George tolerated Jock, he was no lover of the Irish. Perhaps this was due to the war and also the fact that Irish labour had been used to break Welsh strikes in past industrial disputes. He also viewed anyone foreign with suspicion. Today he would have been thought of as being racist but in those days someone from abroad stood out in a crowd. The only thing George and Jock had in common was an interest in cars and a dislike of gambling and alcohol. When Iris went into hospital to give birth to Stuart, Malcolm went to stay with Edna for a week. Edna and Jock lived on the outskirts of a small village near Chepstow, surrounded with countryside, which the 5 year old Malcolm found quite exciting and a new experience. Each day he had to feed the chickens, collect the eggs, and collect firewood from the wood near their house.

Luxton holidays were spent in the south west of England and west Wales. The Gower, and Weston Super Mare, when the children were small, and later in Devon and Cornwall. In the days before fast cars and wide roads this journey was quite a trek. George was not the most patient of drivers and did not like anyone to overtake him, especially if they were queue jumping. The family were always relieved when they reached their destination. On one holiday, on the way to Cornwall, it was necessary to stop halfway and take a B&B. Sadly the boys' bedtime high-jinks resulted in a broken vase. George was not amused and it cost him 10 shillings! When Malcolm left the family home to work in Hampshire their holidays were often in Scotland or abroad, with Benidorm being one of their favourites. Iris and George had nearly 20 years of retirement together. They enjoyed many holidays in this time with a cruise on the QE2 being the highlight. How George could accept spending such a vast amount of money on one holiday is difficult to imagine as all their married life had been spent watching the pennies.

In the 1950s Bishops Walk was on the round of many tradesmen, the greengrocer, the 'pop' man, the milkman, etc. If Iris was given a bad potato by the greengrocer Jack Jones, she was ready for him the following week, and would expect a replacement. The Luxton family were one of the first of their friends to obtain a television and quite a crowd crammed into the living room to see the 'coronation' in 1953. Something strange was in the air in Bishops Walk, as nearly every child in the street was a boy.

George died, aged 80, following a heart attack on the 27th June 1989 at Bishops Walk. His wife stayed at Bishops Walk until 1995 when she moved to a bungalow, 23 Heol Mabon, Rhiwbina, Cardiff so that she could be nearer to Stuart her second son who lived in Lisvane, Cardiff and because Rhiwbina was always somewhere she wanted to live. She moved to Sittingbourne to live with Malcolm and his wife Margaret when it was clear she was unable to look after herself and in more recent years to Kingsfield Nursing Home in Faversham. Iris died on the 2nd May 2015 aged 100.

Iris and George's eldest son, Malcolm Warren Luxton, was born at Northlands Nursing Home, Cardiff, on the 7th December 1944, following a long confinement and weighing in at over 10 lbs. He was baptised at Victoria Park Methodist Church, on the 25th February 1945. Malcolm attended Llandaff Church in Wales Primary School, a school driven by 11+ success. Etched in Malcolm's memory is a school assembly when the junior school pupils and those who "failed" the 11+ had to clap those pupils who had "passed" the 11+ on the stage. It is ironic that Malcolm later spent the majority of his teaching career in Kent, which still continues with the 11+ and Grammar Schools. At eleven years of age, Malcolm went to Kings College School and Canton High School, at 14 following an "overage" exam. Kings College was a small private school run by the Dark family. Malcolm experienced a harsh level of discipline here and was caned in his first year by the head teacher on two occasions, the first occasion for forgetting his P.E. kit!

At eleven he joined the 1st Cardiff Company of the Boys Brigade, under the leadership of the inspiring Tom Cox, where he rose through the ranks and was awarded the Queens Badge at 18. The highlight of each year was the Battalion Summer Camp which was always at some 'exotic' place like Saundersfoot or the Isle of Wight. This experience he replicated, when teaching at the Cornwallis school, where he lead the school trip with 50 of his schoolchildren to the Isle of Wight for a week, for five consecutive years. These years with the BB helped to form his character for future years.

He achieved reasonable O levels for his class at Canton High School, and one A level in Pure Mathematics. Canton H.S. was a very uninspiring school, drifting along under the headship of Harold (Motho) Davies. Careers advice was non-existent in those days, and so on leaving school he applied and was accepted by the Commercial Union Assurance Company in Cardiff as a clerk.

At 18 Malcolm became an officer in the 1st Cardiff Boys Brigade Company but left soon after Tom Cox retired as captain. Like his father, Malcolm was not one to suffer fools gladly so following numerous disagreements over poor organisation with the new captain he joined the 2nd Cardiff BB Company as a leader under the captaincy of Cliff Harris, a very likeable, cheerful and appreciative leader.

He enjoyed the social side the CU job brought him but after three years decided that it was unsuitable for him as a career. His father, George, did not stand in his way, despite the fact that socially it was considered in those days, that once you had a permanent job you should stick at it, and supported him as he trained to be a mathematics teacher at Glamorgan Teacher Training College, Barry. He really enjoyed this time and was torn whether to follow a career in primary or secondary education. However he decided that he was best suited to secondary, given his special aptitude for maths rather than other subjects. Finding a teaching job was easy but most teachers leaving college at Barry had to move to England unless they were Welsh speakers. Malcolm applied to a number of places and finally plumped, for no particular reason, for Hampshire. He travelled to Gosport to see the school on offer and accepted the job as Mathematics Teacher on scale 1 at Bridgemary Secondary School.

He started in September 1969, and to his surprise, without any prior meeting, discussion or preparation, was expected to teach a full timetable to pupils in years one, two and three (now years 7, 8, and 9). How education has changed! The school grew to approximately 2000 pupils and the highlight(!) of his week was teaching year 3 set 13!! Initially, he lived in a bed-sit and survived on Vesta meals, usually curry, but after one year moved into a house with other teachers from Bridgemary School. At the end of the year he moved in with two female teachers, also from Bridgemary. It was whilst at this school, that he was introduced to the game of squash at Lee on Solent Squash Club, which dominated his sporting life for the next 20 years, and Bridge, introduced by maths teacher, John Jones, which consumed a lot of his spare time. He partook in staff 'out of school' activities which mainly meant badminton in the school hall each Wednesday.

Despite thoroughly enjoying his time at this school he decided he should seek promotion, and in 1972 he moved to Maidstone, to take up the position of Head of Lower School Maths at the Cornwallis School, Linton on a scale 3 with the immediate responsibility of organising the Kent Maths Project throughout the school. The school had about 900 students at this time. This was a chaotic time in education with all sorts of new ideas being promoted in various parts of the country. For the first three years in Kent he shared various houses with two other Cornwallis teachers, Richard Blackaby and Clive Leonard in Staplehurst. He then bought his own place, 49 Dixon Close, a maisonette near Maidstone town centre, for £9100. Like his father, he was a keen football fan and started his own football club which played 'friendly' football matches in the Maidstone Sunday League. The headteacher at Cornwallis encouraged him to stay at the school as it grew to 1600 children, with promotions being awarded over the next 15 years.

However, he was determined to lead his own department and was appointed Head of the Mathematics Faculty at the Maplesden Noakes School, also in Maidstone, in 1986. After eight years at this school he retired in 1995. Not one to retire gracefully Malcolm fought and won a seat in the Maidstone Borough Council elections in 1998 for the Liberal Democrats against the sitting Tory councillor, following a successful campaign against Tesco who wanted to build a supermarket nearby. During this time he was instrumental in harnessing residents enthusiasm to set up the North Loose Residents Association so that local people had a stronger say in proposed changes to their area. He continued as a councillor for this area until 2006 following a move to Tudor Rose Cottage, Chestnut Street, Borden in 2003. In 2001 he began part-time work for the AQA Examinations Board as a school assessor, and filled his time with part-time jobs, Lions and DIY.

Malcolm married Margaret Walton, aged 23 (born 30th April 1958), another teacher at the Cornwallis school, daughter of John Walton (local government officer) and Audrey Walton, a teacher, at Thorne Methodist Church, Thorne, South Yorkshire on 22nd August 1981. The register signing was witnessed by Christine Raper, the bride's eldest sister, and Stuart Luxton, the groom's brother.

They began married life living at Malcolm's house 49 Dixon Close, Maidstone. Their first daughter, Rebecca Jane Luxton, was born at the West Kent General Hospital, Maidstone, on Wednesday the 4th August

1982. The house, a maisonette, being on the first and second floors of a three story terrace, was not very suitable once children came along and so the family sold up and bought 9 Shernolds for £31000 in April 1983. Rebecca was followed by Caroline Amy Luxton, also born at the West Kent General Hospital on 29th August 1984 and later by Rhianna Frances Luxton, born at the new Maidstone Hospital on the 18th December 1988. All the girls attended Loose Primary School, (Caroline also attended Brunswick House School) and were Brownies. When they finished primary education both Rebecca  and Caroline went to St Simon Stock Comprehensive School and Rhianna to Maplesden Noakes School. At sixteen, Rebecca transferred to Maplesden Noakes to do her A levels and Caroline chose to go to The Cornwallis School. Education in Maidstone suffers from a commitment to the hated and dated 11+ with grammar schools and hence the secondary schools chosen depended upon their friendships, the reputation of the schools and the gut feeling of Margaret and Malcolm from experiencing the education system in the town. Whether the right choices were made is difficult to say but all the girls achieved good exam results before leaving their respective secondary schools.

Rebecca trained to become a nurse at Anglia Polytechnic University. She then trained as a 'burns and plastics' nurse in Chelmsford and Harley Street, London. She now runs her own clinics 'Luxton Aesthetics' in Essex and Kent and lives in Good Easter near Chelmsford. Caroline trained to become a Social Worker at Northampton University and qualified in 2006. She decided not to take up a career in social work and was offered a job working for the owner of a London chain of maternity shops. After numerous promotions she became their chief buyer. Following a number of job changes she is now a Logistics manager and lives in Pinner, London. Rhianna worked for a large firm of solicitors in Maidstone before becoming a 'custody officer' in Borstal. She has since left that post and rejoined the firm of solicitors. Rhianna's first child, Noah Daniel, born on the 23rd March 2012, sadly died 27 days later at St Thomas' Hospital London on the 19th April with severe heart problems. She now has a son, Cole Noah, born on the 9th May 2013.

Iris and George's second son, Stuart Warren Luxton, was born at Northlands Nursing Home, Cardiff on 29th May 1950, and baptised at Victoria Park Methodist Church. He also had primary education at Llandaff Church of Wales School and then following a successful 11+, at Cardiff High School. He lived at Whiteacres, Rudry Road, Lisvane, Cardiff and now lives at Cami Dels Castellans, Javea, Spain. Stuart worked in the telecommunications industry for BT since leaving school and rose to the position of a Senior Financial Manager working throughout the UK and as a consultant to the China Telephone Company in Ningbo.

He retired in 1996 and was a Lisvane parish councillor. Stuart married (1) Marjorie Richards on the 15th April 1972 at Gelligaer. They were divorced in 1975. (2) Shirley Russell on the 13th August 1977 at Park Place Registry Office, Cardiff. They were divorced in 1981. (3) Maureen Smith (Burgon) on the 25th April 1987 at Bethany Baptist Church, Rhiwbina, Cardiff. There were no children from any of the marriages[214].

---

[214] This chapter has been contributed by Malcolm Warren Luxton who has long supported and encouraged my endeavour to compile a history of our Luxton family.

29

GEORGE LUXTON (1847-1918) MASTER STONEMASON OF CHIPSTABLE, CLEVEDON, WRAXALL AND NAILSEA, SOMERSET

See tree 14

George Luxton, the tenth of eleven children born to Jacob Luxton (1800-1968), stone mason, and his wife Harriet Greenway (1808-1854) of Chipstable, was baptised at All Saints, the parish church on the 1st August 1847. Harriet, the daughter of Charles Greenway and Elizabeth Cleeve, was baptised in the neighbouring parish of Milverton, Somerset, on the 28th February 1808 although both her parents came from Chipstable.

In 1851 when George was three he lived at Paradise Cottage, close to Chipstable parish church, with his parents, Jacob 51, a master bricklayer, his mother Harriet 43 and five of his brothers and sisters. Harriet who suffered with valvular heart disease died, aged 46, and was buried at All Saints, Chipstable on the 20th May 1854. The loss of his mother when he was scarcely seven was a traumatic experience for young George.

Surviving members of the family, still residing in Chipstable in 1861, were living apart. Jacob, a 61 year old widower, who built stone barns in the neighbourhood, was residing with the Parkman family at Dinhill (or Daniel) Cottage. His son George, aged 14, a mason's labourer was living at Larcombe Cottage with his married brother Isaac 23, a building mason, his wife Jane, aged

303

23, and their two infant children, Charley aged 2 and Mary who was born fifteen minutes before the census was taken!

Tragedy struck the family again when Isaac died at the early age of 24 from phthisis, the wasting disease consumption. In Isaac's case he almost certainly died from the 'dust' disease silicosis (once called 'stone cutters' phthisis). Stonemasons worked in dusty atmospheres where they were constantly inhaling particles of stone dust. The sufferer developed a cough, brought up profuse quantities of purulent mucus and was troubled by increasing shortness of breath and wheezing. The victim became increasingly disabled and died.

Following Isaac's tragic death in 1863, George, now sixteen, saw no future in Chipstable. He set out for Clevedon in the company of his younger brother, John (1850-1925). In his possession was Isaac's six inch brass and boxwood spirit level with the initials I/L scratched on the brass[215].

Their elder sister Jane (1842-1878), was already living in Clevedon, where she married William Stock, a labourer, in St Andrews, the twelfth century parish church on the 14th November 1864. Jane performed a motherly role for her two young brothers, providing them with a temporary home. But this must have been for only a short while for Jane, and her husband, William Stock, emigrated in 1865 to Canada, sailing on the S.S. Peruvian from Liverpool to Quebec. They were settled by 1871 at Yarmouth near St. Thomas in Ontario and had at least two sons there before Jane died, aged 36, in Port Stanley, on the 12th November 1878, following complications in the sixth month of pregnancy[216].

---

[215] On the side of the spirit level the wood is impressed E Preston & Sons B'ham, England Improved warranted correct
[216] Information contained in letter dated 29th June 2009 from Susan Freeborn of Calgary, Alberta.

Clevedon, conveniently placed near Bristol, was fast becoming a resort for the gentry who had a growing interest in the seaside break from the city. The Clevedon Enclosure Act of 1799, which enabled local landowners to sell small parcels of land for building, received further impetus with the arrival of the Bristol and Exeter Railway in 1847. There was plenty of work and opportunity in the growing town for a young man like George who qualified as a stonemason in 1866. I have in my possession his large ornate framed certifi-

cate, which certifies that Brother George Luxton was a Legal Member of the Friendly Society of Stonemasons, dated 26th March 1866. In my possession too is his two foot brass rule made by Chesterman in Sheffield. A graphic pen portrait of a mason's life is provided by Charles Dickens in The Mystery of Edwin Drood (1870) in his description of the grim stonemason Durdles:-

"With a two-foot rule always in his pocket, and a mason's hammer always in his hand, Durdles goes continually sounding and tapping all about the cathedral. In a suit of coarse flannel with horn buttons, a yellow neckerchief with draggled ends, an old hat more russet coloured than black, and laced boots of the hue of his stony calling, Durdles leads a hazy gypsy sort of life, carrying his dinner about with him in a small bundle, and sitting on all manner of tombstones to dine."

George and John Luxton were both married in 1869, and between them and their spouses, they produced twenty one children. John, the first to marry, was a nineteen year old labourer, resident in Nailsea, when he married Ellen Hopkins, 19, servant, at Holy Trinity Church, Nailsea on the 5th April 1869. John qualified as a cooper but made his living as a chimney sweep in Nailsea. John and his wife Ellen had eleven children and their descendants still live in Clevedon and Portishead.

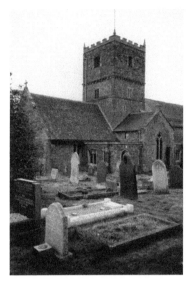

A month later on the 6th May 1869, George aged 22, married Eliza Lilly 23, in St. Andrew's the parish church of Clevedon, built on the bleak promontory of Wainshill, overlooking the Bristol Channel, so that the tower could be used for a beacon fire to help sailors in foul weather[217]. Eliza was the youngest daughter of Thomas Lilly of Vine Cottage, who was the only fisherman listed in the 1841 Clevedon census. He continued to earn his living as a fisherman, but as Clevedon expanded as a holiday resort he launched himself into the profitable bathing machine business in the 1860s[218].

George Luxton, 23, mason and his wife Eliza, 24, lived in Strode Road, Clevedon when the census was taken on the 2nd April 1871. Their son, Charles Henry, born on the 12th April, was baptised at St. Andrew's a month later on the 14th May 1871. Eliza who was already terminally ill with consumption, tragically died at the early age of 25 on the 4th October 1871, and lies buried with her parents in St. Andrew's churchyard where a headstone (in photo on left) commemorates the family.

George, now a widower with an infant son to rear, married for a second time on the 18th May 1875, to Clara Ann Beer, daughter of John and

---

[217] At the wedding one witness, Julia Cowey, was Eliza's sister in law and Emma was a sister, born 1838.

[218] George's marriage was announced in the Western Daily Press, Saturday 8th May 1869-On the 6th inst., at the Parish Church, Clevedon, by the Rev E. H. Fothergill, Mr. George Luxton to Eliza, youngest daughter of Mr. Thomas Lilly, Vine Cottage.

Hannah Beer, shoemaker, in St. James parish church, Bristol. Clara's father, John, came from Yarcombe, in Devon and that is where Clara herself was baptised on the 15th July 1849. Her birth certificate, however, reveals she was born a few miles away at Whitestaunton, Somerset, on the 8th June 1849, and that her mother's maiden name was Hannah Kiddle.[219]

Clara adopted Charles Henry, George's son by his first marriage. She must have found him a handful, because according to Tom, his half brother, Charles was 'a bit of a bad lad' who emigrated to Australia or New Zealand. There is a story too that he married a Maori and that one of his children visited the Clevedon area after the Second World War but I have been unable to substantiate the veracity of this tale.

I find that Charles Luxton, a Protestant, aged 17, farm labourer, was an assisted immigrant aboard the S.S. "Jumna," sailing from London on 31st May and arriving in Brisbane, Queensland, on 23rd July 1889. The ship named after a tributary of the River Ganges, was the first ship completed for the British India Associated Steamers Limited and was designed for the company's Royal Mail Service to Queensland, Australia. She had temporary 'tween deck quarters for emigrants on the outward voyage. On her maiden voyage on 21st September 1886 she caused a considerable stir as the largest vessel yet seen in Queensland waters.

Much of Charles life in Australia remains a mystery. He became a gold miner at Kalgoorlie in Western Australia. Gold was struck there in January 1893 by three prospectors who were travelling to Mount Youle when one of their horses cast a shoe. During the halt the men noted signs of gold and decided to stay and investigate. A gold rush ensued and Charles was one of the hundreds of young men who swarmed the area in search of gold. During the 1890s when the population in the goldfield exceeded 200,000, mostly prospectors, the area gained a notorious

---

[219] A newspaper list of prisoners for trial at the Somerset Quarter Sessions, held in the Shire Hall, Taunton, commencing on Tuesday 1st July 1879 includes a George Luxton on bail for stealing cider at Yatton. I thought he was my George. However a search of the Quarter Sessions Roll ref Q/SR 716 for the mid –summer session 1879, held at Somerset Heritage Centre, reveals that the defendant was in fact a George Loxton, a porter on the G.W.R. who was sentenced to three months hard labour in Taunton Goal! See Western Times, Tuesday 1st July 1879.

reputation for being a "wild west" with bandits and prostitutes. Just when Charles arrived there is unknown to me, but I pick up his trail in the Australian Electoral Rolls for 1903, which records him as a miner at Kookynie (aboriginal for water hole or a spring), located near Coolgarie in the Eastern Goldfields region in Western Australia. Today Kookynie is a ghost town of less than a hundred inhabitants and a tourist attraction, but at is height in 1905, it was a busy gold mining town with a population of around 1500. He was still there in 1906.

By 1907 Charles had become a miner in the Mount Lyell copper mine, near Queenstown, on the west coast of Tasmania. He was a "shift boss" on 20th June 1907 when Patrick Mullins, was fined £1 with costs for assaulting him at the North Lyell Mine at No. 1 engine winze, about 11feet from the bottom[220]. The Tasmania Postal Directory in 1909 lists Chas H. Luxton as an underground manager at North Mount Lyell.

The pneumatic hammer drill, introduced in 1897, and sand blasting, about 1904, both significantly increased the amount of silica dust in mines, causing a rise in lung disease among miners. "Miner's phthisis" was characterised by shortness of breath, cough, fever and cyanosis (bluish skin). With deteriorating health he returned to Queensland where the Electoral Roll for 12th October 1911 lists him as a stockman at Lorraine Station in the Burke district. The 1913 Electoral Roll has Charles Henry Luxton a resident of Winton, a small sheep and cattle town in the outback of western Queensland. He was a secretary of the Winton School of Arts. Interestingly too it was in the nearby Dagworth Station that A.B. "Banjo" Paterson wrote Waltzing Matilda, Australia's unofficial national anthem, the tale of a hungry itinerant worker, or swagman, who gets caught stealing a sheep and chooses death over losing his freedom.

Charles Henry Luxton (1871-1913) was aged 42 years 2 months and 5 days, when he died at Winton Hospital, Queensland on the 17th June 1913. His death certificate is far more informative than its U.K. equivalent. George Luxton, mason and Eliza Lilly are named as his parents and his birthplace Clevedon in Somerset. He had resided in Australia for 24 years. The cause of death was 1.pneumonokoniosis 2fibroid phthisis3exhaustion. The illness had lasted some years. His mother had died of T.B. and it may

---

[220] Daily Telegraph, Launceston, Tasmania, Thursday 20th June 1907.

account for his domicile in Winton as the only treatment at that time was to live in a dry climate. Two of his half brothers were coal miners and his death certificate says Charles was a miner too but it is most likely he was opal mining for Winton has given its name to the Winton Formation, a belt of deeply weathered Cretaceous sedimentary rocks which produces "boulder opal," much of which is extracted in "open cut" mining operations. The Rev. E. Ball, a Methodist minister, conducted his burial service at Winton Cemetery on

the 18th June 1913.G.G. Smith and T.H. James, were two witnesses at the burial[221]. His well preserved headstone reads:-In/Memory/of/Charles Henry Luxton/Born at/Clevedon Somerset England/12th April 1871/ Died at Winton, 17th June 1913/At Rest.

George, and his second wife Clara, had nine children. Ernest Arthur Luxton, the eldest child and my grandfather, was born in All Saints Lane, Clevedon on the 26th November 1875 and baptised in All Saints Church on Boxing Day in that year. Terrace houses for working men were built in Kenn Road in the 1870s and the family were living there when two more sons, William James and Harry Edmund were born in 1877 and 1878. George 33, mason and his wife Clara 31, lived in 1881 in a cottage in Kenn Road, Tickenham, Clevedon, with their sons, Charles 9, Ernest 5, William 3 and Harry aged two. Adelaide Lester, a 45 year old unmarried laundress, and her two year old son, Frank Lester, were boarding with the family. The Luxtons were still resident in Clevedon when a fourth son, Alfred Edward Luxton, was born on the 25th July 1881.

The family were settled in the nearby village of Wraxall, when daughters Kate Louisa was born there on the 24th December 1882, and Ida Laura on the 11th September 1884. Sometime in the late 1880s the

---

[221] See letter of 15 March 2008 from Brian Luxton in Toowoomba Queensland who has helped me unravel details of Charles Henry Luxton's life in Australia.

family moved to Nailsea where the three youngest children were born. Blanche Maud, born on the 25th January 1889 was baptised at Christchurch, Nailsea in April 1889, and she was followed by Thomas John born in 1890, and Emily May in 1892.

The 1891 census records George Luxton, a mason, aged 43, his wife Clara 41 and seven children, William 13, general labourer, Henry 12, Alfred 9, Kate 8, Ida 6, Blanche 2 and Thomas aged 7 months living at 6 The Drove, Nailsea. The Drove was always called the Black Drove because it was made of ashes and pit waste[222]. It was on the north side of the village and joined the road to Clevedon. It is now called Southfield Road but at the junction with Clevedon Road is a large block of flats called Drove Court. These are within fifty yards of where George Luxton and his family lived at the Drove.

The house was overcrowded so Ernest Arthur, their eldest son, aged 15, a baker's apprentice, lived with his maternal grandparents John and Emily Beer at Westcott, King's Hill, near the Butcher's Arms, Nailsea. As soon as they were old enough the girls too left home. Kate Louisa (1882-1949), born in Wraxall on the 24th December 1882, married Isaac Manfield at St. Luke's, Bedminster on 21st January 1903 and in the 1911 census Isaac, a 46 year old hewer in a stone quarry, and Kate 29, with four young children lived in a five room house at Woodview Terrace, Nailsea. When she was widowed she married Samuel Brake, a domestic gardener at Christchurch, Nailsea on 12th August 1922. Sam died and was buried there on 21st October 1939. Kate died at Heathfield Road, Nailsea on

---

[222] See letter of 10th December 1996 from Reginald James Luxton of Nailsea.

the 18th September 1949 and had a married daughter Sheila Hall, living at the same address. Ida Laura (1884-1969), born in Wraxall on 11th September 1884, was a 17year old domestic servant to James Dibsdall, a farmer in Chelvey, Long Ashton in 1901. Interestingly a distant cousin, Thomas Luxton Small, 14 of the Aller branch, was a farm labourer living in the same house. Ida married Herbert Webber, a market gardener, at Christchurch, Nailsea 13th May 1907. They settled in the Castleton, Marshfield area of Gwent where Bert worked as a hedger and ditcher for the River Board. Ida of 4 Caebrandi, Marshfield, died aged 86 on 9th January 1969 and Bert died aged 94, on the 30th August 1974, leaving a family. Blanche Maud (1889- 1961), born in Nailsea on the 25th January 1889, married "Smiler"Alfred Gould who worked as a stone mason on the Tyntesfield Estate, at St. Luke's, Bedminster, on the 20th January 1912. They had a family and Alfred, a Company Sergeant Major in the Great War won the D.C.M. They lived in Jubilee Cottages, near Wraxall Church, where Alfred was Captain of the bell ringers and lie buried close to its tower. On previous page we see Blanch and Alf on Easter Monday 1939 with the tower of Wraxall church in the background. Alfred died in 1956 and Blanche on 28th November 1961. Emily May (1892-1949), the youngest girl, married Albert Price, a miner at Cwmtillery, South Wales in 1918, and I will say more about her in my chapter on her brother Harry.

George and Clara were residing in 1910 at 3 Old Rank, known as The Glass House, Nailsea which was originally built to house the employees of the Nailsea glass works. Old Rank got its name when the area became overcrowded and more

Nailsea Village.

cottages called New Rank were built opposite them. Old Rank has been modernised and is now called Woodview Terrace.

The family moved before the Great War to Rosedene No 89, High Street, a cottage in this old postcard view, adjoining the Queen's Head Public House. In 1911 the cottage with six rooms was occupied by George Luxton, 64, walling mason for a builder, his wife Clara 62, daughter Blanche 23, domestic cook, and youngest son Tom, aged 20, who was a general labourer for a builder. Brit Smallman a housepainter, from St Helens was lodging with the family. The cottage is now demolished and the site is occupied by a block of shops called King's Court[223].

George had to work hard to pay for the upbringing of his large family. Fortunately, masons received a good rate of pay. In 1880 a farm labourer received 17s..6d per week while among tradesmen the mason on 35 shillings received the top pay, ahead of carpenters and plumbers on 33 shillings[224], printers and painters on 32 shillings, smiths on 31 shillings, tinsmiths 28 shillings, bakers 27 shillings, cobblers on 24 shillings.

Much of his working life George was busily employed renovating old churches throughout Somerset. He was especially in demand because of his skills in Gothic free-stone work for the restoration of churches and he was well qualified and skilled at dressing and fitting stone for church pinnacles, gargoyles and other decorative work. In his old age George, from the doorway of his Nailsea home, could see the three fine church towers at Dundry, Backwell and Wraxall which he had spent many years renovating. He was heard to say proudly in his very broad Somerset accent, "I dundry" by which he meant "I done three"[225].

George was closely involved in the late 1880s and early 1890s in renovation work at All Saints, Wraxall parish church[226]. It is one of the best towers around Bristol and from the churchyard the visitor may enjoy a grand view of the Mendips. To start with an elder tree and brambles had to be removed from the stonework of the beautiful grey tower where they were damaging the masonry. In 1892 a pinnacle fell from the tower through the nave roof, narrowly missing the organ. This accident

---

[223] See letter of 1st February 1997 from Reginald James Luxton(1913-2004) of 7 Woodview Terrace, Nailsea, Bristol.
[224] See "The Dictionary of Statistics" by M.G. Mulhall published in 1899 by George Routledge and Sons Ltd.
[225] Related to me by his grandson George E. Luxton (1905-1983) of Barry.
[226] See letter from Mrs Phyllis Horman, 11 Valley Way Road, Nailsea, Bristol dated 30 January 1990.

resulted in the remaining pinnacles being taken down, and reset, and the fourth one being replaced. There were considerable repairs too in the nave roof. The chancel was rebuilt and extended and a new east window was inserted. Other church rebuilding work was undertaken and the churchyard was extended with a new wall. The unusually lofty fifteenth century Preaching Cross in the churchyard was restored in 1893 with a new top.

Georges daughter, Ida Laura (1884-1969), recalled that in the 1890s, when she was a young girl, she would take George's lunch to him while he was working at Wraxall church (in photograph). She was a bit of a 'Tom Boy' and the workmen dared her to go down the tower in a half barrel which was used as a working bucket. To their surprise Ida agreed, but told them she must do it while her father was not watching.

Ida was in the bucket halfway down the tower when her father walked around the scaffolding. He was astonished to see her coming down in the bucket and remarked, "You'll need new knickers after this caper my girl!" "No I won't", she retorted. Ida recalled with a chuckle that she was wearing blue knickers that day.

Clara, George's second wife, was a very strict mother, and with nine children she tolerated no answering back or messing about. She gave her children a good clip when it was necessary. George was generally easy going but at times he displayed a fierce temper. He was training his son Harry to be a mason, when for some reason he made the mistake of showing Harry up in front of the other workmen. Harry, who had an even fiercer temper than his father, threw a hammer which caused a lump behind George's ear. In the course of their altercation, Harry "swung off his father's beard" and then went home to bed, even though it was a fine summer's day. When he got up the following morning, Harry put on his best clothes and left home. He joined the Somerset Light Infantry in February 1896 and fought in the Boer War and returned with medals to prove it. Harry became a coal miner in Cwmtillery, South Wales where he married and had a family. There he died aged 92 and I attended his military funeral on a rainswept Welsh hillside, in January 1970.

George was sometime a soldier, according to his daughter Ida Laura, who remembers that when a girl she played with his black busby. Her face flickered with a smile as she recalled, "What fun we used to have playing with that hat". A search, however, of army records at Kew has failed to uncover any reference to George as a soldier. I'm inclined to think that he was in the First Somerset Artillery Volunteers who wore red coats and black busbys. There was a membership of eighty at Clevedon in 1897.

George was a keen rose grower and was skilled at grafting roses onto wild briars. He grafted a rose successfully onto a cabbage stump on one occasion and had it produce a flower. He also kept a roomful of caged birds, especially canaries and he won an important championship with his birds at the Crystal Palace, the annual national exhibition centre. I have found newspaper reports of other competitions he entered. George won first prize for any other variety of canary at the Clevedon Flower &Poultry Show, held in the Herbert Gardens in late August 1888[227]. He won first prize for his Scotch Fancy in the fourth annual show of the Clevedon Poultry Pigeon Rabbit & Cage Bird Association which opened on the 21st October 1891 at the Skating Rink, Clevedon[228]. He won prizes too at the Portsmouth Poultry Pigeon and Cage Bird Society Show, held at the Volunteer Drill Hall Landport in October 1888,[229] the Bridgwater Poultry Show where George Luxton, of near the Post Office, Nailsea won second prize for his Scotch fancy in February 1889[230], the Shaftesbury Poultry Pigeon and Cage Bird Exhibition held in the Market Hall in October 1889,[231] the Bristol Bird Cage Show & Exhibition held in the Shepherds Hall, Old Market Street, on the 3rd November 1892,[232] the Cardiff and District Fancier's Society in the

---

[227] Weston-Super- Mare Gazette, Saturday 1st September 1888.
[228] Bristol Mercury, Thursday 22nd October 1891.
[229] Hampshire Telegraph, Saturday 27th October 1888.
[230] Weston-Super-Mare Gazette, 9th February 1889
[231] Western Gazette, Friday, 25th October 1889.
[232] Western Daily Press, Friday 4th November 1892.

Cardiff Market Hall on 7th December 1892,[233] the Llandough and Cogan Workingmen's Horticultural Society in the Cogan Board Schools Penarth on the 21st August 1895[234] (where he won a box of Spratt's Patent Cage Food for the best Cinnamon or Scots' Fancy Canary) the Penarth and District Fanciers Society in the Andrews Hall, St. Mary Street on 21st October 1896,[235] the Trowbridge Poultry Show, held in the Market House where George won second prize for his scotch fancy, any colour, cock or hen in October 1897,[236] The Barnstaple Poultry Pigeon Dog & Chrysanthemum Show, held at Barnstaple Market on Tuesday 2nd November 1897[237] the Cardiff & District Cage Bird Society Show, held in the Andrew's Hall, St. Mary Street on Wednesday and Thursday the 9th and 10th November 1898[238] and again in November 1899, and the Exeter and Devon Fanciers' Society, held in the Lower Market, Exeter in November 1901.[239] When he died he left many birds to relatives. His grandson, George E. Luxton (1905-1983) of Barry, visited him at Nailsea and was given five caged canaries to take back to South Wales. Albert Price, George's son-in-law in Cwmtillery also had caged birds from him. A number of these birds termed "mules" were a cross between a canary and a finch. George's love of bird keeping was continued by his sons Ernest, Fred and Harry and other family members.

George suffered for a long time with a bad chest, caused by the stone dust he inhaled in his work as a mason. He was considered as "something of a creaking door" in his latter years and the family were surprised when his wife, Clara, died before him. They were living at the time in the High Street, Nailsea, next door to the "Nags Head" (i.e. Queen's Head Public House) when Clara died aged 67 from cirrhosis of the liver on the 17th May 1917. Clara was buried at Christchurch, Nailsea on the 20th May 1917.Her memoriam below card reads:-

---

[233] South Wales Daily News, Thursday 8th December 1892
[234] South Wales Daily News, Thursday 22 August 1895 & Penarth Chronicle 24 August 1895.
[235] South Wales Daily News, Thursday 22nd October 1896
[236] Warminster & Westbury Journal, Saturday, 30th October 1897.
[237] Exeter & Plymouth Gazette, Wednesday 3rd November 1897.
[238] Western Mail, Thursday 10th November 1898.
[239] Western Times, Wednesday 20th November 1901.

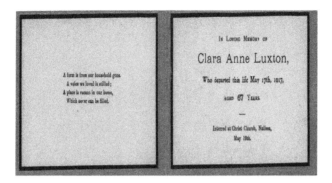

In Loving Memory of

Clara Anne Luxton,

Who departed this life May 17th, 1917,

Aged 67 Years

Interred at Christ Church, Nailsea,
May 19th.

A form is from our household gone,
A voice we loved is stilled;
A place is vacant in our home,
Which never can be filled.

George went to live with his married daughter, Blanche Gould, in Farleigh, a hamlet forming part of the nearby village of Backwell. Blanche's husband, Alfred Gould, worked for the Tyntesfield[240] Estate and they lived in one of a pair of semi-detached houses at Chapel Hill, Backwell Green, Backwell[241].

The house (below) is still there but I don't know the number. That is where George died at the age of 71 from chronic bronchitis and heart failure on the 25th October 1918. James Luxton, his grandson in Nailsea remembered seeing George in his coffin in Blanche's house in Backwell[242]. So many family members were crammed into the cottage for the funeral, Millie Webber, a grand –daughter later recalled she had to sleep under the kitchen table.

George Luxton, aged 71, of Farleigh, Backwell, was buried with his wife Clara, at Christchurch, Nailsea, on the 30th October 1918. It was a few weeks before the Armistice which would bring three of his soldier sons' home from the Western Front.

---

[240] The Rev George T Seymour erected a handsome manor house Tyntesfield at Wraxall in the early 19th century.

[241] See Reginald James Luxton (1913-2004) of 7 Woodview Terrace, Nailsea, Bristol, letter of the 1st February 1997. I have tried to pin point the exact address but there were no electoral rolls made during the First World War so I was only able to check the roll from October 1918 to March 19 19 which lists Alfred Gould Backwell, absent voter, probably on War Service. His wife is listed Blanche Maud Gould, Backwell Green. I also checked March 1919 to October 1919 and this is exactly the same but Alfred Gould is now listed so he must be home from war service. No other information is given.

[242] See letter of 10th December 1996 from Reginald James Luxton.

George and Clara Luxton lie buried in an unmarked grave but I still possess a head and shoulders vignette portrait of George, taken when he was an old man. He displays a flowing white beard which according to his youngest son, Tom, at one time spread down to his waist. See photograph at head of chapter.

30

ERNEST ARTHUR LUXTON (1875-1939) MASTER BAKER OF BARRY, GLAMORGAN

See tree 15

My grandfather Ernest Arthur Luxton was born in All Saints Lane, Clevedon, Somerset, on Friday the 26th November 1875. He was baptised a month later on Boxing Day in All Saints Church at the end of the lane. His father George Luxton
(1847-1918), a master mason, came from Chipstable in the Brendon hills to the north west of Taunton, while Clara Annie Beer his mother, was a native of Yarcombe, Devon, close to its border with Dorset. George and Clara who married in St. James parish church Bristol on the 18th May 1875, were among the migrants who settled in Victorian Clevedon as it developed to cater for the increasing holiday trade.

Ernest was the eldest of nine children but there was an elder half brother, Charles Henry who was baptised in Clevedon on the 14th May 1871. He was the son of George by his first wife, Eliza Lilly, a local girl. Tragically Eliza who was terminally ill with consumption, died aged 25 on the 4th October 1871. She is buried in her parents' grave in St. Andrew's churchyard, Clevedon. Charles Henry who was adopted by Clara, his step mother, later emigrated to Australia in 1889.

The family were residing in Kenn Road, Clevedon when two more brothers, William James was born on the 30th June 1877 and Harry Edmund on the 23rd September 1878. When the 1881 census was taken the couple and their four sons were living at 49 Kenn Road, Tickenham,

Clevedon and later that year they were joined by a fifth son, Alfred Edward who was born on the 25th July.

With so many young children, the house was overcrowded so Ernest was sent to live with his maternal grandparents, John Beer (c.1823-1905) shoemaker, and his wife Emily who lived at Westcott, (inset), a cottage on King's Hill, Nailsea. The 1891 census for King's Hill, Nailsea lists John Beer 69, Bootmaker born Yarcombe Devon, Emily 59, his second wife, born Flax Bourton, Somerset and their grandson Ernest Luxton aged 15, baker's apprentice. I still have John Beer's cobbler's last. His son Jim Beer worked in a brewery in Newport, Monmouthshire and had two sons.

Ernest qualified as a master baker, serving his apprenticeship in Alfred Wickenden's baker's shop[243] and restaurant in Hill Road, near the sea front in Clevedon. Alfred Wickenden ran his business as a baker and confectioner in the building now called the Regent Steak House for about thirty years from 1880 until 1910. He catered for balls, wedding breakfasts and all social functions, also hiring out a large hall for dances and parties. The ground floor was used for the baking and confectionery and upstairs was a dining hall used for large functions. Ernest received a thorough training at Wickenden's. Lord Elton of Clevedon Court, and other wealthy and

---

[243] In 1971 I had the good fortune to meet Thomas Lilly, a retired baker of Nailsea, then aged 86. His daughter Beatrice was the wife of James Luxton a nephew to Ernest. Thomas Lilly knew my grandfather Luxton and was aged about 11 when Ernest left for South Wales. He told me that Ernest served part of his apprenticeship with Thatcher of King's Hill, Nailsea.

influential people resided in the area so meals had to be of a high standard.

Grandfather began his career as a delivery boy and always felt awkward when he had to deliver bread to a local monastery. This was in the former Royal Hotel, Clevedon, which was purchased by the Franciscan Order in 1883. To gain entry to the monastery Ernest had to knock on the stout outer door. A monk would slide back a panel to enquire who was calling. He was then ushered into a waiting room and locked in while the monk went off to find out how much bread was needed. Grandfather always had the irrational fear he would be kept there.

One night when the snow covered the ground between Clevedon and Nailsea, he was walking home and could hear movement behind him. Every time he stopped the noise stopped too. Fearing to look back he began to panic. The noise persisted, and eventually he plucked up courage to see what was following. To his great relief he saw a large but friendly dog, standing and staring at him.

When Ernest completed his apprenticeship he was receiving fifteen shillings a week. South Wales was developing rapidly with the expansion of the coal trade and the improved wages on offer beckoned many young people in the West Country to cross the Bristol Channel. Nowhere was the impact of industrialization greater than in Barry in the last two decades of the 19th century. The sudden influx of people into the villages of Barry, Cadoxton and Merthyr Dyfan transformed them into suburbs of a busy modern town.

My family settled in Cadoxton, the largest of the villages, which in the mid nineteenth century was noted for its fruit and flower growing. Here lived John Spickett (1857-1936), whose father John, farmed 35 acres at Hatch House. Their Spickett ancestors had arrived in Cadoxton from Penmark at the start of 18th century. In 1881 John, 23, married with a young family was living in Whitchurch, Cardiff where he was a grocer, but by the late 1880s he was back in Cadoxton, just in time for the momentous opening of No.1 Dock. A new town was being born to serve the dock which increased the tonnage of coal exported every year until disrupted by the outbreak of the Great War 1914-18. The 1891 census lists him residing in Rock Terrace. These newly built houses were constructed from carboniferous limestone, hauled from Ince's

Quarry on the opposite side of the road. No.7 Rock House, his home and corner shop, was at the end of the row. A zig zag path mettled with cinder ash led to his stone built bakery on top of Cassy Hill. This was the setting in which my grandfather came to live and work.

At Barry work commenced in 1894 on excavating the second dock and there was an influx of navvies and their families into the new boom town. When John Spickett, the baker and confectioner at Rock House, Cadoxton, Barry, offered grandfather a sovereign a week as an 'improver' he accepted because it was five shillings more than he could earn in Somerset. An "improver" is a baker who has qualified and has one year's probation before being fully fledged.

On his arrival in Cadoxton, Ernest lodged with Mr and Mrs Howells, a hedger and ditcher, at 3 Cassy Hill, a house which was occupied by Jack Mancell and family when I was a boy. Unfortunately Ernest's first impression of Barry was not a good one for he arrived in time for the almost "arctic winter" of 1894 and he was snow bound for about six weeks. He was so despondent he wanted to return to Somerset and would have certainly done so if the trains had been running. Luckily, Spickett's Bakery on Cassy Hill was close by so he did not have to travel far to his work place.

In July 1895 when the third annual outing of the Cadoxton Barry District Master Bakers' Association was held at Raglan Castle, athletic sports were held in a field in the vicinity of the castle. E.A. Luxton is listed as coming third in the final of the 120 yards race. The Barry Dock News, a local newspaper which I have scrutinised closely for the years 1890 to 1900 contains other interesting references to my grandfather. He was among the seventy present at the Royal Hotel, Cadoxton on Wednesday 3rd March 1897, when his employer J.Spickett, the President, occupied the chair at the fourth annual dinner of the Barry and Cadoxton District Master Bakers and Millers Association. The proceedings closed at mid-night with the singing of "God Save the Queen". In March 1899 he attended the sixth annual banquet at the Windsor Hotel, Barry Dock. On a Saturday night in May that same year he was at the Royal Hotel, Cadoxton, when the journeyman bakers of the district, under the auspices of the Cadoxton and Barry Branch of the Amalgamated Union of Operative Bakers and Confectioners, held a "very enjoyable and successful smoking concert which was well attended". In January 1900 Luxton & Spickett won third place with a pigeon in the Porth & Rhondda Fanciers' Show held in Porth Town Hall[244]. Finally on the 3rd August 1900 the Barry Dock News reported that at the Penarth Fanciers Show, held on the previous Wednesday, E.A. Luxton, Cadoxton, was very highly commended for his Scotch Fancy Canary.

Ernest, described as a baker resident at 29 Crichton Street, Cardiff, married Florence Sandall of 14 Herbert Street, in St Mary the Virgin Church, Bute Road, Cardiff on the 4th March 1900. I possess a carte print of my grandfather E.A. Luxton taken at the time of his wedding by Williams & Williams photographers, 53 Queen Street, Cardiff. In the head and shoulder portrait he is wearing a three piece lounge suit and his fashionable jacket is cut quite narrow with small high lapels. His white shirt has a starched collar, standing high, and his hair, cut short and close to the head, is parted on one side. He sports a neat moustache.

Florence had first come to Barry in 1894, when she was 17. Her father Thomas Sandall, born in 1842, in the Lamb and Flag Inn, Pinchbeck, Lincolnshire, drove an excavator's engine, the "Runcorn". When his excavating work finished on the Manchester Ship Canal, Tom, his wife, Sarah Jane Shackley, and family travelled to Barry in a pony and trap. The journey took three months and he bought and sold horses on the way! The family settled in a newly built stone fronted house, no. 8 (now renumbered 28) at the top of Church Road, Cadoxton and when Tom's excavator engine, the "Runcorn" arrived by rail he was employed by Tannet & Walker in excavating the Barry No 2 Dock which opened in 1898. "Runcorn Tom," as he was called by fellow navvies, returned north,

---

[244] Evening Express, 1st February 1900.

and settled at Bolton Lee Sands, and Morecombe in Lancashire before dying in Grimsby in 1916.

Ernest and Florence lived at Porth in the South Wales Coalfield for awhile and it seems likely it was in this period when they were newly weds. In later life Florence recalled her surprise at seeing the Welsh colliers, black with coal dust, returning to their homes from the mines to scrub themselves clean in portable tin baths in front of the fire. For a while Ernest suffered with dermatitis and had to give up baking. He found work with Cardiff Corporation and was employed as a mate in a carpenter's shop.

This could not have been for very long. The couple were back in Cadoxton, Barry by 31st March 1901, when the census lists Ernest 25, confectioner baker, and his wife Florence, 22, living at No 6[245] Coldbrook Road which was next door to Rock House, the home and corner shop kept by his employer, John Spickett. Ince's Quarry was still blasting on the opposite side of the road, and early one morning stones went through their roof! The couple soon moved and Ernest was described as a confectioner when their first child, Florence Ethel, was born at 13 St. Oswald Road on the 31st October 1901.

The family returned to Cardiff, where Ernest was employed as a journeyman baker and confectioner, by Jack Banks (1872-1932), a Liverpudlian, who with his West Country wife Amelia, had just settled in Monthermer Road. The Western Mail Directory for Cardiff in 1904 lists Ernest and family living at 25 Bruce Street, Cathays, just two doors away from J. Banks Park Steam Bakery. Two more children were added to the family while they lived at this address. Doris, a beautiful baby with curly hair and brown eyes, was born on the 18th October 1903 but she died aged 3 months at 25 Bruce Street on the 26th January 1904. An inquest held in Cardiff the following day records the cause of death, "Natural Causes probably from convulsions". George Ernest Luxton, a son was born on the 3rd March 1905.In 1907 they moved to 6 Bruce Street.

Family folklore says Ernest was very upset when one of his colleagues was found dead in a mixing machine at Banks Bakery. However, a

---

[245] No. 6 Coldbrook Road is now 13 Coldbrook Road East and Spickett's shop is now Coldbrook Stores. In photo P 325 they are newly built on end of Rock Terrace.

search of old newspapers has failed to find evidence for this death in Cardiff and I now think my grandfather read a news report in the South Wales Daily News, Friday 7th September 1906 which reports the death of a master baker in Northampton who was found dead by his wife in a mass of half made dough! He left Banks Bakery in 1910 and went to his wife's family in Morecombe in the north of England for a while where he was employed labouring on wagons. Because of the fresh air he became "red faced" and his friends in Barry thought it funny to see a "red faced" baker when he returned to work in the town.

The census of Sunday 2nd April 1911 lists Ernest, a baker confectioner, his wife Florence, and their son George, aged 6, living in Cadoxton at 176 Barry Road. Their daughter, Florence Ethel had been a normal healthy child, but she developed a tuberculosis abscess on the brain and despite treatment at Great Ormond Street in London, she died aged ten at 176 Barry Road on the 26th August 1912. She was laid to rest in what was later to be her parents' grave in Barry cemetery. Ernest and Florence were still residing at 176 Barry Road when my father Burt Arthur Luxton, their youngest child, was born there on the 17th September 1913. He was named Burt after a little boy who was being treated at Great Ormond Street when his sister Florence Ethel was a patient there.

Ernest had returned to Barry to work for B.A.Walker who opened his high class bakery & confectionery business at 264 Holton Road in July 1894. Burton Arnold Walker (1867-1936), a Yorkshire man, who arrived in the town from the firm of Messrs T. Walker & Sons, Penarth, bought Spickett's business but not the old bakehouse. When Walker retired about 1914 Ernest Luxton was offered a partnership with Ben Ashton (1885-1965) a baker, and Walker's rounds man, delivering the bread. He decided to go it alone so the business interests were halved between Ashton and Luxton. The bakery round was split, with Ashton keeping the area around the shop in Holton Road and grandfather Luxton, taking over Walker's round outside that area. No.264 Holton Road is still a successful bakery- "The Jolly Baker".

This was just before the First World War, and Ernest moved to the bakehouse behind Wm Price, hay dealer, corn and seed merchant etc. at 94 High Street, Barry. The bakery could be entered through the shop but more usually it was entered through the rear lane. Florence's father, in his will, bequeathed money which enabled Ernest to establish his business.

The family moved about 1915 to a house, situated on the north side of High Street, opposite to No 117, A.F.Hardy, Welford Farm Dairy and Grocer. My father Burt Arthur Luxton, recalls that he attended High Street Infants School at the end of the Great War.

Ernest Luxton was not conscripted for military service during the Great War but when it was ended he had to vacate his bakery in High Street. The lease on the property was short lived, and Aaron Rees the butcher at 93 High Street, wanted to use the bakehouse to bake his meat pies and other products. He took my grandfather to court to repossess it.

On the day he lost the case, grandfather Luxton went to E. Price in Bristol where he bought a new double decker oven. He returned to Cadoxton where Spickett's old bakery on Cassy Hill was derelict and partly roofless. It still belonged to the Spickett family and grandfather knew the owner, Tom Spickett (1888-1962), the Sanitary Inspector, since Tom had been a boy. The derelict bakery was the play place of children and my father, Burt, recalls that he was aged about 5 when he went with his father to look at the old place. He ran around Cassy Common, playing and having a wonderful time, while his father inspected the property. Ernest realised the place had potential for there were too many bakers in High Street and there was more room for stabling the horse on Cassy Hill.

He rented the derelict bakery from Spickett, threw out the old ovens, and installed the new. He returned to his old home at 176 Barry Road in 1918, but when the opportunity offered he decided to live in No 2 Cassy Hill, next to the bakery, both of which he rented from Tom Spickett. Grandfather kept two cats named after Derby winners to catch mice in the bakery.

In this c.1900 photograph on previous page, Luxton's Golden Crust Bakery, (the L shape stone building), lies on the edge of Cassy Common, behind Rock Terrace. Numbers 2 and 3 Hillside Villas, Cassy Hill, where grandfather first lodged, are the semi-detached houses to the left of the bakery. Tom Thomas, the wheelwright's yard, is next to the old School House on the left. In Rock Terrace the two newer looking houses on right, opposite Ince's Quarry, are No.6 where my grandparent's first lived next to Spickett's Rock House. The brick chimneys belonging to Arkell's Brickyard and the old railway arch over which coal rumbled on its way to the docks have been swept away during my lifetime.

Slates were frequently falling off the bakery roof, and it constantly needed repair. Sometime about the year 1925, Tom Spickett told grandfather that he was receiving little real rent from him because of the continual cost of repair. When grandfather offered to pay £100 for the bakery, Spickett accepted. Grandfather stripped the roof about 1932 and bought slates from a demolished church, to re-roof it. The workmen employed to do the roofing, had only half finished when they left the job. It began to rain and the water came into the bakery where grandfather, was baking so his son Burt, then aged about 19, offered to complete the task. He clambered onto the roof and his father who was in the attic, passed the slates up to him. Burt completed the work, but failed to leave an easy way down and only, with great difficulty, did he manage to reach the ground in safety. When the roofer and his men returned, they were astonished to see that the roof was finished and all they had to do was to put the cresting tiles in place!

His Nailsea relatives considered "Ern" as the gentleman of the family. Friends in Barry described him as a 'short quiet man' while his wife Florence was "prim and proper" and a "good looking woman who worked on the bread van". My grandfather's first bread van was horse drawn. When he was in the High Street bakery he had a mare called

Violet which he kept in fields near Barry Castle. Unfortunately she was kicked by another horse and injured in the flank so that she could not fit into the harness any more.

Polly, the next horse, was bought about 1920 from Mr Tommy Box, who delivered milk from his place at the end of Hebble Lane. The mare was a chestnut grey roan. She was lame and Box fooled grandfather into buying her. Ernest and Florence were very upset when they realised they had a lame horse for they stood to lose a great deal of money and they did not want to go into debt. They treated Polly by standing her in a linseed oil mixture. Fortunately Polly recovered and she lived to do many years of faithful work delivering bread. Grandfather would sing the following ditty to Polly on his bread round:-

> Down the road away went Polly
> with a step so jolly
> and I knew she would win
> the pace was killing
> but the mare was willing
> Whoa mare! Whoa mare!
> You've earned your little bit of corn.

Polly was kept in the bakery stable on Cassy Hill. There she would neigh and kick up a fuss at feeding time. She was kept in a loose box and my father, Burt, on coming home from school, would take her two gallons of water and fill the bucket with chaff[246] twice and sometimes more. This would be poured into a food bin, which measured about four foot by five foot. To this would be added a two gallon bucket of bran and the same amount of oats. This would be mixed and placed in the manger trough for her to eat. Polly was sly and occasionally she would stand on your foot and wouldn't move unless you gave her a hard dig in the side with your elbow!

When spring arrived grandfather Luxton rented a field from Mr Thorne, Bowers Farm, on Bells Hill. The field was at the foot of Church Road, where Bastian Close has been built in recent years. A halter and ropes would be placed on Polly and she would be taken from

---

[246] Chaff is a dry hay about an inch long.

the bakery stable and turned loose in the field. She was very excited when let loose. Her performance always attracted a crowd of onlookers. Polly would gallop madly around, lie down and roll over. It would take a week or so before she settled. When my father was about fourteen (1927), he would be allowed to turn her loose in the field after her day on the bread van and he would collect her again about eight in the morning for a day's delivery work.

The residents of Church Road would give Polly a bucket of water when she was let out in the field. If the water wasn't in a clean bucket Polly would refuse to drink it. When Mrs Brown gave her a bucket which had been used for washing the floor, Polly stuck her head in it and snorted, spraying water over Mrs Brown and other bystanders. They told grandfather who said that they must always use a clean bucket. A few people even bought a new bucket just to give Polly a drink of water.

Every six months, or so, my father would take Polly for new shoes to be fitted by Aubrey Evans, the shoeing smith in Newland Street. Polly would return to the bakery prancing proudly with them. In winter the shoes would have holes in them for studs to be fitted, so that Polly could grip the ice in bad weather. Aubrey Evans' bill of about £9 would be paid in bread for a year to his family.

Jim Pearce, Robin's Lane, would give Polly a summer cut every year when she would sometimes be kept in the Murch Field, Coldbrook Road, on a site now occupied by bungalows. My father would help comb and brush Polly. May Day was special. Polly's hooves and harness were blackened with Blossom boot polish, and the brasses on the harness were made to shine when she was taken to pull the bread van in the May Day procession of tradesmen through the town. The bread van would be freshly painted and Polly would be wearing a hat and ribbons.

Polly had some funny habits. She would pick up and eat a ball of clay when roadmen were digging up the road or she would pick up a stone and chew it around to sharpen her teeth. Once when Polly was unwell, grandfather decided to give the horse whisky to drink. When he reached the bakery stable and gave Polly the whisky she wouldn't let the bottle out of her mouth until she had drunk it all. She was fine the next day.

The bread round began at the bakery on Cassy Hill and ran as far as Queen Street, down Windsor Road and back home to Cadoxton. Originally the bread van was a dark blue but grandmother had it stripped down and cleaned with a pumice stone. It was painted a golden beige colour by Tom Thomas, the wheelwright in Church Terrace and A.H. Bletso, painter of 251 Holton Road, did the finer paint work. The name "Golden Crust Bakery" was painted in gold letters on the side and wheat sheaf transfers provided by Ranks Mill, were painted in gold on the van's back doors. To retain the van's beautiful appearance it was varnished over. At a later period the van was decorated with Nisa bread adverts from Spillers[247].

In 1919 when my uncle George Luxton, was aged fourteen, he was taken out of Hannah Street School to work on the bread van. Polly was put into retirement about 1931 after many years faithful service. She lived her last years in a field situated to the left of the Greenyard Farm Cross-road, as you turn right to the Westra. A shed was provided for shelter and there was a stream where she could obtain a drink. With grandfather's permission, a small holder used Polly, once a week to pull his cart of garden produce to Ely market. Polly enjoyed this work and she would be fed lettuce and other vegetables. She always made a fuss when grandfather and grandmother went to visit her and they fed her with sugar cubes.

When Polly was in her prime, grandfather kept a two wheeled trap in a shed which was up against his house, No 2 Cassy Hill, now the home of Richard Hookings and family. This was next to the bakery, and on weekends, with grandfather and grandmother in the front, and their children George and Burt in the back, Polly would pull the trap as far as Weycock Cross or to Red House Farm, Ely which was occupied by my grandmother's brother, Ernest Sandall.

In the late 1920s grandfather bought a blue Morris Cowley, open tourer, from Joe Donovan, who had a garage in Broad Street. It was fitted with a hood which could move up and down and had a spare wheel carried between the front mudguard and the offside door. The car was bought for

---

[247] The old bread van without its wheels ended its days as a chicken coop at the Colcot Arms, Barry.

private use but was used to deliver bread when Polly couldn't get out to work in icy or snowy weather.

When Polly retired about 1931 a second hand Austin 12, registration No WO 1222, was bought from Gay's in Broad Street. It was a black four door saloon, and this was converted into a bread van. A door was cut in the back and bread racks were placed inside. Boards advertising grandfather's name and bakery were clipped over the windows. The car had artillery wheels with a chrome plated radiator which carried the Austin butterfly logo. It was usually driven by Uncle George but sometimes grandfather drove it in the side streets, off Weston Hill.

The cars were kept at the bakery in a garage which has since been converted into a bathroom at "Hill Crest". At the end of the garage I remember there was a small room. It was entered from the lane and was used as a chicken coop.

There were many incidents connected with the bakery. An Albion lorry which had come to deliver flour at the bakery, tried to turn on Cassy Hill Common, but became stuck in the mud. A second lorry which came to the rescue also managed to become bogged down when it too tried to turn. The two lorries were stuck in the bend near Pear Tree Cottage, and although the drivers put ash on the ground, they were stuck there for most of the day.

My grandmother Florence Luxton (1878-1964) was a very energetic woman. It was a disaster if you were ill on a Monday because on that day all the doors and windows were opened whatever the weather. Carpets were brushed and floors were scrubbed and the house was given a good cleaning. Florence, who walked miles, even in her mid eighties, was a fitness fanatic. Periodically she would go on a slimming diet which would involve drinking a mixture of lemons with senna leaves and Epsom salts. The family had gone to live at No 3 Church Terrace about 1929. One summer's day Florence left a quart jug with this mixture in the conservatory while she and grandfather Luxton went on a day trip to Ilfracombe on a P & A Campbell's White Funnel paddle steamer. They frequently went on these paddle steamer trips in the Bristol Channel during the summer months. While they were enjoying themselves a local character, "Fatty" Faulkner, a strongman, and an other workman, employed by Green's the agents for the G.W.R. were conveying flour in a horse drawn cart from Ranks Mill on the south side of No 2 Dock to the bakery. It was a hot day and when they called at No 3 Church Terrace they saw the jug of drink in the conservatory. They thought it was left for them so they drunk it. They were soon taken ill. One was off work for two days and the other was off for a week. A week later when two different delivery men called at Church Terrace my grandmother learnt what had happened to her drink!

On another occasion "Fatty" Faulkner was delivering flour to the bakery when my father who was playing on the cart, slipped, catching his trousers on a projecting bolt. The trousers were ripped along the seam. His brother George sewed it for him so that his mother did not know. She would have scolded him for being careless. Florence was very active and always on the move. She was very much an open air person and spent much of her time out of doors. There was little time for reading and she did not do needlework or embroidery. When a button came off my father's trousers she sewed it back on but he couldn't take his trousers off because grandmother had sewn it to his shirt as well!

One day Florence was making wine at the bakery when she threw the residue out on Cassy Common. The residue was gobbled up by the chickens and chicks that grandfather kept on the common. They were soon drunk. Their antics included standing on their heads, rolling over and looking upside down through their own legs. A number of the younger birds died. Grandfather also kept ducks. One Sunday in the summer, during the inter-war years, his drake and white ducks wandered from the comparative safety of the common on Cassy Hill to St. Cadoc's, the Old Village Church. The Rev. W. Austin Davies, rector of Cadoxton 1920-1940, was celebrating the Eucharist. The ducks, finding the door open, walked down the length of the aisle to the altar, quacking all the way! There was consternation in the congregation and the rector later requested my grandfather "to keep his ducks in on a Sunday!"

Grandfather Luxton owned a large bird cage in the shape of the Crystal Palace. Linnets and finches which had been caught in the wild were kept in it. These birds were cross bred producing "mules" which were good songsters. This was when he was a young man, breeding canaries too. When he was a small boy my father remembers the cage. It was empty then and kept in the bakery loft and "you could almost climb inside it". The cage had been won by his grandfather, George Luxton, in a big bird competition held at the Crystal Palace in London.

Grandfather Luxton kept chickens, ducks, geese and pigeons. At Christmas time many customers would ask grandfather for goose grease which they used to make poultices etc to ward off colds. Rhode Island Red were his favourite chickens because they laid brown eggs which were popular with customers when he sold them on the bread round. He also reared Leghorns which were good layers but because the eggs were white they were less popular with customers who thought they were 'consumptive'. When grandfather was a young man, working for John Spickett, they had delivery of eggs from China. Grandfather had the hens sit on these eggs and some chicks were born. They produced what appeared to be blue hair rather than feathers and he considered them the funniest chickens he had ever seen.

On one occasion he acquired dark brown eggs from the shop opposite to James the pork butcher in Vere Street, Cadoxton. When a number of these eggs hatched they produced large chickens with feathers that ran right down their legs. He identified these as Van Delders. At another time the manager of Arkell's Brickworks, gave grandfather a mallard, but the duck flew high across Cassy Common back to its home pond at the brickworks. My father was sent to fetch it back. When it returned grandfather clipped its wings to stop it flying. But it still flew away lop-sided to its home pond so grandfather let it go. His brother Fred Luxton (1881-1967), who lived in an old cottage called Noah's Ark in Nailsea, sent Ernest black and white pigeons called "Tumblers". They were given this name because of their habit of flying which made them appear to be tumbling out of the sky. The birds created much interest among pigeon fanciers in Barry who had never seen them before. Bird keeping was popular among my Luxton forebears. My uncle George Luxton was given a fine book full of colour plates, illustrating the different breeds of chicken. It was a gift from his Luxton relatives in Nailsea.

One of the most flourishing trade organisations in the town was the Barry and District Master Baker's Association, founded in the early 1890s. The bakers elected a President every year. I have a photograph of my grandfather, wearing the fine gold chain when he was elected President, sometime in the late 1930s. It was published as plate 116 in Volume Three of my 'Old Barry in Photographs' (1990). In this half length shot he is poised at an angle to the camera. His lounge jacket has long lapels and he has a winged starch collar with a black bow tie. I especially cherish the portrait because few photographs of my grandfather survive, as many family pictures stored in the bakery loft were destroyed in a serious fire during the Second World War.

A photograph of the Barry & District Master Bakers Outing to Lyme Regis in c.1936 was used as Plate 104 in my 'Old Barry in Photographs, Volume 11 (1978)'. My grandfather E.A. Luxton and Florence Sandall are 3rd and 4th from left in third row.

In his later life grandfather suffered with a wheezy chest, caused by smoking and inhaling flour dust, in his occupation as a baker. His death, however, resulted from complications following an appendix operation. He died aged 64, at his home 3 Church Terrace, overlooking St. Cadoc's Church in the 'Old Village' on the 13th April 1939. Following his funeral at St. Cadoc's, on the 18th April, Ernest was

buried in the same grave as his daughter, Florence Ethel, in Barry Cemetery. Their grave is marked by a carrara marble cross surmounted on marble steps. The administration of his personal estate, valued at £469..10shillings, was granted at Llandaff to his widow Florence on the 7th October 1939. In the photo my grandfather is wearing his gold fob Watch (now belonging to his grandson Ian, and the author has the chain). My grandmother bought it in Cardiff. It had belonged to a soldier killed in the Great War.

Florence, now a widow, left No 3 Church Terrace, and went to stay with Dai Griffiths and his wife Mary at "Meadow View," Coldbrook Road, before going to stay with relatives in Morecambe. She later returned to Barry where she lodged with the Knot family in Gladstone Road. This is when I first remember her. The rooms were crammed with Victorian furniture. There was a large table covered in a fine table cloth and a healthy potted aspidistra in a jardinière. Glass show cases displayed china, trinkets and vases and in the fire place were three large ebony elephants. Grandmother was a small, sprightly lady with lovely dark brown eyes, and her skin still had something of its fine olive complexion. In 1941 she married Dai Rees, a widower, who had worked in Ranks Mill. Grandmother had a fine modern bungalow built at the corner of Gladstone and Tynewydd Road, and that is where they went to live.

It was rumoured that there was gypsy blood in the Sandall family and Grandmother Luxton certainly loved walking in the open air. When she was well into her eighties she would walk from her bungalow in Gladstone Road, every Friday evening, to visit us at Passat 12 Coldbrook Road. She would then visit the Hills at No 3 Church Terrace and the Browns next door at No 2 to collect their rent money. From there she would walk on to see my

Uncle George and family in the old bakery now converted into a private house called "Hillcrest". When I was teenager I would escort her on this walk from "Passat" to Church Terrace and on to Hillcrest. She had a love of history and on these walks would relate how as a girl of 17 in 1894, she travelled in a pony and trap from the Manchester Ship Canal to Barry. There were sheep grazing then on Cadoxton Common which was later transformed into Victoria Park. Coldbrook Road where I was born in 1941 was then a narrow lane flanked by tall stately elm trees. Grandmother knew many of the pioneers involved in the early days of the town, and was friends with Dan Evans, the founder of the department store, and Harry Press, senior, Fishmonger, and many more. She also loved to relate the story of a snowball fight on Cadoxton Common with Jimmy Wilde, the famous boxer who was the World Flyweight Champion. Grandmother used to deliver bread to him at Ael y Bryn.

Grandmother Luxton died aged 86 on the 1st November 1964. She lies buried with her first husband Ernest, and their daughter, Florence Ethel, in Barry Cemetery.

Sometime before 1946 the old bakery was converted into a house called "Hillcrest" occupied by my uncle George Luxton and his family. The stables in the centre of the property were made into a large living room, but the old bakehouse in the shorter wing which overlooked Rock Terrace below, had not yet been altered. I can remember the old portable bread oven in this bakehouse which had a Newbridge flagstone floor and whitewashed internal walls. There was a low ceiling, through which a vertical wooden ladder against the wall, passed through a hatch into the flour loft above. But about 1950 the bakehouse was converted into a room, and the flour loft was partitioned into bedrooms. A garage, which had adjoined the stable on its Cassy Common side, was converted into a bathroom.

Above is a modern photograph of No 3 Church Terrace, Cassy Hill, where my grandparents lived.

In the view below of Cassy Common, taken from Little Hill c. 1960, Church Terrace overlooks St. Cadoc's Church in the "Old Village". Grandfather lived in No. 3, the second from the right. In the spring of

2018, I met an old lady, who had fond memories of playing on Cassy Common, smelling the freshly baked bread from my grandfather's Golden Crust Bakery.

31

GEORGE ERNEST LUXTON (1905-1983) OF "HILLCREST", CASSY HILL, CADOXTON, BARRY

See tree 15

George Ernest Luxton, the eldest son of Ernest Arthur Luxton (1875-1939) and his wife Florence Sandall (1878-1964), was born on the 3rd March 1905 at 25 Bruce Street, in the Roath area of Cardiff. George, named after his paternal grandfather, was baptised at Christchurch, Nailsea, on the 21st August 1908, while the family were staying with relatives in the West Country. Ernest visited his grandparents, the Beers, as well as his parents when he visited home.

By 1911 the family were back in Barry, where they were living at 176 Barry Road. George attended the nearby Hannah Street School, but when he was 13, he worked two days a week, as a delivery boy, on his father's bread van. At 14, he left school, to work full time on the bread round. He had a quick brain, and in later life regretted his lack of education because, "it would have made life easier." George was a keen motor cyclist and his first machine, an Aerial NY 3656, was registered to Geo. E. Luxton 2 Hillside Villas, Cadoxton on the 16th July 1923.

George married Phyllis Mary King, youngest daughter of Mr & Mrs Harry King, 94 Graving Dock Street, Barry Docks, at St. Cadoc's parish church in the Old Village Cadoxton – juxta – Barry on Boxing Day 1931. The newly wed couple took out a mortgage for £350 on "Alveston," a bungalow, in Pencoedtre Road. Unfortunately George was unable to keep up the mortgage payments and the couple moved back into his parents' house at 3 Church Terrace. They had issue two children, Sonia, born on the 11th September 1934, married Michael Hackett, a commercial traveller, at St. Joseph's Catholic Church, West Terrace, Penarth, on the 17th August 1957. They had two daughters and lived in Solihull. Sonia divorced, and later married Bob Lake, a company director, at Bromsgrove Register Office on the 30th December

1988. In retirement, the couple lived in Aberdovey on the Cardigan Bay coast, before Sonia, aged 64, died of breast cancer at the Priory Hospital Edgbaston on the 11ᵗʰ October 1998. Her brother, Richard George Luxton, born on the 27ᵗʰ August 1945, an apprentice chef, died aged 18, as a result of a motor cycle accident at the notorious humpback bridge in Weycock Lane, on the 22ⁿᵈ May 1964. Richard's untimely death was a tragic loss still felt in the family.

The bakery business which George inherited from his father in 1939, was in financial trouble. Some of the difficulty was due to an irresponsible streak in George's nature. While courting his future wife Phyllis, he would stay for hours at her house in Graving Dock Street, neglecting the bread round. This had been to the despair of his father who saw customers alienated. George frittered away money in high living and the business was soon in debt. By the late 1930s he was spending more than he was bringing in. In the end he couldn't even pay C.H. Lewis, who supplied the yeast. The flour dust, which had adversely affected his father's health, was beginning to get into George's lungs too.

The roof of the bakery was destroyed by a serious fire on a winter night during the war. It was February 1940, my father Burt was driving home on his Sunbeam motorcycle from his work in the Barry Graving Docks, when he saw the glow of a fire on Cassy Common and realised the bakery was on fire. It was briefly reported in the Western Mail:-"Bakery Destroyed by Fire. Messrs Luxton's Bakery in the Old Village, Cadoxton, Barry, was destroyed by fire on Friday evening. The Barry Fire Brigade was engaged for nearly three hours."[248] Herbie Russell, who was working for uncle George, had overloaded the bakery oven. A vast amount of equipment, which included neighbours motorcycles, was destroyed in the blaze. Lost too were my grandmother Luxton's photograph albums of the family which had been stored in the bakery loft. Among them was a large photograph of my father as a boy with fair curly hair and dressed in a Lord Fauntleroy suit. Fortunately my cousin, Sonia, had preserved a photograph of her father George, aged about 18 months with his sister Florence Ethel, who is aged about 6.

Following the inferno, George sold his bread business, but not the bakery, which he converted into a home called "Hillcrest". This was

---

[248] Western Mail, Saturday, 17ᵗʰ February 1940.

during the war and George became a lorry driver, employed transporting cargoes unloaded from American ships at Barry and Cardiff Docks. Because of rationing and food shortages the Black Market was rife and some of the cargoes he carried never reached their intended destination.

George was employed by Sid Thomas, son of Tom Thomas the wheelwright, who kept his fleet of green lorries in what was formerly Ince's Quarry, Coldbrook Road. In his spare time, my father who worked at Barry Graving Dock, would also do jobs for Sid Thomas. One of his tasks was to shorten the trailers of American lorries so that they could travel more easily through the narrow Welsh lanes. He was working in the large black corrugated metal "Corrigan's" shed, which stood at the corner of the un-metalled lane which leads up through the "Stony lands," to Victoria Park, when he could smell oranges. He climbed a ladder to the loft where he uncovered boxes of oranges, hidden under tarpaulin. They had been stolen from an American shipment. Father brought them home where he filled the kitchen sink and bath with lovely juicy oranges. I was a small boy of four and had never seen an orange before. Today when I plunge into a juicy orange I can still recall my first delicious and illicit feast all those years ago! That was one of uncle George's cargoes which went astray in a way which he had not intended. He never did find out what had happened to those oranges!

George was always up to tricks. One day, while my father was in work at Barry Graving Docks, George came to my mother with bags of slag which he sold her for 3 shillings and 6d. Mam bought them for the garden, only for dad to discover that a workman at Sid Thomas's yard was giving them away free!

George's illicit activities finally ended with him in trouble. He was transporting boxes of kippers, unloaded from an American ship at Cardiff Docks, to a depot at Treforest but he tried to smuggle a number of the crates illegally. He was arrested by the Dock Police and put in Cardiff Gaol. Sid Thomas, his employer, and my father, as a householder, had to go to the gaol to bail him out. This was during the war when I was a little boy so I only heard of this escapade much later.

My auntie Phyllis panicked on hearing the news of her husband's arrest. She came to my mother, pleading George's innocence. But what made her pleading really funny was that she also brought bags of bacon and other items which George had stolen. This was in case the police searched George's home. My mother, a young woman in her early twenties, dug holes in the garden vegetable patch to bury these stolen objects. It was a cold night and she was digging until two in the morning to bury it all. My father knew nothing of this until he came home from work much later!

When the war ended, George, continued as a long distance lorry driver, and on his retirement in the 1960s, he was a petrol pump attendant at the Bartax Garage in Broad Street. He was a bald man of 5ft. $6^1/_2$ inches and sturdily built, with bright blue eyes. He possessed a quick brain and ready wit, but had a fierce temper when roused. He died at the age of 78, at Sully Hospital, on the 10th April 1983. His funeral service at St. Cadoc's Church and cremation at Mid-Glamorgan Crematorium in Bridgend, was followed by his daughter Sonia, scattering his ashes on Cassy Common. Phyllis, his wife, born in Peterborough, on the 1st February 1907, died on the 28th September 1984, and was also cremated at Bridgend. Their home at "Hillcrest," which had formally been the bakery, built about 1870 by the Spickett family, came through a clause in my grandmother's will to my father, who sold the property.

I have a photograph of Ernest Arthur Luxton, his wife Florence, and their son George Ernest Luxton, and his future wife Phyllis King, stopping for a summer picnic in Weycock Lane, near Barry c. 1930. George who was eight years older than my father was a fund of family stories and I miss my chats with him.

32

BURT ARTHUR LUXTON (1913-2007) FITTER TURNER AT BARRY GRAVING DOCKS

See tree 15

Burt Arthur Luxton, the youngest of the four children of Ernest Arthur Luxton, master baker, and his wife Florence Sandall, was born at 176 Barry Road, Barry, Glamorgan on the 17th September 1913. The terraced red brick house at the foot of Crogan Hill, was opposite the 150 foot high brick chimney of the town's destructor yard, which was a noted landmark for many years.

One of Burt's most vivid early memories was watching Mr Andrew Palmer drive the Urban Council's steam lorry to and from the destructor yard. The Foden steam lorry was painted in a reddish brown livery and its brasswork was shining. Burt's parents delivered bread to the Palmer family so as a favour, Mr Palmer, gave him a ride in the steam lorry, and as a special treat, Burt, was allowed to pull the cord which blew the steam whistle. A love for engines and machinery was stirred in the little boy and was to remain a feature of his life. His mother though, feared for his safety, and kept the garden gate firmly shut.

Burt was still a small boy, when about 1915, the family moved to live at No. 50 High Street, a three storey gabled house, next door to John George, a carpenter. His father's bakery at the rear of William Price, Hay & Corn Merchant at No 94 High Street was entered by a back lane. The Co-op in Broad Street backed onto the same lane. High Street was busy with traders and Burt attended High Street Infants School before the Great War ended. His father took him to join the flag waving crowd to see the returning soldiers marching up from Barry Docks through the Island Road railway tunnel into Broad Street. He told Burt the War was over, and they went to Barry Island, where a large celebration bonfire was lit on Friars Point. Some of the tanks and guns which came off the ships were placed on display in Romilly Park for many years.

At the end of the First World War, the family moved to No. 2 Cassy Hill, next to his fathers Golden Crust Bakery on Cassy Common. Burt had been a sickly child, and the Common's fresh air and open spaces helped him to get plenty of exercise and healthy living. He had great fun playing on the common and his father made him a tent out of flour sacks. A constant companion was his pet dog 'Pongo', a cross bred Sealyium whose mother "Chum" a thorough bred Sealyium was his parents' dog.

From early childhood Burt played in Tom Thomas, the wheelwright's workshop at the end of Church Terrace. Tom and his son Sid, would send "Bertie" to Cousins, the ironmonger in Main Street, to buy nails, screws, nuts and bolts etc. At other times he would help them light the forge fire or watch Tom making wheels or putting cart shafts in hot water to bend them into shape. He red leaded a farm cart, which was later painted and decorated. The finished cart was taken via the Three Bells Hill to Cadoxton Railway sidings, because the more direct route via Church Road, was considered too steep. It was then put on a railway wagon for delivery to a farm in the Vale of Glamorgan.

One day while he was playing in the wheelwright's shed, Burt failed to notice their family pet spaniel, Topsy, had just had a litter. As he bent down to pick something up from under the work bench, the dog bit him. There was a great fuss and Tom took him to Mrs Thomas to treat the wound.

Tom would arrange with Burt's dad to put wood which was a little wet in the loft above the bakery on Cassy Hill, where it would be left a week or more to dry before being used. Tom enjoyed shooting and on occasion Mr Butler, in Palmerstown, would collect him in his motor cycle and side car. They would be away for the day and on their return would be laden with pheasants and rabbits etc. Tom wanted to train Burt as a wheelwright, but his father turned down the offer because he saw that with the coming of the motor car, the days of the wheelwright were numbered.

In the early 1920s Sid Thomas, and his business partner, Ned Bishop, son of Dick Bishop, butcher, in Main Street, set up the Crystal Springs Lemonade and Soft Drinks factory, in the old smithy, at the rear of the Three Bells Inn. Burt worked there as a boy, putting labels on the "pop" bottles. The local strong man "Fatty" Faulkner was adept at lifting huge crates of bottles off the wagon and carrying them into the smithy. Burt was eleven (1924) when Sid asked him to take the Sunday School class from Cadoxton Wesleyan Methodist Chapel at the "Royal Hotel," to Sully Woods for a picnic. Burt successfully drove the class there and back in the model T Ford lorry which Sid used to convey his lemonade and soft drinks.

Bishop and Thomas later took over Ince's Quarry, opposite Rock Terrace, Coldbrook and this was turned into a yard where the partners ran their lorry transport and cattle business. When Ned emigrated to Canada, Sid Thomas, continued the business alone. The large corrugated iron shed which stood at the corner of the yard, near the path leading to Victoria Park, was built by Mr Corrigan of Treharne Road. In and after the war years my father worked there in his spare time, shortening the trailers of American lorries used in the country lanes around Barry. The money he earned helped to pay off the mortgage on the bungalow.

In the 1920s Burt's parents would go for picnics in the horse and trap to Weycock or to the Red House, Ely, near Cardiff, occupied by his uncle Ernest Sandall who had taken Ruishton & Proctor steam driven navvies to Russia and India and trained workers how to use them. In about 1923 Burt's uncle, Ernest Sandall, gave his mother Florence, a tiger claw gold brooch set with garnets. It came from India and is still in the possession of the family.

A class photograph of my father B.A. Luxton in Standard V Cadoxton Elementary School 1926/7 taken with his teacher, Tom Yeoman, appeared as Plate No 135 in my Old Barry in Photographs, Volume 11 (1978). When Burt left school at the age of fourteen, he helped on the bread delivery round, working with his brother George in the morning, and his father in the afternoon. He was apprenticed to Ben Ashton, the baker for awhile, but through the influence of his brother George's future father in law, Harry King, he was given an apprenticeship as a fitter and turner at Barry Graving Dock and Engineering Co. Ltd. This was in 1929 and Burt was aged $15^1/_2$ when he began work in the Stores where he earned 8 shillings and 4d a week. The apprenticeship began on his 16th birthday, 17th September 1929, and it lasted until 17th September 1934. He was engaged on all classes of repair work to marine engines and boilers etc. both in the marine shop and on board vessels and at the end of his apprenticeship he was found to be, "punctual and attentive to his duties, an efficient and reliable worker and a young man of good character[249]."

In about 1929/30 the family moved to 3 Church Terrace, opposite St. Cadoc's Church in the Old Village, Cadoxton. Burt went to and from Barry Graving Dock on his Raleigh cycle but later when he had completed his apprenticeship he purchased a motor cycle. His first machine was a 500c.c. Rudge Ulster, with a red painted tank which he purchased for £13 from Harry Thomas, in Palmerstown. It had belonged to a coal trimmer, who had left it on a railway line, where it had been cut in half by a coal train! It was repaired and reconditioned, but was too expensive on petrol. He sold it and paid Jack Kemp, the coal merchant in Barry Road, £8..10s for a 250 unit construction New Imperial. It had belonged to a schoolteacher from Neath who had crashed it into a lorry near Eastbrook in Dinas Powys. It needed a new headlight, front wheel and fork. He used it for about two years to ride back and for to the Graving Dock. It had a black frame and the tank was chrome and green with yellow tracing. It was economical to run and Burt rode it to the Brecon Beacons but it was very low geared and too slow.

Burt and his brother, George, went to Alex Thom's in City Road, Cardiff, to buy a Norton, but the smallest 350 c.c. was too big for what he needed. They ended up in Bevans, Duke Street, opposite Cardiff Castle, where Burt purchased a new Sunbeam 250 O.H.V. (overhead valve) for about £70. He traded his New Imperial in for £40 in part exchange. The Sunbeam was brought to Barry in a van and was delivered at 3 Church Terrace on a Wednesday just before his dinner.

---

[249] See letter of 1st October 1934 by J.H. Evans, manager of the Barry Graving Docks and Engineering Co. Ltd.

It was a long stroke Sunbeam painted black and gold with chrome wheels and head light.

Monty Hook, who lived in St. Paul's Avenue, painted the number plates BNY 865. The Sunbeam motorcycle was registered in Burt's name on the 1st July 1936. Burt had this motor cycle for ten years. He drove it to Penarth Seafront where he was introduced to Beryl Leonora Campbell, his future wife and my mother.

This photograph of B. A. Luxton on his new Sunbeam motorcycle was taken by my mother in the Brecon Beacons, on the 2nd August 1937. That was the day they drove the Sunbeam across Wales to Aberystwyth, on the coast of Cardigan Bay. Burt is wearing a khaki coloured gabardine storm coat. It possessed three linings and was double breasted with huge pockets. He recalls that his weight at this time was a constant 10stone 10lbs. In the summer of 1938 they toured southern Ireland on the Sunbeam. They went to Fishguard, caught the boat to Rosslare and toured Wexford and Waterford, and visited Bantry Bay, Kinsale and kissed the Blarney stone before travelling on to Cork and Queenstown (Cobh). There they visited Fort Villas, where my mother was born, and met her uncle Daniel Leonard and other relatives and friends.

I remember riding on the Sunbeam when I was a child. We still possess the black and gold banded scarf my mother knitted for Burt to match the colours of the Sunbeam.

When my parents were courting they would go to the cinema, two or three times a week, usually to the Washington or the Regal in Windsor Road, Penarth where Monty Smith now has a garage. Sometimes too they would go to the Queens in Cardiff to see a horror film.

Burt married earlier than he intended. His father died in April 1939 and his mother went off to Morecombe and then Wakefield to stay with relatives. His brother George and his wife Phyllis gave up their bungalow "Alveston" in Pencoedtre Road, and moved back into 3 Church Terrace. This situation coupled with the onset of World War prompted Burt, aged 25, to marry Beryl, aged 20, at St. Dochdwy's, Llandough near Penarth on the 10th June 1939. Burt had a chance to buy "Alveston" George's bungalow, but decided instead to buy a new bungalow, for £475, built by Jim Norman in Coldbrook Road. He paid Hammond the Estate Agents who represented the Halifax Building Society £75 deposit in cash. The bungalow was named "Passat" after the four masted barque which visited Barry before and after the Second World War. It was initially lit by gas, but just before the war, Burt converted to electricity, which was supplied by the G.W.R.

When Burt married he was earning £3..6 shillings for a 48 hour week. On Monday to Friday he worked from 7 until 5 with a half hour meal break, and on Saturday mornings he worked from 7 until 12. Overtime worked in the evening or on Saturdays was paid time and a half, and Sunday work was paid double time. He worked hard and the mortgage on the bungalow was paid off before the end of the 1940s.

Burt as a skilled dock worker was in a reserved occupation, and he spent the war years at Barry Graving Docks. He survived air raids on the docks and was lucky to escape death as the result of enemy action. When he came home from work he would have tea, before reporting as a "fire watcher" at Cadoxton School. Along with five other fire watchers, he would look out for German incendiary bombs. This duty would last sometimes until six in the morning. Later in the war he was transferred to fire watching at Sid Thomas' yard in Coldbrook, which handled valuable cargoes transported to and from Barry Docks.

In the early years of the war six soldiers were billeted in the corn loft of the old bakery on Cassy Common. They manned an anti aircraft gun, located on the edge of the common, on the site of an old piggery, close to the foot path which led through the Hayfield to the brickyard. Unfortunately it was not in action on the 1st July 1940, the first air-raid on Barry when a German raider dropped a string of bombs, landing 1) Laura Street 2) Top field of the Pleasure Field (now Marlborough Close) 3) Coldbrook Road in front of No 8, the bungalow occupied by Mr and Mrs Tommy Bishop 4) Cassy Common (the crater is still visible) 5) near the Colcot Reservoir. Burt was lucky to escape with his life as he has told me.

A graphic account of the incident was related on Friday 5th July 1940 in the Barry Herald, which carried a report entitled "Air Raid Experiences" following a raid over Wales on the previous Monday night. The raid was about five o'clock in the evening so it was in the daylight which is not evident from a reading of the newspaper account - "Mr and Mrs Alice Norman, who live only a few yards from where the explosion occurred, were in their shelter with their three children and a friend, Mr Burt Luxton, when Mr Norman, Mr Luxton

Damage to Windows in
Coldbrook Road - 2nd July 1940

and their 16 year old daughter Audrey, decided to "go out and watch the fireworks". They had hardly got out of the shelter when the bomb exploded. Mr Norman was knocked off his feet and flung back into the shelter while Mr Luxton was flung into the garage wall, and Audrey lifted into the air[250].

---

[250] Mr Jim Norman's air raid shelter was built into the car pit of the garage and was fitted with beds. My parents' sometimes stayed there with Jim Norman and family during an air raid.

Providence was certainly generous to their eleven year old son, Anthony. The previous night he had refused to leave his bed during a raid, but fortunately that night he got up straight away and went to the shelter. His bedroom was smothered with debris. The houses themselves were partly wrecked, plaster having been pulled off the ceilings, doors blown off their hinges and practically every pane of glass broken. In Mrs Morgan's house the fumes from the bomb changed the colour of a suite of furniture from a pale green to a much darker shade. The house of Mr and Mrs Thomas Bishop, which caught the full force of the blast, was a shambles, even the roof having been shifted an inch or so. Curiously enough, however, the only china damaged was a cup and saucer"[251].

On Wednesday 3rd July 1940, two days after the raid, the Western Mail carried an interesting report which adds further details:-"A woman slightly injured when she was flung to the ground by the blast of an exploding bomb was the only casualty when German raiders dropped bombs on several areas in Wales on Monday night and Tuesday morning. Some houses were damaged by a bomb which landed in the middle of the road, and windows were splintered for a considerable distance. A Western Mail reporter who visited the area where bombs were dropped found that many people had escaped injury, thanks to the Anderson shelters.

A Mr. Luxton who was out of doors when two bombs fell fairly close to him said, "The first bomb fell in a field close behind me. A second later another bomb landed right in the centre of the road not 30 yards away. They were not screecher bombs, and despite violent explosions I remained on my feet."

The woman who was injured, a Mrs.(Emmie) Morgan, was running with her husband (Cliff) to a neighbours Anderson shelter and they were only half way across the road when a bomb fell within 30 yards of them. The couple were flung to the ground, and Mrs Morgan sustained an injury to her leg. When people inspected the damage as dawn broke some found that iron spikes from railings had been hurled about, and that several were embedded in the shelters.

---

[251] Barry experienced air raids on 1st July, 2nd and 6th September 1940, 4th March 1941(the heaviest attack), 30thApril &4thMay 1941 and finally on30th June 1942.

Later on Tuesday morning a German aeroplane was heard passing over the area at a very great height.

An A.R.P. warden told a Western Mail reporter that he heard several thuds in the distance. "It was not guns because there was no corresponding crack of shells. There was a flash of flame," he said.

The German High Command communiqué on Tuesday claimed:- "During the course of air reconnaissance over the Channel a British patrol boat was attacked east of Torquay during the afternoon of July 1 and set on fire.

During the night of July 1 our fighter planes again attacked docks and harbours in the Bristol Channel. Fires and explosions were observed."

At Passat the doors were blown off their hinges, the plaster was pulled off the ceilings, and nearly every pane of glass was broken. Tony Norman recalls his father Jim laying new plaster ceilings in the hall and the dining room. The Barry Herald received a stiff reprimand for publishing its report as local papers were banned from reporting air-raids. The air-raid was not reported in the Barry and District News or the South Wales Echo. No future air-raids on the town were reported in the local press.

Brian Campbell Luxton, the couple's eldest son, was born at "Passat" 12 Coldbrook Road, on the 29th May 1941. The road, on the outskirts of the town, was quiet during and after the war years with few vehicles compared with today's busy traffic, but there were other noises to contend with. Beryl complained that the gas powered  Ruishton engine, used for hauling the drams in Arkell's Brickworks were creating an irritating din. Strangely the noise from the large Cadoxton railway sidings rarely troubled us because it was sufficiently distant. On winter nights the shunting engines and wagons were a familiar and almost comforting sound. This photograph of the author with his mam Beryl was taken by Chas. Farmer 61 Holton Road in February 1943.

Burt was seldom seen by his son Brian during the war years because he was employed long hours carrying out ship repairs at Barry Graving Docks. The Americans had a tremendous impact because they brought new tools and new ways of working which they taught the local workers. One of the ships he worked on repairing was the Jamaica Planter.

In February 1941 the Jamaica Planter, later to be remembered as the "orange boat" struck a mine in the channel, on a voyage from Kingston, Jamaica, to Avonmouth, and was beached in the Old Harbour, near the breakwater. In the process she lost most of her cargo of fruit which consisted mostly of oranges. These were later washed up on the shore and were sour with an oily taste. She was towed from the Old Harbour (photo below) into Barry Graving Docks for repair. While under repair, she suffered further damage in a bombing raid on the docks. After repairs the Jamaica Planter left Barry for Swansea. While in the Barry Roads she was in collision with the American tanker Wellesley and sank. All the crew were saved. I still possess a ginger jar from the Jamaica Planter which my mother used in the war years as a flower vase!

The build up to D Day was especially memorable. Barry Dock was packed with American, British, Greek, Danish and French ships which were loaded and made ready for the invasion of Normandy. In the Bristol Channel a fleet of ships could be seen assembling in "Barry Roads". Everyone working at the docks realised that something big was about to happen because security was strict. When Burt had to take "sizes" for a pump on a Norwegian ship moored at the Cross Berth, near Ranks Mill, he was escorted there by an armed soldier who stood on the deck while he worked below. The soldier escorted him back to the Graving Docks when he had finished taking the measurements.

One ship Burt vividly remembers, was the American Liberty ship S.S. Artemas Ward (Gross 7176 tons). She was in a convoy from the USA and fully loaded with tanks, guns, jeeps, etc when she was

SS ARTEMAS WARD

in collision with another ship in the Irish Sea, on the 24th March 1944. The ship was badly holed aft of the engine room, and the hole was large enough to drive in two double decker buses. She limped into Barry Docks on the 17th April 1944, and after unloading at No 2 Dock, she came into Barry Graving Docks for repairs. In the between decks she was full of sports gear, which had been tipped in by the lorry load. When the ship dry docked hundreds of balls and other sports gear filled the dock. Burt collected a white waterpolo ball which his son Brian used as a football for many years!

The ship was repaired and the American crew fitted guns fore and aft. All excess gear was removed from the ship and she was moored in No 1 Dock where she was primed with explosive scuttling charges which were placed about the holds of the ship. Finally she was loaded with rubbish from the coalpits. On the 16th May the ship's preparation for the invasion was completed. She was inspected and

approved, and on the following day, the 17th May, she left Barry for a brief visit to Oban in Scotland. She was destined for Omaha Beach in France where on the 8th June 1944, she was scuttled as a "block ship," to help create a breakwater for the Mulberry Harbour, so landing craft and small ships could go to the beach head without being in rough water. The crew remained on board. One wrote, "Don't know how long we will be attached to the ship, but our stay will be miserable. The beach head is red from soldiers' blood in this fight for liberty." The Artemas Ward was officially abandoned on the 22nd June 1944, after the harbour was destroyed by a terrific storm which lasted for three days.[252]

One day while the ship was being repaired in Barry, an American soldier from the Artemas Ward, came into the machine shop where Burt was working. He was in a uniform and carried his rifle. Burt's workmates quipped he had come to arrest him. The Yank had two old British pennies with Britannia on the reverse and he asked Burt if he would help him make a souvenir lighter. Burt, collected a three quarter inch brass hexagon nut from the store room, and drilled out the sides so that the coins with the figure of Britannia, could be placed on either side. The Yank then completed making his souvenir lighter. It turned out that he had worked in a dockyard in California before the war. A day or so later when Burt came into the machine shop he found a seven pound tin of pineapples left on his lathe. It was the Yanks way of saying thank you. They were the first pineapples I had ever tasted!

Burt was involved in the repair of at least two L S T in Barry Graving Docks. An L S T was a large ship tank used to unload tanks jeeps and other supplies on occupied beaches during the allied invasion of Europe. With a top speed of only ten knots the Yanks nicknamed L S T "large slow target." One of these U.S.S. L S T 381 took part in the invasion of Gela, Sicily, Salerno and Anzio, Italy in 1943 and 1944. Soon after that it was involved in the assault on Normandy. The ship on a second visit to Normandy on the 15th June 1944 had unloaded and was "perched" high and dry when about 3 a.m.it was attacked by a lone German bomber which dropped a string of four bombs. One of these exploded about fifty feet of the port bow. Another exploded about thirty feet off the starboard quarter. Although the ship was well "ventilated" by shrapnel, none of the crew were injured which was a small miracle. Most of the damage was above the waterline so it continued operations until the 27th June when it arrived off Barry. It rode at anchor for two days and the crew had to shorten or lengthen the anchor chain due to the extreme tide runs about every six hours. It entered Barry Graving Docks on the 29th June 1944 for repairs to the hull and machinery.

---

[252] See Over Here: in Barry. The American Presence in Barry South Wales, during W.W.2. Last Voyages of Liberty Ship SS Artemas Ward compiled by Glenn Booker.

One G. I. Gordon Lease, (ex-boatswain's mate, U. S. Coast Guard), a crew member, recalls the visit to the port. Here is part of his story in his own words:-

LST 381 Barry, Wales - July 1944

> The work on our ship was done in the Barry Graving Dock and involved welding over 150 holes in the hull, repairs to our main engine clutches and both shaft bearings as well as damage to our bottom. I recall the workmen arrived at about 7:00a.m.and worked until dark each day. They had morning coffee with our crew and we had afternoon tea with them.
>
> My most distinct memory of Barry is how friendly the people were. The workers on our ship were always in good humour, even though they were working over twelve hours, every day of the week, with only a couple of short breaks each day.
>
> All the work on our ship was excellent. No problems at all with our clutches or shaft bearings for the next six months when we transferred L.S.T. 381 to the Royal Navy at Roseneath, Scotland on December the 19th 1944. Our crew returned to the U. S. aboard R.M.S. Queen Elizabeth, arriving in New York City on January 3rd 1945[253].

The repairs took three weeks and when the L S T 381 left Barry on the 22nd July 1944 it proceeded to Cardiff and Swansea for degaussing (i.e. the process of decreasing or eliminating an unwanted magnetic field). As Gordon says the Yanks were impressed and greatly appreciated the high quality and quantity of the work done on their ship at Barry Graving Docks. None of the repairs failed and the ship completed many more trips to Normandy and Britany before the wars end.

Another of these vessels L S T 133 was the very first L S T to beach on Omaha Beach, Normandy[254]. On its third trip from the U. K. over to

[253] See Over Here: in Barry, The American Presence in Barry, South Wales, during W.W.2. (May2010). Mr Gordon Lease & L.S.T.381 by Glenn Booker.

[254] See Over Here: in Barry, The American Presence in Barry, South Wales, during W.W.2.L.S.T.133: From Omaha Beach to Barry Docks by Richard Willstatter and Glenn Booker.

LST 133: From Omaha Beach to Barry Docks

USS LST 133, September, 1944 in graving dock, Barry, Wales, all wreckage cut away and a false bulkhead and jury rigged rudder riveted in place for the tow (26 days) across the Atlantic to the Port of New York.

Omaha at about 8 A.M. Mon 15th June 1944, in about mid channel it struck a German acoustic mine. The result was 78 casualties including 41 dead or missing. The ship was dead in the water having lost both rudders and propellers and it had a huge hole in the transom (the back part) of the vessel. Several ships came alongside to assist in removing some of the dead and wounded and finally in towing the ship to Omaha Beach where all cargo (trucks. tanks, etc) and most of the personnel were taken off leaving only about 5 officers and perhaps 25 men on board. On 18th June she was towed by tug to Southampton and remained there, at anchor, for about a week. It was then towed to Lands End and up the Bristol Channel to Barry.

By the time it arrived at Barry Graving Docks in early July, there was an appalling odour created by stale food and bodies trapped in the wreckage, and the ship was covered in a cloud of about a million flies. The yard manager, employed about 30 Welsh and Scottish deaf mutes to wash, clean out, and remove with all sorts of disinfectant the horrid accumulation of bodies and rotting food. It was said the deaf mutes had no sense of taste or smell and were thus able to handle the job. After a week they were done and the yard workers, including my father took over, cut away the wreckage, and riveted on the false bulkhead and the jury-rigged rudder.

By the end of September the L S T 133 was refloated and departed under tow on a 26 day passage to the port of New York, where at the Brooklyn Navy Yard, a new stern had been fabricated. This was towed over to the Bethlehem Steel Yard in Hokoben, New Jersey, where in dry dock, it was "married" to the L S T 133. Then with a mostly new crew the L S T133 went off to the Pacific war and became heavily involved in the Okinawa campaign.

There were few toys made for children to buy, but Brian had plenty, because his father Burt made them out of wood and metal. These included a wooden steam engine, painted green and black, with the cabin painted red. It had a gleaming brass funnel and brass wheels. There was a hobby horse, painted red, which ran on four

wheels, a red tricycle with yellow wheels and a grey and blue painted Bedford lorry, with yellow wheels. Wooden replicas of the passenger liners Queen Mary and Queen Elizabeth were made to float in the bath. There was a stout wooden shield with a good hand grip, painted silver and decorated with a St. George's Cross, and a sword, to go on the Crusades. Tom Thomas, the wheelwright, had taught Burt, how to make wheel-barrows so he made a smaller version for Brian, who was already a keen gardener. In the years following the war Burt proved to be a wizard too at making kites out of bamboo and brown parcel paper. They were decorated with fierce faces, and Burt made them for Brian and his pals who would have a wonderful time flying and manoeuvring them for hours on Cassy Common or in the Pleasure Field, behind the bungalow. Burt also made wooden sledges, one in particular had high long curved runners, and Brian had a great time sledging down the Pleasure Field in the long winter of 1947 and many winters afterwards. My brother Ian is on the tricycle dad made for me during the war.

The war in Europe over, Burt left Barry Docks on the 26th May 1945, to work for the Universal Metallic Packing Company based in Bradford Yorkshire. Once again he was provided with an excellent reference. This time from the Graving Docks general manager, Major Shirley Beavan, who had been the commander of the Barry Home Guard. The new job provided a pension which he could not get at

Barry Docks. His father in law, James Reston Campbell, was the Cardiff area manager, and they worked in South Wales and the West Country maintaining steam engines on ships and in coal mines. Their branch office in the Royal Stuart Buildings in James Street, Cardiff, consisted of one room on the first floor for storage, and one room used as an office on the second floor. It was held on a quarter yearly tenancy from Cardiff Corporation. Burt was to work with the firm for twenty six years.

Burt realised his Sunbeam motorcycle was not suitable for his wife, Beryl, and young son Brian, so about 1946 he bought a Morris motor car, CAX 297. The car had been in collision with a lamp post and was badly wrecked. At that date few had cars and I can recall the excitement when a lorry brought the wrecked vehicle to the bungalow. Burt rigged up a temporary shelter, with a metal corrugated roof at the head of the drive to house the car. For about eighteen months he spent every available spare moment rebuilding the car up from a new chassis. This work continued even on cold winter nights, with the aid of an electric light on a long lead.

Eventually it was ready for the road and I can remember how proud mam and I were when dad drove us to my mother's parents home at 168 Redlands Road Penarth. It was a great little car but quaint to us now, with a running board on each side. The indicators were lighted arms which came out of the side of the vehicle. It was cold too in winter as there was no heating and we used old rugs to keep warm.

We used the car every week end to visit my materal grandparents in Penarth and in spring and summer we would drive to the Leys at Aberthaw. We would park on the railway bridge before you get to the Blue Anchor at Aberthaw. With trowsers rolled up we would wade across the shallow Thaw River where small flatfish squirmed under our bare feet. A brisk walk along the embankment skirting the golf course led us to the "Far Pool" Here two large pools joined the sea when the tide came in. The pool nearest the beach had a sandy bottom and the water was warm in the sunshine. It was there at the age of six, with the help of an old car inner tube that I learnt to swim.

There too, I further developed my love of nature, and in the spring discovered oystercatchers, ring plovers and terns nests with eggs in

356

them on the shingle above the beach. Many small birds nested too in nearby fields and in one there were lapwings nesting. Skylarks twittered in the blue sky the day long and once I found a skylark's nest cleverly concealed with brown speckled eggs deep hidden in long tufty grass. Those week-ends at the Leys, in the late 1940s and early 1950s, were magic times for us. Sadly when I was about 15 a power station was built at the Leys, obliterating the magic of this place but not the memory.

With the sudden and rapid decline of steam engines, Burt was made redundant with a redundancy payment of £1325. Mr. R. Dracup, the managing director of the Universal Metallic Packing Company Ltd; Beehive Works, Edderthorpe Street, Bradford provided an excellent reference on the 19th March 1971:-

> To whom it may concern
>
> Mr. B.A. Luxton was employed by our company as a service engineer. Since joining us in 1945, he has been conscientious and diligent at his work. Through no fault of his own, his services are no longer required.
>
> The company, being a member of a large group, have rationalised an integrated some of its products into other companies and there fore require a substantially reduced labour force.
>
> Mr. Luxton's performance would have ensured his position in the company, had it been carrying on in its past form.
>
> I would not hesitate to recommend him as a responsible person well qualified as a service engineer.
>
> R. Dracup, managing director.

Within a few weeks Burt was happily back in work as a fitter turner for the Water Board, in Penarth Road, Cardiff, and he finally retired, aged 66, on the 4th February 1980.

Because of his skill in metal working, carpentry, plumbing, electrical work, car repair etc. Burt, saved the family a fortune in bills. On his retirement he and his wife, Beryl, thoroughly renovated the old cottage, No 9 Rock Street, New Quay, Ceredigion, which his son Brian bought in 1980. Burt's ship repairing skills soon came in useful too. One day sitting on the pier, he watched as Winston Evans, the coxon of the lifeboat, struggled to remove wire which had become entangled in the propeller of the "Catherine Arden" his blue fishing boat. Dad soon removed the offending wire. Later that day a grateful Winston called at the cottage to give Burt a large lobster he had just caught. The yacht club too came seeking dad's help and the cottage cellar was used to repair masts and other ship kit. My parents stayed at the cottage from Easter to gone bonfire night every year while Brian and Ian and family would join them in the holidays.

A man of restless yet focussed energy, Burt, was a life long gardener with a special love and care for roses. During the war when F.C. Ball, the market gardener, had to clear his roses cheaply to make way for food production, Burt took the opportunity to fill the garden with roses. He successfully grafted standard roses onto wild briars and for more than half a century the garden put on a fine rose display.

Burt was always supportive of his wife Beryl who was the driving force in many organisations. Beryl was a founder secretary of the P.T.A. at Barry Boys' Comprehensive School, Secretary to the Parochial Church Council for Cadoxton – Juxta – Barry, secretary to the local Gardeners Association, founder member and secretary of the Cadoxton Townswomen's Guild.

Both Burt and Beryl were active supporters of the Scout movement for many years and they each received the Medal of Merit, the highest lay honour for non-scouters. In the photograph Beryl and Burt are being presented with their awards at the old St. Nicholas Church Headquarters of the 6th Barry Sea Scouts, on 7th July 1971. Beryl, a good wife mother and homemaker died peacefully at home on 27th February 1994, aged 75. Burt was in the 94th year of his age when he died peacefully at Llandough Hospital on 1st May 2007.

Their second son, Ian Leonard Luxton, was born at Passat, 12 Coldbrook Road, Barry on the 23rd August 1952. He was educated at Barry

Grammar School and Barry Boys' Comprehensive School and graduated in Jurisprudence at Jesus College, Oxford, in 1973. In 1975 he qualified as a Barrister – at – Law at Grays Inn before changing course to become a solicitor on 1st November 1979. He practiced in High Street and Tynewydd Road, Barry for over 25 years before joining Robinsons Solicitors at 2/4 Buttrills Road, Barry as a Consultant in 2009. Ian married Tina Joan Brady (nee Callendar), at Bridgend Register Office, on the 12th April 1980. They live in Dinas Powys and have two daughters, Rachel Leonora, born 15th December 1980, and Tamsin Alexandra, born on the 5th June 1984. Rachel, who graduated with an Honours History degree at Cardiff University, works in the finance industry in Manchester. Tamsin graduated with an Honours degree in Classics at Bristol University, and married Dusty Jones, at Gileston Parish Church in the Vale of Glamorgan on the 29th July 2017. They are blessed with two sons, Renzo and Casper.

33

WILLIAM JAMES LUXTON (1877-1960) AND THOMAS JOHN LUXTON (1890-1972), TWO SOLDIERS OF THE GREAT WAR.

See tree 14

 My grandfather E.A. Luxton had three brothers who were soldiers in the Great War. One of these Harry (1878-1970) is the central character of the next chapter so here I write about Bill who was a gunner and Tom who was a sapper.

Bill or to give him his full name William James Luxton (1877-1960), the second son of George Luxton and his second wife Clara Ann Beer, was born in a terraced house in Kenn Road, Clevedon on the 30th June 1877. We never met but Bill had a reputation in the family of being "over fond of his bottle." He never married and his younger brother Tom, considered him "as something of a tearaway".

There was some desultory coal mining around Nailsea in the late nineteenth century and Bill was a collier when he joined the Royal Artillery at Bristol on the 9th May 1898[255]. His enlistment papers record that he was aged 19 years 11 months and was an Anglican. He stood five foot seven inches and he weighed 124 lbs. with a chest measurement of 34 inches. His complexion was fresh and he had blue eyes and brown hair. There was a coal mark on the bridge of his nose and below his right eye.

Army records reveal that Bill served in India from the 2nd February 1899 to 22nd January 1906. In 1903 he qualified as a first class Gunner and on the 22nd April 1904 he became a siege train specialist at Rookee in India. When he was discharged from the Army on the 8th May 1910 he had completed twelve years service.

---

[255] Attestation of No27773 William Luxton, Royal Artillery WO97/5372

I possess a postcard photograph of Bill[256] in army uniform (shown here). Its divided back is of a type first published in 1902, but as it was taken by Routledge, a Nailsea photographer it cannot be earlier than 1906 as Bill was in India from 1899 to1906. In the oval portrait he is wearing a brass buttoned khaki serge field service jacket with a webbed Slade Wallace waist belt. Moustaches had become large and elaborately dressed and Bill displays a finely waxed and pointed version in the fashion of the day. He could not have been long back in the country when on Christmas Day 1907, William of Nailsea with two pals, Alfred Youde and Arthur Chard from Wraxall, were caught trespassing in search of game at a coppice in Nailsea in the occupation of Lady Smyth. They pleaded guilty at the Long Ashton Petty Sessions held on Friday 17th January 1908. They were each fined 10s. and costs and were given a fortnight in which to find the money.[257]

Bill, a collier, working at Llanwonno, in the South Wales Coalfield, was one of the thousands who heeded the famous call in 1914 of Field Marshall Earl Kitchener-"Your King and Country need you." He was 37 and three months old when he enlisted at Mountain Ash, Glamorgan on the 8th October 1914. He had a tattoo, with a stag and snake up a palm tree on his right forearm, while on his left forearm, he had a tattoo of hands on heart.

Bill, qualified as a first class gunner in India, enlisted in the Royal Garrison Artillery, and was posted with the 44th company at Pembroke Dock. Then on the 27th January 1915 he was posted with the expeditionary force to Malta, where his commanding officer on the 20th May assessed his military character

---

[256] The photograph of Bill Luxton comes from his nephew Reginald James Luxton (1913-2004) of Nailsea.
[257] Western Daily Press, Saturday 18th January 1908.

as very good and wrote, "This gunner joined 102 Company R.G.A. in February 1915. He has, so far, shown himself to be a steady, willing, sober and hard working gunner." Bill promptly blemished his good conduct sheet when he was sentenced to three days in the cell block for "Drunkenness" and being "Drunk in Barracks." While in Malta he suffered with a chill and diarrhoea, and for nine days, from 26th June to 4th July 1916, he was in Vallencia Hospital.

The newspaper, The Aberdare Leader, dated 4th November 1916, carried the following interesting note on Bill, for his friends in Aberdare:-On Thursday last Gunner W. Luxton, of the R.G.A., who had been home from Malta, left for his headquarters at Aldershot. At the outbreak of war he was a Reservist, and joined on October 9th 1914. He had served throughout the South African War. He took part in many engagements in France. His home is at 27, Victoria Street.

He was posted to 108Company R.G.A. on the 7th October 1916, and by the 15th November that year he was at Aldershot with the 249 Battery at the Siege School. In Aldershot, he overstayed his Christmas leave of 1916 by about 46 hours and was punished by the loss of 14 days pay. He was with the 249 Siege Battery in Bristol, when in February 1917, he was again absent without leave for thirteen hours. He forfeited two days pay and was sentenced to seven days in the cell block. Despite these misdemeanours, Bill was made a Corporal on the 17th November 1917, and his pay rose from a shilling a day, to one and eight pence. He was with 249 Siege Battery in France in December 1918, and was demobbed on the 16th January 1919. Bill, aged 42, gave his home address as Beaconfield House, Nailsea, near Bristol. The World War 1 medal card index lists him as Corporal William J. Luxton, Royal Garrison Artillery, Regimental number 46040.

His nephew, Reginald James Luxton, who was a small boy during the First World War, remembered Bill when he was home on leave.

"My auntie Ida (we called her auntie Di De) lived just down the road from us when we lived at Noah's Ark and I remember Bill being on leave and in uniform taking me down to Auntie Di De's and her giving us Turnip Greens to eat. They tasted so horrid I have never eaten any since"[258].

The blood stained bugle Bill gave to his brother Fred, belongs to Fred's great grandson Kevin Brown who lives in Devon. When he was demobbed at the end of the Great War Bill worked in the local Nailsea quarries. He later worked in the quarries at Cheddar where he lodged at Shute Shelve, Winscombe, with a widow, Mrs Webb who had a son and daughter.[259] Bill was deaf in his old age and he died aged 83 at Cambrook House, which was the poor house at Clutton, near Bristol. He was buried at Clutton on the 15th July 1960. His nephew George Luxton showed me Bill's brass twist box when I visited in 1970.

His younger brother Thomas John Luxton (1890-1972), the eighth child of George Luxton, mason, by his second wife Clara Ann Beer, was born in Nailsea on the 28th August 1890 and was baptised at Christchurch Nailsea on the 7th October 1890. Tom who began his working life as a plate layer on the G.W.R. worked on the railways for forty three years before being pensioned. He then supplemented his pension as a jobbing gardener.

When he was 25 Tom married Amy Gladys Cavill also aged 25, daughter of Charles Cavill of Clevedon at Holy Trinity, Nailsea on the 28th February 1916. The World War 1 Medal Roll lists him, Thomas J. Luxton, Royal Engineers Sapper No. 20138.[260] Sappers did all sorts of work; making barbed wire entanglements, repairing the front line, digging communication

---

[258] See letter of 1st February 1997from Reginald James Luxton (1913-2004) 7 Woodview Terrace, Nailsea, Bristol.
[259] See letter, dated 18th March1997 from late Reginald James Luxton.
[260] "Bird Song" a novel by Sebastian Faulk is an evocative account of a sapper's life and experiences in the Great War and vividly relates the kind of war fought by the sappers.

trenches, mending roads, filling in shell holes, and tunnelling under enemy trenches to blow them up. He was made an acting second Corporal and was given a new Regimental No. WR/260139 when he was transferred to a Royal Engineers sub unit working on railway maintenance. For his service he was awarded the British War Medal and the Victory Medal.

The London Gazette for 17th October 1916 Page 10043 reveals that Tom was a second Corporal, with service No20460, when he was awarded the Meritorious Service Medal. This medal was awarded to non commissioned officers below the rank of Sergeant and men, "for acts of gallantry in the performance of military duty."

I have two photographs of Tom and his wife Amy Gladys. In a studio postcard portrait by the Modern photo Co at 57 Castle Street, Bristol, the young Tom, in his soldier's uniform, is standing next to his seated wife. It was probably taken on their wedding day. His cap badge shows he serves with the Royal Engineers and because army stocks of material were short he is wearing a war economy jacket made with no rifle patches or pleats in his pockets. A second postcard shows an older Tom in civilian clothes. He has a moustache and is wearing a flat cap and he is standing with the support of crutches at the back door of his Nailsea home. His wife Gladys is standing at his side. In the 1939 Register Tom, a permanent way heavy worker on railways and Gladys are listed living at Wynshire Terrace, Old Church, Long Ashton.

Football grew in popularity in the industrial areas of north Britain in the 1860s and was brought to Somerset by workers at the coalfields around Radstock. Tom was a keen soccer player. Nailsea F. C. was formed about 1895 and Fred Williams, its treasurer, was the licensee of the Queen's Head which was the pub next door to the cottage where Tom lived with his parents' prior to the 1914-18 war. The club's changing room was in the skittle alley, which would have three long baths filled with hot water on match days. In 1970 when I interviewed

Tom, he recalled with a chuckle, that in 1919 he was just two months back from the Western Front when he played football for Nailsea. He was also a soccer fan and he went to Wembley to see the F.A. Cup Final. Skittles was another passion and he played for a team which won the local league cup in 1957.

My brother Ian and I visited Nailsea, on the 28th March 1970, and we called on great uncle Tom at 4 Clevedon Road Old Age Pensioners Houses. He was about to leave for the Queen's Head, his usual evening haunt. The three of us walked there together. Tom, who had a very broad Somerset accent and a quaint dialect turn of phrase, was equally intrigued with our Welsh accents.

When we met Tom he was nearly 80 years old. He was about 5ft 4 inches but had probably been taller when a young man. He wore glasses for reading which magnified his blue eyes. His ruddy fresh complexion indicated a love of the outdoors and he was a little deaf. Tom very much missed the company of his wife Gladys who had died at the age of 70 nine years earlier. The couple had not been blessed with children but their marriage had been a very happy one. Gladys had enjoyed football and swimming and Tom happily recalled a holiday they had enjoyed in Weymouth in 1929. He could tell us nothing of his grand parents, Jacob and Harriet Luxton. His father George, who had a beard down to his waist, had told him he came from the Wiveliscombe area of West Somerset.

Tom enjoyed his pipe and a "quiet pint of bitter a night"in the Queen's Head, which is in my photograph below, next door to Rosedene, the cottage where his parents' moved to live before the Great War. Tom was a moderate drinker and showed us pictures including one of himself as a young man in the local soccer team. He told us he had been a railway maintenance sub-ganger for forty three years and showed us a card which gave him a right to free railway travel. The G. W. R. awarded Tom a £2 prize in July 1928, for his part in a team of five, who kept their length of permanent way in good order in Nailsea.[261] He gave me his father's brass folding ruler and his six inch boxwood and brass spirit level. This spirit level had formerly belonged to his uncle Isaac Luxton who died in 1863.

---

[261] Western Daily Press, Tuesday 24th July 1928.

Tom also gave me an item of "Trench art," a memento of his time in the trenches on the Western Front. This was his brass field matchbox holder, made from a German shellcase. On the crest it reads 269 R.E. which was the number of his Field Company and on one side it is inscribed Sapper T. Luxton Royal Engineers. The reverse side it is inscribed Vimy, Arras, Ypres, which is the names of the battles in which he fought. With a distant look in his eyes, he recalled the noise, the filth, the uncertainty of life itself in the

trenches, amid the mud and shrapnel. Tom didn't elaborate but it was evident that "Wipers" as the old veterans called the Flanders town of Ypres had given him his most frightening war experience.

Thomas John Luxton of 34 Clevedon Road, Nailsea died aged 81 at Ham Green Hospital, Easton – in – Gordano, on the 31st March 1972 and was buried at Christchurch, Nailsea, on the 7th April 1972.

34

HARRY EDMUND LUXTON (1878-1970) MASON AND COLLIERY HAULIER CWMTILLERY MONMOUTHSHIRE

See tree 14

Harry Edmund Luxton (1878-1970), the third son of George Luxton (1847-1918) and his second wife Clara Anne Beer of Nailsea, was born at Kenn Road, Clevedon, Somerset, on the 23rd September 1878. His father trained him as a mason but made the mistake of showing Harry up in front of other workers. Harry, who had a fierce temper, responded by throwing a hammer which caused a nasty lump on the side of his father's head. In the course of their struggle, he "swung off his father's beard". Despite the fine weather Harry went home to bed. Early the next morning he put on his best clothes and left home.

Sir John Moore, the hero of the Peninsular War, is credited with founding the British Light Infantry Regiments, with their ability to carry out tactical manoeuvres quickly. The senior regiment, was the 13th Regiment of Foot (Somerset Light Infantry), which Harry joined at Bristol, on the 12th February 1896, when he enlisted in the Fourth Battalion. Army records reveal that Private Harry Luxton No. 4536, was aged 17 years and five months on recruitment. A farm labourer for Mr. Thomas, of Nailsea, he was 5 foot 4 ½ inches with blue eyes and brown hair. He had a small scar on the right side of his forehead. His home address was given as Nailsea, Somerset and he was listed as a member of the Church of England.

He was living back home with his parents in the "Glass House," Nailsea, aged 19 years and five months, when he joined the Militia Reserve on 9th June 1898. He was given a good character and was now 5ft 6 inches, chest 33-34, complexion fair, grey eyes and brown hair. Tattoos on both arms were his distinguishing features. Harry saw plenty of action in the Boer War, when he was called to serve on mobilisation with the Colours from the 4th December 1899 to the 12th October 1900.

In the Second Battalion of the Somerset Light Infantry, he was in the force General Sir Redvers Buller V.C. led to break the Boers siege of Ladysmith in Natal. Buller, a Devonian, had won a dare devil reputation in the Egyptian and Zulu wars, and he was respected by his men because he was a real soldier who cared for them. The campaign culminated in the engagement at Tugela Heights on the 14th to 28th February 1900. It was the greatest land battle fought in the southern hemisphere until the Falklands War. Six days of fighting resulted in the Boers being dislodged from the south bank of the Tugela River. After another five days of fighting and some gains by the British, an armistice was called to remove the dead and wounded from the battlefield. During the respite the Boers and British swapped tales and tobacco and drank whisky together. After a further barrage of 76 guns the outnumbered Boers, turned and fled, and the road to Ladysmith was open. The 118 day siege had ended. Fighting continued elsewhere. Harry was somehow incapacitated, and he was invalided to England on the 17th July 1900. On the termination of the war he was discharged from the army on the 11th February 1902, and he was awarded a gratuity of £5 for his service in South Africa. His character was described as "Good" and he was awarded the Queen's South Africa Medal with clasps Cape Colony, Tugela Heights and Relief of Ladysmith[262].

Back in England census night, Sunday, 31st March 1901, finds 24 year old Harry Luxton, a boarder and ordinary agricultural labourer, lodging with John Freeston, a dairyman, at 24 Hastings Road, Croydon. He made his way to the South Wales Coalfield, where he became a miner at Cwmtillery Colliery, Monmouthshire which was in its heyday. It was a hive of activity with over 1600 working there. At its centre were the colliery buildings,' including two winding wheels, surrounded

---

[262] The Queen's South Africa Medal, awarded to participants in the Second Boer War (1899-1902), is a silver medal with a claw and swivel ribbon bar suspension. On the obverse is the face with veiled crowned head and shoulders portrait of Queen Victoria facing left, circumscribed "VICTORIA REGINA ET IMPERATRIX" while on the reverse is a full length helmeted figure of Britannia. The medal is attributed on the edge to "4536Pte. H. LUXTON SOMERSET REGT." The Cape Colony clasp was for service in the Cape between 11th October 1899&31 May1902. The Tugela Heights clasp was awarded to those present at the battle 14&27February1900 and the Relief of Ladysmith clasp for those present at the battle between 15th December 1899 and 28 February 1900.

on either side of the valley, by rows of workers terraced houses and it was there that he found lodging. This photograph of Cwmtillery Colliery was taken c.1905.

He was soon in trouble. On the 21st October 1906 he struck P. C. Edmunds, giving him a black eye. Harry was summoned at Abertillery magistrates Court three days later. P.C. Edmunds, who was the works constable at the Cwmtillery Collieries, stated that he was near the pits on Sunday night, when Harry came up to him, and, without the slightest provocation, struck him a severe blow in the left eye. Harry denied having struck the constable and said that the officer pushed him for no reason, and then tripped and fell. The chairman Alderman S.N. Jones said, "How do you account for the bruise on his eye-put it down to the fall, I suppose?" Harry retorted, "That's how he must have got it." The Bench imposed a fine of £5 on Harry or a month's imprisonment.[263]

Harry Luxton, aged 27, colliery haulier, of 2 Fieldings Terrace, Cwmtillery, married Florrie Price, 22, of 7

---

[263] Evening Express, 24th October 1906.

Winifred Terrace, daughter of Joseph Price, baker, at Blaenau Gwent Church Abertillery, Monmouthshire by Baptist rites on the 22nd December 1909. I possess a cabinet print (shown here) of Harry and his bride taken in Williams & Williams Studios, Cardiff. The newly weds are shown in a studio setting of leafy trees and rustic furniture. Harry is wearing his best suit and has a bow tie and there is an Albert chain and fob watch in his waistcoat. His chequered cap rests on an ornate rustic table. He is standing next to his wife who is seated in a rustic armchair. Florrie is dressed in a tailored suit, laced white blouse and is wearing gloves. She has an enormous wide-brimmed hat, with a crown, which is almost as wide as the brim. It was a style much in vogue for just a few years between 1907 and 1910. The 1911 census reveals Harry a 30 year old colliery haulier below ground, his wife Florrie 23, born in Worcester and their one year old son George, lived in their three room house at 5 Winifred Terrace. He was still there nearly sixty years later.

This photograph is especially interesting because Harry took it with him to the Western Front. On the reverse he has written:-

47069 Bom.^{dier} H. Luxton
B. Battery No110 Brigade

25 Dec   R.F.A.

B.E.F.
France

Harry enlisted in the Royal Field Artillery on the 4th January 1915 and the World War 1 medal roll lists Harry Luxton R.F.A. Bombardier No. 74069. Harry landed in France on the 24th September 1915 and he joined the British Expeditionary Force which the Kaiser had dubbed as a contemptible little army. The British proudly adopted the name and at the end of the war Harry was awarded the 1914/15 Star, the British War Medal and the Victory Medal. I have two studio photographs of Harry in his First World War uniform. One print, taken shortly after his arrival in France, is dated 4th November 1915, and the second (shown next page) was taken in Le Havre France. In both photographs he is wearing a war economy jacket made with no rifle patches or pleats in his pockets because stocks of materials were short. His white lanyard is worn over the left shoulder and he will have a knife on the end of the lanyard in his top pocket. His cap badge of the field gun denotes he serves in the Royal Field Artillery and the chevron on each shoulder shows he was a bombardier. His spurs, cavalry style bandolier, riding breeches, and his puttees, wound from knee to ankle indicate he worked with horses to haul big guns around the battlefield.

It was very common for soldiers to serve in several regiments. Often the last regiment a soldier served in was the Labour Corps, which was formed in January 1917. The Corps carried out the enormous task of building and maintaining the huge network of roads, railways, canals,

buildings, camps, stores, dumps, telegraph and telephone systems etc. The Corps was made up of men who had been medically classified as below the A1 needed to fight in the trenches. Many of them like Harry had fought in the front line. He was Corporal Henry Luxton Regt.No 445629 serving with 784 A.E. Coy Lab. Corps at Nottingham, when he was demobbed and transferred to Army Reserve on the 13th January 1919. When Harry left the army he continued to work with horses as a coal haulier, in the pits of South Wales, and for a time, he worked at the Rose Heyworth Colliery, in the adjacent Ebbw Fach valley.

Harry's youngest sister, Emily May, (inset) baptised at Christchurch, Nailsea on the 7th August 1892 came to stay with Harry and his wife Florrie in Cwmtillery. Within a short time she married Florrie's brother Albert Price, a coal miner, at St. Paul's Church, Abertillery, Monmouthshire on the 28th January 1918. Emily and Albert lived in the same row of cottages in Winifred Terrace, Cwmtillery as Harry and Florrie and they are buried in the same cemetery. Emily died of cancer at 7 Winifred Terrace, on 29th March 1949 and was cremated and interred at St. Paul's, Cwmtillery. Albert was cremated and interred there on 22nd July 1976.

Harry joined the army for a third time, when hostilities began in the Second World War. He was in the army a month before it was discovered he was already in his early 50s! He was sent away muttering, "I killed them in the First War and I can kill them again!" Relatives and friends considered him a 'great character'. He was short of stature, but very wiry and tough with a quick and fierce temper. When a young man he was rather wild and independent. He would sometimes visit Barry to see his brother, Ernest, and old soldier friends like Tommy Simmonds. Harry and Tommy would go off on a drinking spree and be missing for days. On one occasion they caught the train to Newcastle. There they got drunk again before returning to Barry a week later! On another occasion he came on a miner's outing to Barry where he had a great time and too much to drink. When it was time for the bus to leave he did not bother to catch it. Although he was already elderly he was quite happy to sit on the grass at Barry Island, Promenade. Eventually he set off walking and arrived at his sister Ida Laura's house in Castleton, at two in the morning, having walked all the way from Barry. On Bank Holidays Harry would visit his Nailsea relatives. If he did not get involved in a fight on his way there he did going back home. He wore steel knuckle protectors which he called "knuckle dusters". He wore a very heavy gold ring about half an inch wide which he gave to his nephew Reginald James Luxton about 1927. Jim still had the ring seventy years later but never wore it[264].

Harry Luxton, of 5A Winifred Terrace, Cwmtillery, Monmouthshire worked at No2 Cwmtillery Colliery, when he retired on the 18th October 1953. He was then 75 years old! In old age Harry was balding and wore a cap. He had a leg amputated and when he fell down stairs, drunk as some claim, he had a second leg amputated. He learnt to walk on artificial legs when he was in his late seventies. He remained active until the Christmas of 1969, shortly before he died. He lived a very simple life style and was always very generous to visitors to whom he would give objects they admired.

---

[264] See letter dated 18th March 1997 from the late Reginald James Luxton (1913-2004) of Nailsea.

A veteran of the Boer War and the Great War he died in Cwmtillery on the 18th January 1970. Torrential rain fell throughout the day of Harry's funeral on the 21st January 1970. My uncle George Luxton and I drove to Cwmtillery to attend the service. Harry Luxton, junior, and his wife Mary, welcomed us to Harry's terraced house which was packed with friends and relatives. Albert Price, aged 75, a retired miner, suffering with silicosis, was present. He was Harry's brother-in-law, and together we looked at Harry's medals from the Boer War and the Great War. Harry's Boer War medals were later given to his sister, Ida Laura's children. There was talk of a blood stained bugle and two rings, which Harry had removed from dead Germans, by cutting off their fingers. One ring, with a black pearl had been much admired by my grandmother, Florence Luxton. At first she was delighted when Harry offered it to her but promptly returned the ring when she learnt how he had acquired it. Harry eventually offered the ring to his niece, Millie Webber, and when the ring fitted, she kept it. Millie who attended the funeral, told me she too felt sick when she knew the ring's history. She still owned the ring but the black pearl had come out of its mount. Harry cut the other ring off a German officer after he killed him. He said it was him or the German. He gave the ring to his brother in law, Albert Price, in exchange for a few pints of cider. Harry's son, Harry junior. bought it back for £5 after his father's death. Inside the ring is inscribed, MCW to ER Coche June 7th 1913[265].

Because of the rain, the priest wisely held most of the funeral service in the church. The British Legion gave Harry a military burial in Cwmtillery churchyard on the steep hillside which overlooked the raging river in the valley below. There was a simple but moving ceremony by the graveside. As the coffin draped in the union Jack was lowered into the grave the bugler played the Last Post. It was a fitting tribute to an old soldier of the British Expeditionary Force. I read the brass inscription on his coffin:-

Harry Edmund Luxton

Died 18th January 1970

---

[265] See letter, received 12th March 1997 from his daughter in law Mary Luxton in Keswick.

His widow, Florence, born in Bromyard, Worcestershire, on the 8th August 1889, died at Hafod Dawel Home, Nantyglo, on the 3rd April 1972.

Harry and Florrie had two sons, George Arthur Luxton, born on the 15th March 1910, and Harry Luxton, born on the 15th January 1913. I have a postcard photograph of the two boys taken about 1915 by The Studios of Dura Ltd. George Arthur, aged about five, is dressed in a hip length jacket with a sailor collar, which was still popular wear for little boys. He wears knee length shorts, black socks and laced up boots. His younger brother, Harry, is dressed in a new style of thigh length tunic, featuring a low-slung fabric belt, fastened with a large buckle. The broad collar of his tunic echoes the sailor style, but more generally reflects the vogue for broad white collars which turned down over the shoulders. The eldest son, George Arthur Luxton (1910-1964), who worked in the pit for a while, married Gertrude Elizabeth Taylor, at St. Paul's Church, Cwmtillery, on the 29th March 1937. The couple settled in Birmingham where George worked in a car factory. George Luxton of 22 Shutlock Lane, died on the 7th November 1964, leaving a personal estate valued at £700. Their son Keith William Harry Luxton (1938-2007), born in Nantyglo Hospital, on the 11th December 1938 was in partnership with a firm in Birmingham. He lived at 22 Shutlock Lane, Birmingham, and married Jean Claridge, a distant relative of the hotel founder, in Birmingham, on the 24th August 1957. Their son Grenville Luxton, born on the 21st February 1958, graduated in engineering at Cardiff in 1980. Grenville who married Janet Gumbley, was employed by Motor Panels (Coventry) Ltd where he was responsible for the design and development of heating and air conditioning systems in motor vehicles. Harry Luxton (1913-1993), junior, was born so late, the family called him "Lodger". A bright boy, he passed his eleven plus to Aberdare Grammar School, but his father considered that what was good enough for him was good enough for his son too. Harry was sent to the mine. He married Mary Jane Lewis in St. Paul's Church, Cwmtillery, on the 3rd October 1942. For seventeen years he was a miner in Cwmtillery, before moving in 1945 to Kent, to work as a miner. The couple settled in Ramsgate, where Harry who suffered with pneunoconiosis died of a heart attack on the 14th September 1993. His widow Mary gave me a gold medal inscribed "Aber & Blaina School Rugby League winners 1925-26 which Harry won when he played schoolboy rugby for Cwmtillery[266].

---

[266] Harry's widow in letters of 10th December 1993 & 12th December 1994 and in other correspondence and conversation supplied me with photographs of her father in law Harry Luxton together with many personal details.

35

ALFRED EDWARD LUXTON (1881-1967) OF NOAH'S ARK NAILSEA SOMERSET

See tree 16

Alfred Edward Luxton (1881-1967), the fourth son of George Luxton (1847-1918) stonemason, by his second wife Clara Anne Beer, was born in Clevedon on the 25th July 1881 and was baptised in the parish church (inset) on the 28th August that year. Fred was 18, when with three other young men, he fooled around in Tickenham on April Fool's Day 1900. It was a Sunday afternoon, and they falsely represented themselves as travellers to William Doley at the Star Inn, in order to obtain a "quantity of intoxicating liquor." Arthur Chard, one of the young

men, took several stones from the Washing Pound Bridge and placed them in the middle of the road. When they appeared on Friday 20th April, at the Long Ashton Police Court, they were each fined 5s. and ordered to pay £1, the extent of the damage done to the bridge and a further 5s. and costs for obstructing the highway.[267]

Fred married Rosena Norris of Hilperton, Wiltshire, daughter of James Norris labourer, at St. Luke's Church, Coronation Road, Bristol on the 3rd October 1906.

The couple settled at Noah's Ark, Nailsea, where they had ten children, beginning with Muriel Blanche(1907-1941), born on the 4th February 1907 who married Hedley Rogers at Christchurch, Nailsea on 8th June

---

[267] Bristol Mercury, Saturday 21st April 1900.

1935. Muriel died aged 34 on 12th March 1941. She was followed by Elizabeth May, known as Ethel, born on the 6th May 1908, who died aged 44 on the 13th February 1953. Laura Dorothy born on the 21st September 1910, died of TB aged 18 on 28th February 1929. Clara Ann, born on the 18th June 1912, lived in Staffordshire before moving to Northern Ireland where she died the 5th June 1996. Reginald James born on the 21st July 1913, was followed by Barbara Gladys (1914-1994) on the 25th October 1914, who married Ronald Davey at Wraxall on 28th February 1942. They lived in Flax Bourton, Somerset where Barbara died on 20th December 1994. Violet Emmie (1917-2005) born on the 10th June 1917, a switchboard operator, married Ronald Murray at Christchurch, Nailsea on 6th May 1944. She died 5th March 2005. George Albert born on the 17th June 1920, was followed by Arthur William, born on the 19th September 1922 who was aged 9 days when buried at Christchurch, Nailsea on the 29th September 1922 and Leslie Ralph Luxton, born on the 1st November 1923. The 1911 census lists Fred, 31, general labourer, and Rosena, 28, and three offspring Muriel 4, May 2 and Laura 6 months at Noah's Ark.

Fred's wife Rosena came before the magistrates at the Long Ashton Petty Sessions on Friday 12th July 1918, accused of stealing a woodman's axe worth 10s. William Williams, the owner of the axe, said that after trimming the tops of trees that had fallen at the top of Buckland Batch on the 25th June, he had concealed the axe and on returning the next morning it was missing. When questioned about the axe by P C Hart on the 28th June Rosena, said that she had gone to Buckland Batch with her children to "collect dried sticks and chips" and on returning home she picked up the axe by the side of the road. She produced the axe from the top of a high shelf in an outhouse. The Bench dismissed the case but told Rosena that she should have reported the discovery of the axe to the police.[268]

To maintain his large family Fred worked in a great many places and it was nothing for him to walk several miles to work. He considered the worst tramp was from Nailsea to Yatton, and he travelled by foot as far as Bedminster and Portishead, where he helped build the Nautical School. At one time he was foreman at Joseph Coles Quarry, West

---

[268] Western Daily Press, Saturday 13th July 1918.

Town, and he also worked at Messrs Coates Cider factory for nearly twelve years. In the 1914-18 war, Fred and several other Nailsea men, were sent to South Wales to fell timber. His son Jim remembers that the rabbits and pheasants his father caught in the woods were posted home to Nailsea. They were never parcelled up but simply had an address tag tied to their legs! During the Second War Fred worked at Failand where timber was sent to the pits in South Wales and afterwards he went to Wales to work. He retired at the age of 73.

When I was fifteen in 1956, we were returning from a summer holiday in Torquay. My father made a detour to visit his uncle Fred in Nailsea. The visit made a lasting impression on me. Fred, a widower, whose large family had left home, lived at Noah's Ark, one of three cottages in Station Road, close to the village green. An inscribed plaque set high in the wall above his cottage gave the name Noah's Ark 1667, with the outline of an ark. Fred was no less interesting than the cottage. Around him were mementoes of a long and active life. A row of bright candlesticks stood on the mantelpiece. Talking of these led him to display a store of treasures which brought back many memories. One unusual treasure was a silver watch weighing 8 ½ ozs and a matching chain which weighed a pound. It was illuminated by a battery which lit a tiny bulb on the watch face. Next to the candlesticks stood a German bugle, a reminder of the 1914-18 war. It was brought home by his brother, William James Luxton (1877-1960), who served as a gunner in the Great War. Bill told him it was taken from a dead bugle boy and that the dark stains on it were blood. A pipe for the ardent smoker hung on the wall. It was made of clay and held an ounce of tobacco. There was also a row of gleaming powder and shot flasks, and a "frying pan" clock, complete with knife and fork hands. These had been "collected" from a German captured while he was having breakfast in the trenches.[269] Fred also kept canaries and was a pigeon

---

[269] Sadly this clock was binned in 1970.

fancier until he was in his early eighties. In this rear view of Noah's Ark c.1932, on previous page, Fred's wife Rosena is in the garden with her son in law Hedley Roberts.

Countless so called "friends" visited Fred in his later years at Noah's Ark and many of his treasured possessions simply disappeared. His daughter Violet, managed to save the German bugle, which is now in the possession of her grandson Kevin Brown who lives in Devon. His son George had his brass snuff box including one which had belonged to his brother Bill.

Great Uncle Fred was one of Nailsea's best known characters. In his last years he became much attached to his pet turkey "Turk" who was quite a champion egg layer. The unusual pet stayed with Fred continually and even went for walks with him and his little dog "Tiny". Turk clearly hailed from the West Country for on returning from a walk she enjoyed a saucer of cider! About 1962 the Clevedon Mercury featured an amusing article entitled, "Fred, 'Turk' and Tiny in Noah's Ark". Fred at the age of 81 was proud of the fact that he had never had a bottle of medicine "but I have had plenty of cider" he said.

Alfred Edward Luxton of 75 Greenfield Crescent, Nailsea died aged 87 and was buried at Christchurch, Nailsea on the 25th April 1967. His wife Rosena Luxton, died aged 52, on the 1st October 1934 and was buried at Christchurch, Nailsea on the 6th October 1934. Rosena had been closely linked to Nailsea Congregational Church. Her early death left her family bereft and the following poignant obituary appeared in The Daily Western Press on 3rd October 1934:-October 1st. Rosena, dearly loved wife of Fred Luxton, "Noah's Ark" Nailsea. Sadly missed by husband and children. Again on 30th September 1939 the Children inserted, "Treasured memories of our darling mother" in the Bristol Evening Post, Though tears in our eyes do not glisten, And our faces are not always sad, There is never a night or morning But we think of the loved one we had."

Rosena's son, George and Hazel Clarke, were voted most popular boy and girl by the scholars in their school in June 1929. The couple were still pals a decade later in May 1938, when they won a three legged race on Christ Church vicarage lawn, Nailsea. In August 1930 Barbara,

Violet, George and Leslie were awarded packets of seeds in a sweet pea competition among Nailsea Congregational Sunday School scholars. Their mother was a stall holder in October 1930 when the Congregational Church celebrated its centenary with a successful "Autumn Tints Bazaar" in the Nailsea Village Institute. On a disturbing note her daughter Ann, a civil servant in the R.A.F. living at 85 Millbrook Street, Gloucester, was one of three women attacked by a disturbed youth with a hammer in a railway subway at Gloucester in July 1948. He was sent to borstal for three years[270].

Fred's family continued to live in Nailsea and district. Reginald James Luxton (1913-2004), in the 1930s drove a lorry for Messrs Coates of Nailsea's cider factory. On Thursday afternoon 27th August 1936, he was driving his lorry from Bath and was near the Globe Inn, Newton St Loe, a notorious accident spot, when he was caught up in a triple road crash. Frank Bimson, a young motor mechanic was driving his small car from the direction of Wells. As he came out of the Wells Road he was travelling too fast and made no attempt to slow down or stop at a major road. His car struck the lorry, shot up in the air and spun round. Reg's lorry was pulled or pushed to the right and it collided with a car coming from Bristol. Reg was not hurt but four were injured including a Swansea auctioneer and his wife in the Bristol car who were taken to hospital. Bimson was fined £1 and £6 11s 6d costs. His driving licence was also endorsed.[271] Reg later worked as a foreman in Hobbs Quarries and was married to Beatrice Mary, daughter of Francis Lilly, baker. They lived at 7 Woodview Terrace, Nailsea, and had two married daughters Ena and Dorothy, and a son William John Luxton, born 1942, a motor mechanic, with families.

George Albert Luxton (1920-2002), Fred's second son, was in the R. A. F. when he married Evelyn Ethel Haines, the daughter of a coal miner, at Radstock, Somerset and they lived at 49 Moorfield Road, Nailsea. He too worked in Hobbs Quarries. Two of their children, Lesley Angela and Nigel Allen are married and live in Australia. Their youngest son, John Anthony Luxton, who lives in Nailsea, married to Anita Poole. They have two children Anthony James Luxton born on the 23rd July

---

[270] Gloucester Citizen, Thursday, 28th October 1948.
[271] Bath Chronicle & Herald, Saturday, 13th March 1937.

1973 and Sharon Louise born on the 8th October 1976. Fred and Rosena's youngest son, Leslie Ralph Luxton (1923-2008), married Gwynneth Dorcas Hawke, and lived in Kingswood Bristol where Leslie ran a motoring school.

Fred with his dog Tiny

36

JOHN LUXTON (1850-1925) COOPER AND CHIMNEY SWEEP OF NAILSEA SOMERSET AND HIS FAMILY

See tree 17

John Luxton (1850-1925), a cooper and chimney sweep in Nailsea, was the sixth son of Jacob Luxton and his wife Harriet Greenway who lived in Chipstable, a parish in the Brendon Hills of northwest Somerset. The youngest of their eleven children, John was baptised at All Saints the parish church of Chipstable on the 20th October 1850. He was an eleven year old farm servant to Thomas Davys and family at Washer's Farm in the neighbouring parish of Raddington when the census was taken on the 7th April 1861.

His mother had died in 1854 and in 1863 John, aged thirteen, joined his sixteen year old brother George in an eastward migration to Clevedon. Their sister Jane (1842-1878) who married William Stock, a labourer at St Andrew's Clevedon on the 14th November 1864, performed a motherly role for her brothers until they were settled. John was aged 19 when with a friend Henry Hayman, they appeared before the magistrates for stealing gooseberries from the garden of Sarah Sainsbury at Nailsea on the night of 29th May 1870. They were fined 5s..6d each, including costs, but were unable to pay and were sent to prison for seven days.[272]

John was a 19 year old labourer when he married Ellen Hopkins, also 19, servant, daughter of John Hopkins,[273] labourer, at Holy Trinity, Nailsea on the 5th April 1869. The couple settled in Nailsea where John qualified as a cooper but chose to make his living as a chimney sweep. They had eleven children baptised at Holy Trinity beginning with Ellen Elizabeth on the 25th March 1871 who was aged 1 year and 2 months when buried on 16th April that year. She was followed by Elizabeth on

---

[272] See Bristol Mercury and the Western Daily Press, Saturday 4th June 1870.
[273] John Hopkins came from Abergavenny. See letter of 19th March 1983 from Francis John Luxton of Portishead.

the 5th June 1872, Jane Ada born on the 27th February 1874, Ellen Sophia on the 9th April 1876, Eliza (Liza) on the 13th April 1879, Charles on the 12th June 1881, Sarah Ann (Sally) on the 13th July 1884, Louisa Ann on the 11th July 1886, Rosa Ann on the 10th June 1888, Harry Luxton on the 8th June 1890 and William John Luxton on the 11th February 1894.

John's wife Ellen was a stormy character and his life with her must have been tempestuous! She made at least three appearances before the Long Ashton Petty Sessions. On the 13th October 1871, George Winmill, a labourer at the Nailsea Glassworks, was charged with indecently assaulting Ellen in her home while John was at work. The defence argued that Ellen was a consenting party and the magistrates after hearing the evidence dismissed the case.[274] In a second case, Temperance Barrow of Nailsea, was fined 22 shillings and costs for assaulting Ellen on the 19th May 1880.[275] Edward Lock, a young man, was summoned for assaulting Ellen at Nailsea on the 6th February 1896. Ellen told the court that the assault took place at night when she accused Lock of "picking her husband's pocket." Lock struck her and knocked her down. A witness, John Gamlin, said Ellen used "very bad language and put her fists in Lock's face" and Lock only pushed her back. The magistrates dismissed the case and ordered Ellen to pay the costs.[276]

Details of the growing family and its movement between homes can be traced in the Nailsea census. In 1871 John, aged 22, was described as a sweep, his wife Ellen was 21 and daughter Elizabeth Ellen aged one. No Street name is provided. The family were residing at 6 Silver Street, Nailsea in 1881 when John, a 30 year old chimney sweep, and his wife Ellen 31, had four daughters, Elizabeth 8, Jane 7, Ellen 5 and Eliza 2. John, a weekly tenant paid 2 shillings a week rent for his cottage next to the Royal Oak Inn. It possessed a large garden behind, in the centre of the village, adjoining the main road.[277] They had moved to the Heath, Nailsea by 1891 when the census listed John aged 43, chimney sweep and Ellen aged 41 charwoman with six children, Eliza 13, Charles 9,

---

[274] Bristol Mercury, Saturday 14th October 1871.
[275] Bristol Mercury, Saturday 29th May 1880.
[276] Bristol Mercury, Saturday 29th February 1896.
[277] Western Daily Press, Saturday, 5th May 1877.

Sarah A. 8, Louisa 5 Rosa 3 and Harry aged one. The older children had left home. John, a keen gardener, won first prize for his turnips and second for his potatoes at the Nailsea Flower Show, held in the Drill Hall, Nailsea in August 1895.[278] In 1901 the family were once again resident in 49 Silver Street (next door to no.50 The Royal Oak) where John 51 is chimney sweep, Ellen his wife 51 and three sons still at home, Charley 19, assistant chimney sweep, Harry, 11 and Willie aged 7[279]. Below is an early 20th century photograph of Silver Street.

Ellen died, aged 62, and was buried at Holy Trinity, Nailsea on the 7th May 1911. John, a 65 year old widower and chimney sweep, married Amelia Kimmens 47, spinster of Nailsea, daughter of John Kimmens, a deceased farrier, in the Register Office Long Ashton, on the 8th August 1913. Illiterate, he signs the register with his mark. He died aged 75 from chronic bronchitis and heart failure at Long Ashton Infirmary on the 8th January 1925 and was buried at Holy Trinity, Nailsea on the 9th January 1925. His second wife Amelia, died aged 60, from acute bronchitis and heart failure at Long Ashton Infirmary, Somerset on the 4th December 1925. I have been unable to obtain a photograph of John who with his first wife Ellen established an extensive branch of the Luxton family in Portishead and Clevedon.

---

[278] Bristol Mercury, 6th August 1895.

[279] John was illiterate and the census incorrectly spells his name Loxton and his birthplace Chipstable is given as Chepstow!

Their surviving daughters married and had children. Elizabeth (1872-1913), born 5th June 1872 married George Sawtell, a labourer on 24th December 1894. They had a daughter. Elizabeth who had stomach cancer died at North Weston, Portishead on 23rd July 1913. Her sister, Jane Ada (1874-1950), born in Nailsea on 27th February 1874, married Thomas Sawtell, a porter, at St. John's Clevedon on the 12th December 1894. She died aged 76 at 6 Walton Road, Clevedon on the 7th August 1950.

Ellen Sophia (1876-1922), baptised 9th April 1876, had issue a daughter, Emily Sophia Luxton, baptised at Christchurch, Nailsea on 26th April 1896. The mother was a laundress when this infant daughter died of "measles 8 days" at Pill, St. George on 23rd July 1898. Ellen married Ernest Cornelius Churchill, at St. Peter's, Portishead on the 16th June 1900 and in 1911 Ernest, a general labourer, and Ellen, a laundress with children Arthur 10 and Winifred Mary 5 were living in a five room property at North Weston, Portishead. Ernest, a Private in the Somerset Light Infantry, was killed in the Great War. His widow Ellen died aged 46 of T.B.at 5 Honeyland, Weston Road Portishead on the 24th July 1922.

Eliza (1879-1938), known as "Liza," baptised the 13th April 1879, married James Thomas Paynter, at the Copse Road Meeting House Clevedon, on the 29th January 1900. Eliza was a widow, aged 59, with two daughters when she died on the 8th February 1938. Sarah Ann Luxton (1884-1957), known as Sally, baptised 13th July 1884, married Thomas Ryley at the Copse Road Meeting House, Clevedon, on 14th January 1907. She died at the Mendip Hospital, Wells, of influenza bronchopneumonia, on the 11th December 1957, and is buried in Lockwood Cemetery Bath.

Louisa Ann (1886- dead by 1958), baptised 11th July 1886, was a domestic servant when she gave birth to Elsie Rosina Louisa Luxton, a premature baby baptised at Christchurch Nailsea on 26th September 1904. Elsie died, aged two months, at Silver Street, Nailsea on 15th November 1904, and was buried at Christchurch, Nailsea. Her mother married William Paynter on the 10th of November 1907 and the 1911 census finds the young couple at 180 Tyntyla Road, Ystrad Rhondda in Glamorgan, where Will Paynter, is a 24 year old coal haulier, Louisa, 25 with a daughter, May, aged two. By 1939 the family were living in

Hampshire where Will died in Southampton in 1953. Louisa is believed to have died by 1958.

Rosa Ann (1888-1918), the youngest daughter, baptised 10th June 1888, married William Charles Bessant in St. Peter's, Portishead, on the 5th December 1908. The couple had two daughters. Rosa, aged 31, died on the 29th October 1918 from pneumonia and influenza and was buried at North Weston Cemetery Portishead. She was a victim of the devastating flu epidemic which swept through Britain at the end of the Great War.

Their three sons also established branches of the family. The eldest, Charles John Luxton (1881-1948), considered 'a bit of a black sheep'[280] had a reputation for heavy drinking. "On one occasion he was very drunk and went up to the loft to lie down. There he swore that he saw the Devil and the more sacks he put over his head the brighter and bigger the devil's eyes were!"[281] Charles was summoned at the Long Ashton Petty Sessions, for using obscene language on the highway at Nailsea on the 7th May 1902. The Bench imposed a fine of 15 shillings or 14 days in prison. Charles opted for the 14 days in prison![282] He made a second appearance before the court when he was fined 25s. for stealing a watch, a hay-maker had left in his waistcoat on a hedge in a field, adjoining the highway at North Weston on 9th July 1903.[283] Again on 22nd January 1904 he was fined ten shillings for stealing two stone breaking hammers.

Charles Luxton, [284]26, chimney sweep attempted to hang himself on the 24th February 1908 in his father's home in Nailsea where he lived. He had been out of work for nearly six months and was depressed because he could not find employment. But his real problem, as I have already hinted, was the demon drink! Charles, his brother, William John, their father John, and Charles George Cole the P.C. at Nailsea, made depositions on the 28th February at Long Ashton, Somerset before two magistrates and their statements tell the story of that fateful day.

---

[280] See letter from Raymond James Luxton (1930-) of 46 Griffin Road, Cleveden Somerset dated 2nd October 1997.
[281] See letter from Francis John Luxton (1813-88) of 5A Queen's Avenue, West Hill, Portishead dated 19 March 1983.
[282] Western Daily Press, Saturday 17th May 1902.
[283] The Western Daily Press, Saturday 25th July 1903.
[284] Wells Journal, Thursday, 9th April 1908.

Charles rose early on Monday morning 24th February and rode half way to Nailsea station with his father to see a building contractor about a job, but none were on offer. From there he walked to Backwell, where near the George, he asked another building contractor for work, but there was none. It was suggested that he should go to Barrow to see Mr. Childs, the boss. He did this but no work was available. He returned home and on the news, his father said, "Well it is quite time you got some now for I have kept you very near six months and I can't stand it much longer. If you can't get some near you will have to go further away where it is." His little brother came in and told Charles, that Walter Moore wanted to know if he was going to "screen the ashes."

Charles went straight away and worked from about 10:30 till dinner-time. Walter Moore came to the ground and said, "I suppose you want something to drink?" With the 6d he was paid, Charles went to the "Ring of Bells," where he had "a pint of Burton, two penn'orth of bread and cheese and a packet of cigarettes." He returned to work and finished screening the ashes just after 5. He went back to the "Ring of Bells" and asked Mrs Gallop if she had any cider, as beer always affected his head. There was no cider so he had another pint of Burton. Mr. Moore came in and paid for a "pint of old beer" which Charles helped to drink. Charles began to feel as if he didn't care which way it went so he had another.

He went home, but went out in the village again as far as the "White Lion." There he met one or two friends, and "had a drink or two." He came home but could not recall anything of his attempted suicide the next day. "When I came to…I found myself in the cells. I asked the constable what I was there for and he told me and I said I didn't know nothing at all about it. I have been knocked on the head once and can never stand beer. When I drink beer I always get into trouble." Charles signs his deposition C. Luxton in a clear hand.

The story of that fateful night is taken up by his 14 year old brother, William John Luxton. He was in bed about 10 P.M. when John came home. The moon was shining so he could see quite well. John entered the bedroom and lay on his bed with his clothes on for about 20 minutes, He got up and said, "Willie, get out and unlace my boots." Willie replied that if John was not so drunk he could undo his own boots. Charles said, "Never mind." And he lay across the bed again about ten minutes. Rising he said, "There is someone else in this room besides we three (meaning my brother Harry, himself and myself)[285]

He went downstairs, and Willie thinking he was strange in his manner, followed him. Charles went about four stairs down, untied his muffler and tied it to the banisters. He began taking off his belt, but Willie cut it from behind and pushed him downstairs and knelt on him, because he thought he was going to hang himself. Meanwhile, their brother Harry called their father. Willie eventually got Charles into the kitchen. All he said during this time was, "Let me go!" He was sober but had been drinking. Willie signs his statement in a clear hand-W. John Luxton.

Their father John Luxton, 56, chimney sweep, continues the narrative. He was in bed in the kitchen. About 10:30 he heard his son Willie screaming, and he got out of bed when Harry entered the room. He went to the stairs to see what the matter was and he saw the muffler, belonging to the prisoner, tied to the banister. He said to Charles, "Whatever were you so stupid for, why did you want to do it?" Charles replied, "Well father I can't help of it." John asked his son to come to the kitchen for the night. When Charles got into the kitchen and got onto the bed, John held him down but as he was very obstreperous, he knelt on him. After a struggle Charles got the kitchen door open and went across the yard to the pumphouse.

John stood by the door to watch him. Charles went to where the harness for his father's pony was kept, and he saw him take the rope produced from the pony's head strap. John returned to the kitchen, lighted a lamp, and put it on the window sill inside. When he returned to the pump house he found Charles had the rope in his hand, one foot on a load of hay, and the other foot on the harness, near the door. He then put the rope around the rafter by the ridge piece, and pulled it tight. He made a noose with the other end of the rope; put it over his head, around his neck. John begged his son not to be so stupid. Charles retorted, "See if I don't do it then!" and with that he jumped off the top of the door, which he was then standing on, and hung about a yard away from the wall and about two feet from the floor. His jump was about six feet.

---

[285] Charles is referring to the Devil.

As Charles was putting the noose on, John opened his knife, and, as he was hanging, he climbed on the hay, and cut him down. He knelt on Charles on the ground, and took the rope off. He knelt on him for about ten minutes before two men came to his assistance and they remained with him until P. C. Charles George Cole, the Nailsea policeman arrived. The prisoner said several times while all this was going on, "I have trouble and I can't help it." The statement is signed with the X of John Luxton.

P.C. Cole said that about 11 A. M. Willie called to fetch him to his father's house. When he got there he found the prisoner in the pump house leaning against the wall in an exhausted state. He said,"What have you been doing to yourself Charlie?"The prisoner replied, "Not very much but if I can't have my own way I will bloody do it." He found that the prisoner was not injured. P.C. Cole then charged Charles with attempting to commit suicide by hanging himself, and he cautioned him. Charles retorted, "If I can't get work I will do away with myself but they won't leave me alone long enough to do that. If I can't do away with myself I will kill someone else but what I'll swing."

The policeman then took him to the police station and locked him up. The following morning he was remanded until his appearance before magistrates at Long Ashton on the 28th February when the depositions were taken. He was charged that he did, "Unlawfully attempt to hang himself by means of a rope fastened to a rafter in a pump house in Nailsea, with intent thereby to feloniously, wilfully and of his malice aforethought, to kill or murder himself."

Charles pleaded guilty at his trial at the Somerset Quarter Sessions held in the Town Hall, Wells, the 8th April 1908. He was sentenced to twelve calendar months imprisonment with hard labour to be served at Shepton Mallet Goal (in photo) in Somerset. Prisoners sentenced to hard labour were engaged in breaking stones which were used for road building, oakum picking (unpicking old ropes) and other tasks. The prison, which closed in

2013, once held the notorious Kray twins. From his prison record we learn that Charles had been summarily convicted five times between 1900 and 1907-once using obscene language, once drunkenness, once using threats, once stealing a silver watch and chain and once wilful damage. All this goes some way in explaining why he had difficulty in finding employment. His father John's statement ends with an image of a very disturbed young man:-"Two years ago he tried to hang himself from a tree. It took four men to hold him. About six months ago he tried to shoot himself and me. He is often peculiar."[286]

In the 1911 census John Luxton, chimney sweep, and his wife Ellen, both aged 64 (sic) were living in a four room dwelling at the Collier Arms, Kings Hill, Nailsea. Their sons Charles 29, and William 17, who still resided with them, were employed by their father as chimney sweeps.

Charley failed to learn his lesson from his spell in prison. He appeared at the Quarter Sessions at Wells again on the 11th April 1912 for attacking his father with a meat cleaver in the kitchen of their home at Kings Hill on 23rd February 1912. At his committal at Long Ashton, on the 1st March, Sergeant Comer of Clevedon, who had known Charles for about seven years, said that during the past twelve months Charles behaviour had been fairly good but, "He has a very violent temper, especially when under the slightest influence of drink."

Charles, who assisted his father in his business as a chimney sweep had been drinking that day, but he was not considered to be unaware of his actions. He said that on that Friday evening, the 23rd February 1912, he had returned home from work the same as usual. His father told him there was no straw for the pony. Charles said that he had no money to pay for it but would run down to Mr. Baker, which he did and brought back a bundle of straw. On his return his father said, "Oh hast thee been down Ern Baker's ass?" Charles replied, "No I had to wait." John then said, "Well it will have to be one thing or another between you and I Charles tonight. You will have to give up going to Ern Baker's to work or leave my house." Charles retorted, "You don't call yourself a man to call me out of a good place!" This was the spark that ignited the trouble.

---

[286] Somerset Archives calendar of prisoners and witness statements in Q/SR 831.

John was upstairs in his bedroom when he was informed that Charles was up to no good. He went to an adjoining room from where he could see some straw was burning in the yard, close to the pump house door. Charles was putting a bundle of his sweeping canes on the fire. He went down and told Charles not to burn his brushes as it would put him out of work.

Meanwhile Amelia Kimmens, John's house-keeper, had run to seek the help of Mrs. Ashford, a widow, who lived about a hundred yards away in Kings Hill. When Mrs Ashford arrived about 3:30, she asked Charles why he was burning the sweeping rods but he did not reply. When Charles went straight in the kitchen they followed him. He took the top off the stove and put the brush in and poured oil on the stove. In the ensuing struggle between father and son, Mrs Ashford managed to pull the brush out of the fire.

Charles told John he was going to kill him and the donkey, before 12 o'clock that night. Then he said, "I will do it now!" John who had been sitting exhausted by the fire immediately got off the sofa and sat on the kitchen table. Charles leaned over the sofa and picked up the chopper. He said, "I will chop your b….. head in two like a pigs!" John saw the chopper coming and he leaned back as far as he could. The chopper missed his head by about an inch or two and came down about two inches into the table top.

As Charles was aiming a second blow, Mrs. Ashford pulled him away. John managed to walk out of the kitchen, but he struggled as his heart was bad. He stood by the door to get a breath of fresh air. He heard Charles turn up the table he had been sitting on, and he heard him say, "I would like to serve you like this!" He then chopped two legs from the table and scrunched the table up. John afraid Charles would kill him, went with Amelia and Mrs. Ashford to Mrs. Ashford's house. He then complained to the police and with P. C. Hart he went back to his house, only to find that Charles had gone to his lodgings about two or three hundred yards away.

On Saturday the 24th February Charles came to his kitchen about 7:30 P.M. Amelia, Mrs. Ashford, and another son, Harry, were present. John asked him to go away quietly but Charles made for John with his fist. Harry intervened to prevent trouble and Charles was turned out and went away.

About 7:30 A.M. on Sunday he called again and once more threatened to kill him before mid-night.

On Monday the 26th February he had Charles arrested, and he said he feared that if Charles came back to Nailsea he would kill him. Charles was committed at Long Ashton, on 1st March 1912, and at his trial at Wells, on 11th April, he was found guilty and was sentenced to ten months hard labour in Shepton Mallet Gaol.[287] From the Shepton Mallet Gaol Register, No 610 Charles Luxton, aged 29, was described as five foot six and a half inches tall, with brown hair. He was due for release on the 9th February 1913 but with remission, he was released on 21st December 1912. It is not known where he spent that Christmas.[288]

He was a 35 year old bachelor, living at 43 Hadley Street, Sunderland, when he married Ellen Parker, a 30 year old spinster of no. 13 May Street, at St Mark's Church Sunderland, on the 3rd March 1917. A studio photograph taken at the time shows Charles wearing a khaki serge "service dress" uniforn of jacket, trousers, hat and puttees. His cap badge of the field gun denotes he is in the Royal Artillery. The

photograph was likely taken to celebrate his wedding as he stands with his arm around his wife Ellen who is seated at a table. Brides were often married in civilian dress during the Great War and Ellen wears a tailored suit and her broad-brimmed hat with a shallow crown was fashionable in 1917.

Unfortunately Charles Great War enlistment papers were among those destroyed in the London blitz. However, his grandson, Melvin Wallis, possesses a half length body photograph of Charles in uniform,

---

[287] A Calendar of Prisoners tried at the General Quarter sessions HO 140 Piece No. 300 Page 6
[288] Shepton Mallet Gaol Register A/BRI 2/6.

taken in Devon, where he must have been stationed for further training. The photograph is mounted on card and is embossed L.B. Wadge Brook Street Tavistock in the bottom right hand corner. He is smartly turned out and he still has the stiffening wire in his S.D. cap which clearly displays the cap badge of the Royal Artillery. His bandolier marks him as a member of a mounted unit, while the crossed flags signaller qualification worn on his left cuff, denotes he was a skilled signaller. (photograph next Page) Charles kept pigeons for which he won cups and prizes and it's tempting to contemplate that he used pigeons to carry important messages on the front.

Like most soldiers Charles kept mementoes of his war experiences, and Melvin, his grandson, recalls when a boy seeing a pickelhaube, a German spiked helmet, his grandmother kept in a cupboard.

The war over, Charles, in 1921, was a "hand driller" in the shipyard in Sunderland. The dockyard gate was only a few minutes walk from his home at 13 May Street, Millfield, where he lived with Ellen his wife, and their infant son, John Parker Luxton (1920-1932). However, work was irregular in the dockyard, so on the 11th April that year, when he enlisted in the Durham Light Infantry, Charles was 5ft 8 inches with fair complexion, auburn hair and hazel eyes. He claimed he was born on the 6th May 1885, and was aged 35 years and 11 months, when in fact he was almost 40. He also claimed to have served four years in the Somerset Light Infantry but the Military Record Office in Exeter can find no trace of him serving in the regiment. He no doubt made these claims to improve his chances of recruitment. He "served continuously in the emergency" to the 6th July 1921, a period of 83 days according to his army record and was then discharged because of the termination of the engagement.[289] The nature of this emergency is not stated but it was most likely the war in Ireland which terminated in 1921.

Charles, unemployed and depressed in December 1921, attempted suicide. The Hartlepool Mail, Monday 12th December 1921 reported his appearance before the Sunderland magistrates:- "In a case of attempted suicide,

---

[289] See W.O 90 days Emergency Service Attestation Papers for Charles John Luxton Durham Light Infantry 11 April 1921.

Charles John Luxton, an out of work driller, was discharged after it had been stated that he had been found putting a rope around his neck. He was standing on top of a tub, and was only removed after a struggle. Luxton said he had been depressed, and promised not to repeat the offence."

His daughter Joyce (1922-2002), did not get on well with her parents, and was later to recall that Charles 'had a fearful temper and would up end a laid table if things didn't suit him -----".[290] Ellen, his widow, on the other hand, spoke highly of him, and indeed Charles, does appear to have undergone a transformation in later life. He became a 'Methodist lay preacher, did not smoke or drink.'

He was a watchman on the Borough Council when his twelve year old son, John Parker Luxton, died of tubercular meningitis at Sunderland Royal Infirmary on the 30th March 1932. His funeral notice was in The Sunderland Echo and Shipping Gazette, Friday, 1st April 1932 "-Luxton-At the Royal Infirmary, on March 30, aged 12 years, John (Jackie), the dearly loved and only son of Charles and Ellen Luxton (nee Parker). To be interred at Bishopswearmouth Cemetery on Monday, cortege leaving 13 May Street for service in St. Mark's Church at 2 P. M. Sadly missed".

Charles Luxton, aged 67, of 13 May Street, Sunderland, a builder's nightwatchman, died at Highfield, Hylton Road, Sunderland on the 11th July 1948. He was senile, suffering with arteriosclerosis, and had gangrene in both legs. His widow, Ellen, died at 13 May Street, Sunderland, aged 75 on the 14th December 1956.

Joyce, a daughter, born in Sunderland on the 22nd December 1922, married Stanley Wilfred Wallis, a steward in the Merchant Navy, in

---

[290] See letter from Melvin Wallis, 13 Tenby Road, St Budeaux, Plymouth dated 4 November 2011.

Frodingham parish church, Lincolnshire, on the 29th January 1946 and died in Sunderland on the 9th July 2002.

John and Ellen Luxton's second son, Harry Luxton (1890-1944) was a 23 year old general labourer, living at King's Hill Nailsea, when he married Alice Maud Dare at Bristol Register Office on the 2nd November 1912. His wife Alice came from Hazelbury Plucknett, near Crewkerne, and they lived at North Weston, Portishead where Harry worked as a dock labourer at Portishead Docks.

Harry enlisted in the army at Bristol on the 5th October 1914. He was first posted as a driver to the South Midland Royal Engineers (Regiment Number 1405) but fought in France as a gunner with the South Midland (Warwick) Royal Garrison Artillery and landed in France on the 30th March 1915. His discharge papers reveal that gunner Harry Luxton No. 314682 served with the colours three years and 303 days and a further 166 days in the army reserve. He was discharged at Dover on the 16th January 1919 in consequence of "being no longer physically fit for the War Service under paragraph 392 XVI King's Regulations". He was issued with a Silver War Badge No.B99696. When Harry left the colours he was described as 5ft 7$^1/_2$, of fair complexion, with brown eyes and light hair. He had a scar on his left thigh. He was awarded the 1914-15 Star, the British War Medal and the Victory Medal.

His youngest son, Mr Ray Luxton[291] of Clevedon, has sent me a photograph taken c.1914 of Harry in army uniform with his wife Alice Maud and their first three children, Francis and the twins Alfred Walter and Eva

---

[291] See letter dated 2nd October 1997 from Raymond James Luxton (1930-) of 46 Griffin Road, Clevedon, Somerset.

Luxton. There are five more photographs of Harry as a soldier in the Great War including the postcard photograph of him on last page as a driver No.1405 in the Royal Engineers.

His soldiering days over, Harry returned to Portishead, where he resumed his work as a dock labourer. A docker's work was hard and dangerous, and on the 9th September 1925, while unloading grain from a vessel, a two hundred weight sack of maize fell ten feet from the top of a chute, striking down 35 year old Harry of 2 George Street. He suffered serious internal injuries and the St. John Ambulance Brigade conveyed him to the General Hospital in a serious condition.[292]

There is too a photograph of Harry, taken much later in his life when he was a corporal in the St. John's Ambulance Brigade. Harry Luxton of 2 Hollis Villas, Clevedon Road, Portishead, Somerset died aged aged 54 on the 3rd September 1944 at Bristol Royal Infirmary. The administration of his personal estate, valued at £256..2..10d, was granted on the 13th November 1944 to his widow Alice Maud Luxton who died, aged 74, on the 20th February 1960. They are both buried at St. Peter's Church, Portishead. The bill for Harry Luxton's funeral reads:-

F. H. Halliday and Son
High St, Portishead
   Sept.1944
Funeral late Harry Luxton
Funeral arrangements & all
Necessary furnishings, good
Unpolished coffin, fully lined
Etc; Brass fittings & plate.
Fetching from B. R. I.
Motor Hearse+5 cars,
Bearers & Attendance
    £28..15..0
New grave in
Portishead church 4..15..0

   £33..10..0

---

[292] Western Daily Press, Thursday 10th September 1925.

His wife Alice's funeral in 1960 with the same directors cost £60..19..6.

Ten children were born to this couple in Portishead, beginning with Francis John (1913-1988) on the 19th April 1913. He was followed by Alfred Walter (1914-1979) on the 23rd May 1914 and his twin sister Eva Alice (1914-1980), Rose Winifred May (1919-1994) on the 2nd March 1919, Harry Edward George Luxton (1920-1999) born on the 5th September 1920, Kathleen Evelyn Luxton (1922-1994) born on the 22nd February 1922, Marian Edith born on the 17th January 1924, Hubert Douglas Charles (1925-1991) born on the 30th December 1925, Leslie Thomas Luxton (1928-1972) born on the 14th March 1928 and finally Raymond James Luxton born on the 8th April 1930.

This family has members living in Portishead, Clevedon and elsewhere in the country. A family tradition of stone working was continued by two of the sons. Alfred Walter (1914-1979) was a labourer, at the Black Rock Quarry, Weston in Gordano and his brother Hubert (1925-1991) worked as a flagman at the quarry in the 1940s before becoming an omnibus mechanic. The military tradition too was continued when Alfred Walter enlisted in the Royal Tank Corps in 1935/36. After serving more than 22 years he was demobbed and settled in Portishead with his German born wife, Helga Schulte of Luneberg, Germany and their two children Harry and Eveline. His brother Henry (1920-1999) who married Sylvia Henke at St. Saviours in Splott Cardiff, enlisted in the R.A.F. in the late 1930s and served in England until he was demobbed after the war. More recently Raymond James Luxton's son Mark, who lives in Bovington, Dorset served twenty years in the Royal Tank Regiment. The tree has more detail on this branch of the family.

William John Luxton (1894-1952) known as Bill, was the third son and youngest of the eleven children born to John Luxton (1850-1925) and Ellen Hopkins of Nailsea. He enlisted in the Army on on the 6th January 1912 and with Regimental No.6442 he was in the 1st Battalion of the Somerset Light Infantry which embarked for France on the

11th November 1914. Admitted to a military hospital with "Colic" on the 14th January 1915 he was transferred on 8th November 1915 with a new Reg No.3312 to the 7th battalion of the Gloucestershire Regiment. He was discharged from the Army on the 29th November 1916 because of "sickness" under paragraph 392 vvi King's Regulations and he was awarded the 1914 Star, the British Was Medal and the Victory Medal. William would have also received a Silver Badge Award.

 A court case provides a few details. On Sunday night the 10th June 1917, he was involved in a fracas at Portishead esplanade, which resulted in him and three others being summoned at the Long Ashton Petty Sessions with assaulting two youths. William, describing himself as a discharged soldier in the Somerset Light Infantry, said he "had had eighteen months in the firing line." He admitted striking one of the youths because he had struck Lionel Bessant, a soldier, who had lost a leg. The Bench were unsympathetic and they fined him 10 shillings and 2s..6d towards the solicitor's fee[293].

William made a second court appearance on Wednesday 12th November 1919. This was at Bristol Police Court, for stealing wood from Portishead Dock. The court fined him 20 shillings.[294] A dock labourer of 4 Weston Road, Portishead, Bill, slipped and injured his left knee whilst carrying deal planks at Portishead Dock on 11th December 1919. He was granted an award of £1.. 15s a week on 13th January 1921 under the Workmen's Compensation Act.[295]

He married Mary Jane Hearn at St. Peter's Church, Portishead on the 19th October 1919. They had three sons, Samuel William (1921-1979) who was a warder in the Prison Service, Norman George (1929-2009) who worked as a dock labourer and lived in North Weston and Cyril James (1931-) who worked as a hospital porter.

---

[293] Western Daily Press, Saturday 23rd June 1917
[294] Western Daily Press, Thursday 13th November 1919.
[295] Western Daily Press, Friday 10th June 1921.

William John Luxton of 9 Hollis Avenue, Portishead died, aged 59, on the 17th September 1952 at Bristol Royal Infirmary. The probate of his estate valued at £456..17..10d was granted to his widow, Mary Jane Luxton on the 10th April 1953. Mary Jane Luxton died, aged 82, on the 9th January 1979 and is buried with her husband at North Weston Cemetery, Portishead.

The Portishead Luxtons maintained links with their Luxton relatives in Nailsea. Harry Luxton (1890-1944) and his brother Bill (1894-1952) both kept pigeons and they would cycle to Nailsea to visit their cousin Fred Luxton, at Noah's Ark, who was also a keen pigeon fancier. On 23rd July 1926 one of Bill's homing pigeons was shot when it detached itself in flight and landed on a neighbouring property.[296] Members of the family still live in Portishead and its neighbourhood[297]. Again there are more details on the family tree.

---

[296] Western Daily Press, Saturday 18th December 1926.
[297] See letter dated 1st February 1997 from Reginald James Luxton (1913-2004) of 7Woodview Terrace, Nailsea, Bristol.

37

THOMAS LUXTON (C1803 – 1885)
YEOMAN OF PETTON BAMPTON DEVON
AND ALLER IN SOMERSET.

See tree 18

Thomas Luxton yeoman of Petton, in Devon and Aller in Somerset, had two wives and sixteen children, which makes his branch the most prolific in the family. He was baptised at St. Petrock's Church, Petton Bampton Devon on 1ˢᵗ May 1803, when his name was entered phonetically in the register as Thomas Luxon. His parents were Thomas Luxton (1756 – 1817), bullock jobber of New House Tenement, Petton and his second wife, Ann Jenkins. Thomas had a younger brother William, (c.1807-1845) and two sisters, Jenny, baptised at Bampton on the 20ᵗʰ January 1799 who died aged 7 and was buried at Petton on 9ᵗʰ October 1806, and Elizabeth, baptised at Petton on 6ᵗʰ March 1808. Elizabeth almost certainly died in infancy for she is not mentioned in her father's Will made in 1817. There is uncertainty about Thomas' date of birth. His given age in the census returns is inconsistent with his having been born in 1803, the year of his baptism. When he was buried at Aller in 1885 his age in the register was given as 88 which would indicate he was born in 1797.

When his father died in 1817, his home at the west end of New House Tenement, Petton, marked as plot no. 1513 on the Bampton tithe map, passed to Thomas and his widowed mother, Ann. Thomas decided his future lay elsewhere and in the 1820s he settled in Aller, Somerset. There he became a farmer and parish constable[298], married and began a young

---

[298] From medieval times until an Act of 1842 the annual appointment of the petty constable was legally the responsibility of the Court Leet held by the lord of the manor but in some manors the courts were not held annually and the constables (usually two) were chosen or elected by the parishioners and then sworn before J.P.'s in Petty Sessions. The constable was wholly responsible for the maintenance of law and order in the parish.

family. He finally severed his links with Petton by an indenture dated 27th March 1839, when together with his mother, he sold the New House Tenement, for £59 to their kinsman George Luxton (1802 – 1891), mason of Morebath, Devon.

Aller where Thomas settled, lies two miles N. W. of Langport, close to the River Parrett and it was at Oath in this parish that Guthrum the Dane and his followers were baptised after their defeat by Alfred the Great at Ethandune. Thomas married his first wife, Hannah Sawtell, at St Andrew's Church, Aller on 17th December 1827. Thomas signs the register and Hannah makes her mark. Their marriage entry in the Aller register gives his full name as John Thomas Luxton, which a son's marriage certificate transposes as Thomas John Luxton. Most other documentary references are simply to Thomas Luxton. When Eileen Bangay (nee Luxton), on a visit to the parish, asked Thomas's great-grand-daughter Ivy Luxton (1912-2000), why he had made the move to Aller she was told, "We came to Zommerset because we were sheep rustlers!" This could be true but I'm inclined to think Thomas moved because he had already acquired land there and had married and started a family.

The tithe apportionment for the Parish of Aller, dated 14th July 1837, records that Thomas Luxton owned and occupied a house and garden, marked as No 88 on the tithe map, at Ridley Garden, measuring 0-0-7 perches in extent. No tithe was paid for the property. He also owned and occupied Leaseway (No 655), a meadow measuring 2 acres, 1 rod, and 26 perches for which the rector was paid a tithe of 4s 8d. He also occupied Aller Moor (No 43), a meadow, measuring 2 acres 0 rods, 26 perches belonging to Mary Gristock who paid the rector a tithe of 6d while Thomas as tenant paid him 6s 6d.

Thomas, a 35 year old farmer, his wife Hannah, aged 30, and five sons, John 12, Jesse 8, Richard 5, Alfred 4 and Daniel aged 2 were living at Redley, Aller when the census was taken on the 11th June, 1841. Ann Sawtell aged 75, agricultural labourer, who was probably Hannah's mother was living with the family.

Thomas and Hannah had eight children, seven of whom were baptised at Aller but not all of them survived their childhood. They were John

(1829 - 1906), baptised 12th April, 1829, Jemima baptised on 14th July, 1830 and buried at Aller on 29th August, 1830; Jesse Lewis Luxton (1831 – 1907) baptised on 26th August 1831; Robert Lewis Luxton (1834 – 1899) baptised 19th May, 1834, Richard Luxton born C1836. The 1841 Census is the only reference I have found for Richard. Alfred Luxton (1836 – 1924) baptised 6th May 1836, Daniel Luxton baptised 30th December 1838 and William Luxton baptised on 21st June 1843. These last two sons, Daniel aged 5 and William aged 1 ½ died of scarlet fever on 21st June 1843, and were buried at Aller on the same day, the 25th June 1843. Hannah, their mother, aged 37, followed them to the grave in the autumn of the same year when she died of consumption on 7th October, 1843. She was buried at St. Andrew's Church, Aller on the 15th October, 1843.

Four of Thomas and Hannah's sons, married at Trinity Church,[299] Bridgwater and reared family's of their own. The eldest son, John, displayed a degree of literacy when he signed the marriage register, but his three younger brothers were only able to make their mark. John (1829 – 1906) who was a general labourer and ironworker for the Bridgwater Foundry Company, married Sarah Seymour on 29th October 1854. They had at least two children, Hannah in 1855 and John in 1857 who became a cabinetmaker. The couple first settled in Barclay Street and later St. John Street, Bridgwater. John inflicted a fatal kick on Sarah during a domestic dispute in 1887. He was tried for manslaughter at the Quarter Assizes held at Wells but was found not guilty. Aged 80, a timber yard labourer, John, died from "atrophic cirrhosis of the liver" at the Workhouse Union Hospital in Bridgwater on 21st August 1906.

His brother Jesse Lewis Luxton (1831 – 1907) married Ellen Temblett, on 27th March 1859. They settled at 113 St. John Street, Bridgwater where they had at least six children. Jesse was employed in a number of occupations and is variously described as a journeyman sawyer, fitter, general labourer and riveteer on the railway. He died at 113

---

[299] Holy Trinity Church in Taunton Road, Bridgwater was built in 1839 because St. Mary's the parish church was overcrowded. It was demolished in 1958 when Broadway was constructed.

St John Street, Bridgwater from "age and bronchitis 14 days" on 30th November 1907[300].

Robert Lewis Luxton (1834 – 1899), a third brother, who married Mary Ann Tucker, on Christmas Day 1856, settled in Aller, where he was an agricultural labourer and later a farmer at the Drove. The couple had eleven children, including the following farmers- John (1857 – 1945) a dairy farmer at Russ Farm, Aller; William (1859 – 1912) farmer at Boroughbridge, Somerset; George Lewis (1860 – 1951) who farmed at Milton Ash, Yeovil and Albert Luxton (1871 – 1944) of Avon Water, Aller.

Alfred Luxton (1836 – 1924), the fourth brother, married at Trinity Church, Bridgwater, wedded Betsy Lock on Christmas Day, 1859. Alfred was an agricultural labourer at Ridley and elsewhere in Aller. The couple had fourteen children and must have found it difficult to bring up a large family on an agricultural labourer's wages. I will have more to say on Alfred Luxton (1836-1924) and his large family in a later chapter.

I have rendered an outline of Thomas's family by his first wife Hannah Sawtell. Thomas who was now in his forties might have been expected to remain a contented widower, but he was still a vigorous man and within eighteen months of Hannah's death he married for a second time. Thomas and his new bride, Sarah Stacey, married at St. Mary's Church, Bridgwater on 31st March 1845. His second marriage appears to have been unpopular with the children of his first marriage, for a descendant, Mr. Clive Luxton, relates a family story that "Thomas ran away with the dairy maid"[301]. The 1851 census lists Thomas, 47, as constable at Redly, South Street, Aller with Sarah 34, seven children and Ann Sawtell aged 89.

---

[300] The arrival of the Bristol and Exeter Railway line in Bridgwater in 1841 led to the construction of St. John Street and the surrounding area. In 1847 the Oxford Movement created a new church and parish, St. John's in Eastover, to cope with the population growth.

[301] See letter dated 8th February 1995 from Clive Luxton, 6 The Larches, Wrentham, Beccles, Suffolk.

Thomas and his second wife, Sarah, had eight children, who were all born in Aller. Their eldest child, William Inder Luxton (1846 – 1926), baptised 31st May 1846 married Leah Lock at Trinity Church, Bridgwater on 27th August 1868. This couple moved around a lot in search of work. In 1871 William Inder, a 26 year old labourer, his wife Leah 21, born in Curry Rivel, and their infant son William Inder, 10 months old, lived at the Cottage on the Hill, at Aller. They moved to Dorset to work and in 1881 William, 34, gardener, Leah 31 and their nine year old son Alfred Herbert, born in Aller, were dwelling in England Street in the parish of St. James, Poole. They had returned to Somerset by 1891 when William 45, gardener and Leah 42, lived at Pibsbury, Huish Episcopi. By 1901 he was a 54 year old farmer in Church Street, North Highbridge, Somerset with his wife Leah, aged 50, and their son Alfred Herbert 28, who worked on the farm.

He had at least two children, William Inder Luxton, baptised at Aller on 24th July 1870, died aged 6 years 9 months on 21st January 1877. His brother [302] Alfred Herbert Lock Luxton (1872-1952), born on 31st March 1872 married his first cousin Lucy Ella Luxton, on 12th September 1906. The Chard & Ilminster News reported their wedding-At St. Andrews Church Aller, Alfred Herbert Luxton, only son of Mr. I.Luxton, Poplar Farm, Highbridge, to Lucy Ella Luxton, only daughter of Mr. Alfred Luxton. In 1911 they were tenants at Sealey's Farm at Chilton Polden, Bridgwater. It was a very fertile small holding and when the Cossington Manor Estate auctioned their lands in 75 lots at the Royal Clarence Hotel, Bridgwater, in the autumn of 1919 Herbert successfully purchased 5A.1R.37P. of pasture and orchard land and one piece of arable land for £150[303]. He had a serious drink problem, however, and in December 1924 in a drunken state, he attacked his son Gerald, and when his wife and father tried to intervene, he assaulted them too. At Bridgwater Police Court he was sentenced to three months imprisonment with hard labour.[304] His father Mr. Inder Luxton, and his estranged wife, Lucy Ella, successfully brought an action at the Bridgwater County Court in March 1926 to recover £117..18s, the proceeds of a sale held at the Scrubbit's Farm, Chilton

---

[302] Taunton Courier, Wednesday 31st March 1926.
[303] Taunton Courier, Wednesday 5th November 1919.
[304] Western Daily Press, Wednesday 24th December 1924.

Polden[305]. The couple were separated and it was believed that the husband had gone abroad. However, the 1939 Register lists him as a farm labourer (horseman) lodging at 28 Victoria Road, Newton Abbot. Herbert was a retired hospital gardener when he died aged 80, at 76 Halcyon Road, Highweek, Newton Abbot, Devon on 21st March 1952. Lucy died 9th January 1956. Their only son Gerald Inder Luxton (1907-1978), born at Decoy Farm, High Ham, Somerset on 17th September 1907, was a bachelor and retired farm worker, when he died at Portcullis House, Langport on 17th November 1978.

James Frederick Luxton (1847 – 1929), a second son, born to Thomas Luxton and his second wife Sarah Stacey, baptised 30th May, 1847 married Mary Ann Fisher at Aller on Christmas Day, 1869. This couple farmed at Ridley in Aller where they had at least six children. They feature in a later chapter.

Four daughters followed these two sons. Jane (1848-1890), was born in Aller on the 30th June 1848 and in1861 at the age of 12 she was working as a scullery maid at the Manor House, Aller. She witnessed her brother Frederick's marriage in 1869 but by 1871 she was a cook and domestic servant, living in a multi-occupancy single person's accommodation at 7, Goldsmith Street, West Cheap, Lambeth. Jane and William Henry (James) Chappell were living at 74 Gopsall Street when they married at Christchurch, Hoxton, Middlesex on the 10th September 1871.William, was a jobbing printer and lithographer, and the couple lived at 70 Milkwood Road, Brixton, Lambeth in1881. They had at least eight children but half had died before they reached the age of two.

William was probably bi-polar and he made Jane's life a misery. When Jane died in 1890 aged 42, her younger sister Mary (Polly) came to look after them. This head and shoulders portrait of Jane, framed in a medallion must date to the time of her marriage. She is wearing a close fitting, front fastening dress bodice and

---

[305] Taunton Courier, Wednesday 31st March 1926

the neckline is worn high, with a blouse collar and a decorative silk bow. Her elaborate plaited chignon, worn high on the head, is typical of this period. The pendant earings were popular adornments.

Ann Louisa Luxton (1850-1938), daughter of Thomas Luxton, yeoman, was born in Aller on the 14th May 1850. "Anna" emigrated to the U.S.A. about 1873 where she married William Mallard Scott (1834-1901), a carpenter in Sangamon, Illinois on the 29th January 1874. Anna (seated) and her sister Elizabeth are in this studio photograph taken in Langport, prior to her emigrating to the U.S.A. In 1880 Anna and William Scott lived in Lincoln, Illinois with two daughters, Marian (Minnie) born in 1875, and Georgia E. born in February 1878, who became a teacher. They were joined by a third daughter, Mary W. born in December 1882. William Scott died in 1901 and by 1910 Anna was living with her youngest daughter, Mary and her husband Charles McDonald in Seattle, Washington and that is where Anna died on the 30th April 1938.

Elizabeth Luxton (1852-1912), born at Aller on the 6th April 1852, was a 19 year old general servant with the Dibsdall family in Fore Street, Othery, Somerset in 1871. She married Thomas Small of Hewish, at

St. Anne's Church, Congresbury on the 14th August 1875. The couple were living in Chelvey, Somerset by 1881 but ten years later they had moved to The Grove in Nailsea. They were still there in 1901 but their children had left home and in the 1911 census we learn that they had eight children, six were still living and two had died. Elizabeth Small (In photo on left) died aged 60, of an abscess of the colon and exhaustion, on the 23rd September 1912, at The Grove, Nailsea with Thomas at her bedside.

Mary Luxton (1855-1928), born at Aller on the 16th February 1855 was a 23 year old cook and domestic servant to John Cutliffe and family in Friern Basset London in 1881. When her elder sister Jane Chappell died aged 42, leaving four children, Aunt Polly came to help the family. Aged 32 she was living in 1891 at 1 Nelson Square, Camberwell where she was caring for the two eldest boys while the two youngest children were living with their father William and his new wife at 56, Cold Harbour Lane. By 1901 the four children were living at 25 Manaton Road, Camberwell with Aunt Polly who remained in

C.CARTER.   FOLKESTONE.

London to keep house for them. Mary Luxton aged 73 of 168 Mortlake Road, Ilford, Essex spinster died on the 11th October 1928. Probate of her estate valued at £1475..12s..8d was granted to her nephews William Frederick George Chappell, printer and Robert George Chappell, manager. Her gravestone in Aller churchyard reads, "A mother to the motherless." This photograph of Aunt Polly surrounded by ferns was taken in Folkestone where she was in service in the 1870s.

William Luxton, a third son of Thomas Luxton farmer and his second wife Sarah Stacey, born at Aller on the 14th August 1857 died aged seven months from a body wasting disease and was buried at Aller on 4th April 1858.

When their eighth child, Athaliah, was born on the 10th February 1859 she was Thomas's sixteenth child. Thomas must have been at least 56 or perhaps as old as 63. The choice of name was a strange one. Athaliah was named after the only Queen of Judah, a vicious and vindictive woman, who was eventually murdered!

Thomas's second wife, Sarah died aged 46 at Aller, on the 7th February 1861 and was buried on 14th February 1861. The census of later that year lists Thomas as a 62 year old widower and farmer of 20 acres at Redley. His son William Inder is a 15 year old gardener, Frederick 12 an agricultural labourer, Ann 10, Elizabeth 8 and Athaliah 2. Thomas, now a widower for a second time, was to live for nearly another quarter of a century. Athaliah was a toddler when her mother died and her brothers and sisters would have cared for her until she was older. The 1871 census finds Thomas 76, widower and labourer, and Athaliah 11, residing at Ridley Grape Cottage. In the 1881 Aller census, Thomas, an 86 year old widower and agricultural labourer, continued to live at Ridley Grape Cottage, with his 22 year old unmarried daughter Athaliah, next door to his son, Alfred and family. The parish church burial register records that Thomas died aged 88, and was buried at St. Andrews Church, Aller on the 29th October 1885.

Athaliah (on left) who had cared for Thomas in his old age, was a 36 year old General Domestic servant at Bere Farm, Aller in 1891. She married Francis Cullen, a 38 year old widower and labourer, at St. James Taunton on 5th July, 1893. Francis already had older children and by Athaliah he had three daughters. In 1901 they were living in the cottage next door to the shop in Aller, run by the Locks, with their three daughters-Olive Edith (1894-1962) Frances Maud (1896-1974) and Florence May (1899-1983). Francis Cullen died in 1911 and Athaliah died on the 29th September 1928, leaving £355..11s..1d to Olive and Frances who were spinsters at the time of her writing her will.

There is no headstone at Aller to Thomas Luxton and his two wives, Hannah and Sarah, but they produced a healthy and vigorous progeny and there will be more to say on this branch of the family[306].

---

[306] The family tree contains a more detailed record of this branch and their progeny. A special thanks must go to Rosemary Bryant for sharing her knowledge of the Aller branch and allowing me to use photographs from Aunt Polly's photograph album.

38

A SAD TRAGEDY IN BRIDGWATER

See tree 19

Sarah Luxton died in tragic circumstances in Bridgwater, Somerset in the summer of 1887. It was the year of Queen Victoria's Golden Jubilee when the Royal Mail celebrated the event with an attractive set of Jubilee Stamps. The Bridgwater Mercury for Wednesday, 15th June 1887 which described the town's festivities also printed a graphic report of Sarah's death entitled, "Sad Tragedy in Bridgwater."

Sarah was the wife of John Luxton, the eldest of sixteen children born to Thomas Luxton (c.1803 – 1885) of Aller, Somerset. John baptised in St. Andrew's Aller on 12th April, 1829 married Sarah Seymour at Trinity Church, Bridgwater on 29th October, 1854. The couple were dwelling in Barclay Street, Bridgwater when Hannah Seymour Luxton, their daughter was born on 13th July 1855. The family had moved to 91 St. John Street by 1861 when Sarah 34 was head of household with two children, Hannah 5 and John 3 who were both scholars. Her husband John 30 was working with James Creed a 42 year old millwright. They were lodging with Evan Lewis 62, an iron moulder and his family from Neath at 21 Temple Steps, Llangynwyd, Maesteg, Glamorgan. He was back in Bridgwater in 1871 when John Luxton 42, labourer, his wife Sarah 46 and son John 13, scholar lived in Polden Street. In 1880 this son John was a cabinet maker when he married Sarah Ann Bell, the daughter of John Bell, a brickmaker and his wife Maria Hembry, on the 27th December in the Wesleyan Methodist Chapel, King Street, Bridgwater.

Their daughter Hannah, a domestic servant (in photo above), residing in St. Mary Street, Bridgwater, gave birth to an illegitimate son, William John Luxton on 10th December 1880. When the 1881 census was taken, Hannah Luxton, aged 25, was an unmarried domestic servant to the Revd. Henry Mogg aged 74, clergyman in Weston, Bath. Her son, William John Luxton, aged four months was living with his grand parents John, a general labourer and Sarah Luxton at Denners Building in St. Mary Street, Bridgwater.

In the spring of 1996 I knew nothing of Sarah's sad fate when I wrote to Bridgwater Registry Office for her death certificate. It recorded that Sarah died aged 62 on 11th June 1887 at St. John Street, Bridgwater. I was surprised to read that a coroner's inquest registered her death as manslaughter, resulting from a kick inflicted by John Luxton, her husband.

I wrote to Mr. David Bromwich, the librarian in the Somerset Studies Library, Paul Street, Taunton and within the week he replied with a report of the coroner's inquest and the subsequent trial. The reports in the Bridgwater Mercury for 15th June and 20th July 1887 provide a detailed account of events[307].

John who was aged 56 at the time of his wife's death, had at sometime been an engine-driver but was now a labourer. The Bridgwater Police for "upwards of 30 years" knew John Luxton but they had nothing against him. He had a reputation for being a quiet and inoffensive man who "walked lame". He had worked for a Mr. Bowerman and then for Mr. Gough and the Bridgwater Foundry Company and was considered "a trustworthy man in connection with the erection of bridges". John who had been employed in constructing an iron bridge for the Bridgwater Foundry Company in Scotland returned with his wife Sarah to Bridgwater in April 1887.

---

[307] See letter dated 1996 from David Bromwich, Somerset Studies Library, Taunton.

They moved into Starkey's Buildings[308], a small court, which opened off St. John Street. William John Luxton their six year old grandson lived with them. Their new home was an unhealthy confined space with small insanitory cottages crowded together around a brick paved courtyard, containing a community water tap for its residents. Their neighbours generally considered that the couple lived on good terms.

John and Sarah were in the habit of drinking and Mrs. Luxton was reputed to be "a woman of desperate temper when drunk". On the evening of Saturday, 11th June, John had consumed more alcohol than was good for him though he was not actually drunk. Sarah had also had a drop to drink. A blind neighbour, Mrs. Charlotte Wiltshire, spoke with Sarah about 8.15 that evening. She could smell that Sarah had been drinking and could hear her slurred speech. When someone suggested that brandy should be sent for Sarah, John Luxton replied, "I have no money to get her brandy."

There is an inconsistency in times given by witnesses, but the unfolding story is essentially as follows. James Bond, a shipwright who resided next door but one to the Luxtons, was crossing the court at about 9.15 when he noticed the couple sitting together, rather the worse for drink. Bond had been ill for sometime and Mrs. Luxton "chucked him" under the chin and joked about his health. He was about to enter his house when he saw Sarah put her hand on John's shoulder. He heard her say, "John, come back, there's a good fellow". Bond thought she was advising her husband not to go out, and as far as he could gather he heard no angry words. Instantly he got within his door he heard a kind of thud, as if someone were kicking a block of wood or a tree. He went into the house and sat down and had no sooner done so than he heard a noise, as if a chair were being dragged along the floor. It sounded as if it were coming from the Luxton's house.

Blind Mrs. Charlotte Wiltshire was outside her house six doors away, when she heard the Luxton's pushing and wrestling. There was a noise

---

[308] In the nineteenth century speculative builders acquired old town houses with extensive gardens and possibly a courtyard. On the site they built two rows of working class cottages, facing each other across a narrow paved yard. These new properties were usually called 'courts' or 'buildings'. Many were swept away during slum clearance schemes in the 1930s and later date.

as if someone had fallen against a chair. She heard Mrs. Luxton say in a low tone, "oh dear, oh dear, I shall die".

Mrs. Elizabeth Criddle, wife of Henry Criddle, labourer, who resided next door to the Luxton's went out of her house about a quarter after nine to fetch water from the tap. She saw blood in front of the Luxton's front door and went into her house for a light. On returning to the scene she discovered a much larger quantity of blood than she had seen before. Much alarmed, Mrs. Criddle went to Bond's door and called out for help.

James Bond heard Mrs. Criddle cry out, "My God, Mr. Bond, the place is covered with blood". When he came out of his house he saw a great quantity of blood on the bricks at the spot where he had earlier seen the couple talking. The blood extended right up to the Luxton's house. He went with Mrs. Criddle into the unlit house. Sarah was lying full length upon her back on the floor, against the opposite wall to the door. She was quite insensible, and blood was flowing from her left leg, which lay in a pool of blood. John Luxton was leaning against the fireplace, and was not rendering assistance. The house was like a slaughterhouse, and it was impossible to move a step without treading on blood. Sarah sighed heavily when they lifted her up and placed her on a chair. Mrs. Criddle said to John, "My God, you've killed her". He replied, "I haven't killed her, I have only kicked her". Much distressed Mrs. Criddle left to fetch John's sister-in-law, Ellen, wife of Lewis Luxton, labourer, who lived in the same street.

Bond said to John Luxton, "John what have you been doing?" He replied, "I have kicked the ... and she will know better for the time to come." Bond rejoined, "You will get yourself into trouble, the woman is dying". Luxton remarked "let her die," then used an opprobrious epithet towards his wife but did not finish the sentence.

John Wiltshire, Charlotte's husband, came in and they tried to staunch the flow of blood by tying a pocket-handkerchief above the wound as tightly as possible. When Ellen Luxton, the sister in law arrived, she sent for Dr. Kemmis. Bond remained supporting the dying woman in the chair until after the doctor's arrival. He cut off her boot and sent Ellen Luxton for a drop of brandy but when it arrived Sarah

412

was unable to take any. Bond ordered John Luxton out of the house for using bad language and William John Luxton, the grandson, who was there "up to a certain time" was sent to his uncle Lewis Luxton's house. Dr. Kemmis arrived in the house in a remarkably short space of time, about ten minutes after Bond.

Meanwhile John Luxton joined Charlotte Wiltshire, who was sitting on a window ledge outside the Luxton's house. She asked him what he had done. He replied, "I don't know; she fell on me, and I don't know whether I kicked her in her bad leg or not." He was crying and said he would be a teetotaller if his wife would give up drink too. John Wiltshire came out soon afterwards to get some white rags, and as he passed he said "John, it is a bad job, she will soon be gone". John who got up crying said, "Let her die" or "She must die".

Dr. H.M. Kemmis, surgeon, Bridgwater, said he went to the Luxton's house about ten at night. He found the floor of the front room covered in blood. Sarah was sitting in a chair in an unconscious state, and died in a minute or two after his arrival in the house. He examined the left leg and found a very small wound about the centre of the shin. It was a slightly contused wound with a bruise all round. There were large varicose veins all down the leg. The wound was on top of one of these veins that crossed the shin. The haemorrhage had been tremendous. Death arose from loss of blood from the wound, which might have been caused by a kick from a boot such as Luxton wore. He also found a cut, nearly an inch long in the middle of the back of the head, which was probably caused by a fall.

P.C. Gooderidge went to the Luxton's house about 10.15 that night. He found Sarah was dead and the floor of the house was covered in blood. The woman's clothes were saturated in blood too. He went in search of John Luxton, and found him seated on a low wall, outside his brother Lewis' house in St. John's Street. Luxton appeared to be the worse for drink but was not drunk. When the constable asked him if he could account for his wife's death Luxton replied, "No, I can't." He took John inside his brother's house, and charged him with causing his wife's death by kicking her. The prisoner replied "She began to throw the things at me and push me about, and I pushed she; but I don't know whether I kicked her or not". The constable told Luxton he would have to go to the Police Station but the prisoner said he could not walk.

Sergeant Cheriton who joined P.C. Gooderidge, sent for a conveyance to take Luxton to the Station. The sergeant with the light of a lamp examined the boots Luxton was wearing. He observed blood on them and took them off. The clog boots which were produced at the trial had wooden bottoms, with a rib of iron all round and the toe plated with iron.

The toes of the boots had blood marks on them. There was a blood mark on the right knee of the prisoner's trousers, which were also produced in evidence. P.C. Gooderidge searched the prisoner, in the sergeant's presence, and found tobacco and a pipe on him.

Luxton was taken to the police station at about quarter to twelve that Saturday night. Superintendent Lear charged him with killing his wife, and told him what he said would be taken down and given in evidence against him at his trial. Luxton replied, "I say I have not killed her, thank my God. When I came into the house she pushed me and I pushed her. In the struggle I pushed her and she fell down. She had a bad leg for years. Whether I struck her bad leg or not I don't know". The prisoner was lodged in a cell at the Police Station.

At the Borough Police court held on the following Monday, Luxton was charged with the murder of his wife and remanded in custody. That afternoon at 4.00 p.m. the borough coroner P.H.O. Reed, sat in the police court at the town hall to inquire into the circumstances of Sarah's death. Luxton who was accommodated with a seat in Court, sobbed bitterly several times during the afternoon. The jury proceeded to the prisoner's house to view Sarah's body, before returning to the court to take evidence. The coroner in his summing up said there was no reasonable doubt that the husband, kicking his wife in the leg caused the wound. He did not suppose Luxton intended to kill her but unfortunately she had varicose veins and the kick seemed to have been given upon one of them. He advised the jury to find a verdict of manslaughter against the prisoner.

The jury retired to consider their verdict. On returning into court after a brief absence the foreman gave a verdict of manslaughter against Luxton.

The witnesses were bound over to appear at the assizes to be held at Wells, and a committal was made out for the prisoner to be taken to Exeter prison to await his trial. He was then removed to the cells.

A report of the trial was printed in the Bridgwater Mercury for Wednesday 20th July 1887. John Thomas Luxton, to give him his full name, was indicted for "killing and slaying" his wife Sarah at Bridgwater on the 11th June 1887.

Mr. Broadmead, the defence Counsel, argued that her death was due to an accident. He asked the jury to consider it was just likely that Sarah Luxton, violent with the drink she had drunk, might have knocked her leg against a chair or the prisoner's knee. This would have been quite sufficient to burst the varicose vein. After the judge's summing up, the jury, following a short deliberation acquitted the prisoner.

The judge Lord Chief Justice Coleridge said, "I must take it that the jury think he did not cause the woman's death. It is the verdict of the jury and not mine, but it would not have made any difference, for I should have not have given any punishment.

When John Luxton was discharged from custody and left the Court Room in Wells, he returned to Bridgwater, where in 1891, he was a lodger with his brother Jesse and family at 113 St John Street. Employed as a labourer in a timber yard, he ended his days in the Workhouse. John Luxton, a 76 year old pauper, widower, formerly employed as a timber yard labourer, was an inmate in Bridgwater Workhouse in 1901. He remained a habitual drinker, dying of "cirrhosis of the liver" in the Union Hospital Bridgwater on 21st August 1906

The workhouse system continued to operate in this country until 1948. It loomed brutally in the imagination of the poor, and driven by the fear of sinking into still worse misery and destitution, many chose to settle in the colonies. With their lives blighted in Bridgwater by the tragic events of 1887, John's children decided life was better elsewhere.

John (1857-1937) a cabinet maker, and his wife Sarah Ann Bell, and two infant children, emigrated to Canada. Sarah and the children, Emma Jane, and John arrived in Canada on the 18th September 1887 on the Polynesian, sailing from Liverpool to Quebec. The S.S. Polynesian had a bad reputation, as she was said to "roll on wet grass" and was called "Rolling Poly."Sarah and her children must have experienced a great deal of sea sickness on the voyage! Her husband had probably sailed on an earlier voyage. In the 1891 census, they lived in the York area (now Toronto) Ontario, where John continued work as a cabinet-maker. Sarah Ann's two brothers, John and James Bell, had already settled with their families in the same area in 1882, so it is likely that John and Sarah Ann followed her brothers to Canada.

By the time of the 1901 census the family give their nationality as Canadian. In 1911 everyone except Emma Jane, were still living under the same roof at 77 Osler Avenue Parkdale in Toronto. The head of the family, John, was a 53 year old cabinet maker and gluer in the piano factory of Heintzman and Co. Ltd. His wife Sarah is 49, John 24 pattern maker, Arthur 22 electrician, Nellie 20, operator, George 18, a cane maker, Winnie 16, Gordon 13 and Myrtle aged 8. John was also a Sergeant Major in the Salvation Army. The religion listed for John and Sarah is Salvation Army but the rest of the family is Methodist. They remained residents at 77 Osler Avenue. Sadly John aged 80, was accidently hit by a car on 17th July 1937 and died in St. Michael's Hospital Toronto, with a fractured skull, on the following day, 18th July 1937. His wife Sarah Ann, was the informant, and he was interred at Park Lawn, Toronto.

John Luxton (1857-1937) and his wife Sarah Ann Bell had ten children. The eldest two died in infancy. Albert James, born at Oakhampton, Devon on the 26 October 1881 died four days later on the 30th October. Alice Maud Mary Luxton, born in Hamp Crescent, Bridgwater on the 9th October 1882, died aged three of scarlet fever in Albert Street, Bridgwater, on the 7th December 1885. The third child, Emma Jane (1884-1926) and the fourth John (1886-1949), were born in Bridgwater and emigrated with their parents to Canada. Emma, born on 29th September 1884 in Taunton Road Bridgwater, married Alexander McPerson in Toronto, on the 5th September 1906. They had a daughter Lillian in 1907 and a son John in 1909. Emma died in Galt Ontario, on the 20th September 1926.

John (1886-1949), born in Albert Street, Bridgwater on the 27th December 1886, was a pattern maker, when he married his first wife, Jean Crawford Ness (1885-1918) in Toronto on the 21st June 1911. Jean fell victim to T. B. and died on the 23rd January 1918. They had a daughter, Margaret Bell Luxton, born 7th March 1912, who died

19th November 1972. John, for his second wife, married Frances May Cross (1896-1954), in Toronto, on the 5th March 1919. The couple lived at 22 Ashburnham Road, Toronto in January 1947 when John is listed as a pattern maker for the United Steel Corporation. John died in Toronto on the 12th January 1949.

By his second wife John had three more children. The eldest, John David "Bud" Luxton (1919-1942), born in Toronto on the 30th December 1919, was a farm worker living with his parents at 22 Ashburnham Road Toronto, when he attested in Hamilton, Ontario on 6th January 1941, to join the Special Reserve of the R.C.A.F. for the duration of the war. He was keen to fly but had only twice been in an aeroplane, and that was as a passenger. He had no serious illnesses, had never worn glasses. There was a two inch scar between his index finger and thumb on his right hand. He was 5ft 5inch, weighed 148 lbs, and was of medium complexion with blue eyes and brown hair. He was well developed, with a chest of 34 ½ inches when  fully expanded. A later medical at Camp Borden, Ontario on 26th September 1941 when he was 21 records he is now 5ft. 6inch, weighs 160lbs, has dark brown hair, blue eyes and the "hair on his face" is dark brown so he was probably sporting a moustache!

On the 28th May 1941 he qualified as a pilot and was promoted a Flight Sergeant on 8th October 1941. He joined 412 Squadron "on strength for training only" on 10th February 1942 and from the 9th April 1942 to 1st May 1942 was with the R.A.F. Depot Uxbridge 412 Squadron. His interviewing officer wrote:-"A bright lad who is keen to fly. A country type but better than the usual run. Should turn out well after training." Flight Sergeant Pilot John David "Bud"Luxton No.R.84223 with 412 Squadron at R.A.F. Merston, was killed flying his Spitfire VB Merlin engine BL859 in a mid air collision, one mile north of R.A.F. Station Ford during non-operational daytime practise manoeuvres at 11.35 A.M. on 5th August 1942. He was aged 22, and lies buried at Portfield Cemetery, Chichester, West Sussex. His brother, Peter born 28th December 1939, died in March 1944. Their sister Marjorie (1929-2003) born 3rd July 1929, died in Toronto on the 30th March 2003.

John Luxton (1857-1937) and his wife Sarah Ann Bell, also had six children born in Canada. Arthur James Luxton (1888-1965) born in the York district of Ontario, on the 5th December 1888, was single, Methodist, and a labourer living with parents at 77 Osler Avenue when he underwent a medical in Toronto on the 18th October 1917 to enlist in the First Depot Battalion, Central Ontario Regiment "A Company." 29 years 4 months old, he was 5ft.3inch with fresh complexion, blue eyes, fair hair. He had a wart on his right thigh and suffered with kidney trouble. The war over he married Mabel Beatrice Newton (1888-1970) in Toronto, on the 10th September 1919. On 1st January 1921 he was an electrician at 77 Osler Avenue and in January 1947 they lived at 249 Annette Street and he worked for Toronto Hydro. Arthur died in Queen Street Hospital, Toronto, on the 15th August 1965. James Edgar Luxton, the couple's son born 15th August 1925, died in Toronto on the 30th March 2006.

Ellen May (Nellie) Luxton (1890-1961) born in York distict of Ontario on 10th October 1890, married William Arthur Frazer (1889-?) in Toronto, on the 21st June 1915. The couple had two boys and two girls. Nellie died 25th December1961 in Grimsby, Niagara, Ontario.

George William Luxton (1892-1971) born in the York district of Ontario on 29th September 1892, lived with his parents in January 1909 at 77 Osler Street, Toronto Junction when he was a labourer at Pugsley, Dingman & Co. He was a Major in the Salvation Army, when he married Lieutenant Clarice Irene Moyle, in Toronto, in October 1919. They had four children but I do not have details. George's address was Adjutant Salvation Army, 374, Rhodes Avenue, Toronto when his first wife Clarice, died 20th September 1935. He married Nora Doris Smith (1905- 1988) in Coburg, Ontario on the 11th October 1937. Major George Luxton died in Guelph, Ontario on the 26th August 1971.

Winnifred Hannah Luxton (1894-1964) born in the York district of Ontario on the 6th October 1894, married William Henry Drake (1895-1956) in Toronto, on the 8th September 1920. Their daughter, Winnifred Pearl Drake (1923-2000) was born in Toronto on 26th February 1923. William Henry Drake died in Johnstown, Fulton, New York on 12th August 1956 and his wife Winnifred died in Toronto on the 8th October 1964.

Gordon Victor Luxton (1897-1952), born in York district Ontario on 25th September 1897, signed attestation papers to join the Canadian Over-Seas Expedionary Force on 10th January 1916. He was a machinist of 77 Osler Avenue in West Toronto, single; next of kin was his father, John. He was 18 years and 4 months, 5ft 4 ½ inch tall with a 34 inch chest when fully expanded. Complexion fair, eyes blue, hair light brown and he is a member of the Salvation Army. On the 1st June 1921 he resided at 77 Osler Avenue. He married Margaret Annie (Johnson) Atkins (1900-1959) on the 2nd August 1923, in Toronto. In 1940 they lived at 118 Laughton Avenue Apt 1 in Toronto and he was a store-keeper. He was still there in June 1947, store-keeper for A. Cross & Co. There were no children. He died in Toronto on the 15th June 1952 and he is interred at Prospect Cemetery, Toronto.

Myrtle Edna Lucy Luxton (1903-1991), the tenth and youngest child, was born 15th March 1903 in the York district of Ontario. She is aged 8 in the 1911 census living with her parents and siblings at 77 Osler Avenue. She was still there in January 1947 and was a dress maker. In 1965 Myrtle was a dressmaker living at 634 St. Clarens Avenue, Toronto but was residing at 919 Dufferin Street, Parkdale in 1974. Myrtle never married and died in 1991.

John's sister Hannah (1855-1935), on right, and her first cousin William Thomas Luxton, emigrated to Brisbane, Queensland, Australia. It was his second visit to the colony. As a lad he had been attracted by news of a gold rush in South Australia and he had migrated to Adelaide where the photograph below was taken sometime in the 1880s. After several years work there, in which time he met with considerable success, he had returned to Bridgwater[309]

---

[309] An advert in the Morning Post, Tuesday 31st January 1888 must relate to him-A lady wishes to recommend a good indoor servant or working butler, nearly two years excellent character, personal, if required, three previous; English; town or country; Single; age28-apply Luxton, 113, St. John Street, Bridgwater.

but the call of Australia was too strong, and he returned with Hannah on the "Taroba," and after a voyage around the north of the continent, they landed at Townsville Queensland on the 14th January 1889. Later they travelled on to Brisbane where Hannah, a general servant, married her first cousin, William Thomas Luxton (1860-1930), labourer, son of Jesse Lewis Luxton and his wife Ellen Temblett, at St. John's Anglican Cathedral, Brisbane, on the 27th April 1889. Eighteen months later they were joined by their son, William John Luxton, aged 9 who sailed on the "Dorunda" arriving in Brisbane on 5th August 1890.

About 1890 William Thomas Luxton, above, began work with Messrs D. Lanham & Co. in Brisbane, for whom he took charge of the sail and tarpaulin making. While working with them in Brisbane he was secretly a keen member of the old Workers' Political Organisation. It was unsafe for workers to let it become known that they were members of that body, for their jobs would be jeopardised. For secrecy's sake members of the W.P.O. he said, "held their meetings in paddock or bush on Sundays."[310] William Thomas Luxton, sailmaker, and his wife Hannah Seymour Luxton, domestic duties, and their son William John Luxton, tailor are listed living in Cochrane Street, Paddington Brisbane in the 1903 Queensland Electoral Roll.

He was employed there eleven years before accepting a position at the Railway tarpaulin shops in North Ipswich. For about five years they lived at Warwick Road before moving to Woodend. At Woodend he involved himself with the Progress Association and he worked well in its interests. He was a foundation member of the Prince of Wales Lodge M.U.I.O.O.F. (Brisbane). William received leave from his work at the Railway tarpaulin shops, in order to undergo an operation on one of his eyes which had been causing him much trouble. One operation was

---

[310] Queensland Times (Ipswich), Wednesday 9th April 1930, page 8.

successful, but following a second one complications set in, and his health rapidly deteriorated. His two sons-William John Luxton and Albert Henry Luxton-made a hurried trip from Sydney by boat, train, and car and arrived at their father's bedside a few minutes before he died at the Misericordiae Hospital in Brisbane. His funeral took place at Ipswich Cemetery on on Tuesday 8th April 1930. The photograph shows the couple with their grand-daughter, Nona Luxton, in New South Wales at Christmas 1926.

Hannah had four more children in Australia. Two died in their infancy, Thomas Seymour Luxton, aged 5 months, on the 14th October 1890 and Jesse Lewis Luxton who died aged two months, on the 2nd August 1896. Myrtle Seymour Luxton (1898-1935) a typist did not marry and died suddenly aged 36. Hannah's third child, Albert Henry Luxton (1891-1956) born in Cochrane Street, Paddington, Queensland on the 16th July 1891 was a fitter-turner. He joined the army during World War One and later transferred to the Australian Flying Corps and was very highly thought of by Sir Ross Smith as his mechanic when he flew the first flight from London to Austalia. "Bert" married Ellen Amelia Cook in 1920, and they had two daughters, Nona and Olga, who both married and raised families. Bert's brother, William John Luxton (1880-1947) who married Flora Edith Mary Miles, in Sydney in 1922, successfully reared a family of his own. He became a commercial traveller and died in Sydney, Australia in 1947, sixty years after the tragic events he had witnessed as a small boy in Bridgwater[311].

---

[311] Family photographs and much of my knowledge of the family in Australia is derived from Nona E. Henderson of Caringbah, Sydney, Australia. See her letter received 9th January 1996.

William Thomas Luxton's children were all musical. Bert and his brother Will, sang in choirs and their sister Myrtle, taught piano. Both of Will's daughters played piano and sang.

The photograph shows William and Hannah Luxton's house "Williamyr" Woodend Road W. Ipswich, Queensland c.1912.From left William Thomas Luxton (1860-1930), Myrtle Seymour Luxton (1898-1935), Hannah Seymour Luxton (1855-1935), William John Luxton (1880-1947) and Albert Henry Luxton (1891-1956).

39

JESSE LEWIS LUXTON (1831-1907) SAWYER AND GENERAL LABOURER IN RAILWAY FOUNDRY BRIDGWATER SOMERSET

See tree 20

Jesse Lewis Luxton (1831-1907), the second son of Thomas Luxton (c.1803-1885), farmer, and his first wife Hannah Sawtell, was born on the 12th August 1831 and baptised in St. Andrew's, Aller on the 26th August 1831. He was an unmarried 19 year old servant in 1851, dwelling at Ridley, Aller with George Vickery, 48, dairyman and his wife Jane.

Sometime in the early 1850s Jesse and his elder brother, John, went to live in Bridgwater. There he was a sawyer when he married Ellen Temblett, spinster daughter of William Temblett, butcher, at Trinity Church, Bridgwater Somerset after banns on the 27th March 1859. Jesse signed the register with his mark while Ellen signs her name. Ellen was born in the town on the 27th September 1831.

These two photographs of Jesse and Ellen, from Aunt Polly's photograph album, were taken by Hutchings & Orchard Photographers, Old Kent Road, London. They were in business in years 1877 to 1883. Jesse is wearing a morning coat and his turned down shirt collar was the most common style of the 1870s. His oiled hair is fashionably very short on the sides and is combed back on top. Ellen displays her wedding rings so the couple may well have been on a wedding anniversary holiday.

He was known in Bridgwater, if not earlier, as Lewis, but for the sake of clarity I will refer to him as Jesse, to distinguish him from his younger

brother Robert Lewis Luxton (1834-1899) in Aller, who was also known as Lewis. Jesse, 29, a sawyer and Ellen, 29, a laundress were living in 111 St. John Street, Bridgwater in 1861 with their infant son William Thomas. Mary Luxton (1855-1928), his younger half sister, known to later generations as Aunt Polly, was living with them and it is from Aunt Polly's photograph album we have a photograph of Jesse in Royal Naval uniform. His hat tally carries the inscription "H.M.S. Duke of Wellington." He looks to be in his late 20s or early 30s. It was taken by Simco in Langport who were in business between 1859-1880. We have been unable to find any record of him serving in the Royal Navy and it is likely his service was of short duration. See photograph next page.

Jesse was a 36 year old labourer in a foundry, living in 1871 in Poole's Building in Bridgwater, with Ellen, 39, and their three children, William 10, Sally 7 and Louisa 5. The foundry was at the Bridgwater Railway Works. The family was growing and by 1881 Jesse, a general labourer, his wife Ellen and five children were living back at 111 St. John Street. Jesse a 59 year old labourer, in1891, was at 113 St. John Street with his wife Ellen 59, and their sixth, and youngest child Jesse Lewis (1875-1948), a 15 year old labourer. His elder brother, John, 65, labourer and widower, was lodging with the family, following the tragic death of his wife Sarah Seymour (1826-1887).

Ellen, Jesse's wife, died aged 67 from "chronic gastritis sickness and exhaustion," at 113 St. John Street, Bridgwater on the 24th September 1899. Alice Luxton, her daughter in law, of 3 Edward Street, Bridgwater was present at her death. Jesse continued to reside at 113 St. John Street and the 1901 census records him as a 69 year old "Riveter on the Railway." His son Jesse, 26, a railway sheet repairer, his wife Alice, 24, and their daughters Lilian 4, Dorothy 3 and Hilda 2 were living with him. Jesse Lewis Luxton, labourer in a railway works, died from "age and bronchitis 14 days" at 113 St. John Street, Bridgwater on the 30th November 1907. J. L. Luxton, his son of 113, St. John Street Bridgwater was present at his death.

Jesse and Ellen had issue six children, two boys and four girls. Their eldest child, William Thomas Luxton (1860-1930), who married his cousin Hannah Seymour Luxton, in Brisbane, Queensland is detailed in the previous chapter. The eldest daughter, Sarah Ann Luxton (1863-1930), was born in St. John Street on 29th July 1863. Sarah, a domestic servant, aged 16, was charged in 1880, with stealing a silver Geneva watch, valued at 30 shillings, the property of the landlord of the George Inn in Barclay Street, Bridgwater. The local petty sessions dismissed the case, however, as the evidence was insufficient to prosecute[312]. She was a 22 year old, daughter of Jesse Lewis Luxton, engine fitter, when she married William Alfred Kurton, 32, widower, smith, Back Lane, in the parish church Bedminster, Bristol on the 24th January 1886. They lived in Bristol where William died in 1915. Sarah then married George Henry Bowden (1863-1929) widower, and house painter, in Bristol Registry Office, on 14th October 1916. She was a resident in Berks Mental Hospital when she died and was buried at St James Barkham on 11th September 1930.

Louisa Luxton (1865-?), the second daughter, was born in Polden Street, Bridgwater on the 29th December 1865. In the 1881 Bridgwater census Louisa, aged 16, was a domestic servant in the house of Frederick Jones, a 46 year old mariner. She emigrated in 1889 to Queensland, Australia where her brother William also settled but I have no further details of her life.

Rosina (1869-1923), the third daughter of Jesse Luxton, journeyman sawyer, was born in Polden Street, on the 15th February 1869. She was

---

[312] Western Gazette, Friday 12 March 1880

the 22 year old nursemaid to the family of Metford Rowe, a grocer and widower, in High Street, Bridgwater in 1891. Rosina married Henry Wood, a 32 year old tailor, at the Wesleyan Methodist Chapel[313], King Street, Bridgwater on the 24th June 1894. They were known as Harry and Rose. In 1901 Harry was the sub-postmaster in North Petherton where the couple had a son and a daughter.

Elizabeth (known as Bessie), (1871-1936), the fourth and youngest daughter, was born in St. John Street on the 4th December 1871. In 1890 she emigrated to Toronto in Canada where her cousin John Luxton, and his wife Sarah Ann Bell and their three children had settled a few years earlier. Bessie married James Comer (1861-1938), a native of Taunton, in York, Toronto on the 6th January 1891. He had arrived in Toronto in 1884 and set up a milk business there but by 1897 they were farming in Alberta, and were living at Willow Dale, in 1901 and they were at Red Deer, in 1916. The couple had at least eight children. Bessie died at Red Deer, Alberta on the 3rd September 1936.

Jessie Lewis Luxton (1875-1948), the second son and the sixth child of Jesse Lewis Luxton (1831-1907), was born in St. John Street on the 25th April 1875. He was a 21 year old shirt maker, when he married Alice Manley, 20, daughter of John Manley, lamp-lighter, at the Wesleyan Methodist Reform Chapel[314], St. Mary Street, Bridgwater on the 25th July 1896. Alice Luxton died aged 51 on the 2nd April 1928. Jesse Lewis Luxton, widower, died aged 73, intestate at 149 St. John Street, Bridgwater on the 25th November 1948. Letters of administration of his estate valued at £1357..8s..11d was granted to his son William Lewis Luxton of 235, Taunton Road, Bridgwater, accountant. Jesse and his wife are interred in Bristol Road Cemetery, Bridgwater where a headstone commemorates their memory.

Jesse Lewis Luxton (1875-1948), and his wife Alice Manley (1877-1928), had issue nine children, eight girls and one boy. Over-crowded living conditions resulted in the scourge of T.B. and three of the daughters were to die tragically young. Dorothy Mary Luxton (1898-1921) the second daughter, born at 82 Friarn Street, Bridgwater on the

---

[313] This brick built chapel opened in 1816; was enlarged in 1860 and was closed 1980.
[314] The Free Methodists opened a chapel in St. Mary Street by 1855. It closed in 1906.

30th March 1898, was an upholstress aged 22 years and 10 months when she died at 149 St. John Street on the 11th February 1921. She had pulmonary tuberculosis for five months and suffered cardiac failure. Rhoda Luxton (1904-1923), a fifth daughter born at 113 St. John Street on the 14th April 1904, was a machinest in a collar factory when she died aged 18 years and 11 months on the 24th March 1923. She had pulmonary tuberculosis for two months and 21 days and exhaustion for three days before cardiac failure. Freda (1908-1935), a seventh daughter, born on the 4th October 1908 at 113 St. John Street became a house-keeper to her widowed father but died aged 27 on the 27th November 1935 at Chard Sanatorium. Once again the cause of death was pulmonary tuberculosis and Freda was buried at Bristol Road Cemetery where her two elder sisters were already laid at rest. In January 1934 Freda had taken the part of the Fairy Princess in a performance of the children's play, Bold Robin and the Babes, given by about 40 children at the Mariners' Congregational School in St. Mary's Hall, Bridgwater. Her sister Madge played the Wicked Aunt.[315]

The eldest daughter, Lilian Ellen Luxton (1897-1948), born at 113 St, John Street on the 31st January 1897, died aged 51 at 149 St. John Street on the 2nd October 1948. Lilian had no children and she too is interred in Bristol Road Cemetery. Her sister Hilda (1901-1985), born at 113 St. John Street on the 10th January 1901, married a soldier, Archibald George Gillingham, at St. John the Baptist Church, Bridgwater on the 3rd December 1942.She died aged 84 on the 28th July 1985. There were no children.

The fourth daughter, Alice Maud Luxton (1902-1972), born on the 7th April 1902 was assaulted at the age of 14 in Blake Gardens, Bridgwater on 9th September 1916 by John Bridger an old age pensioner of Bailey Street who had molested other girls in the park. He was sentenced to six weeks imprisonment.[316] Alice was a stitcher in a collar factory when she married Ernest Reginald Atyeo (1902-1992), a baker and confectioner, at the Mariner's Chapel[317], St. John Street, according to the rites and ceremonies of the Independants on the 14th May 1928.

---

[315] Taunton Courier, Wednesday 10th January 1934.
[316] Shepton Mallet Journal, Friday 15th September 1916.
[317] The Mariners' Chapel in St. John's Street opened in 1837 and closed in 1960.

Alice died aged 70 on the 18th October 1972 and her husband Ernest died aged 90 on the 9th October 1992. They lie buried at Burnham-on-Sea, Somerset where a headstone commemorates their memory. Their son David (1932-1999) also lived in Burnham-on-Sea.

Rosina (1906-1996), a sixth daughter, born on the 6th October 1906, was a 27 year old machinist in a collar factory, daughter of Jesse Lewis Luxton, railway porter goods department, when she married James Alfred Dyer 22, merchant seaman, in the Registry Office Bridgwater on the 26th January 1935. They lived at 95 Rhode Lane, Bridgwater and had three daughters, Gloria 1936, Mary 1938, and Judy 1939 and a son Noel in 1941. Rosina died on the 14th October 1999.

William Lewis Luxton (1915-1988), the eighth child and only son of Jesse Lewis Luxton and his wife Alice Manley, was born in Bridgwater on the 21st March 1915. Bill, an accountant, married Nita Gwendoline Dyke, 24, at St. John the Baptist, Bridgwater on the 24th September 1939. In this photograph his father Jessie (1875-1948) is seated front left, next to his daughter, Lilian. The couple settled at 235 Taunton Road, Bridgwater and later at 9 St. Saviour's Avenue. There were no children of the marriage. Nita was on her way to 45 Church Road, West Huntspill, Highbridge when she died suddenly from heart disease in Bristol Road, Bridgwater on the 12th October 1983. He died on the 19th May 1988.

Madge Luxton (1919-2005), the eighth daughter and youngest child of Jesse Lewis Luxton and his wife Alice Manley, born in Bridgwater on the 15th July 1919, married Gordon Stewart 23, a soldier, at St. John the Baptist Church Bridgwater on the 24th December 1941. The couple settled at 27 Gloucester Road, Bridgwater where Gordon became a personel assistant in a cellophane factory. He was retired when he died at home from heart failure on the 8th May 1977. Madge who was a retired garage receptionist, died at Milton House, West Street, Bridgwater on the 12th April 2005 after suffering a stroke on the 8th January that year. This couple had issue a son Murray Stewart, who was born in Bridgwater on the 17th April 1949. Murray who is a retired chemistry teacher and his wife Helen live in Bramcote, Nottingham.

40

ROBERT LEWIS LUXTON (1834-1899)
AGRICULTURAL LABOURER AND FARMER
AT ALLER DROVE SOMERSET

See tree 21

Robert Lewis Luxton (1834-1899), fourth child and third son of Thomas Luxton (c.1803-1885) farmer, and his wife Hannah Sawtell, was baptised at Aller on the 19th May 1834. Robert was generally referred to by his second name Lewis. He followed his two elder brothers to Bridgwater in search of work in the early 1850s and like them he was married there. Robert Lewis Luxton, bachelor, labourer married Mary Ann Tucker, spinster, in Trinity Church, Bridgwater on Christmas Day 1856 after banns. Robert and Mary both sign the register with a mark, witnessed by Ellen Temblett and Jesse Luxton his mark. Mary was born in the village of Othery, Somerset.

Lewis's elder brothers remained in Bridgwater to raise families but Lewis and Mary returned to Aller, where Lewis, prospered to become a small-holder farmer. He was an agricultural labourer, living in Redley Street, Aller in 1861 but by 1871 he had moved to Aller Drove, with his wife Mary Ann and seven children. Lewis and his brother, Alfred, gave evidence in a court case against two men charged with damaging the river bank at Aller Moor on the night of 7th January 1873[318]. In 1881 Lewis, aged 48, farmer, continued to reside at Aller Drove with his wife Mary Ann and their five children, next door to his half brother, Frederick James Luxton (1847-1928) and his wife Ann, and their five children.

He was prospering, but could perhaps have done with more land for his grazing animals. At the Somerton Petty Sessions in July 1883[319] Lewis was fined 9s..6d including costs for allowing five heifers and one

---

[318] Western Gazette, Friday 17th January 1873.
[319] Western Gazette, Friday 20th July 1883.

yearling to stray on the highway at Aller Drove and again on the 4th June 1887[320] he was fined 2s. and 6d costs for allowing three yearlings to stray on Oath Road, Aller. He was a persistent offender and he was fined 1s with 6 shillings costs for allowing five yearlings to stray on Aller Drove on 17th April 1889.[321] In July 1898 at Langport Police Court, he was fined 9s..6d, including costs, for allowing cattle to stray at Aller.[322] Perhaps too, he was the Mr. Luxton owner of a stallion, which had been turned into a drove to feed but had strayed onto the highway. It attacked a dray horse from South Petherton Brewery, causing it to bolt and throw off the driver, who broke one of his thighs and was severely bruised.[323]

The couple with their three youngest surviving children, Reuben, Albert and Grace, were still farming at Aller Drove in 1891. In October 1892 Lewis, his brother Alfred, and his son John, were witnesses called at the Somerton Quarter Sessions to testify on the poor condition of the River Parret's banks prior to the Somerset floods of that autumn[324].

Lewis was a member of the Aller Friendly Society which celebrated their annual festival on Whit-Monday. It was a big day in the life of the village. The weather was fine on Whit-Monday 1894, when the day began early in the morning with merry peals from the church bells, as members made their way to Mr. F Burrough's barn. There they were joined by the Barrington Brass Band and a procession formed. After visiting the Rectory and other places they repaired to the parish church where the rector conducted Divine Service and an appropriate sermon was delivered. Then members returned to the barn for a celebratory dinner placed before them by Mr. Lewis Luxton. The chair was filled by the rector and all the village worthies were present. After dinner all the customery toasts were proposed and duly honoured. In the evening the Club members, accompanied by the band, after visiting the Rectory and perambulating the village, assembled for sports in a field lent by Mr. F. Burrough and the rest of the day was spent in racing and other

---

[320] Western Gazette, Friday 24th June 1887.
[321] Western Gazette, Friday 17th May 1889.
[322] Wells Journal, 21st July 1898.
[323] Western Gazette, Friday, 19th April 1867.
[324] Taunton Courier, Wednesday 26th June 1892.

games and in dancing. The whole parish, men, women and children joined in and enjoyed themselves to the full[325].

Mary, predeceased her husband, and as Mary Luxton of Longstone, she died aged 58 and was buried at St. Andrew's, Aller on the 22nd December 1894. Her husband Lewis Luxton, aged 65, was buried at St. Andrew's, Aller on the 22nd July 1899.

LONDON STEREOSCOPIC COMP.

Robert Lewis Luxton (1834-1899) and his wife Mary Ann Tucker, had eleven children, seven boys and four girls. John Luxton (1857-1945), known as Jack, the eldest child, was baptised at Aller on the 19th April 1857. He was a 24 year old labourer of Aller when with three other young men from the village, he appeared before the Somerton Petty Sessions, charged with setting fire to a wagon and its load of reed and straw in the Nine Acre Field, belonging to Thomas Hebrow, gent of Aller, on the night of 5th November 1881. This was probably a misguided celebration of bonfire night but the prisoners were discharged for want of sufficient evidence[326]. Jack and his bride to be, were staying with relatives in St. John Street, Bridgwater when he married Sarah Ann Faulkner (1856-1925) at St. John's Church, Bridgwater on the 10th April 1889. This oval Photograph of him from Aunt Polly's album was taken in London, perhaps shortly after his marriage.

In 1891 John 34, agricultural labourer and his wife Sarah, born the Isle of Abbots, Somerset, lived at Aller Drove, and by hard work he became a farmer. Kelly's Directory of Somersetshire for 1906 lists him as a dairyman living at Aller and the 1911 census reveals John 54, farmer on his own account and his wife Sarah Ann, of 22 years marriage, dwelling in a five room house. This was   probably Russ Farm, a small holding

---

[325] Taunton Courier, Wednesday 16th May 1894.
[326] Western Gazette, Friday 18th November 1881.

where John made his will on the 4th May 1920. "I leave everything I die possessed of and which is in my power to bestow unto my daughter, Gertrude Luxton of Russ Farm." He was predeceased by his wife Sarah Ann Luxton, who died aged 69, and was buried at St. Andrew's, Aller on the 10th August 1925. John Luxton of Russ Farm, Aller, Somerset died on the 13th February 1945, aged 87. Probate was granted in London to his daughter Gertrude Luxton spinster, on the 6th August 1947, when his estate was valued at £934..2s..5d.

Their only child, Gertrude, born at the Drove Aller, on the 14th July 1892, was a dairy assistant at Batt's Farm, Upton, Langport in 1911. The "somewhat sudden" death of Miss Gertrude Luxton of Russ Farm, on Tuesday 1st February 1949 aged 56 who was employed at Aller Dairies, "came as a shock to her many friends and neighbours in Aller where she was well respected and liked by all who knew her.[327]" Gertrude was buried in her parent's grave at Aller on the 5th February 1949 and her funeral was well attended. The administration of her estate was granted in London on the 1st June 1949 to her two aunts, Mary Jane (Polly) Stacey, widow and Edith Scriven (wife of Archibald Scriven) when her estate was valued at £4176..16s..10d.

William Luxton (1858-1912), the second child and son of Robert Lewis Luxton, farm labourer, and his wife Mary, was born at the Drove Aller on the 27th November 1858 and baptised at St. Andrew's on the 12th June 1859. A 24 year old agricultural labourer, he married Lucy Ann Small (1853-1893) in the parish church of St John the Baptist, Bridgwater, on the 7th April 1884. William makes his x and his wife Lucy signs her name, witnessed by John, the groom's brother. In 1891 William 32 agricultural labourer, his wife Lucy 33 and their 5 year old daughter, Edith Maria, lived with his wife's grand-mother, Maria Richards, at Church Path, Aller. Their two children, Vincent (1884-85) and Edith Maria (1886-91) predeceased their mother Lucy, who died aged 35 and was buried at St. Andrew's on the 12th October 1893.

William 36, widower, and "Hay Cutter" married Annie Bacon, 38 spinster, of 25 Cranhill Road, Street, in the Independent Chapel, High Street, Glastonbury, Somerset on the 11th May 1896. Their

---

[327] Taunton Courier, Saturday 12th February 1949.

marriage was reported in the Wells Journal-On the 11th May, at the Independent Chapel, Glastonbury, William Luxton to Annie Bacon, both of Street.

In the 1901 census they are living at the Farm House, Catcott Road, Bridgwater where William is a farmer on his own account. He was farming at Burrow Bridge, Middlezoy in 1911, while his wife worked in the Dairy Shop. William died, aged 54, of "Pernicious anaemia heart failure" at Burrowbridge, Middlezoy, Somerset on the 10th September 1912. Mary Stacey, his sister, who lived at Curry Rivel, was present at his death. William was buried at St. Andrew's Aller on the 14th September 1912.

William Luxton, Burrowbridge, made his will on the 21st August 1912. He left, "All the estate property and effects whether real or personal of which I shall die possessed or over which at the time of my death I shall have any power of disposition unto and to the use of my dear wife Annie" who he appointed sole executive. Probate was granted to his widow Annie at Taunton on the 27th December 1912, when his personal estate, valued at £539..10s was re-sworn at £569..10s. His widow, Annie Luxton, aged 75, of Colford Mental Institution, Norton Fitzwarren, died at Bishop Lydeard Cottage Hospital on the 24th February 1933 and was buried at Aller on the 1st March. Administration of her estate was granted in London on the 1st May to their son Harold William Luxton, charge hand, when her personal estate was valued at £807..11s..10d.

This couple had two children. Dorothy Isabel, born at Moorlinch, a village seven miles east of Bridgwater, on the 15th February 1897, died aged 28 at Weston-Super-Mare on the 12th August 1925. She was buried at St. Andrew's Aller on the 18th August. Her brother Harold William Luxton (1898-1979), born at Moorlinch on the 5th June 1898, a fish dock worker, aged 23, married Emily Lavinia Roskell, 23, daughter of a fish dock foreman, in the parish church of Fleetwood, Lancashire on the 31st March 1921.

Harold set up as a newsagent and in May 1942 applied to extend his retail business of Toys and Stationery and Library, at 238 Smithdown Road, Liverpool adjoining his existing premises at 235.[328] He was a

---

[328] Liverpool Daily Post, Friday 18th May 1945.

retired newsagent, living at 236 Smithdown Road, Liverpool when he died at the Royal Liverpool Hospital on the 14th May 1979. John William Luxton (1924-2007), his son, born on the 21st December 1924, was a 31 year old newsagent when he married Elsie White 30, cashier, in the parish of St. Matthew and St. James, Mossley Hill, Liverpool on the 9th July 1956. John died aged 83 in Liverpool in 2007. His son John H. Luxton was born in Liverpool in 1959. No more is known of this branch of the family.

George Lewis Luxton (1860-1951), on right, the third son of Robert Lewis Luxton and his wife Mary Ann Tucker, was baptised at Aller on the 2nd December 1860. In 1881 he was a servant to Richard Lambert, the 80 year old vicar at the "Vicker's House" Fivehead, Langport. Ten years later he was a sapper in the Royal Engineers, based in the army barracks in Aldershot, where this photograph of him was probably taken. George, a 31 year old farmer, residing at Milton Ash, married Alice Willmington 29 spinster of Green Quarry, Yeovil, daughter of George Willmington, gardener, at the Register Office, Yeovil, Somerset on the 8th April 1896.

In July that year he was the inn-keeper of the White Lion Inn in North Street, Langport. He is listed in 1901 as the 37 year old licensed victualler at the White Lion with his wife Alice, 34, born in Weston Bampfylde and their children Clifford 4 and Dorothy Violet aged 1. Harriet Willmington his mother in law was living with them.

He went bankrupt in September 1908[329] and in October he appeared at Yeovil Bankruptcy Court. George had become tenant of the White Lion Inn at sometime in 1896 with a capital of just over £100. Trade had

---

[329] Western Times, Saturday 12th September 1908.

not been as good as in former years. He was now over £100 in debt and had become insolvent three months ago. Unable to work he was living with friends[330].

In 1911 he is a 48 year old farm labourer, living in an eight room house in Aller with Alice, 44 and their children, Clifford George 14, baker and Dorothy Violet aged 11. Alice Luxton died, aged 75, and was buried at St. Andrew's Aller on the 6th October 1941. George died aged 91 in Taunton, and he was buried at St. Andrew's on the 23rd November 1951.Their daughter, Dorothy Violet Luxton (1900-1989), born in the White Lion Inn, Langport, on the 18th January 1900, married Frederick Edwin Higham, a chemist, at St. Andrew's Aller on the 4th April 1931 and they lived in Liverpool where they raised a family. Her brother, Clifford George Lewis Luxton (1896-1969), son of George of the White Lion Inn, Langport and his wife Alice, born at 6 Green Quarry, Yeovil on the 8th July 1896, is the subject of the next chapter. The

photograph below is of Cliff in the Royal Fusiliers in the Great War.

Ellen Luxton (1863-1929), known as Nell, the fourth child of Robert Lewis Luxton and Mary Ann Tucker, baptised at Aller on the 22nd February 1863, married Cornelius Saunders, house painter of Ash Martock, at South Street Baptist Chapel Yeovil on the 1st February 1894. They had three children, two boys and a girl. Nell was buried at Holy Trinity Ash Martock on 11th November 1929 followed by Cornelius on 17th July 1950.

Her sister Mary Jane (Polly) Luxton (1865- 1959), the fifth child, born at the Drove Aller on the 23rd February 1865, married Charles Stacey, a wheelwright and carpenter, at St. Andrew's Aller on the 26th June 1890. They lived in Curry Rivel and had four children, three girls and a boy. In this photograph dated c.1885-1889 Polly is seated with her sister Edith standing besides her. Polly was a widow in 1949, when she was a

---

[330] Western Chroncle, Friday 30th October 1908.

beneficiary in the will of her niece Gertrude Luxton. She died 21 December 1959 and is buried at St Andrew's, Curry Rivel. Her husband Charles died 16th March 1936.

Edith Luxton (1866-1951), the sixth child of Robert Lewis Luxton and his wife Mary Ann Tucker, born at the Drove Aller on Christmas Day 1866, was a 31 year old dairy woman when she married Archibald Scriven, blacksmith at Sion Independent Chapel Bridgwater on the 17th December 1902. They were farming at Aller in 1935 and had three children.

Edith died aged 83 at Plot Stream Farm Aller on 31st October 1951 and Archibald was 90 when buried on 9th April 1970.

Reuben Luxton (1869-1909), the seventh child and fourth son of Robert Lewis Luxton and his wife Mary Ann Tucker, was born at the Drove Aller on the 13th May 1869. In 1891 he was a 22 year old agricultural labourer working at the Drove Aller. He married Mary Ann Andrews, 21, of the Temperance Hotel, at St. Benedict's Church, Glastonbury, Somerset on the 18th May 1896. His wife was born in Belrothery, Dublin and in 1901 Reuben, a hay tyer, and his wife Mary Ann were living with her aunt in South Street, Aller. This is perhaps where the photo below of Reuben and his wife Mary Ann, with their eldest child Charles, born in 1897, was taken. Mary Ann was pregnant with their son Reuben, when Reuben Luxton, general labourer, died aged 39 from pulmonary tuberculosis at Aller on the 28th February 1909 and she was in attendance at his death. He was buried at St. Andrew's Aller on the 5th March 1909.

In 1911 Mary Ann Luxton, 38 widow, paper agent, lived in a four room dwelling in Aller with her children, Charles 14, Grace 11, Lewis 6 who were in school and baby Rueben aged 2. With a young family to keep she was desperately short of money and in March 1911 sought a loan of £6 from Mr. J.T. Knight of Langport. But he refused. She then sold him a piano and sideboard for £6 to "Buy a pig which had been recommended to her as far better than the one she had at the time." It was further agreed that she could hire the piano and sideboard for 1s. per week. Then in June 1913 he gave her 16s. and 9d so that she could buy a brood of ducks. Subsequently Mary Ann sold the piano which he had bought for £12 and kept the proceeds! Knight then sent his son and another man to collect the sideboard which he had bought for £1. Mary Ann "set to like a fury" and the men fled.

The Judge in the County Court, in November 1913, asked Mary Ann, if it was true she had sold the piano? She replied, "I had to. I had three children to keep." The judge decided that Knight should have possession of the sideboard and that Mary Ann was to pay 2s. and 8d.

In October 1916 she appeared in the County court a second time, when T. Maxwell, a Taunton draper sued her for £2 and 18s and 9d. for goods sold on a debt which had been running for about four years. An order was made for her to pay 2s. per month[331].

Mary Ann, widow, died aged 68 of pernicious anaemia, at Clock House Dairy, Bockhampton, Christchurch, County of Southampton on the 3rd December 1943. This couple had five children but one had died by date of the 1911 census. This was their fourth child, Margery, born at Aller on the 18th January 1907 who died two months later and was buried with a coroner's order at St. Andrew's Aller on the 23rd March 1907.

Charles Andrews Luxton (1897-1970), the eldest child, was born on the 25th April 1897. He was a soldier in the Great War. I do not have details but know that he served in Ceylon and Egypt. Charles was a milling machinist at an engineering works, when he married Maud Simpkins, at Christchurch in the parish of Derry Hill Wiltshire by licence on the

---

[331] Western Chronicle, Friday, 14th November 1913 and 13th October 1916.

14th February 1925. Maude of 3 Old Derry Hill, Calne, wife of Charles Andrews Luxton, engineer's machinist, died aged 48 at the Cottage Hospital Cheltenham on 31st January 1950. Charles of 3 Derry Hill, Calne Wiltshire died on the 7th February 1970, leaving an estate valued at £1209. This couple had two children, Christine Nora Luxton (1925-2005) and Dennis Victor Luxton (1930-2013) who both married and had offspring.

Grace Millicent Evelyn Luxton (1899-1962), the second child of Reuben Luxton and his wife Mary Ann Andrews, born in December 1899 was baptised at Aller on the 8th April 1900. She was a grocer in Aller but went bankrupt in November 1930[332] before settling in Bransgore, Christchurch Hampshire where she died on the 7th August 1962. She left an estate valued at £295..17s..3d to her brother Reuben Luxton, a smallholder.

Lewis Norman Luxton (1904-2002), the third child, born on the 15th June 1904, was a 56 year old baker's roundsman of Bransgore when he married Dorothy Dawkins at the register office New Forest, Hampshire by licence on the 2nd August 1960. Lewis who lived in New Milton, Hampshire died in April 2002. His brother Reuben Luxton (1909-1980), the fifth child was born in Aller on the 5th May 1909. He was a retired dairyman and smallholder in Bransgore, when he died of broncho-pneumonia at the Royal Victoria Hospital, Bournemouth on the 23rd March 1980.

Albert Luxton (1871-1944), the eighth child and fifth son of Robert Lewis Luxton and his wife Mary Ann Tucker, was born at the Drove Aller on the 16th May 1871. In 1891 he was a 19year old agricultural labourer, helping his father farm at the Drove. Aged 31 he married Constance Scriven, 30, spinster dressmaker, daughter of Charles William Scriven, blacksmith at the Little Holloway Congregational Chapel, Aller on the 26th April 1904. Constance was a sister to Archibald Scriven who had married Edith, Albert's sister in 1902. In 1911 Albert and Constance lived in an eight room farmhouse at Henley, High Ham. They had lost a child, Kathleen? But I have found no clues to her identity in the birth index. Albert was a farmer at Henley, High Ham,

---

[332] Western Morning News, Monday 10th November 1930.

Somerset, when he made his will on the 8th August 1917. He gave "all my property to my dear wife Constance Luxton and appoint her the sole executrix of my will." In his retirement he lived at Avon Water in Aller. He died aged 72 at Taunton Hospital on the 8th September 1944 and was buried at St. Andrew's Aller on the 13th September. Probate was granted in Bristol on the 25th April 1945 to his widow Constance when his personal estate was valued at £5298..10s. Constance of Avon Water, Aller, Somerset died aged 87, on the 17th August 1962 and was buried at St. Andrew's Aller on the 21st August 1962. Probate of her will was granted in Bristol to Lloyd's Bank Ltd. when her personal estate was valued at £10,917..3s.

Jesse Luxton (1873-1877), the ninth child and sixth son of Robert Lewis Luxton and his wife Mary Ann Tucker, was accidentally registered as a girl at his birth! He was born at the Drove Aller on the 22nd May 1873 and his mother who was illiterate signed his birth certificate with her mark, which perhaps goes some way to explain the confusion. He died aged 4 of malignant scarlet fever at Aller, on the 3rd January 1877 and was buried at St. Andrew's the following day. Alfred, the tenth child and seventh son, born at Aller on the 23rd April 1875, died aged 1 year and 8 months and he was buried at St. Andrew's on the 17th January 1877.

Grace Luxton (1877-1934), the eleventh and youngest child, born at the Drove, Aller on the 20th August 1877, placed the following advert in the Western Gazette, Friday 13th January 1899-Housemaid (single-handed) wants a situation in a gentleman's family- G. Luxton, Langstone, Aller, Langport. She married Frederick R. Tucker at Aller on the 3rd January 1903 and they had two daughters, Doris and Gwen Tucker. They lived in 1911 a five room property at Longload, near Yeovil, where Frederick was a thatcher, and their daughter Doris Hilda, was aged 5. Grace, wife of Frederick Tucker, small holder, died aged 57 of septicaemia at her home College Farm, Long Load, Ash Martock Yeovil on 11th November 1934. She left £107..1s..4d to her husband Frederick R. Tucker (1873-1961). This concludes my account of Robert Lewis Luxton of the Drove Aller and his progeny.

41

CLIFFORD GEORGE LEWIS LUXTON (1896-1969) MASTER BAKER IN LANGPORT SOMERSET AND THE ARMY SERVICE CORPS IN WORLD WAR 1

See tree 21

Clifford George Lewis Luxton, only son of George Lewis Luxton (1860-1951), innkeeper of the White Lion Inn, Langport, and his wife Alice Willmington, was born at 6 Green Quarry, Yeovil on the 8th July 1896. His father George was a 37 year old licensed victualler, living at the White Lion Inn in North Street, Langport in the 1901 census with his wife Alice 34, Clifford 4 and Dorothy1 and Harriet Willmington, 67, widow, Alice's mother. George went bankrupt in 1908 and returned to Aller where the 1911 census lists him as a 48 year old farm labourer, living in an eight room house with Alice 44 and their children Clifford Lewis 14 baker and Dorothy Violet aged 11 scholar.

When Cliff was very young he started work at Kelway's Nurseries, for 9 shillings a week, but by 1911, when he was aged 14, he was working for E W Brown and Son, bakers of Langport. He is second from left in photograph below.

Cliff was a keen footballer in his youth, and a photograph of him in Aller Football Club in the early 1920s, is published in Somerton Ilchester and Langport in Old Photographs, by Gosling and Sutton Publications 1993.

Eileen Bangay, drew my attension to Cliff's postcard album in which some of the cards relate to his time in France in the First World War, when he was Pte. Clifford George Luxton G/53243 B Coy. 6th Platoon, 20th Royal Fusiliers B.E. F. France. She wrote, "There are a few letters, not much content obviously because everything was censored, but still very moving to handle some of the letters and postcards he sent home to his mam. Piecing his service record together it seems that for some

of the time he was a baker in the field, there were photos of him and his mates. He was injured, though not badly but returned home for convalescence."

I urged Eileen to send copies and this chapter came alive in September 2014, when I received a letter and parcel from Eilleen who wrote:-"As a child I remember Clifford Luxton as a lovely old uncle, but I had no idea at that time of his World War 1 service.

I am sending you a selection of copied letters and photos. Back along I received a rather dirty and battered bundle of papers from a cousin after the disposal of Ivy Luxton's property (i.e. Canterbury Farm) which included long forgotten material left by Cliff in a box in the roof of the house. From these I have extracted some of those sent between Cliff and his mother back in Aller in Somerset during W.W. 1 when he  was in France, and when convalescing. With all the 100 years recollections in the media....it seems appropriate to bring these things together. The letters reflect his rural background, how initially he benefits from the good food and provisions. As you will see Cliff was a local baker from a boy, when he joined up he was attached to the field bakery of the A.S.C. His letters are written in pencil and he is obviously aware of the censor, as stock phrases are repeated, so there are very few interesting bits, and one has to read between the lines rather. I have about 30 scraps of paper, but have included copies of the most legible for your interest."

Cliff's enlistment papers were destroyed in the London blitz so we do not have details of his military career, but we know he was 18 when he enlisted and was attached to the Field Bakery Division of the Army Service Corps. When he joined up he was with several other lads from Aller. He was in the army by March 1915 and was at Woolwich and Charles Street, Plumstead, for his initial training. Cliff is second left, back row with his young pals in uniform, in this postcard post dated 1st April. It reveals the army experience was novel "fun"and he was still waiting for the rest of his army kit:-Dear Ma, This is a photo we had taken while we waited. We had it just for fun. We had been out to get our dinner. We are getting our pants and shirts and socks this week I think. I am sending home a pair of pants and one or two pair of socks for you to wash and darn. I will write as soon as I can. C L.

An undated postcard from Cliff to his sister Dolly, which must have been written at this time of his enlistment, reads:-"I was vaccinated last

Friday, got an arm about three times the ordinary size, am going to the doctor's this afternoon."

Cliff posted his mother Mrs. G. Luxton, High Street, Aller this postcard of the free Woolwich ferry at 8:45 P.M. on the 13th April 1915:-"You asked in your last letter how I liked it, well I liked it fine. I have put on nearly a stone in weight. I have written to Ethel and Frank. We went across the free ferry today the boat on the other side of this card is the one we went on. There is a tunnel under the ferry if you don't like the boat. Has dad finished the garden yet. How is Tango I should like to see her" (Tango was his dog).

In 1914 there was one Field Bakery in every infantry division. Staffed by one officer and 92 men from the A.S.C. It could produce enough bread for more than 20000 men. Because of the nature of their work they did not set up these bakeries near the front, and many in 1914-15 were based in locations like Rouen and Abbeville, and a little nearer the front in St. Omer and Hazebrouck. They tended to be static units that did not move around much. Cliff is standing third from left, in back row with men in his field bakery.[333]

---

[333] Cliff's photograph album is in the possession of Eileen Bangay to whom I am grateful for sharing her knowledge of the Aller Luxton's.

Letter from Cliff to his mother. A.S.C. Charles Street, Plumstead S.E. London (Army Service Corps):-Dear Ma, Just a few more lines. I am sending on three more shillings for Clarke, you did not say whether you got the other three or not. I sent a card to Ethel and on to Mr. White the other night.

I have just come back from the baths. You can have a lovely warm bath or at least soldiers can for three pence and they find you a towel and soap for the three pence. You asked, if I should like a Langport Herald, I see one every week. Frank has one sent up, the pair of pants and three pairs of socks will not come by post. I am sending them with Frank's, and his sister will take them to the bakehouse and Bob will bring them to you.

I had a look around the Arsenal one night. I went into the bullet factory and had one in each different process, about seventeen different processes. I will put them in one of my socks take care of them they will be nice to keep when this is all over, only soldiers are allowed in there, Frank did not go.

We had a route march today and as we were turning back a whole company of Highlanders came, all in full dress with their bagpipes and drums, so we all joined up and marched home to Woolwich in fine style, it looked alright I can tell you.

I suppose you have seen in the papers that they propose to close the pubs earlier up here, well the Arsenal workers say they will down tools if they do. When I went in the Arsenal I saw some of the big shells, I could get inside and stand upright in them they are a tremendous size.

I went into the soldiers club the other night. I did not stop long because it was full up, a smoking concert was in full swing, it was a row when they all joined in the choruses, about two thousand there.

I should like for you to see the tunnel under the Thames here it takes about half an hour to walk through or go across on one of the boats it is all free horses and carts, motor cars bicycles and all.

Ask dad to put some vaseline on my bike. I have had out two teeth and have to have out two more this week and when I am alright I am going to have my photo taken properly, from your loving son CL"

Cliff is second from left in the photograph below. The Territorial badge above his right pocket reveals he was in the Territorial Army before the Great War.

Cliff frequently fails to date his letters but at sometime in 1915 he was moved to digs in Ipswich. He clearly enjoyed his grub there as the

following letter from Cliff to his mother makes clear:-From Pte. C. Luxton, c/o Mrs Kett, 8 Chaldon Street, Ipswich, Suffolk:-

Dear Ma, Just a few lines to let you know that I am having the time of our lives, plenty to eat, yesterday for breakfast we had tomatoes and sausages, and for dinner we had roast beef, peas and potatoes, and peaches and custard after dinner, and bread and butter and lattice for tea, and for breakfast this morning we had a great plate of salt beef about a pound of it. There is nothing for us to do here, so they say we shall be back in London again to Richmond Park to look after the London Scottish, but we do not want that. I weigh 13stone now but I do not know what I shall weigh if we stay here long, about 15 I expect. It is a very old fashioned place here in some parts there is no church parade for us morning so we are going to have a good look around. I forgot to explain that we are fed by the Government, only sleep at our billets. We were going to Felixstowe today, we did not know that we had to get a pass until it was too late. They are very nice people where we are billeted quite close to our cook house, you should see us scoot when we hear the bugle-come to the cook house door boys-with our plates and basins, from your loving son CL"

From there he was moved to 32nd Field Bakery Park Hall Camp, A. S. C. Hut 23, Oswestry, Shropshire. There was a designated temporary post office at Oswestry Park Hall Camp from the 3rd July 1915. Cliff sends a no date letter from the camp:-

"Dear Ma, Just a few more lines to thank you for the fags. I have got a scab behind my ear this morning went to see the doctor this morning, he gave me two days off duty and about six miles of bandages around my head, so I am alright for two days. We hear that we are shifting from here next month, some say to Ireland and others say to the east coast again. I hope the latter is true. If you have the money to spare will you take out a licence for Tango and I will send on the money as soon as I have some. Scotty and Frank were tinned last night. I think this is all for now from your loving son C.L."

In October 1915 Cliff was back in digs in Ipswich, Suffolk, staying c/o Mrs Thurkettle 271 Cauldwell Hall Road. His letter home on the 17th October is especially interesting as it refers to a zeppelin raid on the town. Zeppelin raids on English towns killed 426 and injured 864 people. There were three raids on Ipswich, two in 1915, in April and this one in October, and a third in 1916 in which a man was killed.

"Dear Ma, Just a few lines in answer to yours which I received yesterday. I might be home Tuesday or Wednesday, do not expect me because I might not be able to get it. If I do I will wire and let you know. I worked three half nights this week at 2/6 a night, and Saturday morning from seven to one and had another 9/6 so I am well up. I am going to buy a light pair of boots tomorrow Monday. You asked if the zeps were near us. I should think the blooming things were, it was the first time I felt nervous. They dropped a couple about four hundred yards from our house, shook the whole house and the land lady nearly fainted and by the time I had come downstairs and got to the front door they were just going over the house and up onto the heath. The guns were banging away at them just about. I think this is all for now I will tell you all about it if I come home from your loving son C.L."

He was moved from Ipswich to Aldershot for further training. No date letter from Cliff to his mother. S4/158005, K. Company A.S.C. Room 2.5 Salamanca Barracks, Wellington lines, Aldershot.

"Dear Ma, Just a few lines to let you know that I am still in the land of the living in Aldershot. I am at present in Barracks as you will see by the address, but do not know how long we shall be there, you get shifted about so much down here. You had better write nearly by return of post because I might be here a day or a month. How is Doll getting on, is she better. (His sister Dorothy)

I have got a good job down here, am working in the dining rooms, plenty of food in there, no baking to do. I was loading motors with eats on Saturday, good job that. I and Scotty was sat under the bridge over the canal most of the time smoking. I think I saw Bill Webb here the other day but was not sure so I did not speak to him, I think this is all for now from your loving son C.L."

We do not have an actual date for when Cliff went to France but he was not awarded the 1914-15 Star. However, surviving army records reveal he was with the 46th Field Bakery of the Army Service Corps when he was admitted with pleurisy to a casualty unit on the 14th June 1916. He was transferred to the ward 8 of the Hospital Ship Lanfranc. Cliff was recovered by the close of the year when he wrote another letter to his mother, dated 22nd December 1916.

"Dear Ma, Just a few lines to let you know that I did not leave Aldershot after all. Five hundred of us bakers have been transferred to the ninety eighth Reserve Infantry Training Battalion and are in another barracks here called Badajoo Barracks, not very far from where I was before.

One good thing I am with all my mates that I was with the A.S.C. Could you send me five shillings if you could possibility spare it as I have not been paid this week. You had better register it as there are so many lost lately and send it to the soldiers home, I will put it inside. One good thing they are giving us plenty of food, so the only thing I miss is cigarettes. I was coming home yesterday but it was all stopped at the last moment. I think this is all for now from your loving son C.L."

No date, another letter, damaged page from Cliff:-

"….lines. I have been to bed since dinner, just got up and had a few rounds with the gloves. You ought to have seen me yesterday I was hut orderly, washing up plates and basins, brushing the floor and black leading the stove. I think I should apply for a house maid's job after the war. You asked after Frank's brother. Herb is getting on alright. I saw a letter he wrote himself last week. I think this is all for now from your loving son C.L." Cliff is on the right in photograph below.

Cliff was on the Western Front when he wrote on a Field Service card dated 13-3-1917,"I am quite well." This was followed by two letters written on "Scottish Churches Huts" headed note paper. One dated 15th March 1917:-

"Dear Ma, Just a few lines to let you know I am quite well. We had a nice trip across the water. Address Pte. C. Luxton G/53243, A. P. O. Section 17 39th I. B. D. B. E. F. France. Having plenty of fine weather at present. Remember me to Aunt Sally and Aunt Ede. (Edith Sciven 1866-1951) Tell them I will write as a soon as possible. I think that is all for now from your loving son C. L. "P/S Did you get the card I sent.

Once in France, Cliff in the Bakery Division, was moved around, attached to various battalions. His second undated letter reads:-"

Dear Ma, Just a few lines in answer to yours which I received this evening + to thank you for the papers I got this morning G/32 243 Pte. C. Luxton 32nd Royal Fusiliers A.P. O. Section 17 39 I. B. D. B.E. F. France Do not make a mistake on the Battn. this week You put the 39th on that one anyway it found me alright. Please excuse the writing I am holding the pencil between my fingers to write. I cut my thumb while opening a tin. I think this is all for now from your loving son C. L."

Other letters and Field Postcards show a change in his writing. Obviously everything was censored so no real news could be given by the men. The paper becomes much more damaged, faded and crumbled. Cliff's writing is much less sure and he makes use of the various churches and charities that are in the Field to support and help the men to keep in touch with loved ones.

When Cliff received injuries he informed his parents on a Field Card, dated 29th June 1917, "I have been admitted into hospital sick and am going on well. Letter follows at first opportunity."

He was convalescing in Rouen and a letter, dated 1917 follows on "Soldiers Christian Association" headed notepaper:-Address Pte. C. Luxton, S lines, No 2 Convalescent Camp, Rouen, France:-

"Dear Ma, Just a few lines to let you know that I am still in the land of the living, hoping you are all quite well at home. I am in hospital here (address)-S lines No 2 Convalescent Camp Rouen. You had better write. You had better write as soon as you get this letter as

I do not expect to be here much longer. I have got a lot of sores on my right leg and a small wound just above the ankle, nothing serious. I can walk about; will write again as soon as possible from your loving son C.L."

The second letter, also on "Soldiers Christian Association" headed notepaper is dated 7th June (1917):-

"Dear Ma, Just a few lines to let you know that I am still alive but nearly suffocated, it is very hot this evening, I think it will turn to thunder. How is the hay making getting on around Aller. I have not come across George Stacey yet. My leg is going on nicely.

12th July (1917) address-20th Batl. Royal Fusiliers, S lines, No 2 Convalescent Camp, Rouen, France:-

"Dear Ma, Just a few lines to let you know that I am still in the land of the living, hoping that you are quite well. I got your letter this morning dated the 7th. I wrote to Ethel the day before yesterday. I have not got the letter or parcel you sent to the Batt. The letter might be forwarded on but I do not suppose the parcel will. You did not say if you got the postcard from the other hospital or not. My leg is getting on nicely. I wish I knew I was going to be here as long as I have been, I would have asked you to send some cigs and some money, but it is not safe to send anything but letters until I get back to the base. I drew ten francs the first week I was in here but that does not last long in here and I don't know how long it will be before I get paid again. I think this is all for now. I will write again as soon as possible let me know if you get my letters, from your loving son C.L."

16th July (1917) address the same:-

"Dear Ma, Just a few lines to let you know I received Doll's letter. I expect Charlie was frightened when the Indian shaved him. He is knocking about the globe a bit isn't he."(This is a reference to his cousin Charles Andrews Luxton (1897-1970) who was serving in Ceylon and Egypt.)

30th July (1917):-G/53243 20th Batt. Royal Fusiliers, No11 Convalescent Camp D. Coy. A.P.O. S44 B. E.F.:- "Dear Ma, Just a few lines to let you know…I have had another shift as you see from the address. I do not know how long I shall be here. I came here yesterday so can't tell you much about it yet.

1st August (1917) on notepaper headed Y.M.C.A. "with the Expeditionary Force" 20th Batt Royal Fusiliers, No 11 Convalescent Camp D. Coy. A.P.O. S44 B.E.F. "Dear Ma, Just a few lines to let you know….much the same…

7th August on notepaper headed Y.M. C. A. "with the Expeditionary Force"

"Dear Ma, Just a few lines to let you know…I am still in the Convalescent Camp, but do not write after you get this letter as I expect to be back to the base shortly…

2nd September letter on a scrap of paper:-"Dear Ma, Just a few lines to let you know that I am still in the land in the living, hoping you are quite well. I have not had any letters since I left the Convalescent Camp, but I suppose they will follow me up in time.

Pte. C. Luxton G/53243 B. Coy, 7th Platoon, 20th Battalion, Royal Fusiliers, B. E.F. "I am writing this letter in bed, if you might call it a bed, I think this is all for now your loving son C.L."

At sometime in the autumn of 1917 Cliff returned to the U.K. on leave but he was back on the Western Front by the 4th February 1918. He writes home on Church Army headed paper, 13th February 1918:- "Dear Ma, Just a few lines to let you know that I am still in the land of the living, hoping you are all quite well as it leaves me in the pink. Just getting used to it again. 53243 16th Platoon No. 4 Company 13th Battalion Royal Fusiliers B.E.F. Tell Dad that the razor goes alright, but the other one is no good, I am having it done up again. I have just finished Aunt Ede's butter, had the last for tea tonight. Has Dad had any more rabbits yet, or else is he on with Flo? yet. I think this is all for now from your loving son C.L.

P.S. How is Doll getting on with her new job? (His sister Dorothy)

There are two other letters I quote here which I think date to 1918 but as Cliff does not provide the year they could refer to 1917:-

One is the fragment of a letter to his mother, dated 30th April. He gives his number, the address has changed. G/53243 Pte. C. Luxton16th Platoon, No. 4 Coy, 13th Battalion, Royal Fusiliers British Expeditionary Force. This is followed by two Field Service Postcards on the 5th and 30th June 1918 which both read "I am quite well"

The second letter to his mother is dated the 4th October (1918, I think but it could be 1917?)

"Just a few lines in answer to yours which I received a few days ago but have not been able to write before. I heard from Gert, Frank and Ethel since I last wrote. We are just out of the trenches again after a few of the hottest days I have yet experienced out here. I suppose you have seen in the papers our division was personally congratulated by Sir D, Haigh. We are having a change in the weather this last two or three days it rained a little last night. All for now from your loving son C.L."

Cliff was hit by a large piece of shrapnel in his lower face and jaw. This was at sometime late in the war and he was returned to London for surgery and recovery. He spent several months with his jaw wired up for it to mend; he could not eat properly and was fed by a tube through his teeth. During this time he was at the Third London General Hospital, and for a while at the British Home and Hospital for Incurables at Streatham. We learn from the scraps of letters that have survived that eventually he was well enough to go out and some entertainment and outings were arranged for the troops. Whilst at Streatham he met and corresponded briefly with Florrie Storey and he received several letters from the young lady who lived at 209 Essex Road Islington and she wrote arranging to meet Cliff. He later wrote to his mother that he was going to Streatham to tea.

When he was able to go out and about as a "walking wounded" Cliff wrote to his mother from Ward B4, Third London General Hospital, Wandsworth. Undated letter.

"Dear Ma, Just a few lines to let you know that I am back at the hospital. I have been to the Haymarket this afternoon. I wrote to the paymaster yesterday so as soon as you get it please send me £1 as I am getting short. I went to the Scala last Monday afternoon, "The Black Feather" is on there. I am going to Streatham tomorrow to tea."Another day he writes, "I am going to the Tower this afternoon, a car is coming around to fetch us at 1 o'clock."

Undated letter, probably written sometime in 1919. Address British Home and Hospital for Incurables, Streatham SW 16

"Dear Ma, Just a few lines to let you know I have had a change of hospital. I am now in a home for incurables but do not be alarmed, because I am only here until the end of the month. It is a lovely place, there are only twenty soldiers here. You would think you were in the country here, it is on Streatham Common. I do not know if dad knows it or not. I got the paper yesterday. I have my wires off but not the splints yet. I do not suppose they will be off until I go back to the 3rd London. I think this is all for now from your loving son C.L."

On the 26th May (1919) Cliff received a letter from his mother, addressed to Pte. C. Luxton B.H.H.I. Ward 59 Streatham Sw. 16. He wrote letter dated 24 June 1919:-

"Dear Ma, Just to let you know that I am still here but expect to go back to the hospital next Saturday… having a glorious time lovely weather."

There were letters from his mother, addressed to Pte. C. Luxton, 3rd London General Hospital B4 Ward Wandsworth SW 18. Aller 9th June 1919:-

"My Dear Cliff, Just a few lines in answer to yours so glad to hear that you have the splints off. I hope that when you have your teeth it will be alright for you, shall be longing to know if it is alright.

What did you think of the Houses of Parliament on Saturday. Did you think of the Aller people on Monday, there were between 130 &140 people in the field. I didn't go up all day. I saw them march past the church quite a lot of them, the Bells were ringing nearly all the day.

Aller 11th June. "My Dear Cliff, Just a few lines in answer to yours. I thought I should have seen you home by this time or are they going to keep you up there for the peace celebrations. I haven't heard that they are doing anything here, too busy hay making to think of anything else…but it is going to be a holiday for everybody at Langport and Huish, they are having fine doings on the 19th …"

Aller 16th June:-"My Dear Cliff, So glad to get your letter and to hear that you are getting on so well also to hear that you will be home soon. Frank Goodson is home, he is home for good. Frank Harris and Percy Wilmot is also home. So there is not many of the Aller boys left now when you are home. Alfred is still in Germany."

Aller 18th June "My Dear Cliff,…glad you got the money and also the clothes, how do you like it, will you be able to have your boots mended. There is such a lot of haymaking and Steve (Stephen Charles Luxton (1877- 1950) of Canterbury Farm) is carrying his home field today. Your dad is helping him…"

Pte. Clifford Luxton, Royal Fusiliers was awarded the British War Medal and the Victory Medal for his services in the Great War. Some of his pals did not make it home. In his possession was a memorial card- In affectionate remembrance of Private James Snell, 7th Somerset Light Infantry, youngest son of James Snell, Hollyar's Farm, Aller who was killed in action with a ration party the night of November 24th1917, in France. Aged 36 years.

The 1914-18 Roll of Honour in St. Andrew's Church Aller lists C. Luxton and five more of his Luxton cousins.

In March 1940 Cliff received a letter addressed to Church Street Aller from his old surgeon Mr. W. Warwick James of the 3rd London

General Hospital, Wandsworth, who wrote:-"I have been writing a series of articles and am now writing a book upon the treatment of face and jaw injuries. Information about my old cases is most valuable.

If you will be good enough to fill in and return the enclosed form I shall be most grateful. I am sending this to the address given when you were at the 3rd London General Hospital in the hope it will reach you, Yours sincerely, W.W. James.

Following the Great War Cliff was in business as Luxton & Lock, Bakers and Confectioners in Langport. In the photograph we see him with his bakers/grocers van at sometime in the interwar years. Cliff a 64 year old retired baker of Church Path Aller married his half cousin Ivy Gertrude Luxton 48 spinster, poultry farmer of Canterbury Farm, Aller at the Register Office Bridgwater on the 20th December 1960. Ivy was the daughter of Stephen Charles Luxton (1877-1950) and his wife Bessie Otten. Her father was the son of Frederick James Luxton (1847-1928) who was a half brother to Cliff's grandfather Robert Lewis Luxton (1834-1899). Clifford George Lewis Luxton of Canterbury Farm Aller died aged 72 on the 27th February 1969 and he was laid to rest at St. Andrews Aller on the 2nd March 1969. Administration of his estate valued at £5797 was granted in London to his widow.

42

ALFRED LUXTON (1836-1924)
AGRICULTURAL LABOURER AT RIDLEY IN ALLER,
SOMERSET AND HIS FAMILY

See tree 22

Alfred Luxton (1836-1924), the fifth son of Thomas Luxton (c.1803-1885) yeoman, and his first wife Hannah Sawtell, born at Aller, Somerset on the 15th March 1836, was baptised in the parish church dedicated to St. Andrew on the 6th May 1836. Alfred grew up at Ridley

in Aller where his parents farmed. He began his working life early and the 1851 census lists the 13 year old as an agricultural labourer, living with his parents there. Betsy Lock (1839-1927), a dressmaker, daughter of Charles Lock, gardener, was the Aller girl he chose for his bride, and they were wed at Trinity Church, Bridgwater on Christmas Day 1859. Betsy wrote her name in the register but Alfred could only make his mark. Census returns for Victoria's long reign reveal Alfred, agricultural labourer, and his family's movements about the parish.

The young couple and their infant son Charles, were living at Wheadon's Alley, Aller in 1861 but by 1871 the growing family lived at Horsemead Cottage. Sometime before 1881 they lived at Ridley Street in Aller with eleven of their children. Next door lived Thomas, his 86 year old father, with his youngest daughter Athaliah, aged 22. Alfred and family were still living at Ridley in 1891 but with only four children still at home. When their son, Albert, joined the army in July 1899 their home in Ridley Street was called Mayfield Cottage. Two years later in 1901, Alfred, 65, agricultural labourer and Betsy, 61, a dressmaker on her own account, resided in Mayfield Cottage, next to the village shop which was kept by relatives. John Smith, a 16 year old gardener, was boarding with the couple. In 1911 Alfred, 75, farm labourer, his wife Betsy 61, a dressmaker, married 51 years, still lived in the 5 rooms of Mayfield Cottage, and 7 of their 14 children were still alive.

Alfred Luxton died, aged 87, on 1st February 1924 and was buried at St. Andrew's, Aller on the 6th February. Administration of his will was granted in Taunton on the 15th September 1927 to his son Alfred Henry Luxton, farmer, when his personal estate was valued at £216. Betsy, his wife, born on the 30th September 1839, was also aged 87, when she died. She was buried at Aller on the 31st March 1927.

Alfred and Betsy had 14 children and they must have found it difficult to bring up a large family on an agricultural labourer's wages, even though Betsy eked out the income by working as a dressmaker. There was tragedy too. Albert Ernest Luxton (1862-1878), their second son, a 15 year old labourer, was "accidentally killed by the kick of a horse" at Aller on the 15th July 1878. The sad circumstances of his death were reported in the Langport and Somerton Herald for the 20th July 1878:- Aller Fatal Accident—On Monday last, a lad named Ernest Luxton, about 15 years of age, son of Alfred Luxton, labourer, of this parish, was accidentally killed. He was accompanying another boy with a waggon load of hay, when a bolt came out of the breeching of the shaft horses, and deceased went back to pick it up. His companion, who was riding the forehorse, could account for deceased up to this time, but when he returned to the load or in what way he met with his accident he had no knowledge whatever. One of Mr. Munckton's sons, who was following a few minutes later, found the boy lying in the road quite dead. Although life was quite extinct Mr. Brooke, surgeon, of Langport, was summoned, and promptly attended. At the inquest held on Wednesday, before Dr. Wybrants, coroner for the district, and a jury of parishers, there was no positive testimony as to how the deceased met with his death. One supposition is that he fell while trying to get upon the shaft, and that one or both wheels of the waggon must have passed over his head and neck, killing him instantaneously. Another supposition is that he was first kicked by the horse while attending to the breeching. The jury appear to have taken the later view, for they returned a verdict to the effect that the deceased had been accidentally killed through being kicked by a horse.

Poverty and overcrowded living conditions must have contributed to the deaths of four more children buried at St. Andrew's, Aller-Anna (1861-1882), died aged 22, from phthisis, Lucy (1865-1870) died aged 4 from croup (so named in imitation of the croak or sharp cough which marked the inflammatory disease of the larynx and trachea), Ada Mary (1875-1889), died in Taunton Hospital of cardiac failure following seven weeks of cardiac disease and Herbert (1879-1884) aged 5, who died of three months exhaustion with diseased hips.

Those of Alfred's children who survived into adulthood became economic migrants, moving away from Aller to seek their livelihoods. Charles (1860-1903), the eldest son, a 21 year old printer, living in lodgings in Shoreditch in 1881, married Mary Doster in South Norwood, Surrey in 1884. In 1891 and in 1901 Charles, a numerical printer and his wife Mary, lived at 6 Douglas Terrace, Leytonstone, with seven children. When he died, aged 43, from consumption on the 2nd December 1903, he was a compositor of 15 Wood Street, Leytonstone, in Essex. Arthur, his younger brother born in 1864, married in Cardiff, and was a marine stoker when he died in Hartlepool, Durham from "capillary bronchitis" on the 24th March 1901.

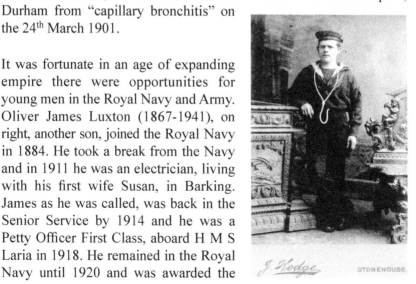

It was fortunate in an age of expanding empire there were opportunities for young men in the Royal Navy and Army. Oliver James Luxton (1867-1941), on right, another son, joined the Royal Navy in 1884. He took a break from the Navy and in 1911 he was an electrician, living with his first wife Susan, in Barking. James as he was called, was back in the Senior Service by 1914 and he was a Petty Officer First Class, aboard H M S Laria in 1918. He remained in the Royal Navy until 1920 and was awarded the

1914 Star, the Victory Medal and the British War Medal for his service in the Great War. He was twice married and settled at Thornton Heath, Surrey where he was an electrician.

Five more sons served in the Hussars. Alfred Henry Luxton (1869-1952), known as Harry, joined the army at 15, after running away from an apprenticeship as a printer in London. He spent most of his life in the 15th Hussars and after that served in the Suffolk Yeomanry where he became a Sergeant Major Instructor. He married twice, had an extensive family and finally settled as a farmer in Suffolk.

William Jesse Luxton (1870-1953), his brother, who joined the 15th Hussars at Taunton on the 1st November 1893, served in India from September 1899 to September 1902.[334] He was discharged from the army on 31st October 1905, after twelve years service and was a gardener at Winsley near Bradford on Avon, when he married Elizabeth Mary Cornwall, a 30 year old spinster, in St. John the Evangelist Staplegrove, Somerset on the 26th October 1904. He died, aged 82, at The Retreat, Woolawington Corner, Bawdrip, near Bridgwater, Somerset on 30th June 1953.

William Jesse was the father of an illegitimate son who was taken to the U.S.A. by his mother shortly after his birth. Jesse Henry Luxton (1907-1999), son of Jesse Luxton, valet, and his wife Annie Jane Luxton, formerly Stacey, was born at 11 London Road, Beccles, Suffolk on 27th May 1907. There is no marriage I can find for this couple in the General Marriage Index. Annie split from Jesse and in 1907 emigrated to the U.S.A. with their infant son. There she married a Mr. White and had two further children. In 1930 Jesse Henry Luxton/White, 22, a nurseryman/florist, was living with his mother and siblings, Edith and William White. His mother Annie, died in Hackettstown, Warren, New Jersey on the 11th March 1970. Jesse married Alice Wayland Hudson (1909-2006). They had a daughter, Alice Wayland White (1946-2005) who married and had issue a child. Jesse died in Peterborough, Hillsborough, New Hampshire on 1st February 1999.

---

[334] Attestation of William Jesse Luxton No3207, Short Service (7 years with the colours, and 5 in the Reserve) WO 97/5372.

Richard Luxton (1872-1914), a third brother, was passed fit for the army at Taunton on 17th December 1889, and at Canterbury, four days later he joined the 18th Hussars[335]. He transferred to the 15th Hussars on 8th February 1890 but by October 1897 he was a groundsman to Mr. Grenfell, Mostyn House, Neston in Cheshire[336]. He married Susan Walsh, an Irishwoman, in Liverpool on the 5th September 1898. In January 1900 "Dick" Luxton as one of the Hussar reservists bound for the war front in the Second Boer War had a "great send off at Parkgate Station"[337] and he served with the 8th Hussars in the South African campaign from 27th July 1900 to 17th February 1901. He was awarded the Queens South Africa Medal and the Kings South Africa Medal and clasps for Cape Colony, Orange Free State, Transvaal and South Africa 01.

When Richard was discharged from the army as medically unfit on the 25th July 1901 he was described as a farm labourer, aged 29 years and 10 months, and his intended place of residence was Neston-cum- Park Gate, Cheshire. His wife Susan, died in 1907, and the 1911 census lists Richard as a widower and builder at Liverpool Road Neston, Cheshire. His step-daughter, Margaret Walsh, and her three children Andrew 5, Oliver 3 and Susan aged 11 months were residing with him. They are surnamed Luxton in the census, but do not appear under that name in the GRO birth index. He was a 42 year old labourer of Liverpool Road, Neston when he died of pneumonia at the Workhouse Union Infirmary, Poulton-cum- Spital on the 20th September 1914.

Andrew Luxton (1877-1952), a fourth brother, was engaged in 1898, as an indoor servant at Bere, in Aller but a dispute arose about his time keeping and he was dismissed. He took his case to the County Court, where after hearing the case, the Judge ordered he should receive £3.. 6s. in wages.[338] In 1911 census he was a domestic coachman to Gerald Apthorp and family, living in a nine room property at Harrietsham, near Maidstone, but he was a coachman at Chiddingstone Causeway, Kennington, Kent when he married Elizabeth Martha Knowles in the

---

[335] Attestation of Richard Luxton No 3562, Short Service (7 years with the colours and 5 in the Reserve) WO 97/5372.
[336] The Cheshire Observer, 30th October 1897.
[337] The Cheshire Observer, Saturday 27th January 1900.
[338] Taunton Courier, Wednesday 24th August 1898.

parish church there on the 24th June 1911.During the Great War he served in the 15th Hussars. One of the "old contemptibles" Private Andrew Luxton (reg. no.3857) first saw action on the 10th September 1914.Later transferred to the Labour Corps, to help service the front line troops, he was awarded the 1914 Star, the British War Medal and the Victory Medal. He was a retired gardener when he died at the Police House, Town Road, Petham, Canterbury on the 4th December 1952.Probate was granted in London on 6th January to Philip Howard Beedle, Police Constable when his effects were valued at £888..6s..01d. This photograph of Andrew with his horse and cart, was sent to his brother Harry in Suffolk at Christmas 1932.

Albert Luxton (1880-1955), the youngest brother, enlisted in the army at Taunton on the 29th July 1899. He joined the 15th Hussars at Shorncliffe on the 2nd August 1899[339] and was posted to the 19th Hussars on the 23rd October 1908. He served in India from December 1900 to October 1908 and was discharged from the army after twelve years service on the 28th July 1911.

Albert was a serving soldier in Aldershot, when he married Emily Bond Woods at Aller, on the 19th October 1910. (See photo below). In the 1911 census the newly wed couple lived at 10 Springfield Terrace, Aldershot. Albert placed the following advert in the Hendon & Finchley Times, Friday, 1st December 1911-Ex-soldier seeks employment as groom, gardener or coachman, aged 30, good references.

At the outset of the Great War Albert rejoined the army on the 21st August 1914. He first served as Private no.3313 in the 19th Hussars

---

[339] Attestation of Albert Luxton No4073 Short Service (Cavalry of the line) WO 97/5372.

but was later transferred to the M.P.S.C. (i. e. the Military Provost Staff Corp) where he was an Acting Sergeant and was awarded the 1914-15 Star, the British War Medal and the Victory Medal. He died at Bottoms Pilsbury, Langport, Somerset on the 26th March 1955.

On their homecoming the brothers must have possessed a rich store of tales to tell their family and friends!

At the Langport and Curry Rivel Agricultural Society's annual dinner held in the Bell Hotel in October 1900, Mr. Meade one of the speakers, spoke of the part West Countrymen were taking in the Boer War and he alluded to one family the Luxtons living in that neighbourhood from which there were five sons serving in South Africa.[340]

In a patriotic age the family's humble contribution to the Empire was acknowledged by Queen Victoria. The Western Gazette in Yeovil, Somerset reported on 24th November 1900:-Aller-It having been represented by the Rector to Her Majesty that Mr. and Mrs. Alfred Luxton, of this parish, now have six sons serving in the Army and Navy, the Queen has been graciously pleased to grant a gratuity of £4.

The photograph shows Andrew John Bond Luxton (1911-1988), a grandson of Alfred Luxton and Betsy Lock, with his wife Margaret Cox and her parents.

[340] Taunton Courier, Wednesday 31st October1900.

43

CHARLES LUXTON (1860-1903) PRINTER OF LEYTONSTONE ESSEX AND HIS FAMILY

See tree 22

Charles Luxton, the eldest son of Alfred Luxton (1836-1924), agricultural labourer of Aller in Somerset, and his wife Betsy Lock (1839-1927), dressmaker, born in Aller on the 29th February 1860, was an economic migrant. He was settled in Shoreditch by 1881 when the census records him as a 21 year old printer, living in lodgings. He met Mary Doster, a Somerset girl from Stoke Gregory, and they married in St Mark's Church, South Norwood, Surrey on the 26th January 1884. The 1891 and 1901 census list Charles, a numerical printer, and his wife Mary, living at 6 Douglas Terrace Leytonstone with seven children. When Charles died of consumption on the 2nd of December 1903, he was a 43 year old compositor, dwelling at 15 Wood Street Leytonstone. Eight children had been born to the couple, three girls and five boys.

Anna Maude, the eldest child, born on 17th November 1886 in Penge, Essex, remained a spinster. She had undergone a distressing experience as a teenager. At the Essex Quarter Sessions held in Chelmsford in May 1901, Arthur Sutton, a 34 year old labourer on bail, was indicted for assaulting her in Leyton on 13th May. The accused who was a married man with five children, emphatically denied the allegations made against him. He said he had been employed as a shunter on the Great Eastern Railway for five years. Sutton was found not guilty and was discharged.[341] Anna was admitted as an inmate of Essex Asylum on 22nd May 1906. The 1939 register lists her as an inmate in Brentwood Mental Hospital, and she died aged 57 in Brentwood on 18th July 1943.

---

[341] Chelmsford Chronicle, Friday 24th May 1901

Her sister Gertrude (1887-?), born in Penge in 1887, is listed in the 1901 census as a 14 year old living with her parents and siblings in Leytonstone. I have failed to trace her after that date. Henry Charles born on the 26th February 1889, was baptised in St. John the Baptist Church, Leytonstone on 8th June that year. Sadly in 1911 Henry, aged 22, described as a former house painter, was an inmate in the West Ham Union Workhouse. He was a 23 year old painter of 97A Acasia Road, Leytonstone when he died of epilepsy at the Essex and Colchester Asylum on the 4th May 1913. Beatrice Emily the next sibling, born on the 24th March 1890, was baptised at St. John the Baptist, Leytonstone on 4th November 1895. She was a 21 year old spinster of 49 Cecil Road, Leytonstone when she married Arthur W. E. Bernard, a 22 year old house painter of the same address, at West Ham Register Office on the 25th April 1911. When her husband, William, joined the Welsh Regiment on 2nd November 1914 her address is given as Llantrisant, Glamorgan. Beatrice of 3 Castell-y- Mynach Road, Beddau, Glamorgan, widow of William Bernard, a colliery engine driver, died at Glamorgan General Hospital, Church Village, on 20th November 1967.

The last four children were boys. Sidney Alfred, born the 24th December 1891 was baptised at St. John the Baptist on 4th November 1895, the same day as his sister Beatrice. During World War 1 he was in Pontypridd, in the heart of the South Wales Coalfield, when he enlisted as Private 28990 in the Welsh Regiment. With service no 60217 he was transferred to the Royal Welsh Fusiliers, 13th Battalion and he was serving in France and Flanders when he was killed in action, on the 8th October 1918. I know more about Ernest George Luxton so will say more shortly. Herbert Andrew, born 26th February 1895, died in West Ham in November 1895. The youngest Arthur Albert Luxton, born in Leytonstone on 27th July 1896, was baptised at St John the Baptist Leytonstone, on 7th March 1897.On the 2nd April 1911 the census lists him as an inmate with epilepsy in an institution in Chalfont St. Peter in Buckinghamshire. Arthur Luxton, aged 16(sic), of 47 Cathall Road, Leytonstone, died of epilepsy at Brentford Asylum, on the 22nd June 1914.

Ernest George Luxton, the sixth child, was born on 2nd November 1892 in Leytonstone. He was a 22 year old driver in the Royal Engineers, (Service

465

No108052) residing in Easton, Winchester, the son of Charles Luxton, deceased printer, when he married Maud Helena Hall, spinster, the daughter of Edward Hall, a blacksmith, in St Mary's, Abergavenny, after banns on 17th November 1915.Maud was born in West Bromwich in the Midlands, on the 21st August 1895. Ernest George became a lance Corporal in the Royal Engineers 508 Reserve and Field Company, with a Regimental No 508024. He served in the Army from 3rd August 1915 to 16th August 1917. He was invalided out of the Army at Chatham with "sickness."A victim of a chlorine gas attack he was awarded a Silver Badge No 225242.

Ernest and his wife Maud, made their in home at 34 Park Street, Abergavenny where he was a circular sawyer when their son John Ernest, was born on the 24th February 1920. He was a farm labourer on 15th January 1922, on their daughter Joyce Doreen's birthday, and a labourer in a market garden, when June Margaret Elizabeth was born on the 13th June 1926.

Ernest George Luxton, a 35 year old road labourer, for the town council, died at home, 34 Park Street on the 3rd May 1929, from what his death certificate calls lobar pneumonia, heart failure and gas poisoning (chlorine). Soldiers on the Western Front faced not only shot and shell but chlorine gas attacks which irritated the throat and chest and left indelible scars on those who suffered it and could cause blindness and death. Ernest George Luxton's early death was a result of his fighting in the Great War. He was another victim, like so many who died, in the years after the conflict. His widow, Maud, of 37 Stanhope Street, Abergavenny, died aged 88 at Nevill Hall Hospital on the 4th October 1983.

Their son John Ernest Luxton (1920-1993) 23, omnibus fitter, of 37 Stanhope Street Abergavenny, married 22 year old Myrtle Maureen Lewis, a munitions worker at Abergavenny Register Office, on the 12th June 1943.John was still residing at 37 Stanhope Street, Abergavenny when he died on the 5th August 1993. Robin Clive Luxton, their son, born at Victoria Cottage Hospital on 18th September 1944, married Eleanor M. Gretton in Pontypool on the 2nd October 1965. He was living at 13 Charles Crescent, Abergavenny at the time of his grandmother Maud's death in the autumn of 1983. Robin, was a resident of Coleford in

Gloucestershire, when he died, aged 66, on the 16th August 2010. His aunt Joyce Luxton was a student nurse, aged 25, of 37 Stanhope Street, when she married 28 year old Ernest Frederick Rowe of Fairfield Road, Bromsgrove, a machinist in an automobile factory at the Register Office in Bromsgrove, Worcester on the 2nd September 1947. Her sister June, a 19 year old student nurse married Ralf Dutton, a draughtsman, at St. Marys, Abergavenny on 16th March 1946.That is the extent of my knowledge on this branch.

44

ANOTHER BRIDGWATER TRAGEDY THE SAD FATE OF ARTHUR FRANK LUXTON (1890-1894)

See tree 22

A dog cart, a two wheeled driving cart with cross seats back to back, was a familiar vehicle on British roads before the advent of the motor car. Then, as now, drink driving was a problem. Arthur Frank Luxton (1890-1894), a little boy in late Victorian Bridgwater, was the victim of a drunken driver in a dog cart. To understand the circumstances of his death we begin with the tragedy that befell his parents' marriage.

 Arthur Luxton (1864-1901), his father, born in Aller, Somerset on the 16th September 1864 and baptised a month later on the 16th October in the parish church of St. Andrew's, was the fourth of fourteen children, born to Alfred Luxton (1836-1924), agricultural labourer, and his wife Betsy Lock (1839-1927), dressmaker. He was a six year old scholar living with parents at Ridley, Aller in 1871 and ten years later he was a 16 year old agricultural labourer living in the parish.

Better economic opportunities were available across the Bristol Channel in South Wales where the rapidly expanding coal trade had led to boom conditions. The young Arthur settled for a while in Cardiff where there was a great deal of house construction, and he made a living as a mason's labourer before qualifying as a journeyman mason. He soon found himself a wife in the bustling seaport when he married the girl next door. Arthur Luxton 24 bachelor, labourer of 139 New Railway Street, Roath, son of Alfred Luxton labourer, married

Mary Ann Rossiter 21 spinster of 140 New Railway Street, Roath, daughter of James Rossiter, deceased mariner, at the Register Office, Cardiff on the 11th June 1889. They both signed the register. The couple were blessed with a child the following year, when Arthur Frank Luxton, son of Arthur Frank Luxton[342], mason's labourer, and his wife Mary Ann Luxton, formerly Rossiter, was born at 19 Maud Street, Roath, Cardiff on the 26th July 1890.

When the 1891 census was taken Arthur Luxton, 26, labourer, his wife Mary 17(sic) and their infant son, Arthur, aged 9 months, were living at 8 Aberystwyth Street, Splott. Within a short while tragedy struck the family. Mary Ann died before 1899, most probably in the early 1890s. Her husband Arthur Frank Luxton, 34, widower, now a merchant seaman, of 8 Darlington Terrace, West Hartlepool, married for his second wife Mary Jane Pearson 25, spinster, daughter of James Pearson, a deceased marine stoker in Hartlepool Registry Office on the 30th September 1899. Sadly Arthur Luxton, marine stoker, died from "capillary bronchitis" at 27 Albert Street, Hartlepool in Durham on the 24th March 1901.

Meanwhile following his mother's early demise the infant boy was despatched to live at 70 Bristol Road, Bridgwater with his maternal grandmother Mary West, the wife of George West, a carter in the employ of the Somerset Trading Company. For the last two years of his life the little boy lived with his grandmother.

Arthur Frank Luxton was just over three and a half years old when he met his untimely death. He left his grandmother's house at 70 Bristol Road, Bridgwater about two o'clock in the afternoon, on Saturday 10th February 1894 in the company of Harriet Pursey, aged between 9 and 10 years old. A dog cart was being driven briskly into Bridgwater by James Hembry, a farm bailiff of Dunwear, shortly before 20 to 3, as the little boy stepped off the pavement to cross the road, opposite 95 Bristol Road. Observers thought it was being driven rather fast, at about 9 to 10 miles an hour. Several adult witnesses saw the offside step of the

---

[342] It's interesting to observe that the father has acquired the middle name "Frank" which is listed on his son's birth certificate but not on his own birth and death certificates.

cart catch the child, knock him down to the ground, and the wheel pass over the child's back. Hembry carried on his drive until witnesses called out to him to stop. He pulled up and on looking around and seeing what had happened he went back. The child walked a little distance before someone took him up and carried him home. A crowd collected at the scene.

Arthur in an insensible condition, reached his grandmother's house, about 20 to 3 and was at once taken to Bridgwater Infirmary. The house surgeon J. D. Wardle, said that the little child in a collapsed condition, was brought to him at the Infirmary at about 3 minutes to 3 o'clock. There was a little blood about the mouth and a bruise about the size of one's hand on the back. There were no other external marks of violence. The child never rallied and died shortly after being brought to the institution. Wardle made a post mortem examination of the body on the following Monday morning, the day of the inquest, and found the cause of death was a ruptured liver.

Just after the child was sent to the Infirmary his grandmother, Mrs West, saw James Hembry in a light dog cart, talking to a Mr. Nicholls nearly opposite her house. Mrs West said to Hembry, "You have driven over my child, and if you have killed or injured it you will have to suffer for it." She also said to him, "You are drinky," and he replied, "I am not drinky." He was sitting on the trap and moved to and fro on the seat. Mrs West called across to two young men, Albert Vernon and Robert Kingdom who were brickyard labourers at Puriton, and asked them if they saw the accident. They replied, "Yes, he has been driving furiously." Hembry heard what was said and denied that he had been driving furiously.

It was not until about 7. 50. on that Saturday evening that Hembry reported to Superintendent Barnett at Bridgwater Police Station. Barnett noted that Hembry was much under the influence of drink and charged him with causing the death of Arthur Frank Luxton. Hembry made a statement:-

"I am very sorry it has happened. I wouldn't have had it happen for anything. I didn't see the child. I was not looking down the road at all. I was looking on the other side of the road. I left home about 11 o'clock in the morning and went to Huntspill on business. I had a drop of cider at Mrs Saunders and when I had done my business I drove home. I should think it was about 4 o' clock when I came into Bristol Road. The mare was going at a pretty good pace, but not very fast. She is a bit fresh

The prisoner was detained on the charge and appeared at the inquest held by Mr. P. U. H. Reed, the Borough Coroner at the Town Hall, Bridgwater on Monday 12th February 1894.

The thirteen man jury viewed the body of the deceased child at the Infirmary and returned to the Town Hall to hear witness statements. Among witnesses of the accident were Alfred Buttle, a horse dealer who was riding down the road, Annie Squire, wife of Thomas Squire, a railway porter, living at 102 Bristol Road, who was sitting on the sill cleaning the outside of her bedroom window facing Bristol Road, and Robert Kingdom and Albert Vernon, two brickyard labourers living at Puriton. The coroner in summing up, said it was astonishing how people differed in their version of an affair. The six or seven witnesses differed in many ways as to what took place. However, he said, all the witnesses agreed Hembry was under the influence of drink. His impression was that Hembry was driving at between 9 and 10 M.P.H. which was too fast, especially for someone under the influence of drink. The witnesses all agreed the man was on the wrong side of the road, and going at 10 M.P.H. and if a drunken man drove at that rate it was negligent and careless. In his opinion Hembry was guilty of manslaughter.

The jury retired to consider their verdict and remained absent for about ten minutes. On returning into court the jury returned a verdict of manslaughter against James Hembry who was remanded in custody.

The death certificate issued by Paul U. H. Reed, coroner, Borough of Bridgwater records Arthur Frank Luxton's cause of death:- "Manslaughter knocked down by a horse and dog cart driven by one James Hembry and a wheel of cart passed over body rupturing liver 25 minutes."

Later that month, at a special sitting of the Bridgwater Borough magistrates, James Hembry, farm bailiff of Dunwear, was charged with unlawfully killing the little boy. After listening to the evidence the Bench considered there was a prima facie case against him.

Mr. Bishop, the defending solicitor, said the prisoner was a man well known in the neighbourhood. He lived with his uncle the late Mr. Edward Durston for 17 years at Dunwear and was now farm bailiff, in the employ of Mr. George Durston at Dunwear. He had always borne a very good character and this was the first trouble of any kind that had ever come upon the family.

The Bench granted bail on the prisoner's own surety of £200, and two other sureties of £100 each from Mr. George Durston, and Mr. Hembry of Pawlett, and committed the prisoner for trial at the next assizes. The prisoner also offered to pay the child's funeral expenses.

The Bridgwater Mercury, Wednesday 13th June 1894, reported the trial at the Somerset Assize held in Wells the previous Thursday, before Mr. Justice Lawrence. The jury, after listening to the prosecution and the defence and the judges summing up, retired to deliberate at half past seven. They returned into court shortly before eight with a verdict of not guilty and the prisoner was thereupon discharged.

This seems an astonishing verdict in light of the evidence of statements made by witnesses. Hembry himself admitted to Superintendent Barnett he had been drinking cider and that he had not been looking down the road. Superintendent Barnett and other witnesses considered he was tipsy, he was driving too fast and knocked the child down on the wrong side of the road! Presumably the judge and the jury thought Hembry had suffered sufficiently and no further punishment was necessary. A modern jury on this evidence would have passed a guilty verdict.

45

SERGEANT MAJOR ALFRED HENRY LUXTON (1869-1952) OF "BROOKLYN" HILL ROAD, WANGFORD, SUFFOLK AND FAMILY.

See tree 23

Sergeant Major Alfred Henry Luxton (1869-1952), the fifth son of Alfred Luxton (1836-1924), farmer, and his wife Betsy Lock, was born in Aller, Somerset on 11th March 1869 and baptised in St. Andrew's the parish church on 11th April. "Harry" as he was known to all the family, joined the 15th Hussars in London on 15th February 1887 aged 18, after running away from an apprenticeship to a printer in the city which he absolutely hated. He signed up willing to serve for a twelve year term and he was to serve in the Regular Army for the greater part of his life. His regimental number was 2437 and he gave his occupation as a carman. He was described as having blue eyes and light brown hair. He was 5ft 6 inches tall, had a mole on his left breast, and his eyebrows met. His complexion was fresh and he was a member of the Church of England.

Harry's service record shows that he served in Edinburgh in 1887, and Glascow in 1889, before a spell in Ireland, from June 1889 to July 1892, moving around barracks at the Curragh, Waterford and Dublin. He was posted to Dundalk on the 16th September 1892 when the picture above was taken. Harry was very young when he "married" an Irish woman who was very jealous. On one occasion she attacked him with a carving knife, so he divorced her as he was in "fear of his life". Fortunately there were no children of the marriage, details of which I have so far failed to locate.

Harry's army account book records that he was successful in improving his reading and arithmetic. He was promoted to Corporal on 5th May 1889, Lance Sergeant 1st July 1892, Paid Lance Sergeant 1st November 1893 and Sergeant on 16th April 1895. He improved his soldiering skills too. A drill certificate, dated 28th February 1893, reveals Lance Sergeant H. Luxton was "thoroughly capable of instructing efficiently in the Firing Exercise as laid down in the Musketry Regulations."Sergeant Luxton also passed a course of instruction at the School of Military Engineering to qualify on the 14th April 1896 "to act as Assistant Instructor in Cavalry Pioneer Duties to his Regiment." A further certificate, dated 28th September 1898, reveals he underwent a course of training at the School of Musketry, Hythe, in Kent where he qualified as a "Serjeant Instructor in Musketry" to a Regiment or Battalion and that he was capable of instructing in the Use and Mechanism of the Rifle Calibre Maxim Machine Gun." This oval photograph of Sergeant Instuctor Luxton, was probably taken in Hythe in Kent in 1898 when he had just qualified. He wears a forage cap (otherwise known as a pill-box cap) and his left index finger is pointing to the crossed rifles and crown insignia on his arm, which denotes he has qualified as a musketry instructor.

There was a spell too in Shorncliffe, Essex in 1898 and on the 1st February 1899 he re-engaged to complete 21 years with the Colours. He was promoted to Squadron Sergeant Major on the 22nd September 1899. This was the day after his embarkation with the 15th Kings Hussars to Meerut, in India, and he was in India throughout the South African Boer War. He arrived in India on the 13th October 1899. Three years later on the 29th November 1902 he sailed from Bombay for England where he disembarked on the 16th December.

On his return he was posted for duty as Sergeant Major Instructor to D Squadron of the Suffolk Imperial Yeomanry.

In August 1903, on the second anniversary of King Edward V11's Coronation, a military parade took place at the Sparrow's Nest, Lowestoft. There was an enormous throng in fine weather to hear the music and join in the the singing. "A contingent of Suffolk Imperial Yeomanry (looking very smart) under Sergeant Major Luxton of Beccles"was included.[343]

During an April afternoon in 1904, the D Squadron (Lowestoft & Beccles) Duke of York's Own Loyal Suffolk Hussars held their annual course of musketry at Yarmouth in which Sergeant Major Luxton (in photo on right) was a winner with 130 points. That evening they held a smoking concert at the Suffolk Hotel, Lowestoft and the evening ended with music and God Save the King[344].A military service was again held at the Sparrow's Nest, Lowestoft on behalf of the Lowestoft Hospital in August 1905, when large crowds attended in fine weather. Members of D Squadron Suffolk Imperial Yeomanry under Sergeant Major Luxton, formed part of the square near the enclosure, and at one side, a platform was erected, the drum-head serving as a temporary lectern.[345]

In June 1908 the Loyal Suffolk Hussars returned home from their fourteen day annual camp on the Berkshire Downs. Sergeant Major Luxton was with the D Squadron (Lowestoft & Beccles detachment) who had won the Regimental cup for being the most efficient and best drilled squadron. They had won this trophy on three successive years.[346]

---

[343] Norwich Mercury Saturday 15th August 1903
[344] Norfolk Chronicle, 23rd April 1904
[345] Evening Star, Monday 14th August 1905.
[346] Eastern Daily Press, Friday 5th June 1908.

There are news reports of smoking contests he attended with the Hussars at the Kings Arms, Halesworth in December 1905 and Public Hall, Beccles in February 1909 and the Fleece Hotel, Bungay in March 1910. He gave evidence at Beccles Petty Sessions in July 1907 against a labourer who had stolen an axe from a Suffolk Imperial Yeomanry encampment, and again at Bungay Petty Sessions in November 1909 to provide evidence against a labourer, wearing the uniform of the Suffolk Yeomanry.

Henry Luxton, Sergeant Instructor of Yeomanry of Hall Road, Lakenham, (in photo on left) a 39 year old bachelor, (sic) married Emma Jessie Baker, 21 spinster of Red House Farm, Rumburgh, Halesworth, daughter of Simon George Baker, farmer (deceased) at the Register Office Norwich, by licence on 29th June 1908. In 1911 Henry 42, Sergeant Major Instructor of Suffolk Yeomanry, his wife Jesse 24, and their children Herbert 2 and Ada 1, his brother in law, Albert Baker, 29, and Jane Butcher, a 16 year old servant, lived in an eight room house at 11, London Road, Beccles, Suffolk. Later that year, on the 30th November 1911, Harry completed his 21 years with the Colours and he was discharged from the Army with a pension at Bury St Edmunds.

Harry and "Jess" as he called his wife, had three children, but Jess had a difficult time in childbirth as all the children were big. Jess was aged 26 and the family were living at Hackford in Norfolk when she died in childbirth at the Norfolk and Norwich Hospital on 11th April 1914. The three children went to live with Alfred and Betsy Luxton, their grandparents in Aller, who were named as their guardians in the army documentation.

Harry went in for farming after retiring from the Army in 1911, but he rejoined when the Great War started. On 2nd October 1914 he signed up with the Army Reserve (Special Reservists) the 15th Hussars. Aged 45 years, he had a new Service Number 26853. A labourer and widower, he was 5ft 6 ½ inches, weighed 12 stone 4 lbs, and had blue eyes and brown hair. He had a mole on his left breast. A warrant dated 29th January 1915 appointed him as Squadron Sergeant Major of the 14th Reserve Regiment of Cavalry.

Alfred Henry Luxton 46 widower, Warrant Officer, at Longmoor Camp in Greetham, Hampshire married for the second time to Harriet Barbara Artis, 34, spinster of Waterloo Farm, Sotterley, daughter of John Artis, farmer in the parish church of St Margaret, Sotterley in the diocese of St Edmundsbury, Suffolk after the reading of banns on 25th January 1916.

There is an excellent photograph of the newly wed pair. Harry in uniform is sporting a waxed moustache and his N.C.O. badge of rank, a crown, is worn on his arm below the elbow. Harriet is wearing a large wide brimmed shallow-crowned hat which was fashionable at this date. Evelyn, Jesse Herbert and Roy the children of the first marriage are photographed with the couple. Evelyn is in a smock dress and her hair is decorated with bows. The boys are wearing a revolutionary new style of clothing-stretchy, knitted jerseys and shorts.

After a period as Sergeant Major Instructor at Longmoor, Aldershot, he went north to train the Northumberland Fusiliers at Alnwick. In total he served 24 years and 280 days. He held both the Long Service Medal and the Meritious Service Medal (with an annuity) and clasp dated 2nd October 1946.

Harry bought Wangford after the 1914-18 war and went in for farming on the Henham Hall Estate, retiring in 1928 when illness put a stop to it.

By Harriet Barbara Artis, his second wife, Harry had two more children. John Alfred Luxton (1920-1977), born on 13th November 1920, was married twice. He was a 19 year old farm labourer when he married "Edie" i.e. Edith Alice Bealing, 20 daughter of Walter Burden Bealing, Cowman, after banns in the parish church of St Peter Stutton, Suffolk on 1st June 1940. Their son Stephen John Luxton, born in 1943, was a Corporal in the RAF when he married 19 year old Joyce Briggs at the Register Office, Lothingland, East Suffolk on 23rd September 1967. The couple, now divorced, have a son Stewart Luxton.

When his first marriage dissolved, John Alfred Luxton, (an infant in photo, left) 34, a general farm worker of Brooklyn, Hill Road, Wangford, married Kathleen Sago 32 spinster of "The Loyal Oak" Wangford, daughter of Alfred Edward Sago (deceased), licensed victualler at the Register Office, Lothingland, County of East Suffolk on 15th October 1955. The couple had a son, Clive Alfred Luxton, born 17th July 1956 and a daughter, Caroline Ann Luxton, born on 25th August 1957. John Alfred Luxton of 6 Hill Road, Wangford Suffolk died 27th July 1997. Probate Ipswich 28th September £14,325.

Barbara Mary Luxton, the youngest child of Harry Luxton and his second wife Harriet, was born on 31st December 1922 and married Albert R Noble at St. Peter and Paul, Wangford, Suffolk on 12th October 1963. An excellent photograph taken in 1924 of Harry Luxton's five children, Roy, Jesse Herbert, in RAF uniform, Barbara, Ada and John, in a Little Lord Fauntleroy suit, is produced next page.

Throughout the Second World War Harry was an active member of the Home Guard which was set up in May 1940 as Britain's "last line of defence" against German invasion. It is said that old soldiers never die and this was certainly the case with Alfred Henry Luxton! When the Second World War began he was already seventy years of age but here he is photographed at Brooklyn, Hill Road, Wangford in his new uniform in the Home Guard. No, not with Captain Mainwaring, Sergeant Wilson, Corporal Jones and Pike and the rest of the Warmlington-on-Sea Platoon

but with his local Platoon in Suffolk! He has a wry smile which seems to be saying here we go again! This photograph must date to early 1940 because he wears a scant uniform with an arm band. I cannot see a cap badge which would denote he was in the Suffolk Home Guard. He has shiny new boots and has his Browning automatic rifle but he is not wearing the rest of his standard HG equipment i.e. gas mask and pouches with leather belt and cross straps or a pair of leather gaiters. Matters improved dramatically in July 1940, when Winston Churchill took a personal interest in the development and equipment of the Home Guard.

Harry Luxton became identified with practically every aspect of village life at Wangford. He founded the Old Comrades' Association, and when the British Legion Branch came into being he was appointed chairman. On retirement 25 years later he was made a life vice-president. He was a rural district councillor for about a quarter of a century, serving first on the Blything Council and then on the Lothingland authority when Wangford was transferred to that area. He retired at the age of 80. The Lothingland Council's new houses at Norfolk Road bear his name. For about 20 years he was chairman of the Parish Council. A manager of both Henham School and Reydon Area School, he was a former treasurer of the Henham troop of Boy Scouts, and served on the Committee of the Wangford Conservative Association. He started a bowls club in the village and ran it for several years. He was also a loyal churchman. For a long time he was Vicar's Warden at Wangford.

Alfred Henry Luxton (1869-1952) had been in poor health since October 1949, when he died aged 83, from prostrate cancer at his home "Brooklyn," Hill Road, Wangford, Suffolk on 21st May 1952. His widow Harriet Barbara Luxton was granted Probate of his Will in Ipswich on 22nd September 1952 when his personal estate was valued at £434..11..10.

Draped with the Union Jack, the coffin was preceded from the house by Mr. E. Gardener, secretary of the Wangford Branch of the British Legion, carrying the standard, with Mr. W. Walker and Mr. H. Peck as escorts. The bearers were four old members, Messrs H. Gardener, Ben Harvey, E. Goddard and W. Blowers. Lining the churchyard path at Wangford, were other members of the branch, the Women's Section with its standard and the Southwold and Reydon branch also having its standard. The Branch chaplain, Vicar and Rural Dean, the Rev.O.E. Thomas officiated, and gave the Legion exhortation at the graveside, where the Last Post and Reveille was sounded by bugler F. W. Levett of Wrentham. Henry's widow, Harriet Barbara Luxton aged 83 died at 5 The Hill, Wangford, on 14th November 1964. Administration of the Will was granted in Ipswich to her son John Alfred Luxton, builder's labourer, when her estate was valued at £3,000.

The above fine photograph of the family gathered at Brooklyn, Wangford must date sometime after the funeral as it shows Jesse Herbert who was in Queensland at time of the funeral. From left to right - John Alfred, his mother Harriet, Barbara, Evelyn, Stephen (John's son) Edie (John's wife), Jesse Herbert and Roy

Alfred Henry Luxton (1869-1952) by his first wife "Jess" Baker, had issue three children. Their eldest Jesse Henry Herbert Luxton (1908-1994) has proved an elusive and interesting character, so I have given him his own chapter.

Evelyn Ada Emma Luxton (1910-1953), was born at 11 London Road, Beccles, Wangford, Suffolk on 27th January 1910. In 1939 she was living at 160 Lambeth Road, Lambeth North. Evelyn was nursing for years before she finally married Frank Arthur Hipperson (1906 - 1957) of Costerrey, Forekoe, Norfolk, in the Paddington Register Office on 25th May 1948. When Evelyn died, aged 43, of bronchitis and broncho pneumonia, at University College Hospital on 17th November 1953 they were living at 18 Bradiston Road, London W. 9. She left £132..0s..10d to her brother Rowland. They had a daughter, Margaret Edna Hipperson, born in Paddington in 1940, who is married with three sons and lives in France.

The third child, Rowland Albert Simon Luxton (1911 - 1976), was born at Bawdeswell, Norfolk on 18th October 1911. When he was 16 "Roy" left home at Brooklyn, Wangford, near Lowestoft for Australia. His ship "Jervis Bay" (Aberdeen Line) departed from London on 7th August 1928 and arrived in Brisbane, Queensland on 8th October 1928. The ship's list describes him as a "Farm Learner." I don't know how long he stayed in Australia but "Roy" was a 43 year old bachelor and gardener when he married Pamela Ellen Peterson, 33, spinster of Southwold in St. Peter and Paul, Wangford, Suffolk on 5th February 1955. He was a retired domestic gardener of Little Priory, Wangford, Beccles when he died outside the British Legion Rooms, High Street, Wangford, on 24th February 1976. This and the next chapter on his eldest son, conclude my account of Sergeant Major Alfred Henry Luxton's family.

Alfred is a Sergeant in the Hussars in this photograph taken with relatives in Aller c. 1895. He wears a Glengarry which was the standard headgear for other rank soldiers up to the 1890s. His uniform is the standard seven button scarlet tunic with standing collar, and edged with white down the left front. The sash worn by generations of British officers in the 18th century is now worn from the left shoulder and he displays a medal. Harry used to recall with pride having ridden on horseback before Queen Victoria in Glascow and also in her Diamond Jubilee Procession.

46

THE EVENTFUL LIFE OF JESSE HENRY HERBERT LUXTON (1908-1994) CIVIL PILOT

See tree 23

Jesse Henry Herbert Luxton (1908 - 1994) the eldest son of Alfred Henry Luxton, Sergeant Major Instructor of yeomanry and his wife, Emma Jessie Luxton, formerly Baker, was born in Rumburgh, Suffolk on 4th June 1908. He was a 16 year old boy recruit in the R.A.F. in Suffolk in 1924 and a family photograph (in previous chapter) shows the young Jesse that year in uniform with his four siblings. I do not have full details of his career in the R.A.F. but he was given a thorough training in aeronautical engineering skills.[347] In the years 1924-

1927 he was an aircraft apprentice, and in 1927-28 he trained as an aero engine fitter. He was an air-gunner and fitter in 1929-31.

Jesse a 21 year old bachelor, No. 364693, air craftsman, (RAF) married Phyllis Emma Allen, 21 spinster of 33 The Hemplands, Lowestoft, daughter of a deceased trawler fisherman at the Register Office, Mutford, East Suffolk, by licence on the 26th October 1929. Sheila Hilda Luxton, a daughter, born in Lowestoft on 23rd July 1930, married George Stanley Cable in the parish church of St. Peter and John, Kirkley, Suffolk, on the 14th March 1953. They live in Lowestoft and have two sons and a daughter and grandchildren.

When I read in the Grantham Journal, dated Saturday, 31st May 1930, a Flying Officer Luxton had been gravely injured and the pilot Flying

---

[347] The Longreach Leader, Friday, 19th October 1951

Officer Nicholai had been killed I thought I had found him. Their Avro plane, on a training flight from the Central Flying School at Wittering in Lincolnshire, had crashed into a wheat field near Stamford. My hunch was squashed, however, by the Dundee Courier, dated 27th May 1930, which reported that the injured airman was Flying Officer P. F. Luxton who I have since identified as Philip Francis Luxton (1902-1947), a grandson of Robert George Luxton, the famous fox-hunting squire at Brushford Barton.

Jesse was probably serving in the R.A.F. in Lincolnshire, however, when he was fined ten shillings at Sleaford Police Court, for driving without rear lights at Ashby on the16[th] October 1931[348] and it seems likely that he too was trained at the Central Flying School at Wittering. He underwent a pilot training course in 1932-33 in which he secured a distinguished pass. Jesse flew the British reconnaissance bi-plane, the Fairey 111F.

The Fairey Aviation Company Fairey 111 was a British reconnaissance bi-plane that enjoyed a very long production and service in the R.A.F. First flying on the 14th September 1917, examples were still in use during the Second World War. The most prolific and enduring of the Fairey 111s was the final model, the Fairey111F which first flew on 20th April 1926.

A two-seat general-purpose version of the aircraft, powered by a Napier Lion W-12 piston engine, came into service with the Royal Air Force. It had a more streamlined engine installation and initially a fuselage of mixed metal and wood construction. This bi-plane remained in front line service with the R.A.F. well into the 1930s and the last front line squadron to fly the Fairey 111 abandoned there use in August 1935.

---

[348] Grantham Journal, Saturday, 31st October 1931.

Two photographs exist of Jesse flying a Fairey 111F sometime in 1932-33. They were both fitted with an all metal fuselage and wings and were the latest production of the bi-plane. On the reverse of the one here Jesse has written, "6000 feet or just over one mile above mother earth, travelling at 120 miles an hour."Following his success at flying Jesse was made a Sergeant-Pilot in a night bomber squadron.

In 1934-37 he was posted as a Sergeant-Pilot in a transport squadron in Cairo. While he was there, Jesse was chosen in 1935, as a navigator for the British government's Valentia plane's goodwill tour to and from South Africa. The Valentia (in picture) was a British bi-plane cargo aircraft built by Vickers for the R.A.F. It flew for the first time in 1934 and was mostly used for transporting troops and equipment in the Middle East. The planes were also operated by the South African Air Force and it seems Jesse was involved in flying one of these planes to South Africa.

He was in the R.A.F. for twelve years, and when he completed his service in 1937, Jesse became an operations manager and chief pilot, for over nine years with Misr Airlines in Cairo. He flew between Cairo and Khartoum in the Sudan and was engaged by British Intelligence to pass on information which might prove useful.

The Second World War began while he was in Egypt and he was divorced. Jesse joined the Royal Air Force Volunteer Reserve on the 5th June 1940, and the London Gazette, dated 5th November 1940, reports he had been made a sergeant. He was a fitter, air-gunner, pilot of night bombers and transport squadrons. This activity took place in Egypt and North Africa.

Jesse was promoted to Flight Lieutenant on the 5th June 1942, and served in the General Duties Branch and was still listed with that unit in July 1943. A good head and shoulders photograph of a mature Jesse in his RAF uniform, displaying his wings and military ribbons which heads this chapter, must date to this time in his life. Flight Lieutenant Jesse Luxton was resident at H.Q. R.A.F. Middle East when he married Elizabeth Honor Sawle, a nursing sister in the Queen Alexandra's

Reserve, based at the 15th (Scottish) General Hospital M.E.F., in St Andrew's Church in Cairo on 1st June 1943. A photograph of the newly wed couple is on the next page. Their daughter Susan Mary Luxton was born in Cairo in 1944.[349]

Adventure was not the prerogative of her husband, although Jesse had visited most of the countries on the western side of the Iron Curtain and flown over the more inaccessible parts of Africa and Asia, Elizabeth's life too had been filled with enough wartime experiences to make the average woman feel grateful for her slightly monotonous but safe existence. Elizabeth was Assistant Matron of St. Stephen's Hospital in London at the outbreak of World War Two. She immediately joined Queen Alexandra's Nurses and was disembarked in France on Thursday 29th February 1940, to serve in Unit 6 General Hospital. Throughout the year of the "phoney war" she was working with the unit and when the Germans finally invaded, only managed to be evacuated in time. Her section was moved to St. Nazaire. On the day that France capitulated, the nurses were transferred to the troop ship Lancastria in the harbour. The Germans bombed the port, and the Lancastria was sunk within half an hour, with the loss of more than 1000 lives.

Mrs. Luxton was among the survivors and after reaching England she was almost immediately transferred to the Middle East. The voyage took nine weeks via the Cape, as for safety reasons the Mediterranean was out of the question, and the ship finally made her way through the Suez and the troops were disembarked at Alexandria. Elizabeth was moved to Cairo and at the beginning of the Western Desert Campaign, joined a Casualty Clearing Station with the Eighth Army. She served through the long series of battles which ended with El Alamein that broke the German power in Africa. Returning to Cairo she met and married Jesse. She was due to join a troopship for the invasion of Sicily, when her daughter Susan Mary was born in Cairo in 1944, so she was demobbed.

They remained in Cairo four years. During these years, apart from his routine flights, Jesse was called out on search parties, and days

---

[349] An article on Douglas Bader in Picture Post 1946 has a photo of two year old Susan daughter of Capt Luxton of Misr Airlines being helped down the steps of an aircraft by her mother. Susan had made four trips between Cairo and the United Kingdom.

would pass before his wife learned where he was, or even whether he was still alive. In the difficult days before the end of the war, she learned the meaning of patience, and the necessity to be philosophical about her husband's sudden absences if she was to carry on.

The couple took a short break from Cairo. A ships passenger list for the Union-Castle Mail Steamship Company Ltd, reveals Jesse 37, manager, Elizabeth 40, housewife, and daughter, Susan Mary, 2 sailing aboard the S.S. Carnarvon Castle from Alexandria, Egypt to Southampton, arriving on the 21st July 1945. They were going to Elizabeth's home Beacon Cottage, St. Agnes, Cornwall. There Elizabeth became pregnant with their son, John Sawle Luxton, who was born in Redruth, Cornwall on the 12th June 1946.

While the family stayed in Cornwall, Jesse returned to Egypt to fly for Misr Airlines a while longer. In April 1946 he was in Heliopolis when he met Neeltje Visser, a Dutch Red Cross nurse, on her way to Indonesia, where she was to be one of the head nurses for the Childrens Hospital in Menteng (prinses Margriet Hospital, Jalan Palm nowadays Jin Surwiryo). She

was in a contingent which had to overstay in Egypt because their aeroplane had engine trouble. After her arrival in Jakarta, Neeltje discovered she was pregnant and tried unsuccessfully to contact Jesse who was probably unaware of her condition. Neeltje too was most likely unaware that Jesse was married and she never married herself, dying in Amsterdam on the 30th July 1981. Their daughter Anne Marie Visser, was born in Batavia (Jakarta) Dutch-Indies, on 9th December 1946.

Shortly after his encounter with Neeltje, Jesse returned to England with his family. They lived for a time in the village of St. Agnes, on the northern coast of Cornwall where Elizabeth's family owned a farm of 100 acres of well cultivated soil which had supported the family for four hundred years. In the photograph Jesse and his wife, Elizabeth Sawle, are enjoying a day out on the beach near St. Agnes in Cornwall with their children Susan and John, in June 1947.

He became general manager of an English flying service, and secretary and airport manager of the Blackpool Aero Club. He was certainly there in April 1948 because a Press Photo from the Blackpool Herald and Gazette, shows Jesse, the pilot, with passengers climbing aboard for the Football Cup Final between Blackpool and Manchester United.

The next turning point in Jesse's life is strongly reminiscent of Norman Luxton, a half century earlier, and we will see the two men were definitely kindred spirits in their sense of wanting crazy adventures. The post World War Two years were miserable economically depressed times in the U.K. In the hope of finding better flying jobs elsewhere Jesse placed an advert in "Aircraft." It was picked up by Captain Gordon F. Lee who had founded Somerset Airways in 1950 at Muttaburra in the Queensland outback. He had named his new venture Somerset Airways because his father's favourite song was "We've come up from Somerset." As his business expanded Lee decided to re-locate the aircraft from Muttaburra to Longreach where it became headquartered in the original QANTAS hangar. He needed a local manager and another aircraft to meet demand. He operated Austers but wanted something bigger and faster. Luxton an ex-R.A.F. navigator and pilot was just the man he was looking for. Jesse advised that he would find a suitable aircraft and ferry it from England. He procured a Percival Proctor 5 which cost £

600. Mr. Lee agreed to buy the aircraft and engaged Jesse Luxton as a manager partner in business[350].

On Saturday 20th October 1951 The Townsville Daily Bulletin, Queensland announced that Somerset Airways, Muttaburra, had purchased a new model Proctor light aircraft in England and were making arrangements for the plane to be flown to Australia. It was to be used for charter flights, taxi work and emergency and ambulance flights in the Central West of Queenland. The pilot was to be Mr Jesse H. Luxton, the newly appointed manager of Somerset Airways "who has had a distinguished and interesting career. He is a Fellow of the Royal Aeronautical Society, Fellow of the Royal Meteorological Society andAssociate of the Technological Institute of Great Britain and speaks French, German and Arabic. He is also a foundation member of the London Light Plane Club, founded in 1926. An experienced engineer, Captain Luxton has had service as such for six years in the R.A.F. He has piloted more than 50 types of civil aircraft, flying more than one and a half million miles in10,075 flying hours in his logs-----." It was further announced that "Somerset Airways intends to establish a workshop service in Longreach to service commercial and private planes, and Mr Luxton and family, including two children, will reside there."[351]

Jesse flew out to Australia single handed, in his Proctor registered G-AIEV, setting out from Blackbushe, Croydon Aerodrome on 1st November 1951. His route passed through Paris, Rome, Athens, Beirut, Basra, Calcutta, Rangoon, Singapore, Sourabaya, and Koepang. At first all went well and he was in line for breaking the record of 23 days for a solo flight from England to Australia, but the plane was damaged at Waingapu on Soemba Island, near Timor, seven hundred miles north of Darwin. A tropical squall struck the aircraft as it was taxing after landing. It lifted the Proctor off the ground and it bounced heavily on one wheel, damaging the under-carriage and the starboard

---

[350] The History of Somerset Airways, Longreach, Queensland by Roy Entsch (2005) has been a valuable help in discovering what happened during Jesse's time at Longreach. Thank you Anne Marie Visser for sending me a copy.
[351] Townsville Daily Bulletin, Queensland 20th October 1951, page 3. See also Brisbane Telegraph, 7th March 1952.

wing spar. Repairs delayed his flight for three and a half months, and it was nearly the end of February 1952 when he was airbourne again.

He struck the Australian coast near Cape Talbot, and made his first landing at Wyndham, on the north coast of Western Australia. He continued to Darwin and then Camooweal, and arrived in Longreach, Queensland in early March. There he was met by the owner of Somerset Airways, Mr. Gordon Lee of Muttaburra. Captain Luxton and Mr. Lee, flew in the Proctor to Brisbane to obtain his Australian flying certificate and to re-register the air-craft VH-ALR for flying in Australia. As the plane landed late on Thursday afternoon 6th March 1952, at Archerfield, Brisbane, at the end of his eventful 13,000 solo flight from England, the Brisbane Telegraph and Longreach Leader were there to describe the event:-

"One of Britain's outstanding war-time transport pilots in the Middle East, Captain Jesse H Luxton, of St. Agnes, Cornwall, landed unheralded at Acherfield late yesterday afternoon at the end of an eventful 13000 solo flight from England.

"As the small silver painted low-winged Percival Proctor monoplane taxied to a hangar, 44 year old Captain Luxton, sporting a cultivated goatee beard and moustache and wearing khaki shorts and shirt, jumped to the tarmac, "not feeling in too bad a trim." Asked why he had taken up a flying job at Longreach in outback Queensland Captain Luxton said, "I want to start my flying in the outback where flying is the real thing and those people need all the services and amenities they can get." The tall bearded aviator said he did not think the heat of Longreach would worry him. He had spent 15 years in Africa, in country very similar to Longreach, and preferred a warm climate.... He laughed at a suggestion that he had grown a beard during his enforced stay on Soemba Island and he said he had worn it for years."

Jesse believed he was the seventh to fly solo from U.K. to Australia. He received a telegram from ex RAF Group Captain "Bush" Banditt congratulating him on his flight and advising him he had become a member of the exclusive Solo Club, just formed for pilots who had flown solo from England to Australia. [352]

---

[352] Brisbane Telegraph, Friday 7th March 1952 & The Longreach Reader 7th March 1952.

There was a write up in the national press, the Daily Telegraph and perhaps the Mirror, about his hazardous flight. The following graphic account of his flight to Australia is derived from a newspaper cutting taken from the Lowestoft Journal, in March 1952.

WANGFORD MAN'S CRASH ON AUSTRALIA FLIGHT
After a flight from Britain, during which his plane was damaged while landing on a jungle island and he had to set up a workshop there to repair his machine, a Suffolk man, whose home is at Wangford, landed at Darwin, Australia, on Monday night.

Forty-three year old Jesse Luxton, eldest son of Mr A H Luxton, of Brooklyn, Hill Road, Wangford, left London on November 1st, hoping to land in Australia 18 days later, but delays resulted in his arriving three and a half months behind schedule.

The most serious setback occurred on November 17th, when, while landing on Waingapu airstrip, on the tiny Indonesian island of Soemba, a gust of wind lifted his plane, dumped it on the ground and damaged the undercarriage.

"I lived among natives in the bush", said Luxton, describing his experience. "I ate dried fish that tasted like fertiliser, coconuts and frog's legs and drank only coconut milk in case the water was contaminated. I found an Indonesian airline agent with a wireless set that did not work because a jeep would not go to charge the batteries. I fixed the jeep, then the radio and wirelessed the Dutch to allow a ship to call as soon as possible.

I took the wings from the plane and in two trips moved it on the jeep through seven miles of bush to Waingapu anchorage. The tail and fuselage section cleared a bridge by only half an inch. I died a thousand deaths getting across - backwards.

At the beach an old Arab horse dealer assisted me. We got the plane aboard his cattle pontoon and floated it a mile off-shore to the Dutch cattle boat Waiklo and it was swung aboard. She took us to Djarkata, where, with the help of a Dutch carpenter, I worked 232 hours in 21 days repairing the plane. I was determined to get here. My wife and family are now at sea on their way to Sydney".

Luxton's father told a reporter that he had been very worried about his son as he had not heard from him for two months. "He always liked adventure and was always very keen on flying", said Mr Luxton. "He joined the RAF as a boy and served for 12 years, leaving to become operations manager in a private firm. He was with them for 13 years before going to Australia, where he is now with the Somerset Airways, Longreach.

"He has been flying practically ever since he was a boy", said Mr Luxton, "and I remember when he was stationed with the RAF in Suffolk, he used to drop me notes on the meadow behind my house". Mr Luxton, Snr, is well known in Wangford and district, having served for 14 years on the Blyth and Lothingland Rural District Councils.

Jesse's arrival in Australia received good coverage in the Australian Press. The Canberra Times, Tuesday 4th March 1952 – page 2 carried the following report:-

Crashed Airman
Repairs Plane,
Reaches Darwin.

Darwin, Monday.

"A British airman who crashed his Percival Proctor plane on a small Indonesian island, dismantled it, and later rebuilt it again in Djakarta, arrived in Darwin tonight. He is Captain Jesse H. Luxton of St. Agnes, Cornwall.

Luxton left England on November 1, 1951, and expected to arrive in Australia on November 18. He severely damaged his plane and had to take it to Djakarta by cattleboat for repairs. Luxton said he lived on coconut milk for the 17 days he spent on the island because he could not eat the native dried fish and feared the water might be contaminated. A Dutch carpenter helped him to repair the plane in Djakarta."

Another paper, the "Barrier Miner" published in Broken Hill N.S.W. on Wednesday 5th March 1952, page 8 also carried a report on the exploits of the "Plucky Airman" while The Argus, Melbourne, 8 March 1952 displays a photograph of the plane and captain Jesse Luxton. It acknowledged the significance of the flight.

"Few aviators have successfully flown the 18000 mile route between England and Australia in a mono-plane, but when the single engine Proctor aircraft taxied up to the control tower at Archerfield aerodrome in Brisbane on Thursday afternoon Captain Jesse H. Luxton stepped down from the cockpit a tired but happy man."

Jesse's wife Elizabeth and family came by sea to Sydney to join him, sailing on the migrant liner Cameronia. Elizabeth found the voyage "pretty grim" with 500 children on board and the food was deadly monotonous. They disembarked in Sydney on 6th April 1952 and there is a photograph of the reunited family in Brisbane the following afternoon when Jesse presented his wife and children with a bouquet of Queensland flowers and a basket of tropical fruit.[353] The family made their home in Longreach where within a fortnight the local paper interviewed Elizabeth. She said, "If you want to make a success of marriage with a professional adventurer, the only thing to do is adopt a philosophical attitude from the beginning." She went on to say that when conditions showed no signs of improvement in post war England they decided to migrate to Australia. The family deliberately chose the outback, hoping to learn something of the way Australians live, and where the tradition of pioneering is strongest.[354]

Howevever the marriage soon fell apart somehow and the wife returned with the children to her family in Cornwall. A ship's passenger list for the Orient Steam Navigation Company Ltd records Mrs E. Luxton 46, and her children Susan 8 and John 7 sailed aboard the S.S. Otranto from Sydney calling at Adelaide and Colombo and destined for arrival in London on the 26th July 1953. Their destination was care of Mrs Skinner, Beacon Cottage, St. Agnes, Cornwall. After his wife and family deserted him the Australian electoral Rolls for 1954, 1958 and 1964 list Jesse living alone as a business partner at Cassowary Street, Longreach. His growing status in his community was confirmed in 1955 by his appointment as a J.P. in Queensland.

---

[353] Brisbane Telegraph, Monday 7th April 1952.
[354] The Longreach Leader, Friday 18th April 1952.

Two people who remembered Jesse at Longreach have supplied me with their impressions. Brian Luxton of Toowoomba, Queensland, was a young man when he was introduced to Jesse, standing beside his aircraft at Longreach airport. "Jesse, he recalls, was a swash buckling character with a short neat goatee beard like the swordsmen in pirate films." His friend a Longreach grazier, who had flown with Luxton added, "Some of Jesse's passengers had a few anxious moments when he tilted the aircraft to drain one of the fuel tanks before switching on the second fuel tank."[355]

One of the first flight's of the Proctor, in March 1952, with Jesse Luxton in command, was to transport a sick child from Muttaburra to Longreach hospital at night. An emergency flare-path was laid at Muttaburra.

In the event the Proctor was deemed unsuitable for the conditions found in Western Queensland. Unfortunately it wasn't long before glue break-away was found in the woodwork of the Proctor, the deterioration being attributed to the dry and hot operating area of central and western Queensland. The plane was sold in November 1954. This photograph of Jesse's Proctor was shot by Jeff Atkinson in September 1956 at Moorabbin when it was owned by Sunraysia Air Taxi Service of Mildura. As a wood bonded aircraft in Australia the Proctor was withdrawn from use in 1962. Meanwhile Somerset Airways expanded, using two-three-passenger Auster aircraft.

Jesse became a living legend in the Queensland outback. The Central Queensland Herald, published in Rockhampton on Thursday 1st March 1956 relates the following flying exploit:-

---

[355] See letters dated 6 May and 22 July 2008 from Brian Luxton in Toowoomba, Queensland, Australia.

ONE-WHEEL LANDING

LONGREACH, February 28-Bush pilot Captain Jesse Luxton "scraped a little paint"off his Auster aircraft when he made a one wheel landing here today.

The Auster, owned by Somerset Airways, of Longreach, had been chartered to fly a station hand from Moothandella station Windorah, 18 miles away.

Luxton was taking off from the station about midday when the port wheel struck an object on the grass strip. The wheel was thrown almost to right angles but, as only one landing was possible, Luxton pulled the plane into the air and headed for Longreach, 185 miles away.

At Jundah, 90 miles from Longreach, Luxton dropped a note wrapped around a tea packet asking police to warn Longreach of an emergency landing. An ambulance and fire tender stood by as Luxton made an almost perfect landing.

Luxton is an almost legendary figure because of his flying exploits in the Far West. A British wartime air ace, he flew to Australia about four years ago and has been flying in the Longreach district for the last 18 months.

When Somerset became a private company in 1956, Luxton was granted a quantity of shares as an incentive. Lee became the commercial director and Luxton was the technical director. As the two major shareholders, Lee with about 11,000 shares and Luxton having about 6000 shares, they set forth to develop Somerset. The need to buy more aircraft necessitated the company going public in 1958. Jesse was now made sole managing director with Gordon Lee as chairman. By this time the company had six Austers. Somerset pilots were carrying doctors, dentists, policemen, undertakers, businessmen and civil servants. They were transforming life in the very rich wool black-soil plains around Longreach which was bogged down with rain in the wet season but was a sea of dust in the dry. In 1958 and 1959 the company disposed of most of their "wood and rag"Austers and purchased two all metal Cessna aircraft.

In 1959 an opportunity arose to become stronger by merging with Bush Pilots Airways which were based at Cairns in North Queensland. However merger negotiations aborted, when Jesse Luxton, the managing director, opposed the merger and talks broke down. Somerset Airways simply soldiered on. Business tribulations created management tensions that led to a split between Lee and Luxton. Later in 1960 the board sacked Jesse Luxton as managing director. Jesse sued the company for wrongful dismissal and the matter was finally settled out of court.

Jesse was always a very poor correspondent. He returned home to visit Wangford, sometime after his father's funeral in May 1952, but the family did not hear from him again. However, I find at some date in or after 1964, he returned to England, and was a clerical officer with the Ministry of Transport, when, aged 61, he married Christina Sheila Luxton (nee Gray), 49 divorcee by licence at Ealing Registry Office in London on 17th October 1969. His new wife Christina, had assumed the name Luxton before their marriage. She too was a clerical officer in the Ministry of Transport and the couple lived at 8 Twyford Crescent, W3. Jesse's half sister, Barbara, and husband were living in Ealing at the time but were unaware that secretive Jesse was there too! Jesse, a retired Civil Pilot of Hillrise, 117 Hastings Road, Battle, East Sussex, died aged 86 at Conquest Hospital, St Leonards on Sea, on 22nd November 1994. His widow, Christina, survived him at the same address.

The mysteries surrounding Jesse's life don't end there. In 1985 I received a 'phone call from an anxious Jesuit Priest in Holland, who was trying to trace a Jesse Herbert Luxton, born 1908, who served in the RAF during the Second World War. He believed that Jesse was probably unaware that he was the father of a 38 year old Dutch woman born about 1947. At the time I was unable to help although I suspected Jesse was related to me. Jesse had served in the RAF and was undoubtedly the Jesse Luxton, the Dutch lady was seeking to contact. He was alive in 1985 and for years I was left wondering if contact was made between Jesse and his daughter in Holland. Then in August 2012, I received a letter from Anne Marie Visser, informing me that she had met her half sister, Susan, and Susan's mother in London in1989. She was given Jesse's address in Hastings, and wrote to him but understood from Susan, who had visited him that Jesse had been badly hurt, falling off a ladder and his health was "very poorly with eyesight and mobility" problems.

This historic photogaph of Jesse's Proctor was taken by Geoffrey Luck as the aircraft arrived at Archerfield, Brisbane, from England in March

1952 as G-AIEV. Shortly after his arrival in Longreach, a reporter on the local paper, Alex Garner, wrote a report of a flight into the Queensland out back with Jesse, and I will finish my tribute to the adventurer with Garner's gripping  account of what it was like to fly with Jesse in his Proctor over the vast Australian bush:-

When I was assigned to cover a meeting in Winton last week, it seemed a long way off, even in this country of great distances, and I had not yet succeeded in accustoming myself to the idea it was part of a reporters duty to travel one hundred miles, sit through a six hour meeting, get a story and return with the material ready for the presses, within a matter of 24 hours or so. There is something so expansive about the size and concept of the West that it staggers the imagination-journeys such as this are part of the everyday business of living, and it is only to newcomers like myself that they present any novelty. The question which immediately arose was-how? Train car or plane? The problem was solved on the spot. The owner of Somerset Airways Mr. Gordon Lee, was travelling over by plane, and Mr. H. G. Behan, and I was able to go along for the ride, picking Mr. Lee up at Muttaburra. So very simple, I was assured, we'd be over there in an hour and a half, take your typewriter and a night–gown, and leave the rest to Somerset, it was as easy as that.

About 10:15 on Wednesday we went to the aerodrome, where the pilot, Captain Jesse Luxton, looking like a black bearded pirate from a more swashbuckling age, was waiting for us. Captain Luxton was taking the Proctor, the four seater aircraft which he recently flew out from England, and there was a short wait while she refuelled. It took longer than we anticipated, and the men filled in the time learnedly discussing the merits of the various types of planes, the mysteries of cloud strata and cross winds, and the way the Coral Sea Battle was won from Longreach. It sounded very impressive but I was so full of excitement at my first trip in a small plane that most of it fell on deaf ears.

At 10:45 everything was ready, so with an attempt at nonchalance I strolled over to the waiting aircraft and allowed myself to be assisted in, hoping the whole time that my rawness would not appear too childish....... The Captain, however, was gallantry itself, and Mr. Behan was gently reassuring from the back seat, so we settled ourselves in, and the self-consciousness I felt earlier vanished in the excitement of taking off. The engine roared into life, the little plane quivered slightly, like a cat stretching itself after a sleep, wheeled round and sped up the runway. I waited a moment or two, wondering when we would become airborne and looked down to see fences and trees gradually assuming smaller proportions. I hadn't even noticed it had been so easy.

We headed north-east to Muttaburra, into the sun. The landscape seemed limitless, losing itself in mists on the horizons that stretched to kingdom-come. Occasionally there was the glitter of an iron roof, the faint expanse of green country, the ochre ribbon of the Thomson, pin-pointed with trees, but most of all there were the great brown plains. They were endless and looked like the floor of some dried out ocean from which all life had vanished, where only the long–still tides have left their timeless imprint on the contours of the land.

Inside the aircraft it was impossible to speak. The roar of the engine ripped the words away from our lips before they were formed. I was aware of the steady efficiency with which the pilot managed the controls, the seeming slowness of our flight, the slight chill above 6,000 thousand feet-and the penetrating glare which rendered glasses useless. But it was the solitude which I liked best. Time had no meaning up here, there seemed no relation between our easy flight and the laboured journeys the horse waggons had made on the sweeping country below, a bare twenty years ago. Up here one was alone in himself, like the man who works in isolated places on the selections, seeing no-one, finding the solitude a blessing rather than a burden. It occurred to me that man come to the West not only because they find the cities have no place for them, but also because, on their own, with nothing but their wits and their native strength, they are able to realise the full meaning of the words "I am a man."

However, reveries played no part in the business of the Captain. I was jolted back into reality when a hoarse voice shouted in my ear:

"There's Muttaburra ahead," and saw the cross of the landing strip beyond the town. We landed uneventually, waited a few minutes for Mr. Lee, who had set out immediately the plane was sighted, and were off again in a matter of minutes, 50 minutes from the time we had left Longreach. Another forty minutes, and Winton came into sight, a dazzle of iron roofs on the plain, and another uneventful landing. When we alighted, the flies were there to greet us, happily renewing old acquaintances with the ones who had accompanied us from Longreach. It was now 12:15, exactly two hours since we set out.

A meal in Winton, and then work. There was no opportunity to see much of the town, where the only thing that appears to grow is the acacia Arabica, the thorny tree that is rapidly becoming a pest. We left for Longreach at about 10AM the following day, a short hop to Muttaburra, morning tea with our host, and then back home. Towards the end I was becoming a little blasé about it all, and started to pray for something exciting to happen. What could be better? A reporter on the spot, complete with type writer and paper, all that was wanted was the incident. Perhaps fortunately, these wishes did not materialise. We made an easy landing and all was well. A perfectly routine trip for Somerset, something less than routine for the Captain, but to one passenger the most rewarding experience in a very long time[356].

---

[356] The Longreach Leader, Friday 4th April 1952 P 8

47

JAMES FREDERICK LUXTON (1847-1929) FARMER OF THE DROVE AND RIDLEY STREET ALLER SOMERSET

See tree 24

Frederick Luxton (otherwise James Frederick Luxton), the second son of Thomas Luxton (c.1803-1885) of Aller and his second wife Sarah  Stacey, was baptised at Aller on the 30th May 1847. In 1851 and 1861 he was living with his family in Ridley Street. He was a 13 year old agricultural labourer at Ridley, when his mother died in 1861. Frederick 23, labourer, married Mary Ann Fisher 25, servant, both of Aller, in St. Andrew's, the parish church, on Christmas Day 1869. They sign the register with a mark indicating they were unable to read and write. In 1871 Frederick, agricultural labourer, and his wife Mary Ann, were living at Aller Drove. Mary Luxton, (Aunt Polly), Frederick's 15 year old sister, a scholar was living with the couple and Sarah Jane, their infant daughter aged one.

They were living there in 1881 with five children but had moved to Ridley Street by 1891, when four children were still living at home. By 1901 Frederick, a 53 year old farmer on his own account, was living with his wife Mary Ann, 58, and their son Stephen, a 23 year old hay-cutter, at Townsend Cottages, Aller. In 1911 Frederick, 65, who continued to farm on his own account, supported by Ann 68, his wife of 40 years, lived in a six room farmhouse in Aller. Frederick "always wore a hat day and night!" according to family folklore, which makes this photograph of him wearing his hat inside his cottage all the more interesting.

Kelly's Directory for Somersetshire in 1914, lists Frederick Luxton as a farmer, and this continues in each edition until his death. The picture below is a postcard view of the house he lived in, known as "Ridley" next to the Congregational Chapel, on Ridley Hill. Ivy Luxton, his granddaughter, the tallest girl in

the picture, helps us date the postcard to c.1925. Fred's wife, Mary Ann, pleaded guilty to driving without a light (presumably a pony and trap) and was fined 5s. and costs at the local petty sessions in September 1901.[357]

Mary Ann Luxton died, aged 82, and was buried at St. Andrew's, Aller on the 28th December, 1925. Her husband James died, aged 81, on the 19th February 1929 and was buried with her in St. Andrew's churchyard on the 23rd February. In his will made on the 21st January 1927 he left his second son, Arthur Richard Luxton, the sum of £300. This was

---

[357] Taunton Courier, Wednesday 11th September 1901.

probably in lieu of land, as by 1927 Arthur who had four sons, was living in Bournemouth. To his eldest son, Adolphus Warfield Luxton, he gave "my house at Aller, the orchard behind it Dobbins Orchards, Long Hill Orchard Penny Hill, the Caxton Blackwithies and the Higher Horsemeads for him absolutely. To my daughter Lena Lock I bequeath my field called Lower Horsemead together with £50. To my son Stephen Charles Luxton my field called Slabb." Probate was granted in London on the 30th April 1930, to his son Adolphus Warfield Luxton, warehouseman, and Henry James Gullidge, gardener, when his personal estate was valued at £1556..16s..6d.

James Frederick Luxton (1847-1929), and his wife Mary Ann Fisher, had five children, two girls and three boys. Mary Ann Fisher was pregnant when she married and the eldest child, Sarah Jane Luxton (1870-1918), known as Sally, was born at Aller on the 22nd February 1870. In 1891 Sally, 21, was a general domestic servant, living in the household of Edward Lutt, a widower and retired wool agent and his six children in Deptford London. Aged 26 and living at 10 Mallet Road Lewisham, she married Henry Dean, 35, bachelor, labourer, at St. Swithian's parish church in Lewisham, Kent, after banns on the 2nd August 1897. This photograph of Sally, by N. Mayer's Photographic Studio, 146 High Street, Hounslow was probably taken just prior to her marriage. Sally's elaborate hat is decorated with a profusion of trimmings including ribbons, flowers and feathers. Her right arm rests on a studio pedestal, and she is holding a cane parasol with a silver top, in her gloved left hand. Sally's life story is tragic. Her husband Henry Dean, died in 1898 and by a second husband, Arthur Edwards, she had a daughter, Lily and three boys. When Arthur, her second husband died, Sally was destitute. For a time she was in West Ham Workhouse, and her three boys were sent to Canada in the early 1900s as a part of Dr. Thomas Barnardo's British Child Immigration Programme. Sally married for a third time to Hénry Waight, a telephone attendant, in St. Thomas

Parish Church West Ham on 20th August 1911. She died of cancer on 15th May 1918.

Lena Luxton (1880-1960), the youngest daughter, born at Aller on the 7th May 1880, married William George Lock (1877-1964) at Aller on the 31st July 1905 and they had a son William Adolphus George Lock (Billy) born on the 22nd August 1906 who married Freda Miller. This vignette photograph of Lena below, was probably taken just before her wedding in 1905. In 1911the family lived at the Hill, Langport where William, aged 32, was a domestic groom and caretaker. Lena, the wife of William Lock, now a gardener, died aged 80 at Whatley Langport on 11th October 1960.

Adolphus Warfield Luxton (1871-1954), the eldest son, was born at the Drove Aller on the 9th December 1871. Aged 34, warehouseman of Whatley, Langport he married Susan Burrows 30, spinster, domestic servant of the Hill, Langport at the parish church Langport on the 4th February 1906. This photograph of the couple below was probably taken at the time of their marriage. The loose draped front of Susan's blouse and dress, is a style that can be dated to mid first decade of the 20th century. The couple had no children. Susan died, aged 74, at North Street, Langport on the 20th November 1950. Adolphus, a retired grocery warehouseman, died, aged 83, at North Street, Langport, Somerset on the 17th February 1954.

Arthur Luxton (1874-1945), the third child and second son of Frederick Luxton and his wife Mary Ann Fisher, was born at the Drove Aller, on the 14th June 1874. At birth he was registered as Ernest Richard Luxton but was later known as Arthur. In 1891, aged 15, he was living at home and cycling daily to Langport, to work at Kelways Royal Nursery as an apprentice gardener[358]. On the 31st March 1901, Arthur, 28, was a lodger living and working with a nurseryman and his family in Ferndown, Hampreston, Wimborne, Dorset, which was then open

---

[358] The nursery is famed for its peonies and even today is a regular Chelsea gold winner.

country on the outskirts of what was to become Bournemouth. Annie Gollop, his wife of later that year was a 25 year old domestic cook in service in the home of William Shey, a commercial traveller and his family in Broadstone, Canford Magna in Dorset. How the two met is not known but Ferndown and Broadstone are not that far apart. He married as Arthur Richard Luxton, 26, gardener of Upham, Hampshire to Annie Gollop 25, spinster of Canford in the parish church of Canford Magna, Dorset on the 22nd June 1901.

By the time their eldest child was born on the 22nd November 1901, the couple had taken a job with accommodation at Winter's Hill in Waltham, Hampshire. Family lore[359] relates that Arthur was the gardener at the "big house" and they lived in a lodge and his wife Annie opened the gates for carriages to go in. Within the decade the couple were settled at 49 Hankinson Road, Winton in Bournemouth, where the rest of

their children were born. The 1939 register lists Arthur, a gardener, and his wife Annie, living with their son Ernest and wife, at 30 Acland Road, Bournemouth. Arthur died at 30 Acland Road, Winton, Bournemouth on the 29th September 1945, leaving an estate valued at £471..7s..3d. Annie Gertrude Luxton, his widow, died in Bournemouth on the 1st February 1953, leaving a personal estate valued at£1117..4s..1d. The photograph on the left shows a young Arthur (Ernest Richard) Luxton as a young man and was probably taken at the time of his marriage.

---

[359] Eileen Bangay their granddaughter has given me this story and has been very helpful on her family history.

In the 1940s photograph above, Arthur (Ernest Richard) Luxton is standing in the centre, and his wife Annie Gollop, is seated in front of him. Lena Lock nee Luxton is standing next to Arthur to the right and Lena's husband, William Lock, is standing next to her, with his hand on his hip. Freda Lock (nee Miller) is standing next to Arthur on the left and her husband Billy Lock is taking the picture.

Arthur Luxton (1874-1945) and his wife Annie Gertrude Gollop had four sons who are in the photograph below of c.1912. Frederick Arthur (1901-1974) is standing, Alfred Sidney (1910-1978) is on the left, Leonard Oliver (1907-1923) is seated in the centre and Ernest William Joseph (1909-1988) is on the right.

Frederick Arthur Luxton (1901-1974), the eldest son was born at Winters Hill, Bishops Waltham, Hampshire on the 22nd November 1901. He was a 27 year old chauffeur in Oxford, when he married Dorothy Edith Hilda Roberts, 24, spinster, domestic servant, daughter of Frederick Charles Roberts, gardener, at the parish church of St. Andrew's Bournemouth after banns on the 26th December 1928. His wife Dorothy was born in Christchurch, Hampshire on the 28th May 1904 and they were living at 53 Rosamund Road, Wolvercote Oxford when she died on 28th August 1970. Frederick, a retired motor cycle

505

dealer, of 18 Guest Avenue, Branksome, Poole died on the 1st August 1974 and he was cremated at North Cemetery Bournemouth on the 7th August. There were no children of this marriage.

Leonard Oliver Luxton (1907-1923), born at Forest View, Hankinson Road, Winton, Bournemouth on the 24th January 1907, was accidentally drowned while bathing in the River Stour at Wimborne. He was a boy scout in the Charminster Road, 36th Bournemouth Scout Troop, camping at Ashington near Wimborne, when despite being a good swimmer, he got into difficulties and drowned while swimming in the River Stour between 7 and 8 o'clock on the evening of Wednesday 8th August 1923[360]

Ernest William Joseph Luxton (1908-1988), the third son, born on the 2nd December 1908, was a 24 year old butcher, when he married Agnes Edith May Keel, 23 spinster daughter of Frederick Charles Keel, commercial traveller in the parish church of St Augustine, Bournemouth after banns on the 18th October 1933. Ernest was cremated at North Cemetery Bournemouth on the 11th February 1988 and his widow Agnes (1910-1995) was cremated there on the 1st December 1995. This couple had two daughters, Jean Eleanor Luxton, born on the 1st April 1943 and Anne Rosemary Luxton, born on the 5th September 1946. Anne a clerk/typist, daughter of Ernest William Joseph Luxton, car park supervisor, Bournemouth Corporation, married David Stanley Rogers, 32, ice cream factory worker, at Winton Congregational Church, Bournemouth on the 27th October 1967.

Alfred Sidney Luxton (1910-1978), the fourth son, born on the 27th September 1910, was a 26 year old cordite worker, when he married

---

[360] The Bournemouth Echo for the 9th and 10th August 1923 provides details from the inquest held on the 9th August.

Mildred Dorothy Bower (b.28.03.1910-d.18.01. 2000) 26, book keeper and cashier, daughter of Ralph Bower, builder's foreman, at Charminster Road Congregational Church on the 27th March 1937. Alfred, a van driver, died in Dorchester on the 4th January 1978 and was cremated on the 12th. This couple had two daughters, Eileen and Gwendolin and the author is grateful to Eileen for her help in compiling this part of the family story and providing photographs.

Stephen Charles Luxton (1877-1950), the third son and fifth child of Frederick James Luxton (1847-1929) and his wife Mary Ann Fisher, was born at the Drove Aller, on the 30th September 1877. Aged 15 he appeared before the Somerton Petty Sessions for throwing a stone between 3 and 4 in the afternoon of Sunday 30th October 1892, after the school children, as they marched in procession from the parish church in Aller to the school-room. He was fined £1 and 7shillings costs, for what the magistrates termed an "expensive pastime.[361]" Stephen, a 33 year old farmer, married Bessie

Otton (1877-1956), spinster, dressmaker of Aller, daughter of Frank Otton, carpenter, in the Independent Chapel, Somerton Somerset on the 5th January 1911. In the census that year Stephen, a 33year old hay cutter, his wife, Bessie, 32, born in Long Sutton, Somerset lived in a three room dwelling in Aller. His sister-in-law, Mary Otton, a 20 year old assistant teacher lived with them. On a Tuesday night in early March 1914, a rick of hay containing between 18 and 28 tons, belonging to Stephen and situated at the rear of his house, caught fire. Fortunately with the help of the Langport Fire Brigade a fair quantity of the hay was saved. The fire was thought to be the work of an incendiary[362].

---

[361] Taunton Courier, Wednesday 9th November 1892.
[362] Taunton Courier, Wednesday 11th March 1914.

In this photograph, taken c.1905 at the back of Canterbury Farm, where he lived, Stephen, (on left) is seated, relaxing with his half–cousin, John (1857-1945), son of Robert Lewis Luxton. They are wearing working men's cloth caps and gaiters. Urban dwellers returning to visit their Luxton family at Aller in mid twentieth century thought their life primitive. They were amazed to find that they had chickens running around the house, no hot or cold running water indoors and an outside toilet.

In January 1917, Stephen, aged 40, sought a conditional exemption from military conscription when he appeared for a second time at Taunton before the Somerset Appeal Tribunal. He was described as a smallholder of "20 acres, 13 and a half of which he owned, and one of which was arable. He bred 20 to 30 pigs a year and he supplied milk to the parishioners of Aller." The Tribunal exempted him from service until the 20th February, conditional upon him performing 20 hours a week helping neighbours. He appeared before the Tribunal again in February when he presented a record of the work he had done for neighbouring farmers and the Tribunal granted him a further six months exemption on the same conditions[363]. However, he was perhaps the sub-Lieutenant Stephen C. Luxton RNV in the Navy List August 1917 Blandford Camp 63 Royal Naval Division Reserves 3rd Reserve Battalion.

In a sale of Aller grass at the White Lion Inn, Aller, by the Council and other owners in April 1941, Stephen realised £49 for the sale of his grass harvested from Kings Sedge, 7a.1r 5p.[364] Stephen Charles Luxton, farmer of Canterbury Farm, Aller died aged 72, on Sunday the 22nd January 1950 in the Tone Vale Hospital Taunton, "after an illness lasting about three months. He was well known and respected in Aller and neighbourhood, having lived in Aller all his life."[365] He bequeathed £100 to his wife Bessie. All of his real estate and the residual of his personal estate he bequeathed to his daughter Ivy Lucy Gertrude Luxton, "for her own use and benefit absolutely." Probate was granted in London 18th March 1950 to the executers Henry James Gulledge, gardener and Clifford George Lewis Luxton, baker and confectioner,

---

[363] Taunton Courier, Wednesday 13th September 1916, 10th January & 7th March 1917.
[364] Taunton Courier, Saturday 19th April 1941.
[365] Somerset County Herald, Saturday 4th February 1950.

when his personal estate was valued at £3383..4s..7d. His widow, Bessie Luxton (1877-1956) died, aged 79, and was buried at St. Andrew's, Aller on the 12th March 1956. Steve Luxton is pictured at Canterbury Farm c.1910-20 in his pony and trap, with S C Luxton Aller painted on the side.

Ivy Gertrude (1912-2000), their daughter, was born at Canterbury Farm, Aller, Somerset on the 9th March 1912. She was a 48 year old poultry farmer when she married her half cousin, Clifford George Lewis Luxton, 64 bachelor, retired master baker, of Church Path, Aller in the Register Office, Bridgwater on the 20th December 1960. Clifford George Lewis Luxton (1896-1969) of Canterbury Farm, Aller died aged 72, on the 27th February 1969 and he was buried at St. Andrew's the parish church on the 2nd March. Administration of his estate valued at £5797 was granted to his widow, Ivy, who continued to reside at Canterbury Farm until her death on 12th November 2000.

48

JOHN LUXEN (LUXON, LUXTON) (1747-1818), YEOMAN OF CORNER HOUSE, PETTON, BAMPTON, DEVON AND TAUNTON, SOMERSET

See tree 25

John, the son of Joseph Luxton (1719-1791), husbandman, and his wife Dorothy Adams, was baptised John Luxen at Petton on the 14th August 1747. He took for his wife Mary Redwood, of the nearby parish of Upton, when they married at Clatworthy[366] Somerset, on the 16th April 1779. Many years later their son Robert stated in a deposition, made on the 11th November 1853, that John, "lived for sometime in Taunton but some years before he died went to reside in the parish of Bampton where he died."[367]

John and Mary's movements on the Devon Somerset border can be traced through the baptismal records of their nine children. They were settled in St. Mary Magdalene parish Taunton, by the 20th January 1782, when their eldest child, John Luxen (Luxton) (1782-1837) was baptised in the parish church. A second son, Joseph Luxon (Luxton) was baptised at St. Mary Magdalene, on the 30th May 1784. The couple had moved house, and were resident in the hamlet of Petton, Bampton when their third son, Robert Luxon (Luxton) (1786-1871), was baptised at St. Petrock's church on the 2nd April 1786. A further four children were baptised at St. Petrock's church Petton. These were Maria Luxon (Mary Luxton) on the 2nd March 1788, William Luxon (Luxton) (1791-1851) on the 1st July 1792, Thomas Luxon (Luxton) (1798-1856) on the 21st September 1798 and Francis Luxon on the 3rd August 1803, who was buried at Petton aged four, on the 14th February 1808.

---

[366] The Clatworthy register describes John Luxon as "of the Parish" but this does not mean he was born there or even a long standing resident. This was frequently done, simply as a means of fulfilling the requirement for the three weeks calling of banns.
[367] The deeds of Petton Farm (formerly Frogpit Farm) were consulted by my brother Ian and myself at the National Provincial Bank in Tiverton on the 21st July 1975.

Their son James Luxon (Luxton) (1796-1869), was baptised at St. Michael's parish church, Bampton on the 24th April 1796. Perhaps this was because services at St. Petrock's were only held once a month and it was held by the living of Bampton. It is intriguing too to speculate why their son, George

Luxon (Luxton) (1802-1891), was baptised at St. Michael's (in photo) in the neighbouring parish of Raddington, Somerset on the 2nd February 1802. It may be that St Petrock's was closed for repair or without a priest, but it is more likely that John was a tenant farmer in Raddington when George was baptised there. A search of the Raddington Land Tax Assessments may provide evidence of John's farming activities in the parish.

With the permission of Mr and Mrs Tooze, the owners of Petton Farm (formerly Frogpit Farm), my brother Ian and I, on the 21st July 1975, visited the National Provincial Bank in Tiverton, where we were locked in the bank vault to examine the farm deeds. An indenture, dated 30th December 1854, revealed that John Luxton (1747-1818) resided at Corner House, Petton which is marked as No 1553 on the Bampton tithe map of 1842 and is described as "Cot. Garden and Orchard measuring 1 acre 1 rod 5 poles."

With the help of property deeds, and especially the 1842 Bampton tithe map and apportionment, we can establish what had been John's property in the parish. One parcel, measuring 5 acres 3 rods and 3 poles at the rent charge of three shillings and three pence, centred on Corner House and the adjoining fields which abutted the road from Petton Cross to Skilgate. The adjoining fields were No 1552 Eastern Close, Meadow, measuring 1 acre 25 P. No 1551 Bottom Piece, Pasture, measuring 3 rods 20 poles, No 1550 Bottom Piece, Pasture, 3 rods 20 poles. He also held No 883, a Plantation, measuring 3 acres 2 rods. Another parcel of land on the north side of the turnpike road between Bampton and Wiveliscombe included two more fields No 1515 Higher Field, Pasture, measuring 2 rods 38 poles and No 1514 Lower Field,

Pasture, measuring 3 rods 15 poles. The adjoining No 1511 was a Cot, Smith's Shop and Garden, measuring 2 rods 5 poles while No 1512 was a Cottage and Garden measuring 30 poles occupied by his son in law, Joseph Brewer, the church sexton at Petton, who was married to his daughter Mary. John also held the eastern part of New House Tenement, marked on the 1842 tithe map as No 1513, a Public House, Garden, measuring 2 rods and 1 pole. It lay on the south side of the turnpike road from Bampton to Wiveliscombe.

The Bampton Surveyors of Highways Rates and Account Books reveal that John made payments for the maintenance of the highways. The rate he paid varied. This was 3 shillings in 1775 to 1780, 5 shillings in 1791, 3 shillings and 6 pence in 1792 and 1800, 2 shillings and 6d in 1794 to 1796, 4 shillings in 1797, 1799, 1802, 1803, 2 shillings in 1798, 6 shillings in 1801, 8 shillings in 1805 and 1809, 12 shillings in 1807, 16 shillings in 1810, £1 and 2 shillings in 1811, £1 and 4 shillings in 1812, £1 and 4 shillings in 1813 and in 1814 16 shillings were due but John was 10 shillings and 6 pence in arrears.

One interesting record shown in the Bampton Surveyors of Highways Rates and Accounts 1766-1816, was a list of occupiers that was unfortunately undated. It occurred, however, just after a section of receipts (dated between 1775 and 1781) that appeared at the end of the volume, separate from the disbursements for the same period. I have therefore tentatively given the year 1775 as the date for this list of occupiers. It includes a valuation of John's property:-

> Occupier: John Luxon
> Tenement: Frogpit Moor
> Yearly value: £10..0sh..0d
> Two 3 rds value: £6..13..4d
> Six days: 3 sh..0d

The Road Surveyors made numerous payments to John Luxton for work he undertook in maintaining the Bampton highways. On the 23rd May 1765 he shared 4sh..8d with three others for repairing "the road near Frogpit Moor towards Cornwood Hill." Other payments for his labour on the Bampton Highways include:-

1776 Dec 3rd: Paid: "John Luxon 25 faggotts wallet": 9d
     1802:   Paid: "John Luxon 42 seams of stones: 3sh..6d."
     1810:   Paid: "John Luxon cleaning drains: 14sh..2d."
     1810:   Paid: "John Luxon 3 days: 4sh..6d."
     1811:   Paid: "John Luxon 7 days work: 10sh..6d."
     1812:   Paid: "John Luxon : 9sh..3d."
     1815:   Paid: "John Luxton for labour as per bill: 1sh..6d."

John's wife Mary Redwood (Maria Redwood) was baptised at Upton Somerset daughter of Francis and Mary Redwood on the 23rd November 1759. Already in her mid forties when her youngest son was baptised in 1803 she named him Francis after his maternal grandfather. She was dead by 1818 as her husband makes no provision for her in his will. A scrutiny of the Petton register reveals Mary Luxon aged 68 was buried 17th May 1812. Her given age is wildly inaccurate as she was about 53.

John Luxton, yeoman, of Corner House, Petton, died, aged 72, and was buried at St. Petrock's Church on the 12th July 1818. I made a copy of his Will in 1989, when it was in the possession of Mr Maurice Hawkins of Venn Farm, Waterrow, Somerset.

In his will made on the 20th March 1818 he bequeathed, "all my lands" except a cottage house called New House with a garden and orchard, to his eldest son John Luxton (1782-1837), a carpenter and joiner who lived in Taunton. New House with its garden and orchard he left to his son William who was to have possession at the end of one year after his father's death. He was to pay his brother John, the executor of the will, the yearly annuity or sum of ten shillings each year for six years. The first payment was due at the end of "two years after my decease." If William died without issue the property was to descend to the youngest surviving son, George Luxton and his heirs.

He further bequeathed £3 to his daughter Mary Brewer, to be paid in two years after his death. Robert his son was to receive £3 payable in three years after his death and was also to receive "my silver watch to be delivered at the time of my interment." At this date a watch would have been hand crafted and cost several guineas. On the whole, only the gentry, factory owners, farmers and tradesmen would have been able to afford one. There was a Clock Club in Bampton in 1808 and it was probably through this cooperative savings club that John was able to afford his silver pocket watch[368]. His son James was to receive £3 payable in four years after his father's decease. Thomas was to receive £3 payable in five years and George was to receive £3 payable in six years. "All rest residue and remainder of my goods, chattels, ready monies, rights and credits.........after payment of my just debts legacies and funeral expenses to give to my son John Luxton," who he made residuary legatee and sole executor of his last will and testament. The Will, signed and sealed by John Luxton, was witnessed by William Cleeve and William Cleeve junior and John Capron who was a whitesmith in Bampton.[369] The Will was proved by the oath of John Luxen (sic) the son and sole executor in the archdeaconry court of Exeter on the 30th January 1819.

The property at Petton, belonging to John Luxton (1747-1818), which he had inherited from his grandfather Robert Luxton (c.1664/69 – 1751), husbandman, was sold by his descendants in the mid nineteenth and early twentieth centuries. John's great-grandson, James Luxton (1827-1905), an innkeeper, of the Green Dragon in Taunton, sold Corner House and the bulk of the land for a total of £550 to Frederick William Collard, of No 26 Cheapside, London, Piano-forte manufacturer. The transaction is recorded in two deeds dated 11th November 1853 and 30th December 1854. A much smaller parcel known as "Ashelford's Plot," at New House Tenement, was sold on the 30th December 1857 for £11 by John's son George Luxton (1802-1891) of Morebath. The purchaser, Thomas Elworthy, yeoman of North Hayne, Bampton, erected a house, Frogmore, on the site and there is a plaque set on the exterior bearing his name and the date 1858. George's daughter, Mary Ann Luxton, matron of the Midland Institution for the Blind, Nottingham, conveyed another plot of New House land for the

---

[368] The increasing pace of life in the early nineteenth century led to a growing demand for pocket watches and clocks. Clock Clubs which were cooperative savings clubs were set up to meet the demand. Farmers, small businessmen, craftsmen & labourers from the more affluent in the local community became members of these clubs which were usually organized by the clock maker with the help of the local publican. In this way members could afford to buy a pocket watch or a longcase clock in oak or mahogany. See Clive N. Ponsford, Devon Clocks and Clockmakers (Newton Abbot) 1985, page 132 on the Bampton Clock Club.

[369] Whites Devon Directory (1850) page 323 lists John Capron as a whitesmith (i.e. tinsmith) in Bampton.

erection of a Bible Christian Chapel by an indenture dated the 11th August 1892. Finally Mary Luxton sold the two houses known as New Houses, Petton by a deed dated the 29th September 1902, to Mr William Hawkins for £134 plus £50 to settle the mortgage debt on the property.

John and Mary, his wife, lie buried at St. Petrock's chapel Petton, but no headstone has survived to mark their burial place. Their eldest sons John (1782-1837) Joseph (1784-alive 1816) and Robert (1786-1871) settled in Taunton in the early nineteenth century, when it had a population of a little over 5000. There they made a living as carpenters, joiners and sawyers. Two of the younger brothers James (1796-1869) and Thomas (1798-1856) were to become farmers at Skilgate, and Upton, in Somerset while George (1802-1891) the youngest, became a stone mason in Morebath. Today their numerous descendants are living worldwide and in the chapters which follow I will say more on these sons and their families.

John's daughter Maria Luxton, baptised at Petton on 2nd March 1788, is also referred to as Mary in later documentation. She married Joseph Brewer (1785-1861) at St. John the Baptist in Bedminster, Somerset on the 15th February 1808. They lived at Frogpit Cottage where Mary and Joseph, a labourer and parish sexton, had nine children baptised at Petton. In the 1841 census Joseph was a 60 year old agricultural labourer, Mary 55 and two children Joseph 10 and Eliza 7 were still at home. Mary's brother William 50, described as a pauper, was living with them. In 1851 Joseph Brewer, is a 69 year old pauper and sexton, Mary, 65 and her brother William is a 63 year old unmarried lodger and pauper. Mary died aged 66 and as Maria Brewer she was buried at Petton on 30th March 1854. In 1861 Joseph Brewer, widower, 78, farm labourer, born in Tiverton, was living with their married daughter, Eliza Penick 28 and her husband James Penick, 30 farm labourer, at Zeal, Bampton. Joseph Brewer 76 (sic) was buried at Petton on the 14th July 1861.

49

JOHN LUXTON (1782 – 1837) CARPENTER AND JOINER OF HIGH STREET IN THE PARISH OF ST MARY MAGDALENE, TAUNTON, SOMERSET

See tree 26 & 29

John, the eldest of nine children born to John Luxton (1747 – 1818) yeoman of Corner House, Petton, Bampton and his wife Mary Redwood, was baptised as John Luxen, at St. Mary Magdalene Taunton on 20th January 1782. When he was still an infant his parents moved to his father's home hamlet of Petton, Bampton and that is where he spent much of his youth in all likelihood. He was resident in Taunton again when his son John Garland alias Luxton, an illegitimate child born to Mary Garland was baptised at St. Mary Magdalene, on Christmas Day 1800.

John qualified as a carpenter and joiner and in 1801 he was a member of the Taunton Loyal Volunteers. This local militia force was formed by a public meeting held in the town in April 1794, when revolutionary France had declared war on Britain and a French invasion was anticipated.

John Luxon married Ann Webb at St. George's Church, Wilton, Somerset on the 30th November 1801. The newly wed pair settled in Taunton where James Luxton (1802 – 1853) their eldest child, was baptised at St. Mary Magdalene on 4th July 1802. Seven more children were baptised at St. Mary Magdalene beginning with Sarah on 16th June 1805, followed by William (1807 – 1878) on 29th March 1807, Mary and John on 4th April 1813, Joseph (1817 – 1879) on 23rd February 1817, Elizabeth on 13th June 1819, and Mary Ann on 11th April 1822.

The family's movement around Taunton can be traced in the baptismal register. When Mary and John were baptised in April 1813, they were living in High Street. John, described as a joiner, was resident in East Street when Joseph was baptised in February 1817. The family continued to dwell there in June 1819 when Elizabeth was baptised, but when Mary Ann, the last of their eight children, was baptised in April 1822, the family resided in Church Square.

John was residuary legatee and sole executor of his father's will which he proved at Exeter on 30th January 1819. He was bequeathed his entire father's land at Petton except New House Tenement. A deposition made by his younger brother Robert on 11th November 1853, stated that following their father's death John "went to reside in Bampton where he resided for some time and he then moved to Taunton where he died"[370].

John died intestate, and as "John Luxton aged 55 of High Street, Taunton", he was buried at St. Mary Magdalene on 24th February 1837. Ann Luxton, his widow, a cook aged 60, resided with her eldest son James, a carpenter, in Fore Street, when the 1841 census was taken. Ten years later, Ann, a 71 year old widow, born in Abenhall in Gloucester, was still living with James and family who dwelt at Twiles Court, St Paul Street, Taunton. It was probably in 1853, when her eldest son James died, that Ann moved to Ilminster, in Somerset to live with her son, John who was a hairdresser. She was living with John and his wife Susan in Silver Street, when the 1861 Ilminster census was taken. Ann Luxton, widow of John Luxton, carpenter, died at the age of 88 from senile decay, in Silver Street, Ilminster on 6th October 1867 and was buried in the Unitarian chapel burial ground on 11th October 1867.

John and Ann's eldest son James Luxton (1802 – 1853), a carpenter in Taunton, married Mary Ann Bennett at St. Mary Magdalene on 23rd June 1822. They lived in Fore Street in 1841, and Twiles Court, St Paul Street ten years later. James inherited the bulk of his grandfather John Luxton's (1747 – 1818) property at Frogpit Moor, Petton. He is the James Luxton listed in the Poll Book Register of 1841 owning the freehold of Frogpit Cottage, Petton.

---

[370] This deposition was among Luxton deeds relating to Frogpitt Farm consulted by my brother Ian and myself in the vaults of the National Provincial Bank Tiverton on the 21st July 1975.

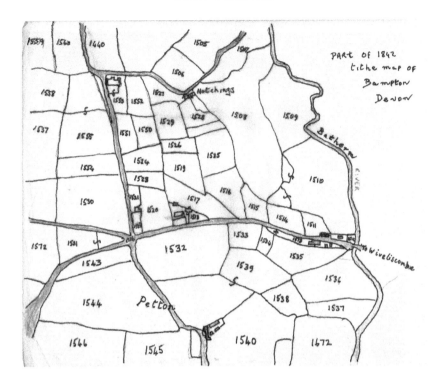

We have a detailed account of his property from the Bampton tithe map and apportionment, made on 22nd August 1842. James owned 5 acres 3 rods 3 poles at the rent charge of 3 shillings and 3 pence. No 883 a plantation measuring 3 a 2r 0p was occupied by James himself. Corner House, which had been the home of John Luxton, his grandfather, was leased to James Haywood. It is marked as No. 1553 on the map and is described as "Cot. Garden and Orchard" measuring 1 acre 1r 5p. The adjoining fields No. 1552 Eastern Close, Meadow, measuring 1 acre 25p, No 1551 Bottom Piece, Pasture, 3 rods 20 poles were all leased to the mentioned James Haywood.

Corner House and these adjoining fields abutted the road from Petton Cross to Skilgate. Two more fields No. 1515 Higher Field, Pasture, measuring 2 rods 38 poles and No. 1514 Lower Field, Pasture, measuring 3 rods 15 poles which formed part of another parcel of land on the north side of the turnpike road between Bampton and Wiveliscombe were also leased to James Haywood. The adjoining No 1511 Cot. Smith's Shop and Garden measuring 2 rods 5 poles were leased to James Warren and

No. 1512 described as a Cottage and Garden measuring 30 poles were occupied by Joseph Brewer the husband of Mary, a daughter of John Luxton (1747 – 1818) of Corner House.

James Luxton (1802 – 1853) carpenter, was resident in St Paul Street, Taunton when he died aged 51 on 30th May 1853. His cause of death is registered as "Gangrene of foot – exhaustion", and he was buried at Taunton on 5th June 1853[371]. He died intestate and this explains why a deposition made by his younger brother Robert was found among the deeds of Frogpit Farm, Petton. The Petton property descended to James' only son and heir, James Luxton (born 1827 – 1905), a Taunton innkeeper who sold it before moving with his wife and daughter to settle in London in the 1860s where he was a coachman before returning to the Taunton area.

William Luxton (1807 – 1878), the second son of John and Ann Luxton, was a carpenter and a successful builder, who married Hannah Paull, at St. Mary Magdalene on 29th March 1832. In the 1841 census for St. Mary Magdalene parish, William aged 30, a carpenter and his wife Hannah, aged 35, lived in Westgate Street, Taunton. William prospered and became a man of property. The Taunton Electoral Rolls for 1853 list him as the owner of a freehold house buildings and land in Westgate Street. Property he had built by the Shire Hall, were sold by auction in January 1860.[372] He applied in April 1860 to the Taunton authorities, for a sewer to be laid from two houses he had recently erected near Park Street[373]. In 1861 he was described as a 54 year old "proprietor of houses" and with his wife Hannah, aged 56, resided at the Market House, 1 Park Villas, near the Compass Inn, Taunton, as a servant of the trustees[374].

The house was used as a venue for business functions. Mr. Moore, a chiropodist from Exeter, for example, stayed at Mr. Luxton's Park Street in the last Monday in every month and would remain until

---

[371] Bristol Mercury, Saturday 11th June 1853 records a brief obituary-Aged 53 in Paul Street, Taunton, Mr. James Luxton.
[372] Taunton Courier, Wednesday 25th January 1860.
[373] Bridgwater Mercury, Wednesday 11th April 1860.
[374] Taunton Courier, Wednesday 9th October 1861. William was a Conservative voter.

Thursday to see clients.[375] In 1860 William resigned as Superintendant, and the Market Trustees at their usual monthly meeting in the Guildhall, elected his successor[376]. He donated five shillings in April 1862, to the fund for sculptured figures to be inserted in the eleven niches of the rebuilt tower at St. Mary Magdalene.[377] In 1871 William, 64, and his wife Hannah, lived in Park Street Taunton. William's obituary was listed in the Somerset County Gazette, 1878-July 18th St. John's Terrace, Taunton Mr. William Luxton aged 70.[378] He left his property to his wife Hannah, who by her Will, made 7th August 1878, bequeathed, "two dwelling houses situate near St. John's Church in Taunton …now in the occupation of myself and Mr. Arthur Burridge, Solicitor, to Augustus Chubb."

John and Ann's two youngest sons, were to follow different occupations to their father and elder brothers. The third son John Luxton (c1808 – 1869), who was baptised on the same day as his sister Mary, 4th April 1813, was a hairdresser in Ilminster, where he married Susan White on 16th December 1833. The couple attended the Unitarian Chapel where their four children were baptised. Joseph Luxton (1817 – 1879), the youngest son, became a prosperous grocer and tea dealer in mid-Victorian Bath. I have more to say on them in a future chapter.

It remains to say a little about the four daughters. Sarah baptised at St. Magdalene on 16th June 1805, a teacher in Midsomer Norton, married Thomas Collier, carpenter in Clutton Register Office near Bristol on 31st May 1838. She died of cancer, aged 36, and was buried at St. Vigor Stratton on Fosse on 18th April 1841. Mary, the next daughter, died aged one and was buried at St. Mary Magdalene 17th April 1814. Her sister, Elizabeth (1819-1860) features in a later chapter. Mary Ann, baptised 11th April 1822, was a 29 year old dressmaker, living with her brother James and family in1851. She married William Wilkinson, whip maker, in Old Church St. Pancras on 1st June 1859. They had two daughters. Mary suffered for a year with breast cancer, before dying at her home, 58 Grove Street, Camden Town, on 22nd March 1864.

---

[375] Somerset County Gazette, Saturday 5th October 1857.
[376] Bridgwater Mercury, Wednesday 8th August 1860.
[377] Taunton Courier, Wednesday 16th April 1862.
[378] Somerset County Gazette, Saturday 20th July 1878.

50

JOHN GARLAND LUXTON (1800-1860)
FOREMAN IN TAUNTON SILK FACTORY.

See tree 26

Mention must be made too of John's eldest child, his illegitimate son, John Garland alias Luxton (1800 – 1860) who married Sarah Goodman at St. Mary Magdalene Church on 14th June 1822. The groom signed the register with his name while his bride made her mark. The couple already had a daughter, Caroline, and Sarah was pregnant with their second daughter, Jane. When the 1841 census was taken John and Sarah lived at Upper High Street, Taunton with eight children and records show that they attended the Paul Street Independent Chapel. Nine children were born to this couple in the years between 1821 and 1840. John, a labourer, his wife, Sarah, and their growing family worked in a silk factory in the town.

Silk weaving had been introduced into Taunton from London in 1778, and the industry soon expanded to include the production of Persian sarsnet and crepe. In February 1826 the New Monthly Magazine, noted there were about 1,000 silk looms in Taunton, employing 2,500 persons. The free import of French Silk in the late 1820s led to four hundred silk weavers being wholly or partially unemployed in the town. This resulted in Petitions to Parliament and public subscriptions to help the unemployed. I do not know if John and his family were among the silk workers thrown out of work at this time.

Tragically, Sarah, aged 41, died in childbirth on Christmas Day 1842. The Taunton census for 1851 records that John, a widower, continued to live with his family in Upper High Street. As John Luxton, aged 61, of Woodford's Buildings, he was buried at St. Mary Magdalene on 9th June 1860.

Caroline (1821-1884), the eldest child, born the 24th May 1821, was baptised on 19th May 1823 at Paul Street Independent Chapel, Taunton. She was a 41 year old shoe binder, HighStreet when she married Anthony Mockridge, 46, widower, a mason, at Taunton Register Office on 5th October 1862. In 1871 they were living at Eastbrook Cottage, Pitminster, Taunton but Anthony was away from home. Caroline was caring for William Luxton, aged 6, described as her grandson. William was in fact the illegitimate issue of Emma, Caroline's younger sister. Ten years on they continue to live at the cottage, where Anthony, 65, mason, Caroline is 59 and their daughter Charlotte 29 unmarried laundress with William Luxton 16 "grandson" mason's labourer. Caroline suffered with chronic Bright's disease before she died at Eastbrook Pitminster on the 8th August 1884. Anthony Mockridge, 76 widower, mason, and his daughter Charlotte, 45 laundress were listed at Pitminster in 1891.

Her sister, Jane Luxton (1823-alive 1891) born on 29th December 1822, was baptised at Paul Street Independent Chapel, the same day as her sister Caroline, 19th May 1823. She married Charles Batson, servant, at Taunton Register Office, on 15th February 1846. In 1851 Charles, a groom, and Jane, with two young children, were living in Cann Street, Shuttern, St. Mary, Taunton. Ten years on, Charles a 36 stableman and family were at 2 Tangier Place, Bishops Hull, Taunton. Charles Batson died and was buried 20th October 1862 and in 1871 Jane, his widow, a 44 year old charwoman, and young son continued to live there. However, the same census lists her staying with the family of Alfred Batson, a gardener, and family in Fulham! In 1881 Jane Batson, widow, 54, was a general servant in the household of a 75 year old widow at East Reach in Taunton. By 1891 Jane, 66, needlewoman, was an inmate of the Taunton Union Workhouse.

The third daughter, Mary Ann Luxton (1825-1889), was baptised at Paul Street Independent Chapel, on 11th September 1825. Mary, 27, a silk throwster, Shuttern, Taunton married James Samuel Seaman, whitesmith, in Taunton Register Office on 14th November 1852. An illegitimate son, Thomas Luxton, born in Bristol in 1849, is listed in 1851 living with his mother in High Street, Taunton. When his mother married he changed his name to Thomas Seaman. He married Mary Jane Long at St Mary Magdalene on 10th March 1872 and they had four daughters by time of 1881 St Mary Magdalene census. His mother Mary Seaman, who suffered with diabetes asthenia (i.e. loss of strength), died at 1 Court Upper High Street, Taunton on 29th November 1889.

Eliza Luxton (1827-1872), the fourth daughter, a silk throwster, baptised at Paul Street Independent Chapel on 27th December 1827, lived in Upper High Street when she married William Turner, a cabinet maker, at Taunton Register Office on 29th August 1852. By 1871 the couple were residing at Tangier, Bishops Hull, St John, Taunton where William now blind, was a French polisher. Eliza aged 44 died with breast cancer at Tangier, Bishops Hull on 8th August 1872 and by 1881 William was lodging with his sister in law, Sarah Josling at 7 Hewers Court, St Mary Taunton.

The fifth daughter Sarah Garland Luxton (1830-1883) a silk throwster, born 23rd January 1830, and baptised at Paul Street Independent Chapel on 25th December 1830, was aged 25, and living at Foundry Square when she married Richard Josling 25, bricklayer in St James Taunton on 11th September 1854. The couple who were illiterate sign with their mark.[379] They lived at Woodfords Court, High Street St Mary Magdalene in 1861 but were at Beadons Court in High Street in 1871 and Hewers Court in 1881. Sarah of High Street died, aged 53, from "Stoppage of bowels- Shock" on 13Th September 1883 and her husband Richard died in 1898. They raised her sister Selina's illegitimate son, John Luxton (1860-1944) who served as a soldier in Egypt.

Maria Garland Luxton, the sixth daughter of John and Sarah Luxton of the parish of St. Mary Magdalene, was born July the 20th 1832, and was baptised on December the 25th that year by Thomas Luke, the minister in Paul Street Independent Chapel. She witnessed her sister Sarah's wedding in September 1854. I have failed to pick up her movements after that reference.

Emma Garland Luxton, the seventh daughter, was baptised at Paul Street Independent Chapel, on 25th December 1835. Aged 20 and living in South Street she married Charles Hooper, 20, shoe maker, in Holy

---

[379] Sarah was not alone, her parents and most if not all of her siblings were illiterate.

Trinity, Taunton on 28th October 1866. I have failed to find details of her later life. Emma had an illegitimate son, William Easton Luxton (1865-1921), who was born at Eastbrook, Pitminster on 4th February 1865 and baptised at All Saint's, Trull, Somerset on the 25th June that year. He was brought up by his aunt Caroline Mockridge, and he was a 21 year old mason, when he married Emma Jane Oaten at Pitminster, on 17th June 1885. They had issue three girls and a boy. William 46, a bricklayer in building trade, and his wife Emma 47 had been married 25 years in 1911. They had four children, three of whom were alive including Frances 19 dressmaker who still lived at home in their five room property at South View, Trull. William of Comeytrowe Road, Trull, died 6th March and was buried at Trull 12th March 1921. His widow, Emma Jane of 5 South View, Comeytrowe Road Trull, died aged 88, on the 6th June 1952.

Selina Garland Luxton (1838-1908), the eighth daughter, a silk throwster, was born in January 1838, and was baptised on 16th April at Paul Street Independent Meeting House. She married William Hayman, a shoemaker in St. James, Taunton, on 13th September 1863. In 1901 William Hayman, 59 boot and shoemaker, Selina 64 and their married daughter, Elizabeth Webb, 23 blousemaker, and her husband Charles 20, a cycle mechanic, lived at 30 East Reach, St. James, Taunton. Selina Hayman died at 30 East Reach, Taunton on 4th May 1908. A coroner's inquest on 5th May, recorded that she "died of a fracture of the skull caused by her having fallen in her bedroom. Misadventure." Her illegitimate son John Luxton (1860-1944), soldier in Egypt is the topic of a future chapter.

John Luxton (1840-1905), their only son and ninth child, was baptised at Paul Street, Independent Meeting House, Taunton, on Christmas Day 1840. In 1861 John, a mason's labourer, was a 22 year old lodger with Edward Curry and family at Barings Buildings, High Street, Taunton. Later that year, on the 11th August, he married Mary Jane Smith, at St. Mary Magdalene. John 30, and Mary Jane, 28, lived in 1871 with five children at Fooks Court, Shuttern. By 1875 they were resident in Spread Eagle Court (also called Spread Eagle Yard) in North Street. One day in May that year a boy named Frederick Davis, of Alma Street, left his coat, valued at ten shillings, and a pocket hankerchief worth six pence, upon the door of the coalhouse in the Spread Eagle Yard where he worked. When it was missed a search was made. James Turner had stolen the coat and Jane (ie Mary Jane) Luxton had pawned it for him at Van Trump's shop for 2 shillings and 6 pence. Turner was sentenced at Taunton Petty Sessions to 21 days imprisonment with hard labour.[380] A James Luxton, Spread Eagle Court was commended for his cage of four birds, any variety, not pepper fed, at the Taunton Ornithological Society Show, held in November 1884 in the Parade Assembly Rooms. I cannot identify him and suspect his name maybe a misprint for John (1840-1905).[381]

The family were still at Spread Eagle Court in 1881 with six children, and they were there on the 1885 electoral register but were at Denmark Cottages, Coal Orchard, St James Taunton, with three children by 1891. John, aged 50, was a mason's labourer, Mary Jane 49, worked at a marine stores, George 18 was a carpenter while 13 year old Florry and 11 year old Albert were silk workers. In 1895 they lived in James Street, when in August, Mary was admitted into Taunton & Somerset Hospital, suffering from a fractured rib.[382] John was aged 63 when he died of "Exhaustion Epithelioma of one month" at 25 Stephen Street, Taunton on 7th November 1905. His widow Mary Jane, aged 85 died at 21 Tancred Street Taunton on the 5th March 1929. They had eleven children.

The eldest Sarah Jane Luxton (1862-1948), baptised at Trull 8th June 1862, married Charles Littlejohns, a mason at St Mary Magdalene, Taunton, on 23rd August 1880. In 1881 the young couple with an infant son Charles, were lodging with a widow at 2 Woodforde's Buildings, St Mary, Taunton. By 1901 they lived in Stephen Street, St. James, Taunton, with five children. Charles died in the spring of 1902 and Sarah Jane, a 46 year old widow, married William Smith, a 53 year old widower and plasterer, of 37 Wyeverne Road, at St Teilo's Church, Cardiff on 18th April 1908.

William John Luxton (1864-1924), the second of eleven children born to John Luxton (1840-1905), mason's labourer, and his wife Mary Jane

---

[380] Tiverton Gazette, Tuesday, 1st June, 1875.
[381] Taunton Courier, Wednesday, 5th November 1884.
[382] Taunton Courier, Wednesday 28th August 1895.

Smith, was baptised at St John's Taunton on the 12th June 1864. He was called John in the 1871 and 1881 Taunton census which appears to be the name he was known by in the family. In 1881 he was a 16 year old shoemaker's apprentice, but had settled in Cardiff by 1883, when he married Ellen White, and as a bricklayer and mason, he raised a family. He turns up as a 30 (sic) boarder and mason's labourer in 1901, when he was lodging with his sister Florrie Harris and family at 8 Laburnam Street, St James, Taunton. I have more to say about him in a future chapter.

Eliza born at Shuttern, Taunton, 17th February 1866, was a collar machinist, when she married Henry Ellett, bricklayer, at St. James, Taunton on 23rd September 1883. She died, aged 25, of syncope haemorrhage at her home Denmark Place, St. James Street, Taunton on 12th June 1889. The next sister, Emma, (in photo) was born at Shuttern, Taunton 31st July 1868. On the 11th May 1878, as a nine year old Emma, living with her mother at Spread Eagle Court, was staying overnight in the home of Mrs Brown in the same court when she was criminally assaulted (today we would call it raped) by 20 year old Charles Roberts, a printer. He was found guilty of a vile act and was sentenced to five years penal servitude at the Somerset summer assize held in August 1878, in Wells.[383] Emma married William Arthur Williams, a mariner, at St James, Taunton 9th September 1889 and they had two daughters.

Her sister Alice, born at Shuttern, St Mary Magdalene, Taunton, on 16th August 1870 was a 20 year old silk worker, living with her sister Sarah Littlejohns and family in 1891, just three doors away from their parents in Denmark Cottages. Alice married Edwin Bishop Harding, carpenter, at Barton Regis Register Office, Bristol on 20th May 1893. In 1911 Alice and her husband Edwin, carpenter, were living with six

---

[383] The Western Daily Press, Bristol, Saturday August 3rd, 1878.

young children at 4 Wilton Street, Taunton in a four room house. Two more children had died. Alice died aged 68 at home in 17 Laburnam Street, Taunton on the 3rd January 1939. She had advanced T.B. and suffered an internal haemorrhage. Edwin died in 1942.

The sixth child, a son, was registered as George Edward Luxton, born in North Street, Taunton 17th April 1872. He was baptised, however, as Edward George Luxton at St Mary Magdalene 22nd December 1872. George, was the name he used in adult life. A carpenter, he married Elizabeth Martin from Barnstaple, in Taunton Register Office on 19th May 1895, and we find him in the 1901 census, aged 28, with wife Elizabeth 28, and three young children, living at Court 5, St James Street Taunton. Like many carpenters he became a builder, and by 1906, while he continued to reside in James Street, he had a workshop at Salisbury Road in Rowbarton, when two young boys broke in and stole an air gun worth 3 shillings[384]. He was in partnership in January 1904, when the Taunton planning department approved the construction of two new houses in Salisbury Street, for Messrs Luxton & Rabjohns[385]. George identified four flooring boards in Taunton Police Court in June 1906, when a chargeman at the GWR engine shed, was charged with stealing them from a property Messrs Luxton & Rabjohns were building in Cyril Street[386].

In July 1910 E. G. Luxton was residing at 51 Winchester Street, St. James Taunton when he won first prize, a pair of high grade boots in a newspaper competition set by Day & Martins, Boot Polish[387]. The 1911 census confirms the couple were residing at 51 Winchester Street, in a six room property, with eight off-spring. Four had died and they had been  married 15 years. He was a "carpenter building worker." Edward George Luxton was still resident there on 3rd August 1915 when he attested to serve in the Territoral Force of the Wessex Division of the Royal Engineers. Before joining up, he had worked as a leading

---

[384] Taunton Courier, Wednesday 16th May 1906.
[385] Taunton Courier, Wednesday 13th January 1904.
[386] West Somerset Free Press, Saturday 16th June 1906.
[387] Taunton Courier, Wednesday 13th July 1910.

carpenter for seven years for H. G. Sevills, 153 East Reach, Taunton. Aged 39 years 8 months he was 5ft 9 inches tall, with a chest of 35 and half inches when fully expanded and weighed 134 lbs. With complexion fair, eyes blue, and brown hair, his eyesight and physical development were good. There was a slight hammer toe, second diget on right foot, and a patch of ezema below his right knee. He was placed in the Royal Engineers 508th (Wessex) Reserve Field Company. His Army service was at home from 3rd August 1915 to 16th August 1917, a period of two years and four days.

George suffered a fracture of his left ankle, and his tibia was dislocated, when he was caught by the pole of a cart swinging round. The fibula too was broken lower down and the tibia reduced and placed in a splint. Admitted to the Kent and Canterbury Hospital on the 17th July 1916 he spent 54 days in hospital and he was moved to other places including the Military Hospital at Shorncliffe. A Court of Enquiry, held on 20th July 1916, decided that Lance Corporal Luxton was on duty and was not to blame for the accident. He was discharged from the Army at Chatham on 16th August 1917, as he was no longer physically fit for war service para 392 xvi Kings Regulations. His Military character was very good and his conduct was very satisfactory in all respects. Aged 41 years and 9 months, he was now 5ft 11 inches tall, and was returning home to 51 Winchester Street, Taunton.

The family moved to Barnstaple where he had a workshop in the Kingsley Hotel Yard, Boutport Street. E.G. Luxton, carpenter & joiner, (Silver Badge) advertised that with 30 years experience he could turn his hand to anything in wood-doors, kitchen dressers, kitchen tables, wood bungalows, windows, class cupboards, shelving and greenhouses. His private address was 11 Lansdowne Terrace, Yeo Vale, estimates were free, drop me a postcard for rock bottom prices, I gave my services in 1915, let me have a chance now.[388] He was employed by Messrs Allens of Pilton as a carpenter and for many years he was the chairman of the Barnstaple Woodworkers Association. George died, aged 74, at 4 Pilton Quay, Pilton East on 3rd September 1946, leaving a widow, three sons and four daughters.[389] His widow, Elizabeth, died aged 83, at Sticklepath, Tawstock, Devon 15th April 1955.

---

[388] North Devon Journal, Thursday 6th October 1921.
[389] North Devon Journal Thursday 12th September 1946.

The seventh child, Frederick Luxton, baptised at St Mary Magdalene, Taunton, 25th April 1875, died aged 11 weeks from bronchitis in North Street, Taunton on 10th June 1875. He was followed by Albert, baptised at St Mary Magdalene on 25th June 1876. Sadly, he died in North Street on 26th January 1877, "of convulsions," aged 9 months. A sister Florry, baptised at St Mary Magdalene, 7th April 1878, married William Harris, a hotel ostler, at St James Taunton, on Christmas Day 1898. In 1901 they were living at 8 Laburnam Street, St James Taunton, with a one year old son and her brother John Luxton, boarder, mason's labourer aged 30 (sic). Florrie, was 38, a widow, when she married Sidney Herbert Crocker, 32 gardener, in St. James Taunton, on the 22nd of June 1921. The widow of Sidney Herbert Crocker, army pensioner, Florrie Crocker, died aged 63 of a coronary thrombosis, at 21 Tancred Street, Taunton on 19th January 1941.

Charles the ninth child, baptised at St. Mary Magdalene on 4th July 1880, died aged 11 months at North Street, and was buried at St. Mary Magdalene on 2nd April 1881. Albert, the tenth and final child, was aged 11, a silk worker in the 1891 census when he lived with his parents and siblings in Denmark Cottages, St. James Taunton.

George Edward Luxton (1872-1946), and his wife Elizabeth Martin, had twelve children. James G. Luxton born 1892, was a nineteen year old dairyman, living at home with his parents in 1911. He attended his father's funeral in 1946. The next child, Henry George Luxton, born at No. 5 Court, James Street, Taunton, 15th January 1897 died from "Diarrhoea 7 days Exhaustion" at James Street, aged seven months on 4th September 1897. His sister Amy Jane Luxton, born at No 5 Court Street, on 4th August 1898, died at home from "convulsions three hours" aged 14 months on 27th October 1899.

Frederick Charles Luxton (1899-1965), the fourth child, was born at No. 5 Court, James Street on 5th August 1899. A baker, he married Florence Minnie Barrow, in Barnstaple Register Office, on 9th January 1923. Florence "well known and highly esteemed"[390] was aged 28, when she died at their residence 2 Bradiford, Barnstaple on 8th July 1928. Their eldest daughter, Phyllis Irene Luxton, born at 5 Buller Road, Barnstaple,

---

[390] North Devon Journal, 12th July 1928.

on 7th April 1923, died aged 17 months on 3rd October 1924. Her sister Joan Margaret Luxton, born at no. 2 Bradiford, Pilton East, Barnstaple on 27th June 1924 was a 21 year old spinster, serving in the WAAF, of 17 Vicarage Lawn, Barnstaple, daughter of Frederick Luxton, baker, when she married Ronald Bridger, 27, clerk, of 7 Alexandra Place in Jesmond Parish Church, Newcastle on Tyne, on 20th May 1946. For a second wife Frederick married Mary Jane Jones (nee West) aged 42, widow, at Barnstaple Register Office on 11th September 1929. Frederick of 17 Vicarage Lawn, a retired baker's roundsman was aged 66 when he died in Barnstaple on 7th December 1965. His second wife, Mary, died in Barnstaple on 7th April 1969.

Edith May Luxton, born at 5 Court, James Street, Taunton on the 13th August 1900, the fifth child of George Edward Luxton and Elizabeth Martin, was listed aged 10 in the 1901 census living at home. She married Arthur Edward Paull, a 23 year old horseman, of Pilton, Barnstaple on 23rd April 1923. She attended her father's funeral in 1946. John Luxton, the sixth child, born at no.5 Court, James Street, Taunton, on 30th December 1901, died aged 15 months of whooping cough and pneumonia on 22nd April 1903. Beatrice Luxton (1903-1994) the seventh child, born at 5 Court, James Street, Taunton 11th March 1903, married John Jewell, general labourer, at Barnstaple Register Office 14th April 1928. Beatrice who died in Barnstaple in June 1994, had a least two daughters, Phyllis and Ethel.

Ivy, the eighth child, born at 5 Court, James Street, Taunton on 22nd May 1905, married Frederick William Hill, Lance Corporal in Prince of Wales Volunteers at Barnstaple 18th December 1929. Ivy is in photograph below with her mother Elizabeth Martin. She too attended her father's funeral in 1946. Ivy died of breast cancer, aged 42, on the 14th August 1947 at 4 Reform Street, Pilton.[391]

Her brother, Harold George Luxton (1907-1982), the ninth child, was born in Taunton, on 22nd February 1907. He was a baker and confectioner of Purley, Surrey when he married Margaret Annie Clark, at St Mary's Thatcham, Berkshire on 27th March 1937. Harold, a retired master baker, of 11 Greenlands Road, Newbury, Berkshire, died 8th December 1982.

---

[391] Photograph and information kindly provided by grandson Colin Hill.

His wife Margaret Annie (1912-1997), retired bakery proprietor, died on 9th December 1997. Their son, Roger David Luxton, was born in Newbury, Berkshire and he was living in the town in 1997 at 12 Howard Road. Ethel Lily Luxton, born at 51 Winchester Street, Taunton on 12th January 1909, was the tenth child. Her father was serving as a Lance Corporal in Royal Engineers when Ethel died at the age of eight on 1st April 1917. William George Luxton, the eleventh child, born at 51 Winchester Street, Taunton on 4th February 1911 died of "exhaustion enteritis" on 7th  August 1911 aged six months. Kitty Elizabeth Luxton, the twelfth and youngest child, born at 51 Winchester Street, Taunton on 28th September 1912, married Robert Malcolm England, clerk, of Sticklepath, at the parish church of St. Mary the Virgin, Pilton, Barnstaple, Devon on 17th December 1932. Kitty England died in Barnstaple in August 1991.

There is a great deal more to find out about the descendants of John Garland alias Luxton (1800 – 1860) and his wife, Sarah Goodman. Their grandson William John Luxton (1864-1924), a mason and bricklayer, who established a branch of the family in Cardiff features two chapters ahead.

Another grandson William Luxton (1865 – 1921), was a mason and bricklayer, living at Eastbrook, in Pitminster and Trull in Somerset. Further research is needed on his family. Perhaps the most intriguing member of this branch, however, was another grandson John Luxton (1860-1944) who was born in Taunton in 1860. He served as a soldier in the 1882 Egyptian Campaign and was in the heroic Nile Expedition of 1884 – 1885 which arrived in Khartoum two days too late to rescue the ill-fated General Charles Gordon and his garrison besieged by the Mahdi and his forces. He is the focus of the next chapter.

51

JOHN LUXTON (1860 – 1944), BRICKLAYER IN TAUNTON AND SOLDIER IN EGYPT

See tree 26

John Luxton who served as a soldier in Egypt had a lamentable start to life. He was born in the Union Workhouse, Taunton, on 19th May 1860, the illegitimate son of Selina Luxton, who on the day he was born signed his birth certificate with a cross.

Selina Garland Luxton, his mother, was baptised at St. Paul Street Independent Meeting House, Taunton on 16th April 1838. Her father John Garland alias Luxton (1800 – 1860), a labourer, and later a foreman in a silk factory, was himself the illegitimate son of Mary Garland and John Luxton (1782 – 1837), a carpenter and joiner, who lived in High Street, Taunton. When the 1851 census was taken Selina aged 12, a silk throwster, was living with her father and mother Sarah and family at Upper High Street, Taunton. Ten years later in 1861, Selina, aged 23, and her son, John, aged 11 months, were living with her married sister Sarah, aged 31, and her husband Richard Josling, aged 30, a mason at Woodfordes Court, High Street, St. Mary Magdalene parish.

The name of John's putative father may be obtainable from Poor Law Union records in Taunton. When John was aged 3 his mother, Selina, married William Hayman (1841-1931) a shoe maker, at St. James Parish Church, Taunton on 13th September 1863. By 1871 Selina was a 31 year old laundress, living with her husband William Hayman 29, bootmaker, and their two young sons Henry 5 and William 2, at Reach, East Street, St. Mary Magdalene parish, Taunton. Her son John Luxton, aged ten scholar, was a visitor, staying with his uncle Richard Josling, a 40 year old journeyman bricklayer, and his wife, Sarah 41 laundress at St. Beadon's Court, High Street, Taunton. In 1901 Selina 64, her husband 59, and their daughter Elizabeth Webb, 23, blouse maker, and husband, Charles, a cycle mechanic, were living at 30 East Reach, Taunton. Selina died, aged 70, in 1908, following a fall in her bedroom which fractured her skull.

John Luxton was 19 and a bricklayer, when he enlisted in the 35th Brigade at Taunton on 18th July 1879, and as Private John Luxton (Reg. No. 1238) he joined the 32nd Regiment of Foot (Cornwall Regiment of Foot) at Portland, on the 23rd July 1879[392]. Enlistment papers state he was a single man, 5 foot $5^1/_4$ inches tall with slight physical development. His chest measurement was 34 inches, complexion fresh, eyes grey, and hair dark brown. John bore two vaccination marks on his left arm from infancy and on joining the army he was successfully re-vaccinated with three more. He had no distinctive marks or scar and he was a member of the Church of England. Henry Hayman, his half brother, whose address was not known and his uncle Richard Josling in High Street Taunton were his next of kin.

For the first year and 56 days of his military service, from 21st July 1879 to 14th September 1880, he was posted at Home as a Private in the 32nd Regiment serving with the Second Battalion of the Duke of Cornwall Light Infantry. His commanding officer wrote that his habits were temperate and conduct was fair.

John during his twelve years in the army saw service in Gibraltar, Malta and Egypt. He saw action in the Egyptian campaign 1882 and the more famous Nile Expedition 1884-85.

His medals and decorations included the Egyptian 1882 and clasp Tel-El-Kebir Bronze Star.

John's foreign adventures began on the 15th September 1880 when he was transferred to the 46th Regiment of Foot (South Devonshire Regiment of Foot), and on the same day, he embarked for Gibraltar. He was stationed there for one

---

[392] See his enlistment papers in the National Archives, London.

year 302 days until the 13th July 1882. There followed a short six day spell in Malta, from the 14th July to the 19th July 1882 in preparation for the invasion of Egypt.

The Egyptian Campaign was in response to nationalist riots, which threatened the safety of the Suez Canal. They broke out in Alexandria Egypt in June 1882. Among the victims were fifty Europeans killed and over sixty wounded, the British Consul among them. On 11th July 1882 the British fleet under Admiral Seymour silenced the enemy forts at Alexandria after a ten and a half-hour bombardment.

Nine days later the Prime Minister and his cabinet decided to send an army under Sir Garnet Wolseley, the original of W. S. Gilbert's "Modern Major General."He was a famous fighting general who was severely wounded in the thigh in Burma, and he had lost the sight in his right eye in the Crimea. Wolseley had had an unbroken run of military successes in the Ashanti and Zulu campaigns and Pte John Luxton was in Wolseley's army, when it landed in Egypt on the 20th July 1882. Wolseley, following a long and completely successful night march, surprised and destroyed the Egyptian Army led by Colonel Arabi Pasha at Tel-el-Kebir on 13th September 1882. The British casualties were over 450. A cavalry dash on Cairo followed the rout and obtained the surrender of the remaining enemy forces.

The Nile Expedition 1884 – 85 is better remembered, if only for the film Khartoum, starring Charlton Heston as General Gordon. Misgovernment throughout the vast areas known as the Egyptian Sudan led to a revolt under the leadership of the Mahdi or Messiah. General Charles Gordon was surrounded and besieged in Khartoum. Four months too late, General Wolseley was appointed to command the Nile Expedition for which scarcely any preparation had been made. He reached Cairo early in September 1884, and was not able to start from Wady Holfa until

5th October. For three months, a most gallant army marched and fought its way against time up the 850 mile course of the uncharted Nile, while all England counted its daily steps. It reached Khartoum on 28th January 1885, but the place had been stormed and Gordon killed two days earlier, after a long and heroic defence.

Private John Luxton's military service in these campaigns in Egypt lasted 3 years 59 days, ending on the 16th September 1885. He had been stationed in Alexandria on the 23rd November 1882, Cairo on the 17th February 1884, and Assouan, on the 1st September 1884. From the 10th October 1882 he had received good conduct pay, an extra penny per day, but he is twice listed in his company's default sheet (the reason is not specified), forfeiting his good conduct pay on the 6th January 1883 and again on the 23rd January 1885.

He had escaped wounds and injuries in the fighting but had fallen foul of syphilis. For this he was in hospital for 62 days from 6th May to 6th July 1883. A doctor's note reads "Contagion severe eyes local. No mercury" indicating he was in the primary stage of the disease, which in his case, manifested itself around the eyes but had received no mercury treatment.

John was back in the UK on the 17th September 1885, and on the 23rd September he was passed into the Army Reserve 32nd Regiment at Gosport. He returned to his native Taunton, where he must have had an inexhaustible store of tales to relate to his family and friends, on his exploits in Egypt and the Sudan.

He wasted no time too in getting married. The banns of John Luxton, bachelor 25, bricklayer, residing in the parish of Clayhidon, and Susan Ann Manley 24, spinster of Clayhidon, were called on 18th and 25th October and 1st November 1885 and the couple wed there in St. Andrew's the fifteenth century parish church the next day 2nd November 1885. The witnesses were Ephraim Luxon (1855-1922), an agricultural labourer, and his wife Sarah Ann Trickey who belong to the Clayhidon family. Ephraim's home in Hemyock was named Egypt Cottage which suggests he may have been in Egypt as a soldier when John was serving there.It is likely too that Susan, a Clayhidon girl, knew the couple already. The banns describe John as residing in the parish, not of the parish as Susan is said to be, so I take it he was just there for the required time to be classed as a resident. I note too that he has "invented" a father John Luxton, bricklayer, no doubt to save the blushes of his bride. Susan, born in Hemyock in 1861, was a domestic servant in Wellington, and married in Clayhidon because it was the home of her mother, and step father, Charles and Sarah Wyatt. The couple's only child, Sarah, born in Taunton, in1887, died in infancy. John's syphilis may account for why no more children were born.

Like many soldiers John found it difficult to adjust to civilian life. At Taunton Police Court, on Wednesday 11th April, 1888, John, an (army) pensioner of High Street Taunton, was charged "with having been drunk and riotous in the High Street on the 2nd April." He was further charged with having assaulted two policemen whilst in the exercise of their duty[393]. P. C. Bourne told the court that while he was on duty in High Street, he received a complaint about a disturbance in the Green Dragon Inn. He succeeded in getting the defendant's brother-in-law out of the house, but Luxton still struck his brother-in-law. When the constable ordered Luxton to go away, John struck him in the mouth. The officer had to put handcuffs on him and needed the assistance of a civilian, before he could get him away. In High Street, Luxton kicked P. C. Osment who had come to assist in the arrest.

John told the court that he had, "been four years in Egypt during the recent campaign, and since his return a little drink had affected him. It was the drink that did it but he could not give up drinking." John was fined 10s and 5s costs, and he told the court that he had his money in his pocket but would rather go to goal. His wife created a slight sensation in the court by imploring him to pay the money and the magistrates ordered Luxton to leave the dock to consult with his wife. Afterwards Luxton came up and asked if he may be allowed to pay the money in the course of the day. The Mayor, who was presiding, told him if he had conducted himself properly in court the fine might not have been so heavy.

John appeared in the Taunton Court again in July 1890, when as John Luxton, Batt's Court, High Street, he was summoned for assaulting

---

[393] Taunton Courier and Western Advertiser, Wednesday 11th April 1888.

George Rowe, a rent collector[394]. Rowe said he went to Luxton's house on 2nd July to collect the rent and he heard a man behind him using bad language. He turned around and Luxton struck him in the eye and he had to have it attended by a doctor. Luxton denied knocking Rowe's head against a door and said that Rowe had no authority to collect rent and that he charged too much. He was fined 5 shillings and costs.[395]

At an inquest held in the Taunton and Somerset Hospital, in October 1898[396] Annie Luxton, the wife of John Luxton, bricklayer of No. 7 Court, High Street, identified the body of her uncle Richard Josling, a mason aged 68, an inmate of the Huish Almshouses in Magdalene Street, who had died as the "result of a wound which he had inadvertently inflicted on himself during the use of a surgical instrument." Richard Josling (or Gosling) had brought John Luxton up and it was probably through his influence that John became a bricklayer.

He remained in the reserve 5 years 300 days until the 20th July 1891, when he was discharged from the army with 12 years service. The census earlier that year finds the young couple at 13 Court, High Street, Taunton where they are listed as John Luxton, mason's labourer, born in Taunton, and Susan A.30, sorter in marine stores, born Woolwich, Kent. Somehow Susan confused the census taker, for in 1901, she says she was born in Taunton, and it's only in the 1911 census, that she puts the correct birthplace of Hemyock. The 1901 census lists John 41, now a labourer in a timber yard, his wife Susan A. a laundress, living at Court no. 7, 11 High Street, St. Mary Magdalene parish, Taunton. By 1911 John Luxton, 51, general labourer in a timber yard, and his wife Susan 50, a rag sorter in a marine store, were dwelling in two rooms at 7 Court High Street, Taunton. They had been married 21 years and had one child who died.

The Town Council at the Taunton Borough Sessions held in June 1942 were granted possession of a flat at 3, Lyngford Crescent[397] occupied by John, aged 83, and his wife Ann, aged 81. The condition of the flat

---

[394] Western Gazette, Friday 11th July 1890
[395] Taunton Courier, Wednesday 16th July 1860. The Courier gives the rent collector's name as John Roe.
[396] Taunton Courier and Western Advertiser, Wednesday 5th October 1898.
[397] Taunton Courier and Western Gazette, 6th June 1942 & 30th November 1946.

had been the subject of an unfavourable comment both by neighbours and the Council's Housing Officer. In the opinion of the Medical Officer the couple were unable to look after themselves properly and because of their carelessness the fire brigade had had to be called to attend a fire at the property. The old couple were reluctant to move into an institution and Mrs. Luxton wrote a moving letter:-

"We owe no rent and we do not interfere with neighbours. As we have broken no law we ask that we may end our days in each others company and in our own little home for which we have always been grateful."

The old couple were settled in 1942 in Holmoor House, Trinity, Taunton where John Luxton of 3, Lyngford Crescent, Taunton, retired labourer in a timber yard, died aged 84, on 9th December 1944.Susan Ann Luxton, his widow, was also aged 84, when she died on the 25th November 1946,[398] eleven days after a fall at her ward, at Holmoor House.

---

[398] Taunton Courier and Western Advertiser, Saturday 30th November 1946.

52

WILLIAM JOHN LUXTON (1864-1924) OF TAUNTON, MASON AND BRICKLAYER IN CARDIFF AND FAMILY

See tree 27

William John Luxton, the second child of eleven born to John Luxton (1840-1905) mason's labourer, and his wife Mary Jane Smith, was baptised at St. John's Taunton on 12th June 1864. He was called John in the 1871 and 1881 Taunton census which must have been the name his parents called him by. In 1881 he was a sixteen year old shoemaker's apprentice but he gave up this career and left Taunton.

The seaports of South Wales were expanding rapidly to cope with the growing demand for steam coal mined in the Welsh valleys. Many young West Country folk migrated to Cardiff. Two of these newcomers, William John Luxton from Taunton and Ellen White from Axminster in Devon, both living at 119 Cairns Street, Cathays, Cardiff married by certificate in Cardiff Register Office on Christmas Eve in 1883. He was a labourer claiming to be 21, the son of John Luxton labourer, and Ellen the daughter of John White, a deceased labourer, claimed to be 18. The entry was corrected on the 1th June 1896 in the presence of William John Luxton who informed the registrar that he was in fact19 at date of the marriage and that Ellen was only 15!

William James, a son for William John Luxton, labourer and his wife Ellen was born on 5th June 1884 at 119 Cairns Street, St. John, Cardiff. Elizabeth Harry the babies aunt was present when the poor little fellow died there aged three months of "meningitis convulsions" on 6th September 1884.

William John (1864-1924) and his wife Ellen were living at 30 Hirwaun Street, St. John's Cardiff in the 1891 census where William was a 26 year old plasterer, and his wife Ellen, 22, born Axminster in Devon.

On the 1st and 2nd August 1900 J. Luxton 30 Hirwaun Street, Cathays, Cardiff, placed the following advert in the South Wales Echo-Found, a Rough Dog; if not claimed in three days will be sold.

They were still living there in 1901 when William, was a 36 year old bricklayer, Ellen 32, with two sons, William J, 14, plasterer's labourer and Ernest Bertie, 9 scholar. Ellen of 30 Hirwaun Street, St. John's, Cardiff, was only 34 when she died of pulmonary phthisis on 31st May 1902. She was laid to rest in St John's Churchyard in the centre of Cardiff, on the 5th June 1902.

William John Luxton, a 45 year old widower, and bricklayer, of 37 Wyeverne Road, Cardiff chose another West Country girl, Jane Betty, from Chard in Somerset, for his second wife, and they were married in the Wesleyan Chapel Victoria Street, Taunton on the 10th April 1909.[399] The year before, William's sister, Sarah Jane Littlejohns (1862-1948), was a 46 year old widow also living at 37 Wyeverne Road, when she married William Smith, a 53 year old widower and plasterer, at St. Teilo's, Cardiff on the 18th April 1908.

The newly wed couple turn up in 1911 at 55 Wellington Street, in Canton, Cardiff where William is a 46 year old bricklayer, Jane 42 born Chard, with their sons William John, 24 blacksmith, Ernest Bert, 19 bricklayer's labourer. Most interesting in this census is that his widowed mother, Mary Jane Luxton, who was born in Trull, Somerset is living with the family. She returned to live in Taunton and died in Tancred Street in 1929. No. 55 Wellington Street was a six room property and family members continued to live there until at least 1932. William John Luxton of 55 Wellington Street, jobbing mason, died aged 60 of throat cancer, at 30A Cowbridge Road in Cardiff on the 27th August 1924. His wife Jennie, otherwise Jane Luxton of 28 Llanblethian Gardens, Cardiff, widow, died on 11th February 1937 at 30A Cowbridge Road Cardiff. Administration was granted in Exeter on 2nd April 1938 to May Manning widow, when her personal estate was valued at £84..8..8.

---

[399] Jane Betty's sister, Louisa Betty was the mother of Lilian Elsie Roles.

The oldest surviving son, William John Luxton, (1886-1951), was born in Cardiff on 13th June 1886, and he was admitted as a pupil at Crwys Road School, Cardiff Boys in 1892. He was employed by Cross Brothers Ltd. in Working Street when he married Lilian Streeter of 9 Cardiff Road at Llandaff Cathedral on 15th September 1913. They made their home at 9 Cardiff Road, Llandaff where their first child, "Jack" that is Francis John Luxton was born on 5th September 1914.

William, a blacksmith, aged 29 years and 5 months, enlisted in the Army in Cardiff on 10th December 1915. Placed in the Army Reserve he was mobilised on the 29th April 1916. A proficient blacksmith he was posted as a sapper in L Company of the Royal Engineers on 2nd May 1916 with a Reg. No.166883. William saw four months service with the Royal Engineers 83 Field Company 20th Division of the Expedionary Force in France from 18th November 1916 to 18th April 1917.

But towards the end of that time on the 19th March 1917 he was admitted to No 34 Casualty Clearing Station with valvular disease of the heart and lumbago. Transferred by sick convoy in No 20 Ambulance Convoy to no 4 Ambulance Train Bay he was back in England at the Chatham, Kent Station, on 30th March 1918.

Demobbed on the 9th March 1919, aged 32, he returned to his home at 9 Cardiff Road. Unfortunately, he had developed mitral valvular disease during his army service. It caused a thirty percent disablement and was attributed to his war service. A weekly pension of 5s..3d was granted to him from 10th March 1919, and he was awarded the Victory Medal and the British War Medal.

At some point the family moved house and are listed at 70 Theobald Road, Canton in the 1937 Western Mail Directory. William John Luxton, blacksmith of 70 Theobald Road, who suffered with rheumatoid arthritis, died aged 64 at Llandough Hospital, Penarth on 28th April 1951. In the photograph on last page we see William with Lilian his wife and their children Thomas and Joan in the garden of their home about 1945. His widow, Lilian Luxton, (1889-1957) died aged 68, of a cerebral tumour at home in 70 Theobald Road, on the 22nd November 1957. They had two sons and a daughter and we see Thomas with his sister Joan and brother Jack, taken in August 1942 in the photograph on the next page.

Their eldest son, Francis John Luxton (1914-1971), born at 9 Cardiff Road, Llandaff on the 5th September 1914, was a 21 year old butcher's shop assistant, when he married Emily Cottle, 18, in Cardiff Register Office on 30th March 1936. "Jack" was a van driver of 46 Waterhall Road when he died of a coronary thrombosis at home on 24th December 1971. Their son Raymond John Luxton, born at 152 Cyfartha Street on 14th February 1937, was aged 22, a photo-engraver of Fairwater, Cardiff, son of Francis John Luxton, salesman, when he married Ivy Williams, 23, in St. Catwg's the parish church of Gellygaer, Glamorgan on 21st February 1959. Their three children were Kevin John, born in St. David's Hospital, Cardiff on 13th December 1961, Russell Mark, born in the Miners Hospital, Caerphilly on 2nd July 1965 and Karen Ann, born 25 Lon Isaf, Bondfield Park, Caerphilly on the 22nd November 1967. Russell, 22, box maker, of 25 Lon Isaf, Caerphilly married Jane Waddon, a 21 year old shop assistant, in Merthyr Tydfil Register Office on 31st October 1987. Raymond's sister Jacqueline Elizabeth was born at 30A Cowbridge Road on 10th May 1945, when her father, who worked for a butcher meat importer, was serving as a Lance- Corporal in the Welch Regiment. Jacqueline, aged 20, married Michael William Harfleet 21, panel beater, in St. John's Canton, Cardiff on 26th March 1966. Raymond was living at 25 Lon Isaf Caerphilly when his father died in 1971.

Thomas (1919-2005), the second son of William John Luxton, blacksmith and ex sapper Royal Engineers, and his wife Lilian, was born at 9 Cardiff Road, Llandaff on 5th September 1919. Like his father before him Tom became a sapper in the Royal Engineers. Tom, in photograph below, was injured by a single bullet shot which passed through both knees. Evacuated out of Dunkirk he was admitted to the Queen Elizabeth Hospital, Edgbaston, Birmingham on the 2nd June 1940. He was a 30 year old ironmonger's maintenance fitter, of 70 Theobald Road, Cardiff when he married

Eunice May Cooksley (1923-1989) 26 in St. John's Canton, Cardiff after banns on 25th February 1950. He was still resident there, when he died aged 85, at Llandough Hospital on 7th February 2005. Their daughter, Pamela Ann, born in St. David's Hospital on 28th November 1950, was aged 23 when she married William Kimmis Kelso 25, bus conductor in St. John's Canton on 28th September 1974. Her brother Stephen Thomas Luxton, born at 70 Theobald Road on 12th July 1954, the son of Thomas Luxton, "Bench Fitter, Ironmonger," married twice. He was a 25 year old lorry driver of 70 Theobald Road when he married a divorcee, 30 year old Calinna Marchant in Conway Road Methodist Church, Cardiff on the 10th November 1979. Stephen, the 40 year old licensee of the Rummer Tavern, 14, Duke Street, Cardiff married Kathryn Elizabeth Burnett 24, hairdresser, in the City United Reformed Church, Windsor Place, Cardiff on the 23rd July 1994. Their son Tomas James Luxton was born 1993, followed by Daniel 1995 and Oliver in 1997. Tomas has his own carpet cleaning business in Cardiff and Daniel and Oliver work in the leisure industry. Stephen was living at 5 Clos Creyr, Meadow Farm, Llantwit Fardre when his father died in 2005 but now lives in Splott. David Thomas Luxton, the third child of Thomas Luxton, fitter, and his wife Eunice, born at 70 Theobold Road on the

14th August 1957, still lives there in 2018. He is a taxi driver.

Joan, the daughter of William John Luxton, blacksmith, and his wife Lilian, was born at 55 Wellington Street, Cardiff on the 13th September

1922. She was a 24 year old of 70 Theobald Road, when she married William Alfred John 31, a labourer, in St. John's Canton, Cardiff on 25th January 1947.

Ernest Bertie Luxton (1891-1960), the youngest son of William John Luxton (1864-1924) and his first wife Ellen White, was born in Cardiff on 29th July 1891. Interestingly, he was baptised at St. Mary Magdalene, Taunton on 10th August 1892 when his parents William John, mason, and Ellen were residing at Coal Orchard, probably with relatives. Like his brother before him he was admitted to Crwys Road School, Cardiff in 1898. A bricklayer's labourer aged 19 in 1911, he was living at home with his parents when later that year he was described as a 21 year old "Range Fitter" on his marriage to Lilian Elcie Roles, aged 22 at Cardiff Register Office on the 15th April 1911. Their granddaughter, Joanna relates- There is a funny story attached to the wedding of my grandparents-- Ernest and Lilian-- gran always used to tell me that she and her husband Bert had eloped and that she got married in a raincoat! I was told later by one of my father's cousins on his mother's side that in fact Bert was supposed to have been engaged to his mother at that time-- Aunty Flossie Roles (one of my gran's sisters). Hence they would not have had consent to marry and the need for him to fib about his age. I understand the families did not know about the marriage for a couple of weeks afterwards.

Bert, as he was called, had several jobs when he first married. He was a coal miner for a while and he also had a short spell in the merchant navy. He signed on as a fireman's trimmer on the "Elonville" of Sunderland, at Penarth, on the 21st February 1913, and was discharged on 4th April 1913. He was described as 5ft. 5 and three quarter inches tall with blue eyes, light brown hair with a fresh complexion.

Ernest B. Luxton (1891-1960) Regimental No 454514 served in the Royal Engineers in the First World War. He was present at the Second

Battle of Ypres in early 1915. In the Pioneer Corps his regiment was based at Haverfordwest, where his wife and two eldest sons went to join him in about 1915. He is described as a sapper R.E. (mason) when their third son James was born on 3rd January 1917. At some point he was transferred to the Northumberland Fusiliers (Reg. No.57866). There appears to be some confusion over the military record, which claims that he was promoted to a Lieutenant, but the medal roll lists him as a Private when he was awarded the British War Medal and the Victory Medal. In the Second World War he was a Corporal (in photo on last page) in the Home Guard.

He had moved by 1920 to 46 Wellington Street, Canton, close to his parents' home. By 1937 the family were in Fairwater, Llandaff and were living at 19 Llangynidr Road, Fairwater but moved later that year to 124 Fairwater Grove East, Llandaff. The 1939 Register too lists the family there. He was a 68 year old retired builders' merchant of 124 Fairwater Grove East, when he died of heart disease and broncho-pneumonia at St. David's Hospital, Cardiff on 19th January 1960. Lilian Elsie (sic) his wife, born 27th July 1887 in Cardiff, widow of Ernest Bert, jobbing builder, 18 Chestnut Road, Fairwater, died aged 91, in St. David's Hospital on 2nd November, 1978. In fact her death certificate is incorrect on her birthplace. She was born in Chard, Somerset, and her middle name Elcie is said to be of French origin. The Roles were of Huguenot descent.

They had four sons. The eldest William John Luxton, son of Ernest Bert Luxton, a kitchen range fixer, was born at 33 Coveny Street, Cardiff on the 19th March 1912. On his fifth birthday his father gave him a Bible, inscribed on the flyleaf-"To Jack from Daddy 19th March 1917 Latbury Camp." I say more about him at the end of this chapter. Their second son Ernest Bert, son of Ernest Bertram (sic) and Lilian Elise (sic) Luxton, mason, of 69 Constellation Street was baptised at St Saviour's Roath on 27th November 1913. He was a 17 year old tile slabber for an ironmonger's firegrates department, when he died of a cerebral abscess and cardiac failure at Cardiff Royal Infirmary on 24th November 1930. The third brother James, the son of Ernest Bert Luxton, a Sapper R.E. (mason) was born at 29 Ann Street, Cardiff on 5th January 1917. In the early part of World War Two, James known as Jim, and his fiancee Phyllis Martin, went to live in Knighton, Radnorshire where they worked in an aircraft factory. In 1942 he joined the army and was assigned to the Highland Light Infantry. He did his training in the commando training grounds in Scotland. An armourer, he attained the rank of Corporal, and was offered officers training, but declined it. In 1944 he was part of the ground forces supporting "Operation Market Garden." His unit had been due to be flown into Arnheim but this was cancelled. One of his most vivid memories was driving a jeep up and down the main supply road. On one occasion he overtook a convoy of about six lorries, and a few days later on his return, he saw the lorries were totally burnt out, having been attacked by German tanks shortly after he had passed them. He remained in Germany, as part of the occupation forces, until late in 1945 or early 1946. He was of 124 Fairwater Grove East, son of Ernest Bert Luxton, mason, a 28 year old serving in H.M. Forces, when he married Phyllis Martin, 23, of 8 Adam Street, Cardiff in Llandaff Cathedral on 19th June 1945. James, a retired checker in a brewery, died aged 66 at his home 124 Fairwater Grove on 17th January 1983. His widow Phyllis born on the 5th March 1922, died on the 16th April 1985, leaving a Will.

Kenneth (1919-1970), the fourth and youngest son, was born in Cardiff on the 1st September 1919. As a child he had severe rheumatic fever which caused spinal problems and damage to his heart valves, so he was unfit for military service in World War Two. His skill and knowledge as an amateur photographer, earned him a job as a radiographer in Glan Ely Hospital in the 1950s. He married Beryl Lloyd- Jones in September 1960, and they set up a mini-market in Finchley Road, Fairwater. Sadly Kenneth died in 1970, due to the earlier damage done to his heart valves. Kenneth and Beryl had two children, Jennie born in August 1961 and Kenneth Jonathon Luxton (known as Jon) born 22nd August 1964. Jon Luxton inherited a condition from his mother called Osteogenesis Imperfecta, and as a result of this he uses a wheelchair. For the last 21 years Jon has worked for the Welsh Government on a part time basis, and also runs his own successful consultancy business. He is labour councillor in Penarth and for the last year has been deputy Mayor of Penarth. Jon has been nominated as Mayor of Penarth from May 2018 (to run to May 2019).

William John Luxton (1912-1977), known as Jack, joined the Army in 1942. He was sent to an army camp near Colwyn Bay for his initial military training, and was later assigned to the Royal Signals Corps. In early 1943 he was posted to Sierra Leone, and he remained there about twenty months. In the autumn of 1943 he and his unit 119 Line Squadron Royal Signals, returned to the UK for further training. He took this opportunity to marry Elise Nora Folkes of 26 Greenfield Road, Colwyn Bay, daughter of Alfred John Folkes, solicitor in Llandaff Cathedral on 6th November 1944. The couple had met when they belonged to the same hiking club in Colwyn Bay. Elise was a Londoner, who had been sent to Colwyn Bay,

as a typist for the Ministry of Food. Shortly after their wedding, Jack was sent to the continent and on to Germany, as part of the invasion forces. He remained in Germany for about a year and was billeted with a German family in Hamburg.

William, a master builder, and his wife Elise, had two daughters, Hazel Jane, born at 68 Connaught Road, on 5th October 1946 and Joanna Lilian, born at 8 Hazel Road Cardiff on the 4th June 1950. Joanna was a 28 year old civil servant when she married 27 year old Grantley Thomas Griffiths, a civil servant in St. Augustine's Rumney, Cardiff on Saturday the 19th May 1979. They were living at 8 Heol Dyfed, Birchgrove Cardiff in 1983.

In 1937 William John Luxton was a building contractor at 124 Fairwater Grove East Llandaff and was still listed there in Kelly's 1955 Directory. He was living at 1, Carter Place, Fairwater, Cardiff in 1960. William John Luxton otherwise Jack of 1 Carter Place, Fairwater, Cardiff, died on the 27th March 1977. Probate of his will was granted in Llandaff on 27th May when his personal estate was valued at £3,113.

The photograph of Jack above, was taken in the early 1960s in his original sports shop at 30 Customhouse Street (opposite the Golden

Cross Pub). He moved about 1969 to new premises at Mill Lane. In the early 1970s I met Jack in his Mill Lane sports shop on the corner of the Hayes near its junction with St. Mary Street. His shop was well known and he had a particularly fine display of fishing rods and fishing tackle on sale. We chatted about our Luxton ancestry and he told me his mother was surnamed Roles and that the family came from Chard. The description of Jack as a building contractor, however, did not seem to fit with the man I knew who kept a sports shop. His identity was confirmed by his wife's death certificate. Elise Nora Luxton, aged 52, of 1 Carter Place, Fairwater, wife of William John Luxton, Sports Shop Proprietor, died from breast cancer at the Radiotherapy Hospital, Whitchurch Hospital on 18th September 1962. In photo below, Jack Luxton, (on the right) is in front of his Sports Shop in Mill Lane, the Hayes, Cardiff. On a more poignant note his death was registered in Brecon because he died while fishing at the top reservoir on the Beacons, off the A470.

53

JAMES LUXTON (1827 – 1905),
INNKEEPER AND HATTER IN TAUNTON
AND COACHMAN IN LONDON

See tree 29

James Luxton (1827-1905), the son of James Luxton (1802 – 1853), carpenter and his wife Mary Ann Bennett, was born in Taunton on the 15th July 1827, and he was baptised at St. Georges Catholic Church, Taunton on the 23rd July 1827[400].

James spent his early working life as a steward in the merchant navy. His ticket no.305477, issued in Bristol on 12th May 1848 records that he first went to sea that year. He was 5ft 4inches with brown hair, a fresh complexion and had blue eyes. When unemployed he resided in Taunton.

When his father died, aged 51, and intestate on 30th May 1853, James, his only son and heir, now described as an innkeeper in Taunton, inherited land at Petton, Bampton which had been held in the family for generations.

On 21st July 1975 my brother Ian and I, with the permission of Mr. & Mrs, Tooze, the owners of Petton Farm (formerly Frogpit Farm), examined the farm deeds kept in the vault at the National Provincial Bank in Tiverton. They revealed that James, an innkeeper[401] in Taunton and his widowed mother, Mary Ann Luxton, disposed of the Petton property to Frederick William Collard of No. 26 Cheapside, London,

---

[400] The Roman Catholics opened a chapel in the Crescent in 1822 then in 1860 they built St. George's Church at the top of Billet Street.
[401] The Taunton Electoral Rolls do not list James Luxton Innkeeper and he is not listed in the 1859 Somerset Directory.

Pianoforte manufacturer[402]. By an indenture dated 11th November 1853 they sold for £280, "All that messuage and tenement containing three ground rooms and two chambers and two gardens and one orchard and one acre and a half of meadow ground lying, adjoining the River Batherm ......formerly in the possession of Humphrey Honeyball and now of Joseph Brewer. Together with the dwellinghouse erected on part of the said lands and fronting the turnpike road now in the occupation of William Greenslade, Wheelwright." James signature, and the mark of his widowed mother, are on a second indenture dated 30th December 1854, by which they conveyed the rest of their Petton property to F.W. Collard for a further £270. This property included Corner House, Petton marked as No. 1553 on the 1842 Bampton Tithe map and surrounding fields No. 1552, 1551 and 1550.

---

[402] Sherborne Dorchester and Taunton Journal, Thursday 23rd February 1860. Mr. Collard, the celebrated pianoforte manufacturer has just died aged 88 years. He came to London from his native Wiveliscombe at the age of 17 with a few shillings in his pocket to the house of Clemente the celebrated player and pianoforte manufacturer in Cheapside: after a time he was taken into partnership, and eventually became the sole proprietor of the business.

The property mentioned in these last two deeds, plus a long parcel of land lying to the north side of the road from Skilgate to Waterhouse, containing about half an acre, is listed in an abstract of title held by Alfred Beverley Collard, dated 4th February 1858.

What the Luxtons did with the money they received from the sale of the Petton property is unclear, but James' widowed mother, Mary Ann Luxton, is listed as a Beer retailer in Upper High Street, Taunton, in the Bristol Post Office Directory and Gazetteer 1859 (page 854). She moved to London where in 1861 she was a 58 year old nurse of a week old baby in the household of William Miller, artist and colourman, at 62A High Holborn West Park Finsbury.

In 1871 Mary A. Luxton, widow, aged 71, upholsterer and her spinster daughter, Mary Ann 46, needlewoman lived in George Court, St. Martin's London. She was a 74 year old widow of James Luxton, builder, when she died of congestion of the lungs at 1 George Court, the Strand, on 20th June 1873. Her daughter Mary Ann Luxton was present at the death.

Her son James Luxton, the licensee of the old established and well known Green Dragon Inn, situated in High Street, Taunton, married Mary Ann Waterman Radnage at Ruishton near Taunton on 20th February 1855. This late 20th century photo shows a stagecoach access and from the steep gable it was probably at one time thatched.

He had decided to leave the Green Dragon by the 6th July 1855, when an advertisement in the Taunton Courier,[403] states he was leaving the

---

[403] Taunton Courier & Western Advertiser, Wednesday 11th July 1855.

inn and invited a potential new tenant "to take the stock in trade, furniture, fixtures etc. at a fair valuation." A week later, on the 13th July, Mr. W. C. Brannon, auctioneer, advertised that he had received instructions[404] from Mr. James Luxton "who is about to remove to Bristol,"to sell "the whole of his useful household goods, furniture and stock in trade on Thursday the 19th July. Particulars to be seen in the large bills. The sale to commence at 11 o'clock to the minute, when the whole will be sold without the least reserve."

James may have moved to Bristol to train as a hatter, for he was back in Taunton as a journeyman hatter, when a son, William James Luxton, was born at New Road, Bishops Hull, near Taunton, on the 9th June 1857 and a daughter Mary Ann Raddenige (sic) Luxton, was born at the Pig Market, High Street, Taunton on the 29th January 1860.

The family moved to London where the 1861 census lists James 34 hatter, Mary 34 dressmaker, and their children William James 4, and Mary Ann 1, living at 29 Litchfield Street, Westminster. Their daughter Mary was baptised at Westminster St. John the Evangelist, Drury Lane on the 6th December 1863.

The saying as "mad as a hatter" refers to the mental and physical side effects hatmakers endured from using mercury in their craft. A lot of men's felt hats were made using hare and rabbit fur. In order to make this stick together to form felt, hatters brushed it with mercury. It was extremely toxic and went straight to the brain especially if it was inhaled. Those infected developed neuromotor problems, like trembing. They became paranoid, got angry and had outbursts. Many developed cardiorespiratory problems and died at an early age.

James, no doubt becoming aware of the health danger, had changed his occupation within the decade. In 1871 James, 43 coach labourer, his wife Mary 41 dressmaker, William James 14 lamp-maker, and Mary Ann scholar, lived in Mercer Street, St Martin in the Field. By 1881, James 53, now a coachman, his wife Mary, 51 and daughter Mary Ann Luxton 21 dressmaker, were living at 15 St. Leonards Street, St. George Hanover Square.

---

[404] Taunton Courier & Western Advertiser, Wednesday 18th July 1855.

The daughter Mary Ann became pregnant. Whether this was in London or Somerset is unclear, but she was in the the West Country when the baby was born. Mary Ann Radnidge Luxton, single woman, was living in Norton Fitzwarren when her son Walter James Luxton, was baptised in All Saints the parish church on 14th October 1888. Sadly he died aged four months, and was buried at Norton Fitzwarren on 16th January 1889. Two years later in 1891, James, a 63 year old groom and cabman, Mary his wife aged 61 and their daughter Mary Ann 31 dressmaker, were living at 198 Vauxhall Bridge Road in the parish of St. Margaret and St. John the Evangelist in Westminster.

Sometime in the 1890s the family returned to live in Taunton where Mary Luxton, aged 69, the wife of James Luxton, cabdriver, died from "cerebral haemorrhage apoplexy" at their home in Bridge Street, Black Horse Lane, Taunton on the 8th September 1899. Her daughter Mary Ann was present at the death. James' son, William James Luxton, carriage lamp maker of Pimlico, was summoned at the Somerset County Sessions, in January 1900 to show why he should not contribute to the support of his father, who was chargeable to the Taunton Union. The son offered to pay 2 shillings weekly which the court accepted[405].

Father and daughter were at the same address in the parish of St. James Within in 1901, where James Luxton, 73, retired, was head of house with his daughter Mary Ann 41, factory hand. Ella Davey a 19 year old factory hand was a boarder with the couple. The daughter, Mary Ann Luxton, 41, spinster, dressmaker of St James Taunton, married George Kidner, 40 bachelor, shepherd of Kingston, son of Anthony Kidner, shepherd in the parish church of Kingston, Somerset on 6th April 1902.

James Luxton, a cab driver, aged 77, died at Cuishuish Cothelstone, a village to the north of Taunton on 13th January 1905. Mary Kidner, his daughter, was present at his death. In 1911 Mary, aged 50, lived with her husband George Kidner, 49, in Cushuish Kingston, Taunton. There were no children. George Kidner, an estate labourer, died aged 70 in 1932, and Mary of Manor Cottages, Cothelstone died aged 75 at Holmoor House, Taunton on 30th January 1935.

---

[405] Taunton Courier & Western Advertiser, Wednesday 31st January 1900.

Her brother William James Luxton (1857- alive in 1911), was a 30 year old lamp maker, of 194 Vauxhall Bridge Road, son of James Luxton, coachman, when he married Mary Ann Young, 25, spinster, servant, daughter of George William Young coachman, in St. Stephen, Westminster after banns on the 17th April 1887. The 1891 census lists William, 33 lamp-maker, and his wife "Rose" Luxton, 28, born Salisbury, living at 193 Vauxhall Bridge Road, close to his parent's home. The couple were still together in 1901 when William, 43, lamp-maker, "Rose" 35 and daughter Emily 8, resided at 13 St. Leonard's Street, Hanover Square. Mary Ann Luxton 48, wife of William James Luxton, fish hawker,[406] died of chronic Bright's disease at 13 St. Leonard Street, Pimlico, on the 28th April 1910. In 1911 William, a 54 year old fish hawker, lived with his 19 year old daughter Emily Alice in two rooms at 9 Warwick Place Mews West, St. Georges, Hanover Square. I do not know what became of this son or his daughter but wonder if they too returned to the West Country or emigrated.

---

[406] In 1888 hawkers were legally distinquished from pedlars by a ruling that pedlars travelled on foot, hawkers by horse or beast of burden

54

JOHN LUXTON (C1808/10-1869),
HAIRDRESSER OF ILMINSTER, SOMERSET
AND HIS FAMILY

See tree 29

John the third son of John Luxton (1782-1837), carpenter, and his wife
Ann Webb, was born in Taunton c.1808-10. He was baptised in the
parish church of St. Mary Magdalene on the 4th April 1813, the same
day as his sister Mary. Mary was aged one when baptised and although
no age is given in John's baptismal entry he was probably aged three or
five[407]. I have no details of John's early life and my next reference to
him is in the rural town of Ilminster, set on the banks of the little river
Ile, five miles north of Chard in Somerset. It was there that John, a
bachelor, married Susan White, a native of Ilminster, in St Mary's (next
page) on the 16th December 1833.

The couple were Unitarians, a Congregationalist sect, tracing their
origins to the Presbyterianism of the seventeenth century. Unitarians
were a controversial religious body because of their rejection of the
doctrines of the Trinity and the Divinity of Christ. John and Susan
worshipped in the "Old Meeting," a chapel in East Street, Illminster,
which contained records of the baptism of four of their children[408]. The
eldest child, Mary Ann, daughter of John and Susan Luxton, born on
the 28th October 1834, and baptised on the 28th November 1834,[409] was
followed by John White Luxton in June 1837, William White Luxton,
born on the 22nd July and baptised on the 11th August 1839, and
Elizabeth Winstone Luxton, born on the 24th February and baptised on
the 21st March 1841.

---

[407] The re-baptism of an elder sibling with a new born child was not uncommon in the
earlier part of the 19th century. John may have been baptised previously but I can find
no earlier entry for him at Taunton.
[408] Their Old Meeting House is now an Arts Centre.
[409] See Ilminster Unitarian register Ba/D to 1837 in Somerset Record Office, Taunton.

The Christmas of 1839 was a heartbreaking one for the Luxtons. Their daughter, Mary Anne, died at the age of five from Scarlet Fever, on the 22nd December while William her infant brother, aged five months, succumbed to the disease on Christmas Eve. Mary Symonds of Ilminster who signs the death certificates with her mark, was in attendance at both deaths. The Unitarian Chapel registers in Ilminster record the burial of Mary Anne aged $5^{1}/_{2}$ and William aged 6 months on the same day, the 27th December 1839.

The family were living in Silver Street, Ilminster, near the parish church of St. Mary's with its pinnacled and beautiful tower rising gracefully above the town, when the 1841 census listed John Luxton 30 hairdresser, his wife Susan aged 35, a milliner, and two children, John aged 4 and Elizabeth aged 3 months. Mary White, 13, a servant, was living with the family. Hunt & Co's 1850 Directory & Topography of the Town of Illminster, lists John Luxton, Silver Street, as one of two hairdressers in the town. When the 1851 census recorded the place of birth, John was a 43 year old hairdresser, born in Taunton, while Susan, aged 45, was born in Ilminster. Their thirteen year old son, John, assisted his father as a hairdresser while Elizabeth, aged ten, was a day scholar. Susan's father, John White, aged 74, an overseer, born in Ilminster, lived with the family. A vintage postcard view of Silver Street is below.

Kelly's Somerset Directory for 1861 lists John Luxton as a hairdresser in Silver Street, Ilminster. The census for that year records John aged 51, hairdresser at 57, Silver Street but incorrectly gives Ilminster as his birth place. His wife Susan was aged 54, and John's widowed mother Ann, aged 80, was now dwelling with the family.

It was probably in 1853 when her eldest son James (1802-1853) died, that Ann moved from Taunton to Ilminster, to live with her son John and family in Silver Street. Ann aged 88 "widow of John Luxton carpenter" had been a widow for thirty years when she died of senile decay at the home of her son John in Silver Street, Ilminster on the 6th October 1867. Her given age was 89 when she was buried in the Unitarian Chapel burial ground at Ilminster on the 11th October 1867. Her death was reported in the Somerset County Gazette, Saturday 12th October 1867:-October 6th, at Ilminster Ann, wife of John Luxton, builder, late of Taunton, aged 89.

In June 1865 John, was foreman of an inquest jury at the Bell Inn, Ilminster concerning the death of Elizabeth White, aged five months, who had died in her mother's arms. After viewing the body and hearing evidence from the mother and the post mortem report, the jury returned a verdict of accidental death.[410] John was granted permission by the Ilminster Petty Sessions to sell fireworks in October 1868[411]. A month later, the same newspaper reported that William Best, an apprentice barber in John's employ, had absented himself from the service of his

---

[410] Western Gazette, Friday 16th June 1865.
[411] Western Gazette and Flying Post, Friday 30th October 1868.

master without permission. The court issued a warrant for Best's arrest.[412] The Western Gazette, a year later reported John's obituary:- November 4th, at Silver Street, Ilminster after a few days illness, Mr. John Luxton hairdresser etc aged 60 years.[413] He suffered a stroke which left him paralysed down his right side and died on the 3rd November 1869, according to his death certificate. He was aged 61 and was buried in the Unitarian burial ground at Ilminster on the 9th November 1869.

In his Will, made on the 29th November 1862, John left his wife Susan all the "Shop Goods that may be in my shop & Dwelling house at the time of my decease" and after her death "the same Shop Goods" he gave to his daughter, Elizabeth Winstone. Susan was also to have "the use of all my Household Goods and furniture" which following her demise, were to be divided equally between his son John and daughter Elizabeth Winstone. John was also to have "the whole of my Stock in trade as a hairdresser." John appointed Susan, his wife, the sole executor of his will, which was proved at Taunton on the 2nd January 1871, when his effects were valued at under £200. In October 1873 the local petty sessions granted a licence to Mrs. Luxton of Silver Street to sell fireworks.[414]

The couple's surviving daughter, Elizabeth Winstone Luxton, married Edgar James Parrett, a 25 year old, Ilminster iron monger, son of James Parrett, Grocer, in the "Old Meeting," Ilminster, according to the rites and ceremonies of the Unitarians on the 20th February 1870. The couple had five children but tragically Elizabeth Winstone Parrett, died, aged 38, at her home, Cornhill, Ilminster from "cardiac Dropsy 3 months Exhaustion" on the 18th January 1881. She was buried at the Ilminster Unitarian Chapel on the 24th January that year. See the photograph of the old chapel below.

The census in 1881 reveals that her widowed mother, Susan, aged 74, was a housekeeper to Elizabeth's late husband, Edgar J. Parrett, aged 37, grocer and ironmonger, and a widower with four children at Market

---

[412] Western Gazette and Flying Post, Friday 27th November 1868.
[413] Western Gazette and Flying Post, Friday 12th November 1869.
[414] Western Gazette, Friday 31st October 1873.

Place, Ilminster. Susan did not long survive as a house keeper for she died at Langport Street, Ilminster on the 1st February 1882 from what her death certificate describes as "Morbus Cordis exhaustion 18 months."

Susan's will, made on the 28th July 1879, left all her "money in the West Somerset Savings Bank" to her grandchildren, Bertha Mary Luxton and Edith Parrett in equal shares. After the payment of her debts funeral and testamentary expenses Susan directed that the residue of her estate and effects were to be divided equally between her daughter Elizabeth Winstone Parrett and the children of her deceased son John. The shares due to the children were to be invested during their minority in a Savings Bank.

Susan, in an interesting codicil to her will, made on the 4th November 1881, left her daughter in law Elizabeth Luxton, the widow of her son John, "my best black dress and jacket." Nellie Luxton, her granddaughter was to receive "my long black silk  dress and jacket," while another granddaughter, "Berdie" Luxton was to have her "satin dress best boots best clothes brush and work box." Susan's other clothes were to be "divided between my late son's children" and her books were to go to her son in law Edgar James Parrett. Her will with the codicil was proved at Taunton on the 7th June 1882 by her son in law Edgar James Parrett of Ilminster, grocer, the sole executor when Susan's estate was valued at £181..9s..5d.

55

JOHN WHITE LUXTON (1837-1871) MASTER HAIRDRESSER OF SOUTH PETHERTON SOMERSET AND FAMILY

See tree 30

John White Luxton (1837-1871), John and Susan's son, was a 24 year old bachelor and hairdresser, residing at the nearby small town of South Petherton in Somerset when he married Elizabeth Davies, aged 27, spinster, and scholastic teacher. Elizabeth who was born in Liverpool, was the daughter of Edward Davies, carpenter. Elizabeth was residing in Mount Street, Taunton, when she married John in the Mary Street Chapel, Taunton, according to the rites and ceremonies of the Unitarians on the 30th January 1862. Both signed the register and were witnessed by John's sister, Elizabeth Winstone Luxton, and his uncle William Luxton (1807-1878), a builder in Taunton.

The newly weds settled in South Petherton where five children were born, beginning with a daughter Ellen on the 1st March 1863. There followed William Joseph Luxton born on the 20th November 1864, Bertha Mary, born on the 20th August 1866, Kate Luxton, born on the 10th January 1869 and John Harold Luxton born on the 19th June 1870. Ellen and Bertha Mary, two of the daughters, were baptised at the Unitarian Chapel in Ilminster on the 31st May 1863 and the 18th May 1873 respectively.

John White Luxton advertised in the Western Gazette, Friday 24th November 1865:- Sacks lent on hire by the West of England Sack Company Limited at halfpenny per sack per week. Agent for South Petherton - J.W. Luxton Agent for the Caledonian Fire and Life Insurance Company.

Penny readings were exceedingly popular all over the country in the mid 1860s. It was a form of popular entertainment that arose in the middle of

Victoria's reign, consisting of readings, music and singing. John Luxton was one of five readers, when the sixth in a series of Penny Readings, took place in mid January 1866 in the new school room in South Petherton "which was again crowded although the weather was very unfavourable." A scene from The Merchant of Venice was capitally given by Mr Luxton. He was also one of the members of the Glee Union that sang while the parish organist, playing on the piano, sang in character "The Broken-hearted milkman," which was encored. The proceedings terminated with the singing of the National Anthem.[415] Mr Luxton sang John Brown in capital style at the February reading and there is record of him singing and reading in penny readings held there in 1864 and 1867.

The 1871 census finds him a hairdresser, living at St James Street, South Petherton with his wife Elizabeth, and five young children. His mother Susan 64, who lived with them, was also a hairdresser and kept a toy shop. John White Luxton, master hairdresser, in South Petherton, suffered with cardiac disease for ten years. Struck down with pneumonia for a week, he died at the early age of 33 on the 5th April 1871. Susan, his widowed mother, was present at his death. Mrs Luxton acted as an agent for S Lazenbury who ran a Dyeing and Glazing establishment in East Street, Bridport.[416]

In 1881 John's widow Elizabeth, aged 45, was a certificated schoolmistress, living at Pensford Hill in the village of Pensford, Somerset, which lies south of Bristol. Three children, William aged 16, a "Page out of employ"," Kate aged 12, and John 10 were scholars, living with their mother. Bertha Mary Luxton, another daughter, was a 14 year old nurse, living in the house of George Langford, a jeweller in Pensford.

Ellen, the eldest child in 1881, was an 18 year old unmarried lodger and draper's cashier, living in the house of Alfred Templar in the parish of St. Peter's Bristol. A 23 year old spinster, of 29 Bathwick Street, daughter of John White Luxton, hairdresser, she married Joseph Goldsworthy 29, time-keeper of Hendford, Yeovil in the parish church

---

[415] Shepton Mallet Journal, Friday 19th January 1866 & Western Gazette 12th January 1866.
[416] Bridport News, Friday 17th November 1871 and in other issues.

of St. John the Baptist, Bathwick, Somerset on the 9th October 1886. Her husband had joined the Dragoon Guards in 1874 and had served a spell in the Army.

In 1891 Elizabeth Luxton, widow, 55, school certificated mistress, lived in the village of Salford, Chipping Norton, Oxfordshire with her unmarried daughter Kate 22, a dressmaker. Ten years later in 1901 Elizabeth, a 65 year old widow, and her daughter Bertha Luxton, a 28 year old assistant schoolmistress, were visitors staying at the Duke of York Inn, Middleton on Hill in Herefordshire. Herefordshite Directories list Mrs Luxton (i.e. Elizabeth) as the schoolmistress at Puddleston Herefordshire in 1900 and 1905.

Bertha Mary Luxton (1866-1945), a 24 year old single woman in 1891, was the assistant mistress at the National School at Pound Green, Kingsnorth, Kent. As we noted earlier, she was with her mother in Herefordshire in 1901. In 1911 Bertha, a certificated schoolmistress, aged 44, was teaching at Latton Cricklade in Wiltshire. Elizabeth, her mother, a 75 year old retired schoolmistress was living with her.

Bertha of the Rest, Noos Mayo, Revelstoke, Devonshire, spinster, died on the 22nd October 1945 at the City Hospital Plymouth. Probate was granted in Exeter on the 11th December 1945 to her sister Kate Lock, widow and nephew Donovan Grant Luxton, motor engineer when her personal estate was valued at £543..18..7d.

Her sister Kate (1869-1960), in 1901 aged 30, was a domestic nurse visiting the family of Edward Jones at 1 Bromley Lane, Kingswinford, Staffordshire. Kate Luxton 36, spinster, of 59 Park Avenue, daughter of John White Luxton (deceased) accountant, married Albert James Lock, 30, bachelor, Sergeant 4th Dragoon Guards, Richards Castle, Ludlow, son of Robert Henry Lock, farmer in the parish church of St. Augustine, Kingston on Hull on the 19th August 1905. Her husband, a butcher by trade, had joined the Army at Shrewsbury on 17th March 1896. He was promoted a Corporal in 1900 and was a Sergeant in 1903. He completed his twelve years in the Army and was discharged on the 23rd April 1908. In 1911 Kate, and her husband, now a prison warder, and three young children were residing in St. Peter's Close, Hereford. Kate Lock, aged 91, widow, died at 27 Manor Road, South Norwood, Croydon on 18th September 1960.

Elizabeth Luxton, a widow for nearly fifty years, was living at School House, Warkleigh, Umberleigh, Devon when she died aged 84, at Umberleigh on the 18th April 1920. Administration of her estate valued at £72..19..6d was granted on the 3rd June that year to her surviving son and one of the next of kin, William Joseph Luxton, of 5 Thornhill Road, Plymouth, commercial traveller.

William Joseph Luxton (1864-1945), the eldest son, was a commission agent for the "Rizene Food Company." A portion of his premises at 6 Nelson Street, Bristol were destroyed and the rest "slightly damaged by water but not sufficiently to check business," when a massive fire in March 1891, destroyed the Albion Glass Factory warehouse in Rupert Street[417]. He was in his office writing at the time, and "mistook the crackling of the timber for the fall of rain but he had soon to make a speedy exit for his personal safety."

He was a 26 year old bachelor and Commission Agent, living at 152 Cheltenham Road, Bristol when he married Augusta Sarah Grant 22, spinster at St. Catherine's Church in the parish of Ventnor, Isle of Wight on the 8th October 1891. The couple settled in 152 Cheltenham Road, Bristol where William, a commercial traveller, made a wide circle of friends. An active Liberal, he was chairman of the St. Paul's branch of the Bristol Operative's Liberal Association. Just before his marriage in October 1891, he presided at a dinner in the Liberal Club in Corn Street, Bristol when he was praised by the toast-master as "a capital fellow, and as a politician, a thorough going and uncompromising Radical (applause). Mr Luxton had done good service as a Liberal in Bristol and especially in St. Pauls." His friends presented him with a handsome marble time piece, accompanied with an address, to celebrate his forthcoming marriage.[418] William was an admirer of W. E. Gladstone and he gave his eldest son Harold, the middle name Ewart, in honour of the great statesman[419]. When the Somerset Agricultural Show was held at Glastonbury in May 1892, W.J. Luxton, the local representative of

---

[417] Western Daily Press, Tuesday 17th March 1891 and Bristol Mercury, Tuesday 17th March 1891.
[418] Western Daily Press, Wednesday, 7th October 1891.
[419] Western Morning News, Thursday 9th June 1938. See his letter in praise of Gladstone.

Orlando Jones, starch makers to the Queen, ran their stand[420]. On 12th January 1894 he advertised the sale of a four wheel Coburg Cart, to suit Grocer or baker, also a set of harness. Then on the 24th October that year he advertised the sale of a Grocery & Provisions business for £110, in a splendidly fitted double fronted shop with marble counters in the main thoroughfare, Bristol.[421]

In December 1899, when they learnt he was moving to Plymouth, friends invited him to a dinner where he was presented with a chiming clock[422] and an address signed by his many friends. In 1901 the Plymouth street directory lists Wm J. Luxton, residing at 5 Thornhill Road. The couple were still there to celebrate their Golden Wedding which was announced in the Western Morning News-Luxton-Grant. October 8th 1891, at Ventnor, W. J. Luxton to Augusta S. Grant, Present address 5 Thornhill Road Plymouth.[423]

William Joseph, was an 80 year old retired commercial traveller, when he died from heart disease at 5 Thornhill Road Plymouth on the 6th November 1945. Following William's death their home was advertised for sale by auction at the Law Chambers, Princess Square, Plymouth on Thursday 23rd May 1946. The property was described as "the well-built freehold residence 5 Thornhill Road, containing two reception rooms, five bedrooms, bathroom W.C. kitchen scullery and usual offices. Garden at rear with entrance to lane."[424] His widow Augusta Sarah Luxton of 70 Bushey Hall Road Watford, Hertfordshire, died on the 10th September 1954. Administration of her personal estate valued at £423..5..6d was granted in Exeter on the 18th October to her son Donovan Grant Luxton motor engineer.

The couple had two daughters born in Bristol. Gladys Augusta Luxton was born at 152 Stokes Croft Road, Bristol on the 31st October 1892, and her sister Doris Isabel was born at the same address on the 24th May 1894. Gladys married Ernest Walker Dexter, wireless engineer,

---

[420] Western Gazette, Friday, 13th May 1892.

[421] Western Daily Press, Friday, 12th January & Wednesday 24th October 1894.

[422] Western Daily Press, Monday 18th December 1899.

[423] Western Morning News, Thursday, 9th October 1941.

[424] Western Morning News, Thursday 23rd May 1946.

Roath, Cardiff in the parish church of Emmanuel, Compton Gifford, Plymouth, Devon on the 1st August 1922. Her sister Doris Isabel married Joseph Charles Wiggs, a 33 year old railway employee of Bushey Hall Road, Watford, in the same church on the 28th June 1924. Joe Wiggs was a well known Herts cricketer. He had served as a lieutenant in the Berkshire Regiment during the First World War and for a time had been a patient at Hyde Park Military Hospital.[425]

The couple also had at least two sons born in Plymouth. Harold Ewart Luxton, the eldest, born at 5 Thornhill Road, Mannamead, Plymouth on the 11th October 1901, was baptised in Emmanuel Church on 12th October 1902. He first went to sea as an apprentice in 1918 and he qualified as First Mate on 18th December 1924 and a Master Mariner on 25th February 1927, initially with the Chellow Steam Navigation Company and later the Clan Line. His merchant seaman records reveal that he was 5ft..6inches tall, with hazel eyes, light brown hair and a fair complexion. There was a scar on the centre of his forehead.

He married Nora Endicott, third daughter of Mr. and Mrs. E E Endicott of Hartley, Plymouth at Emmanual Church Plymouth on 31st May 1929, and they dwelt at 24 Devon Terrace, Mutley, Plymouth but Nora died aged 25, of cardiac failure at Charlton Nursing Home Plymouth on the 12th June 1930. The administration of her personal estate, valued at £986..8..8d, was granted in London the 30th July to Harold Ewart Luxton, merchant service officer. Kelly's Directory 1930 lists Harold Ewart Luxton living at 24 Devon Terrace, Mutley, Plymouth and beer retailer at No 6 William Street. In 1930 Harold established The Chocolate Store at 34 William Street, Devonport.[426] His newspaper advert reads:-

"A Box of Chocolates?" A fully stocked confectioner's shop, situated on one of the main routes to an amusement centre, is of great convenience to theatre and kinema goers. "The Chocolate Store,"taken over in William Street, Devonport, just over a year ago by Mr. Luxton is just such a convenient shop.

---

[425] Western Morning News, Friday 27th September 1929.
[426] Western Morning News, Monday 19th October 1931.

He was a 30 year old widower and confectioner of 34 William Street, Devonport when he married Hettie Bailey (1898-1981), a 31 (sic) year old spinster, at the Register Office, Devonport on the 20th July 1932. The newly weds had a daughter, Heather Celia Luxton, born at Devonport on 23rd April 1933, who died, aged 69, in Colchester on 14th July 2002.

By 1936 Harold was the licensee of the Steam Reserve Inn, William Street, Devonport.[427] Kelly's Plymouth Directory 1937 also lists Harold Ewart Luxton as a beer retailer in William Street Devonport before the war.

Then he re-embarked on his career as a mariner, when on the 7th November 1937, he became second officer on the "Seven Seas Spray," at Swansea where it was loading coal for Valencia in Spain.[428] He witnessed his brother Don's wedding in Plymouth on the 9th December 1944. He later moved to Colchester, in Essex and he was a retired master mariner when he died at his home 13 Hanover Court, Walton on the Naze, on the 16th March 1973. His widow Hetty, born on 6th March 1898 in Tavistock, Devon, died at her daughter's home in Kirkby-le- Soken, Essex on 9th September 1981.

Donovan Grant Luxton, the youngest son, was born at 5 Thornhill Road, Charles, Plymouth on the 29th June 1904, and he was baptised at the parish church of Emmanual in Compton Gifford. From the electoral register we locate him in 1926 at 5, Cornmarket Street, Great Torrington

---

[427] Western Morning News & Daily Gazette, Tuesday 28th July 1936.
[428] Western Morning News, Monday 8th November 1937.

and he was in Paignton in 1930/1. He is listed as a motor engineer at 6 Coburg Street in Plymouth in the 1937 Directory and his garage was on the corner with Milton Street. Press adverts put him there in 1933 and 1941.Donovan was still at Coburg Street during the war but the area was very badly hit during the blitz and although the house Donovan lived in was still standing at the end of the war, it was cleared in the early 1950s for redevelopment. A press advert for 26th September 1946 lists Luxton's Garage in Princess Street but by 12th September 1950, Don Luxton's Garage had re-located to Gibbon Lane, Sherwell, Plymouth and The Plymouth Directory for 1953 records that Don Luxton, motor engineer, had moved to Gibbon Street. An advert of 19th September 1950 is typical:- Motor Cars etc. for Sale. Bargains-1937 Austin 12 four door £310; 1936 Morris 8 4 door £200, 1935 Austin 10, very reliable £135. All taxed ready to drive away. Exchanges. Don Luxton's Garage, Gibbon Lane, Sherwell, Plymouth.[429] The electoral register 1970-75 lists Donovan Grant Luxton at 12 Wellington Street but he is not listed there in 1976.

Donovan, a 40 year old bachelor and motor engineer, of 5 Thornhill Road Plymouth, married Sybil Reed, 26, spinster, Wren W.R.N.S. of 5 Cheltenham Place, Plymouth by licence at the Register Office, Plymouth on the 9th December 1944. Sybil was already pregnant and a son Christopher Marcus Paul Luxton was born at North Friary Nursing Home, Plymouth on the 29th March 1945. Don was on the "juice", however, and the couple were living with his parents. They divorced about 1956 and Sybil moved to London with her son Christopher. Don remained in Plymouth and was a retired motor mechanic, living at 36 Clifton Street, when he died aged 72, in the Freedom Fields Hospital Plymouth on the 13th May 1977. Sybil in her mid 80s in 2002 was in a Home while her son Christopher, a chemical engineer, and his wife Brenda live in Gravesend Kent. They have a daughter Paula Jane Luxton.

---

[429] Western Morning News, 19th September 1950.

56

SERGEANT JOHN HAROLD LUXTON (1870-1901) OF THE IMPERIAL YEOMANRY KILLED AT VLAKFONTEIN TRANSVAAL IN SECOND BOER WAR

See tree 30

John Harold Luxton (1870-1901), the youngest son of John Luxton, Master hairdresser, and his wife, Elizabeth Davies, was baptised at South Petherton on the 12th July 1871, the same day as his older siblings, Joseph and Kate. He was living in Leominster, a commercial traveller, well known in Bristol, where he was a member of the Commercial Travellers' Club and the Bristol Rugby Club before he became a soldier in the Second Boer War (1899-1902). This was a campaign in which the British tried to annexe the Boer Republic of the Orange Free State and the Transvaal. It proved to be the longest and most expensive campaign fought by the British between 1815 and 1914. Twenty five thousand Boer, twenty two thousand British and twelve thousand African lives were lost. Serious weaknesses were exposed in British military tactics. Redvers Buller, the general commanding the British, suffered early reverses in the war and he made an appeal to the government in 1900 to raise a volunteer force of ten thousand mounted infantry who could "ride and shoot like the Boers."

In response to his appeal the Imperial Yeomanry was created on the 24th December 1899. It was a British volunteer cavalry based on members of standing yeomanry regiments but also contained a large contingent of middle upper class volunteers. In late January 1901 John underwent a qualifying examination at the Queen's Hotel, Cheltenham, to join the Second Contingent of the Imperial Yeomanry. One of thirty volunteers from Gloucestershire he was taken to the riding school in Regent Street where his riding skills were tested. He then proceeded to the rifle shooting range at Seven Springs where each man had five shots at the rifle butts from a distance of 300 yards.

Those successful were conveyed back to the Queen's Hotel to be medically examined and if fit were sworn in and attested. John passed and with other successful recruits proceeded to Aldershot to be trained and equipped. The successful candidates were insured for £250 each out of the Gloucester County Fund raised the previous year.

John Harold Luxton as a trooper in the new fighting force, was equipped with a khaki field service uniform, and because he was a horse soldier he wore spurs, a cavalry style bandolier, riding breeches and puttees wound from knee to ankle. He wore a slouch hat and also the cavalry pith helmet which had an elongated blunt back shape. This proved efficient in protecting against being struck on the back of the head. This hat, made from "cork pith" covered in cotton twill and a cotton turban, was often "dunked" in water, before wearing, to create an evaporation effect for cooling the wearer.

John in the 48th Company (North Somerset) 7th Battalion Imperial Yeomanry, was in the Second Contingent, which received extremely poor training before being shipped aboard the "Arundel Castle" to South

Africa. His 48th Company was posted to Klerksdorp in the Transvaal, and it spent the whole of its service in the Transvaal where it took part in some of the severest fighting of the later stages of the war. There John soon proved his worth as a soldier, and in a little over three months, was promoted to Sergeant. From April to November the 48th Company were continually on the trek chasing and fighting the Boers. Their march during the month of May was continually harassed by snipers. The Boers who were virtually all mounted infantry would strike fast in the open veldt behind enemy lines and move away again quickly.

John was in a column from Naauwpoort, under Brigadier-General H.G Dixon, consisting of 230 men from the 7th battalion and other soldiers clearing farms along the line of a march in a wild inhospitable region when they arrived at Vlakfontein, a farm in the Koster district on the 28th May 1901. Dixon was searching for buried guns but the information he had been given proved to be false. That night of 28th May a veldt fire was deliberately started by the Boers and by the morning of the 29th it was blowing directly towards the British camp. It extended for about one and a half miles and undercover of the smoke from the grass fire which was raging Kemp, one of the most daring of the Boer commanders, and his 500 hundred men, were able to come close to the British flank.

In the British camp that morning, the order was given for all mounted troops to parade at 8 A.M. with stripped saddles (no wallets overcoats and nosebags with rifle bandolier and bayonet only). They were ordered to advance, well spread out in skirmishing order, directly towards the veldt fire. When they were a little distance from it they dismounted and the horses were sent to the rear. Trooper Sid Clay of Weston-Super-Mare, in a letter[430] to his brother wrote:- "The Boers had us like a rat in a trap. The artful beggars caught the veldt on fire in front of us and the 48th ...advanced, as we thought to clear them out... We got to about a hundred yards from the fire ... We were laughing and chatting, not thinking there was such a force behind that fire, when, all of a sudden, out they slipped, hundreds of them. We had not got a chance."

---

[430] Bath Chronicle and Weekly Gazette, Thursday 18th July 1901

Suddenly the Boers were galloping all over the place, and were shooting from the saddle. Their bullets roared down like hail, and they were so close, fifty British soldiers were dropped at the first volley.

Another survivor, Trumpeter A. D. Love wrote to his mother in Bristol:- "Luxton, Logan, Gardener and Lee … got a couple of shots in" before they fell in the storm of bullets. The Boers quickly snapped up Dixon's rear-guard and captured two guns. Dixon's fellow commanders lumbered up to reinforce him with pompoms, maxim guns etc. Within a short time they recaptured the two guns and drove the Boers off.

Sergeant Love, in his long letter[431] already quoted says:- "Then came the most touching scene…this was bringing in the dead and wounded. I found my chums and Sergeant Luxton shot through the head…" The British had lost six officers and fifty six men killed and over a hundred wounded while the Boers had forty nine men dead on the field. The next day there was an armistice to bury the dead. At nine o'clock that Thursday night the whole British column retired without a sound, travelling twenty miles to get back to their base camp by next morning. The British wounded were left in the field in charge of the R.A.M.C. The following morning an army of 2000 Boers under Koos de la Rey surrounded where the British had been and the wounded were allowed to go in wagons to Kruggersdorp.

The administration of the estate of Sergeant John Harold Luxton who was killed in the action, valued at £250, was granted on the 14th October 1901 to his widowed mother, Elizabeth Luxton of Puddleston, Herefordshire.

The Hereford Times for Saturday 29th June 1901 under a column in the Transvaal War carries an obituary on Sergeant Luxton:-

Herefordshire Man Killed.
Sergeant J.H. Luxton, of the 48th Company Imperial Yeomanry, who was killed at Vlakfontein on May 29th, was the youngest son of Mrs E. Luxton, schoolmistress, Puddleston, near Leominster. He went as a trooper, and got on so well that he was promoted to sergeant in a little over three months.

---

[431] Gloucester Citizen, Thursday, 11th July 1901

The following resolution was passed by the members of the Bristol branch of the United Kingdom Commercial Travellers' Association (U.K.C.T.A.) on June 22nd 1901 at the Royal Hotel, College Green, Bristol (headquarters of the branch). It was proposed by the Chairman (Mr. D. Beak) and seconded by Mr. F. H. Strong "That a very sincere vote of condolence and sympathy be sent, on behalf of the Bristol branch of the U.K.C.T.A. to Mrs Luxton in the loss she has sustained by the death of her son in South Africa, whilst serving his King and country as a Volunteer in the Gloucestershire Yeomanry."

Sergeant John Harold Luxton, Service No.21203 of 7th Battalion Imperial Yeomanry was awarded the Queen's South Africa Medal with clasps for Cape Colony, Orange Free State, Transvaal & South Africa 1901. He is commemorated on a plaque in Hereford Cathedral, and on a tablet sited on the north wall of the north transept, of Wells Cathedral in Somerset.

57

JOSEPH LUXTON (1817 – 1879)
GROCER AND TEA DEALER IN BATH

See tree 29

Like the formidable Dr. Johnson and the celebrated Welsh bard, Iolo Morgannwg, I am an ardent tea drinker. I take great pleasure from my everyday cup of P.G. Tips and on a summer's afternoon I luxuriate in a cup of Earl Grey. This is why it intrigued me to learn about my kinsman, Joseph Luxton (1817 – 1879), who thrived as a grocer and tea dealer in mid 19ᵗʰ century Bath.

The son of John and Ann Luxton, joiner, East Street, Taunton, Joseph was baptised in the imposing St. Mary Magdalene Church on 23ʳᵈ February 1817. Joseph and his sister Elizabeth born 1819, were settled at 8 Saville Row, Bath, when they celebrated a double marriage in St. Swithin's Church, Walcott on 30ᵗʰ January 1844.

Their late father, John Luxton (1782 – 1837), was a carpenter and joiner when his eight children were baptised in Taunton, but it is evident that in his later career he developed his skills to become a builder for this is how he is described on Joseph's and Elizabeth's marriage licences.

The first wedding to be celebrated was Elizabeth's to Thomas Burrow, bachelor, and confectioner, of 12 Peter Street, Bristol. Joseph described as a grocer of 8 Saville Row, followed his sister to the altar where he married Sarah Howell, spinster of 6 Harley Street, daughter of John Lloyd Howell, gentleman. The double marriage was reported in the Bath Chronicle:- At Walcot Church, by the Rev. S. H. Widdrington, Mr. Joseph Luxton of Saville-row, grocer, to Sarah, 24, daughter of Mr. J H Howell, Harley-street; also Mr. T Burrows of

Ilminster, to Elizabeth, eldest daughter of the late Mr. John Luxton, of Taunton, builder.[432]

By 1871 Thomas and Elizabeth Burrow had a tailor and draper business at Stapleton Road, Bristol. Elizabeth, wife of Thomas Burrow, tailor, died of bronchitis exhaustion at 7 Blackbirds Place, Bristol on the 8th September 1880.

Joseph Luxton was included among the gentlemen sworn on the Grand Jury at the mid-summer sessions at Bath, held in July 1853.[433] He advertised regularly in the Bath Chronicle. This one of Thursday 21st March 1867 was for a cook-Wanted, a strong active Young Woman who understands Plain Cooking, and would have to Assist in the Housework.-Apply to Mr. Luxton, Grocer, Saville Row. Apart from recruiting staff he was an agent too on the behalf of customers and the following is an example:-For Sale, a First Class Piping Bull-Finch, apply to C.H.C., Mr. Luxton's Grocer etc Saville Row Bath.[434]

In November 1853 Sarah Ball, a young girl in service, came in Joseph's shop and asked for a quarter pound of spiced nuts for a customer, Miss Sims, with which he served her. However, it was ascertained that she had not been sent by Miss Sims and when the girl appeared in court she was severely admonished by the bench.[435] On Monday 18th July 1867, Joseph heard the wail of a dog, and on looking out of his shop window, saw that a man had fastened a large iron lock to its tail. The dog was in great pain, and was frothing at the mouth, until the lock was removed by a compassionate by-stander. In court Joseph was praised by the magistrates for giving evidence which led to the punishment of the culprit.[436]

The Bath Street Directory of 1846, lists Joseph Luxton as a grocer and tea dealer, at 8 Saville Row. He was still resident there when the 1851 census described him as Joseph Luxton, 32, grocer and his wife Sarah aged 31 who was born in Bath. They were employing a live in servant,

---

[432] The Bath Chronicle, 1st February 1844.
[433] The Bath Chronicle, Thursday 14th July 1853.
[434] The Bath Chronicle, Thursday 28th January 1864.
[435] The Bath Chronicle, Thursday 24th November 1853.
[436] The Bath Chronicle, Thursday 25th July 1867.

Susan Fry, aged 26, who came from Corsham, Wiltshire. Twenty years later when the 1871 census was taken, Joseph aged 53, grocer and tea dealer, and his wife Sarah, aged 52, were residing at 6 Bennett Street. However, the Bath Street Directory for 1870 – 1871 makes it clear that Joseph still retained his family grocery at 8 Saville Row[437]. At the quarterly meeting of the Bath Town Council in August 1871, the lease of No. 6 Bennett Street, was renewed to Mr. Luxton for £1060 for the term of 75 years at an annual rent of £5.[438]

Sarah, who suffered from "softening of the spinal cord" for 12 years, died aged 59 at 6 Bennett Street, on 2nd June 1878. Joseph, who lived on another year, died at 6 Bennett Street on 5th June 1879. The Bath Chronicle carried a single line obituary – June 5th at 6 Bennett Street, Joseph Lucton (sic) aged 60.

Joseph and his wife Sarah had no children. In his will, made on 15th March 1879, he bequeathed, Elizabeth Burrow, his married sister a £300 legacy but made no bequests to other members of the family. Further legacies were £100 and his gold watch and chain to his friend Robert Davis of Priston Farm, Milverton, Somerset and £200 to his friend Henry Lambert, 10 Fountains Buildings, Bath, artist and photographer.

Joseph bequeathed his dwelling house, shop and premises, No 6 Bennett Street and the household furniture and effects to his assistant, Samuel Chivers, who with his friend Henry Lambert were executors of the Will.

His housekeeper, Priscilla Reed was left a £500 legacy and the following itemised articles all free of duty, viz:-

"One Iron Bedstead, Mattress, Feather Bed, Bolster and two Pillows, my best Chest of Drawers, Towel horse, Two Bedroom Chairs, Night Convenience, Mahogany Pembroke Table, Ditto Card Table, Dressing Table, Six Chairs from Bedrooms like those in the Drawing Room,

---

[437] Bennett Street runs from Belmont to the Circus and Saville Row from Alfred Street to Bennett Street.
[438] The Bath Chronicle, Thursday 3rd August 1871.

Steel Fender in Bedroom, set of Fire Irons in Drawing Room, Chimney Glass and Dressing Glass in Bedroom, Two large China jars painted with birds and three small China Scent Bottles all on the sideboard, the Dressing Room Clock, Carpet in back Drawing room, Rug and Skin Mat, Two Pictures of Children in Drawing Room, Two Pictures by Chimney Glass in Ditto, Portable Writing Desk, Two Silver Table Spoons, Six Silver Tea Spoons, Two Silver Salt Spoons, One pair of Silver Sugar Tongs, Six Plated Dinner Forks, Six Plated Dessert Forks, Six Plated Dessert Spoons, Carved Box for Plate, Six small Knives, Tray, Copper Kettle, Dutch Oven, Two Iron Saucepans, Two pairs of best sheets, One pair of Blankets, Marseilles Quilt, Four Pillow Cases, Four Towels, One Damask Table Cloth, One Toilet Cover, Pair of Red Damask Window Curtains, and Pole in Back Drawing Room and the Furniture of the Bedstead upon which the late Mrs. Luxton slept".

The Will was proved at Bristol on 18th June 1879 when Joseph's personal estate was valued under £2,000.

The picture of Luxton's Tea & Grocery Shop, which is reproduced in a beautiful book on Bath, is from an original wood engraving, in the Bath Reference Library.

58

JOSEPH LUXON (LUXTON) (1784 – ALIVE 1816) SAWYER OF TAUNTON, SOMERSET

See tree 31

Joseph the second son of John Luxton (1747–1818), carpenter and joiner, and his wife Mary Redwood, was baptised Joseph Luxon at St. Mary Magdalene Taunton on the 30th May 1784. Thirty years later Joseph Luxton, bachelor, and Margaret Powell, widow, both of the parish of St. James, Taunton married in the parish church on Monday 29th August 1814. Margaret signs her name but Joseph could only make his mark. His younger brother Robert, a carpenter, and his wife, Elizabeth, witnessed the marriage. Joseph's wife Margaret Powell was born Peggy Gore, daughter of Francis and Elizabeth Gore, on the 9th July 1783 and was baptised at St. James Taunton on the 25th November that year. She married her first husband Robert Powell there, on the 15th April 1805, but there was no issue, and Robert died and was buried at St. James Taunton on the 4th August 1807. The church of St. James was built in St. James Street, to serve the growing population north of the river. It has a 120foot west tower that was rebuilt in 1870-75.

The newly wed couple already had a son Charles Luxton, born in Taunton on the 3rd November 1813. As Charles, illegitimate son of Margaret Powell, widow, he was baptised at St. James Taunton on the 9th January 1814. I believe Joseph was the child's natural father as he married Margaret Powell, just seven months after Charles' baptism and nine months after his birth. Perhaps significantly, Joseph's elder brother John, also had an illegitimate son before his marriage.

Charles Luxton (1813–1885) a lace maker, married Charlotte Townsend at St. James Taunton on the 18th August 1833. They lived in Taunton before moving to Tiverton about 1845 and had at least nine children.

Robert, a second son of Joseph and Peggy Luxton, was baptised at St. James, Taunton on the 21st January 1816. He attended a Sunday

School or a Charity School in Taunton where he learned to read, but not write, according to the Wilton Goal Register (1807-1879) which states, Robert, 22, was sentenced in August 1837 at the Somerset Assizes to three months imprisonment with hard labour for embezzling the property of his master, George Pyne. A local paper, however, gives a different version, saying he was sentenced for stealing a watch, the property of his employer William Hill in Bristol[439].

Robert, a labourer, married Olive Drew, both residing at Lawrence Hill, in the church of St. Philip & Jacob in the parish of Holy Trinity, Bristol on the 2nd May 1841. Both make their mark. Olive, a minor, was a dressmaker, the daughter of Eli Drew, a hatter. She was born in Frampton Cotterel, Gloucestershire. The 1851 census for St. George, Bristol has Robert Luxton 35 agricultural labourer, born Taunton, and his wife Olive aged 27, living at "Holms". The wife's parents, Eli Drew, 55, lodger, hatter, born Iron Acton and Ann 55, born in Bitton, Gloucestershire lived with them.

Labourers were frequently on the move looking for work. Robert, 45, labourer and his wife Olivia, 37, were living by 1861 at 3 Codrington Street, St. Sidwell's in Exeter where they shared a house with two other couples. They were in north Devon by 1871 when the census records Robert, 55, agricultural labourer and his wife Olivia dwelling at no.5 Churchyard, Bideford.

Robert Luxton was a 59 (sic) railway labourer, when he died of cerebro-spinal meningitis at Vinegar Hill, Bideford on 25th November 1872. Mary Mountjoy of Vinegar Hill was present at his death. Olivia, his widow, married George Langmead, a widower and shipwright, at the parish church Bideford on the 15th November 1875.

Joseph and Margaret appear to have had no further children baptised at St. James Taunton and, indeed, it seems possible that Joseph may have died by 20th March 1818 for he finds no mention in his father John Luxton's (1747– 1818) Will. However, one cannot assume that all children are mentioned in wills. Omissions are rarely because the

---

[439] Bristol Mercury, Saturday 12th August 1837.

children are out of favour. It may be that John had made gifts to his son Joseph, the sawyer, during his lifetime.

Joseph may have been alive as late as 1841. When his son Robert married in Bristol in May that year he states his father Joseph was a sawyer. Of course we cannot be certain that Joseph was alive, because the certificate only requires the name and occupation of the father and although it was usual to state if the parent was deceased I have found this was not invariably recorded.

Joseph as a sawyer was a semi-skilled worker. The carpenter would choose and buy standing trees, and they would be felled, and brought to his yard to await the arrival of the sawyer. Sawyers worked in pairs or more and a skilled and exhausting job awaited them. First they had to manoeuvre a tree trunk into position over the sawpit, through the adept use of levers. Then, when sawing began, the 'top sawyer' – the senior man – stood on the tree trunk, holding his end of the saw. The 'bottom sawyer' in the pit underneath, would usually wear a brimmed hat to keep the sawdust out of his eyes.

I have found no burial entry for Joseph at either St. James or St. Mary Magdalene Taunton in years 1813-1841 but a Margaret Luxton aged 45[440] (sic), Burton Square who was buried at St. James on the 30th March 1835 may have been his widow. It may be that Joseph deserted his wife and family after the birth of their second son Robert in 1816 and moved elsewhere. There are clearly some loose ends here which need tidying up.

---

[440] Margaret would have been 52 in 1835.

59

CHARLES LUXTON (1813 – 1885) LACE MAKER TAUNTON AND TIVERTON AND HIS FAMILY

See tree 31

Charles, the eldest son of Joseph Luxton (1784–alive 1816), sawyer, and his future wife Margaret Powell, widow, was born in Taunton on the 3rd November 1813. Described as the illegitimate son of Margaret Powell, widow, he was baptised at St. James, Taunton on the 9th January 1814. He was a nineteen-year-old bachelor, living in the parish of St. James Taunton when he married Charlotte Townsend in the parish church on the 18th August 1833. Neither sign their name but we know that Charles could certainly write.

The first five children of Charles and Charlotte's nine children were born in Taunton, beginning with Eliza Goar,[441] who was born on 18th December 1833. She was an 11 year old when she died in Tiverton on the 14th August 1845. Their eldest son, William Charles (1836–1912), born on the 4th February 1836, was baptised on the 22nd May the same year. Alfred born 8th July 1838, died 19th October 1840. James Rechab (1841–1886) born in Concord Place, St James, Taunton on the 2nd January 1841, died in Tiverton in 1886. The year James was born, 1841, the Taunton census taken on the 6th June, records that Charles, a lacemaker, his wife Charlotte and family, had moved to live in Tancred Street, St. James, Taunton. A second son, named Alfred, born in Taunton on the 22nd April 1843, died at Westexe, Tiverton on the 7th May 1875. His death certificate describes him as aged 33, a private in the Marine Artillery. Alfred, who served on H.M.S. Cossack in the East Indies, died from chronic asthma and bronchitis and his brother James was present at his death.

---

[441] Goar is a corruption of Gore, the maiden name of her grandmother Margaret Powell and it was this pointer that finally confirmed the origins of Charles Luxton

Charles and Charlotte moved with their growing family to Tiverton, sometime between April 1843 when the second Alfred was born, and August 1845 when Eliza Goar died. Tiverton was Charlotte's hometown and this may be why the family made the move, but improved work opportunities in lace making were also a likely reason for moving to the town.

Charles and Charlotte spent the rest of their lives in Tiverton. In 1851 Charles was a lacehand but he had become a draper's porter by 1861. Charlotte worked in John Heathcoat & Co's Lace Factory, for the Heathcoat scroll, contains her signature along with that of other workers in the factory about 1864.[442] Heathcoat had established a factory for machine lace manufacture in the town in 1816 because he feared the Luddites would smash the machinery in his Loughborough factory. The print above shows John Heathcoat's Lace Manufactory in 1836. By the 1890s the Heathcoat Amory Lace Factory employed 1400 hands and 130 children.

---

[442] Tiverton Museum possesses various books, records, documents etc belonging to John Heathcoat & Company, giving details of the firm's activities and employees from 1816 to 1890.

Charles was a Bible Christian preacher. A notebook inscribed "Charles Luxton His Book Tiverton Devon 1846" was in possession of Alfred William Luxton (1920 - 1997) his great grandson in Doncaster. It is a hand-written record kept by Charles, giving details of all the services at his church or chapel in Tiverton from 4th January 1846 to 26th November 1862 when the last entry was made. It is in a very small intricate writing, so small it is difficult to read, even with a magnifying glass. It gives the birth dates of himself, his wife and his children and in some cases their death[443].

Each year ends with a small verse, largely concerned with the ephemeral nature of life and impending death. An example taken from the end of the year 1848 reads:-

"Our wasting lives grow shorter still
As days and months increase
And every beating pulse we tell
Leaves but the number less.
How then ought I on earth to live
While God prolongs the kind reprieve
And props the house of clay
My sole concern, my single care
To watch and tremble and prepare
Against the fatal day."

A further four children were born to Charles and Charlotte in Tiverton. Sadly the first three, Robert, Ellen Margaret and Elizabeth, died in infancy. Emily their ninth child was born 3rd December 1852. She became a silk winder in the lace factory in Tiverton. She never married and died aged 69 at 6 Elm Terrace, Leat Street, Tiverton on 9th February 1922.

The years 1841 to 1852 must have been a harrowing time for Charlotte and the family as the following events show:

---

[443] See letter from Alfred William Luxton, Doncaster, dated 14th July 1987. Alf was an enthusiastic supporter of my endeavours in compiling this family history.

James Rechab born 2nd January 1841
Alfred born 22nd April 1843
Eliza Goar died 14th August 1845
Robert born 12th September 1846
Robert died 20th October 1847
Ellen Margaret born 27th October 1847
Ellen Margaret died 30th July 1849
Elizabeth born 25th February 1850
Elizabeth died 21st September 1851
Emily born 3rd December 1852

As can be seen Charlotte gave birth to Ellen Margaret, just seven days after the death of her baby son Robert, and probably within two or three days of the child's funeral. This event has a parallel in more modern times when Henrietta Lucy Jones (nee Luxton) gave birth in London to a daughter, Sylvia Margaret Jones, on the day her beloved husband was buried.

Charles and family lived in Westexe, Tiverton where in 1861 census Charles 47   Porter, Charlotte 47, lace mender, Alfred 17 labourer and Emily 8. The 1871 census has Charles 57 Draper Porter, Charlotte 57 and Emily 18 both listed as lace workers. In the 1881 Tiverton census Charles Luxton aged 67, general labourer, his wife Charlotte, 67 lace mender and their daughter Emily 28 a "Skeiner in a lace factory" continued to live at Westexe (South). Mary Towell, 21, a "silk winder in a lace factory" was lodging with them.

Charles had heart disease, and when pneumonia set in, he died at his home in Westexe Street, Tiverton on the 8th July 1885. His obituary in the Western Times reads:- July 8, at Westexe South, Tiverton, Charles Luxton, aged 72.[444] His death certificate describes him as a general porter and it may be that failing eyesight in later life prohibited him working as a lace hand. Emily is thought to be the daughter named "Bessie" who was present at his death. It was just over a year later on the 25th November 1886 that Charlotte, aged 73, widow, of Charles Luxton, Draper's Porter, died from bronchitis exhaustion. Emily, the couple's youngest daughter, was present at her mother's death.

---

[444] Western Times, Monday 13th July 1885.

60

WILLIAM CHARLES LUXTON (1836-1912) LACEHAND OF TAUNTON, TIVERTON, CHARD AND NOTTINGHAM

See tree 32

The family continued working in the lace industry but were to move around the country to keep in employment. The eldest son, William Charles Luxton (1836-1912), was a fifteen year old lace hand in 1851 when he lived with his parents and family in Tiverton. He chose for his life partner another lacehand when he married Elizabeth Ellen Newberry at Chard, Somerset, on the 18th February 1854. Elizabeth, the same age as William, was born in Bridport, Dorset on the 3rd August 1836, the daughter of William and Louisa Newberry.

The couple lived in Chard for a quarter of a century and had twelve children born in the town. They were employed as lace hands making "plain net" used for mosquito nets and ladies underwear. The 1861 census lists William, 25, lace hand, Elizabeth, 24, and three infants, residing at 10 Margaret's Hill, Chard. By 1871 the couple had seven children and were living at Chilson Common, Chard. The photograph shows the Perry Street Works, lace mill in Factory Lane, Chard, Somerset.

The family moved to Nottingham in the years 1879-81 because of changing employment opportunities in the lace making industry. They were in St Mary, Nottingham for the 1881 census which lists William, his wife Elizabeth and six of their children living at 5 Belvoir Terrace.

William was a 45 year old lace maker, while his wife Elizabeth was a 44 year old lace mender. Their daughter Matilda, 20, was a "lace cotton winder" and Henrietta 11, Frederick 10, Walter 8, Alfred 5 and Elizabeth aged 3 were scholars. In 1891 William 55 lacemaker, Elizabeth, 54 lace mender, lived at 34 Birkin Avenue in Radford, Nottingham. Four off-spring were still living at home- Henrietta, 21 lace mender, Frederick, 20 lace threader, Walter 18, painter and Alfred 15, general labourer. By 1901 William, 65, lace maker, and Elizabeth, nursing 3 year Henry Wright, were living at 2 Bramcote Street in Nottingham.

William and Elizabeth had eight girls, beginning with Ellen Matilda Luxton, born on the 2nd September 1855. She died aged 3 of malignant scarlet fever at Perry Street, Chard on 16th October 1858. Eliza Jane (1857-1952), the second daughter, born in 1857, (in photo) was a nurse in Bristol Royal Infirmary when she married James Notley 26, machineman, in St. Mark's Church, New Swindon, Wiltshire on 22nd December 1883. They lived in Swindon and had issue one son and four daughters.

The third daughter, Matilda, born in 1861, a lace worker, married George Sydney Jefford, also a lace worker in Nottingham, on the 10th September 1887. Matilda and her husband George, lace maker, are listed living in Liddington Street, Basford in 1891 with their son Albert 10, and daughter, Beatrice aged 1. Matilda died aged 34 of mitral heart disease at 55 Liddington Street Basford on the 29th March 1895. She was followed by Eunice Ellen, born on the 17th January 1863. In the 1881 census Eunice was an 18 year old general servant in the home of Martha Purnall, a china dealer at 7 Cotham Parade, Westbury on Trym, Gloucester. She married Willie James Charlesworth, in the parish church Radford, Nottinghamshire on Christmas Eve 1885.

The next sibling, Lois Ann (inset) born on the 13th January 1865, married John Henry Rice, a railway manager, in Stoke on the 15th August 1898. Lois Ann died on the 30th March 1920 at Blythe Bridge. Two other daughters were to follow, Henrietta born in 1869, who married Thomas Charles Phasey at Radford on the 13th March 1897, dying in Ealing, London on the 29th October 1955 and Elizabeth Emily born on the 26th October 1877. Elizabeth Emily married George Henry Pinkstone, a cabinet maker, in Nottingham in 1904.

William and Elizabeth also had five sons beginning with William James (1859-1929) born 1859, known as James who was a plain net maker. When young he made two appearances before the Chard magistrates. He was aged about 13 and one of five boys, all labourers, who were fined small sums and costs for stealing apples from orchards in the autumn of 1873.[445] Aged 19 James, was one of nine young labourers, who appeared at Chard Petty Sessions, charged with making a bonfire in Perry Street on the 5th November 1878. P.C. Higgins stated that about 8 o'clock that night there was a crowd of people, a heap of wood and some tar barrels in Perry Street. He warned them not to light the fire but the defendants lit the fire and did not leave the place until 10:30. They told the court that they were "enjoying themselves" but the court fined them 1s and 5 shillings costs each[446]. In both of these escapades James was joined by Joshua Hayball who was perhaps a brother to Lydia Hayball, James first wife, who he married in St. Mary's Chard on the 22nd December 1878.[447]

The newly wed couple made the move to Nottingham where the 1881 census lists William, aged 22, lace maker, and his wife Lydia, 21, living at 7 Miall Street, Lenton. Ten years later the couple were living at 87 Norton Street in Radford in Nottinghamshire and Rose Notley 17, their

[445] Exeter & Plymouth Gazette, Friday 17th October 1873.
[446] Somerset County Gazette, Saturday 16th November 1878.
[447] Western Gazette, Friday 3rd January 1879.

niece, a dressmaker, born in Chard was living with them. By 1911 William 52, lace maker, and Lydia, dwelling at 6 Alice Terrace, Dorking Road, Nottingham, had been married 32 years but there were no children. In 1914, William, a twist hand, lived at 35 Belper Road Nottingham. Following Lydia's death, William, 60, lace maker, of 16, Hubert Street married for a second time to Susan Wilkinson, 44, widow, at Nottingham Register Office, on 21st August 1919. William James Luxton of 23 Beckenham Road, died on 20th December 1929 at 700 Hucknall Road, Nottingham. Probate was granted in Nottingham on 9th January 1930 to Frederick Newberry Luxton, lace maker when his effects were valued at£269..13s..11d.

Alfred Charles Luxton, was born at Tatworth, Chard, on the 16th November 1866 where he died of measles on the 1st June 1869. The third son, Frederick Newberry Luxton (1870-1937), was born in 1870, and was living at 70 Walbeck Street when he married Mary Jane Dykes, on the 5th August 1893 in Nottingham. The couple dwelling in 17 Denison Street in 1901, had settled by 1911 at 27 Belper Road, Hyson Green, where he died aged 67 on 9th June 1937. His widow, Mary Jane Luxton of 27 Belper Road, Nottingham died the 12th August 1939, leaving £27..16s..8d to Robert Henry Corner, bricklayer.

The couple had two daughters. Clarice Rosie Luxton (1895-1983) born in Nottingham on the 9th January 1895, married Richard Horobin, a carder & gilder, in the parish church Hyson Green, on 4th October 1915. Clarice died at 45 Milton Road, West Bridgford, Nottingham on 16th January 1983. Her sister, Ivy Winifred Luxton (1903-1939) born at 17 Denison Street, Nottingham on 24th February 1903 married 23 year old Robert Henry Corner, at Hyson Green on 16th April 1927. Tragically Ivy of 60 Wilbert Road in Arnold, Nottingham, committed suicide "by coal gas poisoning whilst the balance of her mind was disturbed" on the 30th June 1939. Her obituary in the Nottingham Evening Post, Tuesday 4th July 1939, reads-Corner- Ivy Winifred, formerly Luxton, died Friday, 30th very suddenly, aged 36. Interment Wednesday 3 P. M. Beeston Cemetery.

The fourth son, Walter Henry Luxton, was born in1873. He was eighteen years old, a painter, and was in the 4th Battalion of the Sherwood Forresters when he joined the Durham Light Infantry in Newcastle on Tyne on 18th January 1891. He was 5ft 6 ½ inches tall with a fresh complexion, brown eyes and dark brown hair and there was a small scar below his left nipple. In religion he was a Wesleyan Methodist. He was admitted to hospital on 6th February 1891 with a severe case of gonorrhaoea and had mercury injections before leaving 28 days later. He claimed discharge from the army on 3rd April 1891.[448] Walter became a painter and decorator in Nottingham, and there is little doubt that the taking up of this calling was instrumental in causing his death in Nottingham on the 15th October 1898, aged 25, from lead poisoning.

He had married Cicely Sampey at St Paul's, Hyson Green in 1893. They had a son Sidney Harold Luxton (1897-1959). His mother, Cicely, married George Edward Parr, a store-keeper, at Hyson Green on 22nd January 1905. In 1911 aged 13 Sidney was living in Newark with his mother Cicely and step-father George Parr. A sapper in the Royal Engineers from 23rd October 1916 he worked in the Railways Troops Department before being discharged through sickness on 3rd February 1919 as someone no longer physically fit for war service. He was issued with a Silver Badge No. B135198. Sydney of 9 Grosvenor Crescent, Arksey near Doncaster died 20th September 1959. Administration of his effects valued at £386 was granted in Wakefield on 2nd December to his widow, Elsie May Luxton.

The youngest son, Alfred William Luxton (1875-1922), was born on the 10th November 1875. Will, as he was known to his parents and siblings, eschewed the softer life enjoyed by his elder siblings and went to work in the coal mines where he moved frequently about the pits of South Yorkshire, North Derbyshire and North Nottinghamshire. Around 1897, aged 22, he must have been working in the Leicestershire coal fields for it was in 1897 that Hannah Mary Ann Wright bore him a son at 21 Britannia Street, Leicester. We have more to say on Alfred William Luxton in the next chapter.

Finally, Vanda Hopwood in the Isle of Wight who is descended from William Charles Luxton (1836-1912) and his wife Elizabeth Ellen Newberry (1836-1919) possesses two cabinet prints of the couple.

---

[448] WO97 3325   23.

The photographs were taken by R Evans & Co at 8 Derby Road, Bottom of Toll Street, Nottingham, sometime in the years 1883 to 1887 when Evans & Co were working at that address. William, in his early fifties, wears spectacles and is bald but has a full beard and moustache. His hair is streaked with grey and the "Albert" chain of a fob watch is in his waistcoat.

His wife Elizabeth is the same age but looks older. She is wearing a mantle or more likely, a dolman which had wide sleeves cut in one with the sides of the garment, making it half coat, half cape. Both were widely worn during the 1880s when the exaggerated bustle made the wearing of a long coat difficult. Her collar and cuffs are of astrakhan, a fur made from closely curled lamb's wool which has a shiny appearance in black and white photographs. She is sporting a large silk bow at her throat and firmly centred on her head is a small soft cap or toque, a type of hat without a brim.

In 1911 census William Charles Luxton, 75, retired lacemaker and his wife lived at 6 Kentwood Road Nottingham with their daughter Elizabeth Emily 33 an office cleaner, and her husband George Pinkstone, a cabinet maker.

Vanda also possesses an evocative photograph of William Charles Luxton with a flowing beard and his wife Elizabeth Ellen Newberry, lace makers, celebrating their 40th wedding anniversary in 1894 with their ten children[449]. The ladies distinctive sleeves, made full at the top and narrow on the lower arm, typify the gigot or "leg-o'-mutton" style, fashionable c.1893-1897.

---

[449] Alfred William Luxton, Doncaster also had a copy of this family photograph. See his letter dated 14th July 1987. He supplied much of the personal details in this chapter.

Standing in back (from left to right.) Matilda (1861-1895) Frederick Newberry, (1870-1937), Walter Henry (1873-1898), Alfred William (1875-1922), Eunice Ellen (1863-1943). Eliza Jane (1857-1952) in the light coloured dress is seated to the left of her father William. Charles William James (1859–1929) with drooping moustache is seated to the left of his mother Elizabeth Ellen. In front row L-R. are Lois Ann (1865-1920), Henrietta (1869-1955), Elizabeth Emily (1877-1912).

William Charles Luxton (1836-1912) of 6 Kentwood Road, Nottingham died aged 76 on the 15th July 1912. Administration of his estate was granted in Nottingham on the 30th July to his widow Elizabeth Ellen Luxton, when his personal effects were valued at £258..19s..2d. Elizabeth Ellen Luxton of 12 Aspley Place, Peverel Street, Nottingham, died aged 83 at her daughter's residence in Stetchford, Warwickshire on the 20th August 1919. Probate was granted in Nottingham to William James Luxton and Frederick Newberry Luxton, lace makers, when her personal estate was valued at £450..18s..9d.

61

ALFRED WILLIAM LUXTON (1875 - 1922) COALMINER, AND HIS FAMILY OF CHARD AND ROTHERHAM

See tree 33

Alfred William, the fifth son of William Charles Luxton (1836 - 1912) and Elizabeth Ellen Newberry, was born on 10th November 1875 at Chard in Somerset. Little is known of his childhood but he was obviously educated and later in his comparatively short life displayed a particular gift of "soap-box oratory". He was still a child when his family moved to Nottingham in the years 1879-81 following work opportunities. His father may well have been induced to move by his wife's family who were lace manufacturers.

His teenage years were troublesome and caused his parents much anguish. At the Guildhall Nottingham on Tuesday 10th May 1892 Alfred of 34 Birkin Avenue, Hyson Green, pleaded guilty to stealing a ferret valued at 10 shillings but not guilty to stealing a ferret valued at a £1. Sergeant Aldridge, however, found the two ferrets in the prisoner's house. His mother told the court that her son "was a great trouble to her" and if the magistrates would set him free she would "send him to America." Alfred had been before the court only a few weeks before for a similar offence and the magistrates sent him to prison for two months hard labour[450].

Matters did not improve. On the 3rd March 1893 he pleaded guilty at the Police Court in the Guildhall Nottingham to stealing a rabbit to the value of 5s. Dr. Littlewood characterised Alfred as a confirmed thief and the court committed him to prison for six weeks hard labour[451]. It got worse. Alfred made yet another appearance at the Guildhall on

---

[450] Nottingham Evening Post, Tuesday 3rd & 10th May 1892.
[451] Nottingham Evening Post, Monday 27th February and 3rd March 1893.

Tuesday 25th July 1893 for assaulting Edward Mann, a cab proprietor in his stable, and demanding money. Without the slightest provocation he struck Mr. Mann a violent blow in his face, bit his nose and then tried to thrust his left eye out. The court sent him to prison for a month[452]. He was still only eighteen.

Whether Will, as he was known to his parents and family, ever worked in the lace industry we do not know but he was soon working in the coal mines where he was to develop strong left wing political tendencies. Those were the days of "hire and fire" and Will moved freely around the coalfields of north Nottinghamshire, north Derbyshire and south Yorkshire to keep himself in employment[453].

He was a 26 year old miner in Mansfield when he met Ada Mather, a parlour maid who was born on 27th February 1881 in Apperknowle, North Derbyshire, marrying her in St. Peter's Elmton, Derbyshire on 21st July 1902. It was about the time of his marriage that he began to be known as Alf. Whether this was at the instigation of his wife or his own choice we do not know.

The earliest evidence I have found for Alfred's left wing sympathies is in a letter he wrote to the Editor of the Derbyshire Times, published Saturday 23rd May 1903 when he was a miner, living at 27 Bradder Street, Mansfield. He describes himself as a working member of the Derbyshire Miners Federation and claims that Messrs Harvey and Haslam, the leaders of the Derby Miners Association, are autocratic and that they are refusing to listen to the 3000 miners residing in Mansfield. He ends his letter with a plea to his fellow miners to join him to work for an Independent Labour representation[454]. In 1911 Alfred was an active member of the Doncaster Trade and Labour Council where he championed better conditions for the working class[455]. The census that year lists Alfred 35, Pit Sinker for a mining

---

[452] Nottingham Evening Post, Tuesday 25th July 1893.

[453] His son the late Alfred William Luxton (1920-1997) of Doncaster has provided me with the more personal details of his father's life. See letter dated 29th August 1996.

[454] Derbyshire Times and Chesterfield Herald, Saturday 23rd May 1903.

[455] Sheffield Daily Telegraph, Wednesday 18th January 1911.

contractor, his wife Ada 30 and four children plus Harry his 13 year old illegitimate son, living at Ulley near Sheffield.

He stood as a candidate in the local Municipal Elections in Rotherham in 1913, appealing to the electorate in the East Ward to "vote for Luxton and the cause of the workers". During the campaign he spoke on the night of Tuesday 21st October to a fairly large crowd gathered at the corner of Bethal Road and Shakespeare Road. In his speech, reported in the Rotherham Advertiser on the 25th October, he passionately pleaded his views on local political questions.

If returned he would see that the roads and footpaths in the East Ward which had been neglected and were a disgrace to the town were put in a decent condition.

Then there was the question of gas. Most of the residents of the East Ward were slot meter consumers who had to pay 3s..4d a thousand units for their gas where as the people who got it "on tick" only paid 2s..3d and employers who used large quantities got it on a sliding scale ranging from 1s..6d to 1s..10d per thousand units. He suggested that the Council used the profits made at the Gas Works to give a reduction to slot meter consumers.

Then there was the question of trams. The Tramways Department was making a good profit and he felt the time had arrived when they ought to have another trial for half penny fares. He was not prepared to say the venture would be a success but only a trial could prove that. This was a question the miners were determined should be dealt with. They felt that they had a right to be carried home from work for a half penny as well as taken to work at that price. It was a remarkable fact that once a man had got to work he ceased to be a workman and had to pay full fare to return home. He knew from his own experience hundreds of men who would ride to work in the morning and walk home in the afternoon and if they were on the afternoon shift plenty of the men would walk to work because the fare was a penny. The problem could be solved by the issue of return tickets so that a man could come home at anytime when his shift finished.

He had visited most of the large towns of this country but Rotherham was the worst place he had seen in its provision of public toilets. There was, he said, going to be some fun in the Rotherham Council Chamber if the needs of the working classes were not given better attention.

If returned he would use every endeavour to secure better housing accommodation for the working classes. At present there were only sixty empty houses in Rotherham but three years ago there were over four hundred. The scarcity of houses meant higher rents. The Corporation had it in their power to erect houses to be let at a reasonable rental and the Council should implement the Housing of the Working Classes Act.

Education was another issue raised and Mr Luxton said he believed in equal facilities all round. His children attended the Doncaster Road Council School, a school which was built at a cost of £15 per head but in Middle Lane they had another school which was built for the children of the businessmen which cost £48 per head. He had been asked by the Teachers' Association if he was in favour of limiting the number of scholars a teacher could take to sixty and his reply was that the number was not small enough. In the Middle Lane School a teacher could not have more than thirty five scholars. One of the reasons that children of today were being so poorly educated was that the classes were too large for any teacher to do them justice. The children of the working classes had a right to equal treatment with those of the Middle and Upper classes.

A resolution pledging the meeting to support the Socialist candidate Mr Luxton was moved and seconded from the crowd and was carried unanimously.

On Saturday 1st November 1913, the day of the election, The Rotherham Advertiser reported, "Mr Luxton has fought vigorously", and although he has the disadvantage of not living in the East Ward, "he has spent a great deal of time there, and his policy is one which has won him many enthusiastic supporters. His main plank, the securing of workmen's fares on the tramways for miners on the afternoon shift will commend itself to many of the electors, who will vote for him on this if no other ground."

The election results were declared shortly after 9pm on the 1st November 1913 and they must have been a bitter disappointment to Alf and his supporters. Mr Henry Maxfield, the incumbent candidate who had represented the ward for the previous nine years was re-elected, with 319 votes to Mr Luxtons 185, a majority of 134 votes. Only 46 per cent, less than half the 1076 electors in the East Ward, had taken the trouble to vote.

Alf continued to champion the the miners. On Friday 13th March 1914, he presided over an attendance of about a thousand striking miners at a public meeting held in the Fairground Rotherham. The miners, who had ceased work at Messrs John Brown & Co's collieries some weeks before, were in an ugly mood, expressing dissatisfaction at the way they had been treated by their own union officials[456].

Like most of his contemporaries Alfred was patriotic, and although he was already near forty, and had a wife and family to support, he enlisted at Rotherham on the 21st July 1915 for four years in the 4th Battalion of the Yorkshire and Lancaster Regiments Territorial Force with Reg. No.265565. A little over five foot six inches he wore glasses and had a chest measurement of 37 inches when fully expanded. His physical development was considered good and he was a member of the Church of England.

Alf's military career was cut short by an accident. In March 1916, while on active service at Clipston, near Mansfield in Nottinghamshire he fell in a trench, twisting his left knee. He was excused duty for four days but the knee continued to give him pain and he suffered with pain in his knee and groin especially after walking. On 31st October 1917 he underwent a  medical examination in Sheffield. He had wrenched the hamstring muscle of his left leg and there was some thickening on the inner side of

---

[456] Sheffield Independent, Saturday 14th March 1914.

his left knee. Although his disability was rated at 20 per cent and was not considered to be permanent he was discharged from the army on the 15th November 1917 because he was "no longer physically fit for war service due to the internal derangement of his left knee joint." His character was "good" and he had served two years and 118 days in the Territorial Force. He was awarded a gratuity of £42..10 shillings with a pension from 31st October 1916.[457] Alf was also awarded a Silver Badge no 274577.

He returned to coalmining, the job he knew best. Alf also resumed his enthusiastic support of the emerging Labour Party, when on 16th April 1919: he presided over a meeting of the party in Rotherham. He said they hoped to enroll at least three thousand new members during the summer, so that when the next general election came they would have a Labour member for Rotherham.[458] A.W. Luxton was elected a vice president at the annual meeting of the Rotherham Labour Party held at the Trades Union Club, College Street on the evening of Tuesday 6th May 1919.[459] The party held meetings at Parkgate and Rotherham to rally support on the 18th May. Alf attended the Rotherham meeting convened at the Theatre Royal and presided over another meeting of the local party in July.

In the Rotherham Municipal election held on 1st November 1919, Alf stood against an Independent in the West Ward. The Sheffield Daily Telegraph commented on Election Day, "A spirited fight was proceeding in the West Ward where Mr. Reginald Dewar, Independent, estate agent, has Mr. A.W. Luxton, coal miner, a leading official of the Labour Party against him." On the 3rd November the same paper commented, "Mr. A.W. Luxton the secretary of the Labour Party ran rather close in the West Ward." Dewar won by 40 votes, 483 to Luxton's 443. The monthly meeting of The Rotherham Labour Party, "were all sorry that Mr Luxton who made such a splendid fight was not returned."

Alfred William Luxton, a forty six year old coal hewer, died of pernicious anaemia and acute bronchitis, at his home 67 Clifton

---

[457] WO 364 First World War Pension Claims.
[458] Sheffield Independent, Thursday 17th April 1919.
[459] Sheffield Daily Telegraph, Wednesday 7th May & 19th May 1919.

Avenue, Rotherham on the 27th February 1922. He was laid to rest at Moorgate Cemetery, Rotherham.

By his wife Ada Mather he had seven children, five daughters and two sons. The first daughter Elizabeth Ellen, born on the 3rd January 1903, married Clement Kendrick on the 7th June 1924 at Rotherham parish church and died at 20 Victoria Avenue, Rotherham on 9th June 1992 as a result of a massive heart attack. The second daughter Ada, born on the 22nd February 1906, married Samuel Didlock in Rotherham on the 10th December 1927 and died on the 28th October 1980. The third daughter, Henrietta Lucy, born on 20th March 1908 at Warsop Vale in Nottinghamshire, married Bernard Reginald Jones on 5th August 1928 at Brentford, London. This couple had two children. Just a few days before the second child, a daughter, was born, Bernard met with a tragic accident on their house-boat home on the Thames at Thames Ditton. He fell overboard and was drowned. Henrietta struggled on alone to bring up her two children until twenty years later she met and married Clifford Corbett on 29th October 1951 at Paddington, London. The fourth daughter Bessie, born on 10th September 1912 at 67 Clifton Avenue, Rotherham, married Artemus Didlock, younger brother of Samuel, her brother-in-law, at St Stephens Church, Eastwood, Rotherham on 20th October 1930. Bessie died on 28th December 1991 at Badsley Moor Lane Hospital, Rotherham from the smoking related disease Emphysema. The fifth and last daughter Annie Lois, (the baby in her mother's arms in photo below) was born on 5th October 1917, at the family home in Clifton Avenue and, after a somewhat wayward period in her teens, married John Henry Eckersley Heyes, at the Rotherham Registry Office on 1st March 1941, her eldest sister Ellen and younger brother Alf being witnesses at the ceremony. Annie Lois, who suffered from Parkinson's disease in later life, died at her home in Rotherham on 19th November 1987.

Alfred William's first born son (in photo with his wife on next page) was born on 5th December 1897 and registered as Harry Wright. He somehow learnt the circumstances of his birth, left home and went to live with his Luxton relatives in Nottingham. Harry Luxton of 67 Clifton Avenue was one of five Rotherham youths who were turners in a shell factory summoned to attend Sheffield Munitions Tribunal on the 3rd March 1916 "for refusing to obey orders and for losing time."

The boys objected to a woman being put on the work that one of them was doing. The Tribunal pointed out that had nothing to do with them as they were still employed at turning. The ring-leader was sacked and fined £3, the rest including Harry were fined 20s[460].

Harry lived and served in the army during World War 1 as Pte Harry Luxton (Reg. No. 29698) in the Kings Own Yorkshire Light Infantry. His service record reveals that when he enlisted on the 6th December 1915, he was living with his father and family at 67 Clifton Avenue, Rotherham, and he names his father as his next of kin. He was an 18 year old fitter's labourer and was 5ft. 1inch with a chest measurement of 34 inches when fully expanded. He served in France and Belgium from 10th November 1916 to 7th January 1919. Transferred in April 1917 as a driver in the Armour Service Corps, he suffered a fractured wrist while driving horses on 17th June and with deafness as a result of gunfire on 17th November. He was stationed at Woolwich Dockyard when demobbed on 6th February 1919. Harry was awarded the Victory Medal and the British War Medal.

Harry was home, either on leave or discharged from serving with the Armour Service Corps in France, when this studio photograph (next page) of Alfred William Luxton and family was taken in Rotherham in c.1918. He displays a gold wound strip on his left cuff, an indication it is sometime after 17th November 1917 when he suffered serious hearing loss as a result of heavy gunfire. L-R. Ada, Lucy, Alfred, Bessie, Harry, baby Annie Lois with mother Ada, Fred and Ellen.

He returned home again briefly in February 1922 for the funeral of his father but left almost immediately afterwards. Harry married Mae Story at Nottingham on 28th April 1923, his two Luxton uncles James and Frederick being witnesses.

---

[460] Sheffield Daily Telegraph, Saturday 4th March 1916 & Sheffield Evening Telegraph, Friday 3rd March 1916.

For some reason Harry Wright reverted to his original name when he emigrated to Canada in 1923, sailing on the SS. Laconia on 6th August, arriving in Halifax, Nova Scotia on 13th August. He was 25 and on his arrival signed a declaration in his own handwriting that his intention was to do harvesting. In return for his services the Canadian government would refund his sailing costs and give him a quarter section of land. Although he did not intend to stay he remained in the country. His wife and young child did not join him until somewhat later, leaving the UK on the child's fifth birthday. His wife bore him eight children and was fated never to see the land of her birth nor her family again. In 1929 under a certificate of entry for a soldier's grant he was provided with land in Red Pheasant, Saskatchewan but in the late 1940s he was resident at Fairmont Hot Springs in British Columbia.

In the Second World War Harry joined the Veterans Guard of Canada. It was necessary to undergo a full physical to join including hearing. He had lost hearing in one ear in W.W.1 (shell blast) and had learned to lip read. This enabled him to pass the test. Harry is centre back row in this 1945-47 photo of the Veterans Guard taken in Medicine Hat, Alberta.

Harry returned to the UK early in 1946 as guard for Italian prisoners of war being repatriated. At this time he visited the family home only to receive a cold reception from his stepmother, and the visit lasted possibly no more than half an hour. He was to return again in 1972, sadly some five years later after his stepmother's death, and was made welcome by his siblings and so peace within the family was restored. Harry died on 23rd June 1974 from a heart attack, just five weeks after his younger brother Frederick Charles. Harry Wright lies in Windermere Cemetery, British Columbia, Canada.

The first son of Alfred William and Ada Mather was Frederick Charles born in Mansfield on 20th March 1904. Fred like his father before him was a law-breaker in his teenage years. A burglar, he broke into the dwelling-house and shop of Richard Fieldhouse, grocer, at 72 Clifton Avenue on the night of Thursday 3rd November and stole a quantity of "chocolate and nuts, value 6s." An 18 year old labourer, he was sentenced to six months imprisonment with hard labour. Detective Emsley said the prisoner was the leader of boys younger than himself, and had got to be a pest in the Clifton district.[461]

Fred, who became a railway locomotive driver, married twice. He married his first wife Edna Ogley on 9th September 1933 at East Retford, Nottinghamshire, the marriage ending in divorce. There was but a single child Doreen, born at Scunthorpe on 29th December 1938. The second marriage was to Ella Katherine Luxton (nee Miller) a divorcee. Ella had changed her name to Luxton by Deed Poll and lived with Fred as his wife for at least five years before they finally married at East Retford Registry Office on 14th April 1972. Fred died

---

[461] Sheffield Daily Telegraph, Thursday 10th November 1921 & Friday 13th January 1922.

after a stroke in 1974. His daughter Doreen now lives in Edmonton, Alberta.

The second and last son, Alfred William, his father's namesake, was born on 15th March 1920 at the family home in Clifton Avenue. His mother told him later in life that he was over fourteen pounds in weight at birth.

62

ALFRED WILLIAM LUXTON (1920 - 1997) ENGINEER AND HIS FAMILY OF ROTHERHAM, YORKSHIRE W.R.

See tree 33

Alfred William Luxton was born on 15th March 1920 in a small terraced house, two up and two down, at 67 Clifton Avenue, Rotherham. He attended Wellgate Primary School, and for a brief period, South Grove Central School before winning a scholarship to the then largely fee paying Grammar School, which he attended from 1931 to 1936. By his own admission he did not make full use of the opportunities afforded there. He left at the age of sixteen and after a few weeks of unemployment obtained a post as trainee draughtsman at Robert Jenkins & Co., Engineers and Steel Fabricators. After a period of works training he joined the Sales Department as a Cost Engineer and through the years progressed to Chief Estimator and then on to Commercial Manager, a position held when he retired in 1979 after 43 years service. This service was interrupted by the outbreak of World War II in 1939.

29 MARCH 1942. EGYPT.

As the war clouds gathered in early 1939 Alf attempted to join all three services but was rejected in each case on medical grounds. Two years later, as the service demands for men grew; Alf was conscripted and ironically given a medical grade of A1. After thirteen weeks infantry training with the Gloucester Light Infantry and five weeks at an Ordnance Depot in Burscough, Lancashire, Alf found himself with a service history of just thirteen weeks, on a draft bound for the Middle East. The convoy in which he sailed was escorted by the two battleships Princess of Wales and Renown which ships, after escorting the convoy as far as Durban, went on to the Far East where within days they were sunk by Japanese dive bombers. In all Alf spent four and a quarter years in the Middle East, serving in Egypt, Libya, Cyrenaica, Palestine, Syria and Greece.

Alf (on left in photo last page) spent the first two years of his overseas service with the Central Ordnance Provision Office, whose concern was to ensure that adequate stocks of military equipment was held at the various depots for the various campaigns. The remainder of his service in the Middle East was with the Graves Registration & Enquiry Service, which was responsible for the location of isolated burials, mainly in the Western Desert, subsequent exhumation, identification and reburial in the military cemeteries which were strung along the north coast of Africa.

Towards the end of November 1944, one month after the first landings in the liberation of Greece, Alf landed at the port of Piraeus in Greece. Within three days the country was in the grip of civil war which was to last something like six weeks before the Communist backed guerrilla forces were finally overthrown. This episode was to be the event which was to lead to his marriage to a young Greek schoolteacher, Vassilikee Liori, whom he met for the first time on 17th January 1945, got engaged to her on 4th March and married on 5th April 1945. This was a whirlwind romance, the wedding taking place eleven weeks after their first meeting. Such is the attitude of the military in time of war that Alf was posted to Egypt on 13th April, just eight days after his marriage. In that short time, however, his wife became pregnant with their first child who was born in Rotherham on 10th January 1946 and given the name of Dimitrius Edward Anthony. Their second child, a daughter Elainie, was born in Moorgate General Hospital, Rotherham at one o'clock in the afternoon on Sunday 1st May 1949, five weeks premature and weighing just four pounds eleven and three quarter ounces.

It was later in life that Alf became a keen genealogist and he helped me to link his branch into the greater Luxton family of Petton, Bampton tree. He was in possession of various memorabilia including a family portrait of his grandparents, William Charles and Elizabeth Ellen Luxton, taken in 1894 to celebrate their 40th Wedding Anniversary.

Alf died at Doncaster on 22nd August 1997 and his widow Vassilikee died in January 2001.

Dimitrius Edward Anthony Luxton, first born of Alfred William Luxton and his wife Vassilikee Liori was born in the Kimberworth Nursing Home, Rotherham in the West Riding of Yorkshire at seven o'clock in the morning on Thursday 10th January 1946. His early years were spent at the Herringthorpe Primary School from where, in 1957, he won a place at Rotherham Grammar School where his father had studied from 1931 - 1936.

After a good academic performance at the Grammar School Tony won an Exhibition to read Medicine at Lincoln College, Oxford. He gained his BA in Animal Physiology on 18th November 1967, going on to complete the clinical part of the course at Radcliffe Infirmary. He gained his BM and BCh on 12th December 1970. After the usual moves to gain experience, Tony finally chose to specialise in the care of the elderly at the Queen Elizabeth Hospital, Kings Lynn. By examination he gained admission, at the age of 29, to the Royal College of Physicians in July 1975 and was elected a Fellow in April 1989. He rose to hold the position of Consultant Physician and is now retired.

It was while at the Radcliffe Infirmary that Tony met his wife to be, Lilian Anne Berry, a Theatre Sister at the Infirmary and a daughter of Raoul Geoffrey Berry and Gladys Lilian. Tony and Anne married at St Mary's Church, Burnham-on-Crouch on 24th April 1971. They have one daughter Melanie Clare Luxton, born in the Mill Road Maternity Hospital, Cambridge on 26th July 1976 who has two children Elena Grace Anne Luxton, born 16th January 2000 and Alfred Robert Will Luxton, born 27th December 2005.

Elainie Luxton married Stuart Jordan in Tickhill Methodist Church, Doncaster on 6th June 1982. They are both retired school teachers and have a son, Matthew Alexander Jordan, born in Doncaster on 27th June 1984 and are grandparents.

63

JAMES RECHAB LUXTON (1841-1886), SOLDIER AND GREENGROCER OF TIVERTON

See tree 34

James Rechab Luxton (1841-1886), the third son of Charles Luxton (1813-1885) lace-maker, and his wife Charlotte Townshend, born in Concord Place, St James, Taunton on the 2nd January 1841, was baptised in the Wesleyan Chapel, Taunton on the 20th January. The census taken later in that same year reveals he was five months old and the family had moved to a new address in Tancred Street, St James, Taunton.

James was a 10 year old lacehand in 1851 when the family had moved to Tiverton in Devon, to work in the lace industry there. He had received some education and was in possession of a Second class school certificate when as a labourer aged 19 years 2 months he attested for the 10th Regiment of Foot (The North Lincolnshire Regiment of Foot) at Tiverton, on the 29th March 1860. Stationed at Aldershot in 1861, he served in the army 14 years 37 days during which period he was 9 years 4 months abroad. His widespread postings reflect the world power that Victorian Britain had become. For 1 year 9 months he was in the Cape of Good Hope, and 1 year 6 months on the remote island of St. Helena in the South Atlantic, made famous for the imprisonment of Napoleon. For three years and seven months he was in Japan which had only very recently been opened up to western influence, and was in the Straits Settlements which included Singapore for one year 3 months.

His name appeared six times in the Regimental Defaulters Book, and he was twice imprisoned in the barrack cells. Once on 23rd to 24th February 1863 for 'overstaying pass' and again for 'absence' on the 5th to 7th March the same year, but he was never tried by court martial and his commanding officer of the 1st Battalion of the 10th Regiment at the time of his discharge wrote in red ink that "His conduct had been very good".

James must have been proud when he was promoted Corporal on the 3rd February 1869, and he was stationed at Yokohama in Japan when on the 29th May 1869, he was re-engaged for the 10th Regiment "for such time as shall complete a total service of 21 years." But it was not to be, for although he was promoted Sergeant on the 5th October 1871, he was unable to complete his 21 years service due to ill health. Sadly the proceedings of a Regimental Board convened in Singapore, on the 16th February 1874 concluded that he was "unfit for further service."

On the 20th April 1874 James underwent a medical examination, conducted at Netley in Cheshire, where army cases of invalids from abroad were examined. Surgeon Major C.D. Madden found that James had "Valve disease of the heart due to a constitutional cause aggravated by service in hot climates first noticed at Singapore in November 1872 when the patient was under treatment for another complaint. He suffered from most serious heart disease which he can never recover from. He can contribute to his maintenance by light work only."

Interestingly, James discharge from the army on the 4th May 1874, was signed by Redvers Buller, who at the close of the 19th century was to be a famous general in the Second Boer War.

A pen portrait of James when he was discharged at Netley, on the 4th May 1874, states he was 33 years 3 months old, 5foot 6inches tall with a fresh complexion, grey eyes and dark brown hair. He had no marks or scars upon his face or other parts of his body. He was a labourer and his listed place of residence is given as Tiverton, Devon but this has been crossed out and replaced with Lambeth, Surrey. Romance was the reason for the change of address. For James Luxton, labourer, married Hannah Maria Hawkins at St. John the Evangelist, Waterloo Road, Lambeth, Surrey on the 11th May 1874. Emily, his sister, was one of the witnesses. The following day, the 12th May 1874 Sergeant James Luxton Reg. No.592 of Ist Battalion of the 10th Regiment of Foot was admitted as a Chelsea Pensioner. The couple were soon back in Tiverton.

We have shown in earlier chapters how the lace making industry compelled members of this branch of the family to move from Taunton, Tiverton and Chard, sometime in the years 1879 to 1880, to Nottingham.

However, not all of Charles and Charlotte's children left their native West Country. The Tiverton census for 1881 lists their son James Rechab Luxton, as a grocer, aged 40, and a Chelsea Pensioner, living in Bampton Street, with his wife Hannah Maria, aged 40, and their children, Charles 5, Alice 2, and Alfred 1. Bessie Hewitt, 14, a nurse and domestic servant, lived with the family. In Kelly's Devon Directory of 1883, James is listed as a fruiterer and greengrocer in Bampton Street, Tiverton. At some point he gave this up to become a rural postman.

James death was sudden. On Wednesday 1st September he did his usual "round" of deliveries as a rural letter carrier, and he spent the afternoon digging potatoes. He retired for the night at his usual time, but about one o'clock in the morning, his wife alarmed at her husband's groans, sent for Dr. Haydon who found life extinct[462]. James had died, aged 45, from valvular heart disease, on the 2nd September 1886 at Villa Franca Cottage, Tiverton. His death certificate described him as a "Rural Postman and Army Pensioner". His widow Maria was present at the death.

In the 1891 census Maria Luxton, 44, silk lace mender, and her five children aged from 5 to 15, were living at 9 Seward's Court, Tiverton. Hannah Maria Luxton, aged 72, widow of James Luxton, rural postman, died of cardiac disease at 3 Heathcoat Square, Tiverton on the 2nd August 1912. Her son Alfred J M Luxton of 205 Chapel Street, Tiverton was in attendance.

James Rechab Luxton (1841-1886) and his wife Hannah Maria Hawkins had three daughters and two sons. Alice, born above the greengrocer's shop in Bampton Street, Tiverton on the 11th May 1878, was a 12 year old silk winder in a lace factory, living in 1891 with her widowed mother at 9 Seward's Court, Tiverton. She was a 29 year old spinster of 3 Heathcote Square, Leat Street, Tiverton when she married Walter Gollop 27, a Private in the Royal Marines, stationed at the Marine Barracks, East Stonehouse at the Registry Office in East Stonehouse, on the 10th January 1910. Walter, a Corporal in the Royal Marine Light Infantry, died in

---

[462] Western Times, Friday 3rd September 1886.

1914. Alice died of cancer on 16th December 1923, at the age of 45, cared for by her sister Emily.

Her sister, Emily, born above the greengrocer's Bampton Street, Tiverton, on the 22nd June 1882, was a 23 year old spinster of Heathcoat Square, when she married Alfred Beamer, 25, Private in the Royal Marine Light Infantry at St Paul's West Exe, Tiverton, on the 14th December 1905. He died, aged 29, on 1st December 1909. She then married John Heard, a coal yard labourer in the United Methodist Church, Tiverton, on the 8th December 1912. Emily died, aged 79, at 4 Moorhayes Bungalows, Tiverton on 7th February 1962.

Jessie, the youngest girl, the daughter of James Luxton, rural postman and his wife Maria was born at Villa Franca Cottage, Tiverton on the 26th June 1886. She was a 23 year old spinster of Heathcoat Square, Tiverton, when she married Charles Kenward, 31 year old Marine in the parish church of St Paul, Tiverton on the 12th April 1910. Jennie Kenwood, widow and retired proprietor of a general store, died in Gillingham Kent on 18th January 1978.

James Rechab and Hannah Maria's eldest child, Charles Frank Luxton (1876-1961) was born in Bampton Street, Tiverton, on the 28th January 1876 and was baptised at St. Peters, Tiverton on 12th February. He was a five year old scholar in 1881, living at home with his parents. In 1891 he was a 15 year old machine boy in a lace factory, living with his widowed mother and brother and sisters at 9 Seward's Court, Tiverton. Charles Frank Luxton, a twenty year old wheelwright, living in Cheriton Fitzpaine, married 19 year old Lucy Rayment, a domestic servant, at the Register Office, Crediton, on the 30th January 1897. Both sign the register, witnessed by John and Richard Rayment. Lucy Rayment was five months pregnant and their son Frank Cecil Luxton, was born at Little Venn, Cheriton Fitzpaine on the 23rd May 1897. His father Charles Frank Luxton was now a Railway Porter.

The young couple and their son moved to Lambeth in London where Charles Frank Luxton, was a Railway Porter when Alice, a daughter was born at 5 Thorne Street, Wandsworth Road, on 18th April 1900.

By 1911 Charles Frank Luxton 35, railway porter, his wife Lucy, 34 and their five young children were living at 10, Riverhall Street,

Lambeth. Two more children had died. A widow and her two young daughters were lodging with the family. He was a railway porter, living at 51 Southville, Houndsworth Road SW8 when his wife Lucy, aged 57, died of pulmonary tuberculosis at Lambeth Hospital on the 26th May 1935. Twenty five years later, Charles, an 85 year old Railway Goods Foreman (retired) of 14 Kettleby House, Barrington Road, Lambeth, died of heart disease and broncho pneumonia, at Kings College Hospital, Denmark Hill, Lambeth on the 5th April 1961.

Charles Frank Luxton (1876-1961) and his wife, Lucy Rayment, had issue of at least seven children. Two were dead by 1911 and I do not have details. Alice, (1900-1987) the eldest daughter, born on 18th April 1900, was a 23 year old shop assistant when she married Arthur William Elliott, a 24 year old pastry cook in Christ Church, Clapham, Surrey after banns on the 3rd June 1923. Mrs Alice Elliott lived at 4 Aspley Road, Wandsworth when her mother died in 1935. The 1939 Register lists her there, "household duties" with her husband Arthur, confectioner and baker. Her sister, Emily (1904-1990), born on 22nd June 1904 at 5 Thorne Street, Lambeth, married Percival Robert Attfield, 25, a silk warehouse porter, at Lambeth Register Office on 18 December 1926. She died in Merton; Greater London, aged 85, in February 1990. The youngest daughter, Jessie (1909-1989), born on the 21st April 1909, was aged 19 when she married Robert George Baker, 21, a carrier's good checker, at Lambeth Register Office on 28th January 1928.

Frank Cecil Luxton (1897-1962), the eldest son, was a postman, aged 18 years and 7 months, when he enlisted in the 8th battalion of the London Regiment at Clapham on the 10th December 1915. He was 5 foot 7 inches tall, and weighed 114 lbs with a chest size of 35 inches when fully expanded. He was made a Lieutenant on 1st July 1917, when transferred to the Royal Irish Rifles and was awarded the British War Medal and the Victory Medal.

He was a 23 year old postman of 2 Undine Street, Tooting when he married Amy Ella Pooley, (1894-1959) a 26 year old spinster at the Congregational Church, Mitcham Road, Tooting, Wandsworth on the 4th July 1920. Amy Ella died, aged 65, on 9th March 1959 at St. Helier Hospital, Carshalston Surrey, leaving £77..14s..10d. Frank Cecil Luxton, a retired postman of 86 Hassocks Road, Streatham died aged 64 from broncho pneumonia at St. James Hospital, Balham, Battersea on the 31st January 1962, leaving an estate valued at £3,185..17 shillings.

The couple had two children. Joyce Doris Luxton, (1921-1999), born at their home 2 Undine Street, Tooting on the 18th April 1921, was a corporal in the W.A.A.F. when she married John David Spurway, (1926-1991), a pilot officer in the R.A.F. at Epsom Register Office Surrey on the 15th December 1947. Joyce died in the New Forest Hampshire in January 1999. Their son Ronald Charles Luxton, (1923-2016) born at 6 Undine Street, Tooting on the 17th March 1923, joined the Royal Artillery in 1942 and was posted to the Reserves on 3rd April 1947 before being transferred to the Royal Signals on 19th October 1951. He was a 23 year old cartographer of 84 Hassocks Road, Mitcham, when he married Joan Olive Wing (1924-2000) 22, spinster, at Christchurch, Croydon on the 21st September 1946. Ronald died in Croydon on the 19th December 2016.

The couple who lived at 169 Mitcham Road, West Croydon, had issue two daughters, Janet Anne on the 7th August 1954 and Ruth Gillian on the 16th June 1959. Both girls trained as teachers and the family were living at 5 Pleasant Grove, Shirley, Croydon when Janet married Robert Geoffrey Fowlds, director of an upholstery manufacturer at All Saints, Spring Park, Croydon on the 27th May 1978. Her sister Ruth Gillian married Bruce Louis Offergelt a trainee accountant in the same church on the 25th July 1981.

Charles Frank Luxton (1876-1961), had a second son, Alfred James Luxton (1902-1967), who was born at 5 Thorne Street, Lambeth on the 14th September 1902. He was admitted in 1918, at the age of 15 as a messenger in the National Union of Railwaymen and was a twenty year old railway porter when he married Sarah Ann Dickens at the Register Office, Lambeth on the 14th August 1923. The couple lived at 67 Frederick Road, Cheam in Sutton and Cheam, Surrey. He was a railway goods loader when Sarah died, aged 40, from pulmonary tuberculosis at Cumberland House, Mitcham, Surrey on 31st March 1941. Alfred James Luxton was a gunner (no.11266887) in the Royal Field Artillery, during the Second World War. He lived at 18 Thoresby Avenue, Tuffley, Gloucester where he died on the 1st May 1967, leaving an estate valued at £4002.

Alfred James Luxton (1902-1967) and his wife Sarah Ann Dickens had three children, Gwendoline, (1924-1986) was an 18 year old assembler in a munition factory when she married a Royal Marine, Peter Michael Fitzgerald on 10th July 1943. She married for a second time to Les James (1924-1999) and died in Gloucester on 5th August 1986. Frank Alfred Luxton, (1927-2014) a son, (see photograph below) born in Stockwell, Lambeth on 8th March 1927, was a nineteen year old soldier when he married Sheila Sizer (1926-2013) an 18 year old waitress, in the parish church of Cheam in Surrey on the 25th August 1945. Frank, a confectioner and pastry cook, of 97 Boscombe Road Cheam had two sons Colin Frank James Luxton in 1949 and David William Luxton in 1951. He married for a second time, to Gloria Pamela O'Connor at the Methodist Chapel, Queen's Road, Peckham on 18th June 1966, and died in Worthing West Sussex on 26th September 2014. His sister, Brenda Margaret Luxton (1930-2012), born 19th April 1930 in Lambeth, died on the 8th May in Shanklin on the Isle of Wight.

Alfred James Massey Luxton (1880-1972), the second son of James Rechab Luxton, market gardener, and his wife Hannah Maria Hawkins, was born at Bampton Street, Tiverton, on the 1st April 1880. In 1891 he was a ten year old machine boy living with his widowed mother at 9 Seward's Court. Alfred was a 32 year old cellarman of 3 Heathcoat Square, Tiverton, when he married Maud Hill 24 spinster of Lotley Water, Upton, daughter of George Hill, woodman at St James Upton, Somerset on the 17th July 1912. Both sign in the presence of Alice Tout and George Hill. The Tiverton Borough Directory for 1937 lists him as Alfred Luxton, shop assistant, residing at 15 Park Terrace. Maud, his wife, died aged 73 at 15 Park Terrace on the 28th April 1964.

Following a long life, Alfred James Massy Luxton, a retired Public School Groundsman, died aged 92 at his home Alexandra Lodge Tiverton on the 14th October 1972. There were no children of the marriage.

Frank Alfred Luxton (1927-2014)

64

ROBERT LUXTON (1786 – 1871)
CARPENTER AND JOINER IN HIGH STREET,
TAUNTON, SOMERSET AND HIS FAMILY

See tree 35 & 38

Robert baptised as Robert Luxon at Petton on the 2nd April 1786, was the third son of John Luxton (1747–1818) yeoman of Corner House, Petton, and his wife Mary Redwood. His father bequeathed him a silver watch which was delivered at the time of his father's interment at Petton on the 12th July 1818 and three pounds payable in three years after his father's decease.

Robert qualified as a carpenter and joiner before he married Elizabeth Turner at St. Mary Magdalene, Taunton, on Monday 5th November 1810. The newly wed couple settled in High Street, Taunton and in the next quarter century they had issue twelve children who were all baptised in the magnificent parish church of St. Mary Magdalene situated near the centre of the town. John (1811–1884) their eldest son who was baptised on the 6th October 1811 was followed by Ann on the 28th November 1813, George (1815–1878) on the 12th November 1815, Robert on the 7th February 1819, Francis Turner (1820 – 1873) on 25th December 1820, Jane Agnes on the 8th December 1822, Elizabeth Grace on the 31st October 1824, James Marshall on the 8th October 1826, Maria on the 13th April 1828, James Turner (1830–1853) on the 12th September 1830, Mary Ann on the 28th October, 1832 and finally a second Robert on the 1st March 1835.

In this photograph the Church of St. Mary Magdalene stands at the end of Hammet Street. A planned development begun in 1778 by Sir Benjamin Hammet opened up a vista of the 165ft church tower. The original tower of 1488-1514 was completely rebuilt in 1858-62. The tower contains a carillon of bells, playing tunes on the hour.

When the 1841 census was taken Robert, a 50 year old carpenter, and Elizabeth a 45 year old laundress, were still resident in High Street, St. Mary Magdalene parish, together with five of their children, Jane 18, Elizabeth 16, James 12, Mary 8 and Robert 6. The family continued to live in High Street in 1851, when Robert, aged 64, was a journeyman carpenter, and Elizabeth, was a washerwoman. Robert their youngest son aged 16; an apprentice cabinet maker, was the only one of their sons still at home. Their married daughter Elizabeth Grace Snook 25, laundress and her husband George Snook, a journeyman carpenter, also lived with them.

It was probably some time after this youngest son Robert left home that the couple moved to Magdalene Lane. The 1861 St. Mary Magdalene Taunton census finds them living at The Almshouse, 4 Magdalene Lane where Robert, aged 74, formerly a carpenter. His wife Elizabeth, aged 71, was formerly a laundress.

That is where they were living when Elizabeth aged 75, died and was buried in the nearby St. Mary Magdalene churchyard on the 6th March, 1865. Her husband, Robert, aged 84, Magdalene Lane died six years later and was buried with his wife on the 17th August 1871. His death announcement in the West Somerset Free Press reads:- August 12th, in the Almshouse Magdalene-lane, Taunton, Mr. Robert Luxton, aged 86 years.[463]

Two of the couple's sons died in childhood. Robert Luxton, aged 14, of High Street was buried at St. Mary Magdalene on the 1st September 1833 and James Marshall Luxton, aged one, was buried there on 28th October 1827. Their youngest son, Robert joined the Army in 1855, where as Gunner Robert Luxton No. 4881 he served as a soldier for 21 years 3 months. This included foreign service of three years three months in

[463] West Somerset Free Press, Saturday 26th August 1871.

China and two years 7 months in India. When Robert completed his Army service, aged 41, on the 5th December 1876 he was described as a cabinet maker, 5ft.7 ½ inches tall with brown hair, grey eyes and a florid complexion. His character was very good and he had four good conduct badges to prove it. Robert Luxton died aged 41 in Plymouth in 1876[464]. I say more about him in a future chapter.

Robert and Elizabeth's daughter Elizabeth Grace, born in 1824, was in London in the 1840s where she signed the register when her sister Jane Agnes married at St. Mary's Haggerston in October 1848. A laundress, aged 23, of Woodforde's Buildings she married George Snook, 20, a carpenter and joiner, in the Baptist Chapel, Silver Street, Taunton on the 27th March 1851. The census in April that year, has the newly wed couple living in High Street, Taunton with her parents. However, by 1861 they were living with four young children in Weston-Super-Mare and the growing family were at 1 Alma Street, in Clifton, Bristol, a decade later. Elizabeth died, aged 53, of chronic phthisis at home in 12 Woodborough Street, Bristol on 4th November 1880.

When the 1851 Taunton census was taken her sisters Maria, aged 23, a dress maker, and Mary Ann, aged 19, a laundress, were living in High Street, Taunton with their aunt Agnes Turner, aged 59, a laundress. Maria 24, a dressmaker, married Alfred Allen 22, grocer of Eastover in the Baptist Chapel, Bridgwater on the 6th March 1853. They settled in Wellington Street, Bedminster, Bristol where they raised a family. Maria Allen died at 39 Queen Square, Bristol aged 67, on the 15th June 1895. Her sister Mary Ann aged 22, of Canon Street married John Oaten, 22, printer, in St. James, Taunton on the 5th November 1854. In 1861 they were living with Maria Allen and family in Wellington Street, Bedminster but were in Shoreditch in the 1870s and Picton Street, Bristol in the 1880s. In 1891 Mary Ann Oaten, a widow, was a laundress living with Maria Allen, her widowed sister at 3 Wellington Road Bedminster but died aged 58 at 42 Eldon Road, Canton, Cardiff on the 11th May 1892.

The six remaining children left Taunton to seek their livelihood in the rapidly expanding London of the early 19th Century. John Luxton

---

[464] Wo/116/146 Kew P.R.O.

(1811-1884), the eldest brother, who qualified as a cabinet maker, led this exodus to the metropolis. He left Taunton as a carpenter around 1832, and settled just off Old Street, Shoreditch London. There he married Elizabeth Pearce at St. Luke's, Old Street, Finsbury on the 11th February 1834. John was made a widower at the early age of 37 when his wife Elizabeth, aged 35, who had been ill two years, died of consumption at their home 11 Norfolk Street, Islington on the 17th August 1849. In 1881 at the age of 69, John was lodging with Joseph Maslin, a police officer and family, at 36 Nicholas Street Shoreditch, and he was to stay a widower for 35 years before his own death at 7 Great James Street, Hoxton, Shoreditch on 13th January 1884. I have more to say on John and his family in the next chapter.

John (1811–1884) was followed to London by at least two sisters who married there. Ann born 1813, was of 122 Old Street, when she married William Chard, a cabinet maker at St. Luke, Middlesex on the 23rd November 1837. Sadly Ann Chard of Macclesfield Street, St. Luke, Old Street was only 27 when she died and was buried 28th May 1840. Her sister Jane Agnes born 1822, lived at 8 Canal Road when she married Samuel Beal, a wood carver, at St. Mary Haggerston, Middlesex on the 30th October 1848. The marriage was witnessed by her sister Elizabeth Grace Luxton. In 1851 the young couple lived with an infant daughter at 26 Pearson Street, Shoreditch and they had moved to 35 Appleby Street by 1861 where Jane 39 is an ironer and daughter Jane A is12. Jane aged 42, the wife of Samuel Beale, a journeyman woodcarver, died of phthisis in Shoreditch Workhouse on the 9th June 1865. Samuel, a widower and chair carver, married 18 year old Sarah Ann Farr at Christchurch, Hoxton on 2nd October 1870 and they had a family. A 42 year old master wood carver Samuel and his new wife Sarah Ann Farr, 19, a milliner born in St. Lukes, the daughter of Joseph Farr, a bootmaker are listed at 20 Leonard Street, Shoreditch in 1871. His daughter Jane aged 21 by his first wife Jane Agnes, is blind.

Three of John's brothers settled in the city. George (1815-1878) a chair maker, was almost certainly resident there by 1837, when he was a witness to his sister Ann's wedding. He had taken a wife Jane by 1850. In 1851 census his wife Jane Luxton, visitor, married 25, born in Middlesex c.1826 and her infant son, George Luxton aged 3 months, were visiting George Leach, 29, and family at 45 St. Nicholas Street

Hoxton. He was involved in a watch and jewellery business. When the 1861 census was taken George Luxton, a 45 year old chair maker born in Taunton, his wife Jane 31 and three young children born in Shoreditch, George 10, Alfred 7 and Clara 5 lived at 16 Craven Street, St. Leonards, Shoreditch.

The family appear to have split as by 1871 his wife Jane 44, dressmaker, born in Paddington, describing herself as a widow, and their son Alfred 17, book binder apprentice, were living at 9 Wood Street, St. Lukes Finsbury. George was found dead at his home, 2 President Place, Old Street, St. Luke on the 3rd March 1878. He was aged 62, and the cause of death was given as syncope (i.e. loss of consciousness from fall of blood pressure). By 1881 Jane, a 55 year old widow dressmaker, born in St Pancras, was lodging with Jesse Burrows and family at 45 Wall Street, Islington. In 1891 Jane 65, seamstress now saying she was born in Bloomsbury, was living with her son Alfred 37, a book binders porter, in James Street, Islington. Jane Luxton aged 74, of 11 Church Street, Islington, widow of George Luxton, cabinet maker journeyman, died at Islington Infirmary on 11th February 1899.

Their daughter, Clara Luxton, 15, was a servant in household of Thomas Mears at St. Paul Crescent, St. Pancras in 1871. Clara married John Clement Ingham (1855-1916) in St. Mary, Islington on 29th April 1877. Her elder brother may be the George A. Luxton 20, grocer's assistant, born in Islington, lodging in High Street, Woolwich in 1871.

Clara's brother Alfred Luxton (c.1854-1925), born in Hoxton, Shoreditch spent regular short spells in the Workhouse in Hackney and St. John's Road Workhouse in Islington throughout his adult life. The earliest reference I have noted was in the Hackney Workhouse when he was aged 21, when he was admitted for two days on 8th September 1875. Again on the 23rd June 1876 aged 22, he was "destitute" and was admitted to the Infirmary. There are many references until his death in the 1920s.

He was a porter aged 23 years 6 months, when he attested on the 10th July 1877 to join the general service infantry. He was 5ft 8inch with a chest measurement of over34 inches, a fresh complexion, hazel eyes and dark auburn hair. He had the letter "A" tattoed on his left forearm and a scar on the right side of the neck. A member of the Church of England he was posted to the 30th Brigade on 13th July 1877. He was discharged from the Army a year later aged 24 years and 6 months with a "bad character" reference. His intended place of residence was Windsor Street, Essex Road, Islington.

Alfred, now a bookbinder, married Eliza Dorey 39, widow, at St Saviour's Church Southwark on the 23rd October 1892. In 1901 he was a 47 year old widower, book binder, living at 28 Hanover Street, Islington. Alfred Luxton, 71, bookbinder journeyman, of 12 Fowler Road Islington died at 182 Westmorland Road, Walmouth on 26th April 1925. His niece F. A. Rogers who lived in Stoke Newington was in attendance.

George's brother, Francis Turner Luxton (1820 –1873), a master chair-maker had moved to London by 1851 as he married his first wife Elizabeth Ann Pritchard, on the 8th June that year at St. John the Baptist Church, Hoxton, Shoreditch, built in 1826 in the late Regency style. They had a daughter, Elizabeth Annie, born on the 15th December 1853 at 32 Somerset Place Hoxton and a daughter Mary Catherine born in 1856.

Rapidly expanding London was over-crowded and Francis and family had to share accommodation with Samuel and Julia Gashier, iron and furniture dealer, at 32 Somerset Place. Tensions arose between them and by the summer of 1857 the two families were involved in a bitter feud which had existed for sometime. Matters came to a head on the morning of the 18th June when Francis asked Gashier if he would take in goods standing in the doorway. A "noise" ensued between them and Francis took up the leg of a chair with which Mrs. Julia Gashier struck him in the face "in a violent manner." The matter was settled in the local Police Court on Monday the 6th July where Francis accused Mrs. Gashier of assault[465]. The presiding magistrate concluded as there had been contention between the two parties he would only fine Mrs. Gashier 5s. with costs. Francis was very dissatisfied by this decision. He moved out of no.32 Somerset Place and in a second appearance

---

[465] Morning Chronicle, Tuesday 7th July 1857.

before the same court[466] he was found guilty of wilfully damaging Mr. Gashier's gas pipe connected to the street lamp. His bad temper cost him a fine of 13s..6d with10s. costs.

Francis's first wife Elizabeth Ann, died aged 33 of epilepsy on the 31st March 1865 at 20 Walbrook Place, Hoxton, New Town, Shoreditch, leaving Francis a widower, with their young daughter Mary Catherine. She was buried at Victoria Park Cemetery, Hackney on the 6th April 1865.

Maria Pritchard who Francis married at St. Mary Lambeth on the 1st April 1866, may have been related to his first wife. Harriet Sophia, a daughter was born to the couple in 1869. When the 1871 census was taken Francis, his wife Maria, and his two daughters, were residing at 22 Watson Place, Shoreditch. Sadly Maria aged 25, was already terminally ill with consumption. She suffered for two years with what her death certificate called "Phthisis Pulmonalis" before she died on 17th November 1871 at 22 Watson Place. Francis himself ill for 3 years was dying with consumption and he died aged 53, on the 21st July 1873 at 13 Wellington Street, Shoreditch.

This photograph is of Francis's eldest daughter Elizabeth Annie Luxton (1853-1926) who married William Brown (1850-1896), a butcher, on the 12th November 1871 in St. Johns, Hoxton. In 1891 they lived at

33 Boston Street, Shoreditch. By 1901 Elizabeth a widow, 48, was an office cleaner, living at 29 Jefford Street, Shoreditch with five children still at home. The 1911 census records her living in three rooms at 272 Hoxton Street. Her eight children were all living.

His daughter, Mary Catherine, baptised at Christchurch, Hoxton 20th July 1856, married William Evans, a tinplate worker, at St. Monica's Roman Catholic Chapel Hoxton Square, Shoreditch 13th June 1880. As Mary

---

[466] Morning Chronicle, Saturday 25th July 1857.

Catherine Evans 51 widow of 19 Culford Road, Hackney she married Thomas William Jeffries, 66 master wheelwright, widower, at St. Peter's Hackey on 28th March 1909. His first wife Mary Ann Luxton (1840-1907) was Mary's first cousin.

Her half sister, Harriet Sophia Luxton, baptised at Christchurch Hoxton 4th April 1869, married John Dean, an iron galvanizer, in St. Mary Haggerstone 2nd August 1891. In 1911 they lived at 31 Clinger Street, Hoxton with 17 children aged 2 to 19. Harriet died aged 59 from gastric influenza at her home 47 Rushton Street, Shoreditch, on 15th February 1929.

A third brother, James Turner Luxton, born in Taunton in 1830, was aged 28 (sic), a cabinet maker, in 1851, lodging with his brother Francis, 30 (sic), chairmaker, at 2 Charles Court, St. Luke, Old Street. A cabinet maker aged 23, he died at Shoreditch Workhouse on the 20th August 1853 from what his death certificate called "Effusion on the Brain" (i.e. a stroke). The Shoreditch Workhouse Register records that his brother Francis Luxton, aged 32 of Somerset Place, Hackney Road, took the body away from the Workhouse for burial. James Luxton of 9 Brunswick Street, was buried at St Mary's, Haggerston on the 27th August 1853.

This then is the family of Robert Luxton (1786–1871) carpenter and his wife Elizabeth Turner who had twelve children born in Taunton between 1810 and 1835. I do not know if any of their descendants still live in Taunton but there appear to be none in the male line. When I went in search of Robert and Elizabeth's grave there was no headstone to mark the spot, but the fine lofty perpendicular tower of St. Mary Magdalene Church towering over 150 foot above their busy lives in High Street, and Magdalene Lane, continues to look down on their unmarked resting place.

65

JOHN LUXTON (1811-1884) CHAIR MAKER OF ST. LUKES FINSBURY AND ST. LEONARDS, SHOREDITCH.

See tree 35

John Luxton (1811-1884), the eldest son of Robert Luxton (1786-1871), carpenter of Taunton, and his wife Elizabeth Turner, baptised at St Mary Magdalene, Taunton on 6th October 1811, led the exodus of his brothers and sisters to the metropolis. He left Taunton as a carpenter around 1832, and settled just off Old Street, Shoreditch London. There he married Elizabeth Pearce at St. Luke's, Old Street, Finsbury on the 11th October 1834. The church, built in the mid eighteenth century to meet the religious needs of London's burgeoning population, has an obelisk spire designed by Nicholas Hawksmoor. John and Elizabeth had seven children. The first four were baptised at St. Lukes, Old Street, Finsbury, but the family had moved houses when the three

youngest were baptised at St. Leonards, Shoreditch. Their youngest son Robert died in 1845 aged 1 year and 9 months from measles and pneumonia.

John was made a widower at the early age of 37, when his wife Elizabeth, aged 35, who had been ill two years, died of consumption, at their home 11 Norfolk Street, Islington on the 17th August 1849. In 1881, at the age of 69, John was lodging with Joseph Maslin, a police officer and family, at 36 Nicholas Street, Shoreditch and he was to stay a widower for 35 years before his own death at 7 Great James Street, Hoxton, Shoreditch on 13th January 1884.

I will make mention of their five daughters before concentrating on their eldest son John (1836-1891) and his offspring. Ann Rebecca Luxton (1837-1916) married James Crofts, labourer, in St James, Shoreditch on 16th September 1860. The widow of James Croft, hawker, of 69 Fellows Street, Shoreditch, Ann died aged 77 of senile decay at Shoreditch Infirmary on 19th May 1916. Ann had 12 children but only 6 were still living in 1911. Jane Agnes Luxton (1839-1912) aged 22, and her sister Mary Ann 20, were servants to Henry Roberts, a pawnbroker, at 2 Lansdowne Place, Islington in 1861. Jane Agnes married George Forty, cabinet maker, at St. John the Baptist Hoxton 17th May 1864. She died aged 73 at Buckland Street, Shoreditch on 5th November 1912.

Her sister Mary Ann Luxton (1840-1907) married Thomas William Jeffries, chimney sweep, at St. Mary Haggerston on 26th January 1862. By 1881 Thomas was a wheelwright, and the couple were living in Shoreditch with four children aged under 10. In 1891 Thomas, 48, wheelwright, and Mary Ann, 50, were living with five of their children at 19 Culford Road, Hackney. The family is at 19 Culford Road Hackney in 1901 where Thomas is a general wheelwright aged 58, Mary Ann 60 and there are three different teenage children at home. Mary Ann died aged 65 (sic) from heart disease, on 25th April 1907, in Hertford, Hertfordshire. Thomas (1843-1920) married her cousin Mary Catherine Evans, a widow, at St Peters, Hackney on 28 March 1909. In 1911 Thomas Jeffries was living at the same address with his new wife Mary Catherine aged 53. They had been married two years.

Mary Ann Jeffries sister, Maria Luxton, was born at 4 Europa Place, St Luke, on 10th March 1842 and baptised at St Leonards, Shoreditch 6th June 1844. The youngest child Eliza Luxton, baptised at St. Leonards on 22nd February 1846 died aged 3 from "anascarca 2 weeks" (dropsy) at 1 Harland Square Shoreditch on 12th February 1849. The photograph next page is of St Leonards.

John (1836–1891) their eldest son, baptised 31st January 1836, became a chair maker in Shoreditch and Islington. He married Adelaide Rostance, at St. James Church, Shoreditch, on the 12th May 1856 and

they had a daughter, Mary Ann Adelaide, born on 6th March 1857, at 14, St. John's Row, St. Luke, before his wife died aged 22, on the 19th May 1859 at St. Bartholomew's Hospital, West London from "obstruction of the bowels peritonitis".

John Luxton, 25, widower, chairmaker, 25 Moneyer Street, son of John Luxton chairmaker, married Jane Kelsey, 18, spincaster, of 51 Holywell Street, daughter of James Kelsey, cordwainer, at St. James Church, Shoreditch on the 25th December 1860. John signs and Jane makes her mark. In 1861 John Luxton, 25, chair maker, born St. Luke's, Jane his wife, born Bethnal Green and Adelaide 4 were residing at 53 Moneyer Street, St. Leonard, Shoreditch. They shared house with another family.

They had ten children, beginning with their eldest son, John who was born at 30 Moneyer Street, Hoxton, New Town, on the 5th December 1864. His mother Jane signed his birth certificate, as she did for all her children, with her mark. A daughter Jane was born at 25 Union Street, Hoxton, New Town, Shoreditch on the 27th October 1866. James, a second son, baptised at St. John the Baptist, Shoreditch on the 1st August 1868, was followed by a brother William who was baptised there on the 18th June 1871.John Luxton, 35, journeyman chair maker, his wife Jane, Adelaide, 14 bonnet box maker, John 6, Jane 4 James 1 resided at 30 Union Street, Hoxton, Shoreditch in 1871 census. They shared the house. At this date Hoxton was one of the worst parts of London with poverty and overcrowding as the salient features of its dark narrow, filthy cluttered streets.

The family had moved to 3 Marson Street, Union Street, Hoxton, New Town, Shoreditch, and John was a labourer, when their son Edward, aged 12 hours, died of convulsions, on the 23rd March 1873. Mary Ann baptised at St. John the Baptist, Shoreditch on 17th July 1874, died aged 3½ on 3rd January 1878 from Tabes Mesenterica. (a wasting disease of the spinal column). Henry baptised at St. John Baptist, Hoxton, on the

4th June 1876 was followed by Richard who was baptised there on the 28th June 1878. The family were still living at 3 Marson Street, when Joseph was born on the 6th October 1880 and George on the 10th September 1882.

The 1881 Shoreditch census for 3 Marson Street lists the family, John 45 chairmaker, Jane 37, boot closer, Adelaide 24, box maker, John 16, labourer, Jane 14, box maker, James 11 and William 9 were both scholars and the youngest children were Henry 4, Richard 2, and Joseph aged 6 months.

The family had moved to 63 Moneyer Street, Hoxton, New Town by the 10th April 1887 when the daughter Jane, aged 20, married James Huntingdon 22, a well borer at St. John the Baptist Hoxton. The 1891 census at that address has John 54, chairmaker, Jane 47, laundress, James 22, fancy brace maker, William 20, cardboard box cutter, Henry 14, gents tie cutter, Richard 12, picture frame maker carver, Joseph 10 and George 8 were scholars. The family occupied a shared property.

It was at 63 Moneyer Street, Hoxton, New Town, Shoreditch that John aged 55, a journeyman chair maker, died on the 15th July 1891 of pleurisy and pneumonia exhaustion, Jane, his widow, was present at the death.

Jane was a 54 year old widow, of 88 Britannia Street, when she married Thomas Bailey 61, widower, and ground worker at Holy Trinity Church, Hoxton on the 17th December 1898. The 1901 census for 88 Britannia Street lists Thomas Bailey 66, sewer man, his wife Jane 57, and three of her sons-Richard Luxton 22, Joseph Luxton 20, George Luxton 18 who are described as tie cutters, her grand-daughter, Adelaide Knight, 16 card box maker, and her grandson John 12, the eldest son of John Luxton and his wife Alice Agombar.

Jane Bailey, aged 64, the wife of Thomas Bailey, a sewerman, of 88 Britannia Street, Hoxton, died at St Bartholomews Hospital in the city of London on the 7th October 1908. Jane was often liberal with her age! The daughter of James and Rebecca Kelsey, cordwainer, she was born in Bethnal Green c. 1834 so she was about 74 when she died. She had successfully steered her children into the next generation.

Adelaide, John's eldest child, the daughter of his first wife, Adelaide Rostance, married George Knight, chair carver/maker, in the parish church of South Hackney on the 4th November 1883. None of John's other children maintained the family connection with chair making. Adelaide, who was a fancy box maker, and her husband George Knight, chair maker, lived with their young family at 3 Marson Street, Shoreditch in 1891 which was formerly her grandparent's old home but she was a widow with a young family at 24 Newton Street, Shoreditch by 1901. She married James Kite, a 40 year old widower and labourer, of 22 Newton Street at St. Anne's, Hoxton, Shoreditch on 28th July 1901 and signs her wedding with a cross. Adelaide Kite, aged 48 of 24 Wilmer Gardens, Shoreditch died of pulmonary tuberculosis at Shoreditch Infirmary on 11th April 1905.

Six of John and Jane Luxton's sons continued to live in the Shoreditch and Islington area of the city. John, (1864-1930), the eldest son, was a fancy box maker's warehouseman, of 63 Moneyer Street, when he married Amy Alice Agombar, the daughter of a silk weaver probably of Huguenot descent, at St. John the Baptist, Hoxton, on the 28th April 1889. In 1891 he is listed as a warehouseman, with Alice, a paper box maker, and one year old son John at 71 Provost Street Hoxton. He is recorded in the same address in 1901 where he is a porter, and Alice, a fancy box maker, with four young children. His widowed mother in law Ellen 47 and his wife's sisters-Louisa 18, board liner, and Harriet 16 a French polisher are living with them.

By 1911 his household is at 21 Myrtle Street, Hoxton where he is a 45 year old packer in a warehouse, Alice a 43 year old cardboard box maker and just Adelaide aged 12 is at home. John, a master window cleaner of 189 Chatham Avenue Shoreditch, died aged 65 on 20th January 1930 from a stroke at 204 Hoxton Street. One wonders if this happened while he was on his window cleaning round? His wife Amy was present but otherwise there is no mention of the circumstances of his death. Amy his wife was living at 59 Mildmay Grove, Islington, with her youngest daughter Adelaide Steadman (1898-1977) when she died aged 93 at Hackney Hospital on 30th November 1959.

Jane Luxton (1866-1907) his sister, born at 25 Union Street Hoxton, married James Huntingdon, a well borer, at St. John the Baptist, Hoxton on 10th April 1887. In 1901 they lived at 3 Curzon Street, Shoreditch, James was a slater and Jane a box maker. Her husband was a dock labourer when Jane aged 40, died at 34 Salisbury Street, Shoreditch on the 6th March 1907.

His brother James (1868-1947), was aged 29, a fancy leather cutter, of 28 Britannia Street when he married Elizabeth Mary Ann Rollason on 10th October 1898, at Holy Trinity Church, Hoxton. In 1901 the couple live at 52 Murray Street, Shoreditch where James, 31, is a leather cutter, and Elizabeth, 27, a blouse machinist with infant son George. By 1911 they are living at 5 Edmunds Place, Hoxton. James 41 is a fancy leather cutter for purses/wallets etc. for Thos. De La Rue. Elizabeth is 37. They have been married 14 years and have five young children listed. Two more have died. The 1939 Register lists James, a leather cutter, living in Levington Street, Finsbury. James died aged 77 in Finsbury on 21st May 1947 and Elizabeth of 15 Birnbeck Way, Greenford Ealing died aged 80 on 31st January 1954, at the home of their son George (1900-1973). He was the second of eight children, four of whom died young, including two in accidents. See Tree 38 for details.

William (1871–1909), a foreman fancy box cutter, of 88 Britannia Street, married Sarah Oughton at St. John the Baptist Church, Hoxton on the 1st August 1896. In 1901 William, 29, fancy card box cutter, and his wife Sarah were living at 113 Packington Street, Islington. Sarah died, aged 33, from a "pelvic deformity and obstructed labour" in Islington on 6th January 1906 and William died of "tubicular disease of lungs 12 months & tubicular disease of larynx 3 months" at 52 Linton Street, Islington on 28th January 1909. In the 1911 census their orphaned son William Horace Luxton (1903-1972) aged seven, was being brought up by his aunt Louisa and her husband Frederick Stratford, a leather bag maker, at 25 Arlington Square, Islington. William, a transport clerk, married Winifred Mead at St John's, Upper Holloway on 3rd September 1927. Their daughter Joy married George Hunn in 1958 and they lived in Harlow, Essex.

Henry (1876–1929), a gentleman's silk tie cutter, of 88 Britannia Street, married Harriet Eliza Bailey, at St. John the Baptist, Hoxton on the 5th April 1896. In 1901 they were at 35 Britannia Street, Shoreditch,

with a daughter Harriet, 4 and were at 18 Britannia Dwellings in 1911 when Harriet, now 14 was a machinist for ties, and his Step-father, Thomas Bailey 74, was a retired sewerman pensioner. His wife Harriet Eliza was aged 50, when she died of breast cancer at 59 Mildmay Grove, Islington on the 25th October 1926. Henry married Ada Bailey 45, spinster at St Jude's, Islington on 29th October 1927. Henry and his second wife Ada are photographed at Folkestone in the summer of 1927. When Henry of 191 Southgate Road, Islington died on the 24th February 1929 he left a personal estate valued at £606 0s 2d. Ada his second wife died aged 88 at Hackney Hospital on 22nd February 1969. His daughter Harriet Eliza married Walter Wilkinson, a policeman at St. Jude's, Islington on 29th October 1921 and they had two sons Victor and William.

Richard (1878–1931), was a belt maker, employed by Mr. Hess in Golden Lane, St Lukes, when on the 1st January 1896, he attested for six years as a militia man for the county of London to serve in the Royal Fusiliers. At 17 years six months he was 5ft 7inches. He weighed 112 lbs with a maximum chest of 33 ½ inches. He had a dark complexion with black eyes and black hair. There was a mole on his left cheek and he was a member of the Church of England. He drilled on enlistment for nine days before purchasing himself out of the army. He was residing at 88 Radnor Street, St. Lukes when on the 18th July 1898, aged 20 and one month, he enlisted in the Kent Artillery Regiment. His weight was the same but he was now nearly 5ft 8 with a maximum chest of 34 inches, complexion fair, eyes brown and hair dark brown. There was an anchor tattoed on his right forearm. Again he purchased himself out after 49 days!

He was a silk tie cutter when he married Annie Morgan at St. Mary's Church, Hoxton on the 26th May 1901. Their first child Annie, born 12th June 1902, was baptised on 6th July 1902, the daughter of Richard & Annie Luxton of 19 Witchampton Street, tie cutter. In 1911 Richard

32, gentleman neck tie cutter, Annie 31 Domestic, Annie 8, Richard 5 and Katherine 1 lived in a three room property at 9 Union Street, Islington. In World War 1 Richard served in the 11th Battalion of the London Regiment before a transfer to the Labour Corps and he was awarded the British War Medal and the Victory Medal.

George (1882–1917) was a 19 year old Private in the Dragoon Guards stationed at York Cavalry Barracks in Yorkshire on census day 31st March 1901. He was also listed as a tie cutter, living at 88 Britannia Street with his mother and family! G. Luxton 88 Britannia Street advertised on 6th April 1905 in the London Daily News, desiring a situation under heading Pressmen, Printers, Canvassers, as an improver, shorthand speed fair. But he was still a silk tie-cutter, living at 94 Church Road, Southgate Road when he married Louisa Mary Rutland at St Philip the Evangelist in Islington on the 6th March 1909. In 1911 the couple were listed as living at 69 Church Road. George of 125 Southgate Road, was admitted to the local infirmary at St. John's Road Workhouse, on 3rd February 1917. He died aged 34 of "broncho pneumonia some days and tumour of the brain some months" at London County Asylum on 25th March 1917. Louisa, his widow, married Alfred John Roper at St Paul's Islington on 30th November 1935. Their son George Francis Luxton (1911-1968) a post office sorter, lived at 5 Carter's Cottages in Compton Square Islington in 1933. He married Maud Ethel Claxton at Woodbridge Chapel, Clerkenwell on 28th December 1935 and they had two daughters.

One son Joseph, born in Shoreditch in 1880, emigrated to Canada at an early age but returned to England before he finally made up his mind to return to Toronto, Ontario. The ship's passenger list for the S.S. Lucania shows he sailed from Liverpool on the 1st February 1908 to New York with final destination listed as Toronto, Canada. He was aged 27 years and 8 months, and listed as a silk cutter. On the 8th June 1910 he married Edith Mary Jones (born1886) in York, Ontario.

The 1911 census lists Joseph, a tie cutter and his wife Edith living at Symington Avenue, Toronto with an infant daughter, Helen, aged 6 months. Doris, a second daughter, was born to the couple before Mary Edith (sic) Luxton died aged 32 in Toronto on the 16th November 1914, one week after an operation for osteo sarcoma of fermur. In later life

Doris corresponded with her Luxton relatives in London. Joseph Luxton, tie cutter, widower aged 43 married Emily Helen Everett, aged 46, the daughter of Thomas Everett and Emily Turner in York, Toronto on the 17th November 1923. Emily originated from Wood Green, London and the couple resided at 202 Symington Avenue, Toronto.

I have made contact with one member of this London Family. Mr. Richard John Luxton, (1934-) project engineer of 17 Green Dragon Lane, Winchmore Hill, who is a grandson of Richard Luxton (1878–1931), in photograph, who was the victim of a tragic road accident, reported in the Islington Gazette, Friday, 1st May 1931

Seven Sisters' Road Accident-Finsbury Park Man's Death
Evidence at Inquest

An inquiry was held by Mr. Danford Thomas, deputy coroner, sitting with a jury, at Islington on Friday, relative to the death of Richard Luxton, 52, who lived at Alexander Road, Finsbury Park.

P.C. Woods, 646n, submitted a plan, prepared by him, of the section of Seven Sisters Road, where the occurrence took place.

Evidence was given that on Saturday night, March 28th, the deceased who, it was stated, staggered after stepping off the pavement, halted, to allow a motor car, going in the direction of the Manor House, to go by. After it had passed he was struck and knocked down by a motor car coming from the opposite direction. He was admitted to the Islington Hospital, where he remained under treatment until his death, which took place on Tuesday.

Dr. Cahill assistant medical supt., said that death was from pneumonia, following gangrene, consequent upon an operation for fracture of the left thigh.

P.C. Jones, who accompanied the deceased to the Royal Northern Hospital, where he was first treated, said when he asked him about the occurrence he replied it was his own fault.

The driver said that when he noticed the deceased he applied his brakes and slowed down. The man appeared to be fooling about. He passed in front of the car and then stumbled back and must have been caught by the left wing.

The coroner-Would you like to say that he fell against the car?

Witness-I can hardly say that he fell against the car. He slipped back into it.

The jury returned a verdict of "accidental death."

See the family tree for more details of this prolific branch of the family.

66

CHARLES WILLIAM LUXTON M.M. (1892-1960), FISHMONGER, WAREHOUSEMAN, ARMY PENSIONER AND GENERAL LABOURER OF SHOREDITCH AND DAGENHAM AND HIS FAMILY

See tree 36 & 37

Charles William Luxton (1892-1960), the second son of John Luxton (1864-1930), fancy box maker's warehouseman, and his wife Alice Agombar (1866-1959), was born at 71 Provost Street, Hoxton, New Town, Shoreditch on the 15th April 1892. There is no mention of the name William on his birth certificate. At 16 Charles joined the Royal Navy as a boy rating, and he was training on the Ganges from 3rd October 1908 to 13th March 1909. H.M.S. Ganges, was formerly the ironclad H.M.S. Minataur. She was moved to Harwich in 1905 as a training ship and stayed there until 1922. Charles character was described as very good but on the 26th October 1909 he was sentenced at Old Street Police Court, to three months imprisonment for stealing a saw. The following day he was discharged from the Royal Navy as "unfit", a "low type of boy and intellectually weak."

He is simply named Charles Luxton, 20, (he was in fact 17) bachelor, fishmonger of 62 Moneyer Street, when he married Ellen Elizabeth Pearson 22, spinster, daughter of William Henry Pearson, labourer, in St. Mary's Church, Hoxton, London after banns on the 27th March 1910. On the 15th April 1910 he was an "Errand Boy" when he was taken into the Royal Navy as a stoker for twelve years. It was his 18th birthday and the still growing lad was 5 ft 6in. with chest 33inch, hair brown, eyes grey, complexion fresh with a scar on the top of his nose. Inconsistently, it seems, the 1911 census describes him as Charles Luxton, 20, and Ellen 23 as cardboard box cutters with a baby son, Charles William, living at 15 Waterloo Street, Finsbury!

However, the Central Criminal Court lists Charles Luxton, stoker, as a habitual criminal in 1914. At the Old Street Police Court on

14th February 1912, he was sentenced to two months imprisonment for stealing tea, and again on the 26th November 1912, he was sentenced for unlawful possession. Finally he was received into custody on 3rd February 1914, together with Benjamin Oxlade, a 46 bricklayer. They appeared at the Guild Hall Police Court on 6th March 1914, accused that on the 26th January 1914 they stole one bale of cloth, and on the 27th January 1914 another bale of cloth, the property of Phillips and Piper Limited, and feloniously receiving the same. The jury found Oxlade not guilty. Charles pleaded guilty and confessed to former convictions. He was sentenced to six months hard labour in Wormwood Scrubs. Charles Luxton, prison number 8484, was 5ft 11 inches tall without shoes, with a fresh complexion, brown hair, blue eyes and had scars on forehead and bridge of nose. There were tattoes of clasped hands on his right wrist. He was released from prison on the 4th August 1914, the day the Great War, which we call World War 1, began. He was described as a stoker of 29 Westmoreland Place, Hoxton.

When he enlisted in the Army at the beginning of the Great War he gave his name as Charles William Luxton, born in the parish of St. Lukes, London and stated he was a porter involved in heavy outdoor work. From now on he is always referred to in official documents as Charles William Luxton. Army documentation provides us with a snapshot of him on his enlistment at Stratford on the 9th August 1914, when he signed on for eight years army service and four in the reserve. He was 22 years and 126 days old, and at 5ft. 11 inches he weighed 145 lbs with a fully expanded girth of 37 inches. His complexion was fresh with blue eyes and light brown hair. Distinguishing marks were a dark mole on his right shin and he had a tattoo of clasped hands on the back of his right wrist. A gunner (Reg. No. 41480) he joined the Royal Garrison Artillery at Newhaven.

Poor cramped and faded handwriting, and the use of abbreviations on his surviving army records makes it difficult to decipher all the details of his military service. For the first two years and 236 days of his service, 9th August 1914 to 1st April 1917, he was based in Britain. In May 1915 he spent sometime in the military hospital in Lewisham but the reason is not stated.

Somehow Charles upset the military authorities and there is a bad character reference on his statement of service sheet. The reason is not clear but there is perhaps a clue in four faded lines of handwriting which I can part read:- 'To be compulsorily posted to France under the M.S. (R. of -----1917 in accordance with ------of 1917.' Underneath in a bold hand is written 'character – bad.' When we realise a soldier could expect to survive for an average of three months on the Western Front, we cannot really be surprised perhaps that Charles with a young family baulked at going there! His elder brother John, who was embroiled in the early battles on the Western Front must have told him how bad it was! I give a brief outline of John's war in next paragraph before continuing Charles story.

His brother, John Luxton (1889-1940), born at 31 Mitchell Street, Holborn on 26th August 1889, was a fur packer before the war. A shoeing smith in the 118th Battery of the Royal Field Artillery, his regiment was in the 1st Division based at Aldershot and was one of the first divisions mobilised for action in France and became embroiled in the Battle of Mons, the Marne and the first battle of Ypres. Home from the Western Front he married Charlotte Eliza Cundale at St John the Baptist Church, Shoreditch on 10th January 1915 and was described as a Farrier Sergeant in the Royal Field Artillery in January 1917. An office keeper in the Air Ministry he died aged 50 on 8th January 1940. He lived at 24A Springfield Upper Clapton and left an estate valued at £184..7s..4d to his widow, Charlotte. They had issue a daughter Mahala and a son John Victor Luxton (1920-1993) who served in the Royal Artillery in the Second World War. John Victor lived at the Grange, 2 Whitehall Farm Lane, Virginia Water when he died on 7th December 1993, leaving an estate valued £15,682.

On the 2nd April 1917 Charles was posted to France with the Royal Garrison Artillery Battalion 297 Siege Battery. Siege Batteries RGA were equipped with heavy howitzers, sending large calibre high explosive shells in high trajectory, plunging fire. The usual armaments were 6 inch, 8 inch and 9.2 inch howitzers, although some had huge railway- or road-mounted 12 inch howitzers. As British artillery tactics developed, the Siege Batteries were most often employed in destroying or neutralising the enemy artillery, as well as putting destructive fire down on strongpoints, dumps, store, roads and railways behind enemy lines.

His involvement in the war on the Western Front came to an abrupt end 119 days later on the 29th July 1917. At sometime in June or early July that year, he suffered a serious gunshot wound to his left upper arm. He was taken to a General Hospital at Etaples on the French coast south of Boulogne, where a medical report for week ending 8th July 1917 states his condition was much improved. From there he was moved to the King George Hospital, Stamford on the 30th July 1917. Consequently his last 206 days in the army were spent as a convalescent, and the reference on his service sheet, 'Passed fit for Gunner duty at home only" must relate to this period. Charles after a service of 3 years and 196 days, was discharged from the army on the 20th February 1918.

A few days earlier at Dover on the 17th February 1918, he was issued with his Silver War Badge and entitlement card. The badge was issued to ex-serviceman, given an honourable discharge, to signify he had 'done his bit' and to prevent accusations of evading military service. It was inscribed 'For King and Empire, services Rendered' and was to be worn on the right lapel  of his jacket, but not on his army uniform. The recipients of these badges were frequently referred to as 'Silver Badge Men' in press accounts of parades and events at the end of the war. Charles' home address is given as 95 Chatham Avenue, Nile Street, Hoxton.

His service record reveals he was awarded the British War Medal and Victory Medal and the Military Medal. Gnr. C.W. Luxton (Reg.no. 41480) R.G.A. is on the list of brave soldiers awarded the M.M. who was gazetted in the Supplement to the London Gazette, 28th July 1917. (See p.7768) The Military Medal (M.M.) was a new medal instituted in March 1916, as an award for distinguished service in the field for warrant officers, N.C.O.'s and lower ranks. Hitherto officers had been awarded the Military Cross and this was the equivalent medal for lower ranks. The ribbon has broad dark blue edges, flanking a central section of three narrow white and two narrow crimson stripes. It is made of silver and has the sovereign's effigy on the obverse and a crowned royal cipher above the inscription 'FOR BRAVERY IN THE FIELD' enclosed in a wreath on the reverse.

Details of Charles act of bravery are wanting but the event for which the award was made was usually some three or four months before. However, I'm inclined to think he won his M.M. due to the action he was in which led to his serious arm injury in June or early July 1917[467]. This was the start of the third battle of Ypres known as Passchendaele, a name which has become synonymous with the horror of the Western Front. It is likely that he was recommended for bravery under very heavy shell fire. Soldiers faced not only shot and shell but chlorine gas attacks which irritated the throat and chest and left indelible scars on those who suffered it and can cause blindness and death.

Charles was a 26 year old night watchman, when he attested to join the R.A.F. on 18th June 1918 for the remaining duration of the war. His official no. was 198229 and his trade description was given as

---

[467] My attempts to make contact with his descendants who perhaps could provide photographs of Charles in army uniform and details of how he won his M.M. have proved abortive.

"Disciplinian."Records reveal his character was very good. Islington, Aldeburgh and Felixstowe were among the stations in which he served and on the 28th August 1918 he was promoted to Corporal.

Details of his time as a gunner are also included in R.A.F. papers which clarify his disability-"gunshot wounds to right shoulder and left arm." The injury appears to have taken an inch off his height, for he is now described as 5ft 10inches and he has lost weight too with a chest measurement of 33 inches. He has fair hair, grey eyes and a fresh complexion. Charles was demobbed from the R.A.F. on 4th February 1919 and his home address was 39, Crondall Street, North Road, Hoxton. Again he was awarded a silver war badge no 7164 to take effect from 1st August 1919.

While he was in the R.A.F. Charles attended a seven day fire-fighting course on the 4th November 1918 at Aldershot. It proved useful when he was recruited as an auxiliary fire-fighter in the London blitz of the 1940s. When his son John French Luxton married on  2nd August 1941, he lists his father's occupation as A.F.S. In this photograph taken during the Second World War Charles is wearing his military ribbons above the left pocket on his Auxiliary Fire Service uniform. He has a distinctive AFS chrome cap badge and his uniform buttons of a white metal were later replaced by black plastic buttons as an economy measure. His daughter Sarah Adelaide, (Sally) born in 1913, is an Aircraftwoman Second Class, Women's Auxiliary Air Force c.1941. The W.A.A.F. were involved in duties such as parachute packing, manning of barrage balloons and were a vital presence in the control of aircraft as plotters in the operation rooms, most notably during the Battle of Britain.

On Christmas Eve 1910 when Charles, and his wife Ellen's first child, Charles William Luxton was born at the City of London Lying-in Hospital, Charley as he was known, was a fishmonger's assistant and the family were living at 34 Peerless Street, St. Luke, Holborn.

When Sarah Adelaide, the second of the couple's nine children was born on the 16th February 1913, they were living at 29 Westmorland Place, Nile Street, Shoreditch and Charley paid his way as a general labourer. They were living at 83 Chatham Avenue, Nile Street, Shoreditch when a third child, John French Luxton was born on the 14th July 1915. Charley who was now a gunner in the R.G.A. named this second son after Sir John French, the commander of the British Expeditionary Force in France.

In this family picture we see John French Luxton (1915-1991), Sally (1913-1989), her husband Henry George Watts, and Eleanor Luxton (1888-1961). The growing family had moved to 39 Crondall Street, Hoxton when Henry William Luxton (1918-1993) was born on the 19th July 1918. Charley, a pensioned gunner Royal Garrison Artillery, was a messenger at the air ministry when Jane Delia, another daughter was born on the 28th February 1920, but he was a packing case dealer when William Henry Luxton was born on the 22nd September 1922, and he continued in this capacity until at least 1st August 1936. Two more sons, Albert Edward Luxton (1925-1973) and George (1927-1992) were born at 39 Crondall Street but the family had moved to 210 Hunters Hall Road, Dagenham Essex when Benjamin James Luxton (1931-1984), the youngest of their nine children was born on the 8th July 1931.

The 1939 Register lists Charles, a disabled pensioner R.G.A. at 30 Union Street Maidstone, Kent. He was probably visiting an old friend, Albert Masters, now blind and incapacitated, who was also born in St Lukes, London in 1892. Charles wife and children are listed at home in 210 Hunters Hall Road, Dagenham. Family birth, marriage and death certificates provide other fleeting references to Charley who was a street fruit vendor on the 5th March 1949 but a garage attendant by Christmas Eve that year. In August 1952, and again in September 1955, he is a night watchman but in June 1958 he is simply an army pensioner.

His grand-daughter, Brenda Luxton, remembers her nannie saying, "that he needed to be kept quiet as he had a plate in his head" and she adds "he used to stay in their front room to play music." Charles Luxton M.M. aged 68, retired general labourer and army pensioner died at 210 Hunters Hall Road, Dagenham, Essex on the 18th September 1960, from lung disease, emphysema & chronic bronchitis and high blood pressure. His widow, Ellen otherwise Eleanor Elizabeth Sarah Rebecca Luxton, aged 73, died at the same home address on the 26th March 1961.

The eldest son, Charles William Luxton (1910-1974), served in the Suffolk Regiment in World War 2 and he was successfully evacuated from Dunkirk. A packing case dealer, he married Catherine Theresa Marson at Romford Register Office by licence on the 19th June 1933. He was a French polisher, working at Jay's Furniture Store in Staines, when their only child Jean Audrey Luxton (with Charles in photo) was born on the 3rd January 1937. Then he drove a lorry for Simmond's Brewery, before working as a stage hand at Bray's Studios and Shepperton Studios, but he was a general labourer of 71A Avondale Avenue, Staines, Middlesex, when he died at Charing Cross Hospital in Hammersmith on the 27th June 1974.[468]

His sister Sarah Adelaide (1913- 1989), was a 23 year old spinster when she married Henry George Watts, a 24 year old French polisher, in the Register Office Shoreditch on the 1st August 1936. They had a hardware shop (in photo) in Heathway, Dagenham before moving to

---

[468] Thanks to Jean and her daughter for information on Charles and the help given me by her grand daughter, Bex Bastable.

St. Neot's Kent, and they bought and sold a marina before buying a small hotel with holiday cottages in Axminster, Devon. Sarah, was the widow of Henry George Watts, a Builders Merchants Director of 58, Queens Gardens, Rainham, Essex when she died on the 25th October 1989.

Jane Delia (1920-1954), her sister, known as Jean (in photo below) died of T.B. at the London Chest Hospital, Stotfield, Bedfordshire on the 2nd April 1954 and left her personal estate valued at £149..6 shillings to her mother. John French Luxton (1915-1991), the second son, was a 26 year old baker, when he married Grace Alma Wood (1923-2004) aged 18 in the parish church Dagenham, Essex on the 2nd August 1941. At the end of World War Two they lived at 3Field Way, Hillingdon. The couple had three daughters Margaret, Alice and Brenda who has kindly provided photographs to illustrate this chapter. John French Luxton was a retired painter and decorator of 118 Appletree Avenue, Hillingdon when he died on the 17th May 1991.

Henry William Luxton, a third son born in 1918, married twice, and was a foreman pile driver for a contractor. He lived in Victoria Road Barking in 1961. William Henry Luxton (1922-1982), a fourth son worked in mines and went to Palestine with the Army where he won a medal. He was a metal process worker in a Tungsten Works, when he married Gladys Ivy Elliott (nee Syer) 1926-2005 at the Register Office in Romford, Essex on the 19th August 1952. Two sons William Henry (1951) and Gary William (1954) were born to this couple in Dagenham and a daughter Sallie Anne (1957) and a son Timothy John (1959) were born in Romford.

Albert Edward Luxton (1925-1973), the fifth son of Charles William Luxton and his wife Ellen Elizabeth Pearson, born at 39 Crondall Street, Hoxton was a 23 year old Winch driver for a construction Engineer, living at 90 Caerleon Road, Newport when he married Bronwen Lily Maud Jones 18, hospital ward orderly of 8 Glanffrwd

Avenue, Ebbw Vale at the Register Office, Bedwellty, Monmouthshire on the 5th March 1949. The couple settled in Ebbw Vale where they had three sons Anthony Paul Luxton (1950), Charles William (1951) and Albert Edward Luxton (1953-1999) who married in the Ebbw Vale area and produced their own families. Sadly Bronwen died of cancer, aged 35, on the 25th June 1966 and her husband Albert Edward Luxton, steel works labourer of 14 Tredegar Avenue Ebbw Vale died in hospital in Abergavenny on the 31st May 1973. Tragically too their son, Albert Edward Luxton (1953-1999), a steel worker, of 1 St Teilos Close, Ebbw Vale, died, aged 47, in a works related accident on the 24th November 1999.

George Luxton, the sixth son of Charles William Luxton and his wife Ellen Elizabeth Pearson, was born at 39 Crondall Street, Shoreditch on the 23rd May 1927. He was in the merchant navy during World War Two and was awarded a merchant seaman's medal. He was a 22 year old labourer for a Public Works Contractor when he married Lilian May Barlow 22, in the Register Office, Romford, Essex on the 24th December 1949. George who became a self employed decorator, and his wife Lilian, had a son George David Luxton in 1951 and a daughter Diana Jean on the 26th November 1954. Diana married Samuel Dougherty, a soldier, in Dagenham Parish Church on 17th May 1980. The family were last recorded in the Dagenham area.

Benjamin James Luxton (1931-1984), the seventh son of Charles William Luxton and his wife Ellen Elizabeth Pearson, was born at 210 Hunters Hall Road, Dagenham Essex on the 8th July 1931. He was a 24 year old pile driver for a contractor when he married Elizabeth Jean Morris (1934-2013) aged 21, in Romford Register Office on the 3rd September 1955. The couple had a son Barry Benjamin John Luxton (1958-2010) and daughters Lorraine Elizabeth 1961 and Beverly Elise 1963. They lived at 17 Kirklees Road, Barking in1964 and were at 1 Treswell Road Dagenham in 1974. Benjamin James Luxton was a retired driver partsman of 1 Treswell Road, Dagenham Essex when he died at Old Church Hospital, Romford on the 27th September 1984. In this happy group of revellers on the last page we see Ellen with sons Charles, Ben and daughter Sally.

67

ROBERT LUXTON (1835-1876) GUNNER IN THE ROYAL ARTILLERY IN INDIA AND SECOND OPIUM WAR IN CHINA

See tree 35

Robert Luxton (1835-1876), the twelfth and youngest child of Robert and Elizabeth Luxton, High Street, carpenter, was baptised at St. Mary

Magdalene Taunton on the 1st March 1835. In the 1851 census, Robert, aged 16, was an apprentice cabinet maker and was the last child of the family still living at home with his father Robert 64, journeyman carpenter and his mother Elizabeth 61, washerwoman, in High Street, St. Mary Magdalene, Taunton.

Robert, a 20 year old cabinet maker, attested for the Royal Artillery at Taunton on the 11th September 1855. He was 5 foot $7^1/_2$ inches tall with a florid complexion, grey eyes and dark brown hair. Gunner Regimental No.4881 served as a soldier for 21 years three months which included spells of three years three months in China, and two years 2 months in India.

A detailed statement of his service reveals that he began as a gunner and driver in the 14th Battalion of the Royal Artillery from the 11th September 1855 to the 31st December 1857, and was a gunner from the 1st January 1858 to the 30th April 1859. On the 1st July 1859 he was transferred as a gunner to the 13th Brigade until the 1st March 1863, a period of 3 years 305 days, and was stationed at Woolwich, Secunderabad, Tien Tsin, Aden, Neemuch and Poona. It was in this spell that he served in the Second Opium War. He was placed on Good Conduct pay at an extra penny a day from the 1st March 1860, and was promoted to Bombardier from the 2nd March 1863 to the 17th June 1863, a period of 108 days. Then on the 19th June 1863 he was tried by

Court Martial[469] and reduced in rank and imprisoned, from the 19th June 1863 to the 2nd July 1863, and forfeited good conduct pay on the 18th June 1863. He was restored as a gunner on the 3rd July 1863 to the 11th July 1865, a period of 2 years 9 months and was restored to good conduct pay at a penny a day from the 3rd July 1864. Again he forfeited his good conduct pay on the 4th January 1865 and was once again awaiting trial from the 12th July 1865 to the 14th July 1865. He was tried a second time by Court Martial and was imprisoned from the 15th July 1865 to the 11th August 1865. Then he was restored as a Gunner on the 12th August 1865 to the 8th September 1867 and was restored to good conduct pay at a penny a day from the 12th August 1867.

Back home in the U.K. he was re-engaged as a gunner at Dover for nine years from the 9th September 1867. He received good conduct pay at 2d a day from the 2nd August 1869, and advanced good conduct pay at 3d a day from 12th August 1871. He was transferred to the 12th Brigade from the 1st September 1871 to the 28th February 1873, followed by another transfer to the Coast Brigade from the 1st March 1873 to the 16th November 1876 and received advanced good conduct pay at 4 pence a day from the 27th October 1873. He completed a further 19 days service from the 17th November 1876 to the 5th December 1876 when he was finally discharged with a total service of 21 years 44 days. At that date he was serving with the 4th Division Coast Brigade of the Royal Artillery at Devonport. He was 41 years and 2 months old and had no marks or scars upon the face or other parts of his body and his intended place of residence was Taunton in Somerset.

Fortunately, the irritating vagueness of the foregoing account of his service record is redeemed to some extent by other documents. The 1871 census reveals he was a 35 year old unmarried gunner, living in barracks, serving with the Battery of the 13th Brigade Royal Artillery in the parish of Maker Cornwall. At some later date he married a lady named Emma but I do not have details of their marriage or any children. More helpful were the proceedings of a Regimental Board held at Devonport on the 16th November 1876. It notes that he had no school certificate and that 'His name appears in the Reg. Defaulters' Book seven times and he has

---

[469] His army records at Kew provide no details of his offence but it was probably related to a drink problem.

been tried by Court Martial twice" It concludes however that 'his conduct has been very good and he is in possession of Four Good Conduct Badges also China Medal and clasp for Taku Forts.'

The aim of the allied French and British expedition in the Second Opium War with China, was to compel the Chinese government at Peking to observe the trade treaties signed between their governments at Tientsin in 1858. This included allowing the British to continue the opium trade in China. An important engagement in this war was the third battle of the Taku Forts, from the 12th to the 21st August 1860, in which Gunner Robert Luxton saw action.

The Chinese opposition was made up of 5000 Qing Army troops who garrisoned the 26 Taku Forts, thirty six miles south east of Tientsin. They were assisted by at least 45 artillery pieces.

On the 30th July 1860 an Anglo-French army landed at Pei Tang-Ho. The force consisted of about 400 men: 200 British and 200 French. Lieutenant General Sir Hope Grant, was the British commander with Charles Cousin-Montauban, Comte de Palikao in charge of the French. A few days later when a reconnaissance force moved towards the Taku Forts for close observation, two British soldiers were wounded by bullets from a Chinese jingal. After a few more days, on the 12th August, the allied force attacked the emplacement. They also built trenches to help protect them from a possible Chinese counter attack. Then the major assault took place on the main Chinese forts. Heavy fighting ensued as the attackers crossed several Chinese trenches and spiked bamboo palisades. The Anglo-French force first tried an unsuccessful attack on the main gate of the fortifications.

After that failed, the allied army resorted to climbing over the walls and entering the main fortress that way. The first British officer to enter the fort was Lieutenant Robert Montresor Rogers, who was later awarded the Victoria Cross for his bravery that day. He was closely followed by a private, John McDougall who was also awarded the Victoria Cross. During the fighting Lieutenant Rogers was severely wounded, fourteen men were killed and one drummer boy and forty-six other men were also wounded. Over one hundred Qing defenders were killed, many were wounded and forty five guns captured. After capturing the main Chinese positions, the force rested for six days then attacked again, resulting in the capture of the remaining Taku forts which were pacified by the

21st August. This third battle of the Taku Forts was one of the last major engagements of the Second Opium War. The fighting ended with the occupation of Peking on the 13th October 1860 and the Chinese acceptance of the trading treaties.

All this had taken place in the early years of Robert's military career. His army record WO/116/146 Kew P.R.O. for the 5th December 1876 lists him as a Chelsea Pensioner No.45556 but his life was drawing to a rapid close. At the date of the Regimental Board's proceedings in Devonport on the 16th November 1876 he was seriously ill and was in a dropsical condition. Like many soldiers he appears to have had a 'drink problem' which may account for his two court martials in the service. Robert Luxton, Pensioner Royal Artillery, died aged 41 from cirrhosis of Liver, 2 years, anasarca (ie a dropsy condition) 2 months, certified by T.E Owen surgeon, at his home 13 Castle Street in St. Andrews Parish Plymouth on the 27th December 1876. Emma Luxton, his widow[470] was present at his death. He was buried in a common grave (Section H no 59, Row 2) on the 31st December 1876 at Ford Park Cemetery, Plymouth.

---

[470] I can find no evidence for this marriage.

68

JAMES LUXTON (1796 – 1869),
"FARMER LUXTON" OF TOWNSHEND FARM
SKILGATE SOMERSET

See tree 39

By the commencement of the 18th century my Luxton forebears had migrated from their aboriginal home in central north Devon, to the hamlet of Petton, Bampton on the Devon side of its border with Somerset. Many family members settled in Somerset and made their lives there. One of these was James Luxton, or "Farmer Luxton" as he was called by his kinsman, Isaac Luxton, the shoemaker who kept a journal.

James was baptised at St. Michael's, Bampton, on the 24th April 1796 where the register reflecting the dialect pronunciation of his surname renders it James Luxon. He was the sixth of nine children born to

John Luxton (1747–1818) yeoman of Petton and his wife Mary Redwood, who married at Clatworthy, Somerset in 1779. The family lived at Taunton a while and at least two of his elder brothers, John Luxton (1782–1837) and Robert Luxton (1786-1871) were carpenters and joiners in St. Mary Magdalene parish, Taunton.

James married Elizabeth Palfrey of Morebath at Morebath, Devon on 31st October 1816 where the first four of the couple's recorded five children were born. John (1816-1896), the eldest, baptised at St. George's, Morebath on 29th December 1816 was followed by Mary (1821-1899), baptised on 27th September 1821, William, baptised 4th January 1824 and George (1825-1901), baptised on the 6th November 1825. James' wife, Elizabeth Palfrey, was born in Clatworthy, Somerset and by the 26th January 1834 the family had moved to the nearby village of Upton, Somerset where their youngest child, James Luxton, (1834–1918) was baptised in St. James, the parish church the son of James and Betsy Luxton, labourer on 26th January 1834.

James and his family farmed the 40 acres at Lotley Water Farm, Upton. In 1841, aged 45, he farmed there with his wife Elizabeth, and two sons, George 15 and James 7. Thomas Palfrey, 51, independant who is probably Elizabeth's brother is also at the farm. The family are still at Lotley Water in 1851 where James, 52, farms 40 acres, assisted by Elizabeth 65, and George 25 and James 17. Ann Marsh 16, a local girl, is the dairymaid.

James Luxton, Upton, farmer is listed on page 899 of the Bristol Post Office Directory and Gazetteer with the counties of Gloucestershire and Somersetshire (1859). Regrettably there are only a few remains of their former house and sheds at Lotley Water today.

Fortunately a unique description of the farm at Lotley Water is provided by the tithe apportionment for Upton, dated 8th May 1838. Sir Humphrey Phineas Davie Baronet was the landowner and Lotley Water was occupied by James Luxton as the tenant farmer. The farmhouse and its fields are identified by numbers so that they can be found on an accompanying tithe map and the field names, their land measurement and type of usage are given:-

310 House and Garden	Pasture	0-1-4
311 Goose Moor	Pasture	0-2-30
312 Orchard	Meadow	0-1-4
313 Drought	Arable	0-3-34
314 Starve Acre	Arable	1-1-18
315 The Cleeve	Arable	4-0-32
316 Little Cleeve	Arable	0-2-23
317 Great Furze Hill	Arable	3-1-9
318 Part of Ditto	Arable	6-0-20
319 Furze Brake in ditto	Woodland	2-0-16
320 The Brake	Woodland	6-2-5
321 Home Meadow nr Bittiscombe	Meadow	2-2-39

		29-0-34

In 1838 Lotley Farm amounted to 29 acres no rods and 34 perches and James Luxton made a tithe payment of £1..5s..0d in total.

By 1861 James, 65, and Elizabeth, 75, were farming the 55 acres of Townsend Farm, Skilgate, with the help of their 27 year old son, James. Elizabeth Sedman, a local girl aged 15, was house servant. James died aged 73 and was buried on 13th June 1869. His widow, Elizabeth Luxton, aged 87, was buried with him at Skilgate on the 23rd February 1873.

James' life was abruptly ended as the result of a tragic farming accident. His kinsman, Isaac Luxton (1815–1876) the shoemaker and parish clerk, of Skilgate notes in his Journal:-

June 7th 1869 – Farmer Luxton Brought (i.e. broke) his both legs
June 8th   – Farmer Luxton Died

James' death certificate reveals he died at Skilgate on the 8th June 1869 as the result of "Injuries by a waggon passing over him, Accident". Information received from W.W. Munkton Coroner for Somerset. Date of Inquest 11th June 1869. Registered 15th June.

The circumstances of James'sad fate were published in the West Somerset Free Post, Saturday, June 12th 1869.

Skilgate

Fatal Accident – On Monday evening, Mr. James Luxton of Skilgate, an old man, seventy three years of age, met with a sad and fatal accident. He appears to have been walking beside a team of three horses which were drawing a waggon. One of the horses started and he, in endeavouring to restrain it, lost his footing and fell, the wheels passing over both legs. On Tuesday morning, medical aid was sent for, and Dr. Edwards with his assistant, Mr. G. Moores, went immediately to Skilgate, but before their arrival the poor fellow had succumbed to the injuries he had received.

Other newspapers provided a more detailed account of the accident. James was contracted by Mr. John Hill Tarr of Frogwell Farm on Monday 7th June to fetch a load of bark[471] from Haddon. For this he used his own wagon drawn by two horses. He was assisted by Thomas Lyddon, an employee of Mr. Tarr, who followed in a cart pulled by three horses. They collected their bark and on the return journey, James was walking by the side of his wagon load of bark, but as they descended Windway Hill the belly-tie of the shaft horse unfastened. He tried to re-buckle it and in so doing fell, the wheel passing over both legs[472].

Thomas Lyddon told the inquest[473] held at Skilgate on the 11th June, that he was following in the cart. As they were descending Windway Hill the hind wheel of the wagon jumped out of the "slipper" to which the deceased had adjusted it. This resulted in the shaft horse being forced along by the loaded wagon, the pace becoming faster every moment. He detached two of his team of three horses and ran with them down the hill to assist. He found James lying in the road with both of his legs broken, the near wheels of the wagon having passed over them just below the knees. He ran for the assistance of Mr. Tarr who had James conveyed to his home. James told him that no one was to blame for the accident but that he was knocked down by some means. Tarr thought that the prime cause of the accident was the decayed state of the harness on the shaft horse. He rode to fetch the doctor. Mr. J. B. Collyns, surgeon of Dulverton, on examining the deceased found that

---

[471] Bark from oak trees was ground in water mills to tan hide into leather.
[472] Western Daily Press, Friday 11th June 1869.
[473] Taunton Courier and Western Advertiser, Wednesday 16th June 1869.

he had lost a good deal of blood which was flowing from an artery of the left leg. Both legs had sustained compound fractures below the knee and were literally smashed. He arrested the haemorrhage but James died at noon the next day Tuesday 8th June from the loss of blood and a shock to the nervous system. The verdict of the jury was "accidental death." Mr. Luxton was greatly respected in the neighbourhood and his death "cast quite a gloom over the parish.[474]"

Mr. Edward S.W. Luxton of Oatway Farm, Brompton Regis near Dulverton, who is a great-great grandson of James Luxton of Townsend Farm "has a long plank table and a grandfather clock which belonged to him when he was at Townsend Farm. I also have his walking stick".[475]

It remains for me to say a word or two about their five children. Their eldest son John Luxton (1816–1896), was a 33 year old servant in1851 to John Blueth, a landed proprietor at Hay Grass, Pitminster near Taunton. He was a porter, when he married Harriet Fry, (nee Long) a straw milliner and widow, with three children in St James, Taunton on the 1st January 1860. John rented out his cottage in Morebath and went to live at 29 High Street, in Taunton.[476] At the the Taunton Petty Sessions held in the Guildhall, John a porter to Messrs Whitmarsh, was fined 8s. for obstructing the Highway, caused by his leaving eight barrels in Hammet Street on 18th October 1867[477]. A cellarman in Pitminster and High Street, Taunton and Bishops Hull he died aged 79 of throat cancer at 37 Alma Street, Taunton on the 6th November 1896.

His sister Mary, born at Morebath in 1821, was an unmarried cook included in the six servants in the household of Alex Luthall, Rector of East Quantoxhead in 1851. Later that year on the 28th April she married Henry Burcher, a maltster, at St. Mary Redcliffe, Bristol. Mary a widow aged 59, in 1881 was a general shopkeeper in East Quantoxhead, Somerset where she died aged 77 on the 10th July 1899. William,

[474] Western Times, Friday 18th June 1869.
[475] See correspondence received from Edward S.W. Luxton the 14th December 1995.
[476] Western Times, Wednesday 15th August 1883 where a Tiverton County Court case of his dispute with Maria Vicary a tenant.
[477] Somerset County Gazette, Saturday 26th October 1867. There were also reports in the Western Gazette and Taunton Courier.

James and Elizabeth's third child, died aged 11 months and was buried at Morebath on the 25th July 1824. Their fourth child, George Luxton (1825–1901), baptised at Morebath on the 6th November 1825, became a farm bailiff for Arthur Capel esquire at Halsdown Farm, Chipstable, and I say more about him in the next chapter. James Luxton, (1834–1918), the youngest sibling, baptised at St. James, Upton, the son of James and Betsy Luxton, labourer on 26th January 1834 married Elizabeth Atkins, daughter of James Atkins a veterinary surgeon in Skilgate at Dulverton Registry Office in 1867. He was a shepherd in Minehead when the 1881 census was taken and in old age retired to Lurban Doverhay, Porlock. James and his wife are buried in Skilgate churchyard where there is a monument to their memory. Again I have more to say on him in a future chapter.

69

GEORGE LUXTON (1825 – 1901) FARM BAILIFF, HALSDOWN CHIPSTABLE, SOMERSET

See tree 39

George, the third son of James Luxton (1796 –1869) and Elizabeth Palfry, was baptised as George Luxon at Morebath, on 6th November 1825. In 1841 George, aged 15, was living with his parents who were farming at Lotley Water, Upton, across the border in Somerset. Ten years later in 1851, he is a farmer's son, aged 25, residing with his parents at Lotley Water.

The marital links[478] between the Luxton and Atkins family at Skilgate received a boost when George Luxton, 27, batchelor, farmer, residing at East Reach, married Ann Atkins, 21 spinster of East Reach, daughter of James Atkins, farmer in St James, Taunton, Somerset on 12th February 1855. Both sign the register and the marriage was witnessed by Frederick Dyer and Mary Atkins. George's brother, James Luxton (1834 – 1918) was to make it a double wedding when he married Elizabeth Atkins, Ann's sister at the Register Office Dulverton in 1867.

George and his newly wed wife settled initially in Skilgate which was Ann's home village and the place where George's parents farmed at Townsend Farm. John the first of their ten children was born at Skilgate on 6th May 1855.

When Rosa Ellen, their second child was baptised at Chipstable on 1st June 1857, George, was a Farm Bailiff at Bulland in that parish. In March 1859 his employer Arthur Capel esq. sent him to Wiveliscombe Fair with a cow to sell. George paid the usual toll at the West Gate,

---

[478] The link up began when John Luxton (1817-1845) son of Isaac Luxton (1789 – 1838) married Mary Ann Atkins the daughter of John Atkins, Blacksmith at Skilgate on 8th March 1843.

Wiveliscombe but he was made to pay the toll again when he returned, even though he had sold the cow! This was the usual practice and it angered farmers and buyers of cattle who felt it was unfair that they had to pay a double toll. On behalf of Mr. Capel, George summoned James Manning the toll collector with illegally demanding and taking a second toll. The local petty session agreed and they fined Manning 5s. and costs. In future a single toll only would be paid[479].

The family had moved again to the neighbouring parish of Huish Champflower, when Elizabeth Anne Luxton was born on 4th April 1859, and Mary, on 10th February 1863. Her parents' lived at West Catford, Huish Champflower when she was baptised in St. Peter's, the parish church, on 15th March 1863. George was a dairyman at Chipstable when Ellen a fifth child, was baptised there on 12th March 1865. A son James born at Chipstable on 1st April 1868, baptised there on the 10th May, was followed by William George born at Huish Champflower on 17th July 1870 who was baptised there on the 28th August.

When the 1871 Census was taken at Chipstable, George Luxton aged 45, agricultural labourer, his wife, Ann Elizabeth, aged 35, born Waltham Green, Middlesex were farming at North Coombe with their children, John 15, agricultural labourer, Elizabeth 11, Mary 8, James 5 and George aged 8 months. Two more children were baptised at Chipstable, Frederick George on 31st August 1873 and Henry George their youngest child on 1st April 1877.

George Luxton, 55, farmer, his wife Ann, 45, and five children Mary, 18, James 14, William 11, Frederick 7 and George, aged 4, were farming at North Heydon in Chipstable when the 1881 was taken. In April 1887 George was one of the two churchwardens' in Chipstable.[480] In Kelly's Directory of Somerset and Bristol 1883 he is listed as George Luxton farm bailiff to Arthur Capel esq, J.P. of Chipstable. This was at the 112 acre Halsdown, Chipstable where the 1891 census lists George 64 farmer, his wife Ann Elizabeth, 54 and four sons, John, 35, James 23, Frederick George 17, and Henry George 14. In March 1891 there

---

[479] Taunton Courier, Wednesday 23 March 1859.
[480] Taunton Courier, 27th April 1887.

was a heavy snowfall which caught farmers by surprise. A local Taunton paper reported that Mr Luxton of Chipstable had dug eight or nine dead ewes out of a snow drift.[481]

George died, aged 75, on 23rd April 1901. His burial at Chipstable on 30th April 1901 is recorded in the parish register and at Bethel Chapel, Waterrow, a non-conformist chapel in the parish. The probate of George Luxton's Will was issued at Taunton on 24th June 1901 to his widow Anne Luxton and his sons James Luxton, farmer of Halsdown Farm and Frederick George Luxton, inn-keeper, Williton, when his personal estate was valued at £333 – 12 – 3d. He gave legacies of £10 to his children, "Rosa Ellen Bucknell wife of Elias Bucknell, Farmer of Treverne Farm, St. Keverne, Helston, Cornwall........ John Luxton of Paddick's Farm, Huish Campflower .....William Luxton if he could be found.......Mary Luxton of Williton.... Henry George Luxton of 13 Roseberry Terrace, Clifton, Policeman." The residue of the capital sum raised from the sale of his estate was to be equally divided between his sons James Luxton and Frederick George Luxton.

Ann Elizabeth Luxton, his widow, of 11 Landford Road, Hotwells, Bristol died aged 88 on 9th October 1925. She was buried at Chipstable on 14th October 1925. The Probate of her Will was issued at Bristol to Henry George Luxton, engineer nutfitter foreman on 10th December 1925 when her personal estate was valued at £277. Anne appointed her daughter Mary Hooper of 25 Clyde Road, Redland, Bristol, and her son Henry George Luxton of 3 Dorset Villas, Westbury on Trym, Bristol to be the executors of her Will made on the 9th July 1921. She gave "all my share and interest in these four closes of land called Lower Pitsham, Great Pitsham, Easter Pitsham and Great Bottoms situate in Skilgate.....and also all the lands and hereditaments which I can at my death dispose of by will...unto and to the use of my son the said Henry George Luxton ....and I give ....all my personal estate ....to the use of my daughter ....Mary Hooper".

John Luxton (1855 – 1926), the couple's eldest son, was a 25 year old gardener at Upton in 1881 where he was working for Noblett H.C. Ruddock, clergyman J.P. He was farming Paddick's Farm, Huish

---

[481] Taunton Courier, Wednesday 18th March 1891.

Champflower in 1900 when he was left £10 in his father's Will. In March 1903 he was summoned at the Wiveliscombe Petty Sessions for cruelty to two pigs by neglecting to feed them properly. After hearing the evidence the Bench decided that even if John had not staved the pigs he had treated them abominably, but they gave him the benefit of the doubt and dismissed the case on a technicality. They could not establish exactly on what day the pigs had died and there was a question as to whether the summons was taken out in proper time.[482] He was John Luxton, labourer of Shute Hills Farm, Chipstable when he failed to appear before the Tiverton magistrates for being the driver of a cart without lights at Bampton on the 27th April 1904. He was fined 6s. which included costs.[483]

John became a cow man at Bathealton, Somerset, but was residing at Braglands Farm, Stogumber, Somerset when he died on 11th December 1926. Probate of his Will was issued in London on the 2nd February 1927 to his nephews Frederick and James Bucknell, farmers. The whole of his estate and personal effects valued at £245 – 4 – 0d were to be equally divided between his brothers George and James Luxton, his sisters Mary Hooper and Rosa Bucknell and other relatives. John, who died aged 71, was buried at Bethel Chapel Waterrow on 16th December 1926.

John's sister, Elizabeth Anne Luxton of Devises, Wiltshire, a domestic cook, died aged 28, from "ulceration of stomach, perforation of stomach, peritonitis, syncopy one day" and was buried at Bethel Chapel Waterrow on 17th December 1887.

Their brother James (1868-1948) shared equally with his brother Frederick George the residue of the capital sum raised on the sale of his father's estate. He was farming at Halsdown Farm, Chipstable when he was named as one of the executors of his father's will in 1901. In the 1911 census he was a 37 year old (sic) unmarried stockman, and boarder, with Samuel Watts and family at Hungry Hill, Ripley, Woking in Surrey. James, a 41 year old stockman at Farm Court Cottages in Leatherhead,

---

[482] Exeter & Plymouth Gazette, Saturday 14th March 1903and Taunton Courier, 18th March 1903.
[483] Western Times, Friday 6th May 1904.

Surrey married Daisy Violet Miller, a 20 year old domestic servant, in Leatherhead Parish Church after banns on the 24th February 1914.

Their daughter Doris May Rose, born at Farm Court Cottages, on the 17th May 1914 married Harold Willetts, a stoker petty officer on HMS Hood in Portsmouth Cathedral on 15th May 1937. James Luxton, a farm labourer, of 16 Prospect Place, Mason's Hill, Bromley, Kent died aged 80 on 7th July 1948 at County Hospital, Farnborough, Kent. The administration of his estate valued at £726..13s..10d was granted in London on 26th November 1948 to Doris Mary (sic) Rose Willetts, the wife of Harold Joseph Willetts.

His brother William George Luxton, born at Huish Champflower on 17th June 1870, was bequeathed £10 in his father's will of 1901, if he could be found. He may be the William George Luxton, Service No.4500 who was a Private in the 6th Battalion Dragoon Guards (Carabiniers) who saw action in the Boer War and was awarded the Queen's South African Medal with clasps for Cape Colony, Orange Free State, Transvaal, South Africa 01, South Africa 02.

Frederick George Luxton (1873 – 1947), another brother, was an innkeeper, assisted by his sister Mary Ann, at the Wyndham Arms, in Williton in 1901[484] when he was named as an executor in his father's Will. They were the innkeepers there in July 1898 when a customer who stole money from the till was fined for theft and in November that year when the Petty Sessions granted an extension of time for one hour on the occasion of a Forresters' dinner.[485] Mary married John Hooper, ironmonger, at the Independent Chapel, North Street, Taunton on the 9th April 1901.By 1911 Mary was assisting her husband John, the inn-keeper at the Wyndham Arms in the High Street, Williton, with their six year old daughter Evelyn Gertrude. She was living at 25 Clyde Road, Redland, Bristol when her mother made her Will on 9th July 1921. I believe she was the Mary Ann Hooper, 71, of 17 Vicarage Road Minehead, widow of – Hooper who died of senile decay at Cotford Hospital, Bishops Lydeard on 19th October 1935. By then Frederick George Luxton had long moved on.

---

[484] His sister Mary Luxton was a hotel proprietor of the Wyndham Arms, Williton when she married John Hooper on 9th April 1901.
[485] Taunton Courier, Wednesday 27th July & 9th November 1898.

 As Trooper Frederick George Luxton, he was a member of the Wellington Troop A Squadron, of the West Somerset Yeomanry Cavalry, which took part in September 1898 in a military tournament at Minehead. Fred won first prize in the tent pegging contest, in which a trooper, riding at full gallop, picked a peg out of the ground. The smartness with which he did this was greeted with applause from the crowd. He came third in the lemon cutting contest. Two lemons were suspended at some distance apart, and the competitor had to cut each in two, the first with a forward and the second with the backward stroke of the sword.[486]

In January 1900 Trooper F.G. Luxton of Williton in A Squadron of the West Somerset Yeomanry, was sworn in as a volunteer at Taunton, to serve in the front in the Boer War. He was one of several civilians who were all good riders and shots who joined up. They were to be drilled at Taunton for a short period before leaving and were armed with the Lee-Metford rifle and bayonet. An army doctor examined the men before they were sworn in by Captain Beaumont, Adjutant of the 4th Yeomanry Brigade.[487] Fred applied at the Williton Petty Sessions on 1st February 1900 for a transfer of the Wyndham Arms to his sister Mary Ann Luxton, "because he had joined the Imperial Yeomanry and was about to start for South Africa." However when the Bench said they could not renew until September, Fred told the Bench that the arrangement did not suit him, and the transfer of the licence was not made.[488]

Fred purchased Shute Hills Farm, near Venn Cross, in the spring of 1903. He had only removed part of his goods there when late in the evening of Wednesday 27th May, the farmhouse was consumed in a blaze. The fire originated in a nearby barn. Fred was awakened about 10 o'clock, and a man was sent to fetch the fire brigade at Wiveliscombe four miles away. There was some delay when it was found that the fire

---

[486] West Somerset Free Press, Saturday 1st October 1898
[487] West Somerset Free Press, Saturday 13th January 1900.
[488] West Somerset Free Press, Saturday 3rd February 1900.

had already destroyed the whole of the horse harness, and the brigade did not reach Shute Hills until 1:15 in the morning. By this time the buildings and the thatch roof of the farmhouse was already ablaze. The brigade pumped the pond dry and obtaining water from the well was a slow process. The buildings were soon gutted and at 9 o'clock on Saturday morning nothing remained but blackened walls. The premises were insured and no livestock or implements were destroyed but several tons of hay was burnt.[489]

Fred Luxton, now a brewer of Chipstable, was fined 10s. including costs in May 1905, when he twice failed to attend the Petty Sessions, "for driving without a light,"the chairman remarking that 5s. of that amount had been added for Fred's contempt of court.[490] Mr. Fred Luxton of Chipstable, was among those gathered in St. Audries Park on Friday 29th October 1909 for the season's first meet of the West Somerset Foxhounds. "A touch of frost had sweetened the air with a blue sky and the sun warmly shining."[491] Again in March 1910, Fred of Chipstable, was fined 7 shillings for not having a dog licence.[492]

With all this woe in his life, it's little wonder that he set sail for Australia that year! He was a 37 year old farmer when he emigrated with relatives, aboard the "Moravian". Fred arrived in Melbourne on 13th September 1910, and moved to Queensland where he took up property in partnership at Killarney, (in photo below) on the 30th September 1910. Here he farmed until illness in 1940 when he moved to live with relatives. He died aged 72, in Nambour Hospital, on 8th March 1947 and is buried at Beerwah, twenty five miles from Nambour.

Henry George Luxton (1877 – 1949), known as George to his family and

---

[489] Taunton Courier, Wednesday 3rd June 1903.
[490] Taunton Courier, Wednesday 24th May 1905.
[491] West Somerset Free Press, Sturday 6th November 1909.
[492] Exeter and Plymouth Gazette, Friday 11th March 1910.

friends, the youngest brother was a 19 year old farm labourer in the 2nd Volunteer Battalion of the Somerset Light Infantry, when he enlisted at Taunton on 10th February 1896 in the Second Life Guards (No. 1999) for twelve years with the colours. (See photograph at end of chapter)

He was 5ft.10 ¾ inches, weighing 161 lbs, chest 36 ½ inches, complexion florid, eyes blue, hair brown, a member of the Church of England and with no distinctive marks. He was appointed to the Second Life Guards at Windsor Cavalry Barracks on 18th February 1896 but clearly army life did not suit him for he was discharged on 21st April 1896 with a total of 72 days service.

A policeman of 13 Roseberry Terrace, Clifton, Bristol he was left a legacy of £10 in his father's will made on 7th September 1900. Henry George Luxton, a police officer in Avonmouth, married Charlotte Evelyn Jex-Blake, spinster of Shipston on Stour, daughter of the late Rev. Charles Jex-Blake at St Mary's Church in the parish of Shirehampton, Gloucestershire on 14th May 1904.

Henry George Luxton was an engineer nutfitter foreman, when he was granted probate of his mother's Will at Bristol on 10th December 1925. He is listed in the Bristol Directories for 1930 and 1940 as residing at 36 St Matthews Road, Cotham. That was his address when he died aged

72 at Bristol Royal Infirmary on 7th August 1949. Charlotte Evelyn Luxton, his widow of 50 Saint Matthews Road, Cotham, Bristol died aged 88 on 17th September 1949 at 7 Victoria Gardens, Cotham. Probate of her personal estate valued at £9,808.16s.11 was granted in Bristol on 24th April 1950 to her niece, Evelyn Gertrude Wills, wife of Arthur Vernon Wills of 340, Park West, Marble Arch, London W2.

Henry George Luxton (1887-1949) in the Second Lifeguards 1896

70

JAMES LUXTON (1834 – 1918), FARMER OF SKILGATE AND LURBAN DOVERHAY, PORLOCK, SOMERSET

See tree 40

James Luxton (1834–1918), the fourth son of James and Betsy Luxton, Upton, labourer, was baptised at Upton, Somerset on the 26th January

1834. James aged 7, lived with his parents at the 40 acre Lotley Water Farm, Upton in 1841 and was still resident there a decade later as a 17 year old farmer's son. The family had moved by 1861 when the census that year records James Luxton 27, unmarried farmer's son, living at Townsend Farm, Skilgate.

There are numerous stories of poaching exploits in the family but the only hard evidence I have found are two escapades involving James. In the first James, and James Atkins, a farrier, of Skilgate, were caught on the 28th December 1868, by James Shorney, a gamekeeper trespassing in pursuit of game in a plantation belonging to Sir H.F. Davie. Luxton carried a gun and they had three dogs with them. When they appeared before the Dulverton Petty Sessions on Wednesday 3rd February 1869 they were fined £3 including costs.[493]

Two years later James Shorney, the game-keeper, caught James for a second time! James Luxton and Francis Jones both of Skilgate were summoned at Dulverton Petty Sessions in October 1871 for trespassing on land in the occupation of Mr George Follett, in pursuit of game. James Shorney, told the court that on the 14th September he was hiding

---

[493] Taunton Courier, Wednesday 3rd February 1869.

in a field cropped with turnips. Shortly afterwards Luxton and Jones and a third man he did not know, came into the field with a dog. They "put up" a hare or a rabbit, but the turnips were too high and they failed to catch it. When he revealed himself they ran away. The Bench fined them 10s. each and costs of 12s. They were cautioned that if they appeared before the Bench again they would be severely punished![494]

One day in May 1870 when he needed to do business in Wiveliscombe, James refreshed himself with a drink or two in a tavern. He left Wiveliscombe in an intoxicated state, and on the turnpike road, near Huish Bridge, his cart containing five bags of oats and himself over-turned. When he had recovered his legs he took out the horse and rode home, leaving the cart and the five bags of oats lying in the turnpike road for two days. He was fined 18s. and 11s. costs at the next Wiveliscombe Petty Sessions for obstructing the highway[495].

His elder brother George (1825–1901), who became a farm bailiff at Halsdown, Chipstable, had already married Ann Atkins in 1855 when James decided to marry her sister Elizabeth Atkins, 24, spinster, Skilgate, daughter of James Atkins, veterinary surgeon at the Register Office, Dulverton on the 10th July 1867. Both sign the register witnessed by the bride's father, James Atkins, and her sister, Wilmott Atkins. In the 1871 census James Luxton 37, farm labourer, lived at Red Croft Cottage, Skilgate with his wife Elizabeth 28, and children Mary 7 Ann 4 Ellen 2 and James 3 months. His mother Elizabeth aged 85, lived with them. James was a retired farm bailiff, living at Lurban[496] Doverhay, Porlock when the photograph (next page) was taken of him with his wife Elizabeth Jane Atkins at Porlock Recreation Ground c.1910.

James, working for Mr. A. Clarke, Selworthy, came fourth in the sheep shearing competion at the Williton & Dunster Agricultural Show held

---

[494] Taunton Courier, Wednesday 11th October 1871 and West Somerset Free Press 7th October 1871.
[495] Western Daily Press, Thursday 19th May 1870 and the North Devon Journal, Thursday 26th May 1870
[496] Lurban is a good example of a delightful Somerset name contraction-Lurban, Lowerbourne and Lowerbourne Terrace are the same place by different names. Lurban was probably easier to say after a few glasses of cider!

in the autumn of 1878.[497] He was a farm bailiff, in the employ of the Holnicote Estate, listed in the 1881 Minehead census as a 45 year old shepherd living with his wife Elizabeth 38, and five children, Mary 18, general servant, Ann Elizabeth 13, John 8, Lucy 5 and Frederick aged 1, at East Myne. Census returns never tell the whole story, however, for while he was at East Myne James was involved in smuggling exploits. These would have been while he lived at East Myne Farm, on the high ground near the coast between Minehead and Porlock. The farm was destroyed in the Second World War when the area was used as a tank training ground.

The family lived by the pack horse bridge in Allerford, Selworthy in 1891, and in the census that year James is a 56 year old agricultural labourer, his wife Elizabeth 49, son John aged 18, shepherd labourer, Lucy 15, Frederick 11, and Margaretta 9. At the Dunster Petty Sessions, Friday 3rd April 1891, James a labourer of Allerford, Selworthy was charged with keeping a dog above the age of six months without a licence. He explained it was a sheep dog which he kept for his master, Mr. Fish's use. P.C. James said that Mr. Fish had two sheep dogs on the farm which held exemptions from license but that Luxton kept the dog in question at his own home. The bench ordered James to take out a licence and the case was dismissed on his paying 2s..6d, the cost of the summons.[498]

By 1896 the family had moved yet again, to Stoke Pero on Exmoor, where the 1901 census has James 66 foreman at West Lucott Farm, supported by his wife Elizabeth Jane aged 57. Their daughter Margaretta is a 19 year old teacher in a National Day School.

---

[497] Somerset County Gazette, Saturday 2nd November 1878.
[498] West Somerset Free Press, Saturday 11th April 1891.

James was a colourful character who loved to wear bright waistcoats[499] (one was canary coloured!) and he was highly respected and immensely popular throughout the Exmoor hill country, where as a talented violinist, he was in great demand for the many local dances and other traditional gatherings which were so much an enjoyable part of rural life at that time.

A vivid description of a Harvest Home at Stoke Pero in which James and his fiddle (in photo) were in big demand has been preserved in a press report.[500] For the Harvest Home thanks giving service held in Stoke Pero at 9 AM on the 17th September 1896 the church "was beautifully decorated by graceful festoons of bracken and rowan branches and the service was very hearty and well attended." Afterwards in spite of rain that swept over the hills there was a large gathering of country people during the afternoon and evening at the farm of Mr. Harding, the churchwarden. Games and races were held in a field and afterwards about fifty people sat down to a substantial tea. In spite of rain, which now came down in torrents, a move was made for the barn, "where Mr. Luxton and his fiddle were in great requisition as the fun waxed fast and furious, and sounds of mirth within soon drowned the voice of the elements outside...Meanwhile the rain still came down pitiless as ever outside and the night was closing in....the festivies were kept up until a late hour of the night."

In his earlier days James was most likely a member too of a church band which was usually made up of farmers, skilled craftsmen and artisans such as builders, thatchers, shepherds, tailors and shoemakers who could afford to buy musical instuments and could arrange time for practice and attend weddings and funerals. By the late 19th century

---

[499] James great-grandson, Edward Luxton of Oatway Farm, Brompton Regis, relates the intriguing oral tradition of his smuggling exploits, Amelia Reeves, James granddaughter remembered he wore bright waistcoats when he played his violin at country dances. In 2018 his violin was in the possession of Suzanna Luxton Nurse his great granddaughter. James' walking stick which appears in two of his photographs is now in the possession of Edward Luxton who says it has lasted very well.

[500] West Somerset Free Press, Saturday 26th September 1896.

most bands were gone, replaced by organs. His is a world we have lost but its way of life has been admirably captured for us in the Wessex tales of Thomas Hardy.

In 1911 James Luxton, 77, a retired farm bailiff, and his wife Elizabeth, 67, were residing in a six room property at Lurban Doverhay, Porlock (in photo of 1910). They had been married 47 years and had nine children, but two were dead. Margaretta, their 29 year old daughter, and Florence Cochrane 27, who were both assistant teachers, were living with them. James Luxton, aged 84, of Lurban Doverhay, Porlock was buried at Skilgate on 13th April 1918. His widow Elizabeth Jane Luxton aged 95 of 3 Lower Bourne Terrace, Porlock, Somerset died on 28th February 1939. She was buried at Skilgate on 4th March 1939.

The photograph below was taken at Horner probably at a meet of staghounds c. 1912. James Luxton (1834-1918) is on the right while his daughter Rhoda Ellen Reeves is on the left, with her son, Harold reaching for an apple.

The Will of Elizabeth Jane Luxton, made on 12th December 1933, was proved in London on 28th August 1939, when Probate of her personal estate valued at £506 13s 1d was granted to her son John Luxton, pensioner police inspector, and her daughter Margaretta Luxton, spinster. She gave her daughter Margaretta, "all my trinkets, jewellery, personal ornaments and wearing apparel and all my furniture and household effects …… in the full confidence that she will dispose of the same in accordance with my wishes". She gave the following legacies to her daughters

Mary Jane Caswell	£25
Lucy Woolley	£25
Rhoda Ellen Reeves	£50
Ann Elizabeth Gooding	£50
Margaretta Luxton	£50

Her interest in four closes of land called Lower Pitsham, Great Pitsham, Easter Pitsham and Great Bottoms at Skilgate which had been bequeathed to her in the Will of her father James Atkins, dated 29th July 1880, she devised to her son John, daughter Margaretta and the children of her late son Frederick James Luxton.

The residue of her property were to be equally divided between her daughters Rhoda Ellen Reeves, Ann Elizabeth Gooding and Margaretta Luxton. A portrait of Elizabeth dressed in black which used to hang in her daughter "Aunt Gert's" front room at Lowerbourne, is now in the possession of Edward Luxton of Oatway Farm. Black was often worn by mature women, this fashionably plain style being enlivened by a neck brooch at the centre of a white frill bow. Her hair piled high in a chignon on top of her head, suggests a c1890 date when taller hairstyles were in vogue. It appears to be crowned by a white frill which cascades at the back to neck level.

Elizabeth has a proud look which is borne out by the following story related by Suzanna Luxton Nurse of Cannington, Somerset:-"My cousin Geoffrey who lives in Porlock went round to Lowerbourne as a child. He remembers aunt Gert's mother ("Mer,"as she was known) saying to him, "I can see you've started school. You're holding your knife like a pen!"

He always tells this story in a very haughty voice which seems to fit the lady in the portrait rather well."[501]

A marble headstone to the east of the chancel at St John's Church, Skilgate bears the following epitaph

In
Loving
Memory of
James Luxton
Died April 8th 1918
Aged 84
Also Elizabeth Jane his wife
Died Feb 28th 1939
Aged 95
And James their son
Died July 2nd 1897
Aged 26

The couple had nine children beginning with an illegitimate daughter Mary Jane Luxton, called "Polly" who was born in Skilgate c1863, but I have been unable to find her birth certificate. Mary married William Caswill, (also spelt Caswell) a widower who was the station master at Morebath, Devon, in Holy Trinity Church, Bridgwater on the 18th July 1892. William of Station House, Morebath who suffered with a brain disorder, died aged 50, and was buried at St Georges, Morebath on 26th November 1909. Mary of 25 Park Street, Tiverton died aged 98, at Belmont Hospital, Tiverton on 18th October 1961.

Her sister, Ann Elizabeth Luxton, was born in Skilgate on the 27th July 1867, and was baptised in the parish church of St. John the Baptist on

---

[501] See letter from Suzanna Luxton Nurse of Cannington, Somerset, dated 23rd March 2011.

5th August 1870. "Annie" as she was known, was employed as a cook in Kensington, before marrying John Gooding, a widower and policeman, in Holy Trinity Church, Paddington on 1st June 1905. In 1911 John 54 police pensioner and door-keeper, with Ann 44, and son John aged 2, lived at 208 Wharncliffe Gardens, St. Johns Wood London.

Rhoda Ellen Luxton, was born in Skilgate on the 4th June 1869, and she was baptised there on the 5th August 1870. She was sent as a child to live with her aunt Mary Burcher, who kept the village shop at East Quantoxhead in Somerset. One of her chores was to carry milk to the "Big House" every morning, then run to school where she often had the cane for being late! Rhoda, 20, domestic servant of Holnicote, the name of the Acland Estate near Porlock, married Noah Reeves, 23, mason, at All Saints, Selworthy on 31st December 1889, and they settled at Luccombe where they raised four daughters Annie, Violet, Amelia, Cristabel and a son Harold.

The eldest son James Luxton (1870 – 1897), born at Skilgate on the 17th December 1870, and baptised there on the 5th February 1871, was living with his grandparents James Atkins, 70, and Mary Atkins at the 30 acre Blindwell Farm, Skilgate in 1881 when he was aged ten. A bright boy he did well in school. In March 1883 and again in 1884 he was awarded £5 by the Ellsworth Exhibition Charity and in October 1884 won a book prize at the Allerford National School[502]. He played right wing for the Selworthy Football Team and won praise in the local press as in this report of a match against Minehead, "It is difficult to pick out the best of the Selworthy forwards but I think if there was any one of them just a little above the rest it was J. Luxton."[503]

In 1891 James, was a 20 year old solicitor's clerk, lodging with Edward Heath, a china and fishing tackle dealer, in High Street, Dulverton. A 26 year old law clerk, he died of tonsillitis and pneumonia, at 3 Billet Street, Taunton on the 2nd July 1897. James was buried in his parents' grave at Skilgate. The West Somerset Free Press, Saturday 10th July 1897, carried the following poignant obituary:- Death of Mr. James

---

[502] West Somerset Free Press, Saturday 24th March 1883 & 29th March 1884
[503] West Somerset Free Press, Saturday, 26th 1891

Luxton- We regret to have to report the death of Mr. James Luxton, eldest son of Mr. James Luxton, Luccott Farm, Porlock, who for the past five years has been engaged as common law clerk to Messrs Reed & Co. Hammet Street, Taunton which took place at his lodgings 3, Billet Street, on Friday morning at the early age of 26. During his residence in the town, the deceased had made a large number of friends, by whom he was much respected while for two years he was a member of the West Somerset Yeomanry Cavalry. Previous to this he had been employed in the office of Mr James Bere of Dulverton. His death is attributed to quinsy and pleurisy.

John Luxton[504] (1872–1941) who was born at Skilgate on the 22nd December 1872 became an Inspector in the Metropolitan Police. The family were living at Winsford, on Exmoor, Somerset when Lucy Luxton was born on the 23rd April 1875 and William on 6th May 1877. William died aged 2 from bronchitis on the 9th June 1879 and was buried at St Mary Magdalene, Winsford on the 19th June 1879. Frederick James Luxton (1879–1932) who was also born in Winsford, near Taunton on the 17th November 1879, became a Detective Sergeant in the Metropolitan Police. Their sister Lucy, born at Winsford, Exmoor on 23rd April 1875 was living in Cannington Somerset when she wed James Woolley, a game keeper in Dodington, at Bridgwater Register Office on 15th May 1902. I have failed tracing her in this country but she is listed alive in her mother's will in 1933.

Margaretta (1882 – 1981) the youngest of the nine children, was born in Minehead on 22nd March 1882, and baptised in St. Michael's Church on the 7th May 1882. In January and March 1900 when the Porlock Amateur Dramatic Society, gave a public performance of Cinderella, the 18 year old

---

[504] Susanna Fleckner "Barton Lodge" Bossington Lane, Porlock, Minehead writes 17th April 1976 "Legend has it that both Fred and Jack were exceedingly good looking with fantastic blue eyes! In fact we have sundry photographs which show that members of the family were good looking and of a somewhat haughty disposition!" Susanna has provided these family pictures.

starred as Cinderella "who in addition to a charming appearance possesses a voice of no mean order."[505]

"Aunt Gert" taught at Porlock School for fifty one years. She went to Lowerborne with her parents and lived in the house for many years. She died aged 99, in Minehead, on 27th October 1981 and her ashes were interred in her parents' grave at Skilgate. Probate of the will of Margaretta Luxton of Blenheim Lodge, Blenheim Road Minehead, Somerset, was granted in Bristol, 28th January 1982 when her estate was valued at £31,943. On last page Margaretta is in photograph with her mother c.1900:-

The two sons of this family, John (Jack) Luxton (1872 – 1941) and his brother Fred James Luxton (1879 – 1932) who served in the Metropolitan Police, and their offspring, are the topics of the two following chapters.

---

[505] West Somerset Free Press, Saturday 3rd March 1900

71

JOHN (JACK) LUXTON (1872-1941) METROPOLITAN POLICE INSPECTOR, ENFIELD, MIDDLESEX

See tree 41

John Luxton, the second son of James Luxton (1834-1918), and his wife Elizabeth Jane Atkins, was born on the 22nd December 1872 in Skilgate where he was baptised on the 26th January 1873. On 26th April 1881, John and his sister Lucy, children of James Luxton, East Myne, Minehead, labourer were admitted as pupils in Allerford, National School, Selworthy.

BLINDWELL FARM
SKILGATE
TAUNTON, SOMERSET

He was a farmer at Blindwell Farm, Skilgate when he under went a medical on the 2nd April 1895 to join the Metropolitan Police. A bachelor, aged 22, he was 6ft. ¾ inches tall and weighed 13 stone 4 lbs. His chest measurement was 37inches, and he had a fresh complexion, blue eyes and dark brown hair. He had no particular distinguishing marks.

John was appointed a police constable in the Metropolitan Police on the 22nd April 1895 and was given the warrant number 804000[506]. At first he was attached to the A. Division which was at Westminster and in 1901, aged 28, was one of 162 single police officers residing in

---

[506] For the career of John Luxton, Police Warrant No.80400 the following documents have been consulted at the P.R.O. MEPO 4/336 MEPO 4/347 MEPO 22/54 and MEPO 4/391.

the Police Barracks at Westminster. On his promotion to Sergeant on the 4th June 1904, he moved to G. Division based at King's Cross. He became Station Sergeant on the 9th November 1907 when he moved to the S. Division at Hampstead, and he became an Inspector on the 20th November 1909 when he moved to N. Division at Islington.

When he resigned from the force on the 3rd December 1923, with a certificate of exemplary service, he was an Inspector at Ponder's End, Middlesex. John, aged 50 had completed 28 years in the Metropolitan Police. He was 6ft 1inches with dark hair, turning grey and with blue eyes and a fresh complexion and was born in Wiveliscombe[507], Somerset on the 28th December 1872. He was to receive a pension of £252..4s..0d per annum, commencing on the 3rd December 1923.

John Luxton (on left in 1901) married Louisa Alice Stevens at St. Nicholas Church, Strood, Kent on the 8th August 1901. Louisa, descended from the Eden family was born at Dunmow, Essex on the 2nd August 1877. She was 5ft. 9$\frac{1}{2}$ inches tall with a fresh complexion, brown hair and brown eyes.

In 1911 John, 38, Inspector of Police, and his wife Louisa, 33, lived in a six room house at 44, Nags Head Road, Ponders End, Enfield. They had been married ten years and had six children but one was dead. Eventually the couple had nine children. The eldest, James Henry Eden Luxton (1902-1970) a gunsmith, born on the 19th February 1902, married late in life and had no children. His sister, Phyllis Elizabeth Eden Luxton, born on the 6th July 1903, married Lister Hey on the 20th September 1930. Phyllis was aged 90 when she died on the 16th May 1994. Her eldest daughter Margaret Hey M.A. (Oxon) became a professor in Columbia University. The next child, Muriel Annie Luxton (1905-1981), born on the 8th June 1905 married William Arthur Atkins,

---

[507] His birth certificate states he was born in Skilgate.

an editor, on the 14th June 1930 and they had two children. Her brother, John Robert Luxton, born on the 28th February 1907, died aged 3 in the Children's Hospital, Great Ormonde Street, London on the 4th December 1910, and he is buried in Enfield Highway Cemetery.

I have more to say later in this chapter on the next two children, Harold William Stevens Luxton (1909-1944) and David George Luxton (1911-2004). Their sister, Lorna Louise Luxton (1914-1981) born on the 20th March 1914, married Dennis Albert Beer, a school teacher on the 27th October 1938 and they had six children. Her brother Peter John Luxton (1915-2007) born in Enfield Middlesex on the 25th November 1915, married Dorothy Kate Gaut at Sidbury Devon on the 10th April 1939. He was a noted sprinter at Ponders End Athletic club before the War. They lived in Sidmouth, Devon and had three daughters. The youngest child, Joan Margaret Luxton (1918-2012), born on the 27th May 1918, married Donald Arthur Buchanan, a school teacher, on the 2nd August 1941. They lived in Cambridge and had a son.

John's wife Louisa Alice Luxton, died from pneumonia, at their home, 44 Nag's Head Road, Ponder's End, Enfield on the 15th April 1928, at the comparatively early age of fifty. Photographs of John and his wife Louisa in c.1901 are on this page. John Luxton police pensioner, married his wife's widowed elder sister, Ethel Eden Williams (Stevens) (1875-1950), 54, dressmaker, in the Register Office, Maidenhead, Berkshire on 16th August 1930. She became step-mother to her sister's eight surviving children to whom she was known as "Aunt Betty."

John Luxton, retired police inspector, made his Will on the 29th November 1940. He gave his one half share and interest in the freehold land at Skilgate, Wiveliscombe, Somerset, left him under the will of his mother, to his son Peter John Luxton. His second wife Ethel Eden Luxton was to receive the income from "all his real and personal estate." After her death he made pecuniary legacies for his children and what was left over to be divided between them. Among other bequests John left legacies of £100 to his daughters Phyllis Hey, Muriel Atkins and sons David George Luxton and Peter John Luxton and £50 to his sons Harold Luxton, James Henry Luxton and daughters Lorna Beer and Joan Luxton.

John Luxton of 44 Nag's Head Road, Ponders End, Enfield, Middlesex known as "Jack" was a very bad asthmatic. He died on the 7th March 1941. Probate of his estate was issued in Llandudno on the 20th May to David George Luxton and Peter John Luxton, mechanical engineers when his personal estate was valued at £1423..0..10d.

Two of John and Louisa's sons established branches of the Luxton family. The elder of the two sons, Harold William Stevens Luxton (1909-1944) was born on the 12th October 1909 at 8a Kingston Street, St. Pancras. Harold, the middle child of nine children, who were very close as siblings, and did many things together. Their father, a Police Inspector, didn't let them get away with much. He attended Enfield Central School between 1921 and 1926 and while growing up he was a choirboy, a violinist, a scout and an athlete, including being a high jumper. Upon leaving school, he became a banker with the Midland Bank (now H.S.B.C.) and he married Phyllis Joyce Kent at St. James Church, Friern Barneton on the 25th July 1936.

He had been very careful with money and had saved enough when married to buy a new semi-detached house at 135 Browning Road, Enfield over looking hilly fields. The land was previously orchards with many of the houses growing fruit trees in their back gardens. This was a blessing in World War Two. At the end of August 1939, he signed up to his local Territorial Regiment just before the war was declared against Germany. This meant that he was called up as a 'Territorial' a few days later, even though he had not yet had the opportunity to train with the regiment. His Territorial Army unit was embodied as the 7th battalion Middlesex Regiment (Duke of Cambridges Own) on the 2nd September

1939, the day after the Germans had invaded Poland, and the day before Britain and France declared war on Germany.

I have a photograph of Harold taken in early September 1939. He is wearing the 1937 pattern khaki woollen battledress, which had distinctive pleated pockets and flaps of material to cover buttons. He is in the "walking out" order of uniform, with no webbing or gaiters. His trousers have a shell dressing pocket, on the right, just below the waist, and the large patch pocket on his left leg, is to hold maps and papers. His upper pockets may well contain a Bible or testament, cigarette packet, tin or case or lighter, army pay book, perhaps some keepsake letters and photographs, a watch and wallet. There are two brass buttons on his khaki side cap. Along with his rifle and other equipment, each soldier was issued with a shrapnel helmet and gas mask.

He was posted all over Britain and arranged for his children, Mary and John, to be billeted in Ullswater, when he was there as Joy was hospitalised at the time[508]. Harold progressed through the ranks, eventually becoming a Sergeant. In preparation for the Normandy landings the regiment took part in exercises at Freckenham, Suffolk. Harold landed in the Sword Beach sector of Normandy on the 8th June 1944. In the next ten days he was with troops holding the ground on either side of the River Orne and near Ranville and what became known as 'Pegasus Bridge.' Their position was under constant shelling by the Germans.

During his time in Normandy, Harold was able to write letters home. His son Harold relates, "The second last letter he wrote home just

---

[508] Their daughter, Patricia Anne, born in the North Middlesex County Hospital on 19th May 1943 died on 30th May 1943.

5 days before he was killed comments on Mistletoe growing in the Apple Trees and Pretty Climbing Sweet Peas in bloom. He says how busy they have all been. How wonderful that in amongst such a busy time fighting a battle one can still take time to observe the mistletoe and sweet peas."

Sergeant Harold William Stevens Luxton (Army No. 6208159) 7th Battalion the Middlesex Regiment, was killed on Tuesday 18th July 1944. This was the day the British and Canadian forces launched 'Operation Goodwood,' a massive attack to secure the remainder of Caen and the high ground south of the city. Early in the morning (before 05.00) the Allies began the attack with an artillery barrage and a bombing raid by the R.A.F. in which for three hours approximately 4500 allied aircraft dropped bombs on enemy positions. Three Armoured Divisions then led the attack in what was a relatively narrow strip of country. The Germans were well dug in and ready waiting. During the afternoon, Harold in 154 Brigade, which formed part of the 51st Highland Division, moved forward to consolidate the advance of the Armoured Divisions. It was during this advance about 17.00 hours while he was liberating the village of Cuverville, Calvados, a short distance to the east of Caen, that Harold aged 34, was killed as a "result of fragments from a German shell." Harold's body rested in a temporary grave in a garden for fifteen months, before it was removed to Ranville War Cemetery which lies to the north of Cuverville. The administration of the personal estate of Harold Luxton of 135 Browning Avenue, Enfield, Middlesex valued at £1512..3s..4d was granted to his widow Phyllis Joyce Luxton on the 4th June 1945. On his death his widow Joyce, received a Midland Bank Pension, until her death in 2007, aged 97.

In March 1948 Joy and their three children, Edith Mary born 1937, Walter John born 1939, and Harold born in Merthyr Tydvil Glamorgan, four months after his father's death, emigrated to Perth, Australia[509]. Prior to the fiftieth anniversary of the Battle of Normandy, Joy was contacted by the municipality of Cuverville. In June 1994 Joy and her children visited Cuverville, where they were the special guests of the

---

[509] I am indebted to Joy and family for much of my information. See Joy's letter of 31st December and other correspondence.

mayor. They were made very welcome and were treated extremely generously with Joy being made an Honorary Citizen of Cuverville. The family were there again on Sunday 18th June 2004, the 60th Anniversary, when Cuverville honoured two soldiers Pte. Martin Philbin and Sergeant Harold Luxton, who had died liberating their village. A plaque was unveiled naming the new Civic Hall 'Salle Philbin-Luxton.'

David George Luxton (1911-2004), the other son, who established a branch of the Luxton family, was born on the 26th February 1911, and was baptised on the 16th April in St. James, Enfield. In School David, like his brothers Harold and Peter, was an outstanding athlete, and like them, he loved music. Harold sang and played the violin while David played the piano.

He married Dorothy Ella Ethel Shinkins at Waltham Abbey, Essex on the 26th July 1940. David, a retired civil servant, and his late wife Dorothy, lived at 58 Balmoral Drive, Bramcote Hills, Nottingham and have two surviving sons. The eldest John Richard Luxton, B.Sc. (Hons) Hull, born on the 9th July 1944, married Jane Ann Bush and was a biology teacher in Leeds. They have two daughters, Katie and Phillipa. His brother, Dr Mark Christopher Luxton M.A. B.M. B. Ch. (Oxon) born in Northwick Park Hospital, Harrow, Middlesex on the 22nd March 1947 went to Jesus College Oxford in the 1960s and became a Consultant Anaesthetist at Queen Hospital, Nottingham. Mark, and family live in Nottingham.

To celebrate his ninetieth birthday on the 26th February 2001 David George Luxton (in photograph) taped the story of his long and active life from his apprenticeship days in mechanical engineering in Enfield, to his distinguished career in armaments manufacture, during and after the Second World War. His son John has transcribed the account which concludes this part of the family story:-

By the end of my apprenticeship at the age of 21 at Enfield, I had worked on many machines in the tool room, including milling, grinding turning, drilling and any other odd machines about the workshop and had a long period on fitting and other jobs in the workshops.

At 19, having learnt French, this enabling me to gain a 1st class grade in Matriculation, but did not go to University as I was still attending college.

For the last 5 months of training I moved over to the planning dept., working with the head of dept. and sitting in at discussions about various jobs, which was very important. I was then transferred to the drawing office.

I did well in O.N.C. getting exemption at mechanicals for doing this and went on to follow the H.N.C. at evening classes at Regent Street Polytechnic. I passed with distinction in the theory of machines and engineering drawing, a good qualification for a post in the drawing office. I then transferred into the workshop, as this was required for one year after the apprenticeship, to gain a full qualification for mechanical engineers. Back to working from 7.30am to 5.00pm and on Saturday mornings!!

After one year I was transferred back to the Drawing Office. This involved 2 years work on tooling up and designs for fixtures and alterations to machines for the Bren Gun, from 1935 to 1937. This was a long job and I had 10 men working under me. I was responsible both for their work and my own. This was completed in March 1937. I was always to have a great feeling for Enfield set as it was in those days in the country. I was able to walk to work leaving home soon after 6 o'clock and knew if I passed Rochford's nurseries as their hooter went I would arrive at the factory on schedule at 7.20am. In good weather I would take my cornbeef sandwiches along the river bank, on one occasion falling asleep and arriving back late! I explained why and that was that!!

I applied for a job as Technical Assistant at a new factory being built at Nottingham, and successfully passed the interview which was held at Woolwich Arsenal. The pay was £325 per year, which was good at the time, with the promise of additional money in the future after satisfactorily passing my time there.

The work involved developing 3/7 anti-aircraft guns, in which I had no experience but I did have experience in jigs and tools. The job also involved interviewing people to do the work. Much of this work I did on my own, and found it very interesting. It was a good management staff to work with.

As assistant manager I particularly enjoyed a spell as night manager a different experience which I did well at.

I then had an interview at the factory for a shop manager's post, and was successful on the second vacancy in the factory, which was in the developing small South Shop which was then being built. The war was hotting up by now. I was now working on 14mm anti-tank guns and the Bofors Gun, an anti-aircraft gun. I blossomed out here and did very well, the manager being very satisfied. In 1940 I was offered a job with the manager as his assistant at a new factory in Newport Mon.. I did not know either the area or the factory. I started on Monday 4th August, having picked out certain staff to take with me.

A fortnight before I had got married and was able to spend a week in a hotel (the Gresham) and a second week in digs before we moved to Newport. For the first month Dorothy and I stayed in a hotel. We then moved in to half a house in a pleasant spot at Stow Hill high above the town.

BUT BUT
The factory was on its first legs and the machines were just arriving. As there were very few suitable men available I was only able to employ women, so the jigs and tools had to be redesigned to be used by women, each doing a single operation.

It turned out to be a well suited team and it proved useful to take the drawing office manager down with me. For the first 14 months it was a hard job with no holidays.

On the September 1941 we were bombed out, which was an unpleasant experience. There was a warning that a raid was likely as an enemy photography plane had been spotted over head during the day only staying for 15 minutes. The town was aware something might happen that night.

Soon the town was lit up like day time with flares from the enemy aircraft. We sheltered down stairs under the table downstairs. A bomb dropped near to our house. The roof was torn off, all the window panes smashed and the lounge door blown into the hall, a real mess!! But we were quite safe. With nowhere to sleep we stayed in a friend's house for a month sleeping under the stairs whilst the repairs were completed!!

On the 14th October I was asked to go to Liverpool, of all places, with no rise in pay but a challenge! I knew Victor Lambert the man in charge. Dorothy packed up the small amount of furniture we had and initially went to live in Caerleon, an old Roman town, 5 miles from Newport, which would be safe. I had to go back into digs. I had small arms experience, but found the factory in strange circumstances, meeting the management and the Head Quarters staff on two sides of a room. Mr Harris the Dept. Director a pleasant enough chap told us that Winston Churchill had given orders that if 5000 sten guns could not be made by December, then all the top management would be sacked. At the time the soldier had little to defend himself with except a bayonet on the end of a piece of $1^1/_2$" tubing!! Clearly a gun was better than this to defend yourself with the war in Europe becoming increasingly serious.

Let's get cracking!!

Managed to get 500 made in 10 weeks. Eventually we were making 80,000 a month, eventually producing a total of a million. I redesigned the gun, which was essentially a Tommy Gun, making a further half a million. I sometimes worked all night and the following day in order to get production moving. Eventually we had two production lines, with each worker, often women, doing one operation each. The trade outside the factory became able to provide many of the components, which speeded up the assembly line. I was to come across some of these guns 30 years later when they arrived at Woolwich for melting down. Some inevitably got into the wrong hands and some have turned up more recently, although I never had one.

By the March the Head manager and assistant manager had moved, but I got used to having new bosses. I then became the manager staying there until 1955, when I was offered the job of an assistant director at Woolwich Arsenal. I don't think I was the person they wanted, but I was selected. The top staff had difficulty in seeing your point of view, but I soon found that the skill of the men was fantastic. I never worked in a more wonderful factory.

Woolwich Arsenal started in the 17 century (about 1670) after the Master General of Ordnance had been killed, whilst a casting was taking place, in gun manufacture. Clearly the moulding was damp. So they built a proper arsenal at Woolwich. The original building was designed by Sir John Vanburgh and is still there. The Arsenal was known in Henry V111 time, as warships were built in the docks, there were jetties for shipping and ropes were also made. Rockets were designed and tested there prior to the battle of Waterloo. I stayed there 10 years until 1965 and enjoyed every minute.

Detonator parts, tanks, rocket launchers, bridges and 30mw generators (at the rate of one a month, one on the stocks and one being dissembled) were some of the items we made. For the last two years I was made Director of the company when I was responsible for over £4 million of service work and had to close down the factory.

A great shame. 3500 people and 200 staff were all successfully found alternative employment. 12000 machines had to be disposed of. This proved quite a problem especially for the larger pieces. Some were offered to Woolwich Polytechnic (with Dr Hayward as director) others to two schools – Chislehurst and Sidcup Grammar School and Dartford Tech. - together with laboratory and chemical equipment. These would be free as all were publicly owned. Many of the smaller items and machines were transferred to other factories. Many American machines were on a lend/lease scheme and a clear list of these was available and so these were all shipped back to U.S.A., even though by now most of them were of little value.

The site was over 900 acres and also housed 15 other contractors. The British Library made use of Wellington Store Houses, which were fitted with racks for thousands of books, whilst the air force had an area for unloading service equipment. Customs and Excise also operated there. To confuse closure arrangements the front area of some 67 acres was owned by the government. To maintain its strategic importance from the early days, the site was self-sufficient, having its own electricity and gas supply with a water source directly from Woolwich Common. The factory was a very historic place and has been well described in a book by Brigadier Hogg and by publications in Woolwich library. Long term planning began to take place for the site which was a complex one to develop not helped by the old main London sewer running across the end of the site into the Thames and also the sewage works at one end. A bridge was built across the Thames at one end and there were all sorts of grand ideas like a film studio, mostly still in peoples minds.

Since by now production had finished, I then had to find myself a job and was appointed director at Nottingham where I knew many of the staff, who were young when I was there in 1935/7. I stayed at Nottingham until 1973. I had a very good relationship with the Unions and whilst the staff were not as skilled as in Woolwich they improved. We made 4.5mm and 37 tank guns and 81mm mortars which were used in the Falklands. One big project was making the light gun. These were made of semi-stainless steel and were formed of two parts which could be transported by helicopter over difficult terrain. We also made several hundred forklift trucks that could go on uneven ground and uphill which were very versatile.

I retired as director in Sept 1973 aged 63, by then I had had enough.

Subsequently the factory closed. It had started its existence in the 1914-18 war for ammunition production and then in producing guns. In the 1920s it was shut and used for some years as a bus depot, which also eventually closed. It was reopened some 6 months before I came from Enfield in 1935.

Whilst much of my life's work was very hard, this did not distract from the enjoyment of it. Dorothy, my wife, had to put up with moving, but was happy with somewhere nice to live. Moving also meant separation from Dorothy and subsequently the children which was always difficult.

During my working life I spent 10 years at home, having to leave when my father was ill, $^1/_2$ year in Nottingham, 14 months in Newport, 15 years in Liverpool, 10 years at Woolwich and 7/8 years in Nottingham, so we were up and down the country all that time, which was all very interesting. I never refused to go anywhere or refused a job. It was very fascinating to see how each factory ticked. All were different. Both Woolwich and Enfield were mature factories, Enfield being where I started my apprenticeship at the age of 16, just after the death of my mother[510]. This was a great tragedy and a very upsetting experience at that time of life. She had nine children, although one had died very young, and had a happy life. My father was very good but rather hard having to bring up eight children but we were all fed and cared for. Dorothy and I had three children but lost Roger at the age of 13. A great tragedy also. Over the years the downs have been compensated by the ups and we have experienced life in the raw in all its perplexities and learnt how people tick. I enjoyed it all although the experience was not always a pleasant one. Still we have survived!! Dorothy is now 87 and we will be celebrating out combined birthdays tomorrow (I am 90) at Langer Hall bringing together the immediate branches of the family.

Eventually in 1974 I was awarded the C.B.E., particularly for all my efforts during the war.

---

[510] Louisa Alice Luxton aged 50 wife of John Luxton, a pensioned Police Inspector, died of pneumonia at 44 Nag's Head Road, Ponders End on the 15th April 1928.

72

FREDERICK JAMES LUXTON (1879-1932)
SERGEANT IN THE METROPOLITAN POLICE
AND FARMER IN CUTCOMBE SOMERSET

See tree 42

Frederick James Luxton (1879-1932), the fourth son of James Luxton
(1834-1918), and his wife Elizabeth Jane Atkins, was born in the parish
of Winsford, near Taunton Somerset on the 17th November 1879.
When the 1881 census was taken he was aged one and was living with
his parents and family in Minehead. On 23rd December 1891 twelve
year old Fred was a star turn when he performed "The Butcher's Boy"
spoken in character, and in very appropriate "get up" at the Allerford
School concert before a crowded room.[511]

Frederick, a 22 year old bachelor and farm bailiff of Syndercombe
Farm, Clatworthy Somerset, married Florence Sellick aged 30, of
Syndercombe Farm, Clatworthy, daughter of James Sellick, farmer in
the Wesleyan Chapel, Minehead on the 24th July 1902. Both signed the
register in the presence of Fenwick Greenslade, a farmer at Parsonage
Farm, Luxborough, who was married to Frances, a sister of Florence
Sellick, and Martha Batchelor. Syndercombe Farm is now underwater
at Clatworthy Reservoir.

For a while Frederick was employed as a porter by the G.W.R. at
Bridgwater, but on the 14th October 1902, he was residing at 55
Cambridge Buildings, Charlwood Street, Westminster, when he
underwent a medical to join the Metropolitan Police Force. He was 22
years of age, 5ft 11$^3/_4$ inches tall, weighed 12 stone and had a chest
measurement of 34$^1/_2$ inches. He had a dark complexion, grey eyes, dark
brown hair and no particular distinguishing marks.

---

[511] West Somerset Free Press, Saturday 2nd January 1892

He was appointed to the Metropolitan Police (Warrant No.89170) on the 3rd November 1902, when he was attached to the S Division based at Hampstead[512]. In 1911 Frederick 30, Detective Metropolitan Police and his wife Florence 39, lived in a five room house at 13 Eaton Road, Hendon. They had  been married 8 years and had three young children. Progress and promotion marked his faithful service and he spent most of his time in the Criminal Investigation Department where he attained the rank of Detective Sergeant (third class) on the 18th July 1911 and second class on the 21st August 1917.

In September 1917 he was transferred from Hendon where he had been for about nine years, to Golders Green Police Station (inset) where he was to remain for the rest of his career. There was plenty of work there for him to do. Golders Green was a hamlet in the early 1900s, but when its tube station opened in 1907, it developed rapidly into a busy suburb with streets of semi-detached houses and a major shopping area. Fred and family continued to live in Hendon, and they were living at "Lynmouth" No. 9 Somerset Road between 1918 and 1929.

The local paper, the Hendon & Finchley Times, carries detailed reports of many of Sergeant Luxton's exploits. Here are just a few of them. In October 1908 John Cheesewright 34 a tall powerfully built man, was charged with stealing cable from a building site at Golders Green. Luxton and another officer, Miles, arrested him in a public house, but as they were leaving Cheesewright, punched Miles in the chest, caught his arm badly in the door, and darted off. Luxton closed with him and a desperate struggle ensued in the street until eight or nine officers arrived to overwhelm him and he was sentenced to 12 months hard labour. There were no police cars in February 1909, when a lady

---

[512] For the career of Frederick James Luxton in the Metropolitan Police, Warrant No.89170 the following documents have been consulted at the P.R.O. MEPO 4/435 MEPO 4/337 MEPO 4/348 P45.

attending her baby in Alexandra Road, Hendon heard thieves in the house. No time was lost in informing the police and although Luxton and another policeman cycled at almost break-neck speed, they arrived too late to catch the villains.

In February 1917, a 13 year old boy broke into a house in Hendon, through a scullery window. He skilfully removed the putty and placed the glass on the lawn. When Detective Sergeant Luxton caught up with him, the boy confessed and said that he learnt the way to get into the house in the "pictures". The boy was sentenced to six strokes of the birch but this did not cure him! In January 1917, he stole a valuable sledge and was sent to a reformatory for three years where he would be taught a useful trade.

In March 1919 Richard Flanagan, a private in a Canadian Railway Troop, was hobbling around in London, absent without leave. He spun a story to a widow that he was war wounded, and had nowhere to go. She let him stay the night and he ran off the next day with £140 worth of jewellery and other valuables. Sergeant Luxton tracked him down, and it turned out that he had been court martialled for wilfully injuring himself to avoid being sent to the Western Front. He had been sentenced to 56 days imprisonment. In October he was sent to France where he was wounded in the right thigh, but this was afterwards found to be a self inflicted wound. He was absent without leave when arrested. Luxton found the stolen property, some of which had been pawned in Aberdare. In April 1919 when Flanagan, was sentenced to six months imprisonment, the Bench at the Hendon Sessions, directed that Detective Sergeant Luxton was

deserving of commendation in tracing the prisoner and the manner in which he had conducted the enquiries which led to the recovery of the property. The photograph shows Temple Fortune Golders Green c 1920

Fred resigned from the force after 25 years service in November 1927, because of ill health, and he was pensioned with an exemplary certificate of service, dated 10th November 1927.

The Hendon & Finchley Times, Friday 28th October, were full of praise for the retiring sergeant and wrote a glowing praise of his career:-

"Next Thursday marks the retirement from the Police Force of Detective Sergeant Frederick Luxton, one of the best known C.I.D. men in the district if not in the Metropolitan area. Mr Luxton joined the service 25 years ago and has spent all but five of them at Golders Green. During that time he has had hundreds of cases through his hands, and has been connected with not a few of what are colloquially known as "good jobs."These included the famous "Goslet murder,"a series of very mysterious rick fires many years ago, and numerous important burglaries.

He has the proud distinction of having been 36 times commended by judges, coroners and the Commissioners of Police for ability, devotion to duty and the manner in which his cases were presented. Affectionately known among his colleagues as the "Old Gentleman." Mr. Luxton was until a season or two ago considered one of the finest cricketers in the Force, his lusty hitting being a feature at one time of police matches. With all his official reserve and somewhat austere bearing, Mr Luxton had a soft spot beneath his waistcoat, and prisoners have found him a kindly and considerate custodian. A man who was recently sentenced to a long term of imprisonment at Middlesex Sessions sent his kind regards by another officer to the "grey haired tec…"with thanks for his courtesy and kindness. Mr. Luxton made very few enemies during his long and eventful career but has a host of friends, all of whom will wish him the best of luck for the future."

His colleagues in the S. Division of the C.I.D. at Hampstead presented him with a twelve piece egg cruet suitably inscribed (in fact it is a six piece one and is with his grandson Edward) and a list of thirty five commendations and awards for meritorious services. Detective Superintendent Ashley of New Scotland Yard in making the presentation said that he had always been ready to give the junior officers the benefit of his considerable experience in dealing with criminals and criminal cases. Mr. Luxton had ever gone out of his way to assist those in need of help...He was an asset to any police division because of the confidence of the Courts which he invariably won and so well deserved. Sergeant Luxton was closely involved in the arrest and conviction of the notorious house breaking gang of burglars led by "Jack the Sailor" sometimes called "Mad Jack" who were charged with house breaking and stealing jewellery in Golders Green in 1920[513].

On his retirement Fred bought Lower House Farm, Cutcombe, Somerset, where he lived with his family[514]. Although plagued by ill health he kept working at the farm until the late autumn of 1931. On medical advice he went to London, hoping that special treatment would make him well again, but to his disappointment and that of his family, it was found that he had an incurable disease. He therefore returned home and gradually his strength failed. Though towards the end he was a great sufferer, he was very patient and never murmured against his lot. Frederick James Luxton, farmer of Lower House Farm, Wheddon Cross, near Taunton made his Will on the 1st December 1931. He appointed Mr Perry the manager of Barclays Bank, Minehead and his old friend Mr Fenwick Greenslade of Westcott farm, Luxborough near Taunton to be his executors. The farm, with the whole of the livestock and other effects, he gave to his wife Florence. Frederick died on Monday the 15th February 1932 and probate of his estate valued at £4182..18s..3d was issued in London on the 24th June. His widow, Florence of Lower House Farm, Cutcombe, Somerset, died on the 18th November 1941. Probate of her personal estate valued at £6416..16s..9d was issued in Llandudno on the 2nd March 1942.

On the north side of Cutcombe Church on Exmoor there is a pink granite monument to Frederick and his wife Florence. It consists of three steps surmounted by a cross. The epitaph inscribed on the steps reads:-

---

[513] Dundee Evening Telegraph, Monday 26th April 1920.
[514] Edward S.W. Luxton of Oatway, Brompton Regis writes in December 1996, "I have the family flint lock gun used by the Luxton's and also a gun won by my grandfather, Frederick James Luxton (1879-1932) in 1900".

In
Loving memory
of
Frederick James Luxton
Lower House Farm Cutcombe
Died 15 February 1932
aged 52 years.
also Florence beloved wife of the above
died 18 November 1941 aged 70 years
Rest in Peace.

This couple had issue four children. There were three daughters. Annie Elizabeth Luxton known as Cissie who married Wilfred Wesley Norman, died aged 88 in Minehead on the 29th August 1995. Her sisters also married farmers. Florence May Luxton known as Florrie, married William Giles Escott, and Dorothy Lucy Luxton married Frederick Edgar Norman[515] and had two daughters.

Their only son Frederick James Luxton, born at 52 Gayton Road, Hampstead, London on the 17th May 1905, farmed at Escott Farm, Stogumber, with his uncle, Bert Sellick at the time of his marriage (on right) to Margaret Elizabeth Whitmore of London at Stogumber on the 26th September 1944. Fred who farmed at Oatway, Brompton Regis, Somerset died on the 3rd May 1985 shortly before his 80th birthday. The ashes of Fred and his wife Margaret are interred with his parents at Cutcombe.

---

[515] Frederick was a son of Wilfred Wesley Norman who married Annie Elizabeth Luxton as his second wife.

Fred successfully continued breeding the pedigree Devon cattle herd inherited from his father. In March 1945 at the annual spring show and sale of tuberculin-tested pedigree Devon bulls held in Exeter, under the auspices of the Devon Cattle Breeders' Society, his "Cutcombe Wanderer" was sold for £103 guineas[516]. He and his wife Margaret had three children. Two daughters Margaret Irene, was born on the 22nd October 1945 and Jane Barbara was born on the 27th May 1955. Margaret is married to Donald Arthur Elliott, a veterinary surgeon and they have two daughters. She continues to breed the Cutcombe herd of pedigree Devons began by her grandfather. Their son Edward Stephen Whitmore Luxton, B. Ed., (left at Oatway on 29th July 1976) born on the 29th October 1947, was a deputy headteacher of a Primary School in Minehead for nearly 34 years and was a churchwarden at Brompton Regis. On retirement from teaching he took on a new job for seven years as a gardener attending the four and a half acres of Hollom House.

Edward is now a game-keeper, looking after two shoots. He lives at Oatway with his wife Sylvia Elizabeth Bale from Withiel Florey. They married at Withiel Florey on the 28th May 1988 and have a daughter, Lucy Elizabeth Luxton, born on the 25th July 1990 and a son Stephen Frederick Whitmore Luxton, born on the 24th September 1991. Sylvia and Edward are chapel wardens of Withiel Florey Church and are on the Brompton Regis with Withiel Florey P.C.C.

---

[516] Exeter & Plymouth Gazette, Friday 9th March 1945.

The author took this photograph of Frederick James Luxton (1905-1985) feeding the chickens at Oatway on the 29th July 1976.

73

THOMAS LUXTON (1798-1856) OF PETTON BAMPTON DEVON AND UPTON SOMERSET

See tree 43

Thomas the sixth son of John Luxton (1747-1818) yeoman of Corner House, Petton and his wife Mary Redwood, was one month old when he was baptised as Thomas Luxon at St. Petrock's Church, Petton on the 21st September 1798. In his father's Will made on the 20th March 1818, Thomas was bequeathed three pounds payable in five years after his father's death.

Thomas, an agricultural labourer, married Ann Cooksley in the neighbouring parish of Upton, in the lovely Haddeo Valley, Somerset on the 15th April 1831. Both parties were illiterate and signed the parish register with their mark. Their five children were all baptised in St. James, Upton, beginning with Elizabeth, the eldest, who was baptised on the 14th May 1837. She probably died in infancy for she is not mentioned in the 1841 census. The couples only son, George Luxton (1839-1916) who was baptised on the 24th February 1839, was followed by three daughters, Eliza baptised on the 26th December 1841, Ann on the 10th August 1845, and Mary Maria on the 19th May 1850.

Thomas and his family lived at Higher Cooksley Cottage, Upton in 1841. The cottage is listed as no.44, a homestead measuring 1acre1 rod 4 perches, in the Upton tithe apportionment, dated 8th May 1838, when Silas Wood Blake esquire was the landowner, and occupier of the farm of over 142 acres. It was mostly pasture and meadow with some woodland but it included a garden or potatoe plot measuring 2 rod .12 perch. Thomas and his growing family had moved by 1851 to West Hensdown in the same parish. The farm of over 144 acres, in the possession and occupation of John Langston in 1838, was again mostly pasture and meadow but there was more arable. The homestead and plantation garden marked as no.468 measured 3 rod..3 perches.

At this date a labourer's cottage usually had a piece of land for growing potatoes and other vegetables and for "the run of a pig." A small orchard provided enough for a hogshead or two of cider and winter storing apples. A labourer's tasks varied and included the thrashing of wheat, oats and barley and making bundles of reed. There was cutting and making of faggots in woodland," "brushing and trimming" of hedgerows and cutting and tying of furze. In the fields the man might be spreading beat ash, lime-mould mixing and dung spreading.

Thomas was a 58 year old labourer, when he died at Taunton Hospital on the 3rd December 1856, following the amputation of a leg for malignant disease. He was buried at Petton on the 14th December 1856. Ten years later his widow, Ann, aged 56, Magdalene Street, daughter of James Cooksley, labourer, married for a second time to James Stone 52 widower, wheelwright, Magdalene Street, at St Mary Magdalene, Taunton on the 12th November 1866.

Thomas's daughters went into domestic service. Eliza (1841-1893) aged 39 in 1881 was an unmarried servant and nurse, in the home of Edward Thomas, a solicitor and his family at Yatton near Bristol. She was a spinster and seamstress, of 1 West Grove, Brook Road, Bristol when she died aged 52 from "cancer of the breast 2 years" on the 8th December 1893. Probate of her Will was granted at Bristol on the 21st December 1893 to her sister Mary Maria Luxton, when her personal effects were valued at £153. Her sister Ann (1845-1898) was a 16 year old nurse maid in 1861 to the three infant children of Thomas Cornish and his wife, who farmed 200 acres at King's Brompton Somerset.

She was a 22 year old spinster and servant in Wiveliscombe, when she married Benjamin Greedy 24, labourer in St. Andrew, the parish church on the 9th April 1867. Benjamin who had been born and raised at Farmer's Cleave, Wiveliscombe brought his bride there. They were still there in 1891 when they had seven sons. Ann and her husband had moved by 1898 to Forty Acres Cottage, North Petherton where Ann died on the 21st July that year[517]. Mary Maria Luxton (1850-1902),

---

[517] See letter from Alec Jones 179 Blandford Road, Efford, Plymouth, dated 27th September 1994.

Thomas and Ann's youngest daughter, a tailoress, died on the 5th April 1902 from "cancer of the breast Exhaustion" at 6 Grove Park Terrace, Stapleton Road Bristol.

Their only son George Luxton (1839-1916) was aged 2 in 1841 when he lived with his parents at Higher Cooksley Cottage. He was a 12 year old house servant in 1851 to Ann Voysey widow and family at Hayne Farm, Upton.

George Luxton, 22, unmarried gunner in Royal Marine Artillery, born Upton Somerset was based on Portsea Island, Hampshire in 1861.He was a Corporal in the Royal Marines, living in Southsea when he married Emma Sturgess in St. James Portsea, Hampshire on the 4th October 1868. His personal Bible, printed at University Press Oxford for the British and Foreign Bible Society, has the following dedication scrawled inside the front cover

Presented to
George Luxton. Corporal R.M.A.
whilst serving on board
H.M.S.Minataur
carrying the flag of
Rear-Admiral Warden C.B.
1868
St. John ch.5 – ver.39

HMS Minataur (in photo dated 1868) was built at the Thames ironworks at Blackwall, and was launched on the 12th December 1863. She took five years to complete due to her being used for experimental armament and rig trials. She was finally commissioned as the Flagship for the Channel Squadron at Portsmouth in April 1867.Minataur went into reserve at Portsmouth in 1887 and was later used as a training ship.

George had retired from the Royal Navy by October 1880, when a drunken 21 year old gunner in the Royal Marines tried to break into his home at West Cottage in the middle of the night.[518] The census that year lists the family living at West Cottage, Albert Road, Portsea. George aged 42, naval pensioner, was foreman of a Dairy Company, his wife Emma was 39 and their three daughters were Florence E. aged 8, Lilian aged 6 and Violet Mabel aged 5.

George, a 48 year old Dairy manager, was admitted as a freemason to the St. Clair Lodge No 2074 Landport on the 16th January 1888. In 1891 George, 52, Foreman to the Southsea Dairy Company, lived with his wife and family at 29 Marmion Road, Portsea. In the summer of 1892, before the family moved to Southsea, about sixty friends were present when George, manager of the Southsea Dairy Co.'s business in Marmion Road, was presented with an inscribed marble clock from employees working under him in "token of the esteem in which he was held."[519] The family moved to 43 Margate Road, Southsea, to a six room house where in 1911 he was a 72 year naval pensioner, with Emma and their 35 year old daughter, Violet Mabel, a shop assistant. Later they lived in a smaller property at Jessie Road.

The late Miss Winifred Luxton of Maidstone, Kent, George's granddaughter, recalls that George died when she was three or four years old. "My memory is of someone who always made a great fuss of me when we visited. I was his first grandchild.[520]" She also recollected that the house in Jessie Road, Southsea was poor when compared with her maternal grandparent's home.

"There was one front room, a kitchen and scullery and an outdoor W.C. Just past the front room was a flight of very steep stairs leading up to the bedrooms. My grandmother never allowed anyone upstairs during the day except when the bedrooms were cleaned. George's wife Emma Sturgess, was born in Bulford, Wiltshire, the daughter of William

---

[518] Hampshire Telegraph, Saturday 9th October 1880.
[519] Hampshire Telegraph, Saturday 20th August 1892.
[520] See letter from the late Winifred Luxton 75, Farleigh Court, Terminus Road, Maidstone, Kent, dated 6th March 1995.

Sturgess, labourer. When young she was playing with scissors and managed to run them in one eye. The eye was removed and she wouldn't have an artificial eye, preferring to wear dark blue glasses to hide the socket."

On her grandmother Luxton's death in 1926, Winifred's father brought home a family Bible which is now lost[521]. Winifred remembered it contained the names of her Luxton grandparents and of all their children.

George Luxton aged 77 of "Kenilworth" 85 Jessie Road, Southsea, Portsmouth pensioned Sergeant in the Royal Marines, died on the 4th March 1916. The probate of his Will was granted to his widow Emma Luxton at Winchester on the 28th April 1916 when his personal estate was valued at £175..16..0d. Emma Luxton aged 85 widow of George Luxton R.M.A. pensioner, died of 1. Morbus Cordis and Arterio – scherosis and 2. Apolexy at her home "Kenilworth" 85 Jessie Road Southsea on the 28th July 1926. Her daughter V.M. Luxton of the same address was present at the death.

George and Emma had six children, five girls and one boy. Her father was serving with the Marines in Dublin when the eldest child, Claudine Georgina, was born in Kingstown, Dublin on the 7th October 1871. Claudine had "Spina Bifida" and the family were back in Hampshire, when after suffering with convulsions for two days she died aged 6 years 3 months, at their home 1 Cambridge Terrace, Eastney. Her sister Florence Emma, daughter of George Luxton, Sergeant in the Royal Marine Artillery and his wife Emma was born at 4 Alma Terrace, Eastney on the 11th February 1873. She was an assistant in a dairy produce shop; when she died aged 28 at the family home 43 Margate Road, Southsea on the 20th July 1901. She was engaged to a young curate in the Church of England, and although she had been suffering with T.B. for a year, her death was sudden.

---

[521] Winifred Luxton in letter dated 15th August 1988, states, "Her sister kept the Bible in a large trunk for years. It was lost when the hotel she was temporarily residing in went bankrupt and she went in search of the trunk and found it was gone,"

The next two children were twin daughters, Lillian and Maud, who were born at 2 Highland Street, Eastney on the 3rd August 1874. Maud died aged 14 days from "infantile debility" on the 17th August 1874. Lillian, a dressmaker was employed at Epsom College. Her younger sister Violet Mabel, born at 2 Highland Street on the 19th August 1875, was an assistant in a sewing machine shop in Southsea. Violet continued to live at Jessie Road after their mother's death in the 1920s. Lillian joined her in the holidays. When they retired they continued living at Jessie Road until they were bombed out in the Second World War. They lived for a time at Cowplain in Hampshire before finally settling at 6 Quarry Crescent, Hastings where Lillian, aged 74, a retired College Linen Mistress, died of breast cancer on 15th November 1948, and Violet, a retired commercial clerk, died aged 79, on the 12th March 1955. They are buried in the same grave in Hastings Cemetery.

George Thomas Archibald William Luxton (1881-1937), the youngest child, and only son of George Luxton, naval pensioner, and his wife Emma, was born at West Cottage, Albert Road, Southsea on the 1st December 1881. He came to be known as Archibald George Luxton. When young Archibald, who was musically inclined played the violin, and took many prizes for singing[522]. He was trained as a coachbuilder, and was living with his parents at 43 Margate Road, when he joined the 1st Hampshire Engineers Unit attached to the 37 Company (Field) Royal Engineers as a sapper at Portsmouth on the 20th February 1901. He gave his age as 20 years and 2 months, but when he told his parents he had joined up, his mother threatened to tell the army he was under age. He warned her that if she did, he would leave home altogether and she would never hear from him again. Emma, decided to remain silent[523]. He was already in the First Hampshire Volunteers.

His medical records that he was 5ft 9inches, weighed 9stone 10lbs and had a maximum chest measurement of 34 inches, a fresh complexion,

---

[522] See letter from his daughter Winifred Luxton of Maidstone Kent dated 11th June 1983. Other letters including one of the 13th August 1983 contain much valuable information which I have used to compile this account.
[523] See Winifred Luxton's letter dated 1st December 1987.

grey eyes, dark brown hair and was a member of the Church of England. Archibald served in the Boer War in South Africa where he won the Queen's South Africa Medal with four clasps South Africa 1901-1902, Transvaal, Orange Free State, and Cape Colony and was discharged from the Army at Portsmouth on the 15th July 1902.

Archibald was a 29 year old estate agents clerk, when he married Annie Harriet Hook Hook aged 31, second daughter of the late James Hook, inspector of machinery, at St. Peter's Church, Southsea on the 23rd February 1911. The census that year lists Archibald George Luxton 29, auctioneers and shipping agents and his wife Annie 31 living in a six room dwelling at 9 North Ham Road, Littlehampton, in Sussex.

At the out-break of the Great War in 1914, Archibald George Luxton F.A.I. was an auctioneer for Messrs Stevens & Sons at 8 Marina Arcade, Bexhill-on- Sea in Sussex and was a Fellow of the Auctioneers Institute. He was one of five members of the business staff who enlisted, and while he was away, the firm continued to pay his house rent at 1 Sea View, Bexhill.

In the Great War 1914-18, Archibald served in the Royal Garrison Artillery as a gunner and acting bombardier with Reg No.7284 in 124 Siege Battery. He was mentioned in dispatches and at the end of the war he was a Lieutenant (Reg No 282284) in 144 Siege Battery. The local newspaper caught a glimpse of him in early October 1918 when Lieutenant A. G. Luxton R.G.A. "who has been lately engaged in anti-aircraft work at the front made a flying visit to Bexhill before going to Portsmouth to see friends."[524] He was awarded the British War Medal and the Victory

---

[524] Bexhill-on-Sea Observer, Saturday, 12th October 1918.

Medal. His address was 24 Sackville Road, Bexhill on Sea in Sussex when he applied for his Victory Medal Emblem on the 18th January 1920.

I have a photograph of him in his second Lieutenant's uniform. It shows a newly commissioned officer for his uniform has a "new" look to it, certainly showing little sign of having been worn on the training field, never mind in active service. His Sam Browne belt is worn from his right shoulder and his cuff rank insignia of one pip, identifies him as a Second Lieutenant. His hat has a crown, stiffened by wire, and a bronze cap badge of the field gun, denoting the Royal Garrison Artillery.

Winifred his daughter bequeathed a framed photograph of her father in his soldier's uniform in the Boer War, his Boer War and World War One medals, together with relevant miniatures, her father's cuff links, the framed copy of his mention in dispatches and his sword to the Royal Artillery Historical Trust. The photo shows guns of the R.G.A. in France.

In the 1920s Archibald continued to work for Stevens & Co at 8 Marina Arcade. He became secretary to the Bexhill Ratepayers Association. An active member of the Bexhill Debating Society, he argued vigorously in the spring of 1922, that the emerging Labour Party was not yet ready for power.[525] In 1928 he was elected as a councillor for the Egerton Park Ward in Bexhill, and the Bexhill -on-Sea Observer for Saturday the 3rd November 1928 wryly commented "Councillor Luxton might have had a larger majority if he had been less aggressive in his language".He appears to have had the Luxton flair for ruffling feathers and the same paper reported that Councillor Luxton had been served with a writ by another councillor "for an alleged libel, arising out of certain Council incidents."[526]

Archibald left Stevens after many years, to open his own antique business. An advert he placed in the local paper on 10th May 1930 was typical:- Furniture antique or modern, china, glass, bric-a-brac, silver, jewellery, pictures, books, stamps etc purchased to any amount. Write or call, Luxton 35a Marina, Bexhill.[527]

Archibald and Annie had two daughters. The eldest, Winifred Marjorie Hook Luxton, was born at 9 North Ham Road, Littlehampton, Sussex on the 30th March 1912. The family moved to 24 Sackville Road, Bexhill – on – Sea where their second child, Mabel Joan Luxton was born on the 29th April 1914. The family remained there for about ten years before moving to 11 Park Road, Bexhill – on – Sea. On the last page there is a photograph of Archibald standing in the porch of his new home where he lived until he died.

For a number of years he was known as Archibald George Luxton only, and he died under these names at the age of 55, from cancer at Tower House, Egerton Road, Bexhill – on – Sea on the 20th February 1937. The probate of his estate, valued at £1825..10s..8d was granted to his widow, Annie at Lewes on the 5th April 1937.

Annie, her daughter Joan and Annie's youngest sister, moved to Cambridge, where they ran a guest house, until Annie's death at 1, West Road, Cambridge on the 22nd December 1951. She is buried in

---

[525] Bexhill-on-Sea Observer, Saturday, 1st April 1922.
[526] Bexhill-on-Sea Observer, Saturday, 30th November 1929.
[527] Hastings & St Leonards Observer, Saturday 26th April & 10th May 1930.

Cambridge. The guest house closed and Joan returned to Bexhill – on – Sea where she ran the Joan Luxton School of Dancing. She suffered a massive heart attack and died at King's Cross Station in 1989[528]. Winifred who settled in Maidstone, Kent in 1960, qualified as a general nurse before becoming a midwife. She retired in 1972 and died on the 2nd March 2006 a few weeks before her 94th birthday. At the age of 83 she was still singing in the soprano section of a local choir.

---

[528] See letter from Winifred Luxton dated 4th December 1989.

74

GEORGE LUXTON (1802-1891) STONEMASON OF PETTON AND MOREBATH IN DEVON

See tree 44

George Luxton, (1802-1891) stonemason, the seventh son of John Luxton (1747-1818), yeoman, of Corner House, Petton and his wife Mary Redwood, was baptised George Luxon at Raddington, Somerset on the 2nd February 1802. In his father's Will made on the 20th March 1818 George was bequeathed, "Three Pounds payable in six years after my decease."

George and his wife Ann(e) were married by 1831, but details of their marriage are wanting. The twosome began married life in Bampton where their eldest child, Ann daughter of George Luxton, mason, was baptised on the 7th August 1831. Ann seems to have died in infancy for she is not mentioned in the 1841 census. However, a "second" daughter Mary Ann, who died in 1911 gives her age as 80, which would make her birth date 1831 so there may be some confusion over a change in name.

The family had moved to Morebath by the beginning of 1836 when Elizabeth their youngest child, was baptised in St. George's on the 22nd January that year. The Morebath tithe, dated 1838, lists George Luxton the occupier of Hosegoods Cottage, barn and burton (probably a chicken coop in this instance) No.191 on the Tithe map and No.190 Garden occupying 1 rod and 31 poles for which 1 shilling and 6d was payable annually to the vicar following the commutation of the tithe. The property belonged to John Pearce.

George Luxton of Morebath, mason, by an indenture made on the 27th March 1839, purchased the "West End of New House orchard and garden" being part of Frogpitt's Moor, Petton for £59 from his relatives, Ann Luxton, widow of Bampton and her son Thomas Luxton (c.1803-1885), yeoman of Aller, in Somerset. George was illiterate and signed the deed with his mark. By the terms of his father's Will, he had already inherited the eastern part of New House Cottage and Orchard, when his elder brother William (1791-1851) died without surviving issue. It had belonged to his great grandfather Robert Luxton, who had bequeathed the property in 1751, to his daughter Mary, who sometime before her death in 1776, had conveyed it to her brother Abraham. Abraham had conveyed the property by an indenture dated the 27th November 1770, to his brother Joseph (1719-1791) who was George's grandfather.

George Luxton of Morebath, is listed in the Poll Book Register for Bampton, as the owner in 1841, of the freehold house named "New House" Petton. On the Bampton tithe map and apportionment of 1842, it is described as Plot No 1513 measuring 2 rods and 1 pole. It was a Public House and Garden leased to William Greenslade and it lay on the south side of the turnpike road from Bampton to Wiveliscombe.

The Morebath census for 1841 records George, and his wife Ann, both aged 40, and their children, Mary 7 and Elizabeth 5 as living at Rhode in the parish. Samuel Endicott aged 15 is a male servant. Ten years later, in the 1851 census Mary who was aged about 17 had left home, but her sister Elizabeth, aged 15, still resided with her parents in Morebath village. White's Devon Directory published in 1850 (page 328) lists George Luxton, stonemason, Morebath. George a 59 year old mason and his wife Ann 63 who was born in Morebath, were living in 1861, at Claypit's Cottage, Morebath.

Claypit's Cottage marked No.519 on the 1838 Morebath tithe map, its nursery No.227 and garden and orchard No.516 occupied an area of 2 rods and 36 poles, for which George annually paid the vicar 2s..6d following the commutation of the tithe. By the 1871 census Clay Pitt (in photograph) is listed as two cottages, no.43 on schedule 1. Clay Pitt is occupied by George Tarr, an agricultural labourer and his family while

schedule, no. 44 is 2 Clay Pitt occupied by George Luxton, 69, mason, his wife Anne aged 74 and Mary Greedy a 14 year old domestic servant.

I visited Mr and Mrs Palfry at Frogmore, Petton on the 21st July 1975. They kindly allowed me to transcribe an old indenture dated 30th December 1857, by which George Luxton of Morebath, mason, sold "All that piece or part of land called "Ashelford's Plot" situated in the parish of Bampton" to Thomas Elsworthy of North Hayne, Bampton, yeoman for £11. Thomas Elsworthy signed the deed and George Luxton made his mark. Elsworthy erected a house called Frogmore on the site the following year, and there is a plaque placed high on the exterior wall, bearing his name and the date 1858. George Luxton was a mason, and it is likely that he was employed in building Frogmore.

The deed itself makes interesting reading for the way in which it delineates "Ashelford's Plot" on which the house was built. It was "bounded on the North by the Turnpike Road leading from the town of Wiveliscombe to the town of Bampton, on the south by land belonging to Robert North Esquire and on the east by an orchard belonging to the said George Luxton and containing by estimation Ten Perches…. And which said piece or plot of land now is and for the last eighteen years has been in the possession of the said George Luxton or his tenants. Together with the fence which divides the said plot of land from the said orchard of the said George Luxton and the large fir tree growing in the said fence."

The two dwelling houses at New Houses Petton, No 1513 on the tithe map, which were in the occupation of William Paul, and William Cleeve, were mortgaged by George Luxton on the 30th September 1867 to Robert Escott, a grocer in Bampton. This was to secure £75 and interest which may have been raised to pay for his old age. However, the 1874 Electorial Register lists George as the owner of a freehold house in Morebath and he may have raised the mortgage to finance the purchase of his Morebath home.

George's wife Ann Luxton of Claypit, Morebath, died aged 82, and was buried at Morebath on the 17th May 1879. On the day of his wife's funeral, George made and signed his Will with a mark. He continued to live at 2 Clay Pitt Morebath where the 1881 census has George Luxton, widower, aged 79, mason, Sarah Greedy, 21, domestic servant and James Endicott, 70, widower and agricultural labourer as a lodger. George mortgaged his New Houses property at Petton to this James Endicott of Morebath labourer for £75 on the 21st July 1883.

Sometime after this he went to live in Tiverton with his youngest daughter Elizabeth, a dressmaker, who had married John Takle, a labourer from Porlock, at St. George's Morebath on the 27th March 1856. John Takle was a general labourer in 1881 when the couple lived at Richards' Buildings, Bampton Street, Tiverton and had at least six children, fiveboys and a girl. They had moved to Beck's Square in Fore Street, Tiverton by 1891 where John, aged 60, was now a gardener, with his wife Elizabeth 55. Just two children, Mary Ann Takle 18, dressmaker, and Lewis (1880-1963) aged 10 scholar were at home. George Luxton, a widower, and retired mason, now an old man of 89 was lodging with the family. He died on the 16th April 1891 shortly after the census was taken and as George Luxton of Tiverton, mason, aged 89 he was buried at Morebath on the 21st April 1891.

George's Will was proved in Exeter District Registry by his daughter Mary Ann Luxton, the executor, on the 2nd June 1892, when his effects were valued at £21..1s. Mary Ann was "to have all my household goods, Houses and land that I am possessed of" while his married daughter Elizabeth Tackle (sic) was to receive, "The sum of £5 to be paid her within six months of my decease."

George's daughter, Mary Ann Luxton, was a 28 year old unmarried sub matron in the Sailors Orphan Girls School and Home, in Hampstead, London in 1861. In 1871 she was the 39 year old matron, of St Pancras Female Charity School. Twenty years later in 1891 Mary Ann Luxton aged 59, remained single, and was the House Superintendent and Matron of the Midland Blind Institution in Nottingham. It was located in Chaucer Street, and the pupils were taught how to make brushes, baskets, mats, cane chairs and knitting etc. From time to time the work of the institution was reported in the Nottingham newspapers. Miss Luxton, the matron, the mayor and many ladies and gentlemen were present on Thursday afternoon 14th December 1882 to hear the inmates sing before the distribution of prizes. Again on the evening of Friday 29th March 1889,

Miss Luxton the matron, and other working members of staff were present when the YMCA gave a concert for the inmates.[529]

Mary Ann Luxton of the Midland Institution of the Blind, Nottingham on the 11th August 1892 conveyed a plot of land at the eastern end of New House tenement, Petton, marked as No.1513 on the tithe map to Trustees for the erection of a Bible Christian Chapel at Petton. The trustees purchased for £2, "All that piece or plot of land being the Eastern end of a certain Orchard or Garden belonging to and part and parcel of a tenement called....New Houses otherwise East end of New House and West End of New House situate at Petton....and numbered 1513 on the tithe commutation map, measuring from East to West 32 feet or there abouts and in width from North to South eighteen feet or there abouts." The Bible Christians placed a railway carriage on the site as a place of worship. However, in 1904, the site was bought by Mr W. Hawkins, for the location of a traction engine repair shed, and the Bible Christian Chapel at Petton, was built in 1901, about 200 yards up the road at Frogpit Moor.

Mary Ann Luxton as the devisee and executor of her father's Will paid £25 of the mortgage on New House on the 2nd August 1895. This left only the sum of £50 as the principal money due on the property. She received the £50 to settle the outstanding mortgage debt, plus a further £134, when by a deed, dated the 29th September 1902, she sold the two houses known as New Houses, Petton to Mr William Hawkins. The New House property had been in the ownership of the Luxton family since Mary's great-great-grandfather, Robert Luxton who had died in 1751. In 1901 Mary Ann 69, now retired, was boarding with her widowed sister Elizabeth Takle, 65, and niece Mary Ann Luxton Takle, a 28 year old dressmaker at 4 Beck's Square Tiverton. Her sister Elizabeth Takle, 83, widow of John Takle, slater, died at 3, Pinkstone's Court, Tiverton on the 22nd February 1919.

---

[529] Nottinghamshire Guardian, Friday 15th December 1882 and Nottingham Evening Post, Saturday 30th March 1889.

Mary Ann Luxton was an 80 year old spinster and retired Matron of a Blind Institution, when she died of heart disease, at 4 South View, Fore Street, Tiverton on the 29th July 1911. Her niece, Mary Ann L. Craig, who also lived at the same address was present at her death.

When I visited Morebath church and churchyard in 1974, I could find no surviving inscription to George Luxton or his wife Ann, who for more than half a century had lived in the parish.

This chapter concludes my narrative on the descendants of Robert Luxton and Jane Daniell, who married at Clayhanger on the 28th August 1704. Well my friends, here ends my genealogical odyssey, from Frogpit Moor with the good, the bad and the ugly. I hope you have enjoyed the voyage.

Brian C. Luxton

APPENDIX A

23andMe supplied me with a DNA kit in July 2016. I gave a saliva sample in a phial & posted it to them in packaging they provided. I received the result about six weeks later. The ancestry composition they send back tells me what percent of my DNA comes from each of 31 populations' world wide. They keep updating information and here is my latest report of 2nd January 2019. I am 100% European and in more detail I am 79.5% British & Irish, 7.4% French&German, O.7%Scandinavian, 12.1%broadly north western European, O.2%broadlyEuropean. The French and German ancestry is estimated to have entered the family sometime in period 1790 to 1850 and the Scandinavian sometime in the period 1670 to 1790. I have 1049dna relatives listed on 23andMe.

All Europeans have Neanderthal ancestry. I have 304 Neanderthal variants in my DNA. This is more than 89% of 23andMe customers. However, my Neanderthal ancestry accounts for less than 4% of my over all DNA. Neanderthals, an ancient breed of humans, named after the site where their bones were first discovered (Neander Valley, Germany), and modern humans, share a common ancestor, thought to be an extinct African hominin named Homo heidelbergensis. Neanderthals left Africa about 200,000 years ago and evolved as a species in Eurasia.

When modern humans started to explore beyond Africa 60,000 years ago they encounted and inter- bred with the Neanderthals who became extinct about 40,000 year ago. They were a lot like modern humans and a study of their bones shows their most distinctive characteristics were their wide, robust bodies, relatively short limbs and projecting mid faces. Skeletal remains found in the Manot Cave in Israel and elsewhere suggest that the two groups likely inter-bred in the Middle East or Europe.

I am descended from a long line of men that can be traced back to eastern Africa about 275,000 years ago. For more than 100,000 years my male ancestors gradually moved northwards, following available prey and resources as shifting climate made new routes hospitable and sealed off others. Then around 60,000 years ago my ancestor was in a small group that ventured across the Red Sea into the Arabian Peninsula. My paternal line had reached the western steppes of Asia nearly 50,000 years ago and a man, my common ancestor in haplogroup R, is likely to have lived in Central Asia between 30,000 and 35,000 years ago. The Ice Age was in full swing, and for thousands of years his descendants roamed the vast steppes where they hunted huge mammals like the mammoth.

My male ancestral path forked off again, between 20,000 and 25,000 thousand years ago in western Asia, at the beginning of the last great peak of the Ice Age. Massive glaciers covered northern Eurasia, but further south in the Iranian Plateau my ancestors flourished. When the Ice Age finally gave way to our warmer climate nearly 11,500 years ago, a new era of migration from the Middle East began.

My ancestor R-L21, an offshoot of the prolific R-M269, lived about 10,000 years ago in the Fertile Crescent where people domesticated plants and animals for the first time. Some of these farmers and herders began to push north about 8,000 years ago into the Caucasus Mountains. They reached the steppes above the Black and Caspian Seas. There, they lived as pastoral nomads, herding cattle and sheep across the grasslands, while their neighbours in the south developed bronze smelting. As bronze making skills spread north, a new steppe culture called the Yamnaya was born. Around 5,000 years ago, perhaps triggered by a cold spell that made it difficult to feed their herds, a group of Yamnaya men, moving west, pushed down the Balkans and to central Europe where they sought new pastures for their herds and metal deposits for their bronze implements. Over time their descendants spread to the Atlantic coast. Over 80% of men in Ireland and Wales carry the R-M269 lineage, of which my R-L21 haplogroup is an off shoot.

My distinct paternal haplogroup R-L21, traces back to a man who lived approximately 10,000 years ago. That is nearly 400 generations ago! It is relatively common only along the western coast of Britain. This fits in well with my Luxton ancestry in Devon. The haplogroup reaches its peak in Ireland where the majority of men carry y-chromosomes belonging to this group. It is known too that many Irish settled in western Britain when the Romans departed in the 5th century. The newcomers moved along the Roman roads & by plotting the stones inscribed in ogham on a map we find them clustering in the west of the country where they have left linguistic clues of their Irish origins.

On my mother's side I am descended from a long line of women that can be traced back to eastern Africa about 150,000 to 200,000 years ago. My maternal line is mtdna haplogroupJ1c2. Haplogroup J first appeared among hunter gather groups in s.w. Asia& Arabia about 35,000 years ago not long after the first known settlers arrived in the region from Africa. They arrived there via the Sinai Peninsula or across the Red Sea by the narrow Bel-el-Mandeb into the tip of Arabia. While some of these settlers travelled far and wide my female ancestors remained in the Middle East for tens of thousands of years. When the climate warmed at the end of the Ice Age approximately 12,500 years ago some of haplogroup J's descendants gradually migrated throughout Europe to the west. My maternal line J1c2 is a relatively young haplogroup that traces back to a woman who lived nearly 10,000 years ago. This was the time when agriculture developed in the Fertile Crescent. These farmers carried daughter lineages of J including my mother's haplogroup J1c2 all the way to the western edge of Europe, becoming entrenched among the Celtic speakers of the British Isles. This fits well too as my mother was born in Cobh in S.W. Ireland.

King Richard 111 who died at the Battle of Bosworth Field in 1485 shares a JC1 common maternal ancestor, a European woman who lived about 13,000 years ago!

APPENDIX B

MY SEARCH FOR THE MEANING OF LUGG

Half a century ago when I began investigating my surname's origin I was intrigued by a reference Peter Berresford Ellis, the Celtic historian, made to the River Lugg in Herefordshire. The title of the book escapes me but he said that its name may have a connection to a

Celtic deity. Excited by a possible Celtic derivation of the name I wrote to Basil Cottle, the author of the popular Penquin Dictionary of Surnames. He promptly replied, dismissing a Celtic connection. My name was Anglo-Saxon and Lugg was an ugly monosyllabic word.

The derivation of Lugg has continued to fascinate me and some years ago I discovered that Lugg was a Medieval measure of land. This led me to compile the following possible derivation.

Nicholas's surname Lug was derived from a medieval English word meaning 'stick/pole/staff,' which was a $5\frac{1}{2}$ yard measuring stick used by the medieval ploughman to goad the oxen and measure the ground his ox team ploughed. A lug is also a measure of land, being the same area as a square perch. A linear perch is $5\frac{1}{2}$ yards and consequently a square perch (or lug) is $30\frac{1}{4}$ square yards. There are 160 lugs to an acre and a ploughman was expected to plough an acre a day, which was equal to walking eleven miles. Perhaps Nicholas received his surname because he was of a tall and thin appearance or more likely because he was a skilled ploughman. It is still remains a possibility but I have been unable to prove that Lugg was in fact a nickname for a ploughman.

More recently in discussions with my friend, Aldon Grisdale, we revived the idea that Lugg may be derived from a river/stream named Lugg. Was there such a River/ stream in the Winkleigh area? Our search drew a blank so the idea remained dormant. Then shortly before completing this book I was on line when I discovered Lawrence Molland's 'A History of the Parish of Winkleigh in the County of Devon,' (1949). Lawrence grew up in the Hollacombe area of Winkleigh and knew the place well. I gasped with delighted surprise when he had Luxton as being possibly derived from the Lug, a tributary stream of the Taw as it flows north through Devon. This inspired me to write the following possible derivation.

Nicholas's surname is derived from the Lug, a tributary stream of the Taw as it flows through Winkleigh. The stream lies in a valley on the south side close to Luxton Barton. River names are amongst the oldest in our landscape and Lug is particularly fascinating. The name refers to the nature and quality of the water. Eilert Ekwall [530] writing about the Lugg (Welsh Llugwy) which flows through central Wales and the border country says the Welsh Llug can be traced to the meaning brilliant, shining or white stream.

Because the water is referred to as brilliant shining there might be, I thought, a reference in the name to a sky/sun deity, and the most popular sun deity of the Celtic world was Lugh, the god of the sun light and harvests. His feast day Lughnasa, the harvest festival, traditionally celebrated on the first day of August, marked the end of the summer and the beginning of the harvest season. Participants resorted to a high hill or waterside where there would be festivity, sports, dancing and the wearing of berries and fruits. Wells and streams played an especially important part in many rituals. Visitors to holy wells or streams would pray for health. They would leave offerings and tie strips of rag to a tree close by as part of the healing ritual. The Lug in Winkleigh may have been used in these rituals and also an old well at

---

[530] Eilert Ekwall, English River-Names (1928), Page 268.

Luxton Barton. The present Luxton Barton, a brick house, was built in the eighteenth century over a well which was probably the main water supply for the old house which lies about twenty yards away. The well is actually a spring, and the cellars of the 'new' house are very damp.

In Medieval times the Christian Church embraced Lughnasa wholeheartedly making it the day on which the fields were blessed in order to ensure a fruitful year after the winter's retreat. A Christianised form of the cult was present in the West Country. In St. Meubred's Church, Cardinam Cornwall a sixteenth century bench end shows this image of Lugh, the three -faced god. His head is decorated with fruit and berries. He looks straight at you and back to last year and forward to the new.

However, as Aldon pointed out there does not appear to be any British surname directly derived from a river name. A further query to North Devon Record Office could provide no additional information. It seems to us that the Lug stream in Winkleigh took its name from Nicholas Lugg when in the early thirteenth century he cleared an assart for his vill at 'Lughsland'. The stream lies partly on the border with Bondleigh, suggesting that it was named to fix the boundary between two estates.

Should anyone have any information different to what I already have stated above then I should be pleased to hear from you.

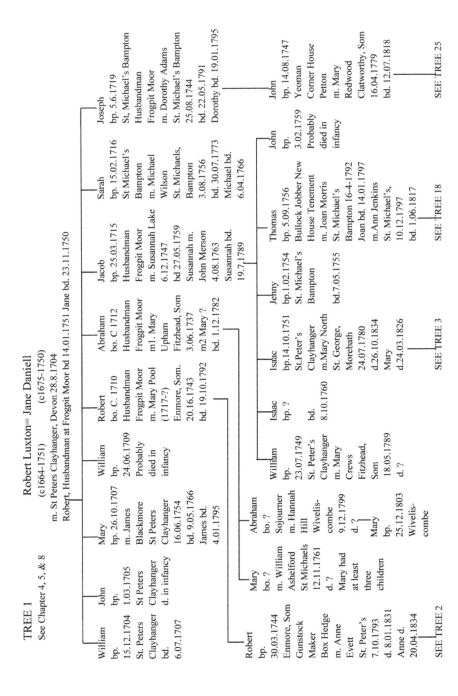

TREE 1
See Chapter 4, 5, & 8

Robert Luxton = Jane Daniell
(c1664-1751)   (c1675-1750)
m. St Peters Clayhanger, Devon 28.8.1704
Robert, Husbandman at Frogpit Moor bd 14.01.1751 Jane bd. 23.11.1750

William
bp. 15.12.1704 St Peters Clayhanger bd. 6.07.1707

John
bp. 1.03.1705 St Peters Clayhanger d. in infancy

Mary
bp. 26.10.1707 m. James Blackmore St Peters Clayhanger 16.06.1754 bd. 9.05.1766 James bd. 4.01.1795

William
bp. 24.06.1709 Probably died in infancy

Robert
bo. C. 1710 Husbandman Frogpit Moor m. Mary Pool (1717-?) Enmore, Som. 20.16.1743 bd. 19.10.1792

Abraham
bo. C 1712 Husbandman Frogpit Moor m1. Mary Upham Fitzhead, Som 3.06.1737 m2 Mary ? bd. 1.12.1782

Jacob
bp. 25.03.1715 Husbandman Frogpit Moor m. Susannah Lake 6.12.1747 bd 27.05.1759 Susannah m. John Merson 4.08.1763 Susannah bd. 19.7.1789

Sarah
bp. 15.02.1716 St Michael's Bampton m. Michael Wilson St. Michaels, Bampton 3.08.1756 bd. 30.07.1773 Michael bd. 6.04.1766

Joseph
bp. 5.6.1719 St, Michael's Bampton Husbandman Frogpit Moor m. Dorothy Adams St. Michael's Bampton 25.08.1744 bd. 22.05.1791 Dorothy bd. 19.01.1795

John
bp. 14.08.1747 Yeoman Corner House Petton m. Mary Redwood Clatworthy, Som 16.04.1779 bd. 12.07.1818
SEE TREE 25

John
bp. 3.02.1759 Probably died in infancy

Thomas
bp. 5.09.1756 Bullock Jobber New House Tenement m. Joan Morris St. Michael's Bampton 16-4-1792 Joan bd. 14.01.1797 m.Ann Jenkins St. Michael's, 10.12.1797 bd. 1.06.1817
SEE TREE 18

Jenny
bp.1.02.1754 St. Michael's Bampton bd.7.05.1755

Isaac
bp.14.10.1751 St.Peter's Clayhanger m.Mary North St. George, Morebath 24.07.1780 d.26.10.1834 Mary d.24.03.1826
SEE TREE 3

Isaac
bp. ? bd. 8.10.1760

William
bp. 23.07.1749 St. Peter's Clayhanger m. Mary Crews Fitzhead, Som 18.05.1789 d. ?

Robert
bp. 30.03.1744 Enmore, Som Gunstock Maker Box Hedge m. Anne Evett St. Peter's 7.10.1793 d. 8.01.1831 Anne d. 20.04.1834
SEE TREE 2

Mary
bo. ? m. William Ashelford St Michaels 12.11.1761 d. ? Mary had at least three children

Abraham
bo. ? Sojourner m. Hannah Hill Wivelis-combe 9.12.1799 d. ? Mary bp. 25.12.1803 Wivelis-combe

TREE 2
See chapter 6

Robert Luxton = Anne Evett   see TREE 1   all baptisms, marriages and burials took place at St Petrock's
(1744-1831)   (1761-1834) bp. at Clayhanger 28.06. 1761 d. of John&Mary.   Petton unless otherwise stated

Gunstock Maker of Box Hedge Petton

Mary (1794-1867)
bp 2.02.1794
m. James Munden
a flax spinner at
Cornworthy, Devon
9.12.1822
Mary d. 15.01.1867
Stoford, Barwick, Som.
James d. 21.07.1869
Park Street, Yeovil

Jane (1796-1867)
bp. 6.11.1796
1851 schoolmistress
at Box Hedge
d. 28.01.1867 aged 70
Heart disease some years
at Bampton
bd. with parents at Petton

John (1799-1829)
bp 3.02.1799
d. 20.01.1829 aged 30
bd. with parents at
Petton

Martha (1801-1879)
bp. 7.06.1801
m. Robert Brimmicombe
a baker on 4.08.1839 at
St.James, Taunton
1871 Schoolmistress
at Box Hedge
d. 27.02.1879 bronchitis

Ann (1804-1868)
bp. 2.12.1804
schoolmistress
with sister Jane
at Box Hedge
d. 27.07.1868 aged 63
of 'natural decay'.
bd. with parents

Mary
bp 17.10.1823 at
Cornworthy. Mary
Chapman died in
1904.

Jane
born 1826 in Bridport,
Dorset
1861 Jane aged 29 was a
schoolmistress in
Yetminster, Dorset. Jane
Swaffield, retired
seamstress died at 30
St.Paul Street, East
Stonehouse in 1913.

Joseph
born c.1821
1841 aged 20 in Stoford

Lucy Luxton Munden
bd.20.05.1839 Barwick, Somerset

TREE 3
See chapter 7

Isaac Luxton = Mary North   see TREE 1
(1751-1834)   (c.1749- 1826)

all baptisms, marriages and burials took place
at St.Petrock's Petton unless otherwise stated

Yeoman at Hutchings Farm, Frogpit Moor, Petton

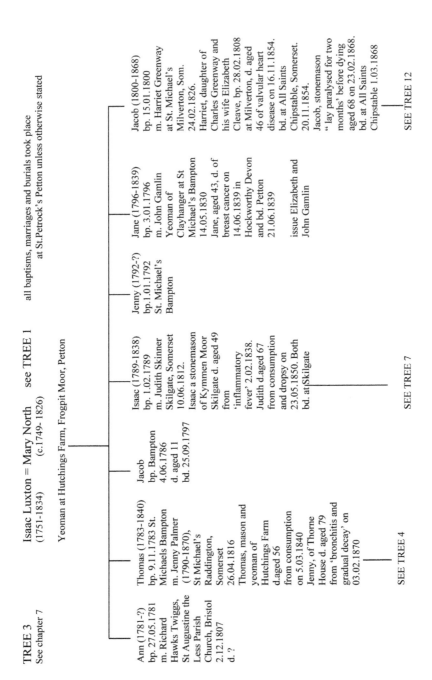

Ann (1781-?)
bp. 27.05.1781
m. Richard
Hawks Twiggs,
St Augustine the
Less Parish
Church, Bristol
2.12.1807
d. ?

SEE TREE 4

Thomas (1783-1840)
bp. 9.11.1783 St.
Michaels Bampton
m. Jenny Palmer
(1790-1870),
St Michael's
Raddington,
Somerset
26.04.1816
Thomas, mason and
yeoman of
Hutchings Farm
d.aged 56
from consumption
on 5.03.1840
Jenny, of Thorne
House d. aged 79
from 'bronchitis and
gradual decay' on
03.02.1870

Jacob
bp. Bampton
4.06.1786
d. aged 11
bd. 25.09.1797

Isaac (1789-1838)
bp. 1.02.1789
m. Judith Skinner
Skilgate, Somerset
10.06.1812.
Isaac a stonemason
of Kymmen Moor
Skilgate d. aged 49
from
'inflammatory
fever' 2.02.1838.
Judith d.aged 67
from consumption
and dropsy on
23.05.1850. Both
bd. at Skilgate

SEE TREE 7

Jenny (1792-?)
bp.1.01.1792
St Michael's
Bampton

Jane (1796-1839)
bp. 3.01.1796
m. John Gamlin
Yeoman of
Clayhanger at St
Michael's Bampton
14.05.1830
Jane, aged 43, d. of
breast cancer on
14.06.1839 in
Hockworthy Devon
and bd. Petton
21.06.1839

issue Elizabeth and
John Gamlin

Jacob (1800-1868)
bp. 15.01.1800
m. Harriet Greenway
at St. Michael's
Milverton, Som.
24.02.1826.
Harriet, daughter of
Charles Greenway and
his wife Elizabeth
Cleave, bp. 28.02.1808
at Milverton, d. aged
46 of valvular heart
disease on 16.11.1854.
bd. at All Saints
Chipstable, Somerset.
20.11.1854.
Jacob, stonemason
"lay paralysed for two
months' before dying
aged 68 on 23.02.1868.
bd. at All Saints
Chipstable 1.03.1868

SEE TREE 12

TREE 4
See chapter 9 & 10

Thomas Luxton = Jenny Palmer　　see TREE 3
　　(1783-1840)　　(1790-1870)
Mason and Yeoman at Hutchings Farm, Frogpit Moor, Petton

Mary (1817-1855)
b. Raddington, Som.
bp. 20.04.1817
Emigrated to
Canada.
d. aged 38 5.10.1855
bd Church of
England Cemetery
St. Thomas Ontario

Jane Palmer Luxton
(1819-1856)
b. Bampton,
bp. Raddington 28.02.1819
m. William Burnett (1826-1881) in Independent Chapel,
North Petherton, Som
29.03.1852.
Emigrated to Canada,
d. aged 37 in St. Thomas
Ontario 29.07.1856.
bd. in Trinity
AnglicanChurch Cemetery St
Thomas Ontario.

Elizabeth (1821-1899)
bp. 6.05.1821
St Petrock's Petton
m. William Isaac Incledon
coachman at Stoke Bishop
Gloucester 2.07.1864.
Elizabeth d. of senile
decay aged 78 at Petton
on 30.03 1899

Thomas (1824-1893)
bp. 2.05.1824
Emigrated to Canada and
farmed near Palmyra,
Ontario.
m. Elizabeth McGugan
at St. Thomas' Church
Ontario 22.12.1853
Elizabeth d. aged 86
31.12.1910.
Thomas d. aged 69 on
19.06.1893. They are bd.
at Duart Cemetery.

John (1827-1906)
bp.7.01.1827 Petton
m. Eleanor Greenslade
at Wellington, Som. 3.10.1850
Eleanor d. 28.03.1900 aged 73.
John d. at Forde Farm Cheriton
Fitzpaine 10.08.1906. and bd. at
Petton churchyard where his
grave is marked by a headstone.

SEE TREE 5

William (1843-1867)
illeg. son b. Bampton
10.10.1843
bp. Petton 29.10.1843. A
mason, he d. aged 24 at
Bampton 8.11.1867
following 'severe
contusions of the legs'
when a wall fell on him.

William Fisher Luxton
(1843-1907)
illeg. son
b. Skilgate Som.
12.12.1843
m. Sarah Jane Edwards
at Strathroy Ontario
4.04.1866.
William d. in
Winnipeg, Manitoba
26.05.1907

SEE TREE 6

Elizabeth Burnett
b. 14.04.1854
Tapper's Lane
North Petherton.
"Bessie"
d. 9.07.1862 aged 8
bd. at Church of
England Cemetery
St. Thomas, Ontario
11.07.1862

Jane (1855-1929)
b. 5.01.1855 in
Ontario
m. Matthew Driver
in Orford, Ontario
17.03.1886.
Matt. d. 1928
Jane d. 19.02.1929
aged 74.
bd. Trinity Anglican
Church Cemetery
Howard Township,
Kent County
Ontario. Issue 5 boys
and 2 girls

Mary (1858-1934)
b. 13.03.1858 in
Orford Ontario
m. Peter Mc Phail
storekeeper and
postmaster Palmyra,
at Orford 4.06.1878
Peter (1843-1922)
and Mary bd. at
Trinity Cemetery,
Howard Township
Issue three daughters

**Margaret Elizabeth (known as
Lizzie)**
b. 18.02.1862 at Palmyra
Ontario
m. William Charles Sifton
(1851-1923) at Trinity
Anglican Church Howard
Township on 13.10.1880.
Lizzie d. 23.11.1964 aged 102
bd. Trinity Cemetery Howard
Township.
Issue included a daughter and
2 sons.

TREE 5
See chapter 16,17, & 18

John Luxton = Eleanor Greenslade   see TREE 4
(1827-1906)   (1826-1900) d. of Thomas & Ann, born 23.07.1826, bp .at Petton 6.01.1827

Mason and farmer at Hutchings Farm, Petton

Thomas Greenslade Luxton (1851-1926)
bp. 18.04.1851 Petton
m. Eliza Jane Mantle at Wesleyan Methodist
Chapel, Tiverton 24.10.1876.
Thomas, a builder, farmer and Bible Christian
preacher d. 21.12.1926
Eliza d. 10.12.1929.
Both bd. at Methodist Chapel Cheriton Fitzpaine
No issue

John Luxton (1854-1932)
b. 31.08.1854
bp. 24.09.1854 at St. Petrock's Petton
m. Eliza Grace Bradford at St Peter's Tiverton
3.10.1884.
John, a tailor. d. 15.01.1932 aged 77
Eliza of Holyoake Street Wellington d. 10.10.1927
Both bd. Rockwell Green Cemetery

Elizabeth Ellen Luxton (1864-1947)
known as Bessie bp. Petton 3.07.1864
m. James Chibbett at Bible Christian
Chapel Tiverton 31.12.1891.
James Chibbett d. aged 65 on 27.09.1928
Bessie d. aged 82 on 30.03.1947
Both bd. St. Decumen's Watchet
No issue

Eve Ellen
(known as Nellie)
b. 24.05. 1886
bp. 20.06.1886.
d. aged 14 from
meningitis on
21.07.1900
bd at St Decumen's
Watchet

Thomas James
b. 15.01.1888
bp Petton
4.03.1888
K. Vimy Ridge
aged 29 on
6.06.1917

Victor John
b. 6.08.1889
Ashbrittle Som.
K. Vimy Ridge
aged 28 on
3.06.1917

Alice Maud
b. 30.10.1890
Ashbrittle, Som.
d. aged 24 from
kidney disease
on 16.10.1915.
bd. Rockwell
Green Cemetery

William Henry
(known as Willie)
b. 1.04.1893 Wivelis-
combe, ironmonger
m. Phyllis Annie
Ashton Richards in
Wellington 27.06.1927
Phyllis d. 10.07.1984
Willie d. 1.03.1986

Ernest Edgar
b. 14.10.1894
m. Olive Victoria
Churchill at All Saints
Wellington 5.10.1924.
Ernest, a baker,
d. 15.12.1968
Olive d. 9.12.1974
No issue

Olive May
b. 6.01.1901
m. Alan William
George Adams
22.08.1921 in
Wellington
Olive d.15.07. 1979

Beverley Thomas John (1931-2017)
b. 2.05.1931. m. Patricia Rose Betty Phillips in Wellington, Som. on
26.12.1953. Patricia d. 19.04.2009. Bev d. aged 86 on 7.11.2017

Deborah Jane b. 27.04.1955
m. William John White at All Saints Wellington 30.07.1983
issue Charlotte and Catherine White

David John b. 2.01.1964
m. Angela Mary French at Paralimi Cyprus on 18.09.2002
They live in Taunton

William Fisher Luxton = Sarah Jane Edwards   see TREE 4

(1843-1907)   (1846-1927)

See chapter 11,12,13,14,&15

Pioneer teacher and journalist in Winnipeg, Manitoba
Illeg. son of Jane Palmer Luxton (1819-1856) b. Skilgate, Somerset on 12.12.1843
Emigrated to Canada in 1855, m. Sarah Jane Edwards at Strathroy Ontario on 4.04.1866
William d. Winnipeg, Manitoba 20.05.1907. bd in St. John's Cathedral Cemetery.
Sarah b. at Komoka Ontario 22.10.1846, d. aged 81 in Minneapolis 3.10.1927

Page 2 ⇧

Harry Addison Luxton
b. 27.07.1870 in
Seaforth Ontario
m. Pearl M. Taylor
Gethsemane Church
Minneapolis, Minnesota
8.07.1899
Harry d. 15.12.1910

Eleanor (Nellie) Luxton
b. Winnipeg 4.08.1873
m. Frederick Kent
Foster in Winnipeg
5.08.1896
Nellie d. in St. Paul
Minnesota September
1967

Norman Kenny Luxton
b. in Upper Fort Gary
(now Winnipeg) on 2.11.1875
m. Georgia Elizabeth McDougall
in Banff Alberta 2.11.1904.
Norman d. in Calgary 22.10.1962
Georgia d. 27.03.1965
Both bd. in Banff Cemetery

Louis Palmer Luxton
b. Winnipeg 29.06.1878
m. Nellie Elsie Manley
(1893-1976) at Trinity
Methodist Church Calgary on
14.04.1914
Louis d. in Banff Alberta
28.10.1961
Nellie d. 30.04.1976 in Calgary.

**William Franklin
Luxton**
b. 16.05.1867
Strathroy Ontario.
Vanished in Yukon
Territory 1916

Olive Eva Luxton
b. 14.03.1915
m. Chas Beil
Canadian sculptor
Olive Beil d. in
Cochrane Alberta
08.03. 1983

Eleanor Georgina Luxton
b. in Banff, Alberta
31.07.1908
d. 22.06.1995. Cremated,
ashes buried in family
plot in old Banff
Cemetery

Elsie Minota Luxton
b. Banff 27.06. 1916
m. Percy Olley about 1954
Minota d.in Chilliwack, British
Columbia 25 .12.2006

William Fisher Luxton
b. Banff 11.11.1919
m. Winifred Clara Hughes in Fort Erie Ontario
22.11.1946
Bill d. in Calgary 22.04.2007

William Fisher Luxton
b.1948. Lives in Calgary and
married with two adopted
sons and a daughter

Constance Luxton
b. 1954, m. Webb now divorced.
daughter living at Carstairs outside
Calgary

Susan Luxton
m. Randy Freeborn & son Michael live in Calgary.
Their son Stephen and family live in New
Hampshire U.S.A.

William Fisher Luxton = Sarah Jane Edwards   see TREE 4

(1843-1907)   (1846-1927)

Pioneer teacher and journalist in Winnipeg, Manitoba   See Chapters 11,12,13,14,&15
Illeg. son of Jane Palmer Luxton (1819-1856) b. Skilgate, Somerset on 12.12.1843
Emigrated to Canada in 1855, m. Sarah Jane Edwards at Strathroy Ontario on 4.04.1866
William d. Winnipeg, Manitoba 20.05.1907. bd in St. John's Cathedral Cemetery.
Sarah b. at Komoka Ontario 22.10.1846, d. aged 81 in Minneapolis 3.10.1927

Olive Luxton (known as 'Ollie')
b. Winnipeg 21.04.1880
m. Edgar Richard Camp Hosking in
St Paul, Minnesota 24.09.1903
Olive d. in July 1966 in a nursing
home in Deerfield, Illinois.
bd. in St. Paul Minnesota.

Issue included Mary
Nell Hosking
b. 12.06.1914
m.. Boyd H. Graeber
at St. Paul Minnesota
16.06.1936
Mary d. aged 96 in
San Diego on
16.09.2010

Susan Mary Graeber   Gail Mesplay
                          in Golden Colorado.

George Edwards Luxton 25.10.1881
b. Winnipeg, Manitoba 25.10.1881
m. Ada Livingstone in
Minneapolis 30.06.1910
George d. 1.11.1962
bd. at Sunset Memorial Park
Minneapolis 3.11.1962

Patricia Jane Luxton
b. Minneapolis 17.05.1919
d. Minneapolis 11.01.1988
in her parents home overlooking
Luxton Park named in memory
of her father.

Harold Malloch Luxton
b. London Ontario 2.02.1884
Shot by a sniper on the Western Front
18.12.1915.
bd. in Kemmel Cemetery, Flanders

See chapter 19

TREE 7

Isaac Luxton = Judith Skinner   see TREE 3
(1789-1838)   (1783-1850)d. of James & Phillis bp.15.06.1783
Mason of Kymmen Moor Skilgate

All baptisms, marriages & burials at
St. John's Skilgate unless stated otherwise

James (1813-1861)	Isaac (1815-1876)	John (1817-1845)	Phillis	Sarah Skinner	Mary Anna	William	Thomas
bp. 29.12.1813	bp. 9.07.1815	bp. 31.03.1817	bp. 9.08.1818	Luxton	bp. 4.11.1821	bp. 16.11.1823	bp. 9.01.1825
mason	shoemaker	mason	m. Charles Ash	bp. 5.03.1820	A domestic	d. aged 2	Mason
m. Mary "Molly"	m. Florence Martin	m. Mary Ann	bricklayer in	A domestic	servant she d.	bd. 30.10.1825	d. aged 24
Melhuish 8.11.1844	(nee Tout) at Kings	Atkins 8.03.1843	St. Margaret	servant, she	of "Bronchitis		17.11.1849
James d. of "Phthisis 2	Brompton Parish	John d. aged 28	Westminster	d. aged 58 at	influenza"		bd. 24.11.1849
years" aged 48 on	Church, Somerset	on 11.03.1845	4.12.1843	Upton, Som.	aged 70 at		
2.12.1861	19.03.1846	Mary Ann Luxton	Phillis Ash	bd. at Skilgate	Petton		
Molly d. aged 57	Isaac d. aged 60 on	m.2 John	d. 3.12.1869	6.10.1878	11.12.1891		
bd 20.04.1873	27.02.1876	Greenslade at	bd. 10.12.1869		bd. at Skilgate		
	bd 4.03.1876	Kingston St Mary	in Bridgwater		17.12.1891		
	Florence d. aged 74	Somerset					
	bd. 9.05.1893	26.06.1851					
See TREE 8	See TREE 9	See TREE 11					

Page 2 ⇧

TREE 8
Page 1
See chapter 20

James Luxton= Molly Melhuish   see TREE 7
(1813-1861)   (1815-1873)d. of John & Molly bp.6 08.1815
Mason of Kymmen Moor Skilgate

All baptisms, marriages & burials at
St. John's Skilgate unless stated otherwise

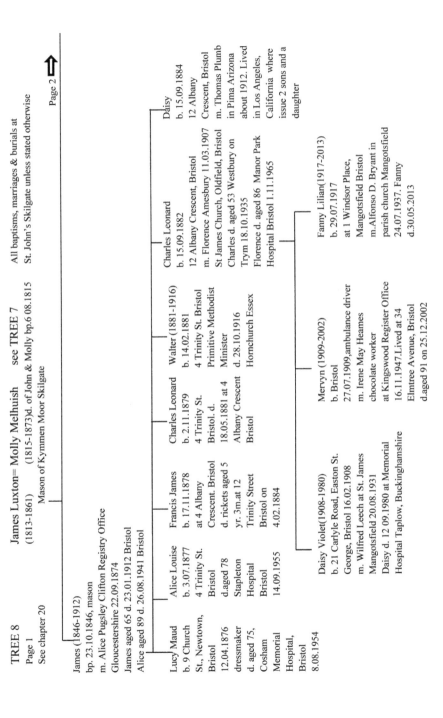

James (1846-1912)
bp. 23.10.1846, mason
m. Alice Pugsley Clifton Registry Office
Gloucestershire 22.09.1874
James aged 65 d. 23.01.1912 Bristol
Alice aged 89 d. 26.08.1941 Bristol

Lucy Maud
b. 9 Church St., Newtown, Bristol 12.04.1876 dressmaker d. aged 75, Cosham Memorial Hospital, Bristol 8.08.1954

Alice Louise
b. 3.07.1877 4 Trinity St. Bristol d.aged 78 Stapleton Hospital Bristol 14.09.1955

Francis James
b. 17.11.1878 at 4 Albany Crescent. Bristol d. rickets aged 5 yr. 3m.at 12 Trinity Street Bristol on 4.02.1884

Charles Leonard
b.2.11.1879 4 Trinity St. Bristol. d. 18.05.1881 at 4 Albany Crescent Bristol

Walter (1881-1916)
b. 14.02.1881 4 Trinity St. Bristol Primitive Methodist Minister d. 28.10.1916 Hornchurch Essex

Charles Leonard
b. 15.09.1882 12 Albany Crescent, Bristol m. Florence Amesbury 11.03.1907 St James Church, Oldfield, Bristol Charles d. aged 53 Westbury on Trym 18.10.1935 Florence d. aged 86 Manor Park Hospital Bristol 1.11.1965

Daisy
b. 15.09.1884 12 Albany Crescent, Bristol m. Thomas Plumb in Pima Arizona about 1912. Lived in Los Angeles, California where issue 2 sons and a daughter

Daisy Violet(1908-1980)
b. 21 Carlyle Road, Easton St. George, Bristol 16.02.1908 m. Wilfred Leech at St. James Mangotsfield 20.08.1931 Daisy d. 12 09.1980 at Memorial Hospital Taplow, Buckinghamshire

Mervyn (1909-2002)
b. Bristol 27.07.1909,ambulance driver chocolate worker m. Irene May Heames at Kingswood Register Office 16.11.1947.Lived at 34 Elmtree Avenue, Bristol d.aged 91 on 25.12.2002

Fanny Lilian(1917-2013)
b. 29.07.1917 at 1 Windsor Place, Mangotsfield Bristol m.Alfonso D. Bryant in parish church Mangotsfield 24.07.1937. Fanny d.30.05.2013

James Luxton= Molly Melhuish   see TREE 7
(1813-1861)   (1815-1873)d. of John & Molly bp 6.08.1815
Mason of Kymmen Moor Skilgate

All baptisms, marriages & burials at
St. John's Skilgate unless stated otherwise

William (1849-1918) bp. 19.04 1849, mason, m.Selina James (1846-1911) in St. Andrews, Christchurch, Clifton 24.11.1874
Selina aged 63 d. at 7 Victoria St. Bristol 22.09.1911 William d. there 2.10.1918

Harriet Ann
b.Glyntaff Street,
Pontypridd 15.10.1875
m. Edwin Dean Huntley
3.09.1919 Bristol Registry Office
Harriet d. aged 85 May 1960
No issue

William James
b. 16.11.1877 at 8 Stanley Terrace, Bristol
m. Louisa Bryant (1880-1956) at
St Michael's, Kingswood, Bristol 22.09.1900
d. aged 29 25.08.1907 – cycling accident
Louisa m.2 John Henry Budd 24.05.1915
Bristol Register Office.

Francis Charles
b. 3.08.1879 8 Victoria Street, Bristol
m. Susie Emma Hall at St. Andrews Clifton 6.08.1906
Francis d. aged 74, 14.01.1954
Retired builder of 147 Stapleton Road, Bristol
Susie d. 15.03.1968

Francis Albert b. 4.08.1907 Bristol
d. aged 64, retired carpenter & shop fitter at
Southmead Hospital, Bristol 24.01.1972

Daisy Kathleen
b. 31.05.1910 at 26 Victoria St.
d. aged 57 on 10.04.1965

Gladys Louisa
b. 16.08.1901 Bristol
m1. Matthew James
Todd 27.08.1924 at
St Gabriel's Bristol
m2.Reginald John
Kimball Siddorn
Easton Register Office
18.02.1942
Gladys d. 16.12.1983
Issue 1 girl & 2 boys
by 1st husband

William Henry
b. 8.07.1907 Bristol, builder & decorator
m. Rose Grace Hope Gourd 27.08.1932
d. 25.10.1981 Appledore Grace d. 17.02.1994

Cynthia Pamela b.12.10.1933 at 50
Southwell St., Clifton, Bristol
m. Ian Michael Green 27.06.1953 at St.
Stephens Southwell. Issue 3 children

Keith Charles b. 4.08.1944 at 50
Southwell Street Bristol m. Jean
Elizabeth Lovell at Hebron Methodist
Chapel Staplehill 11.09.1965

Jennifer b. 5.07.1946 at 170
Downend Road, Bristol. Lives at
Buckland Brewer, Bideford, Devon

Gary Keith Luxton b. 5.04.1966 Tavistock Devon
m. Jo(anna) Dunn at Parkham Bideford 9.08.1989
They live at Northam

Deborah Jean Luxton b. 25.06.1969 Plymouth
m. Stephen Andrew Watts at St. Michael & All Angels Marwood,
Devon 5.09.1992 Issue a son and daughter

Thomas James b. 8.06 2000 Barnstaple   Oliver William b. 11.04.2003 Barnstaple

TREE 8
Page 3

James Luxton= Molly Melhuish   see TREE 7
(1813-1861)   (1815-1873)d of John& Molly bp. 6.08.1815
Mason of Kymen Moor Skilgate

See chapter 20

Sarah Skinner Luxton
bp. 12.09.1852 dressmaker
m. William Blew 16.08.1881
St. Philip & St. Jacob, Bristol
Sarah,widow of William Blew,
farm labourer, d. aged 83 at 15
Armoury Square on 16.01.1936.

Phillis (1855-1920)
bp. 29.07.1855
m. Richard Johnson at St Gabriel's Church,
Bristol 4.10.1897.Phyllis,widow of Richard
Johnson,market gardener, d. of consumption
at 15 Armoury Square Bristol on 10.08.1920.

Francis William Luxton
Known as William, base born at
New Town, Llantarnam, Mon.
21.02.1884
m. Beatrice Ethel Major at Holy
Trinity Parish Church, Bristol
31.05.1914
Beatrice d. 18.05.1940 aged 58
Francis d. 12.12.1948
adopted a daughter Doris Ethel
Luxton who m. John Stone

Mary Ann
bp. 22.08.1858
d. aged 6 months
on 12.04.1859
bd. 17.04.1859

See chapter21 & 22 bp. 9.07.1815, m. Florence Martin (nee Tout)
at Parish Church Kingsbrompton, Somerset 19.03.1846 Isaac, shoemaker & Parish clerk d. aged 60 on 27.02.1876. bd 4.03.1876.
Florence b.30.10.1818 & bp 27.12. 1818 at Brompton Regis.d. of Thomas & Florence Tout. she d. aged 74, bd. 9.05.1893

Levi (1848-1905)
b. 10.06.1848 in Skilgate
m. Lucy Kemp at Wiveliscombe on 10.04.1879
Levi, a rural postman, d. aged 56 on 11.01.1905
Lucy d. aged 74 on 17.02.1918

Isaac Abel (1850-1918)
b. 29.07.1850 in Skilgate
m. Elizabeth Rawle at Independent chapel, Dulverton on 23.08.1888
Elizabeth Ann d. aged 42 on 28.11.1898
Isaac Abel, a retired sergeant in the Metropolitan police,d. aged 69 at County Asylum, Exminster, 7.01.1918

Walter Kemp
b. 19.12.1884
d. 27.11.1885
aged 11 months
& 8 days

See TREE 10

Florence Hilda (1880-1938)
b. 12.01 1880 in Wiveliscombe
d. at Holmoor House, Trinity
Street, Taunton on 5.09.1938

Clement Henry (1880-1957)
b. 10.10.1882 in Wiveliscombe
m. Mabel Elizabeth Harvey at Dulverton Congregational Church on 12.06.1919
A cabinet maker, he d. at The Hayes South St., Wiveliscombe on 5.06.1957
Mabel d. aged 90 on 28.04.1973

Dixon Henry (1925-2013)
b. 7.09.1925 in Wiveliscombe, a civil servant,
m. Hannalore Emma Augusta Warttman at garrison church British Army
of the Rhine at Bad Beynhausen, Westphalia, Germany on 2.06.1947
"Lore" d. 9.03.2000, Dixon was a churchwarden at Wiveliscombe.
d. 19.01.2013

Edward Harvey (1920-2010)
b. 30.03.1920 in Wiveliscombe, an architect,
m. Gladys Daisy Grandfield at St. Andrews, Cullompton
on 12.02.1944. Gladys d. 9.05.1990. Edward of 66 Station
Road, Winterbourne, Bristol d. aged 90 on 13.08.2010

Cecilia Ann
b. 1.12.1946
m. Allan Richard Hearle
at Winterbourne parish
church, Gloucester on
23.01.1971
issue 2 children

Elizabeth Joan
b. 7.03. 1948 at
The Hayes,South
Street,
Wiveliscombe,
Somerset

Still born son
23.09.1959

Lucy & Alexandra twin
daughters b. 11.10.1960
Alexandra d. 11.10.1960
Lucy d. 12.10.1960

Clement Mark
b. 17 04. 1962
d. 19.04.1962

Victoria Emma, adopted daughter,
b. 7.08.1962. Graduate of Exeter
University
married and living in France.
Her daughter Sarah is studying law.

TREE 10   Isaac Abel Luxton= Elizabeth Ann Rawle (nee Hobbs)   see TREE 9

(1850-1918)   (1856-1898) bp.11.05.1856 at Withycombe d. of Richard & Eliza Hobbs, mason

Sergeant in Metropolitan Police

See chapter 23

Mabel (1890-1967)
b. 20.05.1890
Brompton Regis, Som
d. 24.01.1967
South Street,
Wiveliscombe.

Isaac Hubert (1891-1934)
b. 23.05.1891
m. Jessie Maud Stanynought
27.02.1920 at Wandsworth Reg. Off.
Jessie d. aged 47 of TB at 1 Oldchurch
Road, Romford 16.02.1934
Isaac d. aged 43 of TB at
12 Bowes Road, Dagenham 12.11.1934

Thomas George (1892-1978)
b. 29.07.1892 in Bury Bromptom Regis
m. Frances May Denteth (nee Harwood)
at Tooting Parish church South London
19.09.1920
Frances d. 14.01. 1965
Tom d. 20.02.1978

Harold (1897-1989)
b. 30.08.1897 in Bury, Brompton Regis, Som.
m. Maud Woosman at Wandsworth Reg. Off.
7.06.1923 (b. 21.06.1893, d. 1.12.1982)
Harold d. 1.04.1989 in Walden, Lancashire.

Maria Stella
b. 5.06.1926
St. Thomas Hosp.
London
'Marie' m1. Charles
Robert Spiers
12.01.1946 at Old
Carshalton Parish
church, Surrey.
m2. Ian Gould Ronald
Marie had 4 daughters
by first husband.

Frances Mabel
b. 33 Mellison Road Tooting
12.08.1921 m. George
Benjamin Franklin at St.
Mary's Beddington, Surrey
10.03.1945 had issue

Harold James
(1924-2016)
b. 16.07.1924
m. Bertha Bradburn
at Manchester Reg.
Off. 1.09.1944 Jim
died 1.01.2016.

Sylvia Maud (1930-2006)
b. 4.03.1930 in
Withington, Manchester
m. Graham Godsell and
emigrated to New Zealand
in 1952. D. 1.10.2006 issue
2 daughters

Geoffrey William (1931-2002)
b.11.06.1931 at Corbei France
m. Dorothy Eames Butcher
(nee Woolham) at Manchester
Reg. Off. 17.12.1957 No issue,
marriage dissolved 1980.
Geoffrey d.19.09.2001 in
Manchester aged 71

Vivien C.
b. 26.04.1948
Manchester
m. Philip Freakle at
Harringay Register
Office, London
12.07.1972

Sylvia J. b. Manchester 14.03.1951
m. William Redhead at Leicester Reg. Off.
16.04.1977 issue a son and a daughter

Gillian Helen
b. Manchester
7.03.1960

Robert James
b. 14.09.1961
m. Anita Pauline Sharp in
St. Andrews, Mottingham,
Greenwich, 24.08.1985

Geoffrey Stephen
b. 26.10.1966
Bury, Lancashire

Stephen James
b. in Harrow
17.03.1983

Rebecca Anne
b. Eltham, London
20.11.1989

Hannah Rose
b. Eltham, London
28.04.1992

Sophie Nicole
b. Eltham,
London 4.06.1996

John Luxton= Mary Ann Atkins   see TREE 7

(1817-1845)   (1822-?) d. of John & Ann bp.at Skilgate 7. 01.1822. had a family by second husband John

Mason Kyrlmen Moor Skilgate   Greenslade a game-keeper

Page 2

John (1843-1928)=Eliza Reeves(1837-1923)d. of James & Charlotte bp. Wisbough Green 26.02.1837

b. Skilgate 12.05.1843, 'Johnnie Dear', milkman in Limehouse & cattle dealer in Croydon

m. Eliza Reeves at Kensington Parish Church 4.12.1865

Eliza d. aged 86 on 16.03.1923. John d. aged 86 on 15.01.1928. Both bd. at Queens Road Cemetery Croydon

---

William Arthur (1872-1938)

b. 1.10.1872 in Paddington. Gardener.

m. Winifred Corke at Camberwell Reg. Off.
19.09.1902.

Suffered horrendous war experience in WW1.

d. Warlingham Park Hospital, Chelsham, Surrey

27.04.1953. bd. Queens Road Cemetery Croydon

Mary Ann Charlotte

b. 18.04.1870 in Limehouse

'Lottie' d. 29.04.1945 aged

75 bd. Queen's Road
Cemetery Croydon

John James (1868-1947)

b. 4.02.1868 in Limehouse

m. Clara Dolding at St. Augustine's Church

Croydon 14.10.1895. Drove the horsedrawn

dray for Crowley's Brewery

John d. aged 79 18.11.1947

Clara d. aged 83 17.02.1957

Eliza Luxton

b. 7.06.1866

Limehouse, London

m. William Parfitt at

St Augustines,

Croydon 3.06.1895.

Eliza d aged 96 on

11.01. 1963

Doris G.Vera

b.15.06.1900

m.George L.R.

Ritchings in

Christ Church,

Purley

30.06.1923.She

d.22.04.1987

Iris Winifred Audrey

b. 9.05.1909

Coulsdon Croydon

m. George Charles

Parkinson at

Christchurch Purley

4.07.1940.Iris d.

Croydon 1997

Basil William Roy

b. 15.11.1913

Coulsdon, Croydon

bachelor and

prominent member

of Purley District

Council

d. 19.03.1992

Charles Henry

b. 1.02.1907 Croydon

m. Emily May Letford Croydon

Reg. Off. 3.09.1932. Professional

photographer and instrument maker

d. aged 77 10.06.1984

Emily d. 22.11.1988

William Ralph

b. 12.05.1900

Croydon.

bachelor & postman

d. 10.10.1971 Royal

Marsden Hospital

Clara Lily

b. 30.12 1897

Croydon

Spinster and

shop

assistant

d. 20.01.1995

John James

b. 8.04.1896

Croydon,

Corporal in

Suffolk

Regiment.

K. 19.11.1917

Passchendaele

Barbara May b. 30.05.1935 in Croydon, receptionist

m. Bernard Godfrey Miles

at Emmanual Church Croydon 27.07.1957

Margaret Lilian, b. 14.10.1932 in Croydon, librarian

m. Peter Francis William Rutland

at Emmanual Church Croydon 15.11.1958

John Luxton= Mary Ann Atkins   see TREE 7

(1817-1843)   (1822-?) family by second husband John Greenslade, a game-keeper

Mason Kymmen Moor Skilgate|

See Chapter 24

John (1843-1928)=Eliza Reeves(1837-1923)d of James& Charlotte bp. Wisborough Green 26 02 1837

b. Skilgate 12.05.1843, 'Johnnie Dear', milkman in Limehouse & cattle dealer in Croydon

m. Eliza Reeves at Kensington Parish Church 4.12.1865

Eliza d. aged 86 on 16.03.1923. John d. aged 86 on 15.01.1928. Both bd. at Queens Road Cemetery Croydon

---

George (1875-1944)
b. 13.03.1875, 4 Gloucester Terrace, Croydon.
A dairy farmer, m. Annie Maud Collins at Holy Trinity Church,
Selhurst, Surrey, 8.08.1907.
Annie d. 26.09.1941, George of 'Rosedean', Findon Road,
Worthing, Surrey d. 19.06.1944.

A son who
d. very young
bd with mother
at Queen's
Road Cemetery
Croydon

Marjorie Alice (1910-2000)
b. 6.10.1910
m. at All Saints, Merstham
to John William Howard
Shaw.06.06.1938. Marjorie
who lived in Caterham
Surrey d. 6.01.2000
Issue two daughters.

Walter John (1908-1949)
b. Croydon 14.08.1908
m. at Paddington Reg. Off.
to Mildred Ann Redington
28.11.1933.Jack, merchant
seaman torpedoed and 12
days adrift in WW2.
d. aged 41 20 11 1949

Walter Henry (1878-1937)
b. 13.11.1878 in Croydon,a cattle dealer
m1. Nellie Gadsdon at St. Lawrence, Catford, Lewisham, London 27.06.1907.
Walter of 405 Brighton Road, Croydon, d. aged 58 on 3.01.1937.
Nellie m2. Arthur Walter Shoebridge at Maidstone Reg. Off .12.09.1940.
Nellie d. aged 70 on 4.01.1957

Wilfred George (1911-1998)
b. 20.12.1911 m1. Evelyn Leigh at Merstham Reg. Off.
6.09.1939. Marriage dissolved in 1956.
m2. Gertrude Gladys Freda Sansome (nee Orridge)
widow, at Morden Reg. Off, Surrey 11.02.1958. They
lived in Barry, South Wales. Freda d. 29.07.1985.
Wilfred d. aged 87 on 7.08.1998. Both bd. at
Porthkerry, near Barry. Issue by first wife.

Cyril (1920-2009)
b. 10.07.1920
d. 16.02.2009 in Hove
bd. in Hove Cemetery

Peter John b. 30.05.1944 in Croydon. aircraft engineer m. Leslie Ann Leach
in Luton Parish Church 8.08.1970. Emigrated to Canada. Marriage ended.

Christine b. 28.02.1942 in Croydon m. Graham Clarke at St. Albans
Reg. Off 31.05.1963. Lives in London Colney Herts. Issue a son.

Tracy Ann, b. 13.09.1972 Northampton
m. Robert Muter, issue daughter and son

Richard John, b. 26.01.1975 at Forest Park Drive, Oakville Ontario.
In 2009 – Vancouver fine dining restaurant manager

Kate, b. 24.07.1983
m. Canada in 2009

TREE 12
Page 1

Jacob Luxton = Harriet Greenway   see TREE 3

(1800-1868)   (1808-1854)

all baptisms, marriages and burials took place
at Chipstable unless otherwise stated

d.of Charles & Elizabeth Greenway bp. at Milverton 28.02.1808

Page 2

Mason in Chipstable

See chapter 25 &26

Emma Luxton
bp. 13.08.1827
servant
d. aged 16 of
'inflammatory fever'
on 12.08.1843 & bd.
20.08.1843

Jacob Luxton
bp. 10.08.1829
bd. 4.04.1830
aged 8 months

Charles (1831-1911)
bp. 6.02.1831 mason
m. Louisa Byrd at Taunton
Reg. Off. 25.12.1853.
Separated in 1861, Charles
changed his name to Charles
Whitby and d. 26.06.1911
aged 79 Lambeth Infirmary
Louisa d. of pneumonia
7.12.1899

Elizabeth Luxton
bp. 11.08.1833
Servant m.
9.10.1854
William Yeandle
emigrated. to
Canada.Bd. St
Thomas
Ont.1898 . issue

Mary Luxton
b.12.10.1835,
emi. To
Canada
1857.m
George
Johnston 6.1.
1876. d.9.06.
1916 of
Bright's
disease

Isaac (1838-1863)
b. 9.06.1838, mason
m. Jane Vickery at All Saints Chipstable
on 28.07.1858.
d. 22.02.1863 of phthisis
Jane m2. James Smith 19.09.1864.

See TREE 13

Emma Luxton
b. 19.05.1856
in Ufficulme, Devon
m. Henry Moore Bailey
at Uffculme Independent
Chapel 28.07.1887

Willie (1858-1916)
b. Uffculme, Devon on 5.10.1858.
Willie, a miller at Selgar Mills, Halberton
m. Sarah Ann Trott Pine at Tiverton
Independent Chapel 18.08.1887
Willie a farmer at Clavengers Farm
Nynehead, Somerset d. 17.05.1916.
Sarah d. 30.06.1936

Hannah Luxton
b.19.11.1860 in Uffculme Devon
m. William Henry Drew at Uffculme Independent Chapel
on 15.08.1882. Hannah a widow in 1891 lived in Clapham
in 1911 with two adult sons. Hannah Drew d. in Battersea
aged 78 in 1939.

Willie (1905-1980)
b. at Dyke's Farm, Sampford Arundel, Somerset on 16.03.1905
m. Constance Lavinia Willey in Gotham Parish Church, Nottinghamshire on
11.04.1936
Willie a clerical officer in motor taxation department d. in Taunton
16.02.1980
Constance d. 15.02.1990
No issue.

Jacob Luxton = Harriet Greenway   see TREE 3   all baptisms, marriages and burials took place
(1800-1868)   (1808-1854)   at Chipstable unless otherwise stated
d. of Charles &Elizabeth bp.at Milverton 28.02.1808.
Mason in Chipstable

See Chapter 25 &29

Thomas bp.
12.11.1840
d. 9.04.1841
of asthma
aged 5
months

Jane Luxton
bp. 20.03.1842
m. William Stock in
Clevedon Parish Church
14.11.1864.
Emigrated to Canada
1865 sailing on SS.
Peruvian from Liverpool
to Quebec.
d. Port Stanley Ontario
due to complications in
her 6th month pregnancy,
12.11.1878.
Issue 2 sons

Ann Luxton
bp. 8.04.1845
aged 6 in
1851 census
m.Francis
G.Priest,groom
4.06.1866 at
Stratton Audley,
Oxfordshire.
d.19. 4. 1911
from cirrhosis of
liver at home in
High Street
Amersham,
Bucks.issue six
children.

George (1847-1918)
bp. 1.08.1847, mason,
m1. Eliza Lilly 6.05.1869
In St. Andrews Parish Church, Clevedon
Eliza d. of consumption aged 25 on
4.10.1871.
m2. Clara Ann Beer
(bp. 15.07.1849 in Yarcombe Devon)
at St. James Bristol 18.05.1875
Clara d. aged 67 on 17th May 1917 bd.
20.05.1917 at Christchurch Nailsea.
George d. aged 71 on 25.10.1918 at
Farleigh Backwell and bd. 30.10.1918
at Christchurch Nailsea.

See TREE 14

John (1850-1925)
bp. 20.10.1850, chimney sweep,
m1. Ellen Hopkins 5.04.1869
at Holy Trinity Church, Nailsea
Ellen d. aged 62, bd at Holy
Trinity Nailsea 7.05.1911
m2.Amelia Kimmens 8.08.1913 at
Long Ashton Register Office, Som.
John d. aged 75 on 8.01.1925
Amelia d. aged 60 on 4.12.1925

See TREE[17]

Isaac Luxton= Jane Vickery   see TREE 12 page 1

(1838-1863)   (1838-1898) d of William & Joany born 4.11.1838 at Shute Farm Huish Champflower

See Chapter 27

Mason, Larcombe's Cottage, Chipstable.

Page 2 ⇧

Charles (1859-1911) b. 10.03.1859 in Chipstable, mason, coal-tipper & labourer m. Ellen Carpenter at Wiveliscombe, Som 26.07.1880 d. aged 51 at 127 Pearl St., Roath, Cardiff 11.04.1911
Ellen d. aged 66 at 151 Habershon St., Splott, Cardiff 13.03.1928

Mary Luxton
See page 2

Frank Luxton
See page 3

Bessie Ellen Luxton b. 21.10.1880
166 Bute Rd., Cardiff
m. Charles John Mansfield in Roath
Parish Church, Cardiff 25.12.1900
Issue 5 children

Albert Charles (1882-1938) b. 24.05.1882 21 Kingarth St., Roath
m. Violetta Elizabeth Brooks 26.12.1904 at St. Catherines, Canton.
Violetta d. aged 89 7.02.1973
Albert, Chief Dock Foreman G.W.R. Cardiff Docks d. 14.12.1938

Sarah Jane
See page 2

Arthur George
See page 5

Albert William Charles (1906-1997) b. 10.06.1906
m. Elsie Wicks (1909-1972) at Mount Tabor Primitive Methodist Church, Moira Terrace, Cardiff on 11.04.1936. Elsie d.at 182 St. Fagan's Road Cardiff on 19. 12.1972. Albert retired Deputy Operations Officer, General Cargo department, Cardiff Docks. d.aged 91 in Llandaff, Cardiff in August 1997

Philip Ronald, b. 16.05.1937 Cardiff, m1. Sheila Cadwaladr 20.06.1959 at Fairwater Presbyterian Church, Cardiff. Sheila d.
m2. Anna

Keith Frederick, b. 3.06.1939 Cardiff, m1.Joyce Murch 25.05.1963 at Fairwater Presbyterian Church – divorced. m2. Deidre Baldwin b. 1.09.1954 from Taffs Well on 27.02.1998

Andrew David adopted b. 14.05.1965
m. Annabel Elizabeth Smith 28.06.1997 in Cirencester, Gloucestershire

Ross William b. 18.10.1998

Gillian adopted b. 20.12.1966
m. Stephen Allen 14.05.1988 at Brook St. Chapel, Knutsford
issue 3 children

Joanne b. 27.05.1971 m. Gordon Ayres in Cirencester

Helen Kay b. 20.12.1967 Partner.Gareth Barrington Issue 3 children

Robert Keith b. 31.10.1969 m. Nicola Akerman 13.04.1996

Emlyn Thomas b. 25.05.1997   Sunnie Mia Violet b.12.10.98

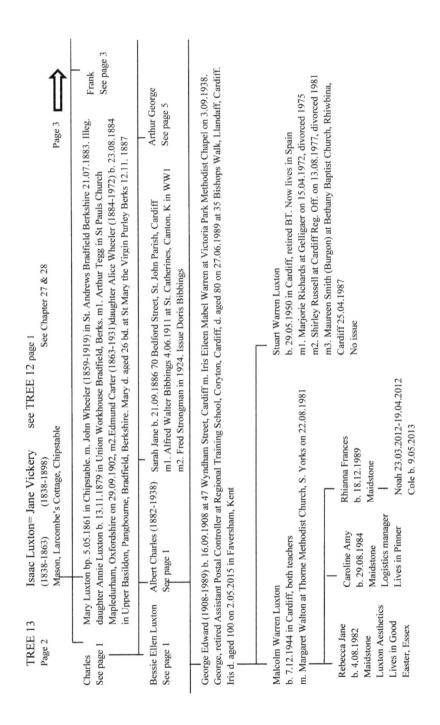

TREE 13
Page 2

Isaac Luxton= Jane Vickery   see TREE 12 page 1
(1838-1863) (1838-1898)   See Chapter 27 & 28
Mason, Larcombe's Cottage, Chipstable

Page 3

Charles
See page 1

Mary Luxton bp. 5.05.1861 in Chipstable. m. John Wheeler (1859-1919) in St. Andrews Bradfield Berkshire 21.07.1883. Illeg. daughter Annie Luxton b. 13.11.1879 in Union Workhouse Bradfield, Berks. m1. Arthur Tegg in St Pauls Church Mapledurham, Oxfordshire on 29.09.1902, m2.Edmund Carter (1863-191)daughter Alice Wheeler (1884-1972) b. 23.08.1884 in Upper Basildon, Pangbourne, Bradfield, Berkshire. Mary d. aged 26 bd. at St Mary the Virgin Purley Berks 12.11. 1887

Frank
See page 3

Bessie Ellen Luxton
See page 1

Albert Charles (1882-1938)
See page 1

Sarah Jane b. 21.09.1886 70 Bedford Street, St. John Parish, Cardiff
m1. Alfred Walter Bibbings 4.06.1911 at St. Catherines, Canton. K in WW1
m2. Fred Strongman in 1924. Issue Doris Bibbings

Arthur George
See page 5

George Edward (1908-1989) b. 16.09.1908 at 47 Wyndham Street, Cardiff m. Iris Eileen Mabel Warren at Victoria Park Methodist Chapel on 3.09.1938. George, retired Assistant Postal Controller at Regional Training School, Coryton, Cardiff, d. aged 80 on 27.06.1989 at 35 Bishops Walk, Llandaff, Cardiff. Iris d. aged 100 on 2.05.2015 in Faversham, Kent

Stuart Warren Luxton
b. 29.05.1950 in Cardiff, retired BT. Now lives in Spain
m1. Marjorie Richards at Gelligaer on 15.04.1972, divorced 1975
m2. Shirley Russell at Cardiff Reg. Off. on 13.08.1977, divorced 1981
m3. Maureen Smith (Burgon) at Bethany Baptist Church, Rhiwbina,
Cardiff 25.04.1987
No issue

Malcolm Warren Luxton
b. 7.12.1944 in Cardiff, both teachers
m. Margaret Walton at Thorne Methodist Church, S. Yorks on 22.08.1981

Rebecca Jane
b. 4.08.1982
Maidstone
Luxton Aesthetics
Lives in Good
Easter, Essex

Caroline Amy
b. 29.08.1984
Maidstone
Logistics manager
Lives in Pinner

Rhianna Frances
b. 18.12.1989
Maidstone

Noah 23.03.2012-19.04.2012
Cole b. 9.05.2013

Page 4

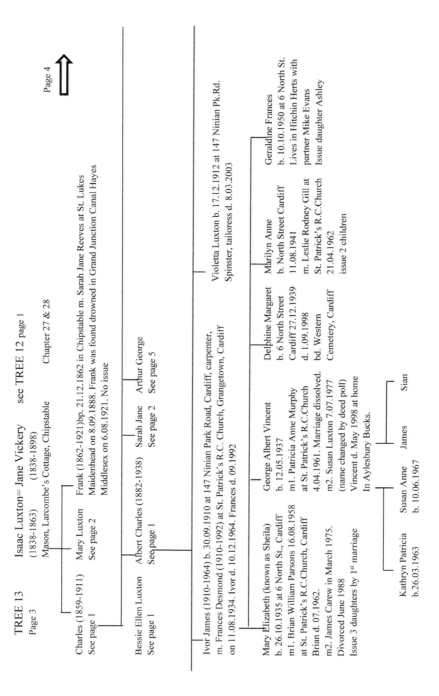

TREE 13
Page 3

Isaac Luxton= Jane Vickery
(1838-1863)   (1838-1898)
Mason, Larcombe's Cottage, Chipstable

see TREE 12 page 1

Chapter 27 & 28

Charles (1859-1911)
See page 1

Mary Luxton
See page 2

Frank (1862-1921) bp. 21.12.1862 in Chipstable m. Sarah Jane Reeves at St. Lukes Maidenhead on 8.09.1888. Frank was found drowned in Grand Junction Canal Hayes Middlesex on 6.08.1921. No issue

Bessie Ellen Luxton
See page 1

Albert Charles (1882-1938)
See page 1

Sarah Jane
See page 2

Arthur George
See page 5

Ivor James (1910-1964) b. 30.09.1910 at 147 Ninian Park Road, Cardiff, carpenter, m. Frances Desmond (1910-1992) at St. Patrick's R.C. Church, Grangetown, Cardiff on 11.08.1934. Ivor d. 10.12.1964. Frances d. 09.1992

Violetta Luxton b. 17.12.1912 at 147 Ninian Pk.Rd. Spinster, tailoress d. 8.03.2003

Mary Elizabeth (known as Sheila) b. 26.10.1935 at 6 North St., Cardiff m1. Brian William Parsons 16.08.1958 at St. Patrick's R.C.Church, Cardiff Brian d. 07.1962. m2. James Carew in March 1975. Divorced June 1988 Issue 3 daughters by 1st marriage

George Albert Vincent b. 12.05.1937 m1. Patricia Anne Murphy at St. Patrick's R.C.Church 4.04.1961. Marriage dissolved. m2. Susan Luxton 7.07.1977 (name changed by deed poll) Vincent d. May 1998 at home In Aylesbury Bucks.

Delphine Margaret b. 6 North Street Cardiff 27.12.1939 d. 1.09.1998 bd. Western Cemetery, Cardiff

Marilyn Anne b. North Street Cardiff 11.08.1941 m. Leslie Rodney Gill at St. Patrick's R.C.Church 21.04.1962 issue 2 children

Geraldine Frances b. 10.10.1950 at 6 North St. Lives in Hitchin Herts with partner Mike Evans Issue daughter Ashley

Kathryn Patricia b.26.03.1963

Susan Anne b. 10.06.1967

James

Sian

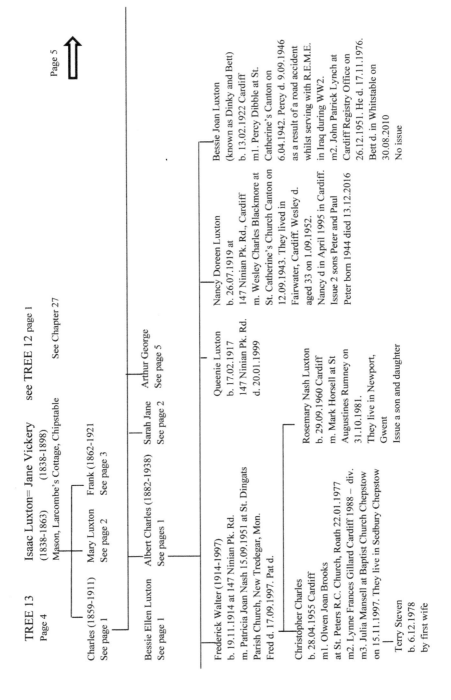

TREE 13
Page 4

Isaac Luxton = Jane Vickery   see TREE 12 page 1
(1838-1863)   (1838-1898)
Mason, Larcombe's Cottage, Chipstable   See Chapter 27

Page 5

Charles (1859-1911)
See page 1

Mary Luxton
See page 2

Frank (1862-1921)
See page 3

Albert Charles (1882-1938)
See pages 1

Sarah Jane
See page 2

Arthur George
See page 5

Bessie Ellen Luxton
See page 1

Frederick Walter (1914-1997)
b. 19.11.1914 at 147 Ninian Pk. Rd.
m. Patricia Joan Nash 15.09.1951 at St. Dingats
Parish Church, New Tredegar, Mon.
Fred d. 17.09.1997. Pat d.

Christopher Charles
b. 28.04.1955 Cardiff
m1. Olwen Joan Brooks
at St. Peters R.C. Church, Roath 22.01.1977
m2. Lynne Frances Gillard Cardiff 1988 – div.
m3. Julia Mansell at Baptist Church Chepstow
on 15.11.1997. They live in Sedbury Chepstow

Terry Steven
b. 6.12.1978
by first wife

Rosemary Nash Luxton
b. 29.09.1960 Cardiff
m. Mark Horsell at St
Augustines Rumney on
31.10.1981.
They live in Newport,
Gwent
Issue a son and daughter

Queenie Luxton
b. 17.02.1917
147 Ninian Pk. Rd.
d. 20.01.1999

Nancy Doreen Luxton
b. 26.07.1919 at
147 Ninian Pk. Rd., Cardiff
m. Wesley Charles Blackmore at
St. Catherine's Church Canton on
12.09.1943. They lived in
Fairwater, Cardiff. Wesley d.
aged 33 on 1.09.1952.
Nancy d in April 1995 in Cardiff.
Issue 2 sons Peter and Paul
Peter born 1944 died 13.12.2016

Bessie Joan Luxton
(known as Dinky and Bett)
b. 13.02.1922 Cardiff
m1. Percy Dibble at St.
Catherine's Canton on
6.04.1942. Percy d. 9.09.1946
as a result of a road accident
whilst serving with R.E.M.E.
in Iraq during WW2.
m2. John Patrick Lynch at
Cardiff Registry Office on
26.12.1951. He d. 17.11.1976.
Bett d. in Whitstable on
30.08.2010
No issue

TREE 13
Page 5

Isaac Luxton = Jane Vickery   see TREE 12 page 1
(1838-1863)   (1838-1898)
Mason, Larcombe's Cottage, Chipstable   See Chapter 27

Charles (1859-1911)
See page 1

Mary Luxton
See page 2

Frank (1862-1921)
See page 3

Bessie Ellen Luxton
See page 1

Albert Charles (1882-1938)
See pages 1

Sarah Jane
See page 2

Arthur George (known as Bert) b. at 32 Rose Street, Roath, Cardiff 11.05.1889. A railway signalman at Cardiff Docks.
m. Daisy Hopkins in St. Saviour, Roath on 1.08.1915. Bert who lost a leg in the course of his work as a railway coupler d. 2.01.1934 and was bd. at Cathays Cemetery, Cardiff. Daisy d. 19.10.1977

Violet May Luxton
b. 26. Walker Road, Splott, Cardiff 16.03.1918
m. William Herbert Rapson at St. Margaret's Roath 27.07.1940. Lived in Cyncoed Road, Cardiff. Violet d. 31.10.1997
Issue David and Linda

Bernard Luxton
b. 12.06.1919 at 28 Walker Road, Splott, Cardiff d. aged 2 of heart failure & laryngea Diptheria 25.04.1922

Mervyn Charles Luxton
b. at Walker Road Splott on 30.09.1923
m1. Annie Thomson at Martyrs North Church Greenoch m2. Doris Painter in June 1989 in South Glamorgan
Mervyn retired pipefitter d. aged 81 on 31.05. 2005 at Llandough Hospital.

Brynmor George
b. 8.08.1947 Cardiff
A lorry driver, he m. Janet Biggar, a Scot at Trinity Methodist Church Penarth on 19.10.1968. They live in St. Athan, Vale of Glamorgan

Heather Dawn Luxton
b. 18.03.1976

Helen June Luxton
b. 3.07.1977

Jonathan Charles Luxton
b. 4.11.1991

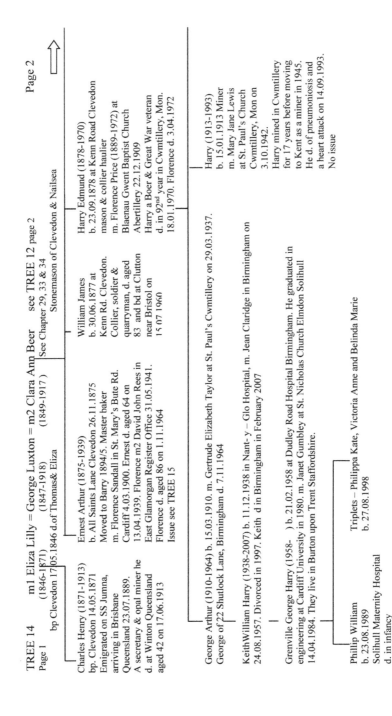

TREE 14 m1 Eliza Lilly = George Luxton = m2 Clara Ann Beer see TREE 12 page 2
Page 1 (1846-1871) (1847-1918) (1849-1917) See Chapter 29, 33 & 34
bp Clevedon 17 05.1846 d.of Thomas& Eliza Stonemason of Clevedon & Nailsea

Charles Henry (1871-1913)
bp. Clevedon 14.05.1871
Emigrated on SS Jumna,
arriving in Brisbane
Queensland 23.07.1889.
A secretary & opal miner he
d. at Winton Queensland
aged 42 on 17.06.1913

Ernest Arthur (1875-1939)
b. All Saints Lane Clevedon 26.11.1875
Moved to Barry 1894/5. Master baker
m. Florence Sandall in St. Mary's Bute Rd.
Cardiff 4.03.1900. Ernest d. aged 64 on
13.04.1939. Florence m2 David John Rees in
East Glamorgan Register Office 31.05.1941.
Florence d. aged 86 on 1.11.1964
Issue see TREE 15

William James
b. 30.06.1877 at
Kenn Rd. Clevedon.
Collier, soldier &
quarryman, d. aged
83 and bd at Clutton
near Bristol on
15 07 1960

Harry Edmund (1878-1970)
b. 23.09.1878 at Kenn Road Clevedon
mason & collier haulier
m. Florence Price (1889-1972) at
Blaenau Gwent Baptist Church
Abertillery 22.12.1909
Harry a Boer & Great War veteran
d. in 92nd year in Cwmtillery, Mon.
18.01.1970. Florence d. 3.04.1972

Harry (1913-1993)
b. 15.01.1913 Miner
m. Mary Jane Lewis
at St. Paul's Church
Cwmtillery, Mon on
3.10.1942.
Harry mined in Cwmtillery
for 17 years before moving
to Kent as a miner in 1945.
He d. of pneumoniosis and
a heart attack on 14.09.1993.
No issue

George Arthur (1910-1964) b. 15.03.1910. m. Gertrude Elizabeth Taylor at St. Paul's Cwmtillery on 29.03.1937.
George of 22 Shutlock Lane, Birmingham d. 7.11.1964

KeithWilliam Harry (1938-2007) b. 11.12.1938 in Nant- y – Glo Hospital, m. Jean Claridge in Birmingham on
24.08.1957. Divorced in 1997. Keith d in Birmingham in February 2007

Grenville George Harry (1958-) b. 21.02.1958 at Dudley Road Hospital Birmingham. He graduated in
engineering at Cardiff University in 1980. m. Janet Gumbley at St. Nicholas Church Elmdon Solihull
14.04.1984. They live in Burton upon Trent Staffordshire.

Triplets – Philippa Kate, Victoria Anne and Belinda Marie
b. 27.08.1998

Phillip William
b. 23.08.1989
Solihull Maternity Hospital
d. in infancy

TREE 14
Page 2

George Luxton = m2 Clara Ann Beer   see TREE 12 page 2
(1847-1918)   (1849-1917)d of John & Hannah born at Whitestaunton Somerset 8.06.1849 bp at Yarcombe
Devon 15.08.1849.

Stonemason of Clevedon & Nailsea   See Chapter 29, 33 & 35

Alfred Edward	Kate Louisa	Ida Laura	Blanche Maud	Thomas John	Emily May
b. 25.07.1881	b. 24.12.1882	b.11.09.1884 Wraxall	b. 25.01.1889	b. 28.08.1890	b. 7.08.1892 at Christchurch
Clevedon	Wraxall	m. Herbert Webber at	Nailsea	Nailsea	Nailsea
m. Rosena Norris	m1. Isaac Manfield at	Christchurch Nailsea	m. Alfred Gould	m. Amy Gladys	m. Albert Price, miner, at
St. Luke's Bedminster	St. Lukes Bedminster	on 13.05.1907.	at St. Lukes	Cavill in Holy	Abertillery Mon. on 28.01.1918.
Bristol 3-10-1906.	21.01.1903	Ida d. 9.01.1969 aged	Bedminster	Trinity Nailsea	Emily May of 7 Winifred
They lived in Noah's	m2. Samuel Brake at	86 in Marshfield Mon	20.01.1912	28.02.1916	Terrace d. 29.03.1949, cremated
Ark Nailsea. Rosena	Christchurch, Nailsea	Bert d. 30.08.1974	Alfred Gould	Sapper in Royal	and interred at St. Paul's
d. 1.10.1934	12.08.1922. Sam bd. at	aged 94	D.C.M. d. 1956.	Engineers in WW1	Cwmtillery.
aged 52. Fred bd.	Christchurch Nailsea		Blanche of Jubilee	& railway under-	Albert was cremated and interred
25.04.1967 aged 86.	21.10.1939. Kate d.		Cottage Wraxall	ganger.	at St. Paul's Cwmtillery on
Both bd. Christchurch	18.09.1949 at		d. 28.11.1961	Tom d. aged 81 on	22.07.1976
Nailsea	Heathfield Road			31.03.1872.	
	Nailsea			Amy d. aged 70 on	
				20.02.1961.	
Issue	Issue	Issue	Issue	No issue	No issue
See TREE 16					

TREE 15

Ernest Arthur Luxton = m Florence Sandall   see TREE 14 page 1
(1875-1939)   (1878-1964)d of Thomas & Sarah Jane b Barrow on Soar Leicestershire on 25
August 1878

Master baker "Golden Crust Bakery" Cassy Common Cadoxton Barry

See Chapter 30, 31 & 32

Florence Ethel (1901-1912)
b. 13 St. Oswald Road,
Barry on 31.10.1901.
Ethel d. aged 10 on 26-8-
1912 from tuberculosis
abscess on
the brain. bd. in parents
grave Barry Cemetery.

Doris Luxton
b. 25 Bruce Street
Roath Cardiff
18.10.1903
d. at 25 Bruce Street
aged 3 months on
26.01.1904 "Natural
Causes probably from
Convulsions"

George Ernest (1905-1983)
b. 25 Bruce Street Cardiff on 3.03.1905
m. Phyllis Mary King at St. Cadoc's
Cadoxton Barry on Boxing Day 1931.
George ex-baker and long distance lorry
driver d. aged 78 on 10.04.1983. Phyllis
(1907-1984) d. 28.09.1984. George's
ashes were scattered on Cassy Common.
They lived at "Hillcrest" Cassy
Common. Cadoxton

Burt Arthur (1913-2007)
b. 176 Barry Road on 17.09.1913.
Burt, a fitter-turner at Barry Graving Dock,
m. Beryl Leonora Campbell at Llandough
near Penarth on 10.06.1939
Beryl d. aged 75 on 27.02.1994. Her ashes
are bd. at Llanina near New Quay, Cardigan.
Burt d. aged 93 on 1.05.2007.
They lived at 'Passat' 12 Coldbrook Road,
Barry.

Sonia Luxton (1934-1998)
b. 11.09.1934
m1. Michael Hackett
at St. Joseph's R.C.Church
Penarth 17.08.1957. They
settled in Solihull – divorced
where issue 2 daughters
m2. Bob Lake at Bromsgrove
Register Office 30.12.1988.
Sonia d. of breast cancer at
Priory Hospital Edgbaston
11.10.1998.
Sonia had issue 2 daughters,
Haley and Julie by her first
marriage.

Richard George Luxton
b. 27.08.1945. Richard
an apprentice chef,
d. as a result of a motor
cycle accident at the
hump-back bridge,
Weycock Barry
on 22.05.1964

Brian Campbell Luxton
b. 29.05.1941 at "Passat"
12 Coldbrook Road Barry
School teacher
m. Edith Mary Jones
(nee Lapton) in Barry Registry
Office on 28.06.2013.
Brian was churchwarden at St.
Cadoc's Cadoxton.

Ian Leonard Luxton
b. "Passat" on 23.08.1952
Graduated in Jurisprudence at
Jesus College Oxford in 1973.
Solicitor.
m. Tina Joan Brady (nee
Callendar) at Bridgend Register
Office on 12.04.1980

Daniel Lewis Brady
From previous marriage
(now Luxton)
b. Aldershot 9.01.1972

Rachel Leonora Luxton
b. 15.12.1980 Cardiff

Tamsin Alexandra Luxton
b. 5.06.1984 Cardiff m.
Dusty Jones 28.07.2017 at
Gileston

Renzo Alexander
Jones b.2. 1. 2013

Casper Emerson
Jones b.29. 12. 2014

Alfred Edward Luxton = Rosena Norris   see TREE 14 page 2
(1881-1967)   (c1882-1934) born Hilperton Wilts. d of James Norris, labourer

of Noah's Ark, Nailsea, Somerset

Page 2

Muriel Blanche Luxton
b. 4.02.1907
bp. At Christchurch
Nailsea where m.
Hedley Ewart Rogers
8.06.1935
Muriel d. 12.03.1941
aged 34

Elizabeth May
Luxton
b. 6.05.1908
bp at Christchurch
Nailsea. Known as
"Ethel" she d. aged
44 on 13.02.1953
bd. at Christchurch
Nailsea

Laura Dorothy
b. 21.09.1910
Laura d. aged 18
from T.B. on
28.02.1929
bd. at Christchurch
Nailsea

Clara Ann Luxton
b. 18.06.1912.
Lived in
Staffordshire
before moving to
Northern Ireland
where she d.
5.06.1996

Reginald James Luxton
b. 21.07.1913. Jim who
worked in Hobbs Quarries m.
Beatrice Mary Lilly at
Wraxall Som. 18.04.1938
"Bee" d. 4.12.2002
Jim d. aged 90 on 25.04.2004

Barbara Gladys Luxton
b. 25.10.1914
m. Ronald James Davey
in All Saints Wraxall
28.02.1942.
They lived in 11
Orchard Close, Flax
Bourton, Somerset.
Barbara d. in Bristol
20.12.1994

Ena Mary Luxton
b. 14.03.1939
m. David Rafferty at
All Saints, Wraxall on
3.04.1961
Live in Nailsea
Issue two married
daughters.David
d.7.09.2017

Dorothy Luxton
b. 16.03.1940
m. Alistair McClean at
All Saints Wraxall
8.08.1964
Live in Isle of Wight
Issue two sons and a
daughter

William John Luxton
b. 24.09.1942
m1. Rosemary Ann Grindle
at All Saints Clevedon
25.09.1965.
Marriage dissolved
m2. Christine McEwan
at Weston Super Mare
Registry Office on
5.11.1976.
William a retired motor
mechanic lives in West
Huntspill.

Judi Louise Luxton
b. 3.03.1967 Bristol
m. Andrew S.
Bowden in
Portsmouth in
October 2004

Hayley Jane Luxton
b. 22.04.1969 Bristol
m Craig Thirkettle in
Swindon October
2003

Theresa Michelle Luxton
b. 30.11.1976

Alfred Edward Luxton = Rosena Norris   see TREE 14 Page 2
(1881–1967)   (c.1882–1934)
of Noah's Ark, Nailsea, Somerset   See Chapter 35

Violet Emmie Luxton
b. 10.06.1917
A switch board operator
m. Ronald Stewart Murray
at Christchurch Nailsea on
6.05.1944.
"Auntie Vi" d. 5.03.2005
Issue 3 daughters and 2
sons

George Albert Luxton
b. 17.06.1920
m. Evelyn Ethel Haines in
Radstock Parish Church Som.
on 30.03.1946
George d. 4.03.2002. Evelyn
d. 2011 Bd. Christ church
Nailsea.They lived at
49 Mdorfield Rd. Nailsea

Arthur William Luxton
b. Noah's Ark, Nailsea
19.09.1922
d. aged 9 days & bd. at
Christchurch Nailsea
29.09.1922

Leslie Ralph Luxton
b.1.11.1923
m.Gwyneth Dorcas Hawke
at Christchurch Hanham
Gloucestershire 12.07.1944.
They lived in Kingswood Bristol
where Leslie ran a motoring school.
Les. d. 6.06.2008

Jill Alyssia Luxton
b. Bristol on 3.05.1950
m. Roger Anthony Goodliffe
at Christchurch, Hanham,
Gloucestershire on 8.04.1972

Lesley Angela Luxton
b. 27.07.1947
m. Stephen Tupper at
Nailsea Methodist Church
on 1.11.1975.
Emigrated to Adelaide
South Australia about 1970
Issue a son and daughter.

Nigel Allan Luxton
b. 20.01.1949
m. Deidre Wright in
Sydney Australia
2.03.1973
They live in Crogee
N.S.W.
No issue

John Anthony Luxton
b. 28.05.1950
m. Anita Poole at
Long Ashton Church
Somerset on 27.01.1973

Anthony James Luxton
b. 23.07.1973

Sharon Louise Luxton
b. 8.10.1976 in Nailsea

John Luxton = Ellen Hopkins   see **TREE 12** Page 2   all baptisms, marriages and burials took place
(1850–1925)   (1850–1911)   at Nailsea unless otherwise stated
d of John & Ann Hopkins, labourer, bp 28.04.1850

Chimney sweep Nailsea

Page 2

See Chapter 36

Ellen Elizabeth Luxton
bp. 25.03.1871
bd. 16.04.1871
Aged 1 yr 2 mths

Elizabeth Luxton
b. 5.06.1872
m. George Sawtell
labourer on
24.12.1894
Elizabeth d. of
stomach cancer at
North Weston,
Portishead on
23.07.1913
Issue a daughter

Jane Ada Luxton
b. Nailsea 27.02.1874
m. Thomas Sawtell,
porter at St. John's
Clevedon 12.12.1894.
Jane d. aged 76 at
6 Walton Rd, Clevedon
7.08.1950

Ellen Sophia Luxton
bp. 9.04.1876
m. Ernest Cornelius
Churchill at
Portishead Parish
Church on
16.06.1900
Ellen d. aged 46 of
TB at 5 Honeyland,
Western Road,
Portishead on
24.07.1922

Emily Sophia Luxton
bp. Christchurch
Nailsea 26.04.1896.
d. of Ellen Sophia
Luxton, laundress, d.
of "measles 8 days"
at Pill, St. George on
23.07.1898

Eliza Luxton
bp. 13.04.1879
'Liza' m. James Thomas
Paynter at the Copse Rd.,
Meeting House, Clevedon
on 29.01.1900.
Eliza, widow, d. aged 59
on 8.02.1938
Issue 2 daughters

John Parker Luxton
b. 7.02.1920 at
4 Cromwell Street,
Sunderland.
He d. aged 12 at
Sunderland Royal
Infirmary on 30.03.1932

Charles John Luxton
b. 7.05.1881 Nailsea,
Som.bp.12.06.1881
'Charley' m. Ellen Parker at
St. Mark's Millfield
Sunderland on 3.03.1917
Charles d. aged 67 on
11.07.1948 in Sunderland.
Ellen d. at 13 May Street
Sunderland on 14.12.1956

Joyce Luxton
b. 22.12.1922 at 13 May
St., Sunderland
m. Stanley Wilfred Wallis
in Frodingham Parish
Church, Lincolnshire on
29.01.1946
Joyce d. at Sunderland
Royal Infirmary on
9.07.2002

John Luxton = Ellen Hopkins   see TREE 12 Page 2   all baptisms, marriages and burials took place
(1850-1925)   (1850-1911)   at Holy Trinity Nailsea unless stated otherwise
d of John & Ann Hopkins labourer bp 28th April 1850

Chimney sweep Nailsea

Page 3

See Chapter 36

Sarah Ann Luxton known as Sally
bp. 13.07.1884
m. Thomas Ryley at the Copse Rd.
Meeting House Clevedon on
14.01.1907.d.11.12.1957 at Mendip
Hospital Wells of influenzal
bronchopneumonia. bd at Lockwood
Cemetery Bath

Louisa Ann Luxton
bp 11.07.1886
m. William Paynter 10.11.1907
Louisa was dead by 1958.
Issue 2 daughters. They were in
Rhondda in 1911 and
Hampshire in 1939.
William d. Southamton 1953

Rosa Ann Luxton
bp 10.06.1888 m. William Charles Bessant
at Portishead Parish Church 5.12.1908
Rosa Ann d. 29.10.1918 from pneumonia
and influenza aged 31.
She was bd. in North Weston Cemetery,
Portishead. Had issue two daughters

Harry Luxton
(1890-1944)
See page 3

**William John
Luxton**
(1894-1952)
See page 4

**Elsie Rosina
Louise Luxton**
bp. 26.09.1904
at Christchurch
Nailsea
Elsie d. aged 2
mths at Silver
St. Nailsea on
15.11.1904.
bd at Christchurch
Nailsea.

Francis John Luxton
b. 19.04.1913 Portishead
m. Mary Amos at St.
Peter's Portishead
26.08.1939.
Francis d. 27.12.1988
Mary d. 1.09.2004
No issue

Alfred Walter Luxton
b. 28.05.1914 Portishead
m. Helga Elizabeth
Augusta Frida Schulte at
Luneburg, West Germany
13.03.1948.
d. 19.06.1979 Portishead

Eva Alice Luxton
(twin to Alfred)
b. 28.05.1914 Portishead
m. George Hook at St.
Barnabus Portishead on
1.11.1938.
Eva d. 9.12.1980
aged 66
Lived in Pill, Bristol
Issue 2 sons and a
daughter

Rosa Winifred
b. 2.03.1919
m. Stanley Delve
at St. Peter's
Portishead
24.08.1946.
Lived in Pill,
Bristol.
Rosa d. in 1994

**Henry (or Harry) Edmund
George Luxton**
b. 5.09.1920
m1. Sylvia May Henke at
St. Saviours Splott Cardiff
on 9.08.1941
Sylvia d. in March 1985
m2. Stella Ackerman-they
lived at 9 Gwendoline St.,
Splott.
Henry d. 25.02.1999.
Issue by Sylvia Henke

Gillian Ann Luxton
b. 24.08.1943 at Glossop
Terrace, Cardiff
m. Hiram Jenkins in
Llanishen Parish Church
on 17.07.1965. They live
in Ystrad Mynach, Glam.

Harry Alfred Walter Luxton
b. 7.10.1952 in British
Military Hospital Hamburg
m. Sally Ann Sparrow at St.
Peter's Portishead 15.07.72

Eveline Helga Elizabeth Luxton
b. 8.11.1959 in Portishead
m. Lawrence Victor Tweedy at
St. Peter's Portishead 4.07.1981
Live in Abbots Leigh nr Bristol

Claire Maria Luxton
b. 21.11.1973 at British Military
Hospital Berlin

Robert Jason Luxton
b. 26.04.1976 at Knoll
Maternity Home Clevedon

John Luxton = Ellen Hopkins   see TREE 12 Page 2   all baptisms, marriages and burials took place
(1850-1925)   (1850-1911)   at Holy Trinity Nailsea unless stated otherwise

↑

Chimney sweep Nailsea

See Chapter 36

William John Luxton
(1894-1952)
See page 4

Harry Luxton (1890-1944)
bp 8.06.1890
m. Alice Maud Dare at Bristol Register Office on 2.11.1912
Harry of Hollis Villas, Clevedon Road, Portishead, Som. d. aged 54 on
3.09.1944 at Bristol Royal Infirmary. Bd. at St. Peter's Portishead
Alice d. aged 74 on 20.02.1960

Marian Ethel Luxton
b. 17.1.1924 in Portishead
m. Hedley Newton in
Weston Super Mare Registry
Office on 1.09.1942. They
lived in North Weston,
Portishead and had three
sons. Marion d. 1.11.1995

Hubert Douglas Charles Luxton
b. 2 George St., North Weston,
Portishead on 30.12.1925
m. Ruby May Lewis at Bristol
Registry Office on 4.04.1963.
Hubert, retired omnibus
mechanic d. at home in Eastville
Bristol on 17.12.1991

Leslie Thomas Luxton
b. 14.03.1928
m. Beryl Cox on 19.11.1953
at St. Peter's Portishead.
They divorced. Leslie who
lived in Clevedon d. aged 44
on 27.07.1972

Raymond James Luxton
b. 8.04.1930 Portishead
m. Moira Ann Baker at
All Saints Kingston
Seymour, Yatton nr Bristol
on 1.08.1955
They live in Clevedon

Kathleen Evelyn Luxton
b. 22.02.1922
m. Thomas Plummer
(1913-1992) at St. Peter's
Portishead on 18.06.1949.
They lived at West Hill
Portishead with two
adopted daughters.
Kathleen d. in October
1994

Geoffrey Charles Luxton
b. 31.08.1963 in Bristol
m. Bernice Caroline Milton
Bristol Register Office
13.02.1988

Beverley Jane Luxton
b. 30.07.1965 in Bristol

Martin Thomas Luxton
b. 8.04.1955 in Clevedon.
Believed to be in
Scotland

Valerie Irene
b. 4.11.1957
in Clevedon
Believed to be
in Scotland

Mark James Luxton
b. 6.05.1958 in Bristol
Served 20 years in
Royal tank Regiment
Lives in Bevington
Dorset m.Michelle
Snelling in Dorset in
2001

Alison Jean Luxton
b 23.04.1962
m. Trevor Raymond
Cranshaw at St. John's
Clevedon on 17.07.1982.
They live in Sandbach,
Cheshire

TREE 17
Page 4

John Luxton = Ellen Hopkins   see TREE 12 Page 2   all baptisms, marriages and burials took place
(1850-1925)   (1850-1911)   at Holy Trinity Nailsea unless
                                                   otherwise stated

Chimney sweep Nailsea

See Chapter 36

William John Luxton (1894-1952)
bp. 11.02.1894
m. Mary Jane Hearn at St. Peter's Portishead on 19.10.1918
William d. aged 59 on 17.09.1952 at Bristol Royal Infirmary
Mary d. aged 82 on 9.01.1979.
They are bd. at North Weston Cemetery Portishead

Samuel William Luxton (1920-1979)
b. 8.11.1920 at Portishead
Prison Officer at Princetown Devon
m. May Matilda Pullinger at
Eastleigh Parish Church, Hants
on 27.04.1946
Samuel d. aged 59 on 9.12.1979
May (1921-1991) d. Dec. 1991

Norman George Luxton (1929-2009)
b. 9.01.1929. dock labourer
m. Primrose Daniels at Weston Super
Mare Town Hall on 18.06.1955
Lived in North Weston, Portishead
Norman d. 25.04.2009
Primrose d. 20.01.2010
They are bd. at St. Peter's Portishead.

Cyril James Luxton (1931-   )
b. 8.03.1931 hospital porter
m1. Phyllis Rosina Sposito at
Bristol Registry Office 21.08.1954
m2. Janet Ena Morgan at Weston Super
Mare Registry Office on 4.07.1970
Janet d. aged 48 on 7.01.1988
Issue by first wife Phyllis

Jacqueline Mary
b. 6.11.1951
Princetown Devon
m. David Anthony Fry
at St. Mary's
Bishopstoke Eastleigh
17.04.1971
David d. aged 33
on 31.07.1982
Jackie lives in
Hayling Island

Colin Raymond Luxton
b. 28.07.1955
m. Jane Elizabeth Sharp at
Western Super Mare on
27.05.1979. Divorced
2.01.1985. By second partner
...Shayne:-

Christine Mary Luxton
b. 13.10.1961
m. Martin Furlong at
Bristol Registry Office
on 12.05.2001
Issue a daughter

Pauline Margaret
b. 20.12.1963

Janet Anne
b. 2.09.1966
m. Christopher
Chambers on
6.07.2002 at
St. Peter's
Portishead
Issue 2 daughters
and a son

William John Luxton
b. 19.09.1954
m. Beryl Lynn Denniss at
Weston Super Mare on
29.09.1973
Live in Portishead

Emma Jane
Luxton
b. 7.11.1979

Richard James
Luxton
b. 17.09.1987

Caroline Luxton b. by 1996
m. Richard Allan Holmes at Weston
Registry Office on 23.04.2011.
Issue a son & daughter

Samantha Louise Luxton
b. 28.12.1973

Thomas Luxton = 2) Ann Jenkins   see TREE 1   all baptisms, marriages and burials took place
(1756-1817)   (1766-1857)   at St Andrew's Aller unless otherwise stated

Bp at Carhampton Somerset 29.06.1766 d of Richard & Ann

See Chapter 37   Bullock Jobber, New House Tenement, Frogpit Moor, Petton, Bampton

Page 2 ⇧

Thomas Luxton (c1797-1885)
He may have been aged as old as six when bp. at Petton 1st May 1803. Settled in Ridley Aller in 1820s, farmer m1. Hannah Sawtell at St Andrew's Aller 17.12.1827. Hannah d. aged 34 of T.B. on 7.10.1843 bd. 15.10.1843

Jenny
bp. 20.01.1799 Bampton
d. aged 7
bd. 9.10.1806 at Petton

Elizabeth
bp. 6.03.1808 at Petton.
Possibly d. in infancy unless she is Elizabeth Thomas who was present in 1845 at William's death

William Luxton (c1807-1845)
Bequeathed New House Cottage, Clayhanger. William, a labourer in Shillingford, Bampton d. 4.11.1845 from T.B. bd. at Petton 9.11.1845

This couple had issue at Aller

John Luxton
bp. 12.04.1829 m. Sarah Seymour at Holy Trinity Bridgwater 29.10.1854 Sarah d. 11.06.1887 aged 62 at St. John Street Bridgwater. John, aged 80, labourer in timber yard d. 21.08.1906 at Union Hospital Bridgwater

See TREE 19

Jemima
bp. 14.07.1830
bd. 29.08.1830

Jesse Lewis Luxton
b. 12.08.1831 m. Ellen Temblett at Holy Trinity, Bridgwater 27.03.1859 Ellen d. aged 67 at 113 St. John Street Bridgwater on 24.09.1899. John, labourer on railway d. at 113 St. John Street on 30.11.1907

See TREE 20

Robert Lewis Luxton
bp. 19.05.1834 m. Mary Ann Tucker in Holy Trinity Bridgwater 25.12.1856. Mary aged 58 bd. 22.12.1894 Lewis, farmer at Aller Drove, d. aged 65 bd. 22.07.1899

See TREE 21

Richard
aged 5 in 1841 in Aller census

Alfred Luxton
b. 15.03.1836 at Aller m. Betsy Lock, dressmaker, at Holy Trinity Bridgwater 25.12.1859 Alfred, ag. lab, d. aged 87 on 1.02.1924. Betsy d. aged 87 bd. 31.03.1927

See TREE 22

Daniel
bp. 30.12.1838 d. aged 5 from Scarlet fever on 21.06 and bd. 25.06.1843

William
bp.21.06.1843 aged 18 months d. of Scarlet fever on day of baptism bd. 25.06.1843

TREE 18
Page 2

See Chapter 37

Thomas Luxton = 2) Ann Jenkins   see TREE 1
(1756-1817)   (1766-1857)

all baptisms, marriages and burials took place
at St Andrew's Aller unless otherwise stated

Bullock jobber, New House Tenement, Frogpit Moor, Petton, Bampton

Thomas Luxton (c1797-1885)
m2. Sarah Stacey in St Mary's Bridgwater on 31.03.1845
Sarah d. aged 44 or 46 on 7.02.1861, bd at Aller 14.02.1861
Thomas d. aged 88 and was bd. at St Andrew's Aller 29.10.1885

Issue by second wife Sarah Stacey born in Aller

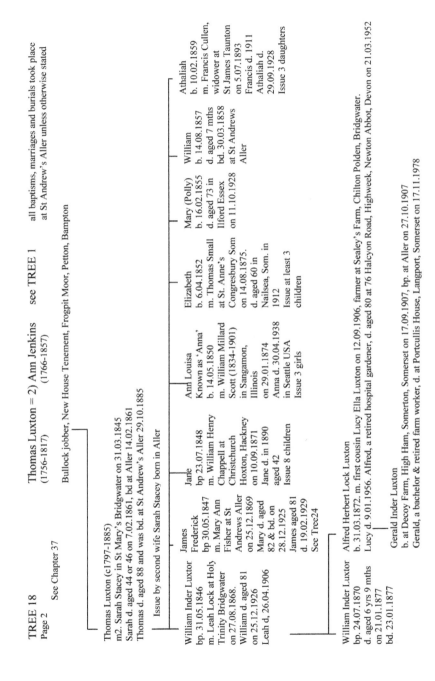

William Inder Luxton
bp. 31.05.1846
m. Leah Lock at Holy
Trinity Bridgwater
on 27.08.1868.
William d. aged 81
on 25.12.1926
Leah d, 26.04.1906

**James
Frederick**
bp 30.05.1847
m. Mary Ann
Fisher at St
Andrews Aller
on 25.12.1869
Mary d. aged
82 & bd. on
28.12.1925
James aged 81
d. 19.02.1929
See Tree24

Jane
bp 23.07.1848
m. William Henry
Chappell at
Christchurch
Hoxton, Hackney
on 10.09.1871
Jane d. in 1890
aged 42
Issue 8 children

Ann Louisa
Known as 'Anna'
b. 14.05.1850
m. William Millard
Scott (1834-1901)
in Sangamon,
Illinois
on 29.01.1874
Anna d. 30.04.1938
in Seattle USA
Issue 3 girls

Elizabeth
b. 6.04.1852
m. Thomas Small
at St. Anne's
Congresbury Som
on 14.08.1875.
d. aged 60 in
Nailsea, Som. in
1912
Issue at least 3
children

Mary (Polly)
b. 16.02.1855
d. aged 73 in
Ilford Essex
on 11.10.1928

William
b. 14.08.1857
d. aged 7 mths
bd. 30.03.1858
at St Andrews
Aller

Athaliah
b. 10.02.1859
m. Francis Cullen,
widower at
St James Taunton
on 5.07.1893
Francis d. 1911
Athaliah d.
29.09.1928
Issue 3 daughters

William Inder Luxton
bp. 24.07.1870
d. aged 6 yrs 9 mths
on 21.01.1877
bd. 23.01.1877

Alfred Herbert Lock Luxton
b. 31.03.1872. m. first cousin Lucy Ella Luxton on 12.09.1906, farmer at Sealey's Farm, Chilton Polden, Bridgwater.
Lucy d. 9.01.1956. Alfred, a retired hospital gardener, d. aged 80 at 76 Halcyon Road, Highweek, Newton Abbot, Devon on 21.03.1952

Gerald Inder Luxton
b. at Decoy Farm, High Ham, Somerton, Somerset on 17.09.1907, bp. at Aller on 27.10.1907
Gerald, a bachelor & retired farm worker, d. at Portcullis House, Langport, Somerset on 17.11.1978

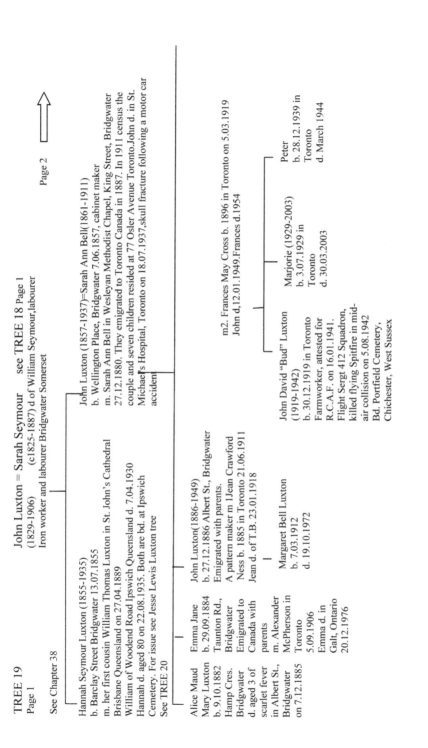

John Luxton = Sarah Seymour   see TREE 18 Page 1
(1829-1906)   (c1825-1887) d of William Seymour,labourer
Iron worker and labourer Bridgwater Somerset

Hannah Seymour Luxton (1855-1935)
b. Barclay Street Bridgwater 13.07.1855
m. her first cousin William Thomas Luxton in St. John's Cathedral
Brisbane Queensland on 27.04.1889
William of Woodend Road Ipswich Queensland d. 7.04.1930
Hannah d. aged 80 on 22.08.1935. Both are bd. at Ipswich
Cemetery. For issue see Jesse Lewis Luxton tree
See TREE 20

John Luxton (1857-1937)=Sarah Ann Bell(1861-1911)
b. Wellington Place, Bridgwater 7.06.1857, cabinet maker
m. Sarah Ann Bell in Wesleyan Methodist Chapel, King Street, Bridgwater
27.12.1880. They emigrated to Toronto Canada in 1887. In 1911 census the
couple and seven children resided at 77 Osler Avenue Toronto.John d. in St.
Michael's Hospital, Toronto on 18.07.1937,skull fracture following a motor car
accident

Alice Maud
Mary Luxton
b. 9.10.1882
Hamp Cres.
Bridgwater
d. aged 3 of
scarlet fever
in Albert St.,
Bridgwater
on 7.12.1885

Emma Jane
b. 29.09.1884
Taunton Rd.,
Bridgwater
Emigrated to
Canada with
parents
m. Alexander
McPherson in
Toronto
5.09.1906
Emma d. in
Galt, Ontario
20.12.1976

John Luxton(1886-1949)
b. 27.12.1886 Albert St., Bridgwater
Emigrated with parents.
A pattern maker m 1Jean Crawford
Ness b. 1885 in Toronto 21.06.1911
Jean d. of T.B. 23.01.1918

Margaret Bell Luxton
b. 7.03.1912
d. 19.10.1972

m2. Frances May Cross b. 1896 in Toronto on 5.03.1919
John d,12.01.1949.Frances d.1954

John David "Bud" Luxton
(1919-1942)
b. 30.12.1919 in Toronto
Farmworker, attested for
R.C.A.F. on 16.01.1941.
Flight Sergt 412 Squadron,
killed flying Spitfire in mid-
air colllision on 5.08.1942
Bd. Portfield Cemetery,
Chichester, West Sussex

Marjorie (1929-2003)
b. 3.07.1929 in
Toronto
d. 30.03.2003

Peter
b. 28.12.1939 in
Toronto
d. March 1944

TREE 19
Page 2   See Chapter 38

John Luxton = Sarah Seymour   see TREE 18 Page 1
(1829-1906)   (c1825-1887)
Iron worker and labourer Bridgwater Somerset

Hannah Seymour Luxton (1855-1935)
b. Barclay Street Bridgwater 13.07.1855
m. her first cousin William Thomas Luxton in St. John's Cathedral
Brisbane Queensland on 27.04.1889
William of Woodend Road Ipswich Queensland d. 7.04.1930
Hannah d. aged 80 on 22.08.1935. Both are bd. at Ipswich
Cemetery. For issue see Jesse Lewis Luxton tree
See TREE 20

John Luxton (1857-1937)
b. Wellington Place, Bridgwater 7.06.1857, cabinet maker
m. Sarah Ann Bell in Wesleyan Methodist Chapel, King Street, Bridgwater
27.12.1880. They emigrated to Toronto Canada in 1887. In 1911 census the
couple and seven children resided at 77 Osler Avenue Toronto..

Arthur James Luxton	Ellen May (Nellie)	George	Winnifred	Gordon Victor	Myrtle Edna
b. 5.04.1888 in York district Ontario.	b. 10.10.1890 York district Ontario	William	Hannah	Luxton	Lucy Luxton
An electrician he enlisted in Army in May 1918	m. William Arthur	b. 29.09.1892	b. 6.10.1894	b. 25.09.1897	b. 8.03.1903 in
m. Mabel Beatrice Newton in Toronto on 10.09.1919	Frazer in Toronto	in York district	York district	in York	York district
d. 15.08.1965 in Toronto	21.06.1915.Nellie	Ontario	Ontario	district	Ontario.
	d.25.12.1961 in	m.1 Clarice	m. William	Ontario	In 1911 census
	Grimsby, Niagara,	Irene Moyle in	Henry Drake	m. Margaret	aged 8.Myrtle,
	Ontario.	Toronto in Oct.	8.09.1926 in	Atkins in	a dressmaker
	issue 2 boys2 girls	1919.m2Nora	Toronto. She	Toronto	d. in Toronto
		Doris Smith	d.8.10.1964 in	2.08.1923. He	in 1991
		on11.10.1937	Toronto	d.15.06.1952	
		in Coburg. He		in Toronto	
James Edgar Luxton		d.26.08.1971			
b. 15.08.1925 in Toronto		in Guelph.			
d. 30.03.2006		issue four			
		children by 1st			
		wife			

Jesse Lewis Luxton = Ellen Temblett   see TREE 18 Page 1
(1831-1907)   (1831-1899) d of William Temblett, butcher, born Bridgwater 27.09.1831

Sawyer & general labourer Bridgwater

William Thomas Luxton
b. 9.11.1860 St. John Street Bridgwater
m. Hannah Seymour Luxton at St. John's Cathedral, Brisbane on 27.04.1889
William d aged 68 in Brisbane on 7.04.1930
Hannah d. aged 80 on 22.08.1935

Sarah Ann Luxton
b. 29.07.1863 at St. John Street Bridgwater
m1. William Alfred Kurton, widower, in parish church Bedminster, Bristol on 24.01.1886. William d. in Bristol on 14.10.1916 in Bristol.
m2. George Henry Bowden (1863-1929) on 14.10.1916 in Bristol.
Sarah, resident in Berks mental hospital bd. 11.09.1930 at St. James Barkham

Louisa Luxton
b. 29.12.1865
Polden Street, Bridgwater
Emigrated to Queensland Australia in 1889 where her brother William settled. No further details.

Rosina Luxton
b. 15.02.1869 in Polden Street, Bridgwater
m. Henry Wood, tailor, at Wesleyan Methodist Chapel King Street, Bridgwater on 24.06.1894.
They lived in North Petherton, Som. in 1901 where Henry was sub Post master. Rosina aged 54 d.of "Paralysis following cerebral haemorrhage 3 years" at Fore Street North Petherton on 1.07.1923.

William John Luxton
b. 10.12.1880 at St. Mary Street, Bridgwater.
Emigrated with parents to Australia
m. Flora Edith Mary Miles in Sydney in 1922.
William d. in Sydney

Thomas Seymour Luxton
b. 13.05.1890
d. aged 5 months on 14.10.1890

Albert Henry Luxton
b. 16.07.1891 at Cochrane St., Paddington, Queensland
m. Ellen Amelia Cook at Congregational Church, Wharf Street, Brisbane on 22.07.1920

Jessie Lewis Luxton
b. 10.06.1896 Brisbane
where he d. aged 2 months on 2.08.1896

Myrtle Seymour Luxton
b. 17.07.1898
d. aged 36 at Ipswich, Queensland on 7.03.1935

Cyra Islay Seymour Luxton
b. 1.05.1923
m. Carmello Barbaro
issue 2 sons

Yvonne Flora Mackinnon Luxton
b. 22.08.1924
m. Keith Alfred Roy Smith M.B.E.
issue 2 sons and a daughter

Nona Elaine Luxton
b. 24.11.1925
m. James Ross Henderson (1923-1982) in Sydney on 26.05.1951
issue a son & daughter and 3 grandsons

Olga Seymour Luxton
b. 29.12.1927
m. Donald Frank Williams in Sydney on 4.09.1954
Olga d. 29.06.2001
Issue 4 daughters and a son

Jesse Lewis Luxton= Ellen Temblett see TREE 18 Page 1
(1831-1907)   (1831-1899)
Sawyer & general labourer Bridgwater

See Chapter 39

Jessie Lewis Luxton
b. 25.04.1875 at St. John Street Bridgwater
m. Alice Manley at Wesleyan Chapel, St. Mary Street, Bridgwater on 25.07.1896
Alice d. aged 51 on 2.04.1928
Jesse d. aged 73 at 149 St. John Street, Bridgwater on 25.11.1948
Interred in Bristol Road Cemetery, Bridgwater

Elizabeth Luxton (known as Bessie)
b. 4.12.1871 at St. John Street, Bridgwater
Emigrated in 1890 to Toronto Canada
m. James Comer (1861-1938) in York, Toronto on 6.01.1891.
By 1897 they were farming in Alberta.
Elizabeth d. at Red Deer Alberta on 3.09.1936.
They had issue of at least 8 children

Lilian Ellen
b. 31.01.1897
113 St. John St.
Bridgwater
d. 2.10.1948
aged 51 at 149
St. John Street
Bridgwater

Dorothy Mary
b. 30.03.1898
82 Friarn St.
Bridgwater
d. 11.02.1921
149 St John St.
Bridgwater

William Harry Luxton
b. at 3 Edward
Street Bridgwater
4. 07. 1899
d. of "bronchitis
6 days" at 113 St.
John Street,
Bridgwater18.03.
1900 aged 8mths.

Hilda
b. 10.01.1901
113 St. John St.
m. Archibald
George
Gillingham at
St John Baptist
Church,
Bridgwater on
3.12.1942
Hilda d. aged
84 on 28.07
1985
No issue

Alice Maud
b. 7.04.1902
m. Ernest
Reginald
Atyeo in
Mariners
Chapel St.
John St.
(Independent)
14.05.1928
Alice d. aged
70 on
18.10.1972
Ernest d. aged
90 9.10.1992
bd. Burnham
on Sea
A son David
Atyeo d.1999.

Rhoda
b. 14.04.1904
at 113 St.
John St.
d. 24.03.1923
at 149 St.
John St.

Rosina
b. 1.10.1906
m. James
Alfred Dyer
in
Bridgwater
Register
Office on
26.01.1935
Rosina d.
14.10.1999
Issue a son
and 3
daughters
Gloria
Mary Judy
& Noel

Freda
b. 4.10.1908 at
113 St. John St.
d. 27.11.1935 at
Chard
Sanatorium

William
Lewis Luxton
b. 21.03.1915
Bridgwater.
An
accountant
m. Nita
Gwendoline
Dyke (1914-
1983) at St.
John Baptist
Church
Bridgwater on
24.09.1939
Lived at 235
Taunton Rd.,
Bridgwater.
William d.
19.05.1988

Madge
b. 15.07.1919
m. Gordon
Stewart at
St. John the
Baptist Church
Bridgwater on
24.12.1941.
They lived at
27 Gloucester
Rd.,Bridgwater
Madge d.
12.04.2005

Murray Stewart
& wife Helen
live in
Bramcote
Nottingham

Robert Lewis Luxton= Mary Ann Tucker   see TREE 18 Page 1

(1834–1899)   (1836–1894)d. of Joseph & Grace, labourer bp at Othery 13.11.1836

Farmer at Aller Drove

Page 2

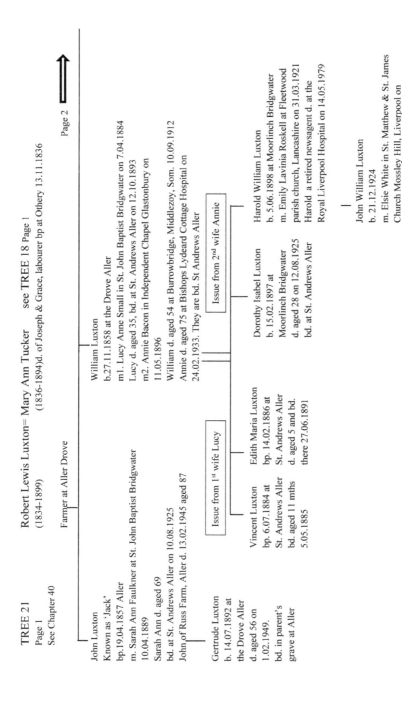

John Luxton
Known as 'Jack'
bp.19.04.1857 Aller
m. Sarah Ann Faulkner at St. John Baptist Bridgwater
10.04.1889
Sarah Ann d. aged 69
bd. at St. Andrews Aller on 10.08.1925
John of Russ Farm, Aller d. 13.02.1945 aged 87

William Luxton
b.27.11.1858 at the Drove Aller
m1. Lucy Anne Small in St. John Baptist Bridgwater on 7.04.1884
Lucy d. aged 35, bd. at St. Andrews Aller on 12.10.1893
m2. Annie Bacon in Independent Chapel Glastonbury on
11.05.1896
William d. aged 54 at Burrowbridge, Middlezoy, Som. 10.09.1912
Annie d. aged 75 at Bishops Lydeard Cottage Hospital on
24.02.1933. They are bd. St Andrews Aller

Issue from 1st wife Lucy

Gertrude Luxton
b. 14.07.1892 at
the Drove Aller
d. aged 56 on
1.02.1949.
bd. in parent's
grave at Aller

Vincent Luxton
bp. 6.07.1884 at
St. Andrews Aller
bd. aged 11 mths
5.05.1885

Edith Maria Luxton
bp. 14.02.1886 at
St. Andrews Aller
d. aged 5 and bd.
there 27.06.1891

Issue from 2nd wife Annie

Dorothy Isabel Luxton
b. 15.02.1897 at
Moorlinch Bridgwater
d. aged 28 on 12.08.1925
bd. at St. Andrews Aller

Harold William Luxton
b. 5.06.1898 at Moorlinch Bridgwater
m. Emily Lavinia Roskell at Fleetwood
parish church, Lancashire on 31.03.1921
Harold a retired newsagent d. at the
Royal Liverpool Hospital on 14.05.1979

John William Luxton
b. 21.12.1924
m. Elsie White in St. Matthew & St. James
Church Mossley Hill, Liverpool on
9.07.1956.He d.in Liverpool aged 83 in 2007

see TREE 18 Page 1

TREE 21
Page 2

Robert Lewis Luxton= Mary Ann Tucker
(1834-1899)   (1836-1894)
Farmer at Aller Drove

See Chapter 40&41

Page 3

George Lewis Luxton
bp. 2.12.1860 at Aller
m. Alice Willmington at Yeovil
Registry Office Som.8.04.1896
Alice d. aged 75, bd. at St. Andrews
Aller 6.10.1941
George d. aged 91 in Taunton
bd. at St. Andrews Aller on 23.11.1951

Clifford George Lewis Luxton
b. 8.07.1896 at 6 Green Quarry,
Yeovil
m. Ivy Lucy Gertrude Luxton his
cousin at Bridgwater Registry Office
on 20.12.1960
Clifford d. aged 72 on27.02.1969
bd. at St. Andrews Aller on
2.03.1969

Ellen Luxton
bp. 22.02.1863 at Aller
m. Cornelius Saunders at South
Street Baptist Chapel Yeovil on
1.02.1894
"Nell" d. in Ash Martock
Somerset in 1929
Cornelius bd. 17.07.1950
issue a son and two daughters

Dorothy Violet Luxton
b. 18.01.1900 in North St.
Langport Somerset
m. Frederick Edwin Higham
at St. Andrews Aller on
4.04.1931
Dorothy d. in Liverpool in
October 1989

Mary Jane Luxton
b. 23.02.1865 at Drove Aller
"Polly" m. Charles Stacey at
St. Andrews Aller on
26.06.1890
Lived at Curry Rivel Somerset
Charles d. 16.03.1936
Polly d. 21.12.1959 according
to their headstone at
St Andrews Curry Rivel
Issue 3 girls & a boy

Edith Luxton
b. 25.12.1866 at the Drove Aller
m. Archibald Scriven at Sion
Independent Chapel Bridgwater on
17.12.1902
Edith, wife of Archibald Scriven of
Plot Stream Farm Aller d. aged 83
on 31. 10. 1951
Archibald d. aged 90 bd. 9.04.1970
Issue 2 sons

Robert Lewis Luxton= Mary Ann Tucker   see TREE 18

(1834-1899)   (1836-1894)

Farmer at Aller Drove   See Chapter 40

Reuben Luxton
b. 13.05.1869 at Drove Aller m
Mary Ann Andrews at St. Benedicts
Glastonbury, Som. on 18.05.1896
Reuben d. of T.B. aged 39 on
28.02.1909
bd. at St. Andrews Aller
Mary d. aged 68 at Bockhampton
Christchurch Southampton on
3.12.1943

Albert Luxton b.16 05. 1871 at
Drove Aller m Constance
Scriven at Little Holloway
Congregational Chapel, Aller,.
on 26.04.1904
Albert d. 8.09.1944 aged 72 bd.
at St. Andrews, Aller 13.09.1944
Constance d. 17.08.1962 aged
87. bd at St Andrews Aller

Jesse Luxton was
accidentally
registered as a girl.
b 22.05.1873 at the
Drove Aller
d. of scarlet fever
on 3.01.1877. bd. at
St. Andrews Aller
on 4.01.1877

Alfred Luxton
b. 23.04.1875 at
Aller
d. aged 1yr. 8ths
bd. 17.01.1877 at
St. Andrews Aller

Grace Luxton
b. 20.08.1877 at the Drove Aller
m. Frederick R. Tucker (1873-
1961),a thatcher at Aller on
1.01.1903.Lived at College Farm,
Long Load, Ash near Yeovil, Som.
Grace d. 11. 11. 1934 leaving issue
2 daughters Doris and Gwen

Charles Andrews Luxton
b.25.04.1897,bp. 6.06.1897 at Aller
m. Maud Simpkins on 14.02.1925
at Christchurch Derry Hill, Wiltshire
Maud d. aged 48 on 31.1. 1950
Charles, 3 Derry Hill, Calne, Wiltshire
d. 7.02.1970

Grace Millicent Evelyn Luxton
b. 28.10. 1899.
bp. Aller 8.04.1900 Grace a
spinster lived in Bransgore,
Christchurch, Hants d. 7.08.1962

Lewis Norman Luxton
b. 15.06.1904,
bp. Aller 28.08.1904
m. Dorothy Kathleen Annie
Dawkins at Register Office
New Forest Hants 2.08.1960
Lived in New Milton Hants
Lewis d. April 2002

Margery Luxton
b. 18.01.1907 Aller
d. aged 2 months
bd. 23.03.1907 at
St. Andrews, Aller

Reuben Luxton
b. 5.05.1909 Aller
d. 23.03.1980 at
Royal Victoria
Hospital
Bournemouth

Christine Nora Luxton b. 12.06.1925
at 79 Old Rd. Studley, Calne
Without, Wilts.
m. Harold William White at
Christchurch in Derry Hill, Wilts. On
7.02.1953
Issue two children Caroline and Ian
White

Dennis Victor Luxton b. 10.03.1930 at 85
Studley, Calne Without, Wilts. d.2013
m. Corrine Ann Lavelle in the R.C. Church
Corsham on 29.03.1958. Divorced in 1976.

Martin John Luxton b. 4.07.1962 Chippenham
Changed his name to Lavelle in 1982. m..Kathy
Issue Ryan, Lewis & Grace Lavelle

Denise Ann Luxton b. 20.11.1964
Chippenham
m. Rupert Swallow in June 1999

Alfred Luxton = Betsy Lock   see TREE 18 Page 1
(1836-1924)   (1839-1927) d. of Charles & Sarah Lock agricultural labourer bp at Aller 27.10.1839

Agricultural labourer of Aller Somerset   See Chapter 42& 43

Page 2 ⇧

Charles Luxton b.29.02.1860 m. Mary Doster (born 1858 in Stoke Gregory Somerset) in St. Marks South Norwood Surrey on 26.01.1884. Charles, a printer, d. aged 43 at 15 Wood Street, Leytonstone, Essex on 2.12.1903

Anna Luxton b. 28.04.1861 d. of phthisis aged 21 on 28.09.1882 bd. at St. Andrews Aller 5.10.1882

Albert Ernest Luxton b.at Aller 2.05.1862 d. aged 15 on 15.07.1878 "accidentally killed by the kick of a horse". bd at St. Andrews Aller 20.07.1878

Anna Maude b. Penge Essex 17.11.1886. Admitted 22.05.1906 in Essex Asylum. Listed as inmate in Brentwood Mental Hospital in 1939 Register.She d. aged 57 in Brentwood on 18.07.1943

Gertrude b. Penge Surrey 1887.

Henry Charles Luxton b. 26.02.1889 Leytonstone bp 8.06.1889 at St John the Baptist Leytonstone. In 1911 census Henry, single, formerly a house painter, inmate in West Ham Union Workhouse, Leytonstone.d. age 23 of epilepsy at Essex & Colchester Asylum on 4.05.1913.

Beatrice Emily b. 24.03.1890 bp at St. John the Baptist Leytonstone on 4.11.1895 m. W.E.Bernard in West Ham 24.04.1911she d.Beddau,Glam 20.11.1967

Sidney Alfred b. 24.12.1891 Leytonstone Served in Royal Welsh Fusiliers in W.W.1. Killed in action on 8.10.1918

Ernest George b. 2.11.1892 Leytonstone m.Maud Helena Hall, born 21.08.1895, in St. Mary's Church, Abergavenny on 17.11.1915 George d. 3.05.1929at 34 Park Street, Abergavenny. Maud d. 4.10.1983.

Herbert Andrew b. 26.02.1895 Leytonstone d. 11.1895 West Ham

Arthur Albert Luxton b. 27.07.1896 Leytonstone bp. St John the Baptist 7.03.1897d.of epilepsy 22.6.1914

Robin Clive Luxton b. 18.09.1944 at Victoria Park Hospital Abergavenny.m Eleanor M. Gretton 2.10.1965 in Pontypool Register Office. He d. aged 66 on 16.08. 2010 in Coleford Gloucestershire

John Ernest Luxton b. 34 Park Street Abergavenny on 24.02.1920. Omnibus fitter, m. Myrtle Maureen Lewis at Abergavenny Register Office on 12.06.1943 John pf 37 Stanhope Street d.5.08. 1993

Joyce Doreen b. 15.01.1922 at 34 Park Street Abergavenny. A student nurse m. Ernest Frederick Rowe at Bromsgrove Register Office on 2.09.1947

June Margaret E. b. 13.06.1926 34 Park Street, Abergavenny. m. Ralph Dutton 16.03.1946 in St. Mary's Abergavenny.

TREE 22
Page 2

Alfred Luxton = Betsy Lock   see TREE 18 Page 1
(1836-1924)   (1839-1927)
Agricultural labourer of Aller Somerset See Chapter 42 & 44

Page 3 ⬆

William Jesse Luxton
b. 3.11.1870 Aller
m. Elizabeth Mary Cornwall in parish church Staplegrove Somerset 26.10.1904 William aged 82 d. at The Retreat, Woolawington Corner, Bawdrip Bridgwater Somerset on 30.06.1953 Elizabeth d. aged 87 at Northgate Lodge Bridgwater 26.04.1961

Alfred Henry Luxton
b. 11.03.1869 Aller
m1. Emma Jessie Baker (1887-1914) at Norwich Register Office 29.06.1908 "Jess" d. in childbirth 11.04.1914
m2. Harriet Barbara Artis (1882-1964) in parish church of Sotterley Suffolk 25.01.1916. Alfred of "Brooklyn" Wangford Suffolk d. on 21.05.1952 Harriet d. 14.11.1964 Issue See TREE 23

Oliver James Luxton
b. 21.09.1867 Aller
m1. Susan Thomas at Bible Christian Chapel East Stonehouse Devon on 25.12.1893 Susan d. aged 65 on 10.12.1925
m2. Mabel George in Croydon Register Office 14.09.1926 Oliver d. in Croydon 5.11.1941

Lucy Luxton
b. 1.12.1865 Aller
d. of croup on 2.10.1870 bd. at St. Andrews Aller on 8.10.1870

Arthur Luxton
b. 16.09.1864 at Aller
m.1 Mary Ann Rossiter at Cardiff Register Office on 11.06.1889. Lived at 8 Aberystwyth Crescent, Splott, Cardiff m 2Mary J. Pearson in Hartlepool 30.9. 1899.Arthur Luxton, marine stoker, d. Hartlepool, Durham on 24.03.1901

Jesse Henry Luxton (1907-1999) son of Jesse Luxton valet and his wife Annie Jane Luxton formerly Stacey b. 27.05.1907 at 11 London Road, Beccles Suffolk . I cannot find a marriage for them. Annie split from William and in that year emigrated to USA. She married a Mr White and had 2 children. Annie d. 11.03.1970 in New Jersey. In 1930 Jesse 22 was a nurseryman/florist in Bergen, New Jersey. He m. Alice Wayland Hudson and they had issue Alice Wayland White (1946-2005) Jesse d. in Peterborough, Hillsborough, New Hants on 1.02.1999

Ivy Luxton
b.16.10.1933 at 72 Frant Road dictaphone typist m. John T. Ledbetter 18.07.1953 at Croydon Register Office

Doris Luxton
b. 13.12.1931 at 72 Frant Road Thornton Heath Croydon d. 2.12.1932

Olive Luxton
b. 30.06.1929 at 72 Frant Road Thornton Heath, Croydon m. Robert Knight at St. Saviours Croydon 17.12.1949 Issue Janette and Julie in Croydon

Elizabeth Luxton
b. 2.08.1927 at 72 Frant Road, Thornton Heath Croydon m. Alfred W.Dix at St. Saviours, Croydon on 3.11.1945. Elizabeth d. aged 80 in Bromley in 2007

Arthur Frank Luxton
b. 26 07.1890 at 19 Maud Street, Roath, Cardiff d. "manslaughter, knocked down by horse and dog cart" at Bridgwater Infirmary 10.02.1894

Alfred Luxton = Betsy Lock see TREE 18 Page 1
(1836-1924) (1839-1927)
Agricultural labourer of Aller Somerset

Page 4

Herbert Luxton
b. 15.01.1879
d. aged 5 from
diseased hips on
22.04.1884
bd. at St. Andrews
Aller on 28.04.1884

Andrew Luxton
b. 29.01.1877 Aller
m. Elizabeth Martha Knowles
in parish church Kennington
Kent 24.06.1911.
"Lizzie" d. aged 78 at
Thornhill Chillenden near
Canterbury 5.04.1952.
Andrew d. Petham Canterbury
4.12.1952

Kathleen Louise Luxton
b. 12.06.1914
Chiddingstone Kent
m. Philip Howard Beadle
in parish church
Nonnington Kent
19.02.1941

Ada Mary Luxton
b. 22.10.1875 Aller
Ada d. aged 13 at
Taunton Somerset
Hospital 14.08.1889.
bd at St. Andrews Aller
on 22.08.1889

Edith Betty Luxton
b. 25.03.1912
Chiddingstone Kent
m. Harry Woodhead
in parish church
Nonnington Kent
12.08.1941. Edith
d.aged 75 in Dover in
2007

Lucy Ella Luxton
b. 1.03.1874 the Drove Aller
m. half cousin Alfred Herbert Lock
Luxton (1872-1952) son of William
Inder Luxton at St. Andrews Aller
12.09.1906.
Lucy d. aged 82 on 9.01.1956.
bd. at St. Andrews 15.,01.1956.
See William Inder Luxton (1846-1926)
for issue

George Inder Luxton
b. at Decoy Farm, High
Ham, Somerset on
17.09.1907.bp.at Aller on
27.10. 1907. Gerald, a
bachelor & retired farm
worker d. at Portcullis
House, Langport, Somerset
on 17. 11. 1978.

Richard Luxton
b. 12.6.1872 Aller
m. Susan Walsh, widow,
at St. Nicholas Church
Liverpool 5.09.1898.
Susan d. aged 48 in
Neston Cheshire
17.06.1907.
Richard d. aged 42 at
Union Infirmary, Poulton
cum-Spital 20.09.1914

Three children,
Andrew b 1906,
Oliver b 1908 and
Susan b. 1910 listed
as his children in 1911
Neston census were
most probably
illegitimate children of
Margaret Walsh, his
step-daughter.

Alfred Luxton = Betsy Lock   see TREE 18
(1836-1924)   (1839-1927)
Agricultural labourer of Aller Somerset

Note Kathleen Constance Luxton an adopted daughter of Alfred Luxton (1836-1924) m. William James Rowland Johns at Aller Som. on 15.03.1948

Albert Luxton b. 5.11.1880 Aller m. Emily Bond Woods at St. Andrews Aller on 19.10.1910 Albert d. at Bottoms Pilsbury, Langport, Som. 26.03.1955 and was bd. at St Andrews Aller 30.03.1955 Emily d. aged 77 in Yeovil Somerset on 25.04.1955 and was bd. at St Andrews Aller on 28.04.1955

Andrew John Bond Luxton b. 29.09.1911 m1. Margaret Eve Cox at Taunton Register Office 16.12.1936, div. 1947 m2. Agnes Margaret Sloley (1908-1991) in Taunton Register Office on 16.05.1953 Andrew of 36 Cleveland Street Taunton d on 14 February 1988. No issue by second marriage.

Geraldine Annie Bond Luxton b. 12.01.1913 Langport Som. bp. St Andrews Aller 27.04.1913 m. Alec Crossman on 21.09.1935 and had issue five daughters and two sons. "Aunty Sis" d. aged 94 on 6.02.2007 bd at St Mary's Huish Episcopi Langport on 16.02.2007

Isabel Ella Bond Luxton b. 17.02.1915 at Langport Somerset bp at St Andrews Aller on 8.06.1919 m1. William George Gosling (1911-1967) at St Andrews Aller on 10.09.1938 William d. January 1967 m2. Ernest W. Bailey on 14.05.1971 No issue of this marriage Isabel d. in Winchester in 2002

Richard Albert Bond Luxton b. 6.07.1920 Langport Som. m1. Joyce Mary Knight at St Cuthbert's Wick Road, Bristol 20.04.1946. Joyce d. 30.06.1972 Bristol W. Gen. m2. Doris Maud Lily Knight (nee Harwood) 1922-1985 d.aged 50 on 15.09.1973 at St John the Baptist, Keynsham, Somerset Richard d. 12.07.1992 in Bath

James Albert Bond Luxton b. 18.05.1947 in Taunton. A music teacher m. Valerie Burgess in Bristol on 11.07.1970

Gordon Bond Luxton b. 11.07.1948m. Christine Joy Bennett in Bristol on 23.05.1970. Lived in Bath divorced.d19.10.2016

Dennis George Bond Luxton b. 22.05.1937 at Greenway Farm Moorlinch, Huntspill, Bridgwater bp. 29.08.1937 Aller. Unmarried in June 1987 and may have changed his name to Cox.

Jean Margaret Bond Luxton b. 18.09.1938 at St Mary Stanley Nursing Home Bridgwater m. John James O'Neill at St John the Evangelist Winchester Hants on 1.07.1961. Jean was alive in 1987

William Inder Bond Luxton b. 28.02.1976 m. Sarah Ewing at Laugharne, Wales or 22.07.2000 Now they teach in N. Somerset

Samuel Bond Luxton b. 24.02.1978

James George Bond Luxton b. 15.12.1981 in Carmarthen.Home address Derlwyn, Llangynog, Carmarthen Now Lives in Cornwall

Emma Bond Luxton b. 31.10.1972 m Matt Taylor in Las Vegas 21.03 2002 sons Noah, Jett

Clare Bond Luxton b. 19.03.1974 m Alex Escott in Bath 6 3 2010

Neve b.11.6 2001

Alfred Henry Luxton = m1. Emma Jessie Baker   see TREE 22 Page 2
(1869-1952)   (1887-1914) "Jess" died in childbirth on 11.04.1914

Sergeant Major Instructor in Suffolk Yeomanry

Jesse Henry Herbert Luxton known as Herbert in the family b. 4.06.1908 Rumburgh Suffolk m1. Phyllis Emma Allen at Mutford Register Office East Suffolk on 26.10.1929. Divorced in or before WW2

m2. Elizabeth Honor Sawle (1905-1993) in St. Andrews Cairo on 1.06. 1943. Divorced after WW2. Elizabeth & children returned home from Australia to farm in St. Agnes Cornwall where she d. 16.08.1993.Jesse made a J.P. in Queensland in 1955.

m3 Christine Sheila Luxton (nee Gray) who had changed her name to Luxton at Ealing Register Office London on 17.10.1969. Jesse, retired Civil Pilot, of 117 Hastings Road, Battle, East Sussex d. 22|11.1994

Issue by Phyllis Emma Allen
Sheila Hilda Luxton b. 23.07.1930 Mutford Suffolk m. George Stanley Cable in parish church of Kirkley Suffolk on 14.03.1953. Lived in Lowestoft Suffolk. Issue Alexander, Roderick & Joanne

Issue by Elizabeth Honor

Susan Mary Luxton b. in Cairo in 1944 m. Richard Roy Barnicoat in the Parish Church of St. Agnes, Cornwall on 22.10.1966 Susan d. in St Agnes on 28.12.2006 Issue Liza, Andrew & Susan

John Sawle Luxton b. 12.06.1946 Redruth Cornwall. Changed his name to Sawle following parents divorce. An air pilot he lives near Truro with partner and two sons by his first wife. Issue Oliver and Thomas Sawle

Jesse also had issue by Neeltze Visser (1910-1981) a Dutch nurse on her way to Indonesia. He met her at Heliopolis Cairo in April 1946.

Anne Marie Visser b. 9.12.1946 in Jakarta Dutch East Indies. Marie lives in Amsterdam

Evelyn Ada Emma Luxton b. 27.01.1910 at London Road, Beccles, Wangford, Suffolk. m. Frank Arthur Hipperson at Paddington Register Office on 25.05.1948. Evelyn d. aged 43 of bronchitis and broncho-pneumonia on 17.11.1953 issue Margaret Edna Hipperson b. 1940

Rowland Albert Simon Luxton b. 18.10.1911 at Bawkeswell, Norfolk m. Pamela Ellen Paterson at Wangford Parish Church Suffolk on 5.02.1955. d. outside British Legion rooms, High Street, Wangford on 24.02.1976. No issue.

Alfred Henry Luxton = m2. Harriet Barbara Artis   see TREE 22 Page 2

(1869-1952)   (1882-1964) m. parish church of Sotterley, Suffolk 25.01.1916

Alfred of Brooklyn, Wangford, Suffolk d. on 21.05.1952

Harriet d. at 5 The Hill Wangford on 14.11.1964

John Alfred Luxton
b. 13.11.1920 Wangford Suffolk,
horseman
m1. Edith Alice Bealing 20, at St
Peters Stutton, Suffolk on
1.06.1940. Divorced.
m2. Kathleen Sago 32 (Peggy) at
the Register Office Lothingland,
Suffolk on 15.10.1955. Peggy
already had issue by her partner
Denis Cox, a merchant seaman,
killed on M.V. Harpagus at
Algiers on 5.08.1943.
Patricia Cox b. 20.08.1943.
d. February 2013.
John of 6 Hill Road, Wangford
d. 27.07.1977
Issue by Edith Alice Beale

Issue by Kathleen Sago

Clive Alfred Luxton
b. 17.07.1956

Caroline Ann Luxton
b. 25.08.1957
Caroline and her partner
Tony Baldock live in
New Zealand and have
issue Kate and Lawrence.

Barbara Mary Luxton
b. 31.12.1922
m. Albert R. Noble at
Wangford Parish Church,
Suffolk on 12.10.1963.
"Bertie" Noble d. aged 97
on 30 07.2011.
Barbara lives in Reyden,
Southwold, Suffolk

Maureen Mary
Luxton
b. 15.04.1941 at
Rectory Lodge
Tattingstone
d. 19.04.1941
aged 4 days.

Stephen John Luxton
b. 6.06.1943 at The Wonder, Tattingstone, Suffolk. Stephen, a corporal in the Air
Force m. Joyce Briggs at Lothingland Registry Office, Suffolk on 23.09.1967.
Divorced

Stewart Luxton, a chef in Provence,
France m. Laure a French girl in France
in February 2004.

Lilly Luxton
b. February 2006 in France

James Frederick Luxton = Mary Ann Fisher   see TREE 18 Page 2
(1847-1929)   (1844-1925) d. Joseph & Ann,born 18.01.1844 bp18.02.1844 West Buckland

Farmer at Aller Drove Somerset

Page 2 ⇧

Sarah Jane Luxton
Known as Sally
b. 22.02.1870 in Aller
m1. Henry Dean at
St. Swithian's parish
Church Lewisham Kent
on 2.08.1897.
Henry d. in 1898
m2.Arthur Edwards
By second husband she
had a girl Lily and
three boys. When
Arthur died Sally was
destitute and the boys
were sent to Canada in
early 1900s as part of
Dr Thomas Barnado's
British Child
Immigration
Programme.m3 Henry
Waight at St.
Thomas, West Ham on
20.08.1911. Sarah d.
of cancer 15th May
1918.

Adolphus Warfield Luxton
b. 9.12.1871 at the Drove Aller
m. Susan Burrows (1876-1950)
in the parish church Langport
Somerset on 4.02.1906.
Susan d. aged 74 at North Street
Langport on 20.11.1950
Adolphus d. aged 83 at North
Street on 17.02.1954. There was
no issue

Arthur Richard Luxton
b. 14.06.1874 as Ernest Richard
Luxton at the Drove Aller
m. as Arthur Richard Luxton to
Annie Gertrude Gollop in parish
church Great Canford Dorset on
22.06.1901.
Arthur d. 29.09.1945
Annie d. 1.02.1953. They lived in
Winton Bournemouth

Frederick Arthur Luxton
b. 22.11.1901 at Winters
Hill, Bishop's Waltham,
Hampshire
m. Dorothy Edith Hilda
Roberts at St Andrews
Bournemouth on
26.12.1928.
Frederick a retired cycle
dealer d. 1.08.1974 in
Branksore, Poole.
Cremated at North
Cemetery Bournemouth.
Dorothy b.
28.05.1904,of 53
Rosamund Road
Wolvercote Oxford
d. 28.08.1970

Leonard Oliver Luxton
b. 24.01.1907 in
Hankinson Road, Winton,
Bournemouth drowned in
the river Stour at
Wimbourne on 8.08.1923.

Ernest William Joseph Luxton
b. 2.12.1908
m. Agnes Edith May Keel
(1910-1995) in St Augustine
Bournemouth on 18.10.1933.
Ernest was cremated at North
Road Cemetery Bournemouth
on 11.02.1988. Agnes was
cremated on 1.12.1995.

Alfred Sidney Luxton
b. 27.09.1910
m. Mildred Dorothy Bower
(1910-2000) at Charminster
Road Congregational
Church on 27.03.1937
Alfred d. 4.01.1978 in
Dorchester and cremated
on 12.01.1978

Jean Elenor
b. 1.04.1943
Bournemouth

Anne Rosemary
b. 5.09.1946
Bournemouth
m. David Stanley Rogers
at Winton Congregational
Church Bournemouth on
28.10.1967

Eileen Beryl
b.21.08. 1941, schoolteacher,
m. Edward Newman Bangay
at Aberdeen Rd.
Congregational Church,
South Croydon on
17.08.1963

Gwendoline Christina
b.24.02.1945 in Poole
m. Leonard William
Onslow at Charminster Rd.,
Congregational Church,
Bournemouth
25.09.1965.Leonard
d. 08.2000

James Frederick Luxton = Mary Ann Fisher   see TREE 18 Page 2
(1847-1929)   (1844-1925)   See Chapter 47
Farmer at Aller Drove Somerset

Stephen Charles Luxton
b. 30.09.1877 at the Drove Aller
m. Bessie Otton (1877-1956) in
Independent Chapel, Somerton,
Somerset on 5.01.1911
Stephen of Canterbury Farm, Aller,
d. 22.01.1950 aged 72.
Bd at St Andrews Aller on 28.01.1950
Bessie d. aged 79 and was bd at
St Andrews Aller on 12.03.1956

Ivy Lucy Gertrude Luxton
b. 9.03.1912 at Canterbury Farm Aller
m. her cousin Clifford George Lewis Luxton at
Bridgwater Register Office on 20.12.1960
Clifford (1896-1969) of Canterbury Farm
d. 27.02.1969.bd at St Andrews Aller 2.03.1968.
Gertrude d. 12.11. 2000.

Lena Luxton (1880-1960) (also called Elena)
b. 7.05.1880
m. William George Lock (1877-1964) at Aller
on 31.07.1905
Issue a son William Adolphus George Lock
(Billy) b. 22.08.1906
m. Freda Miller and they had a son Richard
Lock in 1938. Lena died aged 80 at Whatley
Langport on 11.10.1960

John Luxton = Mary Redwood   see TREE 1
(1747-1818)   (1759-1812) Mary (Maria) d. of Francis & Mary Redwood bp. at Upton Somerset on 23.11.1759
Bd. at Petton 17.05.1812 aged 68(sic) but real age about 53

See Chapter 48   Yeoman Corner House Petton

Page 2 ⟶

John Luxton (1782-1837)
bp 20.01.1782 at St Mary
Magdalene Taunton.
John, a carpenter had
illegitimate issue by
Mary Garland.
m. Ann Webb at
St George's Wilton,
Somerset on 30.11.1801.
John of High Street
Taunton d. aged 55,
bd. at St Mary Magdalene
24.02.1837.
Ann d. aged 88 of senile
decay on 6.02.1867 at
Silver Street Ilminster.
issue

See TREE 26 &27

Joseph Luxton (1784-dead by 1818?)
bp 30.05.1784 at St Mary Magdalene
Taunton.
Joseph, a sawyer. m. Margaret
Powell, widow, at St. James Taunton
on 29.08.1814
Margaret d. aged 45 at Burton Square,
bd. at St. James Taunton 30.03.1835.
Joseph may have d. by 20.03.1818 as
he is not named in his father's will
issue

See TREE 31

Robert Luxton (1786-1871)
bp. 2.04.1786 at St. Petrock's Petton.
Robert, a carpenter/joiner,
m. Elizabeth Turner at St. Mary Magdalene
on 5.11.1810.
Elizabeth d. aged 75, bd. at St Mary
Magdalene 6.03.1865.
Robert of the Almshouse 4 Magdalene
Lane d. aged 84, bd. at St. Mary Magdalene
Taunton 17.08.1871.
issue

See TREE 35

Maria Luxton (1788-1854)
bp 2.03.1788 at St. Petrock's
Petton
m. Joseph Brewer (1785-1861)
on 15.02.1808 at St. John the
Baptist Bedminster, Somerset.
They lived at Frogpit Cottage
where Joseph, a labourer and
parish sexton had nine children
baptised at Petton.
Maria d. aged 66, bd 30.03.1854
at Petton
Joseph 76 bd 14.07.1861 at
Petton

John Luxton = Mary Redwood   see TREE 1

(1747-1818)   (1759-1812) d. of Francis & Mary Redwood bp. at Upton 23.11.1759.bd at Petton 17.05.1812

Yeoman Corner House Petton

William Luxton (1792-1851)
bp on 1.07.1792 at
St. Petrock's Petton.
Bachelor, lived with married
sister Mary Brewer at
Frogpit Cottage.
William d. aged 60 of
"Monomania twenty years,
Pneumonia three weeks" on
11.06.1851.
bd. at St. Petrock's on
15.06.1851.

James Luxton (1796-1869)
bp. 24.04.1796 at St. Michael's
Bampton. James a farmer,
m. Elizabeth Palfrey at St.
George's Morebath, Devon on
31.10.1816.
James d. aged 73 on 8.06.1869
following a tragic farming
accident when he fell and
wagon wheels passed over both
legs. He was bd.at Skilgate
13.06 1869.
Elizabeth d. aged 87.
bd. at Skilgate 23.02.1873
issue
See TREE 39

Thomas Luxton (1798-1856)
bp. 21.09.1798 at Petton. Farm
labourer, m. Ann Cooksley at
Upton Somerset on 15.04.1831.
Thomas d. aged 58 at Taunton
Hospital on 3.12.1856 following
an "amputation for malignant
disease of leg".
bd. at Petton on 14.12.1856
Ann m2. James Stone,
wheelwright at St Mary
Magdalene Taunton 12.11.1866
issue
See TREE 43

George Luxton (1802-1891)
bp 2.02.1802 at Raddington
Somerset.
George, a mason, had m. his
wife Anne by 1831
Ann (c1798-1879) Claypit,
Morebath, d. aged 82,
bd at Morebath 17.05.1879.
George aged 89
d. 16.04.1891.
bd at St Georges, Morebath
21.08.1891
issue
See TREE 44

Francis Luxton
bp 3.08.1803 at
St. Petrock's Petton.
d. aged 4 and bd at
Petton on
14.02.1808.He was
named after maternal
grandfather.

see TREE 25

Page 2 ⇧

TREE 26

Page 1   See Chapter 49 & 50

John Luxton
(1782-1837)

Carpenter in High Street Taunton. Illegitimate issue by Mary Garland

John Garland (1800-1860) alias Luxton
bp as John son of Mary Garland on 25.12.1800 at St. Mary Magdalene, Taunton.
John Garland alias Luxton m. Sarah Goodman (1801-1842) at St. Mary Magdalene
Taunton on 14.01.1822. They lived in Upper High Street Taunton and John, a labourer,
became a foreman in a silk factory.
Sarah d. aged 41 on Christmas Day 1842 in child birth.
John of Woodford Buildings d. aged 61 and was bd at St. Mary Magdalene on 9.06.1860

Caroline Luxton	Jane Luxton	Mary Ann Luxton	Thomas Luxton (c1849-)	Eliza Luxton	Sarah Garland Luxton
b.24.05.1821 bp 19.05.1823 at Paul Street Independent Chapel Taunton. Caroline, a shoe binder, m. Anthony Mockridge, a mason, at Taunton Register Office on 5.10.1862. Caroline who had Brights disease 3 years d. aged 63 at Eastbrook Pitminster 8.08.1884	bp. 19.05.1823 at Paul Street Independent Chapel Taunton m. Charles Batson, servant, at Taunton Register Office on 15.02.1846. Charles d. Oct1862 Jane 66 widow needlewoman was inmate in Taunton Workhouse in 1891 .	bp. 11.09.1825 at Paul Street Independent Chapel Taunton. Mary, a silk throwster, m. James Samuel Seaman, whitesmith, in Taunton Register Office on 14.11.1852.Mary d. Upper High St. 29.11. 1889.	Illegitimate son. In 1851 is listed with mother in High Street Taunton. When his mother m. he changed his name to Thomas Seaman. He m. Mary Jane Long at St. Mary Magdalene on 10.03.1872 and is recorded with four daughters in 1881 St Mary Magdalene census	bp. 27.12.1827 at Paul Street Independent Chapel Taunton Eliza, a silk throwster, m. William Turner, a cabinet maker, at Taunton Register Office on 29.08.1852 Eliza Turner d.aged 44 in Tangier Bishops Hull 8.08.1872.	bp. 25.12.1830 at Paul Street Independent Chapel Taunton. Sarah, silk throwster, m. Richard Gosling, 25, bricklayer, in St James Taunton on 11.09.1854.Sarah d. aged 53 from "Stoppage of bowels-shock" in High Street Taunton 13.09.1883. Richard d. in 1898.

John Luxton
(1782-1837)

see TREE 25

Carpenter in High Street Taunton. Illegitimate issue by Mary Garland

See Chapter 49, 50 & 51

John Garland (1800-1860) alias Luxton
bp as John son of Mary Garland on 25.12.1800 at St. Mary Magdalene, Taunton.
John Garland alias Luxton 20 (sic) m. Charles Hooper in Holy Trinity
John Garland alias Luxton m. Sarah Goodman (1801-1842) at St. Mary Magdalene
Taunton on 14.01.1822. They lived in Upper High Street Taunton and John, a labourer,
became a foreman in a silk factory.
Sarah d. aged 41 on Christmas Day 1842 in child birth.
John of Woodford Buildings d. aged 61 and was bd at St. Mary Magdalene on 9.06.1860

Maria Garland Luxton	Emma Garland Luxton	Selina Garland Luxton	John Luxton
bp. 25.12.1832 at Paul Street	bp. 25.12.1835 Paul Street Independent Chapel Taunton.	b. January 1838 and bp. 16.04.1838	bp 25.12.1840 at Paul
Independent Chapel Taunton	Emma Luxton 20 (sic) m. Charles Hooper in Holy Trinity	at Paul Street Independent Meeting	Street Independent
Maria, a silk throwster,	Taunton on 28.10.1866.	House, Taunton.	Chapel Taunton John, a
witnessed sister Sarah's	Emma Luxton of Pitminster Som. had illegitimate issue	Selina, a silk throwster, m. William	mason's labourer,
wedding in September 1854		Hayman, shoemaker, in St. James,	m. Mary Jane Smith at
		Taunton 13.09.1863. Selina Hayman	St. Mary Magdalene on
	William Easton Luxton (1865-1921)	d. of fracture of skull 4.05. 1908	11.08.1861.
	b. 4.02.1865 at Eastbrook, Pitminster &bp 25.06.1865 at Trull, Somerset.		John d. aged 63
	William, mason, m. Emma Jane Oaten at Pitminster on 17.06.1885.	John Luxton (1860-1944)	"Exhaustion Epitheliona
	William of Comeytrowe Road Trull d. 6.03.21 and bd. at Trull on	b. illegitimate 19.05.1860 in Union	of one month" at 25
	12.03.1921. Emma d. aged 88 on 6.06.1852	Workhouse Taunton. Soldier for	Stephen Street, Taunton
		12 years, served in Egyptian	on 7.11.1905.
		Campaign & the Nile Expedition	Mary Jane d. aged 85 at

Etty Luxton	Louise Florence	Sidney Luxton	Emma Frances		m. Susan Ann Manley at	21 Tancred Street
bp. 30.05.1886	b. 30.12.1887	bp 5.01.1890 at	bp. 6.12.1891 at		Clayhidon Devon on 2.11.1885.	Taunton on 5.03.1929
Pitminster	bp. 29.01.1888 Pitminster	Pitminster	Pitminster m.		John d. aged 84 in Holmoor House	
m. Walter James	m. Henry Charles Vicary,	d. aged 3	Leonard Robert		Taunton on 9.12.1944.	See TREE 27
Vicary at Trull	foreman, at Trull on	bd. 1.02.1893	Bickham at Trull		Susan d. aged 84 in Holmoor	
10.07.1907.	26.06.1912. She d. in	at Pitminster	14.02.1915.		House on 25.11.1946	
Etty d. 27.04. 1934	Bristol 10.12. 1970		She d. 1985		No issue	

John Luxton = Mary Jane Smith   see TREE 26
(1840–1905)   (1844–1929)d of John Smith, a sawyer, she d. aged 85 in Tancred Street Taunton 5.03.1929
bp. at St Paul Street Independent Meeting House 25.12.1840,d in Stephen Street 5.03.1905
Masons labourer Taunton

See Chapter 50 & 52

SarahJane Luxton
bp. 8.06.1862 at Trull
m.1CharlesLittlejohns
a mason, St. Mary
Magdalene, Taunton
23.08.1880.
Charles d. April 1902
2Wm Smith in St
Teilo's Cardiff on 18.
04. 1908.

WilliamJohn Luxton
(1864-1924) bp.12
.06.1864 at St. John's
Taunton. Bricklayer
m. 1 Ellen White in
Cardiff on 24. 12
1883.Ellen 34 bd
Cardiff 5.06.1902.
m.2 Jane Betty Chard
Williamd.27.08.1924
in Cardiff. see tree 28

Eliza Luxton
b. 17.02.1866 at
Shuttern Taunton.
Eliza, a collar
machinist, m. Henry
Ellett, bricklayer, at
St. James Taunton on
23.09.1883.Eliza d.at
Denmark Place,St.
James, Taunton on
12.06.1889

Emma Luxton
b. 31.07.1868 at
Shuttern Taunton
m. William Arthur
Williams, mariner,
at St. James
Taunton
on 9.09.1889

Alice Luxton
b. 16.08.1870 at
Shuttern St Mary
Magdalene Taunton
m. Edwin Bishop
Harding, carpenter, at
Barton Registry
Office, Bristol on
20.05.1893.Alice of
17 Laburnam Street
Taunton d.3.1.1939

George Edward Luxton (1872-1946)
b. 17.04.1872 at North Street, Taunton
bp. Edward George Luxton at St Mary
Magdalene 22.12.1872. George, a
carpenter, m. Elizabeth Martin in
Taunton Register Office on 19.05.1895
George d. aged 76 at 4 Pilton Quay,
Pilton East, Barnstaple, Devon on
3.09.1946
Elizabeth d. aged 83 at Sticklepath,
Tavistock, Devon on 15.04.1955.

Beatrice Luxton
b. 11.03.1903 at
5 Court, James St.,
Taunton
m. John Jewell,
general labourer, at
Barnstaple Register
Office on
14.04.1928.
Beatrice d. in
Barnstaple in June
1994.

John Luxton
b. 30.12.1901
at 5 Court
James Street
d. aged 15
months of
whooping
cough and
pneumonia
22.04.1903

Edith May
b. 13.08.1900
at 5 Court
James Street,
Taunton
m. Arthur
Edward Paull
in Pilton,
Barnstaple on
23.04.1923

Frederick Charles Luxton (1899-1965)
b. 5.08.1899 at 5 Court James Street Taunton
m1. Florence Minnie Barrow in Barnstaple
Register Office on 9.01.1923. Florence d. aged
28 in Barnstaple on 8.07.1928
m2. Mary Jane Jones (nee West) 42, widow, at
Barnstaple Register Office on 11.09.1929
Frederick d. aged 66 in Barnstaple on
7.12.1965. Mary d in Barnstaple on 7.04.1969.
Issue by Florence Minnie Barrow

Amy Jane Luxton
b. 4.08.1898 at
home 5 Court
James St. Taunton
d. aged 14 months
at home from
convulsions 3
hours on
27.10.1899 .

Henry George
Luxton
b. 15.01 1897 at
5 Court James
Street Taunton
d. aged 7months
from "Diarrhoea
7 days
Exhaustion" on
4 .09.1897

James
George
Luxton
b.c.1892
d aged 7months

Phyllis Irene Luxton
b. 7.04.1923 at 5 Buller Road, Barnstaple.
d. aged 17 months on 3.10.1924

Joan Margaret Alexandra Luxton
b. 27.06.1924 at 2 Bradiford, Pilton East, Barnstaple.
Joan Margaret Luxton 21,spinster, WAAF, 17 Vicarage Lawn, Barnstaple,
m. Ronald Bridger,27, clerk of 7 Alexandra Place in Jesmond Parish Church,
Newcastle 20.05.1946

TREE 27

John Luxton = Mary Jane Smith   see TREE 26   (1844--1929)d of John Smith, a sawyer, she d. aged 85 in Tancred Street Taunton on 5.03.1929

(1840-1905)

Mason's labourer Taunton   See Chapter 50

Frederick Luxton
bp. 25.04.1875 at St.
Mary Magdalene,
Taunton
d. aged 11 weeks from
bronchitis in North
Street Taunton on
10.06.1875

Albert Luxton
bp 25.06.1876 at
St. Mary
Magdalene Taunton
d. of convulsions
aged 9 months in
North Street on
26.01.1877

Florry Luxton
bp. 7.04.1878 at St. Mary
Magdalene Taunton
m.1 William Harris at St James
Taunton on Christmas Day 1898.
2 Sidney H Crocker in St. James
Taunton on 22.06. 1921. Florrie
d.aged 63 at 21 Tancred Street,
Taunton on 19. 01.1941.

Charles Luxton
bp.4.07.1880 at
St. Mary Magdalene Taunton
d. aged 11 months at North St.
bd. at St. Mary Magdalene on
2.04.1881

Albert Luxton
b. c.1880 but cannot find his birth
in St Catherines House Index.
Albert aged 11, a silk worker, in
the 1891 census, lived with his
parents and siblings in Denmark
Cottages St. James, Taunton.

Ivy Luxton
b. 22.05.1905 at
5 Court James Street,
Taunton
m. Frederick William
Hill Lance Corporal
Prince of Wales
Volunteers at
Barnstaple on
18.12.1929.Ivy d. aged
42 of breast cancer
14.08. 1947 at 4
Reform Street, Pilton.

Harold George Luxton
b. 22.02.1907 in Taunton
Harold, a baker & confectioner of
Purley Surrey m. Margaret Annie Clark
at St. Mary's Thatcham Berkshire on
27.03.1937. Harold, a retired master
baker, 11 Greenlands Road Newbury,
Berkshire d. 8.12.1992. Margaret
Annie (1912-1997) retired bakery
proprieter
d. 9.12.1997.

| |

Roger David Luxton
b. 31.01.1938 in Newbury
Berkshire was living in the
town in 1997

Ethel Lily Luxton
b. 12.01.1909 at 51
Winchester Street
Taunton. Her father was
serving as a lance
corporal in Royal
Engineers when Ethel d.
aged 8 of acute
meningitis on 1.04.1917

William George Luxton
b. 4.02.1911 at 51
Winchester Street
Taunton
d. of exhaustion enteritis
aged 6 months on the
7.08.1911

Kitty Elizabeth Luxton
b. 28.09.1912 at 51
Winchester Street Taunton
m. Robert Malcolm
England, clerk, of
Sticklepath, at Parish
Church Pilton Barnstaple
Devon on 17.12.1932.
Kitty d. in August 1991 in
Barnstaple.

TREE 28
Page 1

William John Luxton=m1 Ellen White, m2 Jane Betty   see TREE 27   Page 2
(1864-1924)   (1868-1902) d of John White & wife Susan Summerhayes
Ellen d of TB on 31st May 1902,bd at St John's Cardiff
Mason and Bricklayer Taunton and Cardiff

See Chapter 52

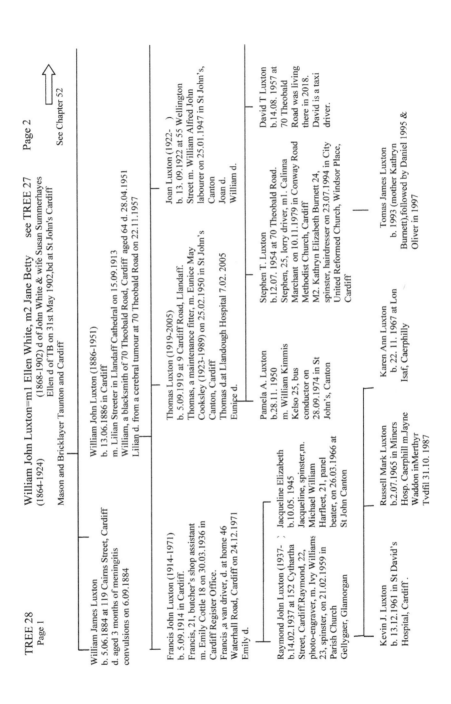

William James Luxton
b. 5.06.1884 at 119 Cairns Street, Cardiff
d. aged 3 months of meningitis
convulsions on 6.09.1884

William John Luxton (1886-1951)
b. 13.06.1886 in Cardiff
m. Lilian Streeter in Llandaff Cathedral on 15.09.1913
William, a blacksmith of '70 Theobald Road, Cardiff aged 64 d. 28.04.1951
Lilian d. from a cerebral tumour at 70 Theobald Road on 22.11.1957

Joan Luxton (1922-   )
b. 13. 09.1922 at 55 Wellington
Street m. William Alfred John
labourer on 25.01.1947 in St John's,
Canton
Joan d.
William d.

Francis John Luxton (1914-1971)
b. 5.09.1914 in Cardiff.
Francis, 21, butcher's shop assistant
m. Emily Cottle 18 on 30.03.1936 in
Cardiff Register Office.
Francis ,a van driver, d. at home 46
Waterhall Road, Cardiff on 24.12.1971
Emily d.

Thomas Luxton (1919-2005)
b. 5.09.1919 at 9 Cardiff Road, Llandaff.
Thomas, a maintenance fitter, m. Eunice May
Cooksley (1923-1989) on 25.02.1950 in St John's
Canton, Cardiff
Thomas d.at Llandough Hospital 7.02. 2005
Eunice d.

Stephen T. Luxton
b.12.07. 1954 at 70 Theobald Road.
Stephen, 25, lorry driver, m1. Calinna
Marchant on 10.11.1979 in Conway Road
Methodist Church, Cardiff
M2. Kathryn Elizabeth Burnett 24,
spinster, hairdresser on 23.07.1994 in City
United Reformed Church, Windsor Place,
Cardiff

David T Luxton
b.14.08. 1957 at
70 Theobald
Road was living
there in 2018.
David is a taxi
driver.

Pamela A. Luxton
b.28.11. 1950
m. William Kimmis
Kelso 25, bus
conductor on
28.09.1974 in St
John's, Canton

Tomas James Luxton
b. 1993 (mother Kathryn
Burnett),followed by Daniel 1995 &
Oliver in 1997

Jacqueline Elizabeth
b.10.05. 1945
Jacqueline, spinster,m.
Michael William
Harfleet, 21, panel
beater, on 26.03.1966 at
St John Canton

Raymond John Luxton (1937-)
b.14.02.1937 at 152 Cythartha
Street, Cardiff.Raymond, 22,
photo-engraver, m. Ivy Williams
23, spinster, on 21.02.1959 in
Parish Church
Gellygaer, Glamorgan

Karen Ann Luxton
b. 22. 11. 1967 at Lon
Isaf, Caerphilly

Russell Mark Luxton
b.2.07.1965 in Miners
Hosp. Caerphill m.Jayne
Waddon inMerthyr
Tvdfil 31.10. 1987

Kevin J. Luxton
b. 13.12.1961 in St David's
Hospital, Cardiff .

TREE 28
Page 2   See Chapter 52

William John Luxton=m1 Ellen White, m2 Jane Betty   see TREE 27 Page 1
(1864-1924)   (1869-1937) born in Chard d of Richard & Jane Betty

Mason and Bricklayer Taunton and Cardiff

Ernest Bertie Luxton (1891-1960)
b. 29.07.1891 in Cardiff and bap. At St. Mary Magdalene Taunton son of William John and Ellen Luxton, mason on 10.08.1892 while his parents were residing at Coal Orchard, Taunton. Elsie Lilian Roles in Cardiff Register Office on 15.04.1911.In W.W.1 he was a sapper in R.E. but was later transferred to the Royal Northumberland Fusiliers.
Ernest, a retired Builders merchants of 124 Fairwater Grove East Cardiff d. aged 68 on 19.01.1960. Lilian Elsie Roles b.27.07.1887 d. 2.11.1978

James Luxton (1917-1983)
b.3.01. 1917 in Ann Street Cardiff
Aged 28 serving in H.M.Forces
m. Phyllis Martin, b 5.03.1922
Cardiff, 23, spinster of
8 Adam Street, Cardiff in Llandaff
Cathedral on 19.06.1945
James d.1983 aged 66 on
17.01.1983
Phyllis d. on 16.04.1985

Kenneth Luxton (1919-1970)
b. 1.09.1919 in Cardiff
m. Beryl Lloyd-Jones Sept 1960
in Cardiff
Kenneth d. 12.1970

Kenneth Jonothan Luxton
b. 22.08.1964

Jennie Z.L.Luxton
b. 1961 Cardiff

Ernest Bert Luxton (1913-1930) bp at
St. Saviour's Roath Cardiff on 27.11.
1913. d. aged 17 on 24.11.1930 at
Cardiff Royal Infirmary from a
cerebral abscess and cardiac failure

William John Luxton (1912-1977)
b. 19.03.1912 at 33 Coveny Street,
Cardiff32 bachelor serving in
H.M.Forces m. Elise Nora Folkes
34, spinster, of Colwyn Bay, in
Llandaff Cathedral on 6.11.1944.
William otherwise Jack of 1 Carter
Place d. 27. 03.1977.
Elise d. aged 52 from breast cancer
on 18.09.1962

Joanna Lilian Luxton (1950-   )
b. 4.06.1950 at 8 Hazel Road, Cardiff
28 spinster, civil servant
m. Grantley Thomas Griffiths, b. 1952
Cardiff, 27, civil servant on 19.05.1979 in St.
Augustines, Rumney, South Glamorgan

Hazel J. Luxton (1946-   )
b. at 68 Connaught Road,
Cardiff on 5.10. 1946

John Luxton = Ann Webb   see TREE 25 Page 1
(1780-1867)   (1782-1837)
d. of John & Mary bp.20.11.1780 at Abenhall, Gloucestershire
d.aged88 of senile decay on 6.02.1867 at Silver Street Ilminster
Carpenter and builder in High Street Taunton

Page 2

James Luxton (1802-1853)
bp 4.07.1802 at St Mary Magdalene Taunton
m. Mary Ann Bennett at St. Mary Magdalene on 23.06.1822.
James of Twiles Court Paul Street Taunton, a carpenter, d. aged 51 of 'gangrene of foot, exhaustion' on 30.05.1853. Mary Ann was a beer retailer in Upper High Street in 1859 and 71 year old widow and upholstress living in George Court St. Martins London in 1871.d. 20.06.1873

Sarah Luxton (1805-1841)
bp 16.06.1805 at St. Mary Magdalene Taunton.Sarah, a teacher in Midsomer Norton, Somerset, m. Thomas Collier, carpenter in Clutton Register Office, Somerset on 31.05.1838. Sarah bd 18.04.1841 at Stratton on Fosse

William Luxton (1807-1878)
bp. 29.03.1807 at St. Mary Magdalene Taunton
m. Hannah Paull at St Mary Magdalene Taunton on 29.03.1832. In 1861 William, a carpenter and master builder was proprietor of houses in Taunton. William d. on 16.07.1878. Hannah d. on 10.11.1886

John Luxton (c1808/10-1869)
bp. 4.04.1813 at St. Mary Magdalene Taunton
m. Susan White in the parish church Ilminster on the 16.12.1833.
John, a hairdresser, aged 61 suffered a stroke which left him paralysed down his right side.
John d. in Silver Street Ilminster on 3.11.1869 and bd. in the Unitarian burial ground on the 9.11.1869.
Susan d. at Langport Street Ilminster on 1.02.1882

See TREE 30

Anne Luxton
b. 23.03.1823 in Taunton bp. at St. George's Catholic Church Taunton on 30.03.1823. Ann (sic) Luxton aged 1 bd at St. Mary Magdalene on 7.04.1824

Marianne Luxton
b. 14.01.1825 in Taunton bp 28.01.1825 at St. George's Catholic Church Taunton. A dressmaker and needle woman, she was living with mother at George Court, St Martin's London in 1871.

James Luxton (1827-1905)
b. 15.07.1827 in Taunton, bp 23.07.1827 at St. George's Catholic Church Taunton. James, an inn keeper of the Green Dragon, High Street, Taunton m. Mary Ann Waterman Radnedge at St. George's Church, Ruishton on 20.02.1855. They moved to London where James was a cab driver. Mary d. aged 69 in Black Horse Lane Taunton on 8.09.1899. James d. aged 77 in Cushuish Cothelstone Bishop's Lydeard, Taunton on 13.01.1905

William James Luxton (1857-)
b. 9.06.1857 at New Road, Bishop's Hull, Taunton
m. Mary Ann Young at St. Stephen's Westminster on 17.04.1887. Mary Ann d. aged 48 of chronic Bright disease at 13 St. Leonard Street, Pimlico on 28.04.1910. William, a lamp maker in 1887-1901, was a fish hawker in 1911 living at 9 Warwick Place Westminster.

Mary Ann Radnege Luxton (1860- 1935)
b. 29.01.1860 at Pigmarket Taunton,
bp 6.12.1863 at Westminster St. John the Evangelist Drury Lane. Mary Ann, a dressmaker, returned to the West Country with parents in 1890s
m. George Kidner, a shepherd, in parish church of Kingston Somerset on 6.04.1902 Mary d. Holmoor House Taunton 31.01.1935 aged 75. Illeg. Infant son Walter James Luxton bd. 16.01.1889 at Norton Fitzwarren

Emily Alice Luxton
b. c 1892 York Street, Westminster.

John Luxton = Ann Webb   see TREE 25 Page 1
(1782-1837)   (1780-1867)
Carpenter and builder in High Street Taunton

See Chapter 49 & 57

Mary Luxton
bp. 4.04.1813 at St. Mary Magdalene
d. aged 1 and bd at St. Mary Magdalene
on 7.04.1814

Joseph Luxton (1817-1879)
bp 23.02.1817 at St Mary
Magdalene Taunton.
Joseph, a grocer and tea dealer, 8
Saville Row, Bath m. Sarah
Howell at St. Swithin's, Walcot,
Bath on 30.01.1844. They lived
at 6 Bennett Street where Joseph
d. aged 60 on 5.06.1879.
Sarah d. aged 59 on 2.06.1878

No issue.

Elizabeth Luxton (1819-1880)
bp 13.06.1819 at St. Mary
Magdalene. Settled in Bath with
her brother. m. same day in
St.Swithins, Walcot to Thomas
Burrow confectioner, of 12 Peter
Street Bristol on 30.01.1844.
They ran a tailor and drapery
business in Stapleton Road
Bristol. Elizabeth d. aged 60 at
7 Blackbirds Place Bristol on
8.09.1880.

Mary Ann Luxton (1822-1864)
Of Church Square, bp 11.04.1822 at
St. Mary Magdalene.
Mary Ann, a dressmaker, aged 29, was
living with her elder brother James and
family at Twiles Court Paul Street in
1851. m. William Wilkinson (1811-
1885), whipmaker, at Old Church, St
Pancras Parish Chapel, Camden on
1.06.1859.Mary died of breast cancer at
58 Grove Street Camden 22.03.1864.
She had issue with William, Mary Ann
in 1860 and Susan Maria in 1862

Fanny Sarah Luxton
b. 24.12.1842 at Hunt Court,
St. Mary Magdalene,
bp. 15.08.1844 at St. Mary
Magdalene, Taunton. Fanny
d. aged 8. 'diseased
mesenteric glands, Peritonis
10 days' in Paul Street

TREE 30
See Chapter 54, 55 & 56

John Luxton = Susan White   see TREE 29 Page 1
(c.1808/10-1869)   (1806-1882)Susannah d. of John White & Mary his wife, born 14.04.1806, bp.18.05.1806 in the
Old Meeting Unitarian Chapel, Ilminster, d. aged 75 in Langport Street Ilminster on 1.02.1882
Hairdresser in Ilminster

Mary Anne Luxton
b. 28.10.1834,
bp 28.11.1834 at Old Meeting
Unitarian Chapel, Ilminster
d. aged 5½ of scarlet fever
on 22.12.1839
bd. in Unitarian Chapel on
27.12.1839

John White Luxton (1837-1871)
bp. June 1837 at Old Meeting Unitarian Chapel
Ilminster. John, a hairdresser in South Petherton
m. Elizabeth Davies 27, Scholastic teacher, in
May Street Unitarian Chapel Taunton on
30.01.1862. John d aged 33 of pneumonia on
5.04.1871. Elizabeth Davies, School House,
Warkleigh Umberleigh Devon d. 18.04.1920

William White Luxton
b. 22.07.1839 in Ilminster
d. aged 5 months of scarlet
fever on 24.12.1839. William
aged 6 months (sic) bd at
Ilminster Unitarian Chapel on
27.12.1839

Elizabeth Winstone Luxton
b. 24.02.1841 in Ilminster
m. Edgar James Parrett, 25, ironmonger in the Unitarian's 'Old
Meeting' Ilminster on 20.02.1870
Elizabeth d. aged 38 on 18.01.1881
bd. at Ilminster Unitarian Chapel on
24.01.1881 Issue five children

Ellen Luxton
b. 1.03.1863 in South
Petherton
m. Joseph Goldsworthy,
time-keeper, in parish
church of St. John the
Baptist, Bathwick,
Somerset 9.10.1886

William Joseph Luxton (1864-1945)
b. 20.11.1864 at South Petherton
m. Augusta Sarah Grant at St.
Catherines Ventnor, Isle of Wight on
8.10.1891. William, a retired
commercial traveller d. aged 80 at
Thornhill Road Plymouth on
6.11.1945. Augusta d. 10.09.1954

Bertha May Luxton
b. 20.08.1866 in
South Petherton.
Bertha, schoolmistress and
spinster d. 22.10.1945 in
Plymouth City Hospital

Kate Luxton (1869-1960)
b. 10.01.1869 in South
Petherton, Som.
m. Albert James Lock,
sergeant 4th Dragoon
Guards, St. Augustines
Kingston on Hull on
19.08.1905. Kate d.
18.09.1960 Croydon

John Harold Luxton
b. 19.06.1870 at South
Petherton. A Sergeant in
the 7th Battalion Imperial
Yeomanry, he was killed at
Vlakfontain, South Africa
on 29.05.1901 during
Second Boer War

Gladys Augusta Luxton
b. 31.10.1892 Bristol
m. Ernest Walker
Dexter in parish church
of Emmanuel,
Compton Gifford,
Devon on 1.08.1927
They lived in Paignton.
Gladys d. 26.09.1971

Doris Isabel Luxton
b. 24.05.1894 Bristol
m. Joseph Charles
Wiggs in parish
church of Emmanuel,
Compton Gifford,
Devon on 28.06.1924
Doris d. 13.04.1965

Harold Ewart Luxton (1901-1973)
b. 11.10.1901 at 5 Thornhill Road, Plymouth.
Harold, master mariner, m1. Nora Endicott 24 in
parish church of Emmanuel Compton Gifford
Devon on 31.05.1929 Nora d. aged 25
12.06.1930. m2 Hettie Bailey, 31 in Register
Office Devonport 20.07.1932. Harold, a retired
master mariner, d. at 13 Hanover Court, Walton-
on-the-Naze on 16.03.1973. Hettie d. 9.09.1981.

Donovan Grant Luxton (1904-1977)
b. 29.06.1904 5 Thornhill Road, Plymouth.
Don, a motor mechanic owning his own
garage in Plymouth, m. Sybil Reed, 26, at
Plymouth Register Office on 9.12.1944. They
divorced about 1956.
Don d. in Plymouth on 13.05.1977

Christopher Marcus Paul Luxton, b. 29.03.1945 at North
Friary Nursing Home Plymouth. An analytical chemist,
m1. Gillian Wendy Anne Nicholls 20.12.1969 Dartford
m2. Brenda Ellen Parker 19.12.1981 Gravesend.
They live in Gravesend Kent and have daughter Jane

Heather Celia Luxton, b. 23.04.1933 at 34 William Street Devonport
m. Colin Charles Smith in St. Mary Parish Church Penzance Cornwall on 16.04.1960
In 1981 they lived at Kirby-le-Soken, Frinton on Sea, Essex

TREE 31
See Chapter 48,58 & 59

Joseph Luxton = Margaret Powell (nee Gore)   see TREE 25 Page 1
(1784-alive 1816)   (1783-1835) born Peggy Gore d. of Francis & Elizabeth on 9.07.1783.bp at St James Taunton 25.11.1783
(known as Peggy, lived with son Charles in Burton Square when she d. in 1835)
Sawyer in Taunton

Charles Luxton (1813-1885)
Family Bible records b. 3.11.1813 in Taunton.
Illegitimate son of Margaret Powell, widow, bp 9.01.1814 at St. James Taunton.
m. Charlotte Townsend at St. James Taunton on 18.08.1833.
Charles, a lace maker and Bible Christian, moved from Taunton to Tiverton about 1845. Charles aged 72 d. at Westexe Street, Tiverton on 8.07.1885.
Charlotte d. aged 73 on 25.11.1886.

Robert Luxton (1816-1872)
bp. 21.01.1816 at St. James, Taunton.
m. Olive Drew in Parish of Holy Trinity (St. Philip & Jacob) in Bristol on 2.05.1841
Robert, railway labourer, d. at Vinegar Hill, Bideford on 25.11.1872
Olivia (sic) m. George Langmead, shipwright, in Bideford Parish Church on 15.11.1875
No issue.

Eliza Goar Luxton
b. 18.12.1833 Taunton, bp 24.08.1834 at St. James Taunton when her parents lived in Burton Square. Eliza d. aged 12 on 14.08.1845. bd. in non-conformist plot at St. Peter's Church Tiverton on 24.08.1845

William Charles Luxton
b. 4.02.1836 in Taunton, bp. 22.05.1836 at St. James Taunton when his parents lived in Concord Place Taunton
William, a lace hand, m. Elizabeth Ellen Newberry at Chard Somerset on 18.02.1854. They moved to Nottingham in years 1879-1881.
William of Kentwood Road, Nottingham, d. 15.07.1912.
Elizabeth d. aged 83, 20.08.1919
See TREE 32

James Rechab Luxton
b. 2.01.1841 Concord Place, St. James Taunton
m. Hannah Maria Hawkins in St. John's Church, parish of St. John Surrey 11.05.1874. James, an army pensioner & rural postman d. aged 45 from valvular heart disease at Villa Franca Cottage Tiverton 2.09.1886
Maria d. aged 72 at Heathcoat Square Tiverton 2.08.1912
See TREE 34

Alfred Luxton
b. 8.07.1838 Taunton
d. aged 2 at Concord Place on 19.10.1840. bd. 25.10.1840 at St. James Taunton

Alfred Luxton (1843-1875)
b. 22.04.1843, bp. at Wesleyan Chapel Taunton.
Alfred, a private in the Marine Artillery d. aged 33 from chronic asthma and bronchitis at Westexe Tiverton on 7.05.1875. bd. in Tiverton 14.05.1875

Robert Luxton
b. 12.09.1846 in Tiverton.
bp. 27.09.1846 aged 2 weeks at Wesleyan Methodist Chapel Tiverton.
d. 20.10.1847

Ellen Margaret
b. 27.10.1847
bp. 7.11.1847 in Wesleyan Methodist Chapel Tiverton
d. aged 2 30.07.1849 bd. non-conformist plot St.Peter's Tiverton 5.08.1849

Elizabeth Luxton
b. 25.02.1850
bp. 24.03.1850 in Tiverton Wesleyan Methodist Chapel
d. aged 9 months on 21.09.1851.bd. in non-conformist Plot St. Peter's Tiverton

Emily Luxton
b. 3.12.1852 Tiverton
Emily Luxton 69, spinster, formerly a silk winder in lace factory d. 9.02.1922 at 6 Elm Terrace, Leat Street, Tiverton

William Charles Luxton = Elizabeth Ellen Newberry   see TREE 31
(1836-1912)   (1836-1919) d. of William & Louisa born Bridport Dorset on 3.08.1836

page 2 ⇧

Lace Worker of Chard and Nottingham

Ellen Matilda Luxton
b. 2.09.1855 in Chard
d. aged 3 of
"malignant scarlet
fever 5 days" in Perry
Street Chard on
16.10.1858. bd at St.
Mary's Chard
19.10.1858

Eliza Luxton (1857-1952)
b. 3.07.1857 in Chard
Eliza, a nurse in Great
Western Railway Hospital
Swindon m. James Notley
at St. Mark's Swindon on
22.12.1883.
Eliza Notley d.aged 95 at
St. Margaret's Hospital
Swindon on 22.07.1952.
bd. at Radnor Street
Cemetery, Swindon.
Issue three daughters and
a son.

William James Luxton (1859-1929)
b. 5.02.1859 in Chard Somerset
William a lace maker of plain net
m1. Lydia Hayball in Chard Parish
Church on 22.12.1878. Lydia d. aged
58 at 16 Herbert Street Nottingham
on 14.04.1918
m2. Susan Wilkinson (nee Mankin)
widow at Nottingham Register
Office on 21.08.1919.
Susan d. 5.12.1926.
William of 23 Beckenham Road
Nottingham d. 20.12.1929

Matilda Luxton(1861-1895)
b. 10.03.1861 in Chard
m. George Sydney Jefford,
lacemaker, in parish church
Radford Nottingham on
10.09.1887
Matilda d. aged 34 of mitral
disease at 55 Liddington
Street, Basford, Nottingham
on 29.03.1895
Issue Albert and Beatrice

Eunice Ellen Luxton (1863-1943)
b. 17.01.1863 in Chard
m. Willie James Charlesworth in
Radford Parish Church
Nottingham on 24.12.1885.
Eunice d. at 58 Vicarage Road
Birmingham on 29.10.1943

Lois Ann Luxton (1865-1920)
b. 13.01 1865 in Chard
m. John Henry Rice, Railway
manager, at Stoke, on
15.08.1898.
Lois d. at Blythe Bridge on
30.03.1920.
bd. at Caversall

Alfred Charles Luxton
b. 16.11.1866 at
Tatworth, Chard
Alfred d. aged 2 from
'measles 4 days' at
Perry Street, Chard on
1.06.1869
bd.5.06.1869 at Holy
Trinity Taunton

Henrietta Luxton (1869-1955)
b. 13.05.1869 in Chard
m. Thomas Charles Phasey in
Radford Parish Church
Nottingham on 13.03 1897
Henrietta Phasey aged 86 d. in
Chiswick on 29.10.1955

William Charles Luxton = Elizabeth Ellen Newberry   see TREE 31
(1836-1912)   (1836-1919)d. of William & Louisa born Bridport Dorset on 3.08. 1836
Lace Worker of Chard and Nottingham   See Chapter 60

Frederick Newberry Luxton b.in Chard Somerset on 22.12.1870. Frederick, a lacemaker, m. Mary Jane Dykes at St. Andrews Nottingham on 5.08.1893. Frederick of 27 Belper Rd. Nottingham d. 9.06.1937. Mary d. 12.08.1939 leaving £27..16s..8d to Robert Henry Corner, bricklayer.

Clarice Rose b. 9.01.1895 in Nottingham m. Richard Horobin in Hyson Green, Nottingham on 4.10.1915 Clarice d. at 45 Milton Rd., Nottingham on 16.01.1983

Ivy Winifred b. 24.02.1903 at 17 Denison St, Nottingham m. Robert Henry Corner at Hyson Green on 16.04.1927. Ivy committed "suicide by coal gas poisoning while the balance of her mind was disturbed on the 30th June 1939."

Walter Henry Luxton (1873-1898) b. 1.01.1873 in Chard. Served in Durham Light Infantry in 1891 but was a painter when he m. Cicely Sampey in St. Paul's Hyson Green, Nottinghamshire on 25.09.1893. Walter, a painter and decorator, d. aged 25 on 15.10.1898 in Nottingham of lead poisoning which resulted from his trade. Cicely m. George Edward Parr on 22.01.1905 in St Paul Hyson Green

Sidney Harold Luxton (1897-1959) b. 9.12.1897. A Sapper in Royal Engineers in W.W.1. Sidney, a railway signalman, m. Elsie May Burnett in St. Peters, Gocots, Lincolnshire on 21.04.1919. Sydney of Arksey, near Doncaster d. aged 61 on 30.09.1959. Elsie d. aged 65 in Doncaster on 26.02 1963

Leslie Stewart Walter Luxton (1925-2004) b. 17.04.1925 at 8 Coulson Road Lincoln m. Vera Hughes in the parish church of Bentley St. Peter Yorkshire on 1.01.1946. Leslie, a chiropodist, who lived in Doncaster died there in October 2004

Alfred William Luxton (1875-1922) b. 10.11.1875 in Chard Alfred, a miner, m. Ada Mather at Elmton Derbyshire on 21.07.1902. Alfred, a coal hewer, d. aged 46 of pernicious anaemia and acute bronchitis at 67 Clifton Avenue Rotherham on 27.02.1922. Ada, b. at Apperknowle, Unstone, Derbyshire on 27.02.1881 d. at Rotherham on 2.06.1967

See TREE 33 for issue

Elizabeth Emily Luxton (1877-1912) b. 26.10.1877 in Chard, Somerset. m. George Henry Pinkstone, cabinet maker, in All Souls Church Radford Nottingham on 21.05.1904. Elizabeth d. of cancer at 6 Kentwood Road, Nottingham on 21.10.1912.

TREE 33
Page 1

Alfred William Luxton = Ada Mather   see TREE 32 Page 2   See Chapter 61
(1875-1922)   (1881-1967)d. of Joseph, a coal miner & his wife Elizabeth, born Apperknowle Derbyshire on
Miner in Rotherham Yorkshire   27.02.1881 d.2.06.1967 in Rotherham

page 2

Illegitimate issue
Harry Wright
b. 5.12.1897 in Leicester
was brought up as Harry
Luxton.
In W.W.1. he served in
Kings Own Yorkshire
Light Infantry.
m. Mae Storey in
Nottingham on
28.04.1923.
He emigrated to Canada
in August 1923 on
S.S.Laconia.
d. 23.06.1974 at Creston
British Columbia. issue
eight children.

Elizabeth Ellen Luxton
b. 9.01.1903 in Mansfield
m. Clement Kendrick in
Rotherham on 4.06.1924
Elizabeth d. 9.06.1992 at
Rotherham.
bd 12.06.1992 at East
Herringthorpe Cemetery
Rotherham

Frederick Charles Luxton
b. 20.03.1904 in Mansfield
m1. Edna Ogley at East
Retford on 9.09.1933.
Marriage dissolved.
m2. Ella Katherine Luxton
(name changed by deed poll)
nee Miller, at East Retford
Register Office Nottingham
on 14.04.1972.
Frederick, a retired railway
locomotive driver, and his
second wife "Betty" lived in
Scunthorpe where Frederick
d. on 17.05.1974.A daughter,
Doreen by Edna Ogley, born
in Scunthorpe 29.12.1938

Ada Luxton (1906-1980)
b. 22.02.1906 in Rotherham
m. Samuel Didlock in
Rotherham on 10.12.1927.
Ada d. 28.10.1980

Henrietta Lucy Luxton (1908-2003)
b. 20.03.1908 in Warsop
m1. Reginald Bernard Jones at
Brentford on 5.08.1928.
He was drowned.
m2. Clifford Corbett in Paddington
on 29.10.1951.
Henrietta d. in Croydon on
10.08.2003

Alfred William Luxton = Ada Mather   see TREE 32 Page 2
(1875-1922)   (1881-1922)
See Chapter 61 & 62   Miner in Rotherham

Bessie Luxton (1912-1991)
b. 10.09.1912 in Rotherham
m. Artemus Didlock at St.
Stephen's Rotherham on
15.10.1930.
Bessie d. aged 79 at
Badsley Moor Lane
Hospital Rotherham on
28.12.1991

Annie Lois Luxton (1917-1987)
b. 5.10.1917 in Rotherham
m. John Henry Eckersley Hayes
(known as Jack Heyes) at
Rotherham on 1.03.1941.
d. in Rotherham on 19.11.1987

Alfred William Luxton (1920-1997)
b. 15.03.1920 in Rotherham
m. Vassilikee Liori, schoolmistress, in Athens,
Greece on 5.04.1945. "Alf" a commercial
manager in an engineering company, and his
wife lived at 33 Lancaster Crescent, Tickhill,
Doncaster.
He d. in Doncaster of stomach cancer on
22.08.1997

Dimitrius Edward Anthony Luxton
b. 10.01.1946 in Rotherham.
Hospital consultant in Geriatics,
m. Anne Lilian Berry, a hospital
theatre sister (b. Eltham London
10.11.1946) in Burnham on Crouch on
24.04.1971.
They live in Kings Lynn. Norfolk.

Elainie Luxton (1949-   )
b. 1.05.1949 in Rotherham. Elainie, a
schoolmistress, m. Stuart Jordon on
26.06.1982 in Tickhill Methodist Church.
Stuart, a schoolmaster, was born in
Fleckney Leicester on 2.09.1947.
This is his second marriage.

Melanie Clare Luxton
b. 26.07.1976 in Cambridge

Elena Grace Anne Luxton
b16.1.2000

Alfred Robert Will Luxton
b27.12.2005

Children have the same biological father who is no
longer part of the family unit.

Matthew Alexander Jordon
b. 27.06.1984 in Doncaster

James Rechab Luxton = Hannah Maria Hawkins   see TREE 31   See Chapter 63

(1841-1886)   (1839-1912)d. of John & Mary Ann bp 9. 02. 1840 at All Saints West Bromwich

d. in Heathcoat Square Tiverton on 2.08.1912

Page2

Soldier, Green Grocer and rural postman, Tiverton

Alfred James Massy Luxton (1880-1972)
b. 1.04.1880 Bampton Street, Tiverton
m. Maud Hill at Upton Parish Church
Somerset 17.07.1912
Maud d. aged 73 at 15 Park Terrace
Tiverton 28.04.1964
Alfred, a retired groundsman, d. aged 92 in
Tiverton on 14.10.1972

Alice Luxton (1878-1923)
b. 11.05.1878 in Bampton Street Tiverton
m. Walter Gollop in East Stonehouse Register
Office 10.01.1910.
Walter, a corporal in Royal Marine Light
Infantry d. 1914.
Alice d. in Tiverton at 125 Westexe 16.12.1923.
Issue Walter & Beatrice

Alice Luxton (1900-1987)
b. 18.04.1900 at 5 Thorne Street, Lambeth.
Alice, a shop assistant, m Arthur William Elliott, pastry cook, at
Christchurch, Clapham, Surrey on 3.06.1923. Alice, household
duties, and husband, confectioner /baker lived at 4 Aspley Road
Wandsworth when 1939 register taken.

Charles Frank Luxton (1876-1961)
b. 28.01.1876 in Bampton Street, Tiverton.
Charles, a wheelwright, m. Lucy Rayment at
Crediton Register Office 30.01.1897. He became a
railway porter in Cheriton Fitzpaine before moving
to Lambeth by 1900. Lucy d. aged 57 on
26.05.1935. Charles, a retired railway goods
foreman d. aged 85 on 5.04.1961

Frank Cecil Luxton (1897-1962)
b. 23.05.1897 at Little Venn, Cheriton Fitzpaine served in
Eighth London Regiment & Royal Irish Rifles in W.W.1.
Frank, a postman, m. Amy Ella Pooley at Congregational
Church Tooting on 4.07.1920 Amy d. 9.03.1959.
Frank d. in Mitcham Surrey aged 64 on 31.01 1962

Ronald Charles Luxton (1923-2016)
b. 17.03.1923 at 6 Undine Street,
Tooting, Wandsworth. Ronald, a
cartographer, m. Joan Olive Wing at
Christ Church Croydon, Surrey on
21.09.1946 Joan d July 2000 in Croydon
Ronald d. 19.12.2016 Croydon

Joyce Doris Luxton (1921-1999)
b. 18.04.1921 at 2 Undine Street,
Tooting, Wandsworth. Joyce, a corporal
in W.A.A.F., m. John David Spurway,
Pilot Officer R.A.F. in Epsom Register
Office on 15.12.1947. Joyce d. in New
Forest in January 1999.

Ruth Gillian Luxton (1959-   )
b. 16.06.1959 at Mayday Hospital
Croydon. Ruth, a teacher, m.
Bruce Lewis Offergelt, trainee
accountant, in All Saints Croydon
on 25.07.1981

Janet Anne Luxton (1954-   )
b. 7.08.1954 at Mayday
Hospital Croydon. Janet, a
teacher, m. Robert Geoffrey
Fowlds, director of upholstery
manufacturer, in All Saints
Croydon on 27.05.1978

James Rechab Luxton = Hannah Maria Hawkins   see TREE 31
(1841-1886)   (1839-1912) born October qtr 1839 in West Bromwich

Soldier, Green Grocer and rural postman, Tiverton

Emily Luxton
b. 22.06.1882 Bampton Street.
m1. Pte Alfred Beamer, Royal Marine Light Infantry at St. Paul's Tiverton 14.12.1905.
He d. aged 29 on 1.12.1909
m2. John Heard on 8.12.1912 in United Methodist Church Tiverton.
Emily d. aged 79 at 4 Moorhayes Bungalows, Tiverton on 7.02.1962

Jessie Luxton(1886-1978)
b. 26.06.1886 at Villa Franca Cottage Tiverton
m. Charles Kenward, marine, in parish church St. Paul Tiverton 12.04.1910.
In 1911 Charles, a sergeant in Marines and Jessie lived in Gillingham Kent.
Jessie, widow & retired proprietor of a general store d. at 73 Chaucer Road Gillingham 18th January 1978.

Jessie Luxton (1909-1989)
b. 21.04.1909
m. Robert George Baker in Lambeth Register Office on 28.01.1928

Alfred James Luxton (1902-1967)
Alfred, a railway porter, born in Lambeth on 14.09.1902,
m. Sarah Ann Dickens at Lambeth Register Office 14.08.1923.
Sarah d. aged 40 of T.B. on 31.03.1941 when they lived in Cheam.
Alfred aged 64 of 18 Thoresby Avenue, Tuffley Glouc. d. 1.05.1967

Emily Luxton(1904-1990)
b. 22.06.04 5 Thorne Street, Lambeth
m. Percival R. Attfield(1901-1981) in Lambeth Register Office on 18.12. 1926 d. aged 85 in Feb 1990

Gwendoline Luxton (1924-1986)
b. 30.06.1924 in St. Thomas's Hospital Lambeth. Gwen, 18, assembler munition factory, m1. Peter Michael Fitzgerald, 26, Royal Marine, at St. Mary's R.C. Sutton Surrey on 10.07.1943
m2. Les James (1924-1999) on 20.06.1970 in Gloucester.
Gwen d. 5.08.1986 in Gloucester.

Frank Alfred Luxton (1927-2014)
b. 8.03.1927 at 66 Thorparch Road, Stockwell, Lambeth. Frank, 19, serving in army,
m1. Sheila Rosalind Sizer, 18, waitress, at Cheam parish church on 25.08.1945.
m2. Gloria Pamela O'Connor at Methodist Chapel, Queens Rd., Peckham on 18.06.1966
Frank was a confectioner and pastry cook. Frank d. 26.09.2014

Brenda Margaret Luxton (1930-2012)
b. 19.04.1930 in Lambeth
m. Albert G. Pocock (1928-2002)
d. Shanklin, Isle of Wight.

Colin Frank James Luxton (1949-
b. 10.08.1949 at Brighton General Hospital. Informant father of 37 Chatsworth Road, Cheam, Surrey

David William Luxton (1951-)
b. 24.01.1951 at 49 Dorking Road, Epsom, Surrey. Informant S.R.Luxton, mother, of 97 Boscombe Road, Worcester Park, Cheam, Surrey.

Robert Luxton = Elizabeth Turner   see TREE 25 Page 1

(1786-1871)   (1790-1865)d. of George & Elizabeth Turner bap. at St Mary Magdalene on 29.08.1790

Carpenter and joiner High Street, Taunton

page 2

See Chapter 64 & 65

John Luxton (1811-1884)=Elizabeth Pearce(1814-1849)
bp 6.10.1811 at St. Mary Magdalene Taunton. John, a cabinet maker, settled
just off Old Street in London about 1832m. Elizabeth Pearce(bap21.06.1814 St.
Sepulchre London)at St. Luke's Finsbury on 11.02.1834.
Elizabeth d. aged 35 from phthisis at 11 Norfolk St. Islington on 17.08.1849.
John d. at 7 Great James Street, Hoxton, Shoreditch on 13.01.1884

Ann Luxton (1813-1840)
bp. 28.11.1813 at St. Mary Magdalene
m. William Chard, cabinet maker, in parish church of St.
Luke, Finsbury on 23.11.1837
Ann of Macclesfield St.Luke d. aged 27, bd 28.05.1840

John Luxton (1836-1891)
bp. 31.01.1836 at St.Luke's,
Old Street, Finsbury.
John, a chairmaker of
Shoreditch and Islington
m1. Adelaide Rostance at
St. James, Shoreditch on
12.05.1856. Adelaide d. aged
22 from obstruction of the
bowels, Peritonitis at
St. Bartholomew's Hospital,
London on 19.05.1859.
m2. Jane Kelsey 18 at St.
James Shoreditch on
25.12.1860
John 55, chairmaker, d. of
pleurisy and pneumonia on
15.07.1891 at 63 Moneyer St
Hoxton, Shoreditch.
Jane Luxton 54, widow,   See TREE 36
m. Thomas Bailey 61,
widower, at Holy Trinity,
Hoxton on 17.10.1898
Jane d. at St. Bartholomews
Hospital on 7.10.1908 age 64

Ann Rebecca Luxton
(1837-1916)
bp. 24.06.1837 at St. Luke's Old
Street Finsbury
m. James Crofts, labourer, in St.
James, Shoreditch on 16.09.1860
Ann, a widow of James Crofts, a
hawker, d. 19.05.16

Mary Ann Luxton
(1840-1907)
bp November 1840 at
St. Luke's, Old St., Finsbury
m. Thomas William Jeffries,
chimney sweep, at St. Mary
Haggerston, Middlesex on
26.01.1862Mary d.aged 65
25.04.1907from heart disease

Jane Agnes Luxton
(1839-1912)
bp. 9.03.1839 at St. Lukes,
Old Street, Finsbury
m. George Forty, cabinet
maker, at St. John the
Baptist, Hoxton,
Shoreditch on 17.05.1864.
Jane, 73, d. at 13 Buckland
Street, Shoreditch on
5.11.1912

Maria Luxton (1842-   )
b. 10.03.1842 at 4
Europe Place, City
Road, St. Luke.
bp 6.06.1844 at
St. Leonard's Shoreditch

Robert Luxton (1843-1845)
b.3.12.1843.bp. 6.06.1844 at
St. Leonard's, Shoreditch
d. aged 1 year 9 months on
28.09.1845 from measles and
pneumonia at 4 King's Road,
Haggerstone, Middlesex

Eliza Luxton (1846-49)
bp. 22.02.1846 at St.
Leonard's, Shoreditch
d. aged 3 years of
"anasarca (dropsy) 2
weeks" at 1 Harland
Square Shoreditch on
12.02.1849

I suspect that two further
infant Luxton burials at
St. Leonards -
Elizabeth,aged 2mths,
KingslandRoad,b.31.03.1
833 and John,aged 2 of
Norfolk Place
b.5.06.1845- belong to
John Luxton and his first
wife Elizabeth Pearce

Robert Luxton = Elizabeth Turner   see TREE 25 Page 1
(1786-1871)   (1790-1865)d of George & Elizabeth Turner bp at St. Mary Magdalene Taunton on 29.08.1790
Carpenter and joiner High Street, Taunton

page 3

George Luxton (1815-1878)
bp 12.11.1815 at St. Mary Magdalene Taunton.
Migrated to London where he married perhaps as
George Luxuom to Jane Topping at Edmonton in
1st qtr 1852. George Luxton 45 chairmaker and wife
Jane 31 and three children born in Shoreditch are
listed in 1861 census at 16 Craven Street St.
Leonard's Shoreditch. The family had split by 1871
when Jane "widower", dressmaker, is head of
household at 9 Wood Street, St. Luke's, Finsbury.
George, aged 62, chairmaker, was found d. at 2
President Place, Old Street, St. Luke, Holborn on
3.03.1878
Jane d. aged 74 at Islington Infirmary on 11.02.1899

Robert Luxton
bp. 7.02.1819 at
St. Mary Magdalene.
Lived in High
Street.d. aged 14.
Bd at St Mary
Magdalene on
1.09.1833.

Francis Turner Luxton (1820-1873)
bp. 25.12.1820 at St. Mary Magdalene Taunton
Francis, a chair maker, m1. Elizabeth Ann Pritchard at
St. John the Baptist at Hoxton, Shoreditch on 8.06.1851.
Elizabeth d. aged 33 of epilepsy at 20 Walbrook Place
Hoxton, Shoreditch on 31.03.1865.
m2. Maria Pritchard at St Mary Lambeth on 1.04.1866.
Maria d. aged 25 from phthisis pulmonalis 2 years on
17.11.1871 at 22 Watson Place, Haggerstone, Shoreditch
Francis d. aged 52 from phthisis 3 years on 21.07.1873 at
13 Wellington Street Shoreditch.

Issue from 1st wife
Mary Catherine Luxton
bp 20.07.1856 at
Christchurch Hoxton
m.1 William Evans,
tinplate worker at St.
Monica's Roman
Catholic Chapel Hoxton
Square Shoreditch on
13.06.1880 m2 Thomas
Wm Jeffries at St,
Peter's Hackney on
28.03.1909.

Issue from 2nd wife
Harriet Sophia Luxton
bp. 4.04.1864 at
Christchurch Hoxton
m. John Joseph Dean,
galvanizer, in parish
church St. Mary,
Haggerstone on
2.08.1891
Harriet d. 15.02.1929
at 47 Rushton Street,
Shoreditch

Issue from 1st wife
Elizabeth Annie
b.15.12.1853
m.William Brown
a butcher on
12.11.1871 at St.
John's Hoxton.
Widow & office
cleaner with five
children at home
in 1911.d.1926

Clara Luxton (c1856-1908)
b. c1856 in Shoreditch
m. John Clement Ingham,
bootmaker in parish church
Islington on 29.04.1877.
Clara Ingham d. of breast
cancer at 19 Newington
Green Road, Islington on
3.05.1908

George Luxton
b. c 1850
aged 10 in 1861
St. Leonard's
census

Alfred Luxton (c1854-1925)
b. c 1854 in Shoreditch
Alfred, a book binder, m.
Eliza Dorey 39, widow, at
Christchurch, Southwark on
23.10.1892.
Alfred Luxton, 71, book
binder of 12 Fowler Road,
Islington d. 26.04.1925

TREE 35   Robert Luxton = Elizabeth Turner   see TREE 25
Page 3   (1786-1871)   (1790-1865)
See Chapter 64 & 67   Carpenter and joiner High Street, Taunton

Jane Agnes Luxton (1822-1865)
bp. 8.12.1822 at St Mary
Magdalene Taunton
m. Samuel Weston John Beal,
carver, at St. Mary Haggerstone
on 30.10.1848. Jane aged 42
d.9.06.1865 of phthisis in
Shoreditch Workhouse.

James Marshall Luxton
bp. 8.10.1826 at St. Mary
Magdalene Taunton
James d. aged 1 of High
Street, bd at St. Mary
Magdalene Taunton on
28.10.1827

James Turner Luxton
bp. 12.09.1830 at St.
Magdalene Taunton
James, a cabinet maker, d. aged
23 at Shoreditch Workhouse
from "Effusion on the brain"
(a stroke) on 20.08.1853.
bd. at St. Mary's Haggerstone
on 27.08.1853

Robert Luxton (1835-1876)
bp. 1.03.1835 at St. Mary Magdalene Taunton.
Robert, a gunner in Royal Artillery for 21 years
3 months was a veteran of Second Opium War.
A pensioner of the Royal Artillery, he d. aged 41
at 13 Castle Street, St. Andrew Parish Plymouth
from cirrhosis of liver on 27.12.1876. An Emma
Luxton widow of deceased was present at his
death. He was buried in a common grave at
Ford Park Cemetery Plymouth.

Elizabeth Grace Luxton (1824-1880)
bp 31.10.1824 at St. Mary
Magdalene, Taunton.
Elizabeth, a laundress, m. George
Snook, carpenter, in Baptist Chapel,
Silver Street, Taunton on
27.03.1851.They settled in Bristol
where Elizabeth d. of Phthisis aged
53 at 12 Woodborough Street on
4.11.1880.

Maria Luxton (1828-1895)
bp 13.04 1828 at St. Mary
Magdalene Taunton
Maria, a dressmaker,
m. Alfred Allen, 22, grocer,
in the Baptist Chapel
Bridgwater on 6.03.1853.
Maria d. aged 67 at 39 Queen
Square Bristol on 15.06.1895

Mary Ann Luxton (1832-1892)
bp. 28.10.1832 at St. Mary Magdalene Taunton
Mary Ann, a laundress,
m. John Oaten, printer, at St. James Taunton on
5.11.1854.
Mary Ann Oaten d. aged 58 of erysipelas of
arm 12 days Septicaema at 42 Eldon Road,
Canton, Cardiff on 11.05.1892.
Issue of at least 6 children

TREE 36
Page 1

John Luxton
(1836-1891)

see TREE 35 Page 1

Page2

Chairmaker of Shoreditch and IslingtonSee Chapter 64 & 66

Issue by 1st wife Adelaide Rostance(c.1837-1859) Issue by second wife Jane Kelsey(c.1834-1908) born Bethnal Green d of James,cordwainer & Rebecca

Mary Ann Adelaide Luxton
b. 16.03.1857 at 14 John's
Row, St. Luke, Finsbury.
m1. George Knight,
chairmaker,in parish church
of South Hackney on
4.11.1883. m2. James Kite
John, a master window cleaner, of
St Annes Shoreditch on
28.07.1901. Mary d. of TB
aged 48 on 11.04.1905

John Luxton (1864-1930)
b. 5.12.1864 at 30 Moneyer Street,
Hoxton, Shoreditch.
John, a warehouseman, m. Amy Alice
Agombar, a silk weaver, at St John the
Baptist, Hoxton on 28.04.1889
John, a master window cleaner, of
189 Chatham Avenue, Shoreditch
d. aged 65 on 20.01.1930.
Amy d. aged 93 on 30.11.1959

Jane Luxton (1866-1907)
b. 27.10.1866 at 25 Union Street,
Hoxton, Shoreditch.
m. James Huntingdon, a well-
borer, at St. John the Baptist,
Hoxton, Shoreditch on
10.04.1887. Jane wife of dock
labourer d. aged 40 at 34 Salisbury
St. in Shoreditch in 1907.

James Luxton (1868-1947)
bp 1.08.1868 at St. John the Baptist,
Shoreditch.
James, a leather cutter, m. Elizabeth Mary
Ann Rollason at Holy Trinity Hoxton on
10.10.1898.
James d. aged 77 in Finsbury on 21.05.1947.
Elizabeth d. aged 80 on 31.01.1954
See TREE 38

John Luxton (1889-1940)
b. 26.08.1889 at 31 Mitchell St. Holborn. He
was a Farrier Sgt in Royal Field Artillery in
1917. He m. Charlotte Eliza Cundale at St
John the Baptist Shoreditch on 10.01.1915.
John d. aged 50 on 8.01.1940. His address
was 24A Springfield, Upper Clapton.
Charlotte E. Luxton d. aged 84 on 7.11. 1965

Charles William Luxton (1892-1960)
b. 15.04.1892 at 71 Provost Street, Hoxton, Shoreditch.
m. Ellen Elizabeth Pearson in St. Mary's Hoxton,
Shoreditch on 27.03.1910. Charles, a gunner in the
Royal Artillery was awarded the Military Medal in July
1917. He d. at 210 Hunters Hall Road, Dagenham, Essex
on 18.09.1960. Ellen d. aged 73 on 26.03.1961
See TREE 37

Alice Harriet Luxton
b.11.09. 1895 at
71Provost Street,
Hoxton, Shoreditch.
d. 7.12 1902 aged 7
at St. Bartholomews
Hospital. Inquest 10th
Dec-Shock from
burns flannelette
clothing ignited at an
unguarded fire on 6th
December.
Accidental

Adelaide Luxton
b. 20.08.1898 at 71
Provost Street, Hoxton,
Shoreditch
m1. Thomas John Wall
attendant in St. John the
Baptist, Hoxton on
17.08.1918
m2. William Steadman at
Christ Church Hoxton on
25.12.1932. Adelaide
alive in Stoke Newington
in 1939 was resident in
Bracknell Berks when she
died at Hestlewood
Hospital, Ascot 2.10.1977

Mahala Adelaide Luxton
b. 99 Shrubland Road
Shoreditch on 22.01.1917.
m John Edmond Fitch at
Christchurch Cockfosters
Enfield after banns on
5.0ę.1943.She was a Mĭs
Eyre in 1965

John Victor Luxton (1920 -1993)
b.11.04.1920 at 91 Albion Road Hackney, father messenger in air ministry
m Rosina Lilian Jane Wright at Christchurch Finchley 20.12. 1941
They lived at 38 Avondale Road Finchley. John V. Luxton of 2 Whitehall
Farm Lane, Virginia Water, Surrey d. 7.12. 1993

Janet Mahala Luxton
b.1.01.1947 at St. Mary Hospital Islington
d. aged 2 of malfunction of the heart on 31.07 1949
at 1a. Argyle Road Finchley

Barbara Jane Luxton b.1.01 1952 at Whittington
Hospital St. Mary's Wing Highgate Hill Islington.
m. Graham Savage at Christ Church, Virginia Water
on 5.04.1980

John Luxton=Jane Kelsey
(1836-1891)   (c.1834 -1908)
Chairmaker of Shoreditch and Islington

See Chapter 64

William Luxton (1871-1909)
bp. 18.06.1871 at St. John the Baptist
Shoreditch. William, a fancy box cutter,
m. Sarah Oughton at St. John the Baptist,
Hoxton on 1.08.1896. Sarah d. aged 33 of
'pelvic deformity and obstructed labour'
on 6.01.1906 in Islington. William d. of
'tubicular disease of lungs 12 months,
tubicular disease of larynx 3 months' at
52 Linton Street, Islington on 28.01.1909.

William Horace Luxton (1903-1972)
b. 28.05.1903 at 10 Canon Street, Islington,
son of William 'foreman (Fancy Box Packing)'
William, a clerk, m. Winifred Mead in St. Johns,
Upper Holloway on 3.09.1927.
William, a retired transport clerk of Waltham
Forest d, on 2.04.1972

Joy Eveline Luxton
b. 7.11.1928 at the Royal Free
Hospital St. Pancras, London.
m. George Hunn in parish church
Waltham Essex on 19.07.1958.
The couple lived at the Ideal
Cottage, Churchgate Street,
Harlow when Joy's father
d.2.04.1972

Edward Luxton
d. aged 12 hours
(of convulsions) at
3 Merson Street,
Hoxton,
Shoreditch on
23.03.1873

Mary Ann Luxton
bp 17.07.1874 at St. John
the Baptist, Shoreditch
d. aged 3½ of "Tabes
Mesenterica" at 3 Merson
Street, Hoxton,
Shoreditch on 3.01.1878

Henry Luxton (1876-1929)
b. at 3 Merson Street, Shoreditch
bp. 4.06.1876 at St. John the Baptist, Hoxton
Henry, a silk tie cutter, m1. Harriet Eliza Bailey at St. John
the Baptist, Hoxton, on 5.04.1896. Harriet d. aged 50 at 59
Mildmay Grove, Islington on 25.10.1926
m2. Ada Bailey at St. Judes, Islington on 29.10.1927.
Henry of 191 Southgate Road, Islington d. on 24.02.1929.
Ada d. aged 88 on 22.02.1969.

Harriet Eliza Luxton
daughter of Henry Luxton,
gentleman's tie cutter and his first
wife Harriet Eliza Bailey was born
at 36 Great Chart Street, Hoxton,
Shoreditch on 15.06.1896.
m. Walter John Wilkinson, Police
Constable, at St. Jude's, Islington
on 29.10.1921.
issue Victor and William

John Luxton=Jane Kelsey
(1836-1891)   (c.1834-1908)
Chairmaker of Shoreditch and Islington

See Chapter 64

Joseph Luxton (1880-alive 1923)
b. 6.10.1880 at 3 Marson Street, Hoxton. Joseph, a silk tie cutter,
emigrated to Canada
m1. Edith Mary Jones (1886-1914) in York Ontario on 8.06.1910.
Mary d. aged 32 in Toronto on 16.11.1914.
m2. Emily Helen Everett aged 46 in York Toronto on 17.11.1923

Richard Luxton (1878-1931)
b. at 3 Marson Street, Shoreditch and bp. 28.06.1878 at
St. John the Baptist, Hoxton.
Richard, a tie cutter, m. Annie Morgan, a box maker, at
St. Mary's Hoxton on 26.05.1901.
Richard, aged 52, d. following a road accident on
31.03.1931. Annie d. in Bethnal Green on 26.08.1957

Doris
who in adult life
corresponded with
Luxton relatives
in London

Annie Luxton (1902-1939)
b. 12.06.1902 at 19
Witchampton Street, Hoxton,
Shoreditch m. Sidney Harold
Nash at Islington Register
Office on 15.08.1925. Annie
d. of stomach cancer on
5.04.1939

Richard Luxton (1905-1975)
b. 7.05.1905 at 21 Newton Street, Hoxton,
Shoreditch. Richard, a civil servant, m.
Margaret Elizabeth Williams at St. James,
Islington on 6.06.1931. Richard d. at Thanet
Kent on 9.12.1975. Margaret, b. in Islington
on 19.05.1909, d. at Ware, Hertfordshire on
19.05.2005, her 96th birthday.

Catherine Luxton (1909-1990)
b. 5.10.1909 in Islington
m. Charles Ludgate at St.
James, Islington on 12.06.1931.
Catherine d. in Southend on Sea
in May 1990

Helen aged 6
months in 1911.
Census at
Symington
Avenue, Toronto.

Susan Eliza Luxton
b. 15.10.1940

Martin Clive Luxton (1944-   )
b. 24.04.1944 in Tottenham
m. Lee Gladys Levy at Wood Green Registry Office, Haringay Civic
Centre, London on 22.03.1966. Lee d. 15.09.2014

Richard John Luxton (1934-   )
b. 31.05.1934. Richard, a project engineer,
m. Shirley Lillian Owers at St. Benet Fink
Church, Tottenham on 23.02.1957.
They live in Green Dragon Lane,
Winchmore Hill, London

Deborah Jane Luxton
b. 8.02.1962 in Wood Green
m. Marc Ellery at St. Paul's,
Grange Park on 21.07.1983

Nicholas James Luxton
b. 16.04.1968 in Enfield,
m. Patricia Costi at All Saints
Greek Cathedral Camden,
London on 23.03.1997

Jennifer Anne Luxton
b. 27.06.1969 at Luton, Beds.
m. Ian Carey D'Souza at
Enfield Registry Office on
31.03.1995

Sandra Lee Luxton
b. 13.12.1971 at Luton
m. Jason David Lyddon at
St. Mary Magdalene,
Enfield on 7.05.1994

Robert Philip Luxton
b.10.03 1959, an analytical
chemist, m. Julie Mitchell in
Enfield Middlesex on 10.08.1985

Elizabeth Rose Luxton
b. 14.01.1989 in Enfield

Angelina Luxton
b. 20.07.1998 in Enfield

Andreas Richard Luxton
b. 18.01.2001 in Enfield

Athena Luxton
b. 14.07.2005 in Enfield

see TREE 35 Page 1

TREE 36
Page 4   See Chapter 64

John Luxton=Jane Kelsey
(1836-1891)   (c.1834-1908)
Chairmaker of Shoreditch and Islington

George Luxton (1882-1917)
b. 10.09.1882 at 3 Marson Street, Hoxton
George, a tie cutter, m. Mary Louisa Rutland at St. Philip
the Evangelist, Islington on 6.03.1909.
George of 125 Southgate Road, Islington d. aged 34 of
bronchopneumonia some days and tumour of the brain
some months at London County Asylum on 25.03.1917.
Louisa m. Alfred John Roper at St. Paul's, Islington on
30.11.1935.

George Francis Luxton (1911-1968)
b. 7.09.1911 at 69 Church Road, Islington
m. Maud Ethel Claxton in the Woodbridge Chapel,
Woodbridge Street, Clerkenwell, Finsbury on 28.12.1935
George of 17 Lombard Avenue, Southbourne,
Bournemouth, a post office sorter, d. aged 55 on
29.03.1968.
Maud (b. 13.09.1913) d. 27.03.1985.
Both were cremated at North Cemetery Bournemouth.

Hilary Frances Luxton (1946-)
b. 28.10.1946 at Redhill County Hospital,
Edgware, Middlesex.
m1. Robert Eric Richardson, accountancy
assistant, at the Methodist Church,
Southbourne, Bournemouth on 20.03.1965.
Marriage dissolved.
m2. Philip Brewer, accountancy assistant, at
Christchurch Register Office, Hampshire on
29.03.1969.

Jennifer Luxton (1949-)
b. 11.07.1949 at 13 Selwyn Court Road,
Edgware, Harrow.

Charles William Luxton M.M. =Ellen Elizabeth Pearson see TREE 36 Page 1

(1892-1960)   (1887-1961)born 1st qtr 1887 d of William Henry Pearson a labourer

See Chapter 66 Army Pensioner and General labourer of Shoreditch and Dagenham   & Ellen his wife in Shoreditch

Page 2

Charles William Luxton
b. 24.12.1910 at the City of
London Lying in Hospital.
m. Catherine Theresa
Marson at Romford
Register Office on
19.06.1933. Charles a
general labourer d. at
Charing Cross Hospital
Fulham on 27.06.1974

Sarah Adelaide Luxton
b. 16.02.1913 at 29
Westmorland Place, Nile
Street, Shoreditch.
m. Henry George Watts,
French Polisher, in
Shoreditch Register
Office on 1.08.1936.
Sarah d. in Rainham
Essex 25.10.1989

John French Luxton
b. 14.07.1915 at 83 Chatham
Avenue, Nile Street, Shoreditch.
m.Grace Alma Wood in parish
church, Dagenham, Essex on
2.08.1941.
John, a painter decorator, d. in
Hillingdon on 17.05.1991

Henry William Luxton
b. 19.07.1918 at 39 Crondall
Street, Hoxton, Shoreditch
m1. Alice Lily Kerby at
Willesden Register Office on
26.08.1940.
Marriage dissolved.
m2. Olive Doreen
Richardson at Romford
Register Office on
29.06.1958. Henry, a retired
pile driver foreman, d. in
Hornchurch Essex on
8.07.1993

Jane Delia Luxton
b. 28.02.1920 at 39 Crondall
Street, Hoxton, Shoreditch
Jane Delia Luxton (otherwise
Jean Delia d. on 2.04.1954 at
London Chest Hospital,
Stotfield, Bedfordshire

Jean Audrey Luxton
b. 3.01.1937 at 30
Twickenham Road,
Isleworth, Middlesex
Jean, a telephonist,
m. Tony Bastable at
St. Peters Staines,
Middlesex on
9.03.1957

Margaret Elizabeth Luxton
b. 1.10.1942 at 3 Field
Way, Ruislip, Middlesex
m. Gordon Irwin Brown in
Uxbridge Register Office,
Middlesex on 22.07.1961

Brenda Joyce Luxton
b. 4.07.1949 at 118
Appletree Ave., Hillingdon
m. Stanley Thomas
Sullivan at St. Catherines,
Feltham, Hounslow on
21.06.1969. Divorced.
Brenda lives in Burnham on
Sea, Somerset.

Henry Edward Charles Luxton
Lived at 115A Victoria Road,
Barking, Essex when his father
d. 8.07.1993

Alice Jane Luxton
b. 17.06.1945 at Hillingdon
County Hospital
m. William Edward Beckett
in Eton Register Office,
Buckinghamshire on
19.07.1963

Charles William Luxton M.M. =Ellen Elizabeth Pearson see TREE 36 Page 1
(1892-1960)   (1887-1961) born in Shoreditch 1st qtr 1887
Army Pensioner and General labourer of Shoreditch and Dagenham

See Chapter 66

William Henry Luxton (1922-1982)
b. 22.09.1922 at 39 Crondall Street, Hoxton, Shoreditch.
m. Gladys Ivy Elliott (nee Syer) at Romford Register Office,
Essex on 19.08.1952
William d. at Rush Green Hospital, Dagenham on 17.06.1982

Albert Edward Luxton (1925-1973)
b. 27.03.1925 at 39 Crondall Street, Hoxton, Shoreditch.
Albert, a winchdriver, m. Bronwen Lily Maud Jones,
Hospital Ward Orderly, at Bedwellty Register Office,
Monmouthshire on 5.03.1949.
Bronwen d. aged 35 on 25.06.1966
Albert of 14 Tredegar Avenue, Ebbw Vale, d. at
Penyvai Hospital, Abergavenny on 31.05.1973

William Henry Luxton
b. 27.11.1951 at 511
Heathway, Dagenham

Sallie Ann Luxton
b. 7.06.1957 at 94
Valentines Way,
Romford

Timothy John Luxton
b. 9.09.1959 at 94
Valentines Way,
Romford

Gary William Luxton
b. 23.07.1954 at 42
Cannington Road,
Dagenham

Anthony Paul Luxton
b. 23.02.1950 at 1A
Mountain Road,
Chepstow.
m. Shirley Davies at
Bedwellty Register
Office on 7.10.1972

Charles William Luxton
b. 27.09.1951 at 210 Hunters
Hall Road, Dagenham
m. Caroline Elizabeth Miriam
Brake at Bedwellty Register
Office 25.11.1972

Albert Edward Luxton
b. 28.03.1953 at Rookery
Maternity Home, Ebbw Vale.
Albert, a steel worker, m. Anne
Rees in Christchurch, Ebbw
Vale on 9.06.1973. Albert
accidental d.24.11.1999

Mark Anthony Luxton
b. 3.09.1973 in St.
James Hospital,
Tredegar

Andrew Paul Luxton
b. 24.11.1977 in
Nevill Hall Hospital,
Abergavenny

Lee David Luxton
b. 3.06.1973 at St.
James Hospital,
Tredegar

Stephen Charles
Luxton
b. 18.07.1975 in
Nevill Hall
Hospital,
Abergavenny

Jeffrey Luxton
b. 7.10.1976 in
Nevill Hall
Hospital,
Abergavenny

Joanne Luxton
b. 22.12.1974
in Nevill Hall
Hospital,
Abergavenny

Hayley Luxton
b. 27.06.1977
in Nevill Hall
Hospital

Charles William Luxton M.M. =Ellen Elizabeth Pearson see TREE 36 Page 1
(1892-1960)   (1887-1961) born in Shoreditch 1887
Army Pensioner and General labourer of Shoreditch and Dagenham

George Luxton (1927-1992)
b. 23.05.1927 at 39 Crondall Street, Shoreditch
m. Lilian May Barlow in Romford Register Office on 24.12.1949.
George, a retired painter and decorator of 57 Roosevelt Way,
Dagenham d. at Oldchurch Hospital on 30.09.1992 when son
George David lived at 51 Poley Road, Stanford le Hope, Essex

Benjamin James Luxton (1931-1984)
b. 8.07.1931 at 210 Hunters Hall Road, Dagenham, Essex.
Ben, a pile driver, m. Elizabeth Jean Morris in Romford
Registry Office on 3.09.1955.
A retired driver partsman of 1 Treswell Road, Benjamin d. at
Old Church Hospital, Romford on 27.09.1984

George David Luxton
b. 21.09.1951 at 396
Commercial Road,
Limehouse, Stepney.
m. Denise Patricia
Broadhurst at St.
Andrews, Hornchurch,
Essex on 1.04.1978

Diana Jean Luxton
b. 26.11.1954 at
66 Heathway,
Dagenham , A nurse,
m. Samuel Dougherty,
a soldier in Dagenham
Parish Church on
17.05.1980.

Barry Benjamin John Luxton
b. 29.03.1958 at Oldchurch
Hospital, Romford.
m. Carole Elizabeth Gunnell
in Barking Register Office on
7.08.1976

Lorraine Elizabeth Luxton
b. 13.08.1961 at 210 Hunters
Hall Road, Dagenham.
m. Bryan Michael Dent in
St. Margaret with St. Patrick,
Barking on 28.02.1981

Beverley Elise Luxton
b. 23.02.1963 at
76 Ivyhouse Road,
Dagenham, Essex

Marie Elizabeth Luxton
b. 21.01.1977 at
Barking Hospital

David Benjamin Luxton
b.12.07.1979 at
Barking Hospital

Paul Barry Luxton
b. 20.08.1980 at
Barking Hospital

TREE 38

James Luxton =ElizabethMary Ann Rollason   see TREE 36 Page 1
(1868-1947)   (1873-1954) b.19.07. 1873 d. of Joseph & wife Ellen at 48 Blackhorse Yard, Aldergate Street
Islington & bp at St Thomas Charterhouse Finsbury 10.08.1873. Joseph was a carpenter.

Fancy leather cutter of Shoreditch and Islington
See Chapter 65

James Luxton
b. 26.02. 1899
at 52 Herbert Street,
Shoreditch
d.of "Diarrhoea
convulsions" at
52 Murray Street on
22.07. 1899 Shoreditch

Elizabeth Luxton
b. 20.09. 1902
Elizabeth, 28,
shorthand typist m.
Wilfred Driskell,
26, Baptist
Minister at Baptist
Church, Chadwell
Heath on
6.04.1931. She
lived at52 The
Crescent, Abbots
Langley, Herts in
1979. Elizabeth d.
16.10.1986 in
Northwood

Grace Luxton
b. 16.10.1906 at 85
Murray Street Shoreditch
m. William James Norman
28, Commercial Traveller
at Greenford Assembly
Gospel Hall, Greenford,
Middlesex on
28.01.1939Grace d. aged
80 in Lewes in 1987

Phoebe Margaret Luxton
b.22.09.1910 at 1 Edmonds Place,
Shoreditch.
A spinster, & lingerie machinist
living at 15 Birkbeck Way Ealing
in 1939 with mother and brother
George.A retired dressmaker, she
d. 17.10. 1979 in Ealing

Joseph Luxton (1913-1920)
b. 6.01.1913 at 5 Edmonds
Place, Shoreditch.
d. aged 7 from Syncope
Fracture of the skull and
other injuries – struck and
knocked down by a motor
car accidental – PM on
7.03.1920 in City Road
opposite No. 215 St. Luke,
Holborn. Inquest held on
10.03.1920.

George Luxton
b. 12.08.1900 at
52 Herbert Street,
Hoxton, Shoreditch.
George, a retired
commercial traveller
in stationery, of
15 Birkbeck Way,
Greenford, Ealing
d. on 29.10.1973

Elsie Luxton
b. on 27.11. 1904
at 7 Bookham
Street, Shoreditch
d.9.04.1906 at 85
Murray Street aged
16 months of
Rickets 1 year
Bronchitis 14 days

William Luxton
b. 6.10.1908 at
85 Murray Street, Shoreditch.
William aged 2 of
5 Edmonds Place, Shoreditch
d. of concussion of brain when
he fell on his head whilst at play
at home on 10.07.1911.
Inquest on 14.07.1911

James Luxton = Elizabeth Palfrey   see TREE 25 Page 2
(1796-1869)   (c.1786-1873)
Farmer at Townsend, Skilgate   See Chapter 68 & 69

Page 2 ⟶

John Luxton (1816-1896)
bp. 29.12.1816 at Morebath,
Devon
m. Harriet Fry(nee Long),
milliner, at St. James,
Taunton on 1.01.1860.
Harriet d. aged 69 at 37 Alma
Street, Taunton on 3.11.1889.
John, a cellarman, d. aged 79
of throat cancer at 37 Alma
Street, Taunton on 6.11.1896

Mary Luxton
bp. 27.09.1821 at
Morebath
m. Henry Burcher,
maltster, at St, Mary,
Redcliffe, Bristol on
28.04.1851.
Mary, a widow and
general shop keeper,
d. aged 77 at East
Quantoxhead,
Somerset on
10.07.1899.

William Luxton
bp. 4.01.1824 at
Morebath
d. aged 11 months
bd. at Morebath on
25.07.1824

George Luxton (1825-1901)
bp. 6.11.1825 at Morebath.
George, a farm bailiff, m.
Ann Atkins at St. James,
Taunton on 12.02.1855.
George, farmer of Halsdown
Farm, Chipstable d. aged 75
on 23.04.1901.
Ann of 11 Landford Road,
Hotwell, Bristol d. aged 88
on 9.10.1925. They are bd.
at Chipstable.

James Luxton (1834-1918)
bp. 26.01.1834 at Upton Somerset
James, a shepherd, m. Elizabeth
Atkins of Skilgate at Dulverton
Register Office on 10.07.1867.
James of Lurban Doverhay,
Porlock d. aged 84. Bd. at Skilgate
on 13.04.1918
Elizabeth of Lower Bourne Terr.,
Porlock d. aged 95 on 28.02.1939.
bd with husband at Skilgate.

See TREE 40

John Luxton
b. 6.05.1855 at
Skilgate. John of
Braglands Farm,
Stogumber, Som.
d. aged 71 on
11.12.1926
bd. 16.12.1926
at Bethel Chapel,
Waterrow

Rosa Ellen Luxton
bp.1.06.1857 at
Chipstable
m. Elias Bucknell,
farmer who farmed at
Trevene Farm
nr. Helston, Cornwall
in 1900
Rosa d. aged 88 at
Trowbridge
Crowcombe, Somerset
on 9.01.1945

Elizabeth Anne Luxton
b. 4.04.1859 at "Winters"
in Huish Champflower.
Elizabeth, a domestic
cook, d. aged 28 of
perforation of stomach and
peritonitis at Old Park,
Devizes, Wiltshire on
10.12.1887. bd. at Bethel
Chapel, Waterrow,
Chipstable on 17.12.1887

Mary Luxton
b. 10.02.1863 in Huish
Champflower.
Mary, 37, Hotel Proprietress
of Wyndham Arms, Williton,
m. John Hooper, ironmonger,
at Independent Chapel, North
Street, Taunton on 9.04.1901.
Mary of 17 Vicarage Road,
Minehead d. 19.10.1935.
Issue Evelyn Gertrude
Hooper

Ellen Luxton
bp. 12.03.1865
at Chipstable
bd. aged 1 year
and 10 months
at Bethel Chapel
Waterrow on
16.12.1866

James Luxton
b. 1.04.1868 at
Chipstable a 41 year
old stockman
m. Daisy Violet Miller
20, Domestic Servant
at Leatherhead Parish
Church Surrey on
24.02.1914. James of
16 Prospect Place,
Masons Hill, Bromley,
Kent d. 7.07.1948

Doris May Rose Luxton
b. at Farm Court Cottages, Leatherhead, Surrey on 17.05.1914.
Doris a waitress 22, m. Harold Joseph Willetts 26, Stoker Petty
Officer on H.M.S. Hood in Portsmouth Cathedral 15.05.1937

James Luxton = Elizabeth Palfrey see TREE 25 Page 2
(1796-1869)   (c.1786-1873)
Farmer at Townsend, Skilgate

See Chapter 68 &69

George Luxton (1825-1901)
Continued (see page 1)

William George Luxton (1870-   ?)
b. 17.07.1870 at Huish Champflower.
William lost touch with his parents and
family. He was bequeathed £10 in his
father's will of 7.09.1900 "if he could
be found".

Frederick George Luxton (1873-1947)
bp. on 31.08.1873 at Chipstable.
He emigrated aboard the 'Moravian'
with relatives to Australia in 1910
arriving in Melbourne on 13.09.1910.
He farmed at Killarney in Queensland
where he died in Nambour Hospital on
8.03.1947. bd. at Beerwah, twenty five
miles from Nambour

Henry George Luxton (1877-1949)
bp. on 1.04.1877 at Chipstable.
Briefly a soldier, he was a policeman when he
m. Charlotte Evelyn Jex-Blake in the parish church
Shirehampton, Gloucestershire on 14.05.1904.
Henry George Luxton aged 72 of 50 St. Matthews
Road, Cotham, Bristol, d. at Bristol Royal
Infirmary on 7.08.1949.
Charlotte (1861-1949) of the same address,
d. at Victoria Gardens, Cotham on 17.09.1949.

TREE 40

James Luxton = Elizabeth Jane Atkins   see TREE 39

(1834-1918)   (1844-1939) d. of James & Mary Atkins, farrier, bap at Skilgate, 10 March 1844

Farmer at Skilgate and Porlock in Somerset

See Chapter 70

Mary Jane Luxton
(known as Polly)
b. C 1863 in Skilgate, Som.
Polly m. William Caswell,
stationmaster, Morebath at
Holy Trinity, Bridgwater on
18.07.1892.
Mary of 25 Park Street,
Tiverton d. aged 98 at
Belmont Hospital, Tiverton
on 18.10.1961

Ann Elizabeth Luxton
b. 27.07.1867 in
Skilgate. In 1880s and
90s she worked in
Kensington as a
domestic cook.
Ann 38 m John Gooding
48 widower, Police
Constable at Holy
Trinity Church
Paddington on 1. 06.
1905. In 1911 John, 54
police pensioner & door
keeper with Ann 44 &
son John aged 2 lived at
208 Wharncliffe
Gardens St John's Wooc
London

James Luxton
b. 17.12 1870 at
Skilgate.
James, a solicitors
clerk, d. aged 26
from tonsillitis 6
days & Pazotitis
pneumonia 2 days
at 3 Billet Street,
Taunton on
2.07.1897. bd. in
parents' grave at
Skilgate

Rhoda Ellen Luxton
b. 4.06.1869 Skilgate
m. Noah Reeves, a
mason, in parish
church Selworthy,
Som. on 31.12.1889.
Rhoda d. 30.08.1961
Issue four daughters
and a son.-
Annie, Violet, Amelia
Christabel & Harold

John Luxton
(known as Jack),
b.22.12.1872
at Skilgate
Jack farmed at
Blindwell, Skilgate.
He joined the
Metropolitan Police
on 22.04.1895.
He completed 28
years in the Force
and was an
inspector when he
retired on
3.12.1923.
m1. Louisa Alice
Stevens at St.
Nicholas Church,
Strood, Kent on
8.08.1901. Louisa
d. 15.04.1928 of
pneumonia aged 50
at 44 Nag's Head
Road, Ponders End,
London
m2. Ethel Eden
Williams(1875-
1950) 16.08. 1930.
John d. 7.03.1941

Lucy Luxton (1875-   )
b. 23.04.1875 at
Winsford, Exmoor, Som.
m. James Woolley, a
game-keeper, at
Bridgwater Register
Office on 15.05.1902.
Lucy was left a legacy of
£25 in her mother's will
dated 12.12.1933.

William Luxton
(known as Willy)
b. 6.05.1877 at
Winsford, Exmoor,
Somerset
Willy d. aged 2
from bronchitis at
Winsford on
9.06.1879. bd. at St.
Mary Magdalene,
Winsford on
19.06.1879

Frederick James Luxton
b. 17.11.1879 in Winsford,
Exmoor, Som. Fred, a farm
bailiff, m. Florence Sellick in
the Wesleyan Chapel, Minehead
on 24.07.1902.
He joined the Metropolitan
Police on 3.11.1902 and was a
sergeant when he resigned on
10.11.1927.
Fred, farmer, at Lower House
Frm., Cutcombe, Som.
d. 15.02.1932.
Florence d. 18.11.1941

See TREE 42

Margaretta Luxton
(Aunt Gert)
b. 22.03.1882, taught
at Porlock School for
51 years. Margaretta
d. in Minehead aged
99 on 27.10.1981.
Her ashes are
interred in her
parents grave at St.
Michael's, Skilgate

John Luxton=m1. Louisa Alice Stevens, m2. Edith Ethel Stevens   see TREE 40
(1872-1941)   (1877-1928)   (1875-1950)
d of Henry & Elizabeth bp29.08.1877 at Dunmow Essex d of pneumonia 15.04.1928

Inspector Metropolitan Police

See Chapter 71

Harold William Stevens
Luxton b. 12.10.1909
m. Phyllis Joyce Kent at St.
James, Friern Barneton on
25.07.1936. Harold, a
Sergeant in the Middlesex
Regiment, was killed at Caen,
France on 18.07.1944 and bd.
at Ranville War Cemetery in
Northern France. Joy and her
three children emigrated to
Perth, Australia.

John Robert Luxton
b. 28.02.1907 at 56 Derby
Buildings, Britannia
Street, St. Pancras.
d. aged 3 from acute
inflammation of bone
marrow and blood
poisoning at
Great Ormond Street
on 4.12.1910.
bd. at Enfield Highway
Cemetery.

Harold William Stephen Luxton
b. 21.11.1944, posthumously at
Merthyr Tydfil Hospital,
Glamorgan, South Wales.
Harold lived in Shoalwater,
Western Australia in December
1977.

Muriel Annie Luxton
b. 8.06.1905
m. William Arthur Atkins
(1900-1954), editor and
journalist at St. James,
Enfield, on 14.06.1930.
Muriel who lived in
Ruislip, d. 21.06.1981.
Issue a son and daughter.

Patricia Anne Luxton
b. 30.05.1943
d. 19.06.1943 at North
Middlesex Hospital

Phyllis Elizabeth Eden
Luxton
b. 6.07.1903
m. Lister Hey on
20.09.1930. Phyllis d.
aged 90 on 16.05.1994.
Issue two daughters.
Margaret Hey, the
eldest, was a professor
in Columbia
University, U.S.A.

Walter John Luxton
b. 9.07.1939 at University
Hospital London
m. Priscilla Meryl Feakes,
school teacher, at St. George's,
Hornsey, Haringay on
18.03.1967

Stewart David Luxton
b. 26.10.1972 in
Melbourne

James Henry Eden Luxton
b. 19.02.1902 in Westminster.
James, a gunsmith, m. Minnie Emily
Sarah May at Enfield Register Office,
Edmonton, Middlesex on 14.02.1953.
James of 31 Ashcombe House Enfield
d.at South Lodge Hospital in Enfield on
24.01.1970
No issue.

Mary Edith Luxton
b. 26.07.1937 in Hertford County
Hospital.
m. Colin Arthur Stevens at St.
Peters, East Victoria Park, Perth,
Australia on 18.06.1952.
Issue one son and two daughters

Julie Grace Luxton
b. 10.05.1970 in
Perth, Western
Australia

See Chapter 71

John Luxton=m1. Louisa Alice Stevens, m2. Edith Ethel Luxton
(1872-1941) (1877-1928) (1875-1950)
Inspector Metropolitan Police

David George Luxton C.B.E. (1911-2004)
b. 26.02.1911.
David a mechanical engineer, m. Dorothy Ella Ethel Shinkins
at Waltham Abbey, Essex on 26.07.1940.
Dorothy (1914-2002) d. aged 87 on 26.01.2002.
David, of 58 Balmoral Drive, Bramcote Hills, Nottingham,
retired Director of the Royal Ordnance Factory awarded the
C.B.E. for his work in the war, d. aged 93 at Derby City
Hospital on 28.05.2004.

Lorna Louise Luxton
b. 20.03.1914
m. Dennis Albert Beer, school teacher, on 27.10.1938.
They lived in Lightwater, Surrey.
Lorna d. 18.07.1881
Issue 6 children

Mark Christopher Luxton (1947-)
b. 27.03.1947 in Northwick Park Hospital, Harrow, M'sex.
In 1960s he read medicine at Jesus College Oxford. Consultant
anaesthetist at the Queen Mary College Hospital, Nottingham.
m1. Gillian Elizabeth Prattent at Lewisham Register Office on
19.11.1970. Jill d. 2.05.1980.
m2. Linette Dufton (nee Waller) in Leeds Register Office on
24.09.1981. Linette d. after a long illness on 14.05.2013.

Roger David Luxton
b. 28.07.1951.
Lived in Sidcup, Kent.
d. 19.02.1964

By 2nd wife Linette

Barnaby Edward Luxton
b. 25.07.1983.
In 2000, Barnaby was
studying catering in a
Nottingham college.

John David Luxton
b. 8.01.1943 at
2 Rutherford Road,
Liverpool. He lived
only a few days.
Father mechanical
engineer in Royal
Ordnance Factory.

John Richard Luxton
b. 9.07.1944.
John, B.Sc(Hons) Hull,
a biology teacher in
Leeds for 34 years
m. Jane Ann Bush B.A.

By 1st wife Gillian

Julian Luxton
b. 23.10.1970.
He lives in
Northampton
with Carolyn.

Joanna Luxton
b. 6.06.1972. She
was working in
2000 for a law firm
in Manchester.

Crispin Luxton
b. 12.08.1975.
He was a
globe trotter in
2000 for a
Bristol
computer firm

Katie Victoria Luxton
b. 1.09.1971 in Leeds,
Yorkshire.
She studied horticulture
at Askham Bryan and
runs a gardening
business

Philippa Sarah Luxton
b. 19.11.1974 in Leeds.
She read for a B.Sc. in rural
resource management at
Bangor University, N. Wales.
Philippa, who taught in a
primary school in Oxford,
m. Noureddine Ben-Aldjie on
2.07.2005 in Leeds Town Hall.
Issue daughter Amina

Ethan Luxton
b.28.05.2004

Soren Luxton
b.15.11.2007

TREE 41
Page 3

See Chapter 71

John Luxton=m1. Louisa Alice Stevens, m2. Edith Ethel Luxton see TREE 40
(1872-1941)   (1877-1928)   (1875-1950)
Inspector Metropolitan Police

Peter John Luxton (1915-2007)
b. 25.11.1915 in Enfield,
Middlesex
m. Dorothy Kate Gaut (1915-
alive in 2002) in Sidbury Devon
on 10.04.1939. They lived in
Sidmouth Devon where Peter d.
aged 92 on 19.12.2007

Joan Margaret Luxton (1918-2012)
b. 27.05.1918
m. Donald Arthur Buchanan (1918- 1987)
school teacher, on 2.08.1941.
They lived in Cambridge and had issue a
son.

Margaret Ann Luxton
b. 31.01.1941 in Sidbury
m. Jeffrey Greenhalgh in
Chorley, Lancs. on 17.05.1963
Issue 3 sons.

Gillian Mary Luxton
b. 26.11.1943 in Worcester
m. John Havard Bamber in
Chorley, Lancs. on 12.03.1966.
Issue a son and daughter.

Elizabeth Joan Luxton
b. 20.11.1950 in Nantwich, Cheshire
m. David John Ford at Abergavenny,
Monmouthshire on 14.10.1972
Issue a son and daughter.

TREE 42

Frederick James Luxton = Florence Sellick   see TREE 40
(1879-1932)   (1871-1941) d.of James & Anne Sellick, farmer,Duddridge, Clatworthy
                                            bp24.09.1871 d. aged 70 on 18.11.1941

See Chapter 72   Sergeant in the Metropolitan Police and farmer at Cutcombe Somerset

---

Frederick James Luxton (1905-1985)
b. 17.05.1905 at 52 Gayton Road,
Hampstead, London
m. Margaret Elizabeth Whitmore of
London at Stogumber Somerset on
26.09.1944.
Jim farmed at Oatway, Brompton
Regis, Somerset. He d. 3.05.1985, a
fortnight before his 80th birthday.

Annie Elizabeth Luxton
b. 15.02.1907 at 111 Warncliffe Gardens,
St. Marylebone
m. Wilfred Wesley Norman at
Minehead Methodist Church
on 22.12.1958.
"Auntie Cis" who lived in
Minehead d. aged 88 on 29.08.1995

Florence May Luxton
b. 19.06.1910 at 13 Eaton
Road, Hendon, Middlesex
m. William Giles Escott,
farmer, at Williton Registry
Office on 17.10.1942
Florence d. 7.04.1977 at West
Somerset and Minehead
Hospital

Dorothy Lucy Luxton
b. 29.01.1917 at 'Lynmouth',
Somerset Road, Hendon, M'sex.
m. Frederick Edgar Norman at
Minehead Methodist Church on
30.09.1939.
Dorothy d. of Jacob Crentzfeldt
disease on 28.09.1984
Issue 2 daughters

Margaret Irene Luxton
b. 22.10.1945
m. Donald Arthur Elliott,
veterinary surgeon, at
Brompton Regis Parish
Church on 25.06.1966.
Issue 2 daughters.

Edward Stephen Whitmore Luxton B.Ed. (1947-   )
b. 29.10.1947 was a deputy headmaster at Minehead
Primary School and church warden at Brompton Regis
m. Sylvia Elizabeth Bale at Withiel Florey Church,
Brendon Hill, Somerset on 28.05.1988

Jane Barbara Luxton
b. 27.05.1955, a partially sighted albino,
trained as a children's nursey teacher for
the handicapped.

Lucy Elizabeth Luxton
b. 25.07.1990
bp. At Withiel Florey Church,
Somerset

Stephen Frederick Whitmore Luxton
b. 24.09.1991
bp. At Withiel Florey Church,
Somerset.

Thomas Luxton = Ann Cooksley   see TREE 25 Page 2

(1798-1856)   (1808-alive1881)born 28.08.1808 d. of Thomas & Elizabeth, bp at Upton 25.10.1812

Farm labourer at Petton Bampton and Upton, Somerset.

Elizabeth Luxton
bp. 14.05.1837 at Upton.
Probably d. in infancy as
there is no mention of her
in 1841 census

George Luxton (1839-1916)
bp. at Upton 24.02.1839
m. Emma Sturgess in St. James,
Portsea on 4.10.1868.
George of 85 Jessie Road,
Southsea, Portsmouth,
pensioned sergeant in the Royal
Marines, d. on 4.03.1916.
His widow Emma d. aged 85 at
home on 28.07.1926

Eliza Luxton
bp. 26.12.1841 at Upton
Eliza, a seamstress in Bristol
d. of cancer aged 52 on
8.12.1893

Ann Luxton
bp. 10.08.1845 at Upton
m. Benjamin Greedy at
Wiveliscombe on 9.04.1867.
Ann d. at Forty Acres
Cottage, North Petherton,
Somerset on 21.07.1898.
Ben d. in Bridgwater
Workhouse on 29.09.1923.

Mary Maria Luxton
bp 19.05.1850 at Upton.
Mary, a tailoress, d. aged
52 of breast cancer at 6
Grove Park Terrace,
Stapleton, Bristol on
5.04.1902

Claudine Georgina Luxton
b. 27.10.1871 in Kingston,
Dublin
d. aged 6 of 'spinobifida,
convulsions 2 days' at
1 Cambridge Terrace,
Eastney, Hampshire on
1.02.1878

Florence Emma Luxton
b. 11.02.1873 at 4 Alma
Terrace, Eastney, Hants.
d. aged 28 of T.B. at 43
Margate Road, Southsea
on 20.07.1901

Lillian Luxton
b. 3.08.1874 at
2 Highland St.,
Eastney
Lillian, a retired
Epsom College
Linen Mistress,
d. aged 74 at
6 Quarry Cres.,
Hastings on
15.11.1948

Maud Luxton
a twin to Lillian
d. aged 14 days
from 'infantile
debility' at 2
Highland St.,
Southampton on
17.08.1874

Violet Mabel Luxton
b. 19.08.1875 at 2
Highland St., Eastney
Violet, a retired
Commercial Clerk, of
6 Quarry Crescent,
Hastings, d. aged 79
on 12.03.1955

**George Thomas Archibald
William Luxton (1881-1937)**
b. 1.12.1881 at West Cottage,
Southsea, Southampton
m. Annie Harriet Hook at St.
Peter's, Southsea on
23.02.1911. In the Royal
Artillery, he fought in the
Boer War and W.W.1. when
he was promoted to lieutenant
George, an auctioneer for an
estate agent and antique
dealer, lived at 11 Park Road,
Bexhill on Sea. He d. aged 55
from cancer on 20.02.1937.
Annie d. aged 73 in
Cambridge on 22.12.1951.

Winifred Marjorie Hook Luxton (1912-2006)
b. 30.03.1912 at 9 North Ham Road,
Littlehampton, Sussex.
Winifred, a retired nurse and midwife, who
lived at 75 Fairleigh Court, Terminus Road,
Maidstone, d. in her 94th year on 2.03.2006.

Mabel Joan Luxton (1914-1989)
b. 29.04.1914 at 24 Sackville Road, Bexhill-on-Sea.
Mabel ran a guest house in Cambridge from 1937-1951.
She returned to Bexhill-on-Sea where she ran the Joan Luxton School of
Dancing. She suffered a massive heart attack at King's Cross Station on
8.04.1989 and d. the same day at University College Hospital Camden.

George Luxton = Ann ?
(1802-1891)   (c.1797-1879)
Stonemason, Morebath, Devon.

see TREE 25 Page 2

See Chapter 74

Ann Luxton
bp 7.08.1831 at Bampton.
There is no mention of her in
the 1841 census so she had
probably d. in childhood.
However, there is plenty of
evidence in the family of
names being adopted later in
life! This I suspect is in fact
the case here and she is Mary
Ann Luxton, the matron on
the right who d. in 1911 aged
80 which would make her
birth date 1831!

Mary Ann Luxton (c1834- 1911)
In Morebath 1841 census Mary
is listed aged 7 living with her
parents.
In 1891 she was the House
Superintendent and matron of the
Midland Blind Institution,
Chaucer Street, Nottingham.
By 1901 Mary Ann, retired, was
boarding in Tiverton with her
widowed sister Elizabeth Takle.
Mary, a spinster, d. aged 80 at 4
South View, Fore Street,
Tiverton on 29.07.1911

Elizabeth Luxton
bp. 22.01.1836 at St. George's,
Morebath, Devon.
Elizabeth, 20, dressmaker,
m. John Takle, labourer, in
St. George's, Morebath on 27.03.1856.
John, a gardener in 1891, was a slater
when he d. in October 1896.
His widow d. aged 83 at
3 Pinkstone's Court, Tiverton on
22.02.1919.

Mary Ann Takle
Aged 18 in 1891
Tiverton census

Lewis Takle
Aged 10 in 1891
Tiverton census